The Tudor Years

Second Edition

Edited by
JOHN LOTHERINGTON

Contributors
HENRY JEFFERIES, PETER SERVINI,
EDWARD TOWNE

With original material by
DAVID GROSSEL, MALCOLM SAXON,
ROY SLOAN

Hodder & Stoughton

Orders: please contact Bookpoint Ltd, 130 Milton Park, Abingdon, Oxon OX14 4SB.
Telephone: (44) 01235 827720. Fax: (44) 01235 400454. Lines are open from 9.00–6.00,
Monday to Saturday, with a 24 hour message answering service. You can also order
through our website www.hodderheadline.co.uk

British Library Cataloguing in Publication Data
A catalogue record for this title is available from the British Library

ISBN 0 340 85774 9

First published 1994
Second edition 2003
Impression number   10 9 8 7 6 5 4 3 2 1
Year   2007 2006 2005 2004 2003

Cover photo reproduced courtesy of the Victoria & Albert Museum, London.

Produced by Gray Publishing, Tunbridge Wells, Kent
Printed in Great Britain for Hodder & Stoughton Educational, a division of Hodder
Headline Plc, 338 Euston Road, London NW1 3BH by J.W. Arrowsmith Ltd, Bristol.

Contents

↠ LIST OF DIAGRAMS ↞

↠ LIST OF ILLUSTRATIONS ↞

⬿ LIST OF MAPS ⬿

⬿ LIST OF PROFILES ⬿

⮌ LIST OF ANALYSES ⮍

⤙ ACKNOWLEDGEMENTS ⤚

Thanks are due to Anselm Eustace for his patient and determined proof-reading.

The Publishers would like to thank the following for permission to reproduce the following material in this book:

Blackwell Publishing, for an extract from *The Reformation and the English*, by JJ Scarisbrick (1984) used on page 438; Chrysalis Books Group (BT Batsford), for extracts from *The English Reformation* by AG Dickens (1989) used on page 438; Palgrave Macmillan, for extracts from *Popular Religion in Sixteenth Century England* by C Marsh (1998) used on page 440.

The Publishers would like to thank the following for permission to reproduce the following copyright illustrations in this book:

The Art Archive, pages 33, 298; © Bettmann/Corbis, pages 2, 13, 82, 86, 131, 157, 188, 197, 263, 265, 325, 407; British Museum, page 107; Cambridge University Library, page 421; Douce. D. Subt. 30, Bodleian Library, page 412; Mary Evans Picture Library, pages 168, 336; © Kevin Fleming/Corbis, page 156; The Fotomas Index, page 402; Frick Collection, New York, page 87; © Historical Picture Archive/Corbis, page 340; © Hulton Deutsch Collection, page 35; © Francis G. Mayer/Corbis, page 81; © Marquess of Salisbury/Hatfield House, Herts, page 415; by courtesy of the National Portrait Gallery, London, pages 23, 32, 54, 59, 72, 84, 180, 217, 226, 254, 391, 410, 414; The Royal Collection © Her Majesty Queen Elizabeth II, page 430; Scala, page 413; Sudeley Castle, Gloucestershire, page 411.

Every effort has been made to trace and acknowledge ownership of copyright. The publishers will be glad to make suitable arrangements with any copyright holders whom it has not been possible to contact.

Preface: How to use this book

1 ⌁ GENERAL

This book has been revised to incorporate recent research and meet the latest demands of the examiners. It is designed to give those starting out on the study of the Tudor period an accessible and thought-provoking introduction to the subject. It is also a workbook containing documents and exercises. As well as providing information, it is structured to help students acquire an awareness and a method so that they can put the limited time they have for further researches to the best use.

2 ⌁ KEY ISSUES

The key issues you will find in the margins are intended to test understanding and to stimulate debate. Written answers to the questions would be an effective way of taking structured notes.

3 ⌁ DOCUMENTS

In some chapters you will find documents interspersing the narrative, along with questions in the margin. These are not just illustrations or separate exercises but an important part of the narrative. They fill a gap in the text; by answering the questions on the documents you will in effect be writing that part of the text for yourself. It is important to note down the facts and quotations you draw from these documents to ensure your notes are complete.

4 ⌁ BIBLIOGRAPHIES

At the end of each chapter there is a short bibliography, with a brief comment on the usefulness of each book. There is a starring system for those that are particularly recommended.

A problem with any reading list is that it becomes almost instantly out of date. One way to keep up with the latest views is to read a journal regularly, with an eye on the reviews section. *History Today* and *History Review* (see www.historytoday.com for both) are the most accessible and attract contributions from leading historians.

5 ~ STRUCTURED AND ESSAY QUESTIONS

There are a number of structured and essay questions at the end of each chapter to show the range possible. It is a good idea to read through these questions before you work on the chapter, to help you to pick out what is most important in the text.

6 ~ EXERCISES

There are a variety of exercises following each chapter to help in developing your ideas and in organising the material. Two types of exercise recur frequently:

- advice on answering structured questions and essays which will help you to develop the skills necessary to select and deploy the necessary information and to construct clear and convincing arguments;
- source exercises. The extracts from documents are longer than those within the text or those normally used at GCSE, so it is necessary to read them two or three times before answering the questions. It is also advisable to review the relevant section of the preceding chapter, and to follow up references to other historians' views which you may want to support or criticise in the light of your own source-based findings.

The Wars of the Roses

INTRODUCTION

The Wars of the Roses between 1450 and 1487 may have seen little of the 'sackage, carnage and wreckage' described in '1066 and All That', but nevertheless the throne did change hands violently no less than five times: in 1461, 1470, 1471, 1483 and 1485. Moreover, three kings died violently: Henry VI in 1471, Edward V in 1483 and Richard III in 1485. Thus these wars were the most serious episode of instability in England between the wars of King Stephen in the twelfth century and the English Civil War in the seventeenth. They were the background to the precarious establishment of the Tudor dynasty which was to stamp its image so firmly on the history of England.

The origin of the Wars of the Roses stretches back to 1399 when King Richard II was deposed by his cousin who became King Henry IV. Henry was the first Lancastrian king. (He was the son of Edward III's second son, John of Gaunt, Duke of Lancaster.) Henry's right to the throne was insecure, but he survived a series of threats to his throne, and when his son succeeded him as Henry V in 1413, the Lancastrian dynasty seemed firmly established. Henry V went on to win the battle of Agincourt and conquer half of France; his authority was indisputable. However, when he died in 1422, his son, who was only an infant, succeeded him as Henry VI. A royal **minority** was always feared as a time when, without the strong leadership of an adult king, the nobility would compete for power and conflict would break out. Henry VI's capable uncles prevented this happening, but the really bad news was that, when Henry grew up, he proved to be a simple, pious man without political understanding or force of character. Under his rule, all the territories in France were lost except for Calais, and he left government in the hands of favourites who were resented by the rest of the nobility – and in particular by the powerful Duke of York, who was also a descendant of Edward III. As resentment and consequent conflict developed, the Duke of York and his followers moved from claiming their rights to claiming the throne. The Lancastrian symbol was the red rose, against the white rose of the Yorkists. The sporadic wars between these two royal houses became known later as the Wars of the Roses.

The Wars of the Roses lasted from the early 1450s until 1487. However, they were not by any means continuous. There were four very distinct episodes, each of which had its own causes and did not necessarily relate directly to previous events.

See page 5

Minority inheritance by a minor, someone under-age

- The first clash was at St Albans in 1455, although more a skirmish than a battle.
- Between 1459–61, there was serious fighting leading to the bloody battle of Towton and the overthrow of the Lancastrian Henry VI by the Yorkist Edward IV.
- Further conflict between 1469–71 saw the temporary return of Henry VI and the eventual triumph of Edward IV.
- Edward's brother, Richard III, succeeded him in 1483, and was likely to have been the murderer of Edward's sons, the Princes in the Tower. Richard was defeated and killed at the Battle of Bosworth in 1485 by Henry Tudor who became Henry VII and founder of the Tudor dynasty.

Two separate issues need to be examined – first, the sequence of events that brought about the overthrow of Henry VI, Edward IV and Richard III, and second, any general causes that underlay the instability of this period.

1 ⌐ HENRY VI AND THE CRISIS OF THE 1450S

PICTURE 1
Henry VI, *anon.*
(HM the Queen)

Henry VI was one of the most unfortunate and unsuccessful of English monarchs. The circumstances of his birth suggested otherwise. His father, Henry V, had destroyed the French army at Agincourt in 1415 and established a huge English empire in France. The Treaty of Troyes (1420) made Henry V heir to the French throne, and the French King's daughter, Katharine, became his wife.

Henry VI inherited this vast empire in 1422, but within 35 years Lancastrian power in France was confined to the port of Calais and English rule was never to return. It would be easy simply to blame Henry VI for these catastrophic disasters. It certainly did not help the English that Henry V's death (31 August 1422) followed the birth of his son (6 December 1421) by only a few months. However, the government of the country during Henry VI's childhood was relatively stable and competent and the English were able to maintain their grip in France.

France was a much more populous and wealthy country than England and English influence was always likely to decline if a stronger and more capable French government emerged. Despite the coronation of Henry VI as King of France at Paris in 1431, the French claimant to the throne, Charles VII, began to consolidate his position in the 1430s. The English had always depended for their success on alliance with the Dukes of Brittany and Burgundy. The Dukes of Burgundy were wealthy and powerful rulers, who controlled much of eastern France and the Low Countries. In 1435, the French and Burgundians allied. The destruction of the Lancastrian empire in France was now simply a matter of time.

Nonetheless, Henry VI's reaction to these events was inept. By 1437, he had taken personal control of the government of the country. His marriage, in 1445, to Margaret of Anjou, was a typical error in political terms. She brought with her no dowry (land or money) and, therefore, no political benefit to the English Crown. Despite the lingering reputation of military invincibility, by August 1450 Normandy was lost to the King of France.

Even more devastating was the collapse of English power in Gascony in the south-west of France, as we shall see. This had belonged to the English monarchy for 300 years, but in July 1451 Bordeaux fell to the French. Dissident Gascons invited the English back the next year and an army was sent under the veteran Sir John Talbot, Earl of Shrewsbury, the most able and feared English general. In July 1453 his army was utterly defeated at Castillion and he was killed. The Hundred Years War had ended in ignominious defeat. Only Calais remained of the English possessions in France.

It would be absurd to blame Henry VI entirely for this. It might even be argued that the campaigns of his father had been foolish and ill-conceived, and that it was unrealistic over the long term for England to challenge France. But Henry VI holds much of the responsibility for the devastating rapidity and finality of the French victory. Traditionally, war with France had been a popular policy in England, which was invariably supported by Parliament. The completeness of the English defeat was a devastating blow. With the exception of Calais, the coast-line facing England was now in enemy hands and there was growing fear of French raids. To compound the problem in the summer of 1453 Henry suffered a complete nervous breakdown, possibly caused by defeat at Castillion.

Defeat in France was not Henry's only problem. Another major source of complaint was his method of governing the country. It was essential that any monarch should attempt to gain support and popularity from all sections of the aristocracy, on whom he was so dependent for assistance in governing the country. There were few paid royal servants and the aristocracy was the main agent of government in the provinces. The main technique for gaining their support was the use of **patronage**. This meant the distribution of titles, land, and government office to the great landowners of the realm. In return, they would enforce royal authority in the shires and provide manpower for the king.

It was essential that patronage should be distributed evenly and fairly. It was in this task that Henry proved singularly inept. In the 1440s he came to rely on a small group of favourites attached to the **Royal Household**. In particular, he favoured the Beaufort family. They were of royal blood and descended, like the King, from John of Gaunt, Edward III's third son. Originally, their line was illegitimate (John of Gaunt had only married the mother of the first Beauforts after they had been born), but the family was legitimised in 1397 and quickly became prominent. By the 1440s the Beaufort family, who became Dukes of Somerset, had accumulated vast amounts of patronage and influence. Even more important was another aristocrat, not of royal blood, the Duke of Suffolk. He owed his ascendancy to his influence over the

KEY ISSUE

How far was defeat in France the fault of Henry VI?

Patronage the granting of posts or other favours to secure support

Royal Household the king's living quarters, but also the centre of much government activity which focused on him

HENRY VI (1421–71)

It is hard to disagree with Professor Pollard's view that Henry was 'perhaps the most unsuited to rule of all the kings of England since the Norman Conquest'. Crowned in London in 1429, and in Paris in 1431, he assumed full regal powers in 1437. In 1440 he founded both Eton College and King's College, Cambridge, and he was piously devoted to both institutions for the rest of his life. He married Margaret of Anjou in 1445, eventually siring an heir (Edward, Prince of Wales) in 1453, but by 1450 the realm was in the throes of the biggest crisis since the reign of Richard II. The territories in France were lost, Henry faced rebellion at home, and key supporters were murdered. Then, at this key time, in 1453, he suffered a mental breakdown; he could not even recognise his own child. He recovered, although it was his wife, Margaret of Anjou, who was by now the effective leader of the Lancastrian cause and Henry was a mere figurehead. With this power vacuum at the centre, war broke out. Henry was captured no less than three times – at the first Battle of St Albans in 1455, at Northampton in 1460, and, following four years of wandering in the north of England after Towton, in 1465. He resumed the throne in 1470–1 after Warwick's rebellion, but the defeat of the Lancastrians at two major battles in 1471 sealed his fate. He was murdered in the Tower of London in 1471. Henry had been the victim of ruthless opponents, but it is hard to disagree with KB McFarlane's rueful conclusion: 'Only an under-mighty ruler had anything to fear from over-mighty subjects'.

King. He and his close allies, Adam Moleyns and Lord Saye and Sele were given land, money and office by the King in a thoughtless and extravagant fashion. They became particularly prominent in East Anglia and the South-east. It seemed that the only criterion for gaining royal patronage was to be a member of the King's Household.

This might not have mattered if these had been men of ability, but they were mostly closely associated with the disastrous events in France. In particular, Edmund Beaufort, Duke of Somerset, was – with some justice – held responsible for the defeats in Normandy. At home there was further strong criticism of these men. The support of the aristocracy was vital if law and order was to be maintained in the shires. A growing number of aristocrats and other ambitious men began to believe that members of the King's Household were unduly favoured and that royal justice was being manipulated in the interests of a faction. Lord Saye and Sele, for example, was entrusted with vast amounts of land and influence in Kent by the King. He became Constable of Dover Castle and Warden of the Cinque Ports. The county, however, was notorious for its disorder and Henry was blamed for this. In his excellent biography of Henry VI, Ralph Griffiths comments: 'To ensure social stability and public order, a circumspect government needed to avoid antagonising prominent **magnates** … Wise, and as far as politics

Magnate a leading nobleman

allowed, impartial patronage was the key to regional control'. Henry's patronage went to a narrow circle of favourites and left other powerful aristocrats out in the cold. Their resentment turned into sullen resistance and finally rebellion.

KEY ISSUE

Why did faction become a particular problem under Henry VI?

2 ∽ OPPOSITION TO THE GOVERNMENT 1450–3

The great favours granted to the house of Beaufort were bound to offend other families of royal blood. By far the most important was the family of Richard, Duke of York. He was descended from another son of Edward III and was one of the greatest landowners in the country. His estates were widely scattered throughout England and also in Ireland. He was particularly well endowed with land on the Welsh borders.

Richard was ten years older than Henry, and there seems always to have been some mutual antagonism. In July 1440, he was appointed Lieutenant-Governor of Normandy for five years. There is no evidence that he made much of what was admittedly a very difficult position. It is clear that Henry favoured the Beauforts over him and that Richard left his position owed a large amount of money by the Crown. He was then sent to Ireland for ten years to recover lands lost to the Irish,

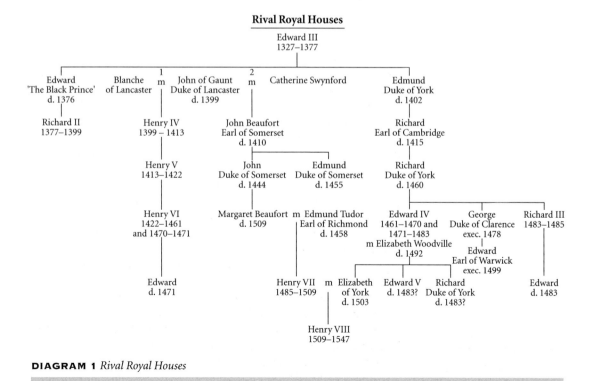

DIAGRAM 1 *Rival Royal Houses*

further emphasising his isolation from the centre of affairs. It seemed likely that Henry would choose a Beaufort in preference to him as his successor should he remain childless.

As for Parliament, at this time it was the King's servant and generally very obedient. The King could summon and dismiss Parliament entirely at his own convenience and **statute** law gave authority to royal policies. However, under normal circumstances, the King was expected to 'live of his own' on the revenues of his own estates and customs duties which were traditionally granted for life. Additional taxation had to be approved by Parliament and this was rarely possible, except for a popular military campaign.

The Parliament which assembled in November 1449 was not compliant. The disastrous situation in France was becoming clear, while foreign trade was at a standstill thanks to an embargo by Philip, Duke of Burgundy. This reduced cloth exports to the Netherlands, which were the basis of English wealth, by one-third.

Parliament blamed these disasters on the clique which surrounded Henry VI. As a result of threatening political unrest, Henry's hand was forced and the Duke of Suffolk was sent to the Tower. He was released in May 1450 and then murdered as he went into exile. His close supporter, Adam Moleyns, had already been murdered the previous January by unpaid and mutinous soldiers at Portsmouth.

Finally, a genuinely popular rebellion broke out in Kent. Disaffection was understandable in this part of England; there was a growing fear of French invasion, and trade with the Low Countries had virtually ceased. Kent was a county with a large number of independent farmers, who were not closely dependent on a particular lord, and there was resentment at the patronage granted to Lord Saye and Sele, one of Henry's most unpopular supporters.

The rebellion broke out in May 1450 under the leadership of Jack Cade who claimed to be connected with the family of Richard of York. The rebels' demands were very specific: first of all that the King's Council should include all the great aristocrats of the country and second they supported Parliament in demanding **Acts of Resumption**. In this way the King would be able to live of his own and would require no parliamentary taxation. A first Act of Resumption was passed in May 1450, but a mob still executed Lord Saye and Sele in July after Henry had fled from London.

There is no evidence that the Duke of York inspired Jack Cade's rebellion. Moreover, despite the King's weakness, his wife, Margaret of Anjou, proved a formidable figure and helped to organise the dispersal of the rebels. But Richard of York did return in September 1450 from Ireland. He was not seeking the Crown, but he wanted to consolidate his position as heir to the throne, and saw an opportunity in Henry VI's political difficulties. He also resented Henry's continued favouritism towards his rival, the Duke of Somerset.

Despite its problems, Henry's regime survived. In part this reflects the power of the monarchy in the fifteenth century. A man like Richard of York may have associated himself with popular discontent, but was

Statute a parliamentary law (as opposed to Common Law, accumulated judicial decisions)

KEY ISSUE

Why was Parliament not as compliant as normal in 1449?

Acts of Resumption parliamentary laws restoring lands to the Crown which the King had previously given away

KEY ISSUE

What was the significance of Jack Cade's rebellion?

clearly essentially a self-interested and disappointed intriguer. Henry also now asserted himself more effectively than ever before in his reign. Parliamentary grievances were addressed by a second and more effective Act of Resumption later in 1450. Henry also made a concerted effort to deal with problems of law and order at a time when, throughout the country, violence was believed to be increasing dramatically. In 1451, he toured Kent and in 1452–3 there were further tours to other areas in which he acted as judge and used his power and influence to enforce the law.

Richard of York did mount a half-hearted conspiracy, but was forced to back down in March 1452. By 1453, the restoration of royal authority was so complete that a Parliament at Reading voted sufficient funds to raise 20 000 men to re-conquer France.

> **KEY ISSUE**
>
> *How did Henry VI restore his authority by 1453?*

3 ✐ ROYAL MADNESS AND THE DRIFT TO CIVIL WAR 1453–9

Despite the weaknesses of Henry's government revealed from 1449 onwards – the sustained challenge to his regime arising from military failure in France, the favouritism towards a small circle of courtiers, the irresponsible distribution of land and office, and the failure to maintain order – it seemed possible by early 1453 that royal authority would be restored. It was hoped Sir John Talbot would re-conquer Gascony, and by then the most unpopular royal servants were dead. Acts of Resumption had been passed and the King had toured the South of England in a fairly successful attempt to restore order.

Two events shattered this progress. In August 1453, news arrived of the disaster at Castillion, which destroyed forever the chance of re-establishing an English empire in France. At the same time, and possibly as a direct result, Henry VI suffered a complete breakdown which lasted for 18 months. Certain diagnosis of his condition is of course impossible, but it seems likely that it was some form of schizophrenia. For the rest of his life, his mental health was always fragile.

The incapacity of the King meant that government of the country had to be reorganised with some urgency. A further complicating factor was the birth of an heir to the throne, Prince Edward, in October 1453. The Queen, Margaret of Anjou, possessed the energy and strength of character that her husband increasingly lacked. Her determination to ensure that their son succeeded Henry as king was to be at the centre of the struggle for power over the next two decades.

Richard of York was an obvious candidate to become 'Protector', who would deputise for the king while his illness lasted, but there were other claimants, such as the Duke of Exeter and Edmund Beaufort, Duke of Somerset. Success in the struggle for power would depend on the attitude of the other great aristocrats. Most important of these was Richard Neville, Earl of Warwick.

> **KEY ISSUE**
>
> *What were the most important consequences of the royal madness?*

PROFILE

RICHARD NEVILLE, EARL OF WARWICK, 'THE KING-MAKER' (1428–71)

Warwick is the exemplar of the fifteenth century 'over-mighty subject'. He was a leading member of the Neville family, who had risen to prominence largely by virtue of their ability to produce children and make successful marriages to great heiresses. Originally their power was concentrated in the North of England, where the need to defend the border against the raids of the Scots created a warlike atmosphere and a large number of experienced fighting men. Richard Neville inherited his family's traditional enmity towards the neighbouring northern magnate family, the Percies. With huge estates centred on the impressive castle of Middleham in North Yorkshire he vied with his Percy neighbours for royal patronage, including the prestigious wardenships of the **Marches** on the Scottish border. He became Earl of Warwick in 1449 and inherited great estates in the Midlands on his marriage to the Warwick heiress Anne Beauchamp. In dispute himself with the Duke of Somerset over land, he was a supporter of Richard, Duke of York in his quarrel with the Lancastrians, and was to be a key figure in the ensuing wars. He was to defeat and capture Henry VI at Northampton in 1460, and helped York's son to take the throne as Edward IV. Warwick, however, was to fall out with Edward in the 1460s over foreign policy and prospective marriage alliances for his daughters. Allied with the Edward's mercurial younger brother George, Duke of Clarence, who had also expected more favours from the King, Warwick rebelled in 1469. In 1470 in a dramatic change of sides Warwick, supported by King Louis XI of France, concluded an alliance with Margaret of Anjou, whereby his younger daughter Anne would marry her son Edward, Prince of Wales, and Warwick would engineer the restoration of Henry VI to the throne. This he achieved, and became known to history as the King-maker, but his triumph was short-lived The following year Warwick was killed at the Battle of Barnet, and the Neville cause was lost.

Marches border territories, either on the border with Scotland or Wales

Given the support of key noblemen, such as Warwick, Richard of York won the power struggle against Henry VI's favourites. In November 1453, Somerset was sent to the Tower, and on 27 March 1454 Richard of York was finally appointed 'Protector and Defender of the Kingdom of England and Chief Councillor of the King'.

York did not govern the country badly, but he could not pretend to have the support of all the great aristocrats. In particular, the Duke of Somerset and Henry Percy, Earl of Northumberland, were bound to be foes of a Yorkist/Neville alliance, and Margaret of Anjou would be suspicious that Richard of York sought the throne.

Everything was thrown into confusion by the recovery of Henry by Christmas 1454. Somerset was released from prison and restored to the vital position of Captain of Calais which gave him control of a garrison of 1000 men. York and Warwick fled to the North and were then summoned to a Great Council at Leicester in May 1455. The estates of the house of Lancaster were concentrated in this part of the Midlands, which increasingly became the centre of royal power.

To defend their position York and Warwick raised an army and marched on London. They clashed with the forces of their opponents at St Albans on 22 May 1455. This was a skirmish rather than a battle, with only a few casualties. But two of the dead were Somerset and Henry Percy, Earl of Northumberland.

St Albans may have seemed a triumph for Richard of York and some benefits were gained. The Earl of Warwick became Captain of Calais and turned it into a Yorkist stronghold. For a few months between November 1455 and February 1456 Richard again acted as Protector as Henry relapsed into insanity.

But there is no evidence of widespread support for the Yorkists and Nevilles. Indeed, they had shed blood and earned the hostility of many other aristocrats. Moreover, Henry may have been in serious decline, but Margaret of Anjou was a formidable and determined antagonist, anxious to protect her son's right to the throne.

The years between 1455 and the outbreak of serious fighting in 1459 are not well documented by contemporary historians and the pattern is not always clear. Some attempts were made to reconcile the opposing factions. In March 1458, there was a 'Loveday' when the victors of the Battle of St Albans met the sons of the men who had been killed and performed a public act of reconciliation. But this seems to have been an isolated incident. More important was the exclusion once again of the Yorkists and Nevilles from government. The Earl of Warwick used his base at Calais to raise funds by piracy, while York withdrew to his estates.

Meanwhile, Margaret of Anjou governed the country increasingly from the Midlands, where there was the greatest concentration of Lancastrian estates. The city of Coventry was her main base. Coventry was a centre of cloth-making and the fourth largest city in the country; its population was loyal to the King. The move to Coventry suggested a lack of confidence amongst the Lancastrians that they could be sure of the loyalty of the people of London and of those aristocrats who were not their personal followers.

In the summer of 1459, a Lancastrian council at Coventry finally decided to accuse the Yorkists and Nevilles of treason. Their response was to raise armies. Richard of York raised a force in the Welsh Marches while the Nevilles drew on their strength in north Yorkshire and Calais. After a skirmish at Blore Heath, they moved to Ludlow shadowed by a larger royal army. The troops from Calais were led by Andrew Trollope, an able veteran of the wars in France. They were shocked to discover that they were expected to fight the King and changed sides. York and Warwick had no option but to abandon the struggle, and on the night

TIMELINE

1421	Henry VI became king
1437	Henry took personal control of government
1445	Marriage to Margaret of Anjou
1450	Jack Cade's rebellion
1451	Loss of Bordeaux
1452	Failure of conspiracy by Richard, Duke of York
1453	Defeat at Castillion Henry had a nervous breakdown Prince Edward born
1454	Richard of York became Protector Henry's recovery
1455	1st Battle of St Albans
1459	'The Parliament of Devils'

Acts of Attainder This legal procedure declared an individual a traitor, and enabled the king to confiscate his property

Does the responsibility for the outbreak of war lie with Margaret of Anjou?

ANALYSIS

Bastard feudalism Feudalism was the holding of land from a lord in return for military service to him. Bastard feudalism was when service was given in return for pay, favours or bribes

Retainers a noble's followers, who made up his retinue

of 12 October they decided to flee. York escaped to Ireland and Warwick returned to Calais.

The rebels had attracted very little support, but their resources were so vast that this had not really mattered. Understandably Margaret of Anjou was determined to follow up the Lancastrian triumph. A Parliament was summoned to Coventry known to Yorkists as the 'Parliament of Devils'. **Acts of Attainder** were passed against the rebels. This legal procedure effectively combined an accusation of treason with the loss of civil rights. The Yorkists and Nevilles were faced with permanent legal condemnation and the confiscation of their estates. Inevitably they would try to reverse this situation, and the Wars of the Roses proper began.

The Causes of the Wars of the Roses

Some historians have tried to find economic or cultural factors in the Wars' origins. It has been argued, for example, that landowners, suffering from falling rents and soaring labour costs, entered into a more acute and pressing competition for patronage to boost their income. However, it can be shown that most of the protagonists were in fact wealthier than their fathers, often benefiting through marriage, inheritance and royal favour.

'**Bastard feudalism**' has also been put forward as a cause. Yet this practice had existed since the beginning of the fourteenth century, so that **retainers** enrolled by cash contracts were familiar well before the crisis of the 1450s. The greatest twentieth-century historian of the fifteenth century, KB MacFarlane, pointed out that the number of retainers rarely exceeded eighty and that they were 'an expression of the Lord's need for service in peace rather than in war'. Rather than promoting instability, retaining created loyalty and helped to organise the social, political, and administrative life of the counties. He argued that 'On the whole, hierarchical bonds of loyalty and service which bound kings, lords, and retainers, made for social and political stability'.

RL Storey, however, widened the argument, suggesting that 'an escalation of private feuds' was the key component. It is not difficult to find examples of such quarrels, the best known being that between the Percies and the Nevilles in the north. AJ Pollard goes further, seeing the root cause of the wars as the excessive influence overall of the upper nobility, whose wealth and power increased from the fourteenth century onwards as many married into the royal family. This did not matter when the war with France was going well, but after 1340, Edward III 'allowed the gap in power and influence [between the King and aristocracy] to narrow'. He argues that this made the government of the country much more difficult unless the monarch was unusually able. It is certainly true that at crucial times, the Nevilles, Stanleys and even Woodvilles determined the course of events.

The violence and instability of the period was much amplified by the weakness at the centre of government, especially when the hapless Henry VI, far from being an unusually able monarch, presided over a corrupt and partial regime. This has been emphasised by a recent authority on the war, Christine Carpenter. Henry V may well have been a hard act to follow – especially at a time when the task of monarchy was more testing than before – but it is difficult to dissent from KB McFarlane's pithy analysis: 'Henry VI's head was too small for his father's crown'.

4 ⌁ THE FIRST WARS 1459–61

These two years saw the most sustained fighting of the Wars of the Roses. In June 1460 after consulting with Richard of York in Dublin, Warwick landed in Kent. Accompanied by York's son, Edward (the Earl of March and later to be Edward IV), he marched to Northampton where the Lancastrian army was defeated and the wretched King captured. The Yorkists then marched to London and summoned a Parliament to meet in October. Its main purpose, of course, would be to reverse the Acts of Attainder and so regain their positions and their estates.

However, when Richard of York returned to England, for the first time he laid claim to the throne. There is no evidence that this had always been his aim. Indeed, he seems to have surprised his closest supporters. It was agreed that he should succeed Henry VI on the latter's death.

This was an unworkable compromise and particularly unacceptable to Margaret of Anjou whose son would be denied the throne. Further fighting was inevitable. In December at Wakefield, Richard of York was killed and it looked as though the Yorkist cause was doomed. Although in February 1461 there was a Yorkist victory under the leadership of Richard's son, Edward (now Duke of York), at Mortimer's Cross, it was cancelled out by defeat for Warwick at the second Battle of St Albans and the recovery of Henry VI by his supporters.

Margaret of Anjou now had Henry as her figurehead and a clear road to London. She failed to seize this outstanding opportunity and withdrew to the North. This seems an inexplicable decision, but her army had mainly been recruited in the North and Yorkist propaganda

TIMELINE

September 1459	Blore Heath – Indecisive
October 1459	Ludford Bridge – Lancastrian victory
July 1460	Northampton – Yorkist victory
December 1460	Wakefield – Lancastrian victory
February 1461	Mortimer's Cross – Yorkist victory
February 1461	St Albans – Lancastrian victory
March 1461	Towton – Yorkist Victory

MAP 1
The main battles in the Wars of the Roses

Hedgeley Moor 1464 ✕

✕
Hexham 1464

Towton 1461
✕
✕
Wakefield 1460

✕ Stoke 1487
✕ Blore Heath 1459

Bosworth 1485 ✕   ✕ Lose-Cote Field 1470

Mortimer's ✕✕ Ludford 1459
Cross 1461

✕ Northampton 1460

✕
Tewkesbury 1471   Edgecote 1469
St Albans ✕✕ Barnet
1455 & 1461   ✕ 1471
London

0   50   100
Scale (km)

✕ Battles

had convinced the population of London that a band of uncontrollable barbarians was approaching the city. Margaret had probably calculated that resistance to the Lancastrians would have been too great.

This hesitancy enabled Warwick and Edward of York to seize London and in March 1461 Edward was proclaimed King. Edward IV was a formidable opponent for the Lancastrians. His energy and appearance – he was a notably handsome man and well over six feet tall – contrasted starkly with the enfeebled Henry VI. He quickly raised an army and marched to meet the Lancastrians.

By far the bloodiest battle of the Wars of the Roses took place at Towton near Pontefract in south Yorkshire on 28–9 March 1461. Estimates of the numbers involved in battles of this period are notoriously unreliable, but the armies at Towton were certainly huge by the standards of the day and may have reached 25 000. The battle was fought in a blizzard and brought complete victory to Edward IV. Margaret of Anjou and Prince Edward fled to Scotland. Henry VI wandered as a fugitive in northern England until his capture and imprisonment by the Yorkists in 1465.

KEY ISSUE

Why were the Lancastrians defeated by 1461?

5 ⌒ EDWARD IV: THE EARLY YEARS 1461–9

Edward had the appearance and physical dynamism of a true king. His record has been much debated. He undoubtedly made serious mistakes leading to the loss of the throne between 1469–71. His methods of government, especially after 1471, anticipate the vigorous and effective approach of the first of the Tudors, Henry VII. On the other hand much of his success appears to be the result of good luck rather than wise policies and his failure to secure the peaceful accession to the throne of his son after his death, as we shall see, must be accounted a great failure.

Edward started his reign facing major problems. In the words of his biographer, Charles Ross, 'Towton had discredited but not destroyed the Lancastrian cause'. Margaret of Anjou and Prince Edward would be invaluable figureheads for any foreign power or discontented aristocrat who wished to challenge the King. There were still Lancastrian strongholds in remote corners of the kingdom. In Northumberland Lancastrians retained control of Alnwick, Bamburgh and Dunstanburgh castles. Twice they were driven out only to return, until their final defeat in the summer of 1464. Harlech Castle remained in Lancastrian hands until 1468.

PICTURE 2
Edward IV, *anon.*
(HM the Queen)

In order to retain the throne, Edward needed broad-based aristocratic support. The Earl of Warwick's reputation as the 'King-maker' is something of an exaggeration; he was less successful in battle than Edward. But his influence was still vast. In the South, he was Captain of Calais, Constable of Dover Castle, and Warden of the Cinque Ports. In the North, Warwick now held the Wardenships of both the Eastern and Western Marches on the Scottish border for the Neville family and so had sole responsibility for the defence of northern England against the Scots. The gentry of north Yorkshire provided a strongly loyal band of personal retainers with a tradition of violence.

During the 1460s, Warwick became estranged from Edward IV. This was partly a consequence of his arrogance and ambition and dislike of other Councillors, such as Sir William (later Lord) Hastings who was Edward IV's most loyal supporter. Edward was, however, the sole author of some of his difficulties. In particular, his marriage to Elizabeth Woodville in 1464 was a crucial and avoidable error.

Romantic considerations generally played no part in the marriages of fifteenth-century kings and aristocrats. A well-chosen bride could bring a beneficial foreign alliance, or valuable land and wealth. The power of the Nevilles, for instance, was based above all on their marriages to wealthy heiresses. Edward, however, was an impulsive and sensual man, and it does seem that romantic considerations determined his decision to marry Elizabeth Woodville. Although her mother, Jacquetta of Luxemburg, came from a great European aristocratic family, her father, the first Earl Rivers, was a minor aristocrat, and the new Queen with her family were disdained as upstarts.

The marriage was to bring Edward no political or economic benefits. The great magnates of the realm had not been consulted at a time when Warwick was actively negotiating a French marriage alliance and he was entitled to feel aggrieved. A further cause of grievance was the huge Woodville family. Elizabeth had two sons by a previous marriage, five brothers and seven sisters. The simplest way to advance their position was to find wealthy marriage partners for them. This cut across the Earl of Warwick's own ambitions. He had two daughters, Isabel and Ann, and wanted suitable husbands for them. Edward IV seems to have opposed Warwick's plan for Isabel to marry his younger brother, the Duke of Clarence.

There was also a growing division over foreign policy between the King and Warwick. Warwick favoured an alliance with France, while Edward IV and the Woodvilles looked to Burgundy. The Netherlands, ruled by the Dukes of **Burgundy**, were the most important market for English cloth and economically crucial. Anti-French policies were universally popular and it does seem that Edward's strategy was sounder than Warwick's. In 1467 a trade treaty was signed with Burgundy and Edward's sister, Margaret of York, married Duke Charles of Burgundy. Warwick's own negotiations with Louis XI of France failed completely and his brother George Neville, the Archbishop of York, was dismissed as **Lord Chancellor**.

Warwick retreated to the North and used his influence amongst his retainers to stir up uprisings against Edward. Meanwhile, his daughter, Isabel, was married to the Duke of Clarence, Edward's volatile and untrustworthy younger brother.

6 ⌐ POLITICAL CRISIS 1469–71

The next two years saw a return to political chaos. Warwick and Clarence initially used Calais as a base. On their return to England they won a victory at Edgecote (26 July 1469), and this was followed by the capture of Edward IV and the ruthless execution of two Woodvilles, Lord Rivers and Sir John Woodville.

However, Warwick's lack of widespread aristocratic and popular support was soon exposed. He was forced to release Edward from Middleham Castle. Edward took steps to counter Warwick's influence in the North by restoring Henry Percy to the Earldom of Northumberland and returning many of his family estates lost after rebellion 50 years previously. Edward next returned to London in October 1469. Neither side was strong enough to defeat the other and uneasy stalemate ensued.

Warwick now proclaimed the Duke of Clarence as his candidate for the throne. They inspired a rising in Lincolnshire in March 1470, but it was easily suppressed by Edward at 'Lose-Cote Field, and in May 1470 they fled to France.

Louis XI of France was nicknamed 'the universal spider', and was a cunning and unprincipled intriguer. It was he who inspired a most

Burgundy A powerful duchy which included modern day Belgium and the Netherlands, and part of eastern France

Lord Chancellor the head of the judiciary and the most important minister of the Crown

KEY ISSUE

How did Warwick become so great a threat to Edward IV by 1469?

unlikely alliance between Warwick and Margaret of Anjou in July 1470. They agreed to restore Henry VI and marry Prince Edward (Henry's son) to Ann, Warwick's younger daughter.

In September 1470, Warwick returned once again to England. He was joined by Clarence and Jasper Tudor, who was the staunchest supporter of the Lancastrian cause. Edward IV has been accused of complacency in the face of these events, but he was unavoidably detained by continued disaffection in Yorkshire. What is strange is the speed with which his authority collapsed. This can be partially explained by the defection of another key supporter, John, Marquis Montagu, who was Warwick's brother and had lost both land and influence as a result of the restoration of the Percies.

In October, Edward was forced to flee virtually penniless to the Netherlands. In the legal phraseology of the day the '**re-adeption**' of Henry VI followed. Henry's new regime was always unstable. The Lancastrians and Nevilles were only united in their opposition to Edward IV, while the Duke of Clarence had gained little power and patronage from his selfish actions. In order to survive, Henry needed a vigour and unity which he was unlikely to find. He also needed an effective foreign policy to prevent Edward securing the foreign assistance he would need to reclaim his throne.

Re-adeption the legal restoration of the king to his throne.

Charles the Bold, Duke of Burgundy, was a wealthy and ambitious ruler married to Edward IV's sister, Margaret. He was naturally worried by Warwick's links with France and the political debts that the Lancastrians owed to Louis XI of France. In 1471, Henry VI's government made a treaty with France and looked set to fight Burgundy. This was neither a popular nor a sensible policy. Burgundy was England's greatest trading partner and popular opinion was always anti-French. Charles of Burgundy's response was to give Edward 50 000 florins and some ships.

On 14 March 1471, Edward landed at Ravenspur on the Yorkshire coast. Initially he found little support, but at least Henry Percy, hostile to the Nevilles, remained neutral and did not hinder him. Edward now displayed his undisputed qualities of boldness and energy. He claimed to be only concerned with recovering his Duchy and built up a following from the vast estates of his close ally Lord Hastings in the Midlands. He was joined by his unreliable brother, the Duke of Clarence, who had gained little from Warwick and the Lancastrians.

Edward marched straight to London. If he gained control of London, it would be hard to dislodge him and it is significant that the citizens, who consistently seemed to have favoured Edward over Henry, admitted him without a struggle. On Easter Sunday (14 April) Edward's forces joined battle with Warwick's at Barnet. In a confused encounter in fog Warwick and Montagu were killed. The power of the Nevilles was broken.

Meanwhile, a Lancastrian army landed at Weymouth and, hearing of Warwick's defeat, began to march to Wales where the Lancastrians had a strong following. Edward IV again showed his decisiveness as a military leader and marched rapidly west. At Tewkesbury on 4 May the

TIMELINE

1464		Edward IV married Elizabeth Woodville
1467		Alliance with Burgundy; collapse of Warwick's negotiations with Louis XI of France
1469	July	Edgecote – Lancastrian/Neville victory
1470	March	'Lose-Cote' Field – Yorkist victory
	October	Re-adeption of Henry VI
1471	April	Barnet – Yorkist victory
1471	May	Tewkesbury – Yorkist victory
		Restoration of Edward IV

Lancastrians were cut off and crushed, and Henry VI's son, Prince Edward, the real hope of the Lancastrian dynasty, was killed. On Edward IV's return to London Henry VI disappeared, almost certainly murdered in the Tower.

Edward's recovery of the throne owed something to good luck, but he must be given great credit for seizing the initiative and taking well-calculated risks. Although there was some sporadic activity by Lancastrians over the next two years, there was now no really convincing Lancastrian claimant to the throne. Henry Tudor, who became the most active Lancastrian leader, had only a remote claim, and there seemed no reason why the Yorkist line should not establish itself permanently.

> **KEY ISSUE**
>
> *Why was the 'Re-adeption' of Henry VI a failure?*

7 ⌐ THE RULE OF EDWARD IV 1471–83

Edward IV was still a young and vigorous man in 1471. He quickly adopted a conciliatory policy towards his former opponents. There were only 13 Acts of Attainder confiscating great estates, six of which applied to the estates of dead men. Twenty-three earlier attainders were reversed. Able men, who had served the Lancastrian cause, entered Edward's service. A good example was John Morton. He had followed Margaret of Anjou into exile, but by 1478 was both Master of the Rolls (a leading judge) and Bishop of Ely; he later became one of Henry VII's most trusted servants. Special favour was given to Edward's younger brother, Richard of Gloucester. He succeeded Warwick as Great Chamberlain of England (controller of state occasions) and in 1471 was given Warwick's confiscated estates in the North. Richard's marriage to Warwick's daughter, Ann Neville, confirmed him as the King's representative in the North and the inheritor of Warwick's great influence.

New monarchy the term coined by historians to suggest that Edward IV (and later Henry VII) used innovative administrative and financial methods to govern the country

Edward's government of the country in these years has been closely scrutinised by historians. Many of his actions have been seen as anticipating the so-called '**new monarchy**' to follow in the reign of Henry VII so that continuity of aims, methods, and personnel between the two men is now often stressed. It is perhaps hardly surprising that two men with similar problems adopted similar policies. It is also clear that no grand strategy lay behind Edward's methods of government. He had no conscious political philosophy, but simply a desire to govern more efficiently.

A *Wales*

Although the government of England was relatively centralised compared to that of many European countries, effective government of the more remote regions remained difficult. (This is dealt with in depth in Chapter 11 'The Frontier Regions'.) The whole of Wales had been conquered by the English only relatively recently and its administration was particularly confused. The remote north and west had been divided into shires, run by Crown appointed **Justices of the Peace** as in England, but the border between Wales and England was still ruled by the Marcher Lords. 'March' simply means border and in this traditionally violent region, all powers of law and administration had been delegated to the Marcher Lords and the King's authority was only nominal.

Edward IV was himself a great Marcher Lord and in 1471 he created the Council in the Marches primarily to administer his own estates. But it was also necessary to combat the lawlessness of an area where no single authority responsible for law and order existed. In 1473, it was decided that the King's eldest son, the Prince of Wales, should live in Ludlow in the heart of the Marches and his Council became the centre of royal authority. (Although only a child, it was hoped he would become the focus of local loyalties.) In 1476, the Prince of Wales was given (in name at least) extensive legal powers in Wales and the Marches by what was known as a General **Commission of Oyer and Terminer**. In 1477 he was technically given control of the Earldom of March and in 1479 of the Earldom of Pembroke. Edward's policy, however, was no more than a series of improvisations. He was not prepared to abolish the Marcher lordships and create new shires with Crown appointed Justices of the Peace, as eventually happened in the reign of Henry VIII. The Prince's household was run by a Woodville, Anthony, Earl Rivers, which created suspicion amongst many other great aristocrats. On the other hand, a serious attempt had been made to co-ordinate and improve the administration of a notably violent region.

See page 278

Justices of the Peace the local, unpaid agents of the Crown. Usually gentry, they sat as magistrates and supervised administration at the shire level

Commission of Oyer and Terminer literally to hear (oyer) and determine (terminer), a commission granted judicial powers

B *The North*

Northern England presented special problems to any monarch at this time. There was a continued threat from Scotland and traditionally the local aristocrats had been given the task of organising the defence of the border. Many of the gentry felt a stronger loyalty to local magnates, such as the Nevilles and Percies, than to the King. Any great aristocrat in the North kept large retinues of retainers, virtually private armies.

Edward's policy in the North was made no change to the system of rule and was arguably short-sighted. First of all, Henry Percy was restored to the Earldom of Northumberland in 1470. The Percies had a great following and he effectively became the King's Lieutenant in Northumberland and an influential figure in Yorkshire.

Even more important was the role given to the King's younger brother, Richard of Gloucester. All the confiscated estates, offices, and influence of the Earl of Warwick passed into his hands. The wardenship

KEY ISSUE

What were the strengths and weaknesses of Edward IV's government of Wales and the North?

of the West March on the border of Scotland, for example, was to be hereditary in his family. Effectively, Edward was not extending royal power, but creating an over-mighty subject and concentrating a considerable amount of power in the hands of Richard of Gloucester. Richard had his own private council and a vast following inherited from the Nevilles. It was this regional influence that enabled him to seize power on Edward's death. It is also likely that the favouritism shown to Richard was one factor in the continued disaffection of Edward's other brother, the Duke of Clarence, whose plotting finally led to his execution (as tradition has it, drowned in a barrel of Malmsey wine) in 1478.

C *Administration and law and order*

Edward's government was intensely personal. He aimed to improve efficiency not through a visionary programme of reform, but by improving the vigour and quality of the government's personnel.

One important example of this was the growing number of letters and warrants issued under the signet, which was the seal carried by the King's secretary. This meant that there was an increasing amount of administration carried out directly by the King and his personal servants, bypassing established government officials. In doing this Edward IV was not making any substantial reform to government; but his closer personal control ensured government operated more effectively, more rapidly and more responsively to his wishes.

The King's Council retained its importance and its functions changed little. There is no doubt that many of Edward's personal servants were capable and effective, but he did lack a strong personal following in the provinces, such as that built up by Richard of Gloucester in the North, and there was always suspicion and jealousy of the Woodvilles. Edward made no consistent effort to restrain the power of the aristocracy. He still relied on the support of great families in the shires, such as the Stanleys in Lancashire and Cheshire. His failure to restrain aristocratic power can be contrasted unfavourably with the far more assertive Henry VII. If the country was not as lawless as in the reign of Henry VI, this simply reflected Edward's more powerful personality. No legal checks were placed on the aristocracy and their followings of retainers. In particular, nothing was done to control **livery**, or **maintenance**. These practices are often seen as examples of excessive noble power used irresponsibly in the provinces.

There is a shortage of good primary source material for this period to illustrate the unchecked power of the aristocracy. However, the 'Paston Letters' are a series of documents written by members of an important gentry family in East Anglia. They are amongst the earliest surviving family letters in English and give an unrivalled insight into the problems and preoccupations of a gentry family of this period, which persisted from the Wars of the Roses into Edward IV's reign.

The Pastons became involved in a complicated legal dispute over property which brought them into conflict with the Duke of Suffolk, who was one of the most powerful men in East Anglia. In 1465, he sent

Livery the badge or clothing showing allegiance by retainers to a particular nobleman. Often provoked the equivalent of gang warfare.

Maintenance the intimidation of a jury by supporters of a powerful man involved in the case

KEY ISSUE

In what ways was the aristocracy a threat to law and order?

a force of armed men against their property. Margaret Paston reported the incident in a letter a few days later.

1465, 27 October.

1 I was at Hellesdon upon Thursday last past and saw the place there, and in good faith there will be no creature think how foul and horribly it is arrayed but if they saw it. There cometh much people daily to wonder thereupon, both of Norwich and of other places, and
5 they speak shamefully thereof …

The Duke [of Suffolk]'s men ransacked the church and bare away all the good that was left there, both of ours and of the tenants, and left not so much but that they stood on the high altar and ransacked the images, and took away such as they might find, and put
10 away the parson out of the church till they had done, and ransacked every man's house in the town five or six times … If it might be, I would some men of worship might be sent from the King to see how it is, both there and at the lodge, ere than any snows come, that they may make report of the truth …

15 And at the reverence of God, speed your matters now, for it is too horrible a cost and trouble that we now have daily, and must have till it be otherwise; and your men dare not go about to gather up your livelihood, and we keep here daily more than three hundred persons for salvation of us and the place …

20 It is thought here that if my Lord of Norfolk would take upon him for you, and that he may have a commission for to inquire of such riots and robberies as hath be done to you and others in this country, then all the country will await upon him and serve your intent, for the people love and dread him more than any lord except the King
25 and my Lord of Warwick.

Q

1. *When Margaret Paston uses the term 'country' (line 23), what does she mean?*
2. *Why do you think that the Duke of Suffolk was able to organise such extensive acts of violence?*
3. *To whom did the Pastons look for assistance? What is the significance of this?*
4. *The letter makes direct reference to the power of the Earl of Warwick. With whom is his power compared and to whom was it passed on?*
5. *Why do you think that the 'Paston Letters' are so valued by historians of the fifteenth century?*

D *Parliament and finance*

Because disputes between monarchs and Parliament eventually came to assume such significance in English history, it is easy to misunderstand the role of Parliament. There is no evidence that Parliament either increased or decreased in importance in the reign of Edward IV. Parliament met six times in 23 years for a total of $84^1/_2$ weeks. Its major task was to carry out the King's business. For example, a Parliament was summoned in 1478 to secure the attainder of Clarence, declaring him a traitor and confiscating his estates. Fifty-four parliamentary statutes were passed in Edward's reign, mostly concerned with economic matters. In 1463, he was granted tunnage and poundage (customs revenues) for life. Apart from this he was expected to 'live of his own', that is, make do with the revenues of his estates and only ask for further taxes if war threatened.

The kings of England possessed limited resources compared with their continental rivals. Edward IV was the first king for 200 years to die solvent, which was an impressive achievement, although owing much to favourable circumstances as well as to good judgment. Inheritance and confiscation brought him much larger estates than those of Henry VI; but in addition Edward exercised closer control to put the royal finances on a sounder footing.

Henry VI had cut deep into his own revenues by making huge gifts of royal lands he could ill afford, and this irresponsible patronage had been a major cause of his unpopularity. A trade recession worsened matters in the middle of the century and greatly reduced customs revenues. Henry VI's annual revenues fell to £24 000 compared with £90 000 in the reign of Henry IV, 50 years before. Edward IV boosted revenue by a series of practical measures. Better foreign relations created an improved climate for trade, and customs revenues increased from an average of £25 000 at the start of his reign to £34 000 at the close. After the Treaty of Picquigny with France in 1475, a valuable pension (meaning an annual payment) of 50 000 gold crowns was agreed by the French King. A commercial treaty with Burgundy in 1478, which smoothed relations with England's most important trading partner, was only one of many successful trading agreements with foreign powers.

Another important source of revenue was the royal estates. In addition Edward's own Yorkist estates were extensive. The further confiscation of estates through Acts of Attainder added the lands of two dukes, five earls, one viscount and six barons. Edward also made money from the profits of wardships. **Wardship** gave the king the revenues of great estates when the heir was a child. Early in Edward's reign, this included the lands of the Duchy of Buckingham and the Earldom of Shrewsbury.

The most significant development in financial policy lay in the use of the King's **Chamber** rather than the **Exchequer** in the administration of the royal estates. The Exchequer traditionally ran the finances of the government, but its methods had become inefficient and cumbersome. The Chamber was the main state room at Court and housed the Lord Chamberlain's department within the Royal Household. Edward adopted a system that had been used on the Yorkist estates. Receivers (rent collectors) and surveyors (to establish what rents were due) were appointed and made directly responsible to the King's Chamber. This meant that money now went directly to the King and not through an inefficient bureaucracy.

Again matters were improved by a more direct and personal approach, which anticipated methods adopted by the Tudors. By 1475 Edward was solvent and did not need financial help from Parliament.

However, there were limits to his achievement. Not all the administrative improvements were effective; on royal estates, such as the Duchy of Lancaster, it proved particularly difficult to implement new ideas. He can also be criticised for distributing rather than keeping forfeited estates, thus letting future royal revenues go to others. Henry VII was a

Wardship A ward was an heiress to an estate. Wardship was where the king, or someone else granted the wardship, was entrusted with the task of protecting the heiress – and had the opportunity exploit her estates

Chamber this was the King's living quarters, where he dined and received visitors. Increasingly it became the centre of government business

Exchequer the government office with the formal responsibility for handling the king's finances. The name comes from the chequered board on which money was counted

far more efficient and single-minded administrator. In his last year royal revenues exceeded £104 000 compared with £65 000 under Edward.

Nonetheless Edward's achievement was outstanding in comparison with what had gone before. He had attained solvency after decades of royal debts mounting up, and annual royal revenues at £65 000 far exceeded the £25 000 under Henry VI. Finally, although Henry VII in turn was to surpass Edward in management of the royal finances, he saw the sense in his methods and was to adopt many of them himself.

KEY ISSUE

What lay behind Edward IV's financial success?

E *Foreign policy*

There was an intimate connection between foreign policy and financial stability throughout the fifteenth and sixteenth centuries. No monarch in any country was able to finance a war without borrowing vast sums and acquiring huge debts. One of the chief reasons for Edward's solvency was his avoidance of major foreign wars. However, luck and chance seem to have played a greater part in this than planning and foresight.

Edward was born at Rouen in Normandy, and his father played a major role in the wars with France. He remained attached to the idea of military success in France. Throughout the fifteenth century France increased in power. Its population and resources greatly exceeded England's, and Louis XI of France was a formidable ruler. Traditionally England had allied with Burgundy and Brittany against France, while Louis harboured territorial ambitions against both these states.

In 1472, Edward negotiated the Treaty of Châteaugiron with Brittany and promised to invade France, but the Bretons were defeated before any English invasion could take place. Despite the traditional popularity of war with France, Parliament was notably unenthusiastic about financing the war and in many ways Edward had a lucky escape.

This did not prevent further diplomatic and military planning. The Treaty of London (25 July 1474) united England and Burgundy in a plan to repeat Henry V's destruction of the French monarchy; Brittany then joined the alliance, and even Scotland – so often a useful ally for France – was neutralised. Parliament provided substantial financial support, and an army of over 11 000 was raised. This would be the largest force ever sent from England to France. By July 1475 Edward was established in Calais.

The seriousness of Edward's invasion plans has been questioned. He may simply have been trying to intimidate the French. Again, he was possibly saved by the lack of commitment of his allies. Charles the Bold of Burgundy had territorial ambitions to the east of his duchy and was reluctant to invade France. Edward's army lacked the experience of previous expeditions and was unlikely to have won great victories.

When the French offered a truce it was quickly accepted. This led later in 1475 to the Treaty of Picquigny. In many ways this was very favourable to Edward; it gave him 75 000 crowns to be followed by an annual pension of 50 000 crowns and freedom of trade with France. In return there was to be a seven-year truce and Louis' son was to marry

Edward's daughter. This French pension ensured that Edward no longer needed substantial grants from Parliament and contributed significantly to his solvency.

On the other hand it does seem that Edward had actively been seeking war and was only saved by good fortune. The death in battle of Charles the Bold at Nancy in 1477 enabled Louis XI to capture territory in Artois and Picardy in northern France. This directly threatened the vital English base of Calais and English trade with the Netherlands. Edward decided not to intervene, and it can be argued that Louis' combination of cunning diplomacy and bribery had completely neutralised England. It was felt that Edward now cared too much for money and a life of ease and luxury.

In his last years Edward further limited his freedom of action on the continent by his decision to invade Scotland. There had been a series of Scottish raids possibly encouraged by the French, to which Edward responded by sending an army to Edinburgh in 1482. Apart from the recovery of Berwick, little was gained. Meanwhile at Arras in 1482, Burgundy and France made peace. One result of this was that Louis stopped paying Edward his annual pension. In addition, French possession of Artois was confirmed and the threat to Calais made real. The marriage alliance with France, which had been agreed in the Treaty of Picquigny in 1475, never took place. Things did not in fact turn out as badly as it seemed they might; Louis died in 1483 and Burgundy had not collapsed completely. Also, Edward had not squandered lives and money on trying to renew the glory days of Henry V, which might well have been futile. On the other hand, there is no sign of coherence or effectiveness in Edward's foreign policy.

F *The end of the reign*

Edward IV died on 25 August 1483 at the age of 41. The cause of his death was probably a stroke, and an increasingly self-indulgent private life may have contributed to this. In many ways he can be regarded as a capable ruler. In his youth he had proved daring and decisive, and his audacious recovery of the throne in 1471 after the 're-adeption' of Henry VI was a remarkable personal achievement.

Much has been made of his financial success, but his personal extravagance, particularly in his later years, may have begun to threaten that. On the other hand, despite his generally unimpressive conduct of foreign policy, he did understand the importance of developing overseas trade.

There was an attractive side to his character. He was the first English king to possess a library, and Court circles encouraged the Caxton printing press. His physical presence and youthful dynamism enhanced the prestige of the monarchy. But he must be blamed for the consequences of his marriage and the succession crisis that followed his death. One major task for any king was to ensure a peaceful succession. The unpopularity of the Woodvilles and Edward's own lack of support amongst the aristocracy as a whole ensured that this would not happen.

TIMELINE

1472	Treaty of Châteaugiron with Brittany
1474	Treaty of London with Burgundy, later also Brittany and Scotland
1475	Treaty of Picquigny with France
1482	Invasion of Scotland Burgundy and France made peace – Edward lost his pension

KEY ISSUE

Was Edward IV just lucky that his foreign policy was not a disaster?

8 ➢ THE REIGN OF RICHARD III

The period between Edward's death and the Battle of Bosworth Field (August 1485) exemplifies the political instability of fifteenth-century England. Edward's brother, Richard of Gloucester, was able to seize the throne from his young nephew, Edward V, and declare himself King Richard III, only to be defeated in battle by Henry Tudor, a remote and virtually unconsidered claimant to the throne.

RICHARD III (1452–85)

Thou elvish marked, abortive and rooting hog! … ,
Thou slander of thy heavy mother's womb!
Thou loathed issue of thy father's loins!
Thou rag of honour! …

(William Shakespeare, *Richard III* Act 1, Scene III)

The reputation of certain English kings is so notorious that they are familiar even to those with no serious interest in history. One such figure is Richard III. His image as the evil hunchback who murdered his nephews, seized the throne and was then killed at Bosworth Field in 1485, is secure in our national mythology. Richard's notoriety seems strange. Many kings have been accused of murder and died violent deaths, but they are not so widely remembered.

It is not in fact difficult to establish why such controversy surrounds Richard III. First of all, William Shakespeare drew an unforgettable portrait of him as a tormented hunchback, which may not bear much resemblance to his looks or deeds, but is familiar to countless people who have never read a serious history book. The above quotation illustrates the venom constantly directed at Richard III by Shakespeare. In turn his sources were Tudor propagandists, such as Sir Thomas More, who portrayed Richard as the archetype of tyranny in order to promote in contrast the virtues of the Tudor dynasty.

Before he became king, however, Richard's reputation was of a loyal, pious, chivalric and courageous nobleman, who enjoyed especial popularity in the North of England. He was Edward IV's youngest brother who had accompanied him back to England from the Netherlands in 1461 at the age of 9. He was later the Duke of Gloucester, and was well rewarded for his support by Edward IV. He married the Earl of Warwick's daughter, Ann, and, following Warwick's fall, took control of the vast Neville estates in the north of England, residing in Warwick's castle at Middleham in north Yorkshire. Edward had made Richard the effective governor of the whole of the North. Richard could offer much patronage and draw on a reservoir of experienced fighting men. Edward had created an exceptionally 'over-mighty' subject with a strong regional base.

PICTURE 3
Richard III, *anon.*

See pages 17–18

After 1478, Richard rarely came to London, and he established his military reputation in the campaign against Scotland. On his brother's untimely death in 1483, at the age of 41, Richard assumed the title of 'Protector', and moved swiftly to seize the person of Edward V, his elder nephew, from the hands of his mother's family, the Woodvilles. Richard then displayed ruthless determination in eliminating his opponents – Hastings, Rivers and Grey were executed in rapid succession – declared his nephews illegitimate, and seized the Crown for himself. The disappearance of his nephews, the 'Princes in the Tower', immediately aroused suspicions as to their fate, and Richard has to appear as the one with the strongest motive to do away with them. His failure to produce the children and the behaviour of their mother reinforce the impression of his guilt, despite the best efforts of the Richard III Society over the years to exonerate him. The Duke of Buckingham who rebelled against him certainly believed that Richard had disposed of the princes, while Richard's frenetic promotion of his northern affinity further aggravated magnate opinion in the south. That, and the failure of his old rivals in the North, the Percies and the Stanleys, to support him, led to his come-uppance at Bosworth Field in August 1485. Thus ended the reign of the man whom the historian Charles Ross has called 'the most vilified of all English kings'.

It is not difficult to explain why Richard III was able to seize the throne. Edward V was still a child and, as Prince of Wales, had lived in Ludlow on the Welsh border under the protection of his Woodville relation, Earl Rivers. The unpopularity of the Woodvilles cannot be overstated. They were regarded as ambitious upstarts and would clearly dominate the young King. Virtually all the great aristocrats disliked them and even Edward IV's most loyal supporter, Lord Hastings, had a grievance against them.

Richard's seizure of Edward V on 30 April and appointment as Protector on 4 May should not be seen as unpopular moves. It is not certain that he initially intended to declare himself King, but it is worth remembering that Edward IV had overthrown his predecessor and was responsible for the deaths of Henry VI and his own brother, the Duke of Clarence. Politics in fifteenth-century England was cruel and violent.

The executions of Lord Hastings (13 June) and Earl Rivers (25 June) suggest that by this time Richard was undoubtedly aiming for the throne. He soon declared that the marriage of Edward IV to Elizabeth Woodville had been invalid so that Edward V was therefore illegitimate and could not rightly be king. Having deposed his nephew, Richard's own coronation followed on 6 July. He could count on fervent support in the North and the passivity of many of the great nobility, who had learned to avoid political commitment after 30 years of instability. It was not Richard's seizure of the throne that shocked contemporaries, but the disappearance of his two nephews, the Princes in the Tower.

Dominic Mancini was a distinguished Italian scholar who spent some time in England in the early 1480s, probably working for the French. His account of the background to the usurpation of the throne by Richard III is an attempt by an intelligent outsider to make sense of these complex events.

KEY ISSUE

What made Richard of Gloucester's usurpation of the throne so easy?

1	By reason of his marriage some of the nobility had renewed hostilities against Edward, and revived hope amongst King Henry's party of regaining the crown, but after their defeat and the complete overthrow likewise of King Henry [VI] and his faction, Edward's power in
5	the kingdom was re-affirmed. The queen then remembered the insults to her family and the calumnies with which she was reproached, namely that according to established usage she was not the legitimate wife of the king. Thus she concluded that her offspring by the king would never come to the throne, unless the Duke of
10	Clarence were removed; and of this she easily persuaded the king … Accordingly whether the charge was fabricated, or a real plot revealed, the Duke of Clarence was accused of conspiring the king's death by means of spells and magicians. When this charge had been considered before a court, he was condemned and put to death. The
15	mode of execution preferred in this case was, that he should die by being plunged into a jar of sweet wine. At that time Richard of Gloucester was so overcome by grief for his brother, that he could not dissimulate so well, but that he was overheard to say that he would one day avenge his brother's death. Thenceforth he came very
20	rarely to Court. He kept himself within his own lands and set out to acquire the loyalty of his people through favours and justice. The good reputation of his private life and public activities powerfully attracted the esteem of strangers. Such was his renown in warfare, that, whenever a difficult and dangerous policy had to be undertaken,
25	it would be entrusted to his discretion and his generalship. By these arts Richard acquired the favour of the people, and avoided the jealousy of the queen, from whom he lived far separated.

Q

1. *Why might Elizabeth Woodville not have been regarded as Edward's legitimate wife (lines 7–8)?*
2. *What does this passage suggest about Edward IV's character and personality?*
3. *How convincing is the explanation of Richard's behaviour? (lines 16–27)*
4. *What are Mancini's weaknesses as a source for this period?*

For all his crimes, Richard was an energetic and capable ruler, but his position was never secure. In late 1483, rebellion broke out in southern England. Its ostensible leader, the Duke of Buckingham, proved ineffectual and was executed, but the antagonism towards Richard in southern England was made plain. The appointment of northerners, such as Sir Richard Ratcliffe, to positions in the South was bitterly resented. English society was intensely parochial and outsiders were always unpopular.

Despite lavish distribution of office and land along with tours of the country, Richard was not able to broaden his political base. The deaths of his son and his wife were further blows. A handful of great men could dramatically shift the political balance. In particular, even in the North he could not rely on the Percies in Yorkshire and Northumberland or the Stanleys in Lancashire and Cheshire. The Percies were traditional rivals of the Nevilles, and Thomas, Lord Stanley, was married to Margaret Beaufort, Henry Tudor's mother.

There was a surprising continuity of personnel in government. Of Richard's 54 Councillors, 24 had served Edward IV and nine were to serve Henry VII. The one innovation of Richard's reign was forced upon him. He had had his own council in the North, but on his assumption of the throne, a separate Council of the North was created as a branch of the Royal Council in 1484. This met four times each year in York and was to last until 1641. Richard did not choose a local grandee as its head, but his nephew, John de la Pole, Earl of Lincoln, who was an outsider.

Richard also needed to neutralise the threat of Henry Tudor, who, at Rennes Cathedral in Brittany on Christmas Day in 1483, pledged to marry Edward IV's daughter, Elizabeth of York. The rise of the Tudor dynasty is one of the more unlikely events of the fifteenth century. The family were originally minor Welsh gentry at a time when to be Welsh was to be considered a foreigner. Henry's grandfather, Owen Tudor, married Katherine, Henry V's widow. One of their sons, Edmund, became Earl of Richmond and married Lady Margaret Beaufort. She was descended from Edward III's son, John of Gaunt, although her line was one of dubious legitimacy. Henry Tudor was their son and inherited his claim to the throne from his mother.

The Tudors became important Lancastrians mainly because Henry VI had few close relatives. Henry's uncle, Jasper, Earl of Pembroke, was amongst the most tenacious and loyal Lancastrians. Edmund Tudor died in 1456 and Henry was born in early 1457. Jasper acted as Henry's guide and protector. For most of the next 20 years, Jasper and Henry were landless exiles, whose estates had been confiscated by Edward IV. Jasper intrigued actively in Wales, where the Tudor name was an advantage.

It would have been impossible for these exiles to have recovered the throne without foreign help. Throughout the 1470s, they depended on the protection of Duke Francis of Brittany. After the execution of Buckingham in 1483, Henry was the only claimant to the throne on the Lancastrian side who had royal blood, and he did have support in England. The Woodville family saw the marriage of Henry with Elizabeth of York (daughter of Edward IV and Elizabeth Woodville) as their only means of recovering influence. A final link was Henry's mother, Margaret Beaufort. Her second husband Thomas, Lord Stanley, was probably aware that a conspiracy was being hatched. After his pledge to marry Elizabeth of York, Henry could present himself as the unifier of Lancaster and York.

The Duke of Brittany abandoned Henry in 1484 and he was forced to flee to France. France was in some disarray after the death of its king, Louis XI. Charles VIII was only 13 years old and his court was divided. But the French were aware that an invasion of England would preoccupy Richard III and prevent England intervening if there was an opportunity to seize Brittany.

See page 277

See page 5

French money enabled Henry to raise 4000 troops, only 400 of whom were English. On 7 August 1485, they landed at Milford Haven in the west of Wales.

As is often the case with decisive battles, it is by no means clear why Richard was defeated. His northern following largely supported him and, while it is true that many great aristocrats did not fight, it may simply be that they did not have time to get to Bosworth. The turning point at Bosworth was Richard's own death. It seems that he recklessly charged Henry and was killed as a result. Almost as important was the desertion of the Stanleys, whose influence in the North-west was vast and whose family links with Henry have been explained. The Percies also did not fight. This may have been because of the cramped battlefield, but might also suggest an element of disloyalty.

Richard's death robbed the country of an effective but cruel monarch. There were plots and pretenders to come, but the fortunes of the House of York were never to recover.

> **KEY ISSUE**
>
> *Why did Richard III lose his throne?*

9 ↶ CONCLUSION: THE WARS OF THE ROSES

No-one would now suggest that the Wars of the Roses were marked by overwhelming violence and disorder. Revisionist historians have rightly drawn attention to the disappearance of town walls, the growing aristocratic practice of building houses rather than castles, the prosperity of the peasantry, and the outstanding quality of the churches of this period.

However, the degree of civil strife is not now seen as negligible. JR Lander estimated that there had been only 13 weeks of fighting in 32 years, but more recently AJ Pollard raised the figure to nearly two years (while conceding that continental wars were far more destructive).

Memories of that scale of conflict accounts for the very real fears, throughout the Tudor years, that if the new dynasty collapsed, England would once again face instability and civil war. No-one could foresee in 1485 that the Tudor dynasty would last more than a century, if only at times precariously, and would transform England, Wales and (more in failure than success) Ireland.

> **KEY ISSUE**
>
> *Which was the greater cause of instability: 'over-mighty subjects' or 'under-mighty kings'?*

10 ↶ BIBLIOGRAPHY

**I Pickering *Lancastrians to Tudors, 1450–1509* (CUP, 2000) is a useful textbook designed for sixth-form study, well presented with numerous documents, and *John Warren *The Wars of the Roses and the Yorkist Kings* (Hodder, Access to History) is a good introduction. **C Carpenter *The Wars of the Roses: Politics and the Constitution in England, c. 1437–1509* (CUP, 1997) is a lively and scholarly view of the whole period. *AJ Pollard *The Wars of the Roses* (Macmillan, 1983) offers a brief and approachable survey of the whole period, and reliable judgments. John Gillingham *The Wars of the Roses* (Weidenfeld & Nicolson, 1988) is worth consulting, if rather dated. JR Lander *Government and Community: England 1450–1509* (Edward Arnold, 1980) covers the ground well, but is also rather dated. *A Goodman *The Wars of the Roses. Military Activity and English Society, 1452–97* (Routledge, 1990) is the best specialist study on the purely military aspects of the wars. R Griffiths *The Reign of Henry VI* (Benn, 1981) is a valuable and exhaustive work of reference that concentrates on the period up to 1461, with many pages of footnotes. *CD Ross *Edward IV* (Methuen, 1974) is the standard biography and a work of real scholarship, as is *CD Ross *Richard III* (Methuen, 1981) with its balanced judgment of this controversial king. BP Wolffe *Henry VI* (Methuen, 1983) is shorter than Griffiths' biography, but a useful supplement to it.

(*Recommended. **Highly recommended.)

11 ⌐ STRUCTURED AND ESSAY QUESTIONS

A *Structured questions*

1. (a) How did the opposition to Henry VI turn into armed conflict?
   (b) Why did it take so long to bring the Wars of the Roses to an end?
2. (a) How had Richard of Gloucester built up such a position of power in England that he was eventually able to seize the throne for himself?
   (b) Does Richard III deserve his reputation as a tyrant?

B *Essay questions*

1. Is 'the Wars of the Roses' an appropriate term for the years 1455–71?
2. Account for the deposition of Henry VI in 1461.
3. How successfully did Edward IV re-invigorate royal authority during his reign?
4. 'His only real achievement was solvency.' Discuss this view of Edward IV.
5. Why was Richard Neville, Earl of Warwick, so important?
6. Why did Richard III take the throne in 1483, and why did he lose it in 1485?

Advice – answering structured questions

Before beginning an answer to any question, read it several times and make sure you are clear what specifically it requires. In the first part of a structured question, there will usually be a particular emphasis on factual knowledge. However, you will not get much credit for simply writing down everything you know about the topic. You must make sure that what you write is *relevant* to the question and *well-*

organised rather than a blow by blow account. The later sections of a structured question are likely to require more *explanation* and *analysis*, where you need to avoid just telling the story and use your knowledge as evidence to back up your argument.

Example question:

(a) How had Richard of Gloucester built up such a position of power in England that he was eventually able to seize the throne for himself?

This requires you to show your knowledge of Richard's career before he became king. The knowledge has to be relevant – showing how Richard built up his power base – and you must exclude irrelevant, incidental detail. Your answer needs to be well organised – divide Richard's career into stages – such as his take-over of the Earl of Warwick's estates, his presidency of the Council of the North, his becoming Protector – and avoid a year by year approach.

A bad start to your answer would be: 'Richard was born in 1452 ...'

A better start would be: 'Richard's first step towards becoming an "over-mighty subject" was when through marriage he acquired the vast land-holdings of the Earl of Warwick in the north of England ...'.

(b) Does Richard deserve his reputation as a tyrant?

This is the part of the question which requires more explanation and analysis. The question is not asking you just to tell the story of Richard's acts of cruelty. To pass a judgment on any historical character, you have to be sure you understand the terms being used and that you see both sides of the argument.

First think about what a tyrant is. It is a ruler who does not himself obey the law and who threatens the life and property of innocent subjects. In what ways did Richard III break the law or threaten innocent subjects?

To show both sides of the argument, write about any ways in which Richard brought benefits to his subjects as well as ways he may have harmed them.

Finally, consider where Richard's reputation comes from. How far is it just Tudor propaganda?

By breaking down the question in this way, you also have a clear *structure* for your answer.

12 ～ SOURCE EXERCISE: WHY DID THE WARS GO ON FOR SO LONG?

SOURCE A
*The attainder of the Yorkist
leaders at Coventry,
November 1459. From
Rotuli Parliamentorum, vol. 5,
page 349*

Wherefore please it your highness, these premises considered, by the advice and assent of your lords spiritual and temporal and of your commons assembled in this your parliament, and by the authority of the same to ordain, to establish and enact, that the said ... Richard Duke of York, Edward Earl of March, Richard Earl of Salisbury, Edmund Earl of Rutland, Richard Earl of Warwick ... for their said traitorous levying of war against your said most noble person, at Ludford ... be declared attainted of high treason, as false traitors and enemies against your most noble person, high majesty, crown, and dignity.... And that they and every one of them, forfeit from them and their heirs, by the same authority, all their estates, honours and dignities, which they or any of them have within this your realm of England, and within Wales and Ireland.

SOURCE B
*The Marriage of Edward IV,
1 May 1464. From the
Warkworth Chronicle, page 3*

Also the fourth year of King Edward, the Earl of Warwick was sent into France for a marriage for the King ... And while the said Earl of Warwick was in France, the king was wedded to Elizabeth Gray, widow, the which Sir John Gray that was her husband was slain at York field (Towton) in King Harry's party; and the same Elizabeth was daughter to the Lord Rivers; and the wedding was privily in a secret place, the first day of May, the year above said. And when the Earl of Warwick came home and heard this, then he was greatly displeased with the king; and after that great dissension rose ever more and more between the king and him, for that and other causes.

SOURCE C
*Polydore Vergil's account of the
internal disorder in the Wars of
the Roses. Three Books of
Polydore Vergil's English
History, H Ellis (ed.), Camden
Society, 1844*

This, finally, was the end of the foreign war, and likewise the renewal of civil calamity; for when the fear of an external enemy, which had kept the kingdom in good exercise, was gone from the nobility, such was the contention amongst them for glory and power, that even then the people were apparently divided into two factions, according as it became afterwards, when those two, that is to say, king Henry, who derived his pedigree from the house of Lancaster, and Richard duke of York, who conveyed himself by his mother's side from Lionel, son of Edward the Third, contended for the kingdom. By means whereof these two factions grew shortly so great through the whole realm that, while the one sought by any manner to subdue the other, and ranged in revenge upon the subdued, many men were utterly destroyed, and the whole realm brought to ruin and decay.

Q

1. *See Source A. How do the attainders at the 'Parliament of Devils' explain the renewal of the civil wars in 1459–61?*
2. *See Source B. What aspects of Edward IV's sudden marriage to Elizabeth Woodville explain Warwick's decision to rebel in 1469–71?*
3. *See Source C. Comment critically on Polydore Vergil's explanation for the continuation of the Wars of the Roses. In particular, to what extent does he exaggerate the impact of the wars?*
4. *How far can these sources help to explain why the Wars of the Roses went on for so long?*

2

The Reign of Henry VII

PICTURE 4
Henry VII, *attr. Sittow*

See Diagram 1
showing the family tree
of the royal houses on
page 5

INTRODUCTION

On 22 August 1485 Henry Tudor defeated Richard III at the Battle of Bosworth and became King of England. As Henry VII he founded the most colourful and best known dynasty in English history. However, he is the least familiar of the Tudors to modern eyes. He was as unfamiliar to contemporaries in 1485. His paternal grandfather, Owen Tudor, was a minor Welsh gentleman, who had the good luck to marry Katherine, the widow of Henry V. Owen's son, Edmund Tudor, married Margaret Beaufort, a descendent of Edward III's son, John of Gaunt. It was uncertain how legitimate the Beaufort line was; there were other better claimants to the throne by right of inheritance. Henry's right to be king came through victory in battle. To some this was taken as a sign of God's judgment; to others it seemed a temporary setback for the Yorkist cause.

Henry had spent the first 14 years of his life (1457–71) in Wales and after the final overthrow of Henry VI in 1471 he had been in exile in Brittany and France. His knowledge of England was therefore very limited. He had possessed neither land nor money in exile and had none of the training or experience an heir to the throne would normally enjoy. He had no experience of government and administration and no close contacts with leading members of the aristocracy.

Nevertheless, he founded a dynasty that lasted more than a century. To do this he had to deal with any possible rivals and gain recognition from foreign rulers as well as his own subjects who were all too used to civil war. He needed to restore stability and order to the country through the effective exercise of royal power. It has been a matter of debate whether he did this simply through the more efficient use of the existing system or whether he made any real innovations. He was also fortunate in that those foreign powers which might have remained a threat became preoccupied by wars in Italy, and he had an adult son to succeed him in the form of Henry VIII.

His own personality remains elusive. He has traditionally been portrayed as a cold and grasping man with a miserly attitude towards money. On the other hand, he appreciated that a king must maintain a lavish and impressive Court and he spent money freely where it suited him. His actions certainly prove him to have been resourceful in his determination to maintain his grip on power.

1 ⌒ SECURING THE THRONE

After the Battle of Bosworth it was essential for Henry to move rapidly to establish his authority. The situation was encouraging. Richard III had had a large personal following, especially in northern England, but his actions had alienated many Yorkists who now readily transferred their allegiance to Henry. Henry also had the distinct advantage of having killed his predecessor in battle, which had removed his main rival as well as showing God's favour.

Henry was crowned on 30 October. In November an Act of Parliament declared his right to be king and passed an act of attainder against Richard III and 28 of his more important followers because they had taken up arms against Henry. This was made possible by Henry dating his reign from the day before the Battle of Bosworth.

In the following January he married Elizabeth of York, the daughter of Edward IV. This fulfilled a promise made to the ex-Yorkists, helped to retain their support and prevented anyone else from marrying her as part of an attempt to claim the throne. The timing of the marriage showed that Henry did not depend on his wife to justify his claim to the throne.

He rewarded his supporters generously. His uncle Jasper was created Duke of Bedford and John de Vere, who was to prove an able military campaigner, was restored to the Earldom of Oxford. Thomas Stanley, whose support had been crucial to Tudor success at Bosworth, was created Earl of Derby and consolidated his position as the most powerful aristocrat in Cheshire and Lancashire. His brother, Sir William Stanley, became Chamberlain of the King's Household.

PICTURE 5
Medal: Henry VII and Elizabeth of York, 1486

HENRY'S SERVANTS: THE MAGNATE JOHN DE VERE, EARL OF OXFORD (1443–1513)

John de Vere was a loyal Lancastrian. He helped to put Henry VI back on the throne in 1470 and after the Yorkist victory in 1471 he fled to France but was captured and imprisoned near Calais. In 1484 he escaped and joined Henry Tudor who, according to Polydore Vergil, was 'ravished with joy' at his arrival. He commanded part of Henry's army at Bosworth in 1485. Henry restored him to his family estates and honours, and he was appointed Admiral of England, Constable of the Tower and Keeper of the Lions and Leopards within the Tower. His attendance at Council and the court had to be balanced by his other responsibilities as a great magnate and as a loyal servant of the King. As the major landowner in East Anglia he exercised the King's authority in the area. For example in 1499 he arrested Ralph Wilford who had attempted to raise rebellion on the Norfolk/Suffolk border, while claiming to be the Earl of Warwick. Oxford was one of the godfathers of Henry's heir, Prince Arthur, and in 1507 the Spanish ambassador wrote that he was 'more in Henry's confidence than any other person'.

Other men who had helped Henry, such as John Morton, Reginald Bray, and Richard Fox were given the highest offices of state and most kept them for the rest of their days.

After the Battle of Bosworth, Henry confined Edward, Earl of Warwick, who was the son of the Duke of Clarence and the Yorkist heir, to the Tower of London. Edward IV's sister, Elizabeth, had married John de la Pole and was the mother of seven sons. Her surviving sons were inevitably drawn into conspiracies and Henry pursued all these rivals of royal blood with great persistence and vigour. William de la Pole was imprisoned for 38 years in the Tower. Archduke Philip, the ruler of the Netherlands, surrendered Edmund de la Pole in 1506 who was executed in 1513, while Richard de la Pole remained in exile until his death.

Henry also seems to have been served by an effective intelligence service. For example, in the 1490s, when Perkin Warbeck first appeared, claiming to be one of Edward IV's sons, his true identity was soon discovered.

What were Henry VII's immediate disadvantages in 1485, and how was he able to overcome them?

2 ⌐ CONSPIRACIES AND RIVALS

We know that the Wars of the Roses ended in 1485, but contemporaries did not. With an insecure claim to the throne and no standing army to enforce his will, Henry faced the possibility of rebellion well on into his reign. There were conspirators who resented the new regime or saw the main chance of seizing power for themselves.

The first attempt at rebellion was led by Viscount Lovell, formerly Richard III's Chamberlain of the Household, and by Humphrey and Thomas Stafford, who were important landowners in Worcestershire. Their uprising in April 1486 was short-lived. One obvious problem was that they lacked a figurehead to be used as the claimant to the throne; the Earl of Warwick was in the Tower and Edward IV's sons were presumably dead.

A more serious threat came in the unlikely form of Lambert Simnel, who was the son of an organ-builder from Oxford. He was the pupil of a priest named Richard Simonds who trained him to impersonate the Earl of Warwick, Edward IV's nephew. Although Henry was able to produce the real Earl from the Tower of London, Simnel quickly attracted widespread support.

Its main centre was Ireland. Edward IV's father, Richard of York, had been the Royal Lieutenant in Ireland during the reign of Henry VI, and Ireland had become a Yorkist stronghold. The great Irish lords, such as Gerald, Earl of Kildare, were anxious to maintain their virtual independence from English control. One obvious way was to produce their own monarch and Simnel was crowned Edward VI in Dublin in May 1487.

PICTURE 6
Perkin Warbeck

See page 37

The other major supporter of Simnel was Margaret of Burgundy, sister of Edward IV and in effect ruler of the Netherlands. Viscount Lovell and one of the Yorkist heirs, John de la Pole, Earl of Lincoln, sought Margaret's help and were given 200 German mercenaries under the leadership of Martin Schwartz, who was an able and experienced soldier.

A combined army of Irish and Germans landed in England in June 1487. At Stoke, on 14 June, the rebels were defeated by Henry's army and Lincoln and Schwartz were slain. As a demonstration of his mercifulness and his contempt for the rebels, Henry VII made Simnel the royal falconer.

A further impostor appeared in Cork in 1491 – Perkin Warbeck. He was the son of a customs officer from Tournai in northern France. He was first welcomed by Charles VIII of France who wanted to ensure that Henry VII did not obstruct his plans to take over Brittany. But after the Treaty of Étaples between Charles and Henry in November 1492, Charles agreed to abandon Warbeck.

Warbeck then went to the court of Margaret of Burgundy who trained him for his role. Again Henry reacted forcefully. A trade war began with the Netherlands, while in Ireland the Earl of Kildare was dismissed from office. In England, Sir William Stanley, the brother-in-law of Henry's mother, was suspected of intrigue and executed in February 1495. All this ensured that Warbeck's landing at Deal in Kent on 3 July 1495 proved to be a complete fiasco.

After a brief stay in Ireland, Warbeck turned to Scotland. He was welcomed by James IV who seized the opportunity to keep the rival power of England divided and thereby weakened. James married

Warbeck off to an aristocratic Scottish wife and supported his invasion of England in September 1496. Henry's response was to negotiate with James through Richard Fox, the Bishop of Durham; his aim was a marriage alliance with Scotland to neutralise the threat from north of the border. James saw the advantages for his own security, abandoned his support for Perkin Warbeck and in 1497 a seven-year truce was agreed which was to become a full treaty in 1502.

See page 38

TIMELINE

1485	Henry VII became King following victory at Bosworth
1486	Marriage to Elizabeth of York
1487	Lambert Simnel as Pretender
	Battle of Stoke – victory for Henry
1491	Perkin Warbeck as Pretender
1495	Warbeck lands in England, then to Ireland and finally Scotland
1496	Warbeck's invasion of England from Scotland
1497	Peace with Scotland
	Warbeck captured

KEY ISSUE

How was Henry VII able to ensure the prevention or defeat of conspiracies against him?

Warbeck returned to Ireland and then moved to Cornwall. He was captured in August 1497 and allowed to stay at court. However, an attempt to escape led to imprisonment in the Tower. In November 1499 he was charged with another attempt to escape and executed. It is possible that he was involved in a plot with the Earl of Warwick who was also executed for high treason in early December.

3 ❧ THE FOREIGN POLICY OF HENRY VII

During the fifteenth century England's international position had declined. After 1453 only Calais was retained on the continent. France controlled much of the Channel coast and threatened to gobble up the still independent Duchy of Brittany, which had traditionally been a useful counterweight to French power and influence.

England's traditional ally had been the Duchy of Burgundy. The Dukes of Burgundy also ruled the Netherlands, which were of immense economic value and strategic importance to the English. The English economy depended on the export of woollen cloth to the port of Antwerp and this trading link was of vital importance to the two states. However, Margaret of Burgundy was a bitter opponent of Henry VII, and she and her son-in-law, Maximilian, the Holy Roman Emperor (who ruled territories in Germany and central Europe), consistently supported the conspiracies of Warbeck in the early 1490s. On the other hand Henry could exploit the close economic relationship between the two states as a means of pursuing his diplomatic aims.

The third major continental power of importance to England was Spain. The marriage between Ferdinand of Aragon and Isabella of Castile had created a dynastic union between the two states and their joint military success against the Moors confirmed the emergence of Spain as a major new power.

In 1485, Henry signed a truce with France. But the death of Duke Francis of Brittany in September 1488 provoked the inevitable crisis. His daughter Anne was still a child and feudal law entitled the French king, Charles VIII, to claim her as his ward. Henry did not want France to gain complete control of the Channel coast and tried to intervene. His attempts to mediate failed and so in September 1489 in the Treaty of Redon he promised the Bretons assistance in resisting Charles VIII. He then sought international assistance and made a treaty with Spain at Medina del Campo in March 1489.

None of these manoeuvres could prevent the marriage of Anne and Charles VIII in 1491, and through that the absorption of Brittany by France. No other European country was prepared to fight France and the activities of Perkin Warbeck further undermined Henry. But Henry made the best of his weak position. Using the traditional English claim to the throne of France to justify invasion, he landed at Calais in October 1492 and began to besiege Boulogne. This was too late in the year for a serious invasion but it was a useful bargaining counter in negotiations with the French.

The result was the Treaty of Étaples in October 1492. Charles VIII was eager to invade Italy and anxious to make peace. He agreed to pay Henry 745 000 gold crowns at a rate of 50 000 crowns per year; and he also agreed not to support any rebels against Henry.

Polydore Vergil was an Italian, who settled in England in the early sixteenth century and wrote a history of the country. Here is his view of Henry's policies in 1492:

KEY ISSUE

Did the crisis over Brittany result in success or failure for Henry VII?

See page 385

There were many who believed Henry to have come to an understanding with Charles before he crossed the sea, partly through fear and partly through a desire to acquire money, and a lasting report of this charge so penetrated into the minds of the public that even today many hold this opinion. Nevertheless, as some argue, it was neither greed nor fear. Henry, a man in general of the most prudent disposition, did not fear the enemy, to whose forces his own were not unequal; nor did he aim to secure cash, but was rather actuated by a desire for honour and for his own safety. For it was at this time that he learnt that Margaret, widow of Charles Duke of Burgundy, had raised from the dead one of the sons of King Edward her brother, a youth by the name of Richard; and that this youth was with Charles to persuade the French king to supply him with arms against Henry.

Line numbers in margin: 5, 10

Q

1. *Who was 'the youth by the name of Richard' (line 12)?*
2. *What events are referred to in the first two lines?*
3. *This document gives a variety of interpretations of Henry's foreign policy. Which do you find most convincing and why?*

Henry's attitude towards the Netherlands was quite clear; he always gave priority to the interests of his dynasty over those of maintaining trade. By 1492, Henry could guarantee that neither Spain nor France would attempt to overthrow him, but Margaret of Burgundy would not abandon Warbeck, and Emperor Maximilian, her son-in-law, resented Henry's peace treaty with France which had been concluded without consulting him. Henry's reaction was to place an embargo in 1493 on all trade with the Netherlands. The Burgundians responded with their own embargo in 1494 and further support for Warbeck.

Fortunately for Henry the deadlock was broken when European diplomacy became focussed on a French invasion of Italy in 1494. (This was the beginning of the Italian Wars which were to last intermittently for half a century.) The Emperor Maximilian and his son, Philip of Burgundy, ruler of the Netherlands, were now much more concerned about this than about Henry VII, and they were also anxious about the harmful effects of economic warfare with England. This led to negotiations, which were completed in 1496. Margaret of Burgundy agreed to abandon all support for Warbeck and faced the loss of her lands if she did not do so. More important was the trade treaty, known as the Magnus Intercursus, agreed in February 1496. This treaty allowed the English to sell goods in all Archduke Philip's Burgundian lands, with the exception of Flanders (in the area of modern Belgium). Duties and tolls were to be no higher than the prevailing rate of the past 50 years. By 1502 Flanders was included in the treaty as well. Trade flourished freely and the threat to Henry from the Netherlands had been neutralised.

KEY ISSUE

How was Henry VII able to neutralise the threat from Burgundy?

See page 35

The price for this treaty was that Henry joined an anti-French alliance, the Holy League, but this was no more than a gesture and did not seriously interfere with the policy of peace with France, which continued to be the basis of Henry's foreign policy.

The next threat came from north of the border when Perkin Warbeck landed in Scotland in 1495. There had been a precarious peace beforehand – in 1486 Henry had concluded a three-year truce with James III of Scotland and his successor, James IV had renewed that in 1493 – but there were too many ancient rivalries and long-running border disputes for James IV to resist offering support to Warbeck. However, the truce that ended that episode became a full alliance – the Treaty of Ayton – in September 1502. The alliance was confirmed by the marriage of James to Henry's daughter Margaret in August 1503, and Henry's northern border was secure for the remainder of the reign.

In contrast with closer neighbours, there was a natural affinity between Spain and England as both could use the other as a counterweight to France. The natural cement for such a relationship would also be a marriage alliance. The Treaty of Medina del Campo (1489) illustrates the priority given to relations with Spain early in Henry's reign. Henry's young son Arthur was to marry Catherine of Aragon, the equally young daughter of Ferdinand and Isabella, the rulers of Spain.

In October 1501, Arthur and Catherine were married, but Arthur died in April 1502. This was a personal and a diplomatic disaster for Henry VII, and threatened the survival of the Tudor dynasty, which now depended solely on Arthur's younger brother, Prince Henry. However, the marriage alliance with Spain was revived by the ensuing treaty of 1503, which arranged for Catherine to marry Henry. Then that marriage was postponed as the situation changed dramatically in Spain.

The marriage of Ferdinand and Isabella was a dynastic union between the separate states of Aragon and Castile. Isabella died in 1504, and this threatened the break-up of the union. Catherine of Aragon no

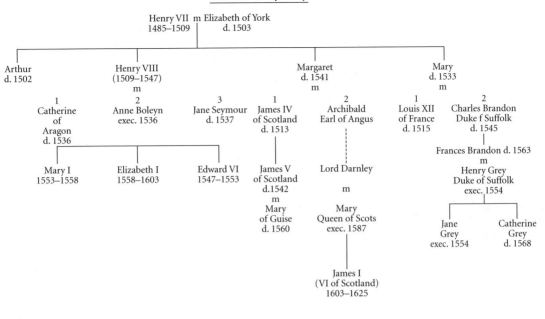

The Tudor Dynasty

DIAGRAM 2 *The Tudor Dynasty*

longer seemed such a diplomatic catch. In the immensely complex diplomacy of the years, Henry abandoned Ferdinand and tried to establish good relations with Ferdinand's son-in-law and rival, Archduke Philip, now ruler of Burgundy (and so also the Netherlands). Philip was trying to take Castile from Ferdinand in the name of his wife, Joanna, the eldest daughter of Ferdinand and Isabella, and therefore Isabella's heir.

After Philip and Joanna were shipwrecked in England in 1506, Philip agreed a trade treaty (the so-called Malus Intercursus) and handed over one of Henry's Yorkist rivals, Edmund de la Pole, the Earl of Suffolk. But the Malus Intercursus never came into effect, and then Philip's death later in 1506 enabled Ferdinand to regain control of Castile, which wrecked Henry's policy. Ferdinand allied himself to France in the League of Cambrai in 1508 and left England isolated.

> **KEY ISSUE**
>
> *How well managed were England's relations with Spain under Henry VII?*

4 ⌐ HENRY'S DOMESTIC POLICIES

It was necessary for Henry to fulfil certain requirements if he was to retain the throne. He needed to surround himself with able and effective Councillors, upon whose loyalty he could rely. He also needed to establish a secure financial base, which would both enhance his prestige and enable him to enjoy greater independence and freedom of action. Most difficult of all, he had to secure the acceptance of royal authority

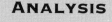

ANALYSIS

Was Henry VII's Foreign Policy a Success or a Failure?

It would be easy to dub Henry's foreign policy a failure. The French acquisition of Brittany and the ultimate failure of the Spanish alliance were certainly two blows. On the other hand, Henry's priorities must be understood. His main aim was to secure his dynasty and his own experience showed how vital foreign support could be for any usurper. His policies ensured that the major powers in Europe had abandoned support for any rival claimants to the throne by the mid 1490s. Moreover, he never faced an active alliance of hostile powers. This was partly a matter of good luck and the preoccupation with Italy, but it also reflected his diplomatic skill and the respect for him overseas.

A valuable contrast can be drawn with Edward IV. Edward still harboured fantasies that the English empire could be re-established in France. Henry's own invasion of France was a mere negotiating ploy and he never forgot that the need to maintain good relations with France was the basis of his policies. He can also be commended for his policy towards Scotland. The Treaty of Ayton and the marriage of his daughter to the King of Scotland benefited both the nation and the dynasty.

Above all Henry's avoidance of war must be commended. England was not powerful enough to wage war and could afford to be a bystander in the conflicts in Italy. This ensured that even exclusion from the League of Cambrai did not prove disastrous, since all its members were preoccupied in Italy. RB Wernham has summarised Henry's policies neatly: 'Peace with France and Scotland, reinforced by the reinsurance policy of alliances with Spain and the Netherlands, provided a pattern of relationships behind which England and the Tudor dynasty could prosper unmolested by Yorkist conspiracies or foreign interference'.

throughout the country at a time when the machinery of law enforcement was weak and reliance on the co-operation of the nobility inevitable.

A *Central administration – the Royal Council*

Henry's Council was the focal point of the government of the country. Its tasks were to advise the King on policy, to help in the administration of government and to administer justice. Henry was a frequent attender at meetings and it was he who made the final decisions.

At first sight Henry's Council seems an absurdly unwieldy body. During his reign, he appointed 227 Councillors, but only about two dozen were regular attenders. It was similar in composition to those of his predecessors, containing clergy, nobility, knights and lawyers. Thirty of them had also served the Yorkist kings as Councillors. An example is John Morton who attended virtually all the Council meetings for which records survive. He was Lord Chancellor from 1486 to 1500 and later became Archbishop of Canterbury. His career started under Henry VI and he then served Edward IV and was a member of his Council. Henry tended to make greater use of men with a background in the law or administration, especially in the offshoots of the Council that were set up in his reign. Rather than having inherited their position, they were professionals. For example, Sir Thomas Lovell trained and practised as a lawyer before committing himself to Henry's cause in 1483 and probably attended more meetings of the Council than anyone except Morton. Sir Richard Empson and Edmund Dudley, who were prominent on the 'Council Learned in the Law', were also lawyers. In the words of JR Lander: 'Loyalty and ability were the only criteria of service – mighty lord, bishop, doctor of canon or civil law, or official, all were there, but only at the King's will'.

KEY ISSUE

Was there anything new in the way the Royal Council worked under Henry VII?

The Council lacked a formal structure in the modern sense. There were no committees or sub-committees but during Henry's reign some offshoots did appear. For instance, a group of Councillors would meet in a room known as 'Star Chamber' to hear cases, often about disorder and violence involving powerful men who might over-awe existing courts. Myths grew up around the Star Chamber that it was a powerful separate institution (which it was not – it was just the room Councillors used) and that it was an instrument of tyranny (when in fact it prevented powerful men disrupting ordinary law and order).

Other courts were established. The 'Court of Audit' supervised the accounting of much of the King's finances, and the 'Court of Requests' handled cases brought by the poor. The 'Council Learned in the Law' supervised all the King's royal and landed rights over his subjects. It collected debts owing to the King and was also involved in drawing up and supervising **bonds** and **recognisances**. Acting without a jury and with a virtually free hand in fixing penalties, it was widely hated and did not survive the King's death. Its two leading members, Empson and Dudley, were believed to be corrupt and participants in a system of royal blackmail. They did not long survive Henry VII's death either – Henry VIII was to win some easy popularity when he had them tried and executed.

Bonds legal contracts whereby an individual promises to pay a given amount when called upon to do so

Recognisances pledges of money guaranteeing good behaviour

B *Financial administration*

If Henry has left any clear image for posterity, it is of a man obsessed with money. There is an underlying basis of truth in this view. It would not be fanciful to suggest that Henry's early poverty may have ensured that he had a firm grasp of the importance of money. It is also obviously true that the political strength of the Crown was, to a great degree, determined by its financial strength. His achievement was to be all the greater as he had no experience to help him. In the words of SB Chrimes, 'no man has ascended the throne with such a lack of financial experience and resources as did Henry VII'.

Henry's most important source of revenue was the royal estates, which had significantly increased in size as a result of the bringing together of Lancastrian and Yorkist lands, the death of many great landowners in previous years and the confiscation of other estates. Unlike Edward IV, Henry made few grants of land to political supporters and by 1509 the royal estates were probably larger than ever before. They now provided revenue of £42 000 per year, which was four times as much as in 1433.

Henry could also raise revenue from his position as feudal overlord of the great aristocrats, who in theory still held their land from the King in return for military or financial services. The most important element in this so-called feudal or **prerogative** revenue was wardship. If a great landowner died and his heir was still a child, the child became a ward of the king and the estates passed under royal control. This was the most important source of prerogative revenue. In 1503 Sir John Hussey was appointed the first surveyor of the King's wards to exploit their estates more systematically. The exploitation of the King's other feudal rights was a complex process. At first a series of commissions investigated means of increasing revenue; eventually in 1508 Edward Belknap was appointed the first surveyor of the King's prerogative.

> **Prerogative** the powers in the hands of the monarch, not subject to decisions by Parliament or anyone else

Remaining revenue came largely from Parliament. As was traditional, Henry was granted customs duties for life by Parliament and this completed his normal peacetime, or ordinary revenues. Extraordinary revenues in times of war and national crisis had to be voted as taxes by Parliament or raised by borrowing and Henry did his best to avoid both. He came close to fulfilling the fifteenth-century maxim that 'the King must live of his own' and avoid taxing his subjects.

The fifteenth century had seen significant changes in the methods of financial administration. Traditionally revenues had been channelled to the Exchequer but under Edward IV and Richard III, revenues were increasingly directed to the Royal Household, or Chamber. This system was speedier and placed revenues directly at the King's disposal.

Untrained in estate management and with more immediate worries of security, Henry did not at first use the new methods, but from 1487 he returned to the Chamber system, helped by the work of Sir Reginald Bray and Sir Thomas Lovell, who was Treasurer of the Chamber until 1492, when he was succeeded by Sir Thomas Heron. By the end of Henry's reign 80% of revenue went directly to the Chamber. Money was then immediately available for royal use and the Jewel House in the Tower of London became, in effect, a kind of crude royal bank where financial reserves were stored.

Henry involved himself directly in the affairs of the Chamber. Until 1503 every entry of a receipt was initialled by him and after 1503 every page. The receivers who collected royal revenue made frequent appearances before the King and his Council, and Henry must take personal credit for the growing efficiency of financial administration.

Henry's management of royal finances, in an age when all European monarchs constantly suffered from shortage of money, raised revenue from the royal estates from about £10 000 p.a. in the last years of

HENRY'S SERVANTS: THE ADMINISTRATOR

SIR REGINALD BRAY (C.1440–1503)

Reginald Bray was born in Worcester in the 1440s. By the mid-1460s he was working for Sir Henry Stafford and his wife Lady Margaret Beaufort, the mother of the future Henry VII. His work included the collection of rents, settling disputes between tenants, and overseeing the property interests of his employers. Lady Margaret used him to recruit support for her son's cause against Richard III, and in 1485 he was responsible for collecting money to pay Henry Tudor's soldiers. Henry rewarded him with a knighthood and appointed him Chancellor of the Duchy of Lancaster. His strength was in the administration of finance and estates. In 1488 he was appointed to a commission to overhaul the administration of all Crown lands. He later became a leading member of the Council 'Learned in the Law' which kept a tight grip on money owed to the King and he played a major role in the development of the Chamber as a centre of royal finances, holding regular meetings with officials. By the 1490s he was recognised by a number of foreign envoys as one of the leading men in the kingdom. Bray reaped the rewards of his career. He was made a Knight of the Garter and accumulated estates and offices that made him one of the richest men in the kingdom.

PROFILE

Edward IV to £42000 per year. Feudal prerogatives were more rigorously exploited. Taxation and customs revenue also increased and the French subsidy was paid to Henry from 1492 until his death in 1509. By the end of his reign his annual revenue amounted to £100000 compared with £65000 in the last years of Edward IV.

The sophistication of Henry's financial system must not be exaggerated. The Chamber accounting system was crude, there were no innovations and no new sources of revenue were discovered. He merely continued Edward's policy of more effective exploitation of the royal estates. His methods were more dependent on diligent supervision than clever administrative techniques, but any monarch who could lend £300000 to the mighty house of Habsburg and leave one year's unspent income to his son, as Henry did, must be considered an effective financier.

> **KEY ISSUE**
>
> *Why were the royal finances so important, and how did Henry VII improve them?*

5 ∽ THE PROBLEMS OF ORDER AND SECURITY

To represent him in different parts of the country, Henry VII relied when he could on members of his family on whose loyalty he could

<table>
<tr><td>

PROFILE

</td><td>

LADY MARGARET BEAUFORT
(1443–1509)

Margaret Beaufort was descended from Edward III. In 1453 she married Edmund Tudor, half-brother to Henry VI. Their son, Henry Tudor, was born in January 1457 when she was still only 13. She had no more children although she was married twice more – to Sir Henry Stafford (d.1471) and Thomas, Lord Stanley (d.1504). Before 1483 she adapted to the prevailing political situation, but after Richard III's accession she began to work actively on her son's behalf. She played a leading role in organising the rebellion against Richard and helped to arrange the marriage between Henry and Elizabeth of York. She was lucky to escape imprisonment and continued to send money to her son. After 1485 she was rewarded with estates and given royal status. Her son's trust was shown from the beginning when she was granted the wardship of the young Duke of Buckingham and initial custody of the Earl of Warwick, the nephew of Edward IV. She frequently accompanied Henry on his progresses and had accommodation near the King in all the main royal houses. In the Tower, for example, her rooms were next to Henry's chamber and the Council chamber. There was considerable overlap between the royal Council and her council, and tasks were sometimes transferred from one to the other. Her house at Collyweston became a centre for royal authority in the Midlands. Here she administered justice on the King's behalf, settling disputes and running what has been described as the 'unofficial council of the Midlands'. Foreign envoys commented on her influence over Henry. She gained a reputation for piety and as a patron of education. She translated a number of religious works and commissioned the printing of others. Advised by Bishop John Fisher, she set up professorships of divinity at the universities and contributed to the Cambridge colleges Jesus and Queens'. She founded Christ's College, Cambridge, basing it on an earlier foundation associated with Henry VI. She died on 29 June 1509, two months after her son, and was buried in Westminster Abbey.

</td></tr>
</table>

count. There was his uncle Jasper, Duke of Bedford and above all his mother, Lady Margaret Beaufort. He also used bishops and professional administrators who depended on him for their authority rather than on an inherited power base. However, without a standing army, a police force, or a modern civil service, no king could rule without the co-operation of the nobility, and their loyalty and subservience had to be maintained.

Under Henry, no aristocrat enjoyed a regional power-base similar to that of Richard III before he became King, and Henry kept the great Yorkist estates in his own hands. No marriages united two great aristocratic families in his reign. The Duke of Buckingham was only seven in 1485, the Earl of Northumberland was killed in 1489 and his heir was only ten years old, so two of the greatest families were left without an effective head. Henry himself only created three new peerages and the number of peers declined from 50 to 35 in his reign. Henry preferred to use the Order of the Garter as a reward for loyal service.

However, Henry was not hostile to the nobility as long as they posed no threat. They were his natural companions and attended him at Court where they had an important role in public ceremonies and service and in private recreation.

A *Retaining*

Retaining was an important feature of aristocratic life. Large numbers of retainers boosted a nobleman's prestige as well as his real power. In return the retainer received the patronage and support of an influential man. Many retainers were household servants, others were recruited for military purposes and many were themselves landholders who were prepared to do whatever service was required of them.

The King relied on these noble retinues as the basis of his armed forces. When he wanted a nobleman to carry out a particular service, it was often his retainers who enabled him to fulfil the royal command. However, it was open to abuse. Too many retainers could be a threat to the King if a nobleman rebelled, and rival groups of retainers were a threat to public order. In addition, the problem of maintenance (the intimidation of juries by retainers) undermined the legal system and the King's authority. Henry followed Edward IV in aiming to control retaining by distinguishing between legal and illegal activity.

Four statutes dealt with the problems of livery and retaining. The earlier ones, such as that of 1487, essentially re-stated Edward IV's measures of 1468. In 1504, the most significant statute was introduced. The first purpose of the statute was to reiterate the prohibition of illegal retaining; a system of 'placards' or licences was introduced. If the King himself had signed or sealed one of these 'placards', retaining could take place. This measure was to apply for the remainder of Henry's reign.

There is no evidence that this statute was enforced with great frequency. The only peer known to have been prosecuted was George Neville, Lord Burgavenny; Sir James Stanley, who was an uncle of the second Earl of Derby, was also fined heavily. Both fines were, however, suspended, and it seems that the statute was mainly used as a means of intimidation. No written evidence of illegal retaining, which is commonly found before 1485, has come to light for the reign of Henry VII.

Henry must, therefore, be regarded as more successful than his predecessors in controlling the nobility through a judicious mixture of threats and patronage. The later career of Lord Burgavenny illustrates the distinction between legal and illegal retaining. He may have been a target for Henry because of his earlier involvement in the Cornish Uprising of 1497, but by 1510 he was sufficiently restored to favour to be made Constable of Dover and Warden of the Cinque Ports. In this position, he was licensed to retain as many men as he needed to meet the threat of the French.

B *Attainders, and bonds and recognisances*

Henry's concern was to maintain his dominance over his most powerful subjects while retaining their co-operation. Certain weapons were available to him at the beginning of his reign, the most well known being the process of attainder. An Act of Attainder prevented a disloyal subject and his descendants from possessing or inheriting land. During Henry's reign, there were 138 attainders and only one Parliament (1497) failed to pass any. Forty-six attainders were eventually reversed. This was a relatively small number; the terms of reversal were often very harsh and did not include the complete restoration of lands. Henry's use of attainder was far more ruthless and severe than had been Edward IV's.

Bonds and recognisances were not a new practice. Edward IV had placed six peers and one peeress under political bonds, but under Henry there was a massive extension of the system. The English peerage consisted of 62 families; of these 36 were placed under bond to Henry at some point during his reign.

After 1502 the system became widespread. Henry effectively placed the aristocracy on probation in return for loyalty and good behaviour. The case of Lord Burgavenny has already been mentioned. He was fined the vast sum of £70 000 for illegal retaining. This was an impossible sum for him to pay, but the King used this offence and the threat of this vast fine hanging over him to force him in turn to enter a recognizance of £13 000 that he would pay the King £500 a year for ten years. The Earl of Kent owed Henry money when he succeeded to the earldom. He was made to agree to a bond whereby he undertook to sell no land and give office to no man without royal consent or forfeit £10 000 should he break this bond.

Bonds were rarely actually used to raise cash and were often cancelled, or suspended; their value was as a threat hanging over the nobility. Henry inherited a system sporadically used by his predecessors and converted it into an organised system of coercion.

KEY ISSUE

By what means, and how effectively, did Henry VII keep the nobility under control?

6 ⌐ GOVERNING THE PROVINCES

Despite his harsh treatment of the aristocracy, Henry relied on them to enforce his will in the provinces. Although there were occasional royal progresses through the country, inevitably Henry spent most of his time at Westminster. He had few paid servants; a small number worked in the Exchequer, the Duchy of Lancaster and the customs service, but it has been estimated that there was only one paid official for every 4000 inhabitants, while in France the figure was one for every 400 inhabitants.

To a great degree, therefore, Henry relied on the co-operation of aristocratic families with strong local roots. The most famous of these families was the Percy family in Yorkshire and Northumberland, but the Stanleys in Lancashire and Cheshire, the Howards in East Anglia, and the Berkeleys in Gloucestershire were equally important.

It was still difficult to assert royal authority in the North. The murder of the Earl of Northumberland, while trying to collect taxes in 1489, gave Henry an opportunity to modify his approach. His principal officers became Lord Dacre, who came from a great local family, and Thomas Howard, Earl of Surrey. Surrey was an outsider and had no great estates in the North. His authority came from being appointed by the King and not from any power base he possessed in the area. In 1501 a council took over, headed by the Archbishop of York, again someone who owed his authority in this matter to the King.

In Wales a council was created under Prince Arthur. On his death the Bishop of Lincoln became its president, and again he was not a local landowner with a local power base but depended for his authority on the King.

Henry's other important agents in the provinces were the Justices of the Peace. As leading members of local society they saw it as their responsibility to exercise authority on the King's behalf and in their own interests. It was in their interests to maintain law and order, and it boosted their prestige to be chosen by the King to do so.

The King was obviously keenly interested in their work and concerned that they should do their job properly. Every Parliament of his reign passed at least one statute concerned with the work of JPs. These included measures to deal with rioting and the intimidation of juries. An Act was also passed allowing complaints against JPs to be made to the King's judges or the King himself, although this system seems to have been little used.

The King also increased his control by appointing members of his household to local offices and by making use of his own position as the country's greatest landowner. Tenants of crown lands could not be retained by anyone else and the King recruited leading landowners into his own service, establishing his own bands of retainers in almost every county.

> **KEY ISSUE**
>
> *How did Henry VII maintain control over the provinces?*

7 ↩ PARLIAMENT

Henry VII summoned seven Parliaments, five of which met in the first ten years of his reign. In the 24 years of his reign Parliament was actually in session for only a little over a year and a half.

Parliament's structure was now fairly firmly fixed; by 1489 it was accepted that an Act of Parliament was only valid if both the **House of Lords** and **House of Commons** had agreed to it. Measures of taxation now had to be initiated by the House of Commons, but the Lords enjoyed far greater prestige and power. Above all the King held the whip hand; it was he who summoned and dissolved Parliaments.

House of Lords upper house of Parliament, the members being nobles, bishops and the most important abbots

House of Commons lower house of Parliament, with MPs representing the shires and boroughs (usually historically important towns). The number of voters was very restricted, and local land-owners dominated the selection of MPs

Tunnage and poundage import taxes on tuns (barrels) of wine and pounds weight of other goods

Fifteenths and Tenths taxes on a fifteenth of the value of personal property and a tenth of landed property

Subsidy a parliamentary tax on property and income

KEY ISSUE

How did Parliament support the work of the King? Did it restrict his authority in any way?

Parliaments played no role in the day-to-day government of the country and were summoned for three reasons: for taxation, to make laws, and for general consultation. Over taxation Parliament's authority was undisputed. Henry's first Parliament granted the customs dues of **tunnage and poundage** for life as was now traditional. The other major Parliamentary taxes were **Fifteenths and Tenths** which could only raise about £30 000. Henry's attempts to replace these with a directly assessed **subsidy** failed. A major reason for Henry's declining use of Parliament in his last years was his growing financial independence and reliance on income from his own lands and the ruthless exploitation of all other sources of revenue.

Parliament's legislative role was important. Acts of Parliament, known as statutes, were considered the highest form of law and could be enforced in the law courts. They were now regularly printed which allowed for a stricter interpretation of statute law.

Parliament also provided a forum for the statement of royal intentions and their discussion by the governing class, who in return could state their own views and pursue their personal ambitions with Henry. Essentially his Parliaments were co-operative ventures between the monarch and the governing elite.

8 ⌐ THE COURT

Henry was willing to spend large sums of money on his court and the entertainments that it provided since it was the setting for his public appearances and these had to impress his own subjects and foreign visitors. Part of the good impression was due to those around the King and so he encouraged the attendance at court of his leading subjects.

Attendance at court had its benefits. It meant access to the King and this could lead to promotion. Individuals we tend to see as professional administrators were also courtiers. For example, the lawyer Thomas Lovell started his royal career as Esquire of the Body, i.e. a personal attendant on the King, at the same time as he was appointed Chancellor of the Exchequer.

An important role at court enabled a man to advance his own dependants and to build up his influence. Giles, Lord Daubeny, was Henry's Chamberlain from 1495. In a conversation recorded around 1505 the comment was made about him: 'Look how strong he is in the king's court of his household servants, for the most part of his (i.e. the King's) guard be of those that were my lord Chamberlain's servants before'.

This meant that rivalries arose at court. Fluid groups seem to have emerged. Lord Daubeny named his 'singular good lords and friends',

Bishop Fox, the Earl of Oxford and Sir Thomas Lovell as overseers of his will, referring to 'the trust and confidence that I have and long have had in them'. When Sir George Plumpton was advised on how to avoid losing his estates he was told to avoid such 'as are belonging to Mr Bray' and instead to rely on a group including Fox and Lovell.

Court rivalry may have contributed to the arrest and execution of Sir William Stanley on suspicion of supporting Perkin Warbeck in 1495. Another possible victim of court **faction** was Lord William Courtenay. He was the son of the Earl of Devon, one of Henry's companions in exile, and had been at court since 1499 and given an annuity for his 'daily and diligent attendance' on the King. Nevertheless he was arrested in 1502 and remained a prisoner for the rest of the reign.

Stanley's fall may help to explain an institutional development at Henry's court. As Chamberlain of the Household, Stanley controlled access to the King, and his treason struck at the heart of Henry's security. Henry's response may have been the development of the Privy Chamber as a separate department, with the right of entry restricted to Henry's personal servants headed by the **Groom of the Stool**. This move to some extent set Henry apart from the rest of the court.

> **Faction** a political grouping pursuing a common interest, usually in competition with other groups. Lacking in the lasting organisation or ideology of a political party.

> **Groom of the Stool** literally the manservant who looked after the king's toilet. Being a confidential servant, he was often an important figure despite the menial task and could wield considerable influence.

Henry VII and the Historians

Francis Bacon published *The History of the Reign of Henry the Seventh* in 1622, in the reign of James I. He emphasised Henry's love of money and the distance he set between himself and his subjects. Bacon had suffered from political intrigue at court and admired the apparent lack of it in Henry's reign. His aim was to present an example of an effective ruler. Although he had access to some original sources, Bacon invented almost all his quotations and was more concerned with making his point than with accuracy. Nevertheless, aspects of his portrait can still be seen in modern views of Henry and are occasionally referred to by text-books and examiners.

Modern interpretations begin in 1893 when JR Green published his *Short History of the English People*. In it he introduced the idea of the 'despotism of the new monarchy'. By this he meant that after the Wars of the Roses the English kings strengthened their power at the expense of their subjects' liberties. Green identified Edward IV as the founder of the 'new monarchy' but later historians shifted the emphasis to the Tudors, and Henry VII became the king who had brought England out of the Middle Ages and set it on the road to being a strong unified nation state.

In the mid-twentieth century historians began to emphasise more the continuities and to criticise the idea that the Middle Ages had ended with Henry VII and his establishment of a 'new monarchy'. For example, the historian of the fifteenth century, JR Lander and the Tudor specialist GR Elton both saw Henry continuing the work of his Yorkist predecessors. By 1972 the leading biographer of Henry VII could write: 'He could bring an essentially medieval spirit and practice of government to its highest point of effectiveness without in any important way changing its character' (SB Chrimes *Henry VII*). In 1985 A Grant challenged this view. He acknowledged continuity but laid greater emphasis on the differences between Henry and the Yorkists. His restoration of order, handling of foreign policy, local government and the nobility brought in real change. '… His victory over Richard III in August 1485 deserves to be re-established as a major turning-point in English history.'

These interpretations tended to be favourable to Henry VII. The most recent views have been more critical. Steven Gunn, for example, has challenged the idea, started by Bacon, that Henry presided over a court with no politics or faction. Christine Carpenter has been more provocative. She criticises him for his attitude to the nobility. They should have been the allies of the King but Henry did not trust them enough, was too extreme in use of bonds and often bypassed them in favour of household officials or local gentry when dealing with local government. This undermined a system in which the King ruled with the co-operation of the nobility. Those people that he did trust he trusted too much. She points to evidence that in some areas at least the King's favourites could exploit their positions and break the law with impunity. These favourites also squabbled among themselves and this contributed to the faction fighting identified by Gunn. So Carpenter, while acknowledging a difference between Henry and his predecessors, sees this as a change for the worse and more likely to destroy rather than restore stability. Henry survived not due to any restoration of order but to military success, skilful handling of foreign policy and the good fortune of leaving the throne to an adult male.

KEY ISSUE

What was the key to Henry VII's success as a ruler?

9 ᕲ BIBLIOGRAPHY

**A Grant *Henry VII: the Importance of his Reign in English History* (Routledge, Lancaster Pamphlets, 1985) provides a short and clear argument for Henry's reign marking a new era. **R Turvey and C Steinsberg *Henry VII* (Hodder and Stoughton, 2000) and R Lockyer *Henry VII* (Longman Seminar Studies, 1997) both provide good accounts. *SB Chrimes *Henry VII* (Methuen, 1977) is the standard biography, rather dry but useful for reference. *C Carpenter *The Wars of the Roses* (Cambridge University Press, 1997) has a chapter on Henry VII in which she puts forward her critical view of the king. It would be best to consult this last, after the basics are clear. Susan Brigden *New Worlds, Lost Worlds* (Penguin, 2000) has two early chapters that provide good background.

(*Recommended. **Highly recommended.)

10 ⌐ STRUCTURED AND ESSAY QUESTIONS

A *Structured questions*

1. (a) What disadvantages did Henry Tudor have when he won the throne in 1485?
   (b) How did Henry Tudor overcome these disadvantages in the first years of his reign?
2. (a) What developments took place in central administration during Henry VII's reign?
   (b) How effectively did Henry VII manage his finances?

B *Essay questions*

1. How far was Henry VII's foreign policy dictated by the need for dynastic security?
2. 'Henry VII's policy towards the nobility was one of repression and control.' How true is this statement?
3. How successful was Henry VII in restoring royal authority in England?
4. 'Ruthlessness and attention to detail brought him success.' How adequately does this describe the reign of Henry VII?
5. Was there anything new about the monarchy in Henry VII's reign?

11 ⌐ SOURCE EXERCISES

(i) Henry VII's Title

After the coronation of King Henry, a parliament was held at Westminster. In this parliament, the sovereignty was confirmed to our lord the king, as being his due, not by one, but by many titles: so that we are to believe that he rules most rightfully over the English people, not so much by right of blood as of conquest and victory in warfare. In the very same parliament a discussion took place relative to his marriage with the Lady Elizabeth, in whose person it appeared to all that every requisite might be supplied, which was wanting to make good the title of the king himself.

SOURCE A
From the continuation of the Croyland Chronicle, *a contemporary account of the events of the reigns of Richard III and Henry VII*

Our Holy Father Pope Innocent VIII, understanding the long and grievous debates that have been in this realm of England between the House of Lancaster and the House of York, and wishing all such division to be put apart approves and confirms the matrimony made between our sovereign lord King Henry VII of the House of Lancaster and the noble princess Elizabeth of the House of York.

And His Holiness also confirms the right and title of the crown of the said our sovereign lord Henry VII and the heirs of his body as well by reason of his undoubted title of succession as the right of his noble victory and election of lords spiritual and temporal of his realm and the act and authority of parliament.

Furthermore he declares that if it please God that the said Elizabeth should die without issue, then any children of Henry and any future wife shall be the right inheritors to the same crown and realm of England.

SOURCE B
From the Pope's bull issued to the people of England

Q

1. *Explain the reference to 'the Lady Elizabeth' in Source A.*
2. *Compare and contrast Sources A and B in the way that they deal with Henry VII's claim to the throne of England.*

(ii) Was Henry VII an avaricious King?

As the King is entitled to have two reasonable *aids*, one for the making knight of the Prince of Wales deceased and the other for the marriage of the Princess Margaret, now married unto the King of Scots; … the Commons in this present Parliament … have humbly asked his Highness to accept the sum of £40 000 … And his Grace, right well pleased with the said loving offer, is content to accept the sum of £30 000 only.

SOURCE A
Act of Parliament 1504

The petition of me, Edmund Dudley, the most wretched and sorrowful creature, being a dead man by the King's laws and prisoner in the Tower of London …

Since the last will of the late King Henry VII was that restitution should be made to all persons that he had wronged … I have searched my books touching all such matters that I knew about and below have written such persons as I think were much more harshly treated than the causes required …

The intention of the King was to have many persons at his mercy. Many persons were bound to his Grace for great sums of money, some by recognisance and some by a simple bond without any condition, payable at a certain day. These manner of bonds should not be considered real debts for I truly believe the King's inward mind was never to collect them.

SOURCE B
The Petition of Edmund Dudley. Dudley was arrested and executed in the first year of the reign of Henry VIII. He wrote this in prison.

Henry wished (as he said) to keep all Englishmen obedient through fear. All of his richer subjects who were found guilty of any fault were harshly fined in order to make the population less well able to undertake any upheaval …

There came on the scene two astute lawyers, Richard Empson and Edmund Dudley. The King rapidly appointed them as judges. The pair, probably realising that they had been given the job by the King not so much to administer justice as to strip the population of its wealth, by every means fair and foul competed with each other in extorting money.

Henry, in the year before his death, learning that there was widespread complaint concerning the plundering in which the two judges daily indulged, is said to have decided to restore what the two had illegally seized. When he realised he was going to die, he laid down in his will that all were to be given back such possessions as had been illegally carried off to the treasury by those two most brutal extortioners.

SOURCE C
Polydore Vergil Anglica Historia. *Vergil was an Italian in the service of the Pope. He visited England on official business in the reign of Henry VII and was asked by the King to write a history of the country*

Q

1. *Study Source A. Using your own knowledge, explain the phrase 'two reasonable aids' in the first line of the source.*
2. *Study Source B. How valuable is this source as evidence of Henry VII's attitude towards finance?*
3. *Study sources A–C and use your own knowledge. 'Henry VII was notable for the avarice he displayed in exploiting his subjects financially.' Explain why you agree or disagree with this opinion.*

3

Henry VIII, 1509–29

PICTURE 7
Henry VIII, *anon.*

INTRODUCTION

Henry VIII was born on 28 June 1491. He became heir apparent on the death of his brother Arthur in April 1502 but there is no evidence that he was given any responsibility in government while his father was still alive. On his accession in April 1509 he was still 17. He was in many ways genuinely talented. He was tall and strong, gifted musically and more than competent academically.

The early years of his reign have attracted less interest than the events of the 1530s and 1540s. Much of the King's energy and the resources of the kingdom were concentrated on an apparently futile attempt to reproduce the victories of Henry V in France. He wished to become a great king in a very traditional way.

The other striking feature of this period is the dominant position of Cardinal Wolsey. By 1515, Wolsey had established himself as the King's chief minister and he maintained this position for the next 15 years. Any assessment of Henry's reign needs to take Wolsey's achievements into account. This includes his contribution to foreign policy, his handling of government and his relationship with the nobility. Recurrent questions are the extent to which he or Henry was in real control in those years and what factors brought about his fall from power.

1 ↪ HENRY'S ACCESSION

Canon law the law of the Church, governing also a wide variety of personal and moral concerns, such as marriage.

See pages 38–9

Henry's elder brother, Prince Arthur, had been married to Catherine of Aragon, the daughter of Ferdinand of Aragon and Isabella of Castile, the rulers of Spain. It is not certain that the marriage had been consummated. Following Arthur's death Henry VII made a treaty for the marriage of Henry to Catherine; at this time Henry was 12 years old and Catherine was 17. **Canon law** did not allow marriage to the wife of a dead brother and permission from the Pope was required before any marriage could take place.

Henry VII did not wholeheartedly commit himself to this match and continued to seek alternative brides for his son until his death. As soon as Henry succeeded to the throne, though, he married Catherine on 11 June 1509. There were good reasons for haste. The sooner Henry VIII could produce children the more stable the Tudor dynasty would be. It also helped to maintain the alliance with Spain.

By 1509 some of Henry VII's methods had become deeply unpopular. Edmund Dudley and Sir Richard Empson were the two men most closely associated with his ruthless financial demands and legal controls over the aristocracy and gentry. Henry VIII had Empson and Dudley arrested in April 1509, and they were executed a year later. This freed him from association with the most unpopular aspects of his father's government. The 'Council Learned in the Law', through which most of the work of Empson and Dudley had been conducted, was abolished, and some of the bonds imposed by Henry to keep noblemen under control were cancelled.

See page 41

2 ⌐ HENRY'S AIMS AND PRIORITIES 1509–12

In foreign policy Henry's aggressive posture contrasted dramatically with his father's caution. On his accession he swore publicly that he would attack France and he meant it. His role model was Henry V, from nearly a century before, whose glorious victory at Agincourt and subjugation of half France Henry wished to emulate. He took the stability of England much more for granted than his father had ever done.

Alongside Henry's personal ambition, there were good reasons for this new policy. The aristocracy was still essentially militaristic in character, and war would give them a chance to win glory and booty in battle. It was seen as the king's duty to win honour for himself and his country and Henry was drawn to this role.

Opportunities would also be available for the dispensation of patronage. Henry VII had been notoriously mean in granting aristocratic titles; in 1509, the Duke of Buckingham was the only hereditary duke in the kingdom. By 1514, Thomas Howard had been restored to the Duchy of Norfolk, taken from the family for their support of Richard III in 1485, and Charles Brandon had been created Duke of Suffolk. Both men had played important parts in the military campaigns of these years. The popularity of Henry VIII was undeniably increased by his aggressive posture of national leadership and lavish distribution of patronage.

There were aspects of the situation in Europe which made it a favourable time for Henry's plans. Louis XII of France, Ferdinand of Spain and Maximilian, the Holy Roman Emperor, were rivals for control in Italy and Henry could present himself as an ally to either Ferdinand or Maximilian, both of whom had an interest in curbing French power at home. But there were also dangers in siding with Ferdinand and Maximilian against France. France was a much more powerful country than England and a war was bound to wreck the national finances. In addition, both Ferdinand and Maximilian were old hands at diplomacy and quite capable of exploiting Henry's enthusiasm for their own purposes.

Henry had inherited most of his father's advisers. He was still young and it might be assumed that major decisions were initially made by senior Councillors such as Richard Fox, Bishop of Winchester, and

KEY ISSUE

Why did Henry VIII want war, and in whose interests was it?

CHARLES BRANDON, DUKE OF SUFFOLK (?–1545)

Charles Brandon was the son of Sir William Brandon, Henry VII's standard bearer who was killed at Bosworth. Tall and strongly built, he was one of Henry VIII's earliest and closest companions and took a leading part in the jousts and entertainments at court. He was knighted in 1512, created Viscount Lisle in 1513, and then made Duke of Suffolk. When Louis XII of France died, Suffolk was sent to bring back his widow, Henry's sister Mary. She promptly insisted that Suffolk marry her. At first Henry was furious, but he relented and the couple were allowed to return to a second ceremony celebrated with a tournament. In the French campaign of 1523 he was made commander of the English army to which he contributed a large number of his own followers. In 1529 Henry sent him on an embassy to Francis I of France, with secret instructions to ask for the French king's opinion of Wolsey and Campeggio. It is difficult to associate Suffolk with any faction. He got on well enough with Wolsey, but tension seemed possible with the Howards. They may have resented him building a rival influence in East Anglia, partly on the basis of land that had previously belonged to the Duke of Norfolk's son. However, he cooperated with Norfolk in dealing with disturbances in East Anglia in 1526 and 1528. There was a brawl in Westminster in 1532 between Suffolk's and Norfolk's retinues, apparently prompted by Suffolk's opposition to Henry VIII's proposed divorce from Catherine of Aragon. Suffolk's wife Mary, Henry's sister, withdrew from the Court, but Suffolk could not escape some involvement. He had to preside at Anne's coronation and on a number of occasions had to take unwelcome messages to Catherine of Aragon.

Having been widowed, he married Catherine Willoughby in 1553; she brought him lands and influence in Lincolnshire which he made use of in 1536 when he put down the Lincolnshire Rising. He still carried out duties as a leading courtier and Councillor. Henry trusted him to the end. In 1544 he was discussing with the King whether Bishop Gardiner should be investigated for treason, and a year later a letter from William Paget to Edward Seymour indicated that it was still worthwhile for ambitious courtiers to be on good terms with Suffolk. He commanded the army that captured Boulogne in 1544. He died in 1545 and was buried at Henry's expense in St George's Chapel, Windsor. Suffolk has not always had a good press. In the 1940s Garrett Mattingly described him as 'the beef-witted hero of a thousand tourneys', and more recently D MacCulloch has referred to 'Suffolk's few brain cells'. But he was a survivor, and was one of the few to retain the King's favour throughout the reign.

William Warham, Archbishop of Canterbury. They were both men of vast experience closely associated with the very different approach of Henry VII. But it was their duty to implement Henry's policies and not create them. If the King was determined to fight a war, war would be fought.

3 ⟿ WAR WITH FRANCE

In 1511 Henry joined the so-called Holy League against France, which Ferdinand, the Pope, the Swiss, and the Venetians had just formed. Henry agreed with Ferdinand on a joint expedition to San Sebastian in northern Spain in April 1512. There seems little doubt that Henry was out-classed in the diplomacy that lay behind this, and the expedition was clearly organised for the benefit of Ferdinand rather than Henry. Ferdinand captured Navarre and, having achieved his objectives, made peace and abandoned Henry.

The obvious base for any offensive against France was Calais which had been in English hands for over 150 years and made an ideal base for transporting troops. In April 1513 Emperor Maximilian agreed to join the English attack on France. Henry led the most imposing English army to have been seen in France since the Battle of Agincourt in 1415. In August it marched on the fortress of Thérouanne. A French force sent to relieve the town was forced to flee in undignified fashion in the so-called Battle of the Spurs, as they spurred their horses so hard to get away, giving Henry a genuine if insignificant victory. Thérouanne surrendered which brought little benefit to the English but pleased Maximilian whose territories had been threatened by the town.

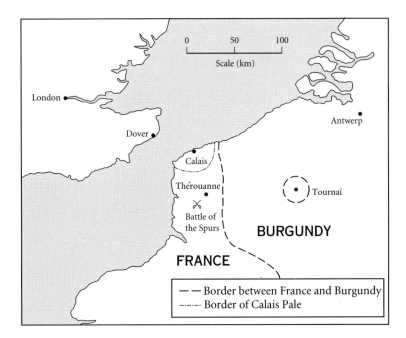

MAP 2
Henry VIII's invasion of France, 1513

The next English target was Tournai, a French city 100 miles from Calais and entirely surrounded by Maximilian's lands, which stretched from the Netherlands into northern France. It was undoubtedly a wealthy city, but again it seems that its capture would be of benefit to Maximilian rather than Henry. On 23 September, the city surrendered, passing under English rule for the next five years. The English were forced to maintain a garrison and entirely re-build the defences of the city at great cost.

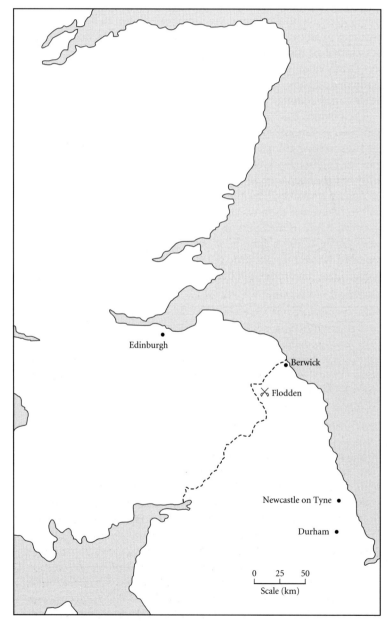

MAP 3
*The Scottish defeat
at Flodden, 1513*

In one sense Henry had simply been fighting France in the interest of countries other than his own. On the other hand, he had flexed his muscles and proved that England could organise a large and well-equipped army. He had proved himself a true king in the traditional manner, and Tournai was at least a valuable possession for diplomatic bargaining.

Ironically, Henry had nothing to do with England's greatest military triumph in 1513. James IV of Scotland, despite being married to Henry's sister, Margaret, had decided to take advantage of Henry's distraction in France and invaded northern England. Acting as regent in Henry's absence, Catherine of Aragon sent an army north, and on 9 September at Flodden Field the Earl of Surrey annihilated the army of James IV. Surrey was rewarded with the title Duke of Norfolk which his family had lost in 1485. James himself was killed along with much of the Scottish aristocracy, and Catherine sent his bloodied coat to Henry in France as a token of victory.

KEY ISSUE

What did Henry VIII gain from the wars against France and Scotland in 1513?

TIMELINE

1511		England joined the Holy League against France
1513	August:	the Battle of Spurs and surrender of Thérouanne
	9 September	English victory over the Scots at Flodden
	23 September	the capture of Tournai

THOMAS WOLSEY (1472/3–1530)

The campaign of 1513 was the first major undertaking to be organised by Thomas Wolsey. Born in 1472 or 1473, Wolsey was the son of a butcher, educated at Magdalen College, Oxford, and ordained priest in 1498. He rose rapidly in the service of Henry VIII and after the success of 1513 he became Henry's leading adviser. He was appointed Lord Chancellor, supervising government administration and the law courts, frequently sitting as a judge himself. He became Archbishop of York, second to William Warham, Archbishop of Canterbury, in the church hierarchy, but was appointed Papal Legate (i.e. acting as the Pope's representative), which gave him full authority over the English Church. His influence with the king, combined with his undoubted ability and extraordinary capacity for hard work, enabled him to dominate foreign and domestic policy for the next 15 years. On one busy diplomatic visit to France Cavendish describes Wolsey working constantly at his desk for 12 hours at a stretch, without rising once to eat or to relieve himself. Wolsey also had a reputation as a patron of education, art and music and his early relations with Henry were helped by common interests in these areas. His patronage was part of the ostentation that was a feature of his character and he spent his enormous income lavishly. Recent excavations have shown that his new palace at Hampton Court was planned according to Italian designs new to

PROFILE

PICTURE 8
Cardinal Thomas Wolsey, *anon.*

England, considered especially appropriate for a prince of the Church. His power and the way he paraded it caused envy among other leading subjects. At times it seemed that his household rather than the royal court was at the centre of affairs, prompting John Skelton's lines: 'The King's court should have the excellence but Hampton Court [Wolsey's palace] hath the pre-eminence'. Wolsey, however, was always aware that he depended on the King for his eminence. At the end of his life he claimed: 'I have often kneeled before him in his privy chamber on my knees the space of an hour or two to persuade him from his will and appetite; but I could never bring to pass to dissuade him therefrom.' Perhaps he worked so hard at doing everything himself in order make himself indispensable and to prevent any rival emerging. In the late 1520s the King grew impatient that Wolsey was unable to secure him the divorce from Catherine of Aragon he was determined to obtain, and when it became clear that Wolsey had finally failed to win the Pope's co-operation, he was dismissed. His enemies at Court, led by Anne Boleyn, whom he called 'that midnight crow', had won out. He retired to his diocese of York in 1529, from where he was summoned back to London to face treason charges in 1530, but died at Leicester on the journey south.

His recent biographer, Peter Gwyn, has presented a portrait of Wolsey as a man with an almost phenomenal range of interests who, as Henry's servant, governed the country successfully and with the willing co-operation of the ruling elite and who made real progress in areas such as the administration of law and social policy. Other historians have not been quite so generous but there is a growing acceptance that in his own terms and in the context of his time Wolsey's career could be accounted a success story.

4 ⌒ FOREIGN POLICY 1514–25

Wolsey's first diplomatic achievement was peace with France in 1514. Ferdinand of Aragon and the Emperor Maximilian had proved to be unreliable allies and the peace settlement with France did not include them. The treaty was to England's advantage: England kept Tournai and the French pension originally paid to Henry VII after the Treaty of Étaples was renewed. In addition, Henry's younger sister Mary was to marry the ageing Louis XII. However, the death of Louis on 1 January 1515 and the accession of Francis I, as determined to seek glory as Henry had been, ended any chance of lasting peace in Europe.

Francis launched a renewed invasion of Italy in the first summer he was king. He won a great victory at Marignano in September 1515, as a result of which he took control of Milan and consolidated French power in Italy. Wolsey made funds available to both Emperor Maximilian and the Swiss in an attempt to build an anti-French coalition, only to see Francis consolidate his position and (temporarily) make peace with his enemies by 1517.

In 1517 Wolsey sensibly opened negotiations with the French. With the French triumphant in northern Italy and no other power in a position to challenge them, a peace policy was the only realistic option. There was also the opportunity to dress the peace up as Christian unity. Increasingly concerned about the threat from the **Ottoman Turks**, Pope Leo X proposed a universal peace in Europe followed by a crusade. Recognising that Wolsey would have a key role in the negotiations, Pope Leo agreed to Henry's request to appoint Wolsey as Papal Legate, i.e. the Pope's personal representative in England. Armed with these legatine powers, Wolsey was now supreme in England in church and state, under the King, and his prestige as a diplomat on the European stage was enhanced.

On 2 October 1518, in London, English and French representatives agreed to a treaty binding the great powers to perpetual peace. Twenty other powers were eventually included in this agreement, which became known as the Treaty of London. On 4 October it was agreed that Henry should return Tournai to France in return for 600 000 crowns (in any case the city had brought more expenses than advantages) and it was also agreed that Mary, Henry's daughter, should marry the son of the French King.

It was a brilliant recovery after three years of diplomatic disaster. England was the pivot of the Treaty of London as each state made their agreement individually with England and not with each other. Therefore, at no cost, Henry and Wolsey were established as the peacemakers of Europe, and England had secured an influence in Europe out of all proportion to its real power and wealth. Wolsey had pulled off the amazing double achievement of winning for himself the reputation as peace-maker, which he seems genuinely to have wanted to be, and yet also gratified Henry's desire for honour and glory.

The Treaty of London did not represent a new golden age of peace, however, as hoped for by some commentators at the time such as Erasmus. Within three years war had again broken out between Francis I and the new Emperor Charles V, who had succeeded his grandfather, Maximilian. The point at issue was control of the Duchy of Milan which was of great strategic importance as the 'shield' of Italy and which Francis had seized in 1515.

The events that followed provide evidence of the central position in diplomacy that Wolsey had engineered for Henry and himself. On 26 May 1520 Emperor Charles V met briefly with Henry on his way from Spain to the Netherlands. The meeting had to be brief because Henry was about to embark for the most glamorous and spectacular of his meetings with Francis I at the Field of the Cloth of Gold, which was located in the no-man's land between Calais and French territory. A retinue of 5000 accompanied Henry, and nearly two weeks of wrestling, dancing, and jousting was exactly the kind of lavish celebration in which Henry most delighted, despite the embarrassment when he lost to Francis in a wrestling match. The two kings parted on 23 June and

Ottoman Turks the Ottomans were the Muslim ruling dynasty of Turkey, who had conquered much of South-eastern Europe and were to reach the gates of Vienna in 1529.

See page 390

exchanged vows of peace. Henry then hurried to Gravelines further north to meet Francis's enemy, Charles V, once again. The Field of the Cloth of Gold had been a magnificent show of friendship, but it meant nothing compared with the diplomatic manoeuvring behind the scenes.

The following year Francis re-opened hostilities against Charles. On 2 August 1521 Wolsey sailed to Calais to try to negotiate a peace settlement between France and the Emperor Charles V. On 14 August he went to Bruges where he negotiated a treaty with the Emperor. This committed England to war with France if fighting continued. Henry and Charles would mount a joint campaign and Mary Tudor was to marry Charles instead of the son of the French King. After this meeting Wolsey returned to Calais and the peace conference.

His behaviour has been much discussed. Scarisbrick has argued that Wolsey always wanted peace and that there was an underlying conflict with Henry. Wolsey's consolation was to delay the commitment to war until May 1522. Peter Gwyn has argued that Wolsey was not looking for peace, but was a tough and uncompromising negotiator, who hoodwinked the French about England's neutrality, while conducting serious negotiations with Emperor Charles V. Neutrality would seriously diminish Henry's role as a major international figure whereas an alliance with Charles might bring material gains and would be popular with the Pope, who was keen to expel the French from Italy. (Wolsey is likely to have wanted to serve papal interests when he could, with himself having an eye one day to being a candidate for the papal throne.) Wolsey certainly enjoyed the reputation as peace-maker, but there is no clear evidence which can finally prove what his underlying motive was. In any case, he was forced to adapt his policy to the changing situation in Europe and, although he could influence the King, he knew ultimately he had to give Henry what he wanted as well.

War was declared on 29 May 1522 and lasted for three years. In August 1523 the Duke of Suffolk crossed to Calais with a substantial army. The initial plan was to attack Boulogne, but Charles V persuaded the English to march on Paris. Initially no opposition was met and the army advanced to within 70 miles of the city, but this was over-ambitious with extended supply lines, and the campaign disintegrated.

The expense of the campaign and the failure of Charles V to offer effective support brought growing disenchantment with the war. In 1524 negotiations were re-opened with the French. As before, Wolsey used the alliance with Charles as a means of bringing pressure to bear on the French.

His approach to the French was put on hold following news of the Battle of Pavia in northern Italy in February 1525. Charles V's army destroyed the French force, and Francis himself was captured. There now seemed a chance that Henry could recover the lost territories in France and even claim the French throne. Another invasion was planned and a forced loan, called euphemistically the 'Amicable Grant', was demanded from the English people. However, it proved impossible to raise sufficient money and gather the forces necessary for a cam-

KEY ISSUE

What influence did England have in European affairs 1514–22, and how was it achieved?

paign to have greater success than in 1523. Moreover, Charles V clearly had no enthusiasm for Henry's plans, and, in August, Wolsey negotiated the Treaty of The More with the French. England abandoned territorial claims in France, and the French resumed an annual pension to Henry of 100 000 gold crowns.

TIMELINE

1514	Peace and marriage alliance with France
1515	Francis I victory at Marignano – takes Milan
1518	Treaty of London declaring perpetual peace
1520	Field of the Cloth of Gold
	Negotiations with Charles V
1521	Calais peace conference
1522	War against France declared
1523	Duke of Suffolk's failed campaign in France
1525	Capture of Francis I by forces of Charles V at Pavia

Wolsey and Foreign Policy

ANALYSIS

According to John Guy, foreign policy has been seen as Wolsey's main area of interest because of an accident of survival. It is simply that there is more material available for the study of his foreign policy than for domestic affairs. Nevertheless, the conduct of foreign policy during his years in power may provide information both on his own ideas and aims and on his relationship with the King. It is possible to identify four main interpretations.

English diplomacy between 1515–25 failed to bring great gains to the country, but it did thrust the country into a major role that its wealth and population scarcely justified. Whatever his other motivations, a major aim for Wolsey was to boost Henry's honour and influence. For all the setbacks as the kaleidoscope of European politics shifted, Wolsey still managed to maintain an independent and active role for England, and win the glory, honour and prestige which meant so much to the King.

1. In 1929 AF Pollard put forward the view that Wolsey's policy was simply to follow the papacy. His ambition was to become Pope and so he led England in whatever direction suited Rome. Superficially there was some justification for this view but by the 1960s it was effectively challenged. DS Chambers, in an article in 1965, showed that Wolsey did not seriously consider becoming pope. He did not try to build up any kind of support for himself in Rome and never visited the city. Far from co-operating with the papacy, he was criticised by Pope Leo X for not keeping him informed of events and in 1518 took over the Pope's initiative for a general peace so the credit went to himself and King Henry.

2. In the 1960s JJ Scarisbrick suggested that Wolsey's aim was to be a peacemaker. This was due to a genuine desire for peace in accord with **humanist** ideals and a more practical desire to save money. He emphasised Wolsey's diplomatic activity which he saw as his means to attain his goal. The fact that England was frequently at war was due not to the absence of such a policy but to its failure. Scarisbrick has since modified his views. One objection is that it pays more attention to what Wolsey said than what he did. In acknowledging Wolsey's failure in maintaining peace, however, he did point to an important factor that Pollard had tended to ignore and that was that Henry also had a say in what happened in policy.

3. In the 1980s Susan Doran, drawing on the researches of Dana Scott Cambell, put more emphasis on Henry's role. Wolsey's aim was to increase and maintain his own power, but to do this he had to follow a policy that pleased Henry and, as a secondary factor, the Pope, since it was to them that he owed his position.

4. More recently historians (e.g. John Guy and Peter Gwyn) have developed this emphasis on pleasing Henry. Wolsey is now seen primarily as the King's servant, his main aim being to fulfil Henry's ambition to be a great European ruler. Peace was often the practical alternative because England was more likely to make an impression in diplomacy than in the expensive option of war. However, if Henry was set on military expeditions or if an appropriate alliance offered any chance of success Wolsey was prepared to go to war.

Finally, it should be remembered that in foreign policy more than any other area, Henry and Wolsey were at the mercy of circumstances beyond their control. Whatever their long-term aims might be, in practice they could only react to the actions of the other European rulers. England rarely had the initiative in such affairs.

5 ↪ DOMESTIC AFFAIRS UNDER WOLSEY

A *The courts*

Wolsey played an active role in all aspects of government. After his appointment as Lord Chancellor in December 1515, he presided over the **Court of Chancery** and the **Court of Star Chamber** which both saw a dramatic expansion in their work at this time. In Wolsey's 14 years as Lord Chancellor, it is estimated that over 9000 cases were brought before the two courts. In particular the Court of Star Chamber became far busier, dealing with about 120 cases each year, compared with only about a dozen in the reign of Henry VII. It is with this court that Wolsey was most closely associated.

Despite all his other responsibilities, he sat as a judge in the Court of Star Chamber several times each week. The value of Wolsey's work in Star Chamber has sometimes been questioned. It is true that he attracted so much business to the court that it could not cope and overflow courts had to be established, and that he failed to organise the court in an effective manner, leaving this task to his successors. On the other hand, recent historians, such as John Guy, have given Wolsey credit for his genuine support for 'impartial justice'. This simply means that when anyone could not obtain justice through the regular court system, they could take their case to the Star Chamber regardless of their wealth or status.

Like Henry VII, Wolsey was prepared to attack abuse of power by the aristocracy and such traditional problems as illegal retaining and bribery of Justices of the Peace and sheriffs. Great aristocrats were brought before the Star Chamber and punished; in 1515 the Earl of Northumberland was sent to the Fleet Prison and in 1516 Lord Burgavenny was accused of illegal retaining.

It is nonetheless true that Wolsey's more ambitious schemes to re-organise the administration of the law never really bore fruit. A scheme of 1526 to send commissioners to every shire to hear cases was never implemented, but a permanent committee was established at Whitehall in Westminster in 1519 specifically to hear cases brought by the poor, and Wolsey clearly did try to make himself accessible to all the King's subjects. According to the Venetian ambassador Guistinian he had 'the reputation of being extremely just: he favours the people exceedingly, and especially the poor: hearing their suits and seeking to despatch them instantly ...' As a lawyer, Wolsey may not have been an innovator or a reformer, but he was diligent and saw the need that great men should be subject to justice as much as their inferiors.

> **KEY ISSUE**
>
> *Did Wolsey achieve anything as a judge?*

B *Enclosure*

Essentially enclosure involves the conversion of land from crop growing to sheep rearing and is associated with the practice of clearing people off the land for this purpose. In the late fifteenth and early sixteenth centuries, there was anxiety about the depopulation of the countryside. This is illustrated by three Acts of Parliament (1489, 1514, 1515), which were concerned with rural depopulation. The anxiety was probably over-done. Enclosure was concentrated in parts of the south Midlands and was, in the words of Professor Scarisbrick, 'slow, erratic, and piece-meal, and as much the work of peasants as of big men'.

> See pages 350–2

In 1517–18 Wolsey encouraged an enquiry into enclosure, whose returns provided material for the Court of Chancery to take legal action against those who had ignored the three statutes. Between 1518–29, legal action was taken against 264 persons, and some were forced to rebuild houses and return land to arable farming. The overall effect of these prosecutions may have been small, but the nature of Wolsey's actions was unprecedented. Proceedings were taken against nine noblemen, three bishops, 32 knights, 51 heads of religious houses, and several Oxford colleges. Wolsey was quite prepared to challenge the wealthiest and most powerful elements of society and to question the right of landowners to do exactly as they pleased in their own counties.

Wolsey's motives are interesting. His actions brought him no financial advantage and evidence of the unpopularity of his policy among the ruling classes was clear in the Parliament of 1523, when Wolsey, anxious for taxation to be agreed, had to make concessions and accept all existing enclosures. It seems that his attempt to combat enclosures had been prompted by an awareness of what would today be called food security, ensuring there would be sufficient grain production even in years of poor harvests, plus a desire to avoid the disorder which could accompany the hardship brought about by enclosures.

KEY ISSUE

How did Wolsey tackle the problem of enclosure, and why was he concerned about it?

C *Parliament*

There were six parliamentary sessions between 1510 and 1515. The main reason for this was that Henry needed money to finance his extravagant foreign policy. He did well out of these parliaments, partly due to Wolsey's development of a new method of taxation. The traditional Fifteenths and Tenths were based on a fixed sum that had to be raised by each community and this sum did not always relate to the real wealth of the community. In 1513 the 'subsidy' was developed. This was based on an assessment of personal wealth and banded according to the ability to pay and proved a far more effective tax than its predecessors.

Wolsey used the new tax four times and raised far more revenue than had been possible with sole reliance on Fifteenths and Tenths. Between 1513–16, the subsidy raised £90 000, while the clergy contributed a further £40 000 to the royal coffers.

Apart from finance, the Parliament of 1515 was dominated by concern over Church matters. A London merchant named Richard Hunne, who had been charged with heresy, was found dead in the custody of the Bishop of London. The City of London was sensitive to any attack on one of its number by the Church, and it was possible that the bishop's officials would be charged with murder. The bishop tried to protect his officials by claiming **benefit of clergy**. This was a topical issue. Benefit of clergy had been restricted by an act of 1512 and was due for renewal in the Parliament of 1515.

Benefit of clergy the clergy could not be convicted of capital offences. The test of clerical status was to read a verse from the Bible, so in effect 'benefit of clergy' was available to anyone who was literate

The bishops in the House of Lords blocked the renewal of the act and two debates were held before Henry in which the bishops defended their position. The affair ended with a joint meeting of both Commons and Lords at which Wolsey knelt before Henry to assure him the Church had no desire to limit the power of the Crown. Wolsey's role in this appears to be that of mediator. The Act of 1512 was not renewed, but a point of principle as to the pre-eminence of the Crown against the Church had been asserted, and the complaints of Parliament had found an audience.

The Parliament of 1523 was the only Parliament to be summoned while Wolsey was Chancellor. Inevitably the main argument was over money. War had been renewed with France, and Wolsey initially demanded over £800 000 on top of 'loans' of £260 000. It appears that Wolsey tried to bully Parliament by maintaining the session well into the summer. He did obtain some extra money, but at the cost of abandoning his campaign against enclosure and creating much ill feeling. It would be going too far to suggest on the available evidence that there was outright antagonism between Wolsey and the leading figures in the country, who sat in Parliament, but there was probably some insensitivity on his part.

KEY ISSUE

How effective was Wolsey in his dealings with Parliament?

D *The Amicable Grant*

The conflicts of 1523 were swiftly followed by one of the most complex and controversial disputes of this period. The 'Amicable Grant' was to be a non-refundable contribution by the English people to finance the war in France. This new demand followed the forced loans and high parliamentary taxation of the previous three years. Popular reaction was swift and hostile. There were disturbances concentrated around the important cloth-making centre of Lavenham in Suffolk and extending to London and Kent.

There is no evidence that this resistance was stirred up by aristocrats, although many probably disliked Wolsey, and the Dukes of Norfolk and Suffolk were happy to make it clear that the money would be almost impossible to collect. Opposition seems to have been spontaneous and based on poverty and inability to pay rather than on innate hostility to Henry's policies. No money at all was collected, and peace was made with France. The Amicable Grant can be viewed as a humiliation for Henry and Wolsey, but it also suggests flexibility and realism in the face of united opposition. It is also possible that the campaign in France had been more or less abandoned before the unpopularity of the Amicable Grant became clear.

KEY ISSUE

Was the 'Amicable Grant' simply an error?

6 ⤳ WOLSEY AND THE CHURCH

As Archbishop of York, Wolsey ranked second in the English Church to William Warham, the Archbishop of Canterbury. However, as we have seen, in 1518 the Pope appointed him a Papal Legate, technically known as a **legate *a latere***. He now outranked the Archbishop of Canterbury and could exercise authority over the whole of the Church in England and Wales. If improvements in the Church were necessary, Wolsey was in an excellent position to implement them.

At first sight Wolsey presented a poor image as a reformer. He was an obvious example of a man who had entered the church as a career move rather than through any spiritual commitment. He was preoccupied with affairs of state, was a **pluralist** and had two illegitimate children. However, according to his servant Cavendish, he also heard two masses a day and, however busy he was, always said the daily office, the prayers to which he was committed as a priest.

Legate *a latere* the most powerful type of papal representative. *A latere* means 'from the side of the Pope'.

Pluralist someone who technically had more than one post, usually in the Church.

Wolsey summoned a council of bishops at Westminster in March 1519 to consider reform, and in November held a meeting of the heads of the religious houses. Both these meetings led to the issuing of sets of regulations, although they were effectively the rewriting of existing rules rather than anything new. In the late 1520s Wolsey was negotiating with the Pope for permission to create a number of new English bishoprics. The appropriate buildings and revenues would come from closing down some monasteries. At the same time he was given permission to join together monasteries where the number of inmates had fallen below 12. Wolsey's fall meant that these plans came to nothing.

During the 1520s he closed 29 religious houses (monasteries and convents) and used the proceeds to finance the foundation of Cardinal College at Oxford and a grammar school at Ipswich. The closures led to protests from the houses involved and their supporters, and Wolsey was accused of ignoring other people's interests. Nevertheless, his work was seen as a major contribution to education and his regulations for the new college aimed to ensure a balance between traditional learning and the new humanist emphasis on the classics and the Bible. At Wolsey's fall, the Ipswich school was closed and the college refounded by Henry as Christ Church.

> **KEY ISSUE**
>
> *How seriously did Wolsey take his responsibilities as England's leading churchman?*

7 ⌐ WOLSEY AND THE ARISTOCRACY

Wolsey was a man from a humble background, who came to control vast patronage and massive wealth. It is argued by some that this aroused antagonism from the great nobles on the King's Council, who saw Wolsey as an upstart and a barrier to their own advancement. At the same time Wolsey dominated policy-making and only communicated decisions to the Council after he and the King had made them.

In fact this tension between Wolsey and the King's noble Councillors may have been exaggerated. Wolsey's biographer, Peter Gwyn, cites a number of instances where Wolsey consulted the Council as a whole or individual members of it. The nobility continued to exercise their traditional roles. For example, the Dukes of Norfolk and Suffolk were frequently called on as military commanders and in 1525 and 1528 were active in dealing with unrest in East Anglia. These two dukes have been seen as helping to bring about Wolsey's fall, but before then much evidence points to good working relations with Wolsey. In a letter of 1528, for example, Norfolk, in the course of dealing with public business, takes time to help Wolsey in the foundation of his school at Ipswich.

The execution of the Duke of Buckingham in May 1521 is sometimes seen as evidence of Wolsey's hostility towards him. Buckingham was the country's leading aristocrat; he had royal blood and at least as good a claim to the throne as the Tudors. Polydore Vergil was the first to suggest that Wolsey engineered his fall to prevent Buckingham exploiting anti-French feeling in an attempt to remove Wolsey.

This interpretation of Wolsey's actions is now largely rejected. Buckingham seems to have been an intelligent but arrogant man. He had spoken against the King, resenting both Henry's failure to appoint him to the prestigious office of Constable of England and for permitting Star Chamber action against his follower, Sir William Bulmer, for wearing Buckingham's livery in the presence of the King. There is also evidence that Buckingham was raising troops and that accusations of treason were not wholly groundless. Far from targeting Buckingham, Wolsey had warned him of the possible consequences of his words.

Wolsey undoubtedly had a dominant role and was more the King's partner in ruling than anyone else. However, he tried to carry out the role through co-operating with, rather than antagonising, the political élite.

8 ⌐ WOLSEY AND THE ROYAL COURT

To understand the political importance of the Court we must look at the King's Household which formed its centre. Closest to the King was the Chamber, headed by the Lord Chamberlain. By Henry's reign this was a series of apartments, doubling as home and offices, designed to serve the King's private and public needs.

The diagram below shows a typical arrangement, although details varied from palace to palace and at different times. The hall was where the servants and less important officials dined and it also provided a spacious setting for major entertainments. Behind the hall was the watching chamber (or guard chamber) and beyond that the presence chamber which held the throne and canopy. These were areas for court ceremonies and entertainments, and here too the King dined in state.

The King's Rooms at Hampton Court 1535

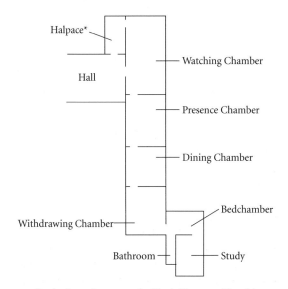

On the floor above were the King's library and jewel-house.

*a stair or ramp connecting two rooms on a different level

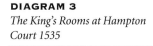

DIAGRAM 3
The King's Rooms at Hampton Court 1535

Beyond that was the Privy Chamber which was the King's private area. This first emerged in the 1490s and here the King was served by a small staff of personal servants headed by his most intimate bodyservant, the Groom of the Stool.

This was the situation that Henry VIII inherited but while he maintained the private nature of the Privy Chamber, he changed the character of its personnel. He built up a circle of close companions with whom he spent his time publicly and privately, and these were not obscure bodyservants but younger members of the peerage or established members of the Court. In 1518 their new status was recognised when the office of Gentleman of the Chamber was created. In ten years a staff of menial servants had been transformed into an official circle of intimate and high-ranking companions.

David Starkey has argued that Wolsey continually sought to control the Privy Chamber which might otherwise rival his own influence over the King. The Gentlemen of the Privy Chamber, known as the minions, had daily contact with Henry while Wolsey's work kept him at Westminster or one of his palaces such as York Place or Hampton Court. The minions were expelled from Court in May 1519. One interpretation is that Wolsey brought this about to protect his position. The excuse given was their irresponsible behaviour which reflected badly on the King, but the French and Venetian ambassadors saw it as Wolsey removing his rivals.

The minions returned before the end of the year but the wars of 1522–5 kept many of Henry's companions away from Court as they were employed as commanders and ambassadors. When the wars finished Wolsey's next ploy, according to this interpretation, was to secure the Eltham Ordinances of January 1526. These were economy measures which reduced the number of Gentlemen of the Privy Chamber from twelve to six. The most politically active were removed and the survivors were of no importance.

This interpretation is persuasive but it has been challenged, most strongly by Peter Gwyn. The contrast between Privy Chamber access and Wolsey's isolation may be too great. For much of the year Henry and Wolsey seem to have had regular weekly meetings; at other times they communicated by letter almost every day. In 1518, when fear of disease kept Henry out of London, he insisted that arrangements be made so messages could be sent every seven hours.

The expulsion of the minions was only temporary. Some had returned to Court within a few months and a number of them ended up in offices that represented a promotion. An alternative explanation of their removal was that their frivolity had brought criticism from senior Councillors, not just Wolsey, and they were being sent away for appropriate experience in royal service. The use of courtiers on military and diplomatic missions was usual and did not reflect some conspiracy by Wolsey. By the same token, the Eltham Ordinances were simply an economy measure, and here again many of the Gentlemen were promoted. For example, Sir William Compton, the Groom of the Stool for ten years, became Under-Treasurer of the Exchequer.

KEY ISSUE

How far was Wolsey in control of government during his period in office?

9 ⌐ THE DIVORCE

In 1509 Henry VIII had married his elder brother's widow, Catherine of Aragon. Although against the law of the Church, a papal **dispensation** had been granted by Pope Julius II. Catherine was five years older than Henry, a pious and loyal wife, to whom her husband had been genuinely devoted at first. Her problem was simply that she did not produce a son and heir. A daughter, Mary, was born, but five other children died in infancy, and after 1518 there were no more pregnancies. Henry needed a son to secure the succession and salve his pride.

Henry saw the failure of his marriage to secure a son as divine punishment and proof that the marriage was not valid. He gradually convinced himself that no papal dispensation could overcome the biblical ban on marriage to a dead brother's wife. Henry did have a case in

Dispensation
exceptional permission not to observe canon law

The Divorce Case

ANALYSIS

Strictly speaking Henry was not seeking a divorce but an annulment. This means a declaration that he had never been truly married to Catherine of Aragon. Henry based his case on the Old Testament where it says: 'And if a man shall take his brother's wife it is an unclean thing ... they shall be childless' (Leviticus 20:21). Some scholars assured the King that in the original Hebrew it said 'without sons'. Henry claimed that no pope could set aside this prohibition. In granting the dispensation to marry Catherine of Aragon, Pope Julius had gone beyond his authority. Henry's case was not especially strong. Another part of the Old Testament seemed to commend such a marriage (Deuteronomy 25:5), and most contemporary opinion supported the Pope's authority in such a case. In addition Henry's case depended on the first marriage having been consummated, since otherwise there was no impediment of affinity (being related) requiring a dispensation. Catherine always maintained, privately and publicly, that the marriage had not been consummated.

There was an alternative argument based on a technicality. The marriage *ceremony* of Catherine and Arthur had set up an impediment to her re-marriage to Henry that needed a different form of dispensation. Henry could have claimed that he had been given the wrong kind of dispensation. This legal technicality would not have challenged generally accepted interpretations of Scripture, it avoided a direct challenge to the Pope's authority, and it would not matter that the marriage had not been consummated. Wolsey brought this argument to Henry's attention, but the King refused to use it. He seems to have been genuinely convinced of the righteousness of his argument and felt it was his best chance of getting an annulment.

PICTURE 9
Anne Boleyn, *anon.*

canon law, but it was not a strong one and informed legal opinion largely opposed him. It would require a favourable international climate for any divorce to be granted by the Pope.

It was at this point that Anne Boleyn seriously aroused the King's attention. Born in 1501, she had spent several years at the courts of Burgundy and France. Her sister had already been the King's mistress, but Anne had different ideas. Either her sense of honour or a realistic appraisal of the situation led her to hold out against Henry's entreaties; she refused the role of mistress and by 1528 Henry had promised her marriage once he had divorced Catherine.

Securing the divorce was a task for Wolsey – Henry's confidential servant, the Pope's representative in England and a skilled diplomat. But things did not go smoothly. Catherine refused to cooperate. She appealed to the Pope and also sent an appeal to her nephew, the Emperor Charles V. In June 1527 news arrived that the Emperor's troops had sacked Rome and that Pope Clement was Charles' prisoner. Henry had already signed a treaty with Francis I of France. Now Wolsey himself went to France for a series of extended negotiations aimed at recruiting French help in the divorce case, supporting Francis in his campaigns against Charles, and possibly gaining the Pope's agreement to Wolsey running the Church on his behalf during his imprisonment.

During Wolsey's absence Henry uncharacteristically took action without consulting him. He sent messages directly to the Pope and discussed policy with leading Councillors such as the Dukes of Norfolk and Suffolk and Viscount Rochford, Anne Boleyn's father. However, Wolsey seems to have lost little if any ground. Henry's initiative had little effect, and Wolsey was still considered the man most likely to negotiate the divorce. Hopes rose when, in September 1528, the Pope's representative, Cardinal Campeggio, finally arrived in England to preside with Wolsey over a legatine court to decide Henry's case.

The court opened on 18 June 1529. Three days later, at the Battle of Landriano in northern Italy, Charles V's forces defeated the French and ensured that Italy and Pope Clement would remain in his power. Campeggio, following confidential instructions from the Pope that he was not to settle the case, adjourned the court on 31 July. It did not meet again, and Pope Clement recalled the case to Rome. In August the Treaty of Cambrai brought Francis, Charles and the Pope together as allies. That destroyed any remaining illusion that the Pope might view the divorce with sympathy.

KEY ISSUE

Why did Wolsey fail to secure the divorce?

10 ✎ THE FALL OF WOLSEY

Wolsey had failed in this, the King's 'Great Matter', and his career was finished. In October he was dismissed from the Lord Chancellorship and allowed to withdraw to his diocese of York. Evidence emerged that he was still communicating with French and Imperial agents, and in November 1530 he was arrested for treason. He died at Leicester Abbey on his way to London to face the charges.

The simplest explanation for Wolsey's fall comes from Peter Gwyn. He argues that Wolsey was Henry's servant, whose duty it was to fulfill his master's wishes. Through no fault of his own, his diplomacy failed and failure to get the divorce inevitably brought about his dismissal. In addition he was particularly vulnerable because of his close association with the Papacy.

David Starkey and Eric Ives both argue that Wolsey was a victim of factional intrigues organised by leading aristocrats, such as the Duke of Norfolk, around the person of Anne Boleyn. Anne, it is argued, had to secure political dominance to challenge the popularity of Catherine of Aragon. In the summer of 1529 it became clear that Wolsey had failed, and this enabled Anne and her faction to bring Wolsey down at a time when Wolsey had little close contact with the King. Ives argues that the fall of Wolsey was 'first and foremost Anne's success'.

The faction theory gives the impression that Wolsey had enemies who were organised and simply waiting to attack him, and tends to see Henry as a figure being manipulated by others. This may play down Henry's role. The divorce was crucial. Here was an issue which affected Henry more closely than anything else, and for the first time he was prepared to get involved not just in making policy but in deciding the details of how it should be carried out. He insisted that his arguments be used in obtaining the divorce rather than the more diplomatic, and possibly more realistic, alternative suggested by Wolsey. He was prepared to take action without consulting Wolsey, and it was not until September 1527 that the Cardinal realised that Henry intended to marry Anne Boleyn. Henry had taken control; when Wolsey's rivals turned against him they were following his lead. Previous co-operation may not have counted for much when the opportunity arose for advancement at the Cardinal's expense.

George Cavendish was a servant of Wolsey, and his view of this issue is highlighted in the biography he wrote of his master in the 1550s. Here he is writing of Wolsey's departure for France in 1527:

> You have heard how several of the great nobles and lords of the Council lay in ambush with my lady Anne Boleyn to espy a convenient time to catch the Cardinal in a trap. At last they thought the time had come that they were waiting for, supposing it best to cause him to travel beyond the seas in this matter. They said (to encourage him) that it was more suitable for his high discretion, wit and authority to achieve a perfect peace among these great and most mighty princes of the world than anyone else. Their purpose was only to get him out of the King's daily presence that they might have convenient leisure and opportunity to attempt their long-desired enterprise and by the aid of their chief mistress (my lady Anne) to slander him so unto the King in his absence that he should be rather in his high displeasure than in his accustomed favours, or at the least to be in the less estimation with his majesty.

Q

1. *How does this extract illustrate the importance of access to the King?*
2. *What role does Anne Boleyn have in this extract?*
3. *Which modern interpretation of Wolsey's fall seems most justified by this extract?*
4. *How valuable is Cavendish's account to an historian studying Wolsey's career?*

Following Wolsey's fall, one of the people whom he counted on to look out for his interests was another of his servants, who had transferred to the King's service - Thomas Cromwell. Cromwell never betrayed his old master, but gradually won the confidence of the King and was to become his chief minister as Wolsey had been, although as the King's Secretary rather than enjoying the trappings of Church and state. Wolsey had done his best to make the existing system work well to serve the interests of the King and the realm. Cromwell was to oversee one of the most radical transformations in English history during the next phase of Henry's reign – the Reformation.

11 ⌐ BIBLIOGRAPHY

*K Randell *Henry VIII and the Government of England* (Hodder, Access to History, 2001) is a sound introduction aimed at sixth-formers. Wolsey dominates this period and **J Guy *Cardinal Wolsey* (Headstart History Papers, 1998) is an excellent introduction that provides a balanced assessment based on recent research. *P Gwyn *The King's Cardinal* (Pimlico, 2002) is a long and detailed book that is well worth consulting. It presents a very favourable view of the cardinal, perhaps excessively so. JJ Scarisbrick *Henry VIII* (Methuen, 1981) is a useful account of the whole reign. Make good use of the index. *D Starkey *The Reign of Henry VIII. Personalities and Politics* (Vintage, 2002) stresses the new character of Henry's court and the role of court politics, and is often an entertaining read.

(*Recommended. **Highly recommended.)

12 ⌐ STRUCTURED AND ESSAY QUESTIONS

A *Structured questions*

1. (a) What were the arguments for and against an aggressive foreign policy at the beginning of Henry VIII's reign?
    (b) How successful was Henry's foreign policy up to the end of 1513?
2. (a) Why did Henry VIII want a divorce?
    (b) Explain Wolsey's failure to obtain the divorce.

B *Essay questions*

1. How believable is the claim that Wolsey's foreign policy was guided by a desire for peace?
2. 'Wolsey's domestic policies showed great promise but little achievement.' How far do you agree with this judgement?

3. 'Throughout his career Wolsey was completely dependent on the King.' To what extent do Wolsey's actions show this to be true?
4. To what extent does faction explain Wolsey's fall from power?
5. Who achieved more in foreign affairs: Henry VII or Wolsey?

13 ∽ SOURCE EXERCISES

(i) Henry VIII: 'The Age's Splendour'

I have no fear but when you heard that our prince, now Henry VIII had succeeded to his father's throne, all your melancholy left you at once. What may you not promise yourself from a Prince with whose extraordinary and almost divine character you are acquainted? When you know what a hero he now shows himself, how wisely he behaves, what a lover he is of justice and goodness, what affection he bears to the learned, I will venture to swear that you will need no wings to make you fly to behold this new and auspicious star. If you could see how all the world here is rejoicing in the possession of so great a prince, how his life is all their desire, you could not contain your tears for joy. The heavens laugh, the earth exults, all things are full of milk, of honey, of nectar. Avarice is expelled the country. Liberality scatters wealth with bounteous hand. Our king does not desire gold or gems or precious metals, but virtue, glory, immortality. The other day he told me 'I wish I were more learned'. 'But learning is not what we expect of a king,' I answered, 'merely that he should encourage scholars.' 'Most certainly,' he replied, 'as without them we should scarcely live at all.' Now what more splendid remark could a prince make?

SOURCE A
Letter from Lord Mountjoy to Erasmus on Henry's accession in 1509. William, Lord Mountjoy was a nobleman with a passion for scholarship. He had been a pupil of Erasmus and was friends with many of the leading scholars in England

But Henry, before he was crowned, hearing that his subjects everywhere cursed Richard Empson and Edmund Dudley, charging these two lawyers with being the most savage extortioners, who eagerly plundered all secular and ecclesiastical wealth, and seeking to have both of them and their accomplices brought to summary justice, consulted his counselors on this matter before he undertook any other business. Then, as his own opinion agreed with that of his advisers, he ordered the wretched extortioners and their accomplices to be arrested, so that they might pay the deserved penalty; so that by granting the first favour sought of him, he might please his subjects, who were already well-disposed towards him … Richard and Edmund, after being convicted of many crimes, were convicted and beheaded. By this act all the wrath of the people was appeased, and everyone was grateful to the monarch for the punishment of the evil-doers.

SOURCE B
Polydore Vergil
Anglica Historia

SOURCE C

George Cavendish The Life of
Wolsey. *Cavendish was one of
Wolsey's servants. He entered
his service in about 1522 and
wrote his biography in the
1550s*

The king was young and lusty, disposed all to mirth and pleasure, and to follow his desire and appetite, not inclined to work in the busy affairs of this realm....The other ancient counsellors would, according to the office of good counsellors, often persuade the king to attend the council, there to hear what was done in weighty matters, which pleased the king nothing at all, for he loved nothing worse than to be constrained to do anything contrary to his royal will and pleasure; the almoner Wolsey knew this very well, having a secret intelligence of the king's natural inclination, and so fast as the other counsellors advised the king to leave his pleasure, and to attend to the affairs of his realm, so busily did the almoner persuade him to the contrary which delighted him much and caused him to have the greater affection and love to the almoner.

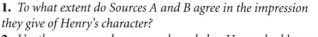

1. *To what extent do Sources A and B agree in the impression they give of Henry's character?*
2. *Use the sources and your own knowledge. How valuable are Sources A, B and C as evidence of Henry VIII's character and aims in the early years of his reign?*
3. *What impression is given of the young King Henry VIII in these sources?*

(ii) The King's Great Matter: Henry's motives in his quest for a divorce

Now let us return to the King who was greatly troubled in conscience because many learned theologians secretly informed him that he lived in adultery with his brother's wife to the great peril of his soul, and told him farther that the court of Rome could not dispense with God's command and precept.

The common people, being ignorant of the truth, and in especial women, said that the King wanted another wife for his own pleasure. The King, like a prudent prince and wanting all men to know his intent and purpose, caused all his nobility, judges and counsellors, with many other persons, to come to his palace of Bridewell and there to them said, as near as my wit could bear away, these words following.

'... If our true heir be not known at the time of our death, see what trouble shall fall on you and your children. The experience thereof some of you have seen after the death of our noble grandfather King Edward IV and some have heard what manslaughter continued in this realm between the Houses of York and Lancaster, by which this realm was almost destroyed ...

And although it has pleased God to send us a fair daughter, yet it has been told us that neither is she our lawful daughter nor her mother our lawful wife…Think you, my lords, that these words touch not my body and soul…And for this only cause I protest before God and in the word of a prince, I have asked counsel of the greatest clerks in Christendom, and for this cause I have sent for this legate (Campeggio) as an impartial man, to know the truth and to settle my conscience.

And as touching the Queen, if it be judged by the law of God that she is my lawful wife, there was never a thing more pleasant nor more acceptable to me. For I assure you that if I were to marry again, as long as the marriage was valid, I would surely choose her above all other women.'

To see the reaction of the hearers of this oration was a strange sight, for some sighed and said nothing, others were sorry to hear the king so troubled in his conscience. Others that favoured the queen much sorrowed that this matter was now opened, and so every man spoke as his heart served him, but the king ever laboured to know the truth for the discharge of his conscience.

SOURCE A
From The Chronicle of Edward Hall, *published in 1547. This incident took place on the 8 November, 1528. Hall was a lawyer from London whose book celebrated the Tudor dynasty and its success in ending the Wars of the Roses.*

And above all things there is no one thing that causes princes to be more wilful than carnal (sexual) desire and foolish love. The experience is plain in this case for what laws have been enacted, what noble and ancient monasteries overthrown and defaced, what differences of religious opinion have arisen, what executions have been committed, and what changes of good and ancient laws have been brought about by the will and wilful desire of the prince (Henry VIII) almost to the desolation of this noble realm.

SOURCE B
From George Cavendish Life and Death of Cardinal Wolsey. *Cavendish had been a servant in Wolsey's household and a close attendant on the Cardinal. His book was written during the reign of the Catholic Queen Mary. Here he is commenting on the effect of Henry's relationship with Anne Boleyn.*

Q

1. *Study Source A. Using the source and your own knowledge explain the significance of the phrase 'manslaughter continued in this realm between the Houses of York and Lancaster'?*
2. *Compare Sources A and B. How reliable are these sources, and to what extent do the authors of the two disagree about the reasons for Henry VIII seeking an annulment of his first marriage?*

4

Henry VIII: The Reformation

Henry VIII's reign was of immense importance in the history of the English Church. When he came to the throne England was an integral part of the Roman Catholic Church, owing spiritual allegiance to the Pope and participating to the full in the traditional practices of that Church. Henry himself had made a show of his piety and had taken up the pen in defence of Catholic doctrine and the Papacy against Luther when he wrote his *Assertio Septem Sacramentorum* (Defence of the Seven Sacraments). For this he received the title of Defender of the Faith. However, with his plans for a divorce frustrated, Henry built up diplomatic pressure on the Pope through a series of measures restricting the powers of the papacy in England. When that did not work, the measures were intensified and became a declaration of independence from the Church of Rome. By the time of Henry's death the English Church had renounced any link with, or allegiance to, Rome; the King had declared himself Supreme Head of the Church; a variety of traditional practices had been banned; and, with enormous implications for the social and economic as well as religious life of the country, the monasteries and other religious orders had been dissolved and their property confiscated by the Crown. Henry himself remained largely Catholic in his beliefs except for his repudiation of the authority of the Pope, and he still regarded much of the doctrine of the continental Protestant reformers as heresy. However, his desire to punish the papacy and its supporters, and the influence of those at Court who sympathised with Protestantism, meant that, despite periods of conservative backlash, the Protestant revolution in belief had begun in England.

1 ⟿ THE PARLIAMENT OF 1529

See page 72

Writs legal commands issued by a court or sovereign authority

From 1527 to 1529 Cardinal Wolsey had been attempting to secure for Henry an annulment of his marriage to Catherine of Aragon. Wolsey's failure in this matter was made clear in July 1529 when Cardinal Campeggio adjourned the court that was hearing the case in England and the Pope recalled the case to Rome. Shortly after the adjournment, **writs** were issued for the Parliament that was to meet in November. This was the first of seven sessions of what has become known as the Reformation Parliament. It was not finally dissolved until April 1536.

We do not know precisely why Henry decided to summon a Parliament at this point. Both the French and Imperial ambassadors reported in October that the coming Parliament was to be used against Wolsey, but by the time it opened the Cardinal had been dealt with. In November, a committee of the House of Lords, with two Commons members, was to draw up a list of 44 articles attacking Wolsey and his policies, but beyond presenting it to Henry and sending a copy to the Commons nothing was done.

The timing of the writs implies that the summons to Parliament was somehow linked to the failure to settle the divorce question and that Henry hoped to make a new beginning with the help of his subjects. According to the Imperial ambassador, Chapuys, Catherine certainly thought the Parliament would be used against her. But if this was the case then it did remarkably little in the matter for more than two years.

The 1529 session of Parliament has been seen as demonstrating the **anti-clericalism** of the time. The main source for this is Edward Hall, a London lawyer and Member of Parliament. Hall was also a historian of the early Tudor period, a great supporter of the Tudor dynasty and a man of strong reforming sympathies. His account stresses the Commons' determination to attack the clergy's greed. This resulted in three Acts of Parliament dealing with fees charged by the clergy, pluralism and non-residence. Their significance should not be exaggerated. They were only three out of 26 Acts of Parliament passed in this session and seem to have been the result of pressure from particular interest groups. The Mercers Company of London, for example, had pushed for some action but only as the fifth of a five-point programme otherwise concerned with trade.

In their final form the Acts would have had little impact. However there was a reaction from the bishops in the Lords who objected to interference from lay people. This may be the true significance of the episode – not that a rampant anti-clericalism was being directed against the Church, but rather that the Church leaders could feel that they were under attack and were being put on the defensive. By the end of 1530 the attack was to come not from specific interests in the Commons but from the King.

> **Anti-clericalism**
> hostility towards the clergy, usually on the basis that they abused their privileges

> **KEY ISSUE**
>
> *How general was the demand for a reformation of the Church?*

2 ⤙ HENRY VIII AND THE SUPREMACY

Despite the failure of Wolsey's best efforts to secure him his annulment, Henry continued to pursue his case, hoping to gather enough support to persuade the Pope of the justice of his cause. At the suggestion of an as yet obscure Cambridge academic, Thomas Cranmer, royal agents were sent to universities across Europe to win backing for the King's cause in addition to the pronouncements that were made on his behalf by Oxford and Cambridge early in 1530. Eight of these universities came out in his favour, though this may have been in response to bribes or political influence. The European reformers were also canvassed for their views and provided differing answers. On the whole, the more radical Swiss reformers were favourable but the majority of Lutheran theologians in Germany maintained the validity of his marriage.

By 1531 Henry had developed his ideas. He could be more confident of a favourable verdict if the case was heard in England and not in Rome, and by one of his own clergy, and he now began to demand this as of right. He claimed that no case could be taken out of any court in England to the courts in Rome, without royal permission. This *privilegium Angliae*, it was maintained, had been recognised by the Popes themselves. The fourteenth century **Statute of Praemunire** had been an expression of this principle which, though neglected, could yet be applied more consistently.

More radical was the idea that Henry need acknowledge no superior on earth, Pope or Emperor, and that within his realm it was his duty to exercise supreme headship over the Church – that is, Royal Supremacy. In October 1528, William Tyndale had published his book *The Obedience of the Christian Man and How Christian Rulers Ought to Govern*. In it he set out the view that the ruler is supreme on earth, answerable only to God, in full charge of his subjects' temporal and spiritual welfare and commanding their total allegiance. Because of the heresies it contained, the book was banned in England, but Anne Boleyn possessed a copy and through her it came to Henry's notice. At her instigation he read through it and was suitably impressed – 'This book is for me and for all kings to read.'

KEY ISSUE

What was the basis of Henry's claim to Supremacy?

By September 1530 Henry's scholars had prepared a manuscript known as the *Collectanea Satis Copiosa*. This was a collection of proofs and precedents, drawn from Scripture, the early Church, and British history, that claimed to show that Henry, like his predecessors, could indeed claim **imperial** authority.

Imperial acknowledging no superior

3 ⌐ THE ENGLISH CLERGY UNDER PRESSURE

In January 1531, Henry threatened to use the Statute of Praemunire against the whole of the clergy of southern England, represented by the **Convocation** of Canterbury. The threat was only lifted when, in seeking a general pardon for any possible offence of this kind, they promised to pay Henry a fine of £100 000, the amount of a clerical subsidy. No doubt there was a financial motive in all this. Henry had no reserves of money and the possibility of an expensive international policy arising from the divorce case was present. But he also seems to have been using the occasion to show that he was fully prepared to come down heavily on the clergy and that it would be in their best interests to co-operate fully in his policies.

Convocation the parliament of the Church

But there were other implications as well. When asking for pardon the clergy had also asked for a clearer statement of their liberties. Henry's response was to demand that he be recognised as 'sole protector and also Supreme Head of the English Church', and that this should include a 'cure of souls', that is, some direct responsibility for the spiritual welfare of his subjects. He had gone too far. Despite considerable pressure, Convocation refused to accept such a claim and it was only with reluctance that they were willing to concede to him the role of 'singular protector, only and supreme lord and, so far as the law of Christ allows, even Supreme Head'. Both sides could claim a minor victory. Henry had asserted himself and not been totally rebuffed, but the qualifying clause on the law of Christ meant that the clergy could justly maintain that there was in fact no change in the situation. Later, in May 1531, the Convocation of York received the same pardon as that of the Convocation of Canterbury, on payment of £18 000.

Substantial pressure on the Pope was attempted early in 1532. In January a Bill in Restraint of **Annates** was introduced into Parliament. The bill set out to put an end to the practice on the grounds that it took money from the country. It also stated that if the Pope refused to accept any appointments made by the King, then consecration of a new bishop should still take place with any papal action ignored. Although this would have made little practical difference, it was nevertheless an attack on papal authority. The bill faced considerable resistance, both in the Lords where all the bishops voted against it, and in the Commons, where the King thought his presence necessary to ensure a favourable vote. The resulting Act was not to come into operation for a year and then only if Henry chose to give it his official assent. A copy was sent to Henry's agents in Rome who were instructed to show it to the Pope and let him know that, if he wished to avoid its possible consequences, the answer lay in co-operation with the King of England.

> **Annates** the first year's income from a bishopric which went to the papacy

At the same time, the English clergy were coming under pressure and again Parliament was to have a role to play. The starting point was the Commons' Supplication Against the Ordinaries (i.e. petition against those in ecclesiastical authority). This was a complaint about the extent and nature of the Church courts, which dealt with many personal affairs, such as wills and marital status, as well as the activities of the Church itself. The Supplication may have been introduced into the House by Thomas Cromwell, Henry's secretary. By working through Parliament more weight could be given to the claim that Henry had the support of his country in his policy. Henry was presented with the Supplication on 18 March and then passed it on to Convocation for consideration.

The representatives of the clergy at first upheld the Church's legislative powers and their practices in the Church courts. However, with the possibility of parliamentary action against them and under pressure from some of the King's noble Councillors who attended their meeting, Convocation gave way. Several bishops were absent, others expressed serious reservations, and there was strong resistance from the lower clergy. Nevertheless, on 15 May the Submission of the Clergy was passed in Convocation.

PICTURE 10
William Warham, Archbishop of Canterbury

According to the terms of the Submission, Convocation could only meet at the King's command, could enact no ecclesiastical legislation without royal consent and royal assent was to be sought for existing legislation. The Submission of the Clergy was a definite attack on the independence of the Church and on papal authority. That this was a turning point was recognised by Sir Thomas More, who resigned as Lord Chancellor on 16 May. He was in favour of moderate reform, but

See page 87

KEY ISSUE

How did Henry manoeuvre the English clergy into submission?

he could not accept the King's policy when it threatened to split the universal Church.

4 ⌐ THE SETTLEMENT OF THE DIVORCE

In mid-1532 events began to move more swiftly. In August, the Archbishop of Canterbury, William Warham, died. Henry now had the opportunity to appoint an archbishop of his own choosing, one whom he could expect to back him in all his policies. The man he chose was Thomas Cranmer.

PROFILE

PICTURE 11
Thomas Cranmer,
Archbishop of Canterbury

THOMAS CRANMER (1489–1556)

Until 1529 Thomas Cranmer must have seemed destined for an uneventful life as a Fellow of Jesus College, Cambridge. At a chance meeting with Stephen Gardiner and Edward Fox, who were both involved in pursuing Henry's annulment, he suggested that the King should seek the opinion of university theologians across Europe rather than rely on the canon lawyers. This led to a meeting with Henry, Cranmer entered the royal service and in 1530 he went to Italy on a diplomatic mission. In 1531 he produced the English translation of the results of the researches he had suggested, before going as ambassador to the court of Emperor Charles V. He was summoned from that post to become the Archbishop of Canterbury in 1533. He became convinced that supremacy in the Church rested in the secular ruler and this became a guiding principle in his life. (It would be a problem in Mary's reign when the ruler herself accepted papal supremacy.) He also showed an early interest in Protestant ideas and demonstrated his loyalty to the new religion in 1531 when, despite being a priest, he married the niece of a Lutheran theologian in Germany. Throughout Henry's reign Cranmer used his influence as far as possible to encourage Protestant reform, but he was always limited by the bounds set by the King himself. Henry must have known of his archbishop's sympathies but he tolerated them, and, according to Cromwell, Henry would never believe ill of Cranmer, whatever accusations were made against him. On two occasions in the 1540s Henry intervened when the archbishop's enemies tried to bring him down on charges of heresy and it was Cranmer's hand that he clasped as he lay dying. With the accession of Edward, Cranmer could set about the establishment of a truly Protestant church in England. On Mary's accession he was found guilty of heresy and under considerable pressure denied his Protestant beliefs. However, he publicly withdrew this denial on the day of his execution, and famously thrust his hand that signed it first into the flames.

Cranmer was more suited to being a scholar than a martyr. His library, which covered a wide variety of subjects, was larger than that of Cambridge University and used by other reformers to study texts they could not find elsewhere. He had a generous and gentle nature. He risked the anger of Henry VIII when he wrote to him on behalf of Anne Boleyn and Thomas Cromwell when they had been condemned. Although his 1552 *Prayer Book* was to be modified under Elizabeth, Cranmer did more than anyone else to establish the liturgy of the Church of England and the language of it, which was to have so profound an effect on the culture as well as religion of England.

By January 1533, Anne Boleyn knew she was pregnant and by the end of the month she and Henry were married in a secret ceremony. The pregnancy and marriage indicate that by now Henry was prepared to seek a radical solution to his problem. Cranmer was consecrated archbishop in March. The Pope thought it timely to make a diplomatic concession so had approved his appointment, but Cranmer took pains to declare, when taking his consecration oath, that his first loyalty was to the King. He now set about his immediate task and presided over a court at Dunstable to hear the case between Henry and Catherine. In May Cranmer declared Henry's union with his first wife to have been no true marriage and that consequently his sole and legal wife was Anne Boleyn. It may have been something of an anti-climax in September when the longed-for child proved to be a girl, Elizabeth, and not the male heir for which Henry was waiting.

5 ↷ THE BREAK WITH ROME

Cranmer's action was a direct challenge to the Pope but Henry now went beyond simple disobedience and the years 1533–6 saw the breaking of all links between England and Rome. It could not have been an easy decision to make. We should remember the radical nature of what Henry was doing, mentally as well as politically. Though he might criticise the Pope and even try to bully him, it took Henry a long time to believe that he really could revolutionise the relationship between church and state.

A peaceful succession might depend on his marriage and he had to have adequate authority to back him up – hence his refusal to countenance any hints from Pope Clement that he should simply go ahead with marrying Anne and hope Catherine would retire gracefully. On at least two occasions in 1530 Henry consulted a gathering of nobility, bishops and judges as to whether he could ignore the Pope and simply have the divorce case settled in England, and on both occasions he was told that it could not be done.

Henry had come to his decision, and he now needed someone to carry it out. This role fell to Thomas Cromwell. Cromwell had previously served Cardinal Wolsey but on his master's fall had come to the King's notice and entered his service. In a short time he had risen high in the King's favour.

PICTURE 12
Thomas Cromwell, *after Hans Holbein*

THOMAS CROMWELL (C. 1485–1540)

Cromwell's father was a blacksmith who also ran an alehouse in Putney. Cromwell travelled abroad, where he may have been a soldier, and visited Italy where he came into contact with Italian political thought concerning the supremacy of the state over the Church. Returning to England, he joined Wolsey's household around 1513. On Wolsey's fall from power he continued to defend the Cardinal, speaking up for him in the Parliament of 1529 and acting as a go-between for his master and the King. Cromwell was obviously a man of ability, skilled in the law, with some knowledge of languages and a genuine interest in scholarship that was reflected in an extensive library. He also knew how to get on at Court. The Imperial ambassador Chapuys indicated something of this when he wrote: 'Cromwell asked and obtained an audience from King Henry, whom he addressed in such flattering terms and eloquent language – promising to make him the richest king in the world – that the King took him into his service'. The details may not be accurate but the general idea was believable. By 1531 he was a member of the King's Council and in 1534 became the King's Secretary and Master of the Rolls. He was now at the centre of affairs. He was created Baron Cromwell in 1536 and gained the leading office in the Household as Lord Great Chamberlain in 1539. In 1540 he was made the Earl of Essex.

Cromwell's role has been extensively debated. GR Elton and AG Dickens presented a picture of a man who dominated the 1530s as the creator of the Royal Supremacy, architect of a revolution in government and the promoter of religious reform. This view has been widely challenged. Cromwell did not think up the ideas behind Henry's Supremacy, although he was responsible for their effective implementation and his supposed changes in government had a much more limited effect than Elton supposed. More recently George Bernard has played down his role even further and sought to demonstrate that even in the details of executing policy he was following the orders of the King. He has also questioned Cromwell's reputation as a reformer who attempted to bring about religious change until stopped by the King. He maintains that there is little direct evidence for Cromwell's religious beliefs and he was simply following royal policy. However, Cromwell's contemporaries certainly believed in his commitment to reform. He was accepted as a kindred spirit by the likes of Cranmer, he used his own money to finance an English Bible, and the charges of heresy that brought about his downfall may have been exaggerated but they were evidently credible.

In a series of Acts of Parliament mainly in 1533 and 1534, the independence of the Church of England from papal authority was established:

April 1533

- **The Act in Restraint of Appeals** was passed. By this Act no appeals were to be made from England to Rome in any matters concerning wills, marriages, or payments to the Church; cases were to go no further than the Archbishop. It was with the backing of this Act that Cranmer was able to decide the King's case at Dunstable and it may have been the active preparation of the act that partly decided the timing of the consummation of Henry's relationship with Anne.

March 1534

- **Act of Dispensations** – ordered an end to any payments to Rome. Any dispensations that might have come from Rome were now to be issued by the Archbishop of Canterbury.
- **Act for the Submission of the Clergy** – repeated details of the submission of 1532.
- **First Succession Act** – declared the succession to the throne lay first with the male heirs of Anne Boleyn and then of any subsequent wife. After them the crown would go to Princess Elizabeth and her children and finally to other daughters that might yet be born. Subjects had to be prepared to take an oath accepting these rules and the legitimacy of the King's marriage to Anne Boleyn. Any words or actions that threatened the King or his title or slandered his marriage would be accounted high treason.

November 1534

- **Act of Supremacy** – declared that Henry was Supreme Head of the Church in England. It was not claimed that Parliament had the authority to make the King Supreme Head. The Act was supposedly just a recognition of his neglected right to be such, derived from the ancient laws of England.
- **Treason Act** – made it high treason to threaten Henry, Anne or his heirs in words, writing or deeds or to deny him his titles or to accuse him of being a heretic, tyrant or usurper.
- **Act of First Fruits and Tenths** – the first year's income from church offices and a tenth of all clerical income was to be paid to the King.

> **KEY ISSUE**
>
> *Why did Henry attack papal authority like this, stage by stage?*

In 1536 the process was rounded off with the Act Against Papal Authority which removed any form of authority the Pope might have had even in matters of heresy.

6 ⌁ OPPOSITION

These changes did not take place without argument or opposition. The Treason Act was passed shortly after the affair of Elizabeth Barton, the

PICTURE 13
Bishop John Fisher

'Nun of Kent'. Since 1527 she had spoken out against Henry's marriage to Anne Boleyn, declaring that it would lead to his being deposed. In 1534 the judges maintained that there was no case against her in law; her execution was only secured by an Act of Attainder. This meant that Parliament declared her a traitor and, therefore, subject to the death penalty.

The Treason Act was passed so that Henry could move against his more eminent opponents, without having to go through the time-consuming process of getting Acts of Attainder passed by Parliament. Five Carthusian monks suffered death for denying Henry's Supremacy, and in June 1535, they were followed by John Fisher, Bishop of Rochester. He had been a scholar, the founder of St John's College, Cambridge and a much respected and conscientious bishop. A staunch supporter of Queen Catherine and for a long time a prominent opponent of Henry's policies, he had been implicated in the Elizabeth Barton affair. He may also have been communicating with the Emperor Charles V. The Pope had incautiously made him a cardinal, at which Henry grimly commented that by the time the cardinal's hat arrived in England there would be no head to put it on. The former Lord Chancellor, Sir Thomas More, was more discreet but his silence spoke volumes. Henry was convinced that he would become a rallying point of opposition, so he was tried, convicted on the basis of trumped-up evidence, and executed on 6 July 1535.

There were other expressions of discontent. The clergy had shown some resistance in both 1531 and 1532, and Parliament too was the scene of profound disagreement, in the debates over the Act in Restraint of Annates, for example. According to George Throckmorton, MP for Warwickshire, he and other members used to meet at the Queen's Head in Fleet Street to discuss the changes, and they had links with known opponents such as More and Fisher and also the Imperial ambassador. Edward Hall, although a supporter of Henry's policies, nevertheless testifies to the existence of much sympathy for Catherine. In April 1532, another MP, Thomas Temys wanted the Commons to ask the King to take Catherine back as his rightful Queen. Throughout the reign examples occur of individuals speaking out against the changes that had taken place and criticising Henry and his advisers.

At no point was this opposition strong enough to force Henry to call a complete halt. To begin with, the method used to implement the changes made opposition difficult. The changes came in stages and it was difficult to say at just what point one should try to halt the process. Bearing in mind the circumstances of this Reformation, many people may have had real doubts about the permanence of the changes. It was not unknown for kings and popes to quarrel, or for kings to bring pressure to bear on popes by asserting their own authority. Was there not a chance that when the divorce problem had been resolved or forgotten, then normal relations would be resumed?

Opposition to royal policy could be difficult to justify, since this opposition might bring disorder which was feared above all. People

SIR THOMAS MORE (1478–1535)

Sir Thomas More was a successful lawyer from London who, as a young MP in 1504, had frustrated one of Henry VII's tax demands, which had landed More's father in the Tower for a time. Under Henry VIII More was employed by the King on diplomatic missions and in 1517 joined the King's Council. He later became Speaker of the House of Commons, and in 1529 succeeded Wolsey as Lord Chancellor. Royal service brought with it the friendship of the King who, according to More's son-in-law, often summoned him privately to discuss 'matters of astronomy, geometry, divinity and such other faculties and sometimes of his worldly affairs', and used to visit More informally at his house in Chelsea.

Parallel to his political career was a spiritual and academic life. Early in his career More spent some time with the Carthusian monks in London and, although he decided to remain a layman, intensive prayer and spiritual reading were part of his daily routine and became features of his household at Chelsea. His last works, written in prison, included prayers and meditations. He was also a Christian humanist, who supported the 'new learning' and enjoyed an international reputation in this field. He counted a number of England's leading scholars as his friends and was very close to the Dutch humanist Desiderius Erasmus. More's Chelsea household, visited by many scholars and regarded as a centre of culture and learning, was painted by Holbein. In 1516 More completed *Utopia*, an account of a mythical, perfectly organised island society across the Atlantic, which could be contrasted satirically with the corruption of Christian society in Europe. By the late l520s, his attention had turned mainly to combatting heresy, and he published a series of works attacking Luther and his English followers. Once he was made Lord Chancellor, he used his influence to secure the arrest and conviction of a number of heretics, even that of a friend, John Petit.

When More became Chancellor, Henry had apparently promised him that he would not be asked to have anything to do with the divorce. More's opinion was well known. The Submission of the Clergy, against which More had fought hard in Council, finally showed him that he could no longer expect to have any influence in the King's affairs, and so he resigned. In April 1534 he was sent to the Tower for refusing to take the oath accepting the Act of Succession, as that would have involved recognising the Royal Supremacy, but he would not explain his refusal, arguing that he could not be convicted on the basis of silence. He was, however, put on trial in July 1535 and found guilty with the help of false evidence given by Sir Richard Rich who claimed that More had denied the King's Supremacy in conversation with him. Once convicted, More made it clear that he did not think Henry could deprive the Pope of his authority and destroy the unity of the Church. He was beheaded on 6 July, declaring on the scaffold that he died the King's good servant, but God's first.

PROFILE

PICTURE 14
Sir Thomas More,
Hans Holbein

wanted good government, with as little disturbance as possible. It would have to be a pressing need that allowed any strong resistance to the source of that government. And Henry was that source, the anointed King. People expected to follow where their superiors led them. To obey was their first duty, and if they were led astray then the fault was not theirs but their leaders'. There were of course those who did dissent but they could be dealt with. Intimidation, of whole groups or individuals, the threat of the treason legislation – these could be, and were, effective checks and they were applied with considerable success during this period.

While there was only limited opposition, what is absolutely clear now is that there was no upsurge of support for the Reformation in its early stages. There were Protestants in key positions of influence, but very few in the country at large. It used to be thought that anti-clericalism, as in the battle between the City of London and the Bishop of London over the Hunne case, had prepared the way for the Reformation, but battles such as that over privileges were the usual stuff of politics and did not amount to enthusiasm for the overthrow of the traditional structure of church authority in England. Many of those who had campaigned for the reform of the church were, like Thomas More, its staunchest defenders when it came under fundamental attack. The Reformation was a revolution from above. There was no popular movement one way or another, at least not until the fabric of people's religious experience was more directly affected by the Dissolution of the Monasteries.

See Chapter 15 on the pre-Reformation Church

See page 66

KEY ISSUE

How did Henry minimise opposition to the break with Rome?

7 ⌁ THE DISSOLUTION OF THE MONASTERIES

It has been estimated that in the early sixteenth century there were 700–800 religious houses ranging from those with only a handful of inmates to the great monasteries such as St Mary's in York or Westminster in London. Their importance can be judged in a number of ways. Twenty-seven abbots and priors had the right to attend meetings of Parliament, and the office of abbot could bring influence and prestige. In economic terms the religious communities in England and Wales are reckoned to have controlled approximately 10% of the country's wealth and individual houses could still provide the economic centre for their area, employing a large number of estate workers. In addition they were important religious and social centres, providing hospitality for travellers, and alms for the poor.

A *The process of Dissolution*

In spite of this, the years 1536–40 saw the end of the monasteries. In January of 1535 Thomas Cromwell was created Henry's Vicegerent in Spirituals, an appointment which enabled him to exercise the royal authority in the English Church. Almost immediately he sent out commissions to make a full survey of all property held by the Church and by the summer these findings had been brought together in the *Valor Ecclesiasticus* (the Ecclesiastical Valuation). In September he sent out another set of commissioners to conduct a visitation, that is a full inspection, of all the religious houses in the kingdom.

Visitations in themselves were nothing new, but previously they had normally been the responsibility of the local bishop, had not been so hastily conducted and had been mainly concerned with reform. It is obvious from the speed with which Cromwell's visitors acted and from the tone of some of their letters that they knew what they were looking for and were determined to find it. Cromwell soon built up a dossier illustrating the corrupt morals and spiritual laxity of the **regular clergy** and these findings were presented to Parliament early in 1536. These reports, combined perhaps with the King's own intervention, were enough to secure the passing of an Act for suppressing, that is closing down, the smaller monasteries – those worth less than £200 a year. Their buildings, estates and other forms of income, were now the property of the Crown. The dispossessed inmates could either transfer to other houses or join the **secular clergy**.

Now there appeared some popular reaction against the process of the Henrician Reformation. In October 1536, the people of Louth, in Lincolnshire, rose up in protest at the changes that were being imposed and they were joined by other communities. The Lincolnshire rising was soon put down, but not before the movement had spread to Yorkshire, where the lawyer, Robert Aske, soon assumed leadership of the rebellion which now took the title of the Pilgrimage of Grace. The pilgrims entered York and Hull, took the castle of Pontefract, and moved to Doncaster. At the River Don they were met by the Duke of Norfolk, who had come north to deal with the trouble. He listened to their complaints and in return for their dispersal, promised that their demands would be investigated and that they would receive a pardon. However, a further outbreak of trouble in the north-west gave him the opportunity to break the promise (which neither he nor Henry seem to have had any intention of keeping) and the main leaders of the Pilgrimage were captured and eventually executed.

Even those who would see the Pilgrimage as essentially a political movement or the result of economic distress cannot deny the strong religious element. The title of 'Pilgrimage', its banner of the Five Wounds of Christ, the songs the pilgrims sang and the demands they made all point to support for the old order in religion as an ideal that many had in common. There were fears for the future of the parish churches and their possessions, condemnation of the reformers, support for the Pope's spiritual supremacy, and the request that the dissolved monasteries be restored. Some suppressed houses were re-opened during the Pilgrimage, and a number of monasteries were closely associated with the movement. After it had been put down, the heads of five abbeys and one priory were executed because of the support they had given to the Pilgrimage.

Commissioners were now sent round the remaining, larger monasteries to 'invite' their surrender to the Crown. Failure to agree to such a

Regular clergy monks, that is clergy who abided by monastic regulations

Secular clergy clergy active 'in the world' outside monasteries, such as parish priests and bishops

KEY ISSUE

Why were the smaller monasteries dissolved first?

See pages 312–13

KEY ISSUE

What brought about the Pilgrimage of Grace?

surrender could have unhappy consequences – the Abbot of Glastonbury, for example, was hanged. Co-operation led to the provision of pensions and the possibility of preferment in the Church outside the monasteries. In 1539 a second Act of Dissolution was passed. This legalised the Crown's possession of all those monasteries that had already surrendered to Henry and those few that had yet to do so. The last surrendered in 1540.

B *Reasons for the Dissolution*

Both Henry and Cromwell may have resented the continued existence of the monastic orders, which were part of international organisations and had superiors based abroad, in the now independent English Church. However, it is unlikely that either Henry or Cromwell saw the monasteries in general as centres of resistance to the King's Supremacy. Most of them seem to have given way with as little fuss as the rest of the Church in England, and some monasteries took pains to stress their new allegiance in letters of loyalty to the King. The public reason for the Dissolution of the Monasteries was corruption and the waste of resources. The unspoken reason was the wealth which could be confiscated from them.

The selective closure of individual monasteries, or groups of them, was not unprecedented. Monasteries and nunneries had been closed in the past with papal approval and their resources directed to other, normally educational, uses. The mere act of closing some monasteries, therefore, did not obviously mean a move away from Catholicism. It could in fact be seen as a genuine attempt at eradicating those abuses which disfigured some religious houses, and so highlighting the good work of those that remained. This was the official line that was expressed in 1536 in the first Dissolution Act. The reason given for the suppression of the smaller monasteries is the 'manifest sin, vicious, carnal and abominable living' to be found there and the need is stressed for the encouragement of the good work of the greater monasteries. This could partly explain Parliament's agreement to this first – and, as they then thought, only – stage in the dissolution process.

Cromwell and his supporters objected to monasticism as a misguided form of spiritual life as well as a waste of human and financial resources. They wished to do away with monasticism altogether. The Dissolution was associated with the attack on traditional religious practices, such as going on pilgrimages and the veneration of images and relics in the belief they had spiritual powers. Reports of Cromwell's commissioners contain many references to these practices; the exposure of fraudulent relics and the dismantling of shrines went hand in hand with the dissolution process. Monasteries were also too closely associated with the practice of praying for the dead to appeal to radical reformers who were now moving towards a denial of the doctrine of **Purgatory**. In 1538 the Abbess of Godstow attempted to avoid the dissolution of her house by assuring Cromwell 'that there is neither Pope nor Purgatory, Image nor Pilgrimage, nor praying to dead saints, used or regarded amongst us'.

Purgatory the punishment and purification after death before a soul became suitable for admission to heaven

There was a body of thought, expressed particularly in Cromwell's circle, that the spirit if not the letter of the founders' intentions would be better served by re-directing the resources vested in the monasteries. In 1539 an Act was passed in Parliament enabling the King to create new bishoprics:

> It is not unknown the slothful and ungodly life which has been used amongst all those who have borne the name of religious folk, and so that from henceforth many of them might be turned to better use as, for example, God's word might be better set forth, children brought up in learning, clerks educated in the universities, old servants to have livings, almshouses for poor folk, readers of Greek, Hebrew, and Latin to have good wages, daily alms to be ministered, mending of highways, support for ministers of the Church; it is thought therefore by the King's Highness most expedient and necessary that more bishoprics and cathedral churches shall be established instead of these aforesaid religious houses …

Q

1. *What judgement does this extract make on the religious orders and how does it differ from the official statements in 1536?*
2. *In what ways does this preamble suggest that the money from the monasteries should be used?*
3. *Does this extract help to explain why many people accepted the dissolution of the monasteries?*

Little was done to fulfil this aspect of the reformers' ambitions.

This failure to re-invest monastic resources in practical religious activities was because, for Henry at least, his financial needs had been a main motive behind the Dissolution. In 1534 a plan had been suggested that would have enabled the Crown to profit from Church wealth. If this had been put into effect it would have meant all the income of the Church going to the Crown. Archbishops and bishops would have been paid salaries, monasteries granted money according to the number of inmates and the considerable surplus would have remained at the King's disposal. The plan was too radical at that time, but it shows that by the early 1530s the Church was being seen as a potential source of money for the Crown.

Some advice that Henry was later to present to the rulers of Scotland on dissolving monasteries supports this view. Any plan, he says, should be kept secret and the first move should give the impression of being simply motivated by reform. Leading clergy should be won over by promises of the worthy use of monastic resources and this, combined with an attack on the morals of the monks, should make for a quiet and easy Dissolution. Certainly in England the eventual use of monastic resources and Henry's failure to live up to any promises made or implied seem to show that he had practised what he now preached.

KEY ISSUE

Were the monasteries dissolved simply because of the greed of Henry VIII?

C *Some consequences of the Dissolution*

The Dissolution resulted in about 9000 monks and nuns being forced to find some alternative way of life. Many of the men could be absorbed into the rest of the Church, joining the ranks of the secular clergy. Those who were unwilling, or unable, to make such a change had to rely on pensions provided by the government from the proceeds of the Dissolution. These pensions were calculated according to the wealth of the house to which they had belonged. The senior members of the system did fairly well, but the average allowance seems to have been about £5 per year which did not compare well with wages elsewhere. Nuns got even less, certainly not enough to live on, and at the same time the King's insistence that vows of chastity remained in force meant that they could not turn to marriage as a way of finding support. In a society where the independent single woman was unknown their plight was serious. Ordinary employees of the monasteries were not so badly affected. Most of these would have been estate workers and they would be required under any new owners.

The immediate area around the monastery may well have suffered from the loss of monastic charity. In 1538, Thomas, Lord Audley, who wished the Benedictine monastery at Colchester to remain as a college for secular clergy, gave the importance of their charitable work as the reason.

For the government, the Dissolution was undoubtedly a financial success. In 1536 a Court of Augmentations was set up to deal with the new income that it had generated and in the ten years between the first closures and Henry's death, the monasteries provided the Crown with over a million pounds. Some of the money came from the gold, silver and jewels that many of the monasteries had possessed, but the bulk of the income came from the monastic estates. Whether Henry or Cromwell wished to keep all the estates as a permanent addition to the Crown's resources is debatable; but, given the scale of royal expenditure, particularly following the renewal of war in the 1540s, this was not to be the case. By 1547 almost two-thirds of the land had passed out of Crown hands, realising total proceeds of about £800 000. There was still income to be had from the estates which remained in Crown hands but this varied greatly from year to year.

A limited amount of money went on the kind of educational enterprises for which many of the reformers had had such high hopes. Wolsey's Oxford college was re-endowed as Christ Church, two college halls at Cambridge were merged and re-founded as Trinity College, and five Regius Professorships instituted at each of the universities. Six new bishoprics were also founded. These were Gloucester, Peterborough, Oxford, Chester, Bristol and Westminster, though the last did not survive beyond 1550. The huge gap left by the monasteries, such as in caring for the poor, was not quickly filled.

While the Church suffered a loss of land and revenue, laymen profited. Whether or not they had sought the Dissolution, they were ready to take advantage of the opportunity to acquire more land, and it was the nobility and gentry who gained most from this redistribution of wealth. Not only did it give them a chance to increase their landholdings, it also gave them, through their new estates, a greater control of Church patronage. In the past a monastery had often appointed parish priests. When the estates were transferred to laymen this role was seen as part of the property, so the new landlord continued to make these appointments.

Some buildings survived to act as cathedrals or parish churches; others were adapted to secular uses, but most fell into decay. The disposal of the contents led to the loss of numberless examples of medieval art, either by dispersal and disappearance, or by being melted down or otherwise destroyed for the value of the materials. The loss to scholarship of the monastic libraries caused some concern even at the time. The antiquary John Leland, with Henry's encouragement, tried to salvage something from the destruction, but we can only guess at what ended up on the rubbish heap.

> ### KEY ISSUE
>
> *Apart from the King, who gained and who lost from the Dissolution?*

8 ~ THE RELIGIOUS REFORMATION

A *The situation in the 1530s*

In breaking away from the Roman Catholic Church, Henry had enlisted the help of a number of men who saw the Royal Supremacy not as an end in itself but as the means to a wider programme of reform. This group included the Archbishop of Canterbury, Thomas Cranmer, and others who were promoted to the bench of bishops during this period – Edward Foxe (Bishop of Hereford, 1538), Hugh Latimer (Worcester, 1535) and Nicholas Shaxton (Salisbury, 1535). Although it would be wrong to describe all of them at this stage as Protestant or Lutheran in their ideas, their reformist stance certainly seemed to be taking them in that direction.

At the same time, the diplomatic situation seemed to favour the reformers. In 1533 serious negotiations had been opened with the German Lutheran princes in the hope of gaining their help in distracting the Emperor from any possible action against England in support of his aunt, Catherine of Aragon. They had demanded adherence to Lutheran teaching as expressed in the Wittenberg Articles as a condition of any alliance. But Henry, although he might seek a Lutheran alliance and even turn to Luther for support in his divorce case, was not yet prepared to go as far as the German reformer in doctrine. The King kept the title of Defender of the Faith which he had won by attacking Luther's theological position, and he clung to many of his inherited beliefs.

B *The Ten Articles*

It was against this background that the Ten Articles were produced in July 1536. They were drawn up at Henry's request by Convocation and issued on his authority as Supreme Head. The introduction to the Articles stated that they were considered necessary because a variety of religious opinions had emerged in the country. A concern over unity is understandable following the unsettling changes of the early 1530s.

The fact that much of the wording of the Articles is directly based on that of the Wittenberg Articles has been taken as demonstrating some concessions in the direction of the Lutherans. If this is the case then the concessions were strictly limited and were simply taking advantage of

Eucharist the ceremony derived from the Last Supper, with the consecration of bread and wine

Transubstantiation the Catholic belief that in the Eucharist the bread and wine are physically transformed into the Body and Blood of Christ, even thought the outward appearance of the bread and wine remain the same

areas where there was some common ground, with statements vague enough to satisfy both sides.

For example, the statement in the Ten Articles on the **Eucharist** could be interpreted in a Lutheran way but could just as well be seen as supporting Catholic teaching on **transubstantiation**. The most that it says is that the body and blood of Christ is 'verily, substantially and really contained and comprehended' in the bread and wine. There is no reference to a complete change of substance (Catholic) nor to the continued existence of the substance of bread and wine alongside that of the body and blood (Lutheran).

Only three sacraments were discussed: baptism, the Eucharist and penance, the only ones the Lutherans were prepared to accept. However, the other four were simply passed over in silence, not rejected.

The practice of praying for the dead was clearly commended. This would be rejected by Lutherans, who denied the validity of such prayers. The Ten Articles, then, did not signify any decisive doctrinal change, but their ambiguity in certain areas did mean that they could be credited with a partially reforming character.

The following year a committee of bishops produced *The Institution of a Christian Man* (also known as the *Bishops' Book*). Henry allowed its publication and recommended it to the clergy, though he had, on his own admission, only flicked through it and was later to make extensive criticisms of it. All seven of the sacraments were mentioned in this book, a concession to the conservatives that was qualified by the statement that the reinstated four were of lesser status, with no foundation in Scripture. But on the whole the book can be seen to follow the general tone of the Ten Articles and cannot be judged as having either furthered or hindered the reformers' cause.

C *The Royal Injunctions*

In 1536, acting as the King's Vicegerent in Spirituals, Cromwell issued the First Royal Injunctions to all the clergy of the realm. These started by stating clearly the clergy's duty to preach regularly in support of the Royal Supremacy. As well as this, clergy were told not to encourage devotion to particular images or saints, and to dissuade people from the practice of making pilgrimages. This, together with the order that everyone should learn the Lord's Prayer, Creed and Ten Commandments in English, certainly showed the influence of the reforming party. The remaining Injunctions concerned clerical behaviour, attention to duty, providing money for charitable and educational purposes and maintenance of church fabric.

Two years later, a second set of Injunctions was issued which went further. Priests had now, in at least four sermons a year, positively to discourage people from venerating images or relics, and if they had previously supported such practices, were now to recant. Perhaps most important for the reforming party was the order that an English translation of the Bible was to be placed in every church and everyone was to be encouraged to read it.

KEY ISSUE

How radical were the Ten Articles and the Royal Injunctions issued by Cromwell?

The English Bible

The official Bible of the Catholic Church was the Latin translation known as the Vulgate, produced by St Jerome in the fourth century. In England since the fifteenth century the Bible in English had been one of the demands of the **Lollards** and so became associated with heresy. From the 1520s the Protestant reformers put a greater emphasis on the Bible in their teaching, which they argued should be the sole source of religious beliefs rather than the tradition of the Catholic church. Their attitude is summed up in Cranmer's preface to the English Bible of 1539: in the Scriptures, he wrote, people may 'learn all things that they ought to believe, what they ought to do, and what they should not do'. Since this was the case, the reformers wanted the Bible available for all to read, and that meant translating it into English. Drawing on the work of Christian humanists such as Erasmus (who had published an edition of the New Testament in the original Greek in 1516), Protestants could claim that their translations were more accurate in many respects than the Vulgate of the Catholic Church. In the early 1520s William Tyndale, having failed to get the support of Bishop Tunstall of London, moved to the Continent where he translated the New Testament and part of the Old. The early editions were published in a small format that made them easy to hide and they were smuggled into England and distributed in large numbers. They were the basis for the growth of Protestantism. Tyndale was executed for heresy near Brussels in 1535. His work was the origin of many later translations but never achieved any official status; Henry VIII rejected his marginal notes as 'pestilent glosses'. In 1535 Miles Coverdale published the first complete English Bible based mainly on existing translations. Although it was a private venture, it had Cromwell's support. In 1539 the Great Bible was published, authorised by the government. Henry was depicted on the title page giving the Bible to his bishops and nobility and through them to his people. However, the title page shows ordinary people not reading the Bible for themselves but having it read to them by the clergy. That was not just because of illiteracy but also a matter of social control. In 1543 an Act of Parliament attempted to limit Bible reading to the clergy, nobility, gentry and merchant classes. Henry feared people were treating the Bible too lightly, and might choose to interpret it for themselves. That could inspire religious strife, or, worse still, resistance to his own authority to determine what his subjects should believe.

ANALYSIS

Lollards English heretics active over the 150 years before the Reformation, who anticipated Protestantism in their attack on the separateness of the priesthood, and who translated the Bible into English and circulated it in manuscript

See page 430

D *A conservative reaction*

In 1538 John Lambert was accused of denying the 'real presence', the physical presence of Christ, in the Eucharist. Henry himself, dressed all

Sacramentaries those who denied that there was any physical presence of Christ's Body and Blood in the Eucharist

in white, presided at his trial and after displaying his own skills in theology, ordered Cromwell to read Lambert's sentence of death by burning. This episode was followed by a royal proclamation against **sacramentaries**, unlicensed books and married priests. Clerical celibacy had already proved a block to any agreement with the German Lutheran princes when Henry had informed their embassy that that was one of the points on which he would make no concessions. In the same letter he had asserted his belief in the legitimacy of private Masses and that the laity should receive Communion under one kind (receiving the bread only) and not, as most Protestants demanded, under both kinds (receiving both bread and wine).

Henry's negotiations with the Lutherans were part of his attempt to find allies against a possible attack from the Emperor Charles V and Francis I of France. However, he would not give way on his traditional religious beliefs and perhaps put more trust in demonstrating the orthodoxy of his Church, and showing any invader that there was no religious justification to attack him.

In May 1539, a committee of bishops was set up to discuss a possible statement that would ensure religious unity. The committee consisted of four conservatives and four radicals so little progress was made. In June, the Duke of Norfolk introduced into the House of Lords six questions which, following discussion and Henry's intervention, were transformed into the Six Articles that formed the basis of a new act of Parliament.

Q

1. *What view of the Eucharist is described in articles 1 and 2?*
2. *Using information from earlier in the chapter, comment on the acceptability or otherwise of these articles to the reforming party.*

First, that in the most blessed sacrament of the altar, … is present really, under the form of bread and wine, the natural body and blood of our Saviour Jesus Christ and that after the consecration there remains no substance of bread or wine, nor any other substance but the substance of Christ, God and man.

Secondly, that Communion in both kinds is not necessary for all persons; …

Thirdly, that priests may not marry by the law of God.

Fourthly, that vows of chastity or widowhood, by man or woman made to God, ought to be observed by the law of God, …

Fifthly, that is meet and necessary that private Masses be continued and admitted in this the King's English Church …

Sixthly, that confession to a priest is necessary to be retained and continued, used and frequented in the Church of God.

This was a clear defence of essential Catholic doctrine. The penalties in the Act were severe. For example, to dispute the first article in any way would be considered heresy and punishable by burning, and any solemn denial of the other five was punishable by death.

Reformers in England and Europe saw this as a setback. It was known as 'the whip with six strings'. Bishops Latimer and Shaxton resigned their sees in protest. Cranmer, however, remained in office, although he sent his wife back to Germany. His belief in the Royal Supremacy overrode any doubts he must have had about some of the Articles.

Four years later, the conservative orthodoxy was reinforced by the publication of *The Necessary Doctrine and Erudition of a Christian Man*. This was subjected to Henry's personal scrutiny before publication, and hence is known as the King's Book. In this book all seven sacraments were said to be of equal weight, the doctrine of transubstantiation was upheld, and demands for Communion under both kinds dismissed. The Lutheran teaching of **'justification by faith alone'** was rejected. Prayers and Masses for the dead were deemed acceptable, although any financial abuses arising from a belief in Purgatory were firmly condemned.

Although the doctrinal position did not change, further inroads were made or planned on some of the ceremonies and practices of the Church. Late in 1541, for example, Henry repeated his order that all shrines should be dismantled and declared that there should be lighted candles only before the Blessed Sacrament, and not before images of the Virgin or saints. He also encouraged Cranmer in his plans for an English liturgy (the 'script' for services) in place of the traditional Latin liturgy. He also allowed the publication, in May 1544, of an English translation of the litany, a sequence of prayers to God and the saints. At the end of the reign the dissolution of the **chantries** was planned. Although the intention was to gain the wealth invested in them, such a move could easily be associated with an attack on the doctrine of Purgatory.

9 ⌐ CONCLUSION

If consistency is looked for in Henry's religious policies, then the result will be disappointment. To the end he remained susceptible to change and persuasion. He never abandoned his affection for his Archbishop of Canterbury, Thomas Cranmer, though he must have known of his marriage and on a number of occasions differed from him on doctrinal questions. Cranmer, for example, insisted on rejecting or correcting most of Henry's criticisms of the Bishop's Book of 1537. And throughout the 1540s, Cranmer continued to pursue reformist ideas within his diocese and in his clerical appointments. In 1543, when Cranmer was accused of heresy by his own clergy, Henry's response was to order the Archbishop himself to investigate the charges. Similarly, when accusations were made against the King's wife, Catherine Parr (well known for her reforming sympathies), she personally sought Henry's pardon and his anger was redirected against the accusers.

It was easy to see in Henry someone whose religious views were unpredictable and inconsistent. Partly this can be explained by the fact that he did not feel constrained to declare himself totally for or against any one set of prescribed beliefs. Partly too this was the result of his being, in theology, an amateur, and a lazy amateur at that. Turning to theology only in fits and starts, he had neither the time nor perhaps the inclination to develop what others would have considered a coherent body of doctrine. He reacted to events rather than planned a Reforma-

Justification by faith alone A soul is 'justified' when it is made fit to enter Heaven. Roman Catholics believed in 'justification by faith and works', the works being good works such as pilgrimages or alms-giving. Protestants believed that human 'works' were as nothing compared with God-given faith – so they taught 'justification by faith alone'

Chantries endowments for a priest to say Mass for the dead

KEY ISSUE

Does 'Catholicism without the Pope' best summarise the religion of England at the end of Henry's reign?

tion, most obviously in the way his need for a divorce brought him to break with Rome in the first place. It was to be in the reign of his son, Edward VI, that there was to be the first attempt to make England a fully Protestant nation.

10 ⌐ BIBLIOGRAPHY

*Keith Randell *Henry VIII and the Reformation in England* (Hodder, Access to History, 2001) and *DG Newcombe *Henry VIII and the English Reformation* (Routledge, Lancaster Pamphlets, 1995) provide good introductions. *J Guy *Tudor England* (Oxford University Press, 1990) is an excellent textbook for the whole period, and particularly good on this topic. Richard Rex *Henry VIII and the English Reformation* (MacMillan, 1993) is not such easy going but has some good themed chapters, e.g. popular religion. **AG Dickens *The English Reformation* (Batsford, 1989) is the second edition of a classic account of the Reformation and is very positive on the Protestant achievement. **JJ Scarisbrick *The Reformation and the English People* is an early example of revisionism, emphasising the Reformation as a change imposed from above. *C Haigh (ed.) *The English Reformation Revised* (Cambridge University Press, 1987), especially Haigh's own contributions, develops some of the revisionist ideas.

(*Recommended. **Highly recommended.)

11 ⌐ STRUCTURED AND ESSAY QUESTIONS

A *Structured questions*

1. (a) What were the stages by which Henry VIII brought pressure to bear on the English clergy?
    (b) What was significant about the events of January and March 1533?
2. (a) What were the main events in the Dissolution of the Monasteries from 1535 to 1540?
    (b) Were the monasteries dissolved only because of Henry's greed?

B *Essay questions*

1. Why was there so little resistance to Henry's Reformation?
2. How important was the role of Parliament in Henry's Reformation?
3. To what extent was England still a Catholic country in 1546?
4. 'The Dissolution of the Monasteries was a disaster for many but a golden opportunity for a few.' Is this true?
5. 'There was no blueprint for the Henrician Reformation; it just evolved stage by stage.' How accurate is this view?

Advice – narrative and analysis

In structured AS questions, the first question may primarily call for a clear statement of relevant knowledge. However, you need to consider very carefully what a specific question requires. A rule of thumb for A-Level essays is the less narrative the better. Re-telling the story can bring in much redundant material and obscure the argument when what is needed is clear, balanced analysis. However, some questions seem to demand narrative. Take, for instance, Question 5 above: ' "There was no blueprint for the Henrician Reformation; it just evolved stage by stage." How accurate is this view?'

At first sight it might appear to be a statement which is generally accurate, and its truth could be demonstrated by telling the story of the Henrician Reformation showing how one development led to another. However, it would be much better to organise the essay thematically. And a more balanced argument will result if any principles or strategies behind the Henrician Reformation are clarified and placed against the view of it as just one development leading to another.

To assist in this, plan to write each paragraph of the essay as if in answer to an appropriate question. The following are questions to illustrate this approach. Complete the list, decide which order the questions should come in and then write the essay.

(a) *Was there a consistent aim or principle which lay behind the legislation of 1533–6 or were the various acts just bargaining counters with the Pope?*

(b) *How important was the financial motive in the Henrician Reformation?*

(c) *Was a reformation necessary for the Crown to exploit the Church?*

(d) *Why were reforms, such as the Dissolution of the Monasteries, made piecemeal rather than all at once? Because the government's plans were unformed or because there was a need to acclimatise the nation to change?*

(e) *Did Cromwell have a clear view of where the Reformation was going or did he just adapt to circumstances and his master's whims?*

12 ⌐ SOURCE EXERCISES

(i) The Royal Supremacy

The Duke of Norfolk answered that the Pope had no jurisdiction except in matters of heresy ... The Duke said that on the tomb of King Arthur (I did not know of whom he spoke) there was some writing that he had copied out for me. It said: 'The Lord Arthur, Emperor of Britain, France and Germany'. I said I was sorry he was not also called Emperor of Asia and that he had not left King Henry his successor.

The Duke said that two days ago he was informed that the Pope had sent some very injurious mandates, which, if the Pope came himself to put into action in person, nothing would save him from the fury of the people. He then said that in the past popes had tried to usurp authority and that the people would not suffer it – still less would they do so now. The king had a right of Empire and recognised no superior. There had been an Englishman who had conquered Rome, i.e. Brennus, that the Emperor Constantine had reigned here and the mother of Constantine was English.

SOURCE A

From a letter of the imperial ambassador, Chapuys, to Charles V, Jan. 1531

Where by divers sundry old authentic histories and chronicles it is manifestly declared and expressed that this realm of England is an empire, and so hath been accepted in the world, governed by one supreme head and king having the dignity and royal estate of the imperial crown of the same, unto all sorts and degrees of people divided into spiritualty and temporalty, be bounden and owe to bear next to God a natural and humble obedience; he being also institute and furnished by the goodness and sufferance of Almighty God with plenary, whole and entire power ... to render and yield justice to all subjects within this realm, in all causes, matters, debates and contentions happening to occur or begin within the limits thereof ...

SOURCE B

From the preamble to the Act in Restraint of Appeals, 1533

SOURCE C

Claims of this kind were not new. The question of royal authority and the idea of imperial power had occurred before in Henry's reign. In 1512 a statute was passed limiting the privilege of benefit of clergy. The statute was denounced as an attack on church liberties by Richard Kidderminster, the Abbot of Winchcombe, in 1515. Following a public dispute, Henry VIII made this declaration

By the ordinance and sufferance of God we are king of England, and the kings of England in time past have never had any superior but God alone. Wherefore, know you well that we shall maintain the right of our crown and of our temporal jurisdiction as well in this point as in all others ...

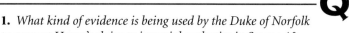

Q

1. *What kind of evidence is being used by the Duke of Norfolk to support Henry's claim to imperial authority in Source A?*
2. *How persuasive does this evidence seem to be?*
3. *What does this preamble have in common with Source A?*
4. *How does Source C affect the view that Henry VIII had been a loyal son of the Roman Catholic Church before the divorce question arose?*
5. *Why do all these sources appeal to the past to support Henry's claim to the Royal Supremacy?*

(ii) Henry VIII and St Thomas Becket

Henry VIII took a particular dislike to the memory of St Thomas Becket. He had been Lord Chancellor of England in the reign of Henry II, and in 1162 the King chose him to be Archbishop of Canterbury. Before long Becket had argued with Henry II over the rights and liberties of the Church and in December 1170 he was killed in Canterbury Cathedral by four of the King's knights. Within three years of his death he had been declared a saint and his shrine at Canterbury became one of the most popular pilgrimage sites in England. The gifts left by the pilgrims also made it one of the richest.

As it now clearly appears that Thomas Becket, sometime Archbishop of Canterbury, stubbornly to withstand the laws established against the enormities of the clergy by the King's highness' most noble ancestor, King Henry II, fled into France and to the Bishop of Rome, maintainer of these enormities …

And further that his canonization was made only by the Bishop of Rome because he had been a champion to maintain his usurped authority …

… the King's Majesty, by the advice of his council, hath thought expedient to declare that, notwithstanding the said canonization, there appeareth nothing in his life whereby he should be called a saint, but rather esteemed to have been a rebel and a traitor to his prince.

Therefore his grace commands that from henceforth the said Thomas Becket shall not be esteemed nor called a saint, but Bishop Becket, and that his images through the whole realm shall be removed from all churches, chapels and other places, and that from henceforth the days used to be festival in his name shall not be observed nor the prayers in his name be read but erased out of all books.

SOURCE A
From a Royal Proclamation of 1538

All the wealth in the world would not be enough to satisfy Henry's ambition … from which has come the ruin of the abbeys and the spoiling of every church in which there is anything to take … St. Thomas is declared a traitor because his relics and bones were adorned with gold and stones.

SOURCE B
A comment from the French ambassador de Marillac, c. 1538

After he [Henry VIII] had summoned St Thomas, the Archbishop of Canterbury into court and caused him to be declared a traitor, he has ordered his bones, which were kept in a golden shrine to be disinterred and burnt and the ashes to be scattered to the winds … And in addition to this he has taken possession of all the offerings given by the generosity of different kings, some of them of England, and of other princes, which were attached to the shrine and were of immense value.

SOURCE C
Papal Bull issued against Henry VIII by Pope Paul III, 1538

SOURCE D
From Miles Coverdale to
Thomas Cromwell, March 1539

This is to inform you that one Nicholas Hyde and one John Gryce of Henley upon Thames came to me, reporting that in a glass window of Our Lady's chapel in the church of the said Henley the image of Thomas Becket, with the whole false story of his death, is allowed to remain. Not only this, but that all the beams and candlesticks, whereupon tapers and lights used to be set up to images, remain still untaken down.

1. *What motives are suggested in Sources A and B for the campaign against the memory of Thomas Becket?*
2. *How reliable are these sources as evidence of Henry's motives?*
3. *What do Sources C and D tell us about the significance of the campaign against Thomas Becket?*

Henry VIII: Government and Politics 1529–47

5

INTRODUCTION

In 1953 GR Elton published a book entitled *The Tudor Revolution in Government*. In it he maintained that, along with the Reformation, the 1530s saw a crucial change in the way in which England was governed, the centre of power moving away from the King's Household and into bureaucratically organised government departments. He attributed that change to the conscious design of Thomas Cromwell. The thesis he put forward was always controversial, but Elton's view dominated the interpretation of the period for several decades. In recent years Cromwell's role as an innovator and statesman has been increasingly challenged, and David Starkey has shown that power remained where it was at the start of Henry's reign – at the heart of his Household.

Historians have also debated the nature of the politics of the reign and the extent to which the Court and policy-making were dominated by the King himself or by rival groups of politicians. Henry was a powerful character, but he was subject to influence and persuasion, and the question is whether he was systematically manipulated by organised factions.

Politics was also played out in other areas – in Parliament and in the provinces, and Henry needed to command general support in both these areas if he was to make his rule effective. Henry certainly made significant use of Parliament and so contributed to its development.

But parliamentary history and administrative reform were not what Henry would have thought important. He would build his reputation on the role he played in Europe and thought not in terms of a developing nation state but of personal triumphs in the dynastic and political struggles of his age. In the 1540s he renewed war with France, in which he squandered the fortune acquired through the Dissolution of the Monasteries, and achieved little.

1 ∽ THE TUDOR REVOLUTION IN GOVERNMENT

According to Professor Elton, during the 1530s a system of government centred on the King in his Household gave way to a system of departments, freed from the vagaries of royal control and run according to a formal routine. Each department would be able to function following the rules laid down for it, without requiring the intervention of monarch or minister. This was the 'Tudor Revolution' and it affected three main areas: the Council, the royal finances, and the role of the King's principal secretary.

A *The Privy Council*

From 1529, the problem of Henry's marriage dominated royal policy and the King was personally committed to finding a solution. He now drew about himself a small group of councillors who became a 'Council Attendant' upon the King. Such an inner circle had existed before Wolsey's domination of the Council but it did not have any official status. It was still part of the Council as a whole. However, by 1540 the informal group around the King had become a new institution – the Privy Council.

The Privy Council consisted of about 19 members, and its separate and permanent status was marked by the appointment of a clerk to record decisions. Its activities were predominantly those of advising on and executing policy rather than the administration of justice. At the same time, the judicial aspects of the Council's work were continued by Star Chamber and the Court of Requests. Although the former consisted of the same personnel as the Privy Council, with the addition of the two chief justices, both it and the Court of Requests were now to be considered as separate institutions, with their own clerks and set times of meeting.

See page 64

Professor Elton saw this as part of Thomas Cromwell's master-plan. Cromwell had an important role to play on the Council. By 1533 he appears to have been responsible for drawing up the agenda for Council meetings, possibly conducting the meetings and afterwards implementing the decisions. He kept his own record of Council decisions and it is probable that all the clerical work for the Council, including minuting, was carried out by Cromwell's staff. In June 1534 Cromwell made a note for himself: 'To remember the King for the establishment of the Council'. It would seem credible that he was responsible for any change.

A few weeks after his death, the Privy Council consolidated its new status with the following decision:

Q

1. *Why is the appointment important in the history of the Privy Council?*
2. *How well does this appointment fit Elton's theory of a Tudor Revolution?*

That there should be a clerk attendant upon the said Council to write, enter and register all such decrees, determinations, letters and other such things as he should be appointed to enter in a book, to remain always as a ledger, as well for the discharge of the said councillors touching such things as they should pass from time to time, as also for a memorial unto them of their own proceedings.

This view that Cromwell had transformed the Council has come in for criticism. The courts associated with the Council, Star Chamber and the Court of Requests, had been developed by Cardinal Wolsey. In both cases we find Cromwell not creating anything new but making a contribution to a development that had already started. They had gained their distinct identities before the Privy Council had fully emerged.

As for the Privy Council itself, one criticism of seeing it as Cromwell's achievement is that it represents an ideal that was sought after by others, especially some of the nobility. This ideal was that government should not be in the hands of a single great minister, but conducted by a small and primarily noble council. In October 1529, for example, the Duke of Norfolk told the Imperial ambassador Chapuys that government would in future be managed by the Council and not by an individual. That Council, moreover, would consist of 'those who from birth and circumstances were more competent'. To some extent, we see this happening on Wolsey's fall, when Henry gathered a small group of Councillors about him to help find a way out of his marriage problem.

As yet, however, there had been no formal change. It was events which were to drive on the development of the Council, rather than Cromwell following a blueprint. The important date would appear to be 1536, the year of the Pilgrimage of Grace. It was a time of danger to the King and also a time when Cromwell, under attack from the rebels, had to take a back seat while the Council assumed a more prominent role. Lists of Council members at this time indicate that membership was now greatly restricted in numbers. It is possible, therefore, that the 1536 crisis had heightened the importance of a small, select Council which could react swiftly and effectively in need. As well as being smaller, there are indications that membership of this Council depended on holding certain qualifying offices. This seems to have been the case by the spring of 1537 when a Council list shows that of fourteen members all but one were important office-holders.

The new importance of offices as a sign of status is demonstrated by the Act of Precedence of 1539. This laid down the order in which people would sit in Parliament and in sessions of the Privy Council and shows clearly that seniority was based upon the holding of particular offices. Ten of the eleven offices mentioned in the Act were almost always held by noblemen, and so this ensured a good proportion of noblemen on the Privy Council. So the Privy Council that emerged by 1540 seems to qualify, by reason of its size and membership, as a manifestation of the noble council sought after by the Duke of Norfolk and his like.

Rather than the Privy Council being Cromwell's creation, it looks as if it was an idea which pre-dated him and which was brought into being by circumstances rather than his design. Its development was then halted by Cromwell's return to prominence for what remained of the 1530s when the Privy Council remained dependent on his staff for all its secretarial work. In this way he kept control, and it was important for him to do so since the kind of people who were on the Privy Council proved to be his political enemies. He was a skilled politician and not likely to establish an important government body that virtually guaranteed membership to people who were his political rivals. It was to be his enemies on the Council who brought about his downfall in 1540. Only

> **KEY ISSUE**
>
> *How significant had the Privy Council become by the late 1530s?*

then was the Privy Council, freed from Cromwell's domination, able to complete its emergence as an institution with the appointment of its own secretary.

B *Finance*

The financial system based on the Household continued into the reign of Henry VIII. Royal revenue was paid to the Treasurer of the Chamber in cash and stored away in one of the King's strongrooms, such as the Jewel House at Westminster. Regular audits were held by members of the Royal Household or specially commissioned Councillors. The advantages of the system were that close supervision by the King was possible, a realistic assessment could be made of the money at his disposal, and that money was readily available in cash. This system continued up to the 1530s with very little modification. Meanwhile the Exchequer continued to function, dealing particularly with income from customs and from the administration of justice. However, although it was acknowledged as being effective in its accounting and collecting, it could also be very slow and cumbersome.

With his influence growing and the flow of royal income increasing as a consequence of the Reformation, Cromwell set about the creation of organised financial departments, beginning in 1536. The Office of General Surveyors, first seen in 1515 handling Household income, now became a permanent department. In the same year the Court of Augmentations ('court' here just means government department) was set up to handle the income from confiscated monastic lands. Augmentations, whose modern collecting and accounting procedures compared favourably with the Exchequer, became the model for further departments (or courts). In 1540 the Court of Wards was set up to handle royal revenue from wardship. After Cromwell's death, the Court of First Fruits and Tenths, which collected the King's ecclesiastical dues, and the Court of General Surveyors, overseeing landed wealth, were organised on similar lines in 1541 and 1542. By the end of Henry's reign, therefore, there were six financial departments functioning independently of the Household and of each other, and, in contrast to the earlier Household arrangements, working within specific areas.

Were these changes due to a master plan prompted by Cromwell's belief in formal and independent departments? His handling of the Court of First Fruits and Tenths does not support this view. He kept it very much under his own control, treating it almost like his own Household department and using its resources to finance his policies. It only became a 'free-standing' institution after his death. As well as this, the creation of these departments can be seen as an obvious response to particular needs. The 1530s saw an increase in royal income in a number of areas and so the new departments were set up. Nor, in daily practice, should the contrast between old and new be over-emphasised. Personnel could move with ease from one department to another or between the new departments and the Household, or even work in two areas at once. This broke down any tendency to clear-cut differences

PICTURE 15
Henry VIII dining in his Privy Chamber

between them. Finally, the whole system was later found to be too cumbersome, and extensive reforms were introduced in the 1550s.

The Privy Chamber continued to play an important role. The new departments collected royal revenue and paid out routine expenses, but they did not keep the surplus. This, according to a government memorandum of 1537, was every year to 'be laid up for all necessities' and the places where it was laid up, or stored, were the King's Privy Coffers. These were Henry's stores of cash, kept in his main palaces, but particularly in Whitehall, and administered by members of his Privy Chamber under the King's direct supervision. Hoarding and spending were still very much a Household affair.

KEY ISSUE

How far did control of the royal finances become bureaucratic under Cromwell?

C *The Secretary*

By the beginning of the Tudor period the role of the King's secretary was already regarded as a public office rather than simply that of personal assistant to the King. The secretary read and summarised letters to the King and helped to draft and write the royal replies. He was also in charge of the signet, the King's private seal which was used to authorise royal orders to government departments.

When Thomas Cromwell took office the secretary was essentially a member of the Household, whose importance lay in access to the King combined with an intimate knowledge of royal affairs. Cromwell managed to exploit it to the utmost and extended his influence to virtually every area of public life. As far as Professor Elton is concerned, he took the secretaryship out of the Household and made it one of the offices of state. Its new status was recognised in the 1539 Act of Precedence where it was listed as one of the 'great offices of the realm', though in precedence the least.

But the new status did not persist. In 1540 Cromwell resigned the office which was then divided between two holders, and the secretaryship was officially restored to its pre-Cromwellian point in the order of precedence, although it did later regain its importance as circumstances changed once again. Cromwell did not institute any lasting formal changes. His use of the secretaryship was purely personal.

D *Was there a Tudor revolution in government?*

Evolution now seems as valid a concept as revolution. Some changes were simply the result of reacting to events. A vast increase in sources of wealth led necessarily to the creation of departments to handle that wealth, and, like the Privy Council, these departments were not fully institutionalised until Cromwell had left the scene. To some extent Cromwell may have acted as a brake on any bureaucratic development as he dominated different areas through his own household system. His own staff provided the Privy Council secretariat, and the treasurer of First Fruits and Tenths was effectively Cromwell's personal servant. At the same time the Household retained an important role in finance.

The distinction between Household and bureaucratic offices may not have been so clear in the 1530s and 1540s when the two areas could share the same personnel — the Privy Council met in the room opposite the King's bedroom, and councillors and secretaries shared the Household privilege of eating at the King's expense. Cromwell himself had been able to exploit the Household offices of Master of the Jewels and the King's secretary in his rise to power, and later in his career he became **Lord Great Chamberlain** as part of his plan of keeping control of that important area of political life.

Professor Elton did modify aspects of his original theory but he continued to argue for Cromwell's commitment to introducing a new style of government and to see him as the initiator and driving force of the policies of the 1530s. This view has also been criticised. George Bernard, for example, believes references to the King's orders occur so often in Cromwell's letters and papers that they show Henry's direct control of policy. Frequent notes by Cromwell that he should find out the King's wishes indicate that, far from carrying out his own masterplan, he was often simply doing what Henry told him to do.

2 ⌁ ROYAL AUTHORITY AND THE LOCAL COMMUNITY

Control of the provinces was important, especially at a time of change when it was necessary to have royal policy first of all communicated to the provinces and then put into effect. The raising of troops and the administration of the King's justice both needed adequate representation of the royal will in the local community.

KEY ISSUE

How important did Cromwell make the role of the King's secretary?

Lord Great Chamberlain the officer in overall control of the King's Household

KEY ISSUE

What substance is there in the thesis that there was a Tudor Revolution in Government?

Cromwell believed that the King should have closer control over all people and all areas within his realm, and he worked hard at putting this ideal into practice. The changes he made to bring the whole of England and Wales into one uniform system of law and administration under royal control were of considerable importance and are discussed elsewhere. These measures included the establishment of the Council of the North to administer royal policy in that area and the inclusion of Wales in the shire system. But, while these moves were aimed at making

See page 286

Royal Progresses

ANALYSIS

A royal progress was the King's summer tour. Accompanied by his court, he journeyed through parts of his kingdom for several weeks, normally between June and October. The route was decided in spring and copies sent to all those involved. Most progresses took place in the south of England, and the majority of properties visited were owned by the King. However, a significant number were owned either by courtiers or the Church. At the Dissolution of the Monasteries almost all the monastic houses taken over by the King were properties he had previously used on progresses.

The primary purpose of these progresses was recreational. All the progress houses were in areas of good hunting. But there was also a political motive. In 1535 the Imperial ambassador referred to Henry 'hunting and visiting with a view to gaining popularity with his subjects'. When he hunted the King was often joined by a number of the local nobility and gentry. The shared activity strengthened the ties between the King and his leading subjects in the locality. Ties were also strengthened by staying at courtiers' houses. This was a major expense and could cause considerable inconvenience, as Henry could be accompanied by a retinue of up to 800. In 1535 Sir Nicholas Poyntz demolished and rebuilt a whole wing of Acton Court when he was visited by Henry. When he visited Wolfhall in 1539, Edward Seymour had to move his own servants out of the house and into a barn. Such visits were a great honour and rooms used by the King or Queen continued to be known by names such as the 'Queen's Great Chamber' long afterwards.

Sometimes there might be specific political needs. Henry's early progresses took him further afield than most later ones, so his subjects could see their new king. His 1535 progress has been identified as a move to boost support for his religious policy since he visited those in favour of reform. After the Pilgrimage of Grace Henry promised a progress in the North. It finally took place in 1541 after the discovery of another conspiracy in Yorkshire. It was as much a military display as a progress and included 1000 soldiers and artillery.

Assizes court sessions held in the shires, presided over by circuit judges who travelled the country

Quarter-sessions the assembly every three months of all the JPs of a shire

KEY ISSUE

How far did the Tudor monarchy control the provinces?

sure the whole country shared the same system, to the system itself Cromwell made no change.

The officers who were most regularly involved in administering the localities for the King were the Justices of the Peace (the JPs). Their duties increased steadily as they were called upon to enforce new statutes. In 1542 the Justices of **Assize** were given the authority to hear any charges against the JPs, and a year later it was ordered that the Court of King's Bench should in future receive a transcript of the **quarter-session** proceedings in each shire. The nature of the Justices of the Peace had changed little but the amount of work they did was increasing and was seen to require greater supervision.

The gentry and nobility of the area, often joined by the leading churchmen, were the JPs and other local officers of the King. They were chosen because they were the natural leaders of their locality. Their work was unpaid and could be onerous. However, to be associated with the royal authority in this way enhanced their own position and was seen as an essential part of their role in society. The King could not afford a system of fully-paid royal officials so he needed the co-operation of the leaders of the counties. (Henry VIII had just over 1000 paid officials serving him, in comparison with the 40 000 who served the king of France.) Special efforts were made to build up a network of personal relationships between the King and individuals in the provinces. These 'King's men' could be linked to their monarch by a variety of means – patronage, the granting of lands and titles, or positions at Court that brought prestige but no duties requiring residence.

People who were important figures in Court and Council were also important in their local areas. Most members of the Privy Chamber were also Justices of the Peace, and courtiers were sent to act on commissions or to raise troops for the King, often from their own followers. The officials of the Privy Chamber provided a substantial proportion of the army when the King went to war.

3 ⌐ PARLIAMENT

Another important link between the centre and the provinces was Parliament. In a Parliament the King's subjects could express their opinions on aspects of royal policy and demonstrate their willingness, or otherwise, to pay for it. The King used the meetings to present his policies to his people, win their consent to them and then send them away to enforce these policies in their own communities.

Although the House of Lords enjoyed a greater status and prestige than the Commons, in parliamentary business the two houses were equal. Consent to taxation and legislation had to come from both houses. The Commons had already claimed with some success a number of privileges. In 1523 the then Speaker, Sir Thomas More, made the first recorded request that members should be allowed to speak freely on any matters put before them and, generally speaking, the spirit of the request was observed through Henry's reign. Such freedom was not without its limits and members still needed to watch their words. Later in the reign, one Thomas Broke found himself up before a panel of bishops to answer for his criticism of the Act of Six Articles.

From 1529 to 1536, the sessions of the Reformation Parliament took place almost annually; and in the next 11 years only four did not witness a Parliament in session. By contrast, Parliaments had been held in only five of the first twenty years of the reign. It has been argued that Thomas Cromwell was particularly keen to use Parliament, especially in securing the breach with Rome. This may be exaggerated. After all, in matters of such high importance the King wanted to be sure of the consent of his important subjects and that any policy could be effectively enforced. For both of these Parliament was the obvious instrument. It contained the leaders of the political nation and its statutes, the Acts of Parliament, were generally regarded as the highest form of positive, or man-made, law in the realm, which could be enforced with the fullest sanctions. The King could simply declare himself to be Supreme Head of the Church, but he needed an Act of Parliament to allow him to chop someone's head off for denying it.

After being involved with such major changes, many historians have argued that Parliament was not to be the same again. It had ventured into areas, such as religion, that it had not previously dealt with, and consequently there was a feeling that Parliament's scope had been widened and there were now no areas from which it could be excluded. According to Professor Graves: 'By 1540 King-in-Parliament had emerged as the sovereign legislator … Its laws were not only supreme but omni-competent'.

Since Parliament's role was recognised as important, care was taken to ensure its efficient co-operation during sessions. After Parliament had been summoned in 1539, Cromwell wrote to Henry that he 'and other your dedicate councillors be about to bring all things so to pass that your Majesty had a never more tractable Parliament'. The methods were not exceptional – the use of direct royal influence in a few areas and the promise of co-operation from influential landowners in others would ensure the return of a sufficient number of councillors and royal 'men of business' to the House of Commons.

The Crown could still face opposition in Parliament. Individuals who were known to oppose the royal policy sometimes had to be persuaded to absent themselves from the House, as happened to Sir George Throckmorton in 1534. This happened also to members of the House of Lords who might cause trouble for government legislation. Henry also used his personal authority to bring pressure to bear. Groups of MPs might be summoned to his presence to be made aware of his feelings. Occasionally he even went down into the House itself. In 1532, for example, criticism of the Annates bill led to Henry forcing the House to vote on the bill in his presence, and in 1536 he may personally have delivered the bill for the Dissolution of the Monasteries.

By its role in a period of particularly important and wide-ranging legislation, Parliament as an institution gained a new prestige and a foothold in areas of competence that would later be expanded. This

KEY ISSUE

What effect did Henry VIII's reign have on Parliament?

enhancement of Parliament's status was of particular importance to the House of Commons, and it became more usual than before to introduce bills in the Commons, partly prompted perhaps by Cromwell's presence there at a crucial stage. The new significance of the Commons was reflected in the greater number of government men that could now be found there and also perhaps in the fact that by the end of Henry's reign it had acquired its own Journal, that is an organised system of records. It had increased in size as well, with the addition of members from the shires of Wales and the Marcher territories and the creation of 14 new parliamentary boroughs. The Lords had also seen a major change in the removal of all the abbots from its benches; the bishops remained but the lay peers now enjoyed a substantial majority.

ANALYSIS

Patronage and Faction

Patronage was the system in which the patron bestowed gifts and rewards on his client, who in turn supported his patron, and it permeated the whole of Tudor society. If a man had an office at his disposal, he gave it to someone he knew or to someone who had been recommended to him. At the summit of this pyramid of patronage was the King himself, the ultimate source of all honours, and without his patronage there was no way to the top. The person who found favour with the King gained rewards for himself and became a channel of that favour for others. Attached to every successful careerist was a band of clients who relied on him for their current positions and future prospects. In return they gave him service and support.

Much of Tudor politics, therefore, was bound up with search for patronage. People sought access to the King but in doing so they rarely tried to act alone. Individuals came together in alliances that are known as factions; and the consequent struggles between these groups have been given the name faction politics. Professor Ives has defined a faction as a group of people who have come together to seek 'objectives that are seen primarily in personal terms' as opposed to parties with longer lasting organisations and beliefs. But it is also possible to see other motives contributing to factions, such as loyalty to an individual or a shared sympathy for religious reform. Membership could shift and change in response to events. Professor Ives sees faction as a continual phenomenon in the sixteenth century, but he admits that there were times when the struggles between the different groups became more violent and intense. Many historians have seen Henry VIII's reign as such a time.

4 ⤳ POLITICS AFTER WOLSEY

Wolsey's fall created a gap that no one person was able or called upon to fill. Henry was left with a continuing problem – how to set aside Catherine of Aragon and marry Anne Boleyn – but with no effective way yet suggested by which he could arrive at a solution. Individuals rose or fell in the King's favour depending on their attitude to the King's divorce and the extent to which they could help bring it about.

According to the French ambassador the result of Wolsey's fall was that: 'The Duke of Norfolk is now made chief of the Council and in his absence the Duke of Suffolk, and above everyone Madamoiselle Anne'. Norfolk may have enjoyed some influence with Henry at this time, and he certainly seems to have tried to keep Wolsey away from the King in case he regained royal favour. However, although Norfolk was willing to go along with Henry's attempts at divorce and could accept the rejection of papal authority, he was able to do little to advance the King's cause. Suffolk did not support the divorce. He gave Henry his loyalty and service but stayed in the background.

THOMAS HOWARD, 3RD DUKE OF NORFOLK (1473–1554)

Thomas Howard was the son of the Duke of Norfolk who, after fighting for Richard III at the Battle of Bosworth, regained his family's title and fortune through loyal service to Henry VII. The third Duke continued the same tradition. His career started as a military leader when he assisted his father in the Scottish campaign of 1513. In the early 1520s he was Henry's representative in Ireland, launched raids on the French coast and led an army against the Scots. But he also knew that real power required involvement at the very centre of political affairs and during this time he was constantly trying to return to court. He was at court by 1524 when his father died and he became the 3rd Duke of Norfolk; he had already taken over his father's office of Lord Treasurer.

During Wolsey's years of power, Norfolk continued to serve Henry and cooperated with the Cardinal, regardless of any private reservations he may have had. However, when his niece Anne Boleyn aroused Henry's affections, Norfolk could take a more prominent role and showed no hesitation in helping to remove Wolsey from office. He advanced his position further in 1533 when his daughter married Henry's bastard son, the Duke of Richmond. Norfolk survived the fall of Anne Boleyn in 1536, pronouncing the sentence of death on her himself, but it must have shaken his security. However, in the same year the Pilgrimage of Grace meant that the King needed him again as a military leader, and he was able to counter any suspicions of his loyalty by his harsh treatment of the Pilgrims. He was not at ease during these years. He disliked

Cromwell as a low-born upstart, disapproved of the changes in religion and felt that the nobility were being denied the role in government to which their birth entitled them.

Once again the King's marriage to one of his nieces, Catherine Howard, seemed to ensure for him a position of influence but her subsequent execution for adultery was a serious setback and he had to write a grovelling letter to Henry disowning his nieces and their behaviour. He continued to serve Henry as a Councillor and military commander, against the Scots in 1542 and the French in 1544. At home he was closely associated with Stephen Gardiner as a leading conservative in religion but he was realist enough to propose a marriage alliance with his opponents at court, the Seymours.

In 1546 his son, the Earl of Surrey, spoke carelessly of his father's right to be regent for the future Edward VI and claimed royal descent for his family. Father and son were arrested and sentenced to death. Surrey was executed, but the night before Norfolk's execution was due to take place, Henry died. The sentence was never carried out and the Duke stayed in the Tower until he was released at the beginning of Mary's reign. Once again he joined the Royal Council. In 1554 he led the troops sent to put down Wyatt's rebellion but the desertion of his soldiers meant that his last act of service to the Crown was a failure. He died later that year. Norfolk was in most respects a very traditional figure. He served his monarch as a soldier and he expected as of right to have a role in the King's councils. He was traditional also in his beliefs. He had no time for new ideas: 'It was merry in England before the New Learning came up; yea, I would all things were as hath been in times past.'

Stephen Gardiner, the Bishop of Winchester, had emerged as a leading player in trying to secure the divorce. As one of Henry's agents in Rome he was willing to put pressure on the Pope and was later to defend the Royal Supremacy in the church. However, he remained a traditionalist in his religious beliefs, and his defence of clerical privilege in Convocation in 1532 cast him under a temporary cloud.

More obviously successful in winning the King's favour were those who provided the solution to his problem, and foremost among these were Thomas Cromwell and Thomas Cranmer. Cromwell was ambitious, able and hardworking and he replaced his old master, Wolsey, in the sense that he took much of the responsibility for carrying out Henry's policies. Cranmer, soon to be Archbishop of Canterbury, was not so ambitious, but he fully supported Henry's plans and helped to provide the material that justified Henry's Supremacy.

At the centre of affairs was Anne Boleyn and her family. She herself was an influential figure, and her ideas had to be taken into account. In 1532 Gardiner had bought his way back into favour by giving her one of his manors. Her rise had helped her father's elevation to the title Earl of Wiltshire. Her brother George, following expulsion in one of

Wolsey's reforms, had been readmitted to the Privy Chamber in 1528 and, as Viscount Rochford, was from 1529 one of the two noblemen in the Privy Chamber as well as being a member of the Council.

The success of the divorce policy meant defeat for others. Sir Thomas More, who succeeded Wolsey as Lord Chancellor, had made no secret of his disagreement with Henry over the divorce and, as the direction of Henry's policy became clear, More felt obliged to resign his office in 1532. Henry Courteney, Marquis of Exeter, a member of the Privy Chamber and the Council, and Lord Darcy both supported Queen Catherine and were suspicious of the possible religious implications that might follow from the divorce. Henry could tolerate such opposition only so far. When Lord Darcy proved too outspoken he was banned from attending Parliament in 1534. More's continued refusal to give even token support resulted in his execution.

<table>
<tr><td>

KEY ISSUE

How clearly divided into factions was the Court after the fall of Wolsey?

</td></tr>
</table>

5 ⌐ THE FALL OF ANNE BOLEYN

On 7 January 1536, Catherine of Aragon died. Henry and Anne danced together in celebration. Pregnant with what she hoped was the longed-for son, she must finally have felt secure as Henry's wife and Queen of England. But Anne certainly had her enemies. Catherine of Aragon's supporters still hoped to have Princess Mary restored to the succession. Now that Catherine was dead, Henry would be spared the embarrassing consequences of any implied restoration of his first queen that might have accompanied such a move. Religion was also a motive. Anne and her supporters were closely identified with the reforming movement in the English Church. Not only had her marriage depended on the rejection of the papacy, but she also showed signs of a strong commitment to some of the new trends in religion. She encouraged the reading of the Bible in English and actively supported the appointment of reforming churchmen such as Cranmer and Latimer.

Anne's relationship with Henry may have been undergoing some strain at the start of 1536. On 29 January she miscarried; the baby may have been a son. Henry is said to have called it a judgement of God on an unlawful marriage, but even if this report were true it is likely to have been the result of his bitter disappointment rather than a considered view.

Anne's situation was made more vulnerable by the existence of a rival for Henry's affections. Jane Seymour had been a lady of the Court since the early 1530s but did not seriously attract the King's attention until 1535 or 1536. The affair was first noted by the Imperial ambassador, Chapuys, in February, and in the following month she was given rooms near the King. Her brother Edward was already an established figure at Court, and in March he was appointed to the Privy Chamber.

Although Anne complained about Henry's affair, she would not have thought of it as a fatal threat. Henry appeared still to be committed to their marriage until late April. An encounter with the Imperial ambassador was arranged 18 April for an implicit and unprecedented acknowledgement by Chapuys of Anne's status, and in a letter of 25 April Henry referred to her as 'our most dear and most entirely beloved wife, the Queen'.

Within a week events had taken a different turn. On 30 April, Cromwell had Mark Smeaton, a musician in the Privy Chamber, arrested and interrogated. Under torture he confessed to adultery with the Queen. On the following day Henry Norris, Henry's Groom of the Stool, was arrested and sent to the Tower, to be followed within the next few days by Anne herself, her brother, Lord Rochford, and two other members of the Privy Chamber, Sir Francis Weston and Sir William Brereton. They were accused of adultery, with the Queen, and in Rochford's case incest.

In prison, Anne wondered which of her words or deeds could have prompted the accusations, and these comments were immediately reported to Cromwell and became evidence. She had unwisely talked about what might happen when the King died. She was accused of conspiracy to bring about the King's death so that she could marry one of her so-called lovers. Smeaton's was the only confession to be obtained but they were all found guilty and sentenced to death. The men were executed on 17 May. On the same day Cranmer declared the King's marriage to Anne to be invalid, so barring their daughter Elizabeth from the succession. Two days later Anne herself was put to death, beheaded as a last favour, in the French fashion, with a sword rather than an axe. On the following day Henry was betrothed to Jane Seymour and their marriage took place on 30 May.

We cannot be certain of the explanation of these astonishing events. One view is that the whole process was engineered by Thomas Cromwell. He had already had his differences with Anne, largely over issues of patronage and also of foreign policy where his support for a pro-Imperial stance was at odds with the Boleyns' French sympathies. In addition, when he saw the conservatives and Seymours ready to act, he had to join them in order to stay on the winning side. This helps to explain why it was not just Anne who was executed. He also had to remove significant members of her faction.

This view has been challenged, particularly by George Bernard. He maintains that the differences between Cromwell and Anne have been overstated and are not credible as motives for such action. Nor do the targets of this plot form a coherent group that would make sense as the victims of a faction struggle. Anne's fall may have been the result of a genuine accusation. According to a contemporary French account, the Countess of Worcester had been accused by her brother of sexual misconduct, and she had replied by accusing Anne of the same behaviour. The accusation then had to be investigated. Smeaton's confession then made further accusations seem more likely to be true. Whether the accused were guilty or not, the trials and execution may have been conducted in good faith by most, if not all, of those concerned. It is true that individuals benefited from Anne's fall but, although they may have taken advantage of events, it does not follow that they set them in motion. This does not rule out faction struggle entirely. But it does play down the extent to which factions consciously and successfully manipulated the King.

KEY ISSUE

What brought about the fall of Anne Boleyn?

6 ⌐ CROMWELL'S TRIUMPH AND HIS FALL

The benefits for Cromwell were soon apparent. At the end of June he replaced Anne's father as Lord Privy Seal and on 8 July was ennobled as Baron Cromwell of Wimbledon. He also recommended two of his followers for the Privy Chamber – Ralph Sadler and Peter Mewtas. The former was also awarded the estates of the executed Brereton.

Mary Tudor's supporters had gained little, although the new Queen did show more sympathy for her. An act of June 1536 specifically banned Catherine of Aragon's descendants from the succession and also did the same to any descendants of Queen Anne.

Later in 1536, some of Mary's supporters, having failed in the struggles at Court, attempted to topple Cromwell, restore Princess Mary and reverse the religious changes, by resorting to armed uprising when they took part in the Pilgrimage of Grace. Lord Darcy's loyalty to Catherine's cause has already been noted, and Lord Hussey had been Mary's chamberlain. Their involvement in the Pilgrimage resulted in their execution in June 1537.

In 1538 Henry ordered action to be taken against a number of potential opponents. This was prompted by the actions of the exiled Reginald Pole, a Cardinal and Henry's cousin. He had written condemning Henry's religious policy and attempted to raise foreign support for the Pilgrimage. A series of arrests and executions followed, including the Marquis of Exeter, Pole's brother Lord Montague, two members of the Privy Chamber, Sir Nicholas Carew and Sir Edward Neville. Even Pole's aged mother, Margaret, Countess of Salisbury, went to the block.

In January 1539 Cromwell was made Chief Noble of the Privy Chamber. His followers Thomas Heneage and Anthony Denny became Groom of the Stool and Chief Gentleman respectively. Cromwell also removed opponents on the Privy Council. Foremost among these was the Duke of Norfolk, who had no sympathy with the changes he saw taking place around him and disliked Cromwell as a low-born upstart. Temporarily excluded from the Privy Council but still actively criticising Cromwell, and his religious policies in particular, was the Bishop of Winchester, Stephen Gardiner. In 1538 he returned from a stint as ambassador at the French court and was keen to build up relations with that country rather than follow Cromwell's plan for a German alliance. This conservative faction saw their chance of toppling Cromwell in 1540 when a combination of circumstances led to a weakening of his influence.

Jane Seymour had died in October 1537, shortly after giving birth to Henry's son, Edward. The King was sincere in his mourning but very soon turned his attention to finding a new wife and this time decided to use his marriage to serve his international interests rather than choose according to his personal affections. Diplomatic isolation made a German alliance desirable, so he settled on Anne, the sister of the

Duke of Cleves, and a marriage treaty was signed in October 1539. A painting by Holbein and some reassuring reports from his agents convinced Henry that Anne would be personally as well as politically acceptable to him, but when he met her on 1 January 1540, he disliked her on sight.

Since the political situation demanded it, he went through with the marriage, but it was never consummated – Henry did not have the inclination and Anne apparently had no idea of what was involved. Meanwhile the international situation had eased, Henry was left with a wife he did not want and Cromwell, whether justifiably or not, had to bear most of the blame. Henry wanted another divorce and Cromwell had to arrange it.

On the face of it nothing could be simpler than annulling an unconsummated marriage, but for Cromwell there was a distinct complication, because an alternative candidate for the King's hand had already been brought forward. Catherine Howard was the niece of the Duke of Norfolk and had apparently been introduced to Henry at the house of Stephen Gardiner. She was young, lively and co-operative and had so captivated the King that it was obvious to Cromwell that if he got Henry his divorce, then his enemy's niece would be the next Queen with a consequent strengthening of his conservative opponents.

Even so, Cromwell might yet have survived, even with Catherine as Queen, for he was still high in the royal favour. In April 1540 he was created Earl of Essex and Lord Great Chamberlain, a post which he could use to extend his influence in the main Household departments. He demonstrated his value as a minister by managing to get a large subsidy from Parliament at a time when it was much needed.

However, his opponents played on Henry's desire to assert the orthodoxy of his Church in the face of religious disunity in the country. The details of what happened are not clear. An investigation into heretics in Calais seemed to show that Cromwell had allowed them to stay there. Cromwell's known sympathies in religion were enough to give substance to the charges of heresy that formed part of the attack made on him by his enemies. The King's impatience with the slow progress in getting his divorce tipped the balance. On 10 June Cromwell was arrested in the Council Chamber and taken to the Tower. His written appeals to the King, refuting the charges of treason and heresy, were ignored. On 28 July, having been condemned by an Act of Attainder, he was executed, acknowledging no guilt, and claiming that he died 'in the catholic faith of the Holy Church'. On the same day Henry married Catherine Howard.

KEY ISSUE

How far were Henry's fourth and fifth marriages responsible for Cromwell's ruin?

7 ∽ POLITICS IN THE 1540S

Cromwell's fall had been personal and was not accompanied by the removal of his clients. Any ascendancy the conservatives may have gained due to the Howard marriage was soon lost. In November 1541, information was laid before the Council concerning Catherine's persistent adultery. It appears no-one had the courage to tell the King until Cranmer, trusting to his special relationship, gave Henry a paper with details of the affair while he was at Mass. A more cynical view might stress Cranmer's opposition to the Howards, especially in matters of religion, and his satisfaction at being able to remove one of the main channels of their influence. When Henry had recovered from the shock of the revelation, he appointed a commission to investigate the accusations. Catherine's two lovers, one of whom was one of the King's favourites in the Privy Chamber, were executed in December, while Catherine and her accomplice, Lady Rochford, were beheaded the following February.

It was a blow to the Howard interest, especially in the Privy Chamber, from which Catherine's relatives were expelled, but the Duke of Norfolk speedily joined in the condemnation of his niece and, once again, the after-effects were limited. The conservatives made another attack on the reformers in 1543, this time taking Thomas Cranmer as their target. Using evidence provided by some of the clergy from Cranmer's own cathedral, Gardiner, in the Privy Council, accused him of heresy. But Gardiner had misjudged Cranmer's relationship with the King. When Henry was informed of what had happened, he sent for the Archbishop and, instead of taking him to task for his heretical views, put him in charge of the investigation into his own activities. The harsh words he kept for those who had attempted to destroy Cranmer.

The reformers were given further encouragement following the King's sixth and final marriage, in July 1543, to Catherine Parr. The new Queen was openly committed to the new ideas in religion, to the extent that a work she wrote – *The Lamentations of a Sinner* – had to wait until after Henry's death before it could be published. Her household became a centre for the discussion and practice of new ideas in religion at Court.

Catherine's role as an active supporter of the new religion is confirmed by the efforts made by the conservatives to associate her and her attendants with out-and-out heresy. In the summer of 1546, a Lincolnshire woman, Anne Askew, was arrested and interrogated on a charge of heresy. Her own guilt was soon established but her interrogators then tried unsuccessfully to force her into including members of the Court in her confession, citing the Countess of Hertford and the wife of Sir Anthony Denny. The conservatives then decided to try a direct attack on the Queen, but she threw herself on the King's mercy, admitting that she might have spoken out of turn on religious affairs but that she had discussed theology with Henry because she knew he had such an interest in the subject. In future, like a dutiful wife, she would accept her husband's judgement in such matters. She survived.

Court politics had increasingly taken on an air of religious dispute. The man who is seen as leading the reforming alliance was Edward Seymour, Earl of Hertford, who combined liberal doses of ambition and greed with his religious commitment. In 1536 the marriage of his sister, Jane, to Henry had boosted an already successful career at Court which was then consolidated by his military activities in the 1540s. Closely allied to Hertford was John Dudley, Viscount Lisle, who had seen a rapid rise in 1542–3 when he gained his peerage, a place in the Privy Chamber and, with his appointment as Lord Admiral, on the Privy Council. By December 1546, the Imperial ambassador had this to say about them:

> Four or five months ago was a great persecution of heretics … which has ceased since Hertford and the Lord Admiral have resided at court.

KEY ISSUE

What does this tell us of Hertford's importance at this time?

By the end of the reign two leading conservatives had been removed from the scene. The first was Stephen Gardiner, Bishop of Winchester. Late in 1546 his opponents turned the King against him, apparently by telling Henry that the bishop had refused to agree to an exchange of lands with the Crown. Henry later removed Gardiner from the list of future Councillors for his son because, he said, the bishop was too troublesome and difficult to control.

The removal of the Howards was a more dramatic affair. On 2 December Norfolk's son, the Earl of Surrey, was accused of disloyalty to the King. (Surrey, incidentally, was reckoned to be one of the two greatest poets of his generation; the other, Sir Thomas Wyatt, had also ended up in the Tower, suspected of adultery with Anne Boleyn, but had survived.) If the evidence against Surrey is to be believed, he had on a number of occasions spoken rashly of what should happen on the King's death and of his own family's right to act as regents for the young Edward. On 12 December 1546 Surrey and his father were both sent to the Tower. Surrey's trial took place in the following January and

TIMELINE

1536	The fall of Anne Boleyn
	Henry VIII married Jane Seymour
1537	Act of Parliament banning descendants of Catherine of Aragon and those of Anne Boleyn from the succession
	Jane Seymour died in childbirth
1540	Henry VIII married Anne of Cleves (January)
	Cromwell created Earl of Essex (April)
	Cromwell arrested and later executed (June)
	Henry married Catherine Howard (July)
1541	Catherine Howard executed
1543	Henry VIII married Catherine Parr
1546	Duke of Norfolk condemned for treason and narrowly escapes execution
	In his will Henry VIII confirmed the order of succession from Edward and his heirs, to Mary and her heirs, and finally Elizabeth and her heirs.
1547	Death of Henry VIII

he was tried on only one of the many charges brought against him, that of quartering the arms of King Edward the Confessor with his own, so claiming royal status. He was found guilty and executed on 19 January 1547. Norfolk had already confessed to knowing of his son's treason and was condemned to die on 28 January. He was, however, saved by the King's death the preceding night which invalidated the warrant for his execution. Norfolk had survived many u-turns in royal policy and favour, but this was his luckiest escape.

This shift in the balance of power played into Hertford's hands. Two leading opponents had been removed from the Privy Council and from Henry's favour at a crucial time. It was crucial because, late in December 1546, the King asked to see his will to make what would be his final amendments.

The King set out his final decision on the order of succession as well as naming the Regency Council that would advise his son. The Crown was to pass first to Edward and his heirs, then Mary and her heirs, and then to Elizabeth and her heirs. The will also named the members of a Regency Council of 16. Gardiner and Norfolk were removed. A clause was included which enabled the Council to put into effect grants of offices and titles which Henry wanted to be made but did not live to implement. The use made of this clause in the next reign gave members of the Hertford faction the opportunity to 'reward' themselves and to 'buy' the support of other significant figures where necessary.

The composition of the Regency Council has commonly been seen as favouring Hertford and the supporters of reform. In fact, consciously or not, Henry achieved a balance in religious views. For example, the reforming Thomas Cranmer was matched by the traditionalist Bishop Tunstall of Durham. Some individuals have been identified as committed reformers on the basis of association rather than specific action. Sir Anthony Denny is an example. As Chief Gentleman of the Privy Chamber he is more likely to have been on the list because he was a trusted and loyal servant. Henry chose the regency Councillors on how competently they would be able to serve his son.

> **KEY ISSUE**
>
> *To what extent was religion of importance in the faction politics of the 1540s?*

ANALYSIS

The Dry Stamp and Henry's Will

From the autumn of 1545 the usual process for getting the royal signature was by using the Dry Stamp. This produced an impression of the King's signature which was then inked in by an official in the Privy Chamber. At the end of each month a register was drawn up of all the documents that had been signed in this way.

It has been argued, for instance by David Starkey, that the effective control of the royal signature by Hertford's allies in the Privy Chamber enabled them to alter Henry's will without his knowledge. The date on the will is 30 December, but other evidence suggests it was not signed (i.e. dry-stamped and inked) until late January when Henry was actually dying and in no position to make changes. The register of documents places the will just before

27 January. In addition the will names Sir Thomas Seymour as a Councillor although he was not appointed to the Privy Council until 23 January. Between 30 December and the actual signing in late January, it is claimed, changes were made to the will in favour of the Earl of Hertford and the reforming group at Court.

However, Professor Ives has shown that, despite the late entry in the register, the will was signed on 30 December. He bases his argument on a detailed analysis of the usual process of signing and registering documents and of the circumstances in which this took place. Nor is the example of Thomas Seymour particularly significant. Others were also included in the Regency Council who were not Privy Councillors in December 1546. Moreover, if there had been any attempt to change the will this would have been more obvious in the final content of the document. Henry VIII's will does represent Henry's true intentions.

8 ~ FOREIGN POLICY

A *The 1530s*

In the years after 1529, Henry's divorce dominated English foreign policy. Embassies were sent to Rome to put the King's case for a divorce. Others were sent to the French King. In October 1532 a meeting at Boulogne and Calais was arranged for the two Kings but the relationship lacked firm foundations since their ultimate aims were so different. Henry seems to have hoped that, if pressure on the Pope did not produce the desired results, then he would gain French support for his split from Rome. Francis' main concern was to recruit the Pope as ally against the Emperor Charles V.

The year 1533 saw a growing division between Henry and Francis. In 1533, negotiations were set in motion for some form of alliance between England and the Schmalkaldic League. This was a group of Lutheran princes who had repudiated the Pope and were hostile to the Emperor. However, lack of religious agreement meant there could also be no political agreement with them. In contrast the death of Catherine of Aragon in January 1536 removed a major cause of tension between Henry and her nephew Charles V, and after the execution of Anne, whose marriage Charles could never be brought to recognise, there seemed a real chance of some reconciliation.

It did not last. In June 1538, the Pope brought Charles and Francis together in a joint declaration of co-operation against the enemies of Christendom, which included the King of England. By the end of the year Pope Paul III was preparing to publish the Bull of excommunication against Henry and sent Cardinal Reginald Pole on a mission to encourage Charles and Francis to take up arms against England.

The threat of invasion seemed very real in 1539, and Henry and Cromwell responded accordingly. In early February a survey of the kingdom's defences was ordered and work started on an extensive campaign of building and refurbishment of fortifications, largely financed from the proceeds of the Dissolution and often using building materials from the plundered monasteries. Henry himself made a long tour of the new defences, and most of the work, on the south and east coasts at least, had been completed within two years. The navy, in which Henry had often shown an interest, and which he had built up from his father's seven ships to a fleet of more than 40, was put on a war footing. In May, 16 500 soldiers marched through London and paraded before the King at a review at his palace of St James.

In January 1539 negotiations were opened with the Duke of Cleves on the possibility of a marriage with one of his daughters. In some ways it seemed the ideal alliance. The Duke, who was in dispute with the Emperor, had, like Henry, broken away from the Roman Catholic Church, but he had not adopted Lutheranism, although he was connected by marriage with some of the German Protestants. An agreement was signed in October and the marriage between Henry and Anne of Cleves took place in the following January 1540. Despite his personal aversion, Henry went through with the marriage since at the time Francis and Charles seemed threateningly close to one another. The two rulers were meeting in Paris on the same day that Henry met Anne for the first time.

See page 118

But the prospect of a European crusade against Henry proved to be an illusion and when, in February 1540, the Duke of Norfolk went on an embassy to France, Henry could be reassured that Francis and Charles were once more drawing apart and assuming their more usual hostile attitude to each other. The Cleves marriage was unnecessary and Henry could safely set aside his new Queen without jeopardising his security.

KEY ISSUE

Did Henry VIII achieve anything in his foreign policy in the 1530s?

B *Foreign policy: France and Scotland 1541–7*

As the hostility mounted between Francis and Charles, Henry was once more seen as a desirable ally in any approaching conflict. It was Charles V who came to a deal with Henry. In June 1542 they agreed on a joint invasion of France, to take place in the following year.

Before Henry could commit his forces he had to make sure of his own safety at home and, in particular, this meant the security of his northern border. An unsatisfactory attempt at improving relations with Scotland failed when the Scottish King James did not attend a meeting with Henry. As a result the Duke of Norfolk led an army on a raid across the Scottish border. In response, a Scottish army invaded England only to have its 10 000 men routed by an English force of 3000 at Solway Moss, with the capture of a number of leading Scottish nobles. Shortly afterwards, in December, James V died, leaving as his heir his daughter, Mary, all of six days old.

In July the Treaties of Greenwich called for peace between the two kingdoms and arranged for the future marriage of Mary, Queen of Scots, and Prince Edward. However, by the end of the year the treaties

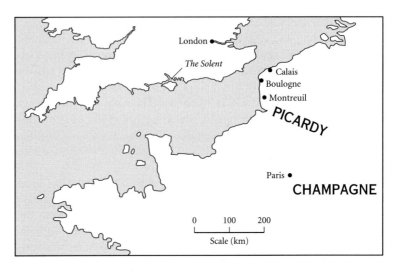

MAP 4
Henry VIII's invasion of France, 1544

had been rejected by the Scottish Parliament. In May 1544, the Earl of Hertford led an expedition into Scotland which resulted in the burning of Edinburgh, the devastation of much of the Lowlands and the strengthening of anti-English feeling in the country. If the aim had been to further the English cause in Scotland, it had failed; but in the more limited terms of keeping the Scots too occupied to intervene in the English invasion of France, either by attacking England or sending an expedition to France, it could claim to have had some success. Hertford led another raid of the same kind late in 1545 but Henry's reign ended with Scotland still engaged in a pro-French policy.

While all this had been happening Henry's main interest was elsewhere. In June 1544, an army of 40 000 went over to Calais where they were joined by Henry himself, marking by his presence the area of policy which he considered most important. On 14 September Boulogne surrendered, and four days later Henry made a triumphant entry into the city and immediately began ordering the strengthening of its fortifications.

Charles V, however, felt Henry had not provided enough support for his campaign and made peace with Francis on the same day that Boulogne fell to the English. Henry was now alone in his war against France and negotiations started almost immediately for a peace settlement, but were stalled by Henry's insistence that he should keep Boulogne and also that France would sever her ties with Scotland.

In July of 1545 the war was carried into English waters when a French fleet sailed into the Solent but caused little damage beyond the affront to English honour and the sinking of the *Mary Rose* (due not to gunfire but the disorganised reaction to the appearance of the French). A landing on the Isle of Wight was easily repulsed and the French attempt to recapture Boulogne failed. Both sides were ready for peace and the Treaty of Campe was signed in June 1546.

Henry was to keep Boulogne for the next eight years but it was then to be given back to the French in return for the payment of £600 000, and the French promised to resume the payment of an annual pension to Henry worth £35 000 a year. When the new fortifications built by Henry were taken into account, Francis got Boulogne back at a bargain price.

In terms of material costs, during these last years of Henry's foreign policy, England had paid a high price for very little gain. War was getting to be increasingly expensive both because of inflation and the greater numbers and more up-to-date weapons that were required. Apart from taxation Henry had access to the money he had made from the Church, but this was not inexhaustible. The expenses of these years also led to the debasement of the coinage which transformed a sound currency into one widely regarded with suspicion.

However, we should not look at the issue purely in account book terms. Henry was fulfilling his role as the warrior king, leading his troops in war, though now he had to be carried in a litter rather than riding on horseback. For him, to participate in great events, matching himself with the other rulers of Europe, was an end in itself. The prestige that it brought was sufficient reward.

The point is made by a set of four paintings that still exist in the Royal Collection. Two of the paintings deal with his first campaign against France in 1513 and illustrate his meeting with the Emperor Maximilian and his victory at the Battle of the Spurs; the other two record his departure for and arrival at the Field of the Cloth of Gold. Although the subjects come from the early part of the reign, the pictures were actually painted in the mid-1540s. What we have in these pictures is an affirmation by Henry, at the very end of his life, of those aspects of his reign that he still considered to be important – the ambitious European venture to which he returned in the 1540s.

> **KEY ISSUE**
>
> *What was gained and what was lost in the wars against Scotland and France in the 1540s?*

9 ⌐ BIBLIOGRAPHY

*K Randell *Henry VIII and the Government of England* (Hodder, Access to History, 2001) is a sound introduction aimed at sixth-formers.
*GR Elton *Reform and Reformation* (Methuen, 1977) is a good start to

finding his views on Cromwell and the Tudor Revolution as well as providing a good basic text on the reign of Henry VIII. The essays in C Coleman and D Starkey *Revolution Reassessed* (Oxford University Press, 1986) provide some effective criticisms of Elton's views but may need to be read in small doses. A very useful reference book for checking details of the different parts of government remains *P Williams *The Tudor Regime* (Oxford University Press, 1981). **D Starkey *The Reign of Henry VIII. Personalities and Politics* (Vintage, 2002) sees Henry's reign primarily in terms of faction politics and this view is reinforced by E Ives *Anne Boleyn* (Blackwell, 1986). He develops the theme in **E Ives 'Henry VIII: the Political Perspective' in D MacCulloch (ed.) *The Reign of Henry VIII. Policy, Politics and Piety* (Macmillan, 1995). Challenges to this view have so far appeared mainly in journals. A good survey of foreign policy is in S Doran *England and Europe 1485–1603* (Longman Seminar Studies, 1986) and D Potter contributes an essay to D MacCulloch (ed.) *The Reign of Henry VIII. Policy, Politics and Piety* (Macmillan, 1995) that presents a realistic picture of England as a second-rate power. For details of, and sound comments on, Parliament in this period use *MAR Graves *The Tudor Parliaments* (Longman, 1985) or MAR Graves *Early Tudor Parliaments* (Longman Seminar Series, 1990).

(*Recommended. **Highly recommended.)

10 ⌐ STRUCTURED AND ESSAY QUESTIONS

A *Structured questions*

1. (a) What was the Tudor Revolution in Government?
   (b) To what extent was the Privy Council the creation of Thomas Cromwell?
2. (a) What were patronage and faction?
   (b) Why did Anne Boleyn fall from power?

B *Essay questions*

1. Did Thomas Cromwell achieve anything of permanence during the 1530s?
2. Can the government of England during the 1530s be fairly described as a tyranny?
3. To what extent was Henry VIII himself in control of events and how far was he manipulated?
4. Was religion or power the dominating factor in politics in the years 1534 to 1547?
5. How successful was Henry's foreign policy from 1529 to 1547?

11 ⌐ SOURCE EXERCISE: WAS HENRY VIII MANIPULATED?

So long as Queen Anne, Thomas Cromwell, Archbishop Cranmer, Master Denny, Doctor Butts, with such like were about him, and could prevail with him, what organ of Christ's glory did more good in the Church than he? ... Thus, while good counsel was about him, and could be heard, the King did much good. So again, when sinister and wicked counsel, under subtle and crafty pretences, had gotten once the foot in, thrusting truth and verity out of the prince's ears, how much religion and all good things went prosperously forward before, so much, on the contrary side, all revolted backward again.

SOURCE A
John Foxe had supported religious reform in the reign of Henry VIII, and on the accession of the Catholic Mary in 1553, had to flee the country. While in exile he collected and published accounts of the Protestant martyrs in England which he later published in his Book of Martyrs *with additional material on earlier martyrs and the European reformers*

The England of Henry VIII, in fact, experienced the politics of manipulation in an acute form. This was due, on the one hand, to the King's character, and, on the other, to the reconstructed Privy Chamber of 1518. For Henry VIII, behind Holbein's image of the archetypal strong king, was profoundly open to influence.

SOURCE B
From D Starkey The English Court *1987*

[In 1540] the failure of the Cleves marriage exposed Henry once more at his most vulnerable point. Catherine Howard, Norfolk's niece, had been placed before a ready King, and the bait worked quickly. Cromwell was about to be trapped ...

His fall was very like Wolsey's. He was hustled out from below, the victim of a conspiracy waged by the same Norfolk, aided by Gardiner and his fellows, who used Catherine Howard as Anne Boleyn had been used before, as their pawn.

SOURCE C
From JJ Scarisbrick Henry VIII *1968*

About eight months after Cromwell's death, Marillac reported that Henry was very gloomy and malevolent; that he suspected that his very ministers had brought about Cromwell's destruction by false accusations 'and on light pretexts'; that he had said so to their faces; that he now knew that Cromwell had been the most faithful servant that he had ever had. At the time, probably, Henry had never fully understood how and why Cromwell was suddenly swept away. The King had been stampeded by a faction bent on a coup d'etat and swept along by it like the suggestible man that he was. It is no contradiction to say this so soon after asserting his complete absorption in, and command of, the policies which some have said Cromwell was furtively trying to foist upon him. For Henry was often this: a vulnerable and volatile thing, just at the moment when he seemed most assured and thrustful.

SOURCE D
From JJ Scarisbrick Henry VIII *1968*

But one thing Henry was not was someone who could be easily manipulated, whether by an individual or a faction, and even those he fell head over heels in love with, such as Anne Boleyn and, to a lesser extent, Catherine Howard, though they obviously affected what he did, were never able to manage him to any significant extent …

Despite the efforts of his most outstanding modern biographer [reference is to JJ Scarisbrick], the prevalent view is that Henry was a King who was easily manipulated; indeed, so weak was he that he needed to be manipulated for anything to happen. This view has been attacked here. It was Henry who made Wolsey, and it was Henry who destroyed him, just as he was to make and destroy Thomas Cromwell. He made all the important decisions and appointments. In every sense he ruled.

SOURCE E
P Gwyn The King's Cardinal: The Rise and Fall of Thomas Wolsey *2002*

Some would argue that Henry was a powerful personality to whom faction was a source of strength, allowing him to play one group against another, keep them in suspense and get the best service from both; episodes, notably in the 1540s, can certainly be read in this way. Others see factions following where the King led, not leading him; undoubtedly this did occur from time to time. But neither is an adequate perspective overall. A full portrait must reveal a monarch who could dismiss Wolsey and then complain 'everyday I miss the Cardinal of York more and more', who was prepared to execute his closest friend when he would not admit adultery with his wife, who had Thomas Cromwell beheaded, only to say that he had been persuaded 'on light pretexts' to destroy the best servant he ever had, who told Cranmer that he would not be able to save him once he was arrested, a king who from time to time could successfully be 'bounced' into decision, be it over the assault on the independence of the Church, the decision to cohabit with Anne Boleyn, or the coup against her.

SOURCE F
Eric Ives Henry VIII: the Political Perspective *from Diarmaid MacCulloch (ed.)* The Reign of Henry VIII *(1995)*

Scattered through his papers are notes that Cromwell regularly made of things to do. Typically they begin in a secretary's hand and end with additions, often even greater in length, in Cromwell's own writing. Cromwell cannot have made these notes for any purpose other than to serve as reminders for himself; they were not meant for anyone else's eyes, apart from his own and those of his secretaries. They may therefore be regarded as especially revealing. A good deal of business is simply listed. But, significantly, Cromwell often makes a note of the need to know what the king wants done …

It is difficult to see why Cromwell should have made such essentially private notes for his own use in this form if he were in effect making decisions and ruling the country himself. There would have been no need to remind himself to learn the king's pleasure if he was not in actual fact doing so. These remembrances strongly suggest that the minister did not act without knowing what the king wanted. They show that the king was very much in command, that Cromwell referred constantly to him on any questions that needed judgement. Henry was asked to decide who was to go abroad and when, to say at what moment ambassadors should be brought to see him, and to determine what answers should be made to letters, messages and requests from abroad. Henry was asked for instructions on how the principal opponents of the king's policies – the nun of Kent, More, Fisher – should be dealt with. The strong impression is of a minister doing the daily executive work of government, drawing his master's attention to the need to fill vacant posts, but asking the king for guidance on how to act in all issues of importance. There is no sense whatsoever here of a minister acting on his own initiative, or manipulating his master, or making substantial suggestions to the king, or trying to temper the king's proposals.

SOURCE G
GW Bernard Elton's Cromwell in the journal History *October, 1998*

Q

1. *What reservations might one have about Source A, bearing in mind the author and context?*
2. *Explain Starkey's reference to the Privy Chamber in Source B.*
3. *See Source E. What is Gwyn's view on Henry VIII's character?*
4. *How well does Gwyn's view fit in with the view expressed by Scarisbrick on Sources C and D?*
5. *Summarise the different interpretations of Henry VIII given by sources B to G.*

Advice: assessment

To what extent was Henry VIII himself in control of events and how far was he manipulated?

In order to make a judgment about an individual's performance, you need to be clear on:

● the criteria by which you are judging them
● how the judgment might vary at different times during their career
● how the judgment might apply in different areas of policy
● what pressures they were working under and how much freedom of manoeuvre they had.

In the case of Henry VIII there have been many views expressed on whether or not Henry was manipulated. See Chapters 3, 4, and 5, and the above historiographical exercise, for the necessary material to answer the above question. In planning your answer, consider the following:

● What is meant by 'manipulation'? Are there areas where you would prefer to use the words 'influence' or 'persuasion'?

- Remember you are dealing with 40 years of a man's life. Do you expect consistency of outlook and behaviour over this length of time?
- Was Henry more vulnerable in some areas than in others? Were there some areas where he took a particular interest in what was happening?
- Why might people want to manipulate Henry?
- Were there times when the structure of the political scene made manipulation more likely?

Edward VI
1547–53

6

INTRODUCTION

Edward's accession to the throne at the tender age of ten kindled memories of minorities in the previous century, periods of instability associated with the Wars of the Roses. But for the small minority of Protestant zealots Edward was potentially the new Solomon, David, even Josiah, the biblical king who had purged his land of idols, while conservatives such as Bishop Gardiner of Winchester feared the worst from one whose tutors, even under the traditionalist Henry VIII, were Protestant evangelists fresh from radical Cambridge.

Protector Somerset, the King's uncle, fought hugely expensive foreign wars, dissolved the chantries and introduced a moderately Protestant settlement in 1549, which went beyond anything which Henry VIII would have permitted. He stretched the nation's precarious finances to the limit, exhausting the Treasury and **debasing the coinage**, and eventually fell when he was accused of failing to take seriously enough two major rebellions in 1549. He became a focus of opposition and was executed in 1552, by which time the Duke of Northumberland had emerged as the new ruler. Northumberland cut back spending, and made peace with both France and Spain. He also introduced a more unambiguously Protestant *Book of Common Prayer* in 1552, and was involved in a futile attempt to settle the throne on his daughter-in-law Lady Jane Grey when Edward died. This plan collapsed and Mary Tudor made a triumphant entry into London, backed even by the Protestant elements in the political community whose first concern was to preserve the Tudor succession, as laid down by Henry VIII's will.

Edward's brief reign raises several obvious problems for the historian: his own role in policy-making, the merits or demerits of his two chief ministers, the extent to which the Reformation was successfully introduced into England. There is also the question of whether the rebellions and the political and economic instability of this period signified a wider and more deep-seated 'Mid-Tudor Crisis'. For all the change at the time which historians focus on, there were considerable elements of continuity as well in Edward's short reign. Above all, the able civil servants trained by Thomas Cromwell maintained their grip on day-to-day administration. The same point could indeed be made of his half-sister's reign which followed (1553–8). Although Mary was trying to re-weave both religious and diplomatic policy in completely different ways from her predecessor, it may be that their reigns throw up similarities as well as differences.

Debasing the coinage reducing the amount of precious metal in coins so that the Crown could mint more to meet its financial needs. But it devalued the money, resulting in inflation

PICTURE 16
Edward VI, *anon.*

1 ⁓ PROTECTOR SOMERSET

Henry VIII's will provided for a Council, but named no individual regent, although it did leave open the possibility of a Protector. On 12 March 1547, Edward Seymour, Earl of Hertford and Edward VI's uncle, obtained letters patent giving him near-sovereign powers as Lord Protector of the Realm and Governor of the King's Person. This gave him the right to appoint whom he wished to the Council. He also quickly secured advancement for himself to become Duke of Somerset.

PROFILE

EDWARD SEYMOUR, DUKE OF SOMERSET AND LORD PROTECTOR (C. 1506–52)

Somerset was born the son of a Wiltshire knight and climbed the greasy pole towards success largely on the strength of his being brother to Jane Seymour, Henry VIII's third wife and mother of the future Edward VI. He was in royal service during the 1520s and 1530s, and in 1541 he was sworn of the Privy Council and advanced to the Earldom of Hertford. He achieved steady success as a place-seeker: Knight of the Garter in 1541, Lord High Admiral in 1543, and Lord Great Chamberlain by 1547. In the process he amassed extensive estates in Somerset and Wiltshire, some of it extorted from William Barlow, Bishop of Bath and Wells. With the fortune he made from royal service, he was able to build his own palace, Somerset House, knocking down part of a densely populated part of London including a cloister of St Paul's Cathedral in the process. He was not simply a place-seeker, exploiting his family ties to the throne – for instance, he achieved a decisive victory over the Scots at Musselburgh at the end of Henry's reign.

At the end of 1547 Somerset was made Lord Protector, responsible for government until such time as the young King came of age. Soon Somerset became unpopular: partly through his autocratic methods, ruling through a small group of cronies, partly through the ruthlessly engineered downfall and execution of his brother Thomas, and partly through his perceived failure to maintain law and order in the face of the mounting rebellions he faced over religious and social issues. In fact, his attitude to rebels was no different to that of any other member of the Tudor upper class, and he showed caution in suppressing the two major risings in 1549. A sensible ruler, and conscious of the exhaustion of the Treasury through foreign wars, he waited until he was sure the rebellions could not be contained locally and that the government could deploy the armed force necessary. However, his rivals on the Council used his alleged hesitancy in dealing with the rebellions to allege that he in reality sympathized with the rebels, having been influenced by the so-called 'Commonwealth Group' of radical social and economic thinkers. While Somerset knew some of this group, including Hales and Latimer, and indeed appointed a few of their number to investigate conditions in various parts of the country, his views never coincided with theirs.

By 1550 Somerset was in the Tower, deposed as Protector. Yet by October 1551 he had been released, pardoned and was beginning to claw back some of the influence that he had lost. Soon, however, he was re-arrested on a charge of conspiracy to murder his successor, the Duke of Northumberland, and was beheaded on Tower Hill. Since then he has had a mixed press. An older generation that included AF Pollard saw him as a high-minded idealist, a friend of the poor and an opponent of religious persecution. While only a handful of heretics perished during his period of government, the image of the 'good duke' has been seriously dented by more modern commentators. Michael Bush, for instance, effectively destroyed his reputation in *The Government Policy of Protector Somerset*, characterising him instead as self-seeking, ambitious and arrogant. As far as his concern for the poor goes, Susan Brigden comments: 'As the soldier who had left the poor in the Borders to live like animals in their ruined homes; as rack-renter, sheep-master and encloser; as the ruler who presided over the Vagrancy Act which imposed slavery upon those who, willingly or not, left their homes, he was ostensibly an unlikely social reformer'. Somerset remains an object lesson for public figures of how historians' views of their subjects can change sharply from one generation to another.

> ### KEY ISSUE
>
> *Was Somerset suited to high political office?*

Once in government Somerset neglected the Council, except to use it from time to time as little more than a rubber stamp. He preferred to work through his own household, sometimes referred to as his 'new' council. Of its leading members – Smith, Stanhope, Cecil, Wolf, Thynne and Gray – only one (Smith) was a member of the King's Council.

Two of Somerset's early measures can be used to put this unfavourable impression to the test. The first concerns his treatment of his brother Thomas, the Lord Admiral, who was executed for treason on 20 March 1549. Thomas's marriage to the widowed Queen, Catherine Parr, in April 1547 had raised some eyebrows. Following Catherine's death shortly afterwards, Thomas was accused of trying to seduce the 15-year-old Princess Elizabeth, and there were even rumours by December 1548 that she was pregnant by him and he planned to marry her. Thomas had sought for himself a higher position in the state, being disappointed at not being named to the Regency Council formed in 1547. He flew into rages at his brother's neglect of him. Finally, he was accused of plotting to abduct the boy King and make himself Protector in the place of his brother, Somerset. He had unwisely sought Sir Thomas Wriothesley's support, but the latter denounced him and gained re-admission to the Council as a reward. Clearly, Thomas was volatile and a threat to the regime, but Somerset's treatment of his brother shows the ruthlessness of which he was capable.

The second such measure is the Act of Parliament moderating Henry VIII's savage treason laws. To deny the Royal Supremacy in writing – or three times in speech – would still constitute treason, but no offence could be proved without two witnesses. In some ways then, this new Act could be seen as a bid for personal popularity. However, a closer examination of the Act shows that it was still fairly repressive, for the dice were heavily loaded against the accused who had no right to confront hostile witnesses, no counsel of his own, and little chance to prepare his case. Moreover Thomas Seymour, and indeed Somerset himself, were to discover that an Act of Attainder could be used in the last resort if the 1547 Act did not apply.

However, before a full picture can be arrived at it will be necessary to look closely at Somerset's better-known policies with regard to foreign affairs, religion, social reform, and the 1549 rebellions.

2 ᴄ SOMERSET'S FOREIGN POLICY

For the Protector, as he surveyed his responsibilities in 1547, the most important task was to face the twin challenge in foreign affairs of a hostile France and an unpredictable Scotland. Henry VIII's legacy in foreign policy was not just commitments against these two traditional enemies, but also a growth of conscious national feeling, especially since the break with Rome. Englishmen's insularity, their sense of being in a world apart, had markedly increased. There was also the expense of embarking on modern warfare, which tended paradoxically to bind England more closely to the continent in a military sense, for the best firearms were to be had from Antwerp, and foreign mercenaries, needed to supplement the tiny standing forces, could only come from the continent too. Hence the need to borrow heavily in order to sustain a military campaign: in 1549 alone £250 000 was borrowed, half of it from abroad.

Somerset was determined to bring about a union of the royal houses of England and Scotland, asserting a claim to the Scottish throne that went back to the time of Edward I. He hoped, rather idealistically, to marry the ten–year-old Edward VI to the five–year-old Mary, Queen of Scots, who had become queen when only a few weeks old in 1542. This would, he hoped, consolidate the Reformation in Scotland and finally secure England's northern border from attack. But by March 1547, the pro-English Protestant party had collapsed to all intents and purposes, and on 31 July their last stronghold, the castle of St Andrews fell to a French force. It had been sent over by the new King Henry II, keen to cut a dash on the European stage by extending French influence in Scotland. Moreover he aimed to recover Boulogne from England immediately, although Henry VIII had agreed to return it to France by 1554. For the French there was also the prize of a marriage between the Dauphin Francis and the Queen of Scots. For Somerset it was an urgent priority that Scotland should not fall into the hands of the French, giving them easy access through this 'postern gate' into England.

An English army invaded Scotland in 1547 and enjoyed early success at the Battle of Pinkie Clough, a mere nine miles from Edinburgh, but Somerset had neither the military strength nor the funds to remain in Scotland in force. Thus he decided to leave a string of garrisons to guard strongpoints along the border and up the east coast as far as Dundee. These were designed to prevent concentrations of Scottish troops, to intercept French reinforcements and, more indirectly, to encourage the fledgling Scottish Reformation. Unfortunately the English fleet could not seal off Scotland completely and several of the forts were difficult to resupply. The Protector's worst fears were confirmed in June 1548 when a French force landed at Leith with 6000 troops and spirited the child Queen away to France where she arrived in August. Somerset responded by sending up an army to relieve the garrisons, but the supply routes were over-extended and almost all of them had had to be withdrawn by the autumn of 1549. The long effort to control Scotland seemed to have been counter-productive. Scotland had a pro-French government and a French army was poised on England's northern border. Meanwhile Henry II declared war on England on 8 August 1549 and proceeded to attack Boulogne.

It hardly needs to be said that the costs of the Scottish campaign were vast: out of £1 386 000 spent on military affairs during Edward VI's reign £580 000 was spent by Somerset on this one campaign. He spent £351 000 on troops alone – 50% more than Henry VIII had spent in five years. Somerset paid for the wars by the usual expedients: he debased the coinage (£537 000 was raised in this way between 1547 and 1551), he tapped some of the resources released by the dissolution of chantries and colleges in 1547 (£110 000 had come from this source by Michaelmas 1548), he obtained a grant of parliamentary taxation (£335 000 was raised in this way during Edward VI's reign, of which £189 000 went for war and defence) and he resorted to the usual steps of Crown land sales and borrowing. The Protector's legacy in foreign affairs to his successor was failure in Scotland, a continuing struggle against France, and extremely strained finances.

> **KEY ISSUE**
>
> *Was Somerset's foreign policy a total failure?*

3 ↝ SOMERSET AND RELIGION

Ever since 1546 the Catholic faction in English politics had lacked effective leadership. Norfolk was in prison, Gardiner, the Bishop of Winchester, had been excluded from Henry VIII's Regency Council, and Tunstall, the Bishop of Durham, was too old to influence events. Wriothesley alone was the most effective member of the conservative group.

Meanwhile Protestant expectations from the new government grew apace as preachers exiled for their radicalism under Henry VIII, like Becon, Turner and Hooper, returned. Foreign reformers also sought refuge in England, especially after the Battle of Mühlberg in 1547 when the Emperor Charles V destroyed the forces of the Protestant princes and cities in Germany and ensured that Strasbourg was no longer a Protestant haven. Thus England became a major centre of Protestant theology as the continental reformers arrived: Bucer from Strasbourg, who became Regius Professor of Divinity at Cambridge; John a Lasco from Poland, who settled at a London church; Peter Martyr Vermigli who secured the Regius Professorship at Oxford; Bernardo Ochino; and John Knox, recently released from a French galley.

In their wake fresh signs of religious radicalism appeared in England: subversive preaching, the suppression here and there of the Mass (in 1548 alone 31 tracts appeared against the Catholic Mass), and **iconoclasm**. Services were said in English rather than Latin, while ballads, sermons and plays all seemed to herald a new Protestant dawn. Indeed the Council was so worried by this ferment that they re-imposed censorship in August 1549. It must be borne in mind, however, that total numbers of Protestants remained small – perhaps one-fifth of Londoners and smaller numbers concentrated overwhelmingly in the South, where Kent, Essex, Sussex and Bristol were particular centres. The printing presses were busy too; out of 394 books printed during the Protectorate no less than 159 were written by Protestant reformers.

> **Iconoclasm** the destruction or removal of statues or other representations of the Virgin and saints, lest the image be worshiped rather than God

The government's response seemed, by contrast, rather cautious. Edward VI himself had, of course, already been brought up to be a Protestant and many of Somerset's supporters were men of pronounced Protestant sympathies. Yet Mary Tudor's evident public Catholicism was tolerated and Somerset seems to have been keen to avoid antagonising Charles V, who could have caused difficulty by intervening in Somerset's Scottish campaign. The initial religious steps taken by Somerset's government were, therefore, rather hesitant. Thomas Cromwell's 1538 'Injunctions' were re-introduced, with some additions which encouraged iconoclasm and the use of the Bible in English, but they went little further than that. The reading of Cranmer's Homilies was also encouraged; these were sets of prepared sermons with a strong Protestant slant, for example the homily 'On Justification' which taught the Lutheran doctrine of justification by faith alone. Finally, some of the emphatically Catholic legislation from Henry VIII's reign was repealed – Parliament met on 4 November 1547 to revoke the Act of Six Articles of 1539 which had affirmed the doctrine of transubstantiation, the *King's Book* of 1543 which reinforced it, and the Act for the Advancement of True Religion also of 1543, which had limited Bible reading to an upper-class male preserve.

See page 135

See page 94

See page 97

The remaining Catholics in the political nation were not slow to oppose these measures. Gardiner took the lead by pointing out that the re-issued 'Injunctions', the 'Paraphrases' and the 'Homilies', all contravened Henry VIII's religious laws from his last years. His case was of course much weakened by the repeal of Catholic legislation mentioned above. His protests led to a spell in the Fleet Prison from September 1547 to January 1548, followed by confinement to London. In June 1548 he was sent to the Tower and eventually deprived of his bishopric in 1551. Gardiner probably avoided a worse fate through his scrupulous regard for the law, but he was not the only one to suffer persecution. Edmund Bonner, the Bishop of London, was deprived of his See (sacked) in October 1549, while 1551 brought the resignations of Bishops Vesey of Exeter, Day of Chichester and Heath of Worcester. Naturally these vacancies enabled ardent Protestants to take their places – the likes of Ridley, Coverdale, and Hooper.

The first real measure against the Catholic Church came in the Chantries Act of 1547, which completed the attack on the Church's corporate property begun by Henry VIII. A total of 2374 chantries and chapels, 90 colleges and 110 hospitals were dissolved. The reasons were partly doctrinal, as chantries were a clear expression of the Catholic doctrine of Purgatory, which encouraged good works such as the founding of chantry chapels where prayers were said to keep the soul of the benefactor out of Purgatory. The motive was also clearly financial, for money was sorely needed for the Protector's wars against both Scotland and France. The cash yield from the chantries was in fact around £160 000, a sum about 20% of that yielded by the Dissolution of the Monasteries. There were 2500 priests made redundant, of whom 2000 were found benefices. While the total number of schools seems to have been reduced slightly, most were re-founded, hence the 'Edward VI' schools in various parts of the country. The Chantries Act itself put of course its own gloss on the motives for the new law:

See page 383

… considering that a great part of superstition and errors in Christian religion hath been brought into the minds and estimation of men … by devising and phantasing vain opinions of Purgatory and Masses satisfactory to be done for them which be departed, the which doctrine and vain opinion by nothing more is maintained and upholden than by the abuse of … chantries and other provisions made for the continuance of the said blindness and ignorance; and further considering and understanding that the alteration, change, and amendment of the same, and converting to goodly and godly uses, as in erecting of grammar schools to the education of youth in virtue and godliness, the further augmenting of the universities, and better provision for the poor and needy, cannot in this present Parliament be provided and conveniently done, nor cannot nor ought to any other manner person be committed than to the King's Highness, whose Majesty with and by the advice of his Highness' most prudent Council can and will most wisely and beneficially, both for the honour of God and the weal of this His Majesty's realm, order, alter, convert and dispose the same. …

Q

1. *According to this document, what seems to have been the main religious motive for dissolving the chantries?*
2. *What does the extract claim to be the main practical reason for the attack on the chantries?*
3. *Does this document just obscure an underlying financial motive for the dissolution of the chantries or does it clarify other motives?*

Various other more minor religious measures followed: an Act allowing priests to marry was eventually passed in February 1549, and around 20% of priests did so, giving them of course a vested interest in continuing the Reformation, as did ownership of former monastic and chantry land for the gentry. Earlier in 1547 another Act authorised the giving out of Communion in both kinds, but the major piece of religious legislation of the Somerset years was the *Prayer Book* of 1549 and its attendant Act of Uniformity. In some ways the new *Prayer Book* leant towards Protestantism: it was in its full title the *Book of Common*

Prayer, that is for priest and people in common, and suggesting the Lutheran idea of the 'priesthood of all believers', as opposed to the Catholic view of the priest as an intermediary between God and lay-men. Yet on the central issue of the Eucharist the more moderate Catholics could derive some comfort from the ambiguity of the *Prayer Book's* phrasing, which meant it did not contradict the essentials of the Catholic Mass.

Radical Protestants like Bucer, Ridley and Hooper called for further changes, but Gardiner (from the Tower of course) could detect no actu-al harm in the new *Prayer Book*. For him it was in no way ideal, but it was acceptable and he seized eagerly on its ambiguities. Somerset had, in fact, despite his own radical religious views, deliberately sought an unclear settlement in order to avoid upsetting Charles V.

Indeed he even assured Charles V that the *Prayer Book* was a conser-vative reform, and there was in reality a good deal about it that was conservative: priests still wore traditional vestments and there was still a railed-off altar at the east end of the church for the priest alone instead of a more Protestant Communion table in the centre at the heart of the congregation. Worshippers would also find other familiar features of Catholic ritual largely intact, such as candles on the altar, prayers for the dead if not chantry Masses, and commemoration of the Virgin Mary and other saints. Conservatives could feel reassured that the line would now be held after so much had been lost: clerical celibacy, Com-munion in one kind only, images and wall paintings, and a variety of ceremonies such as creeping to the Cross on Good Friday. Yet few Eng-lishmen could have supposed in 1549 that the pace of religious reform would quicken following a series of events that led to Somerset's fall in the autumn of that year and his replacement by Northumberland.

> **KEY ISSUE**
>
> *How far could Somerset's religious measures be described as Protestant?*

4 ᔧ SOMERSET, SOCIAL REFORM AND THE 1549 REBELLIONS

See page 6

Popular disturbances in 1549 engulfed much of the country. They were the most serious law-and-order challenge to be faced by a government since Cade's Rebellion in 1450. In May there was unrest in Somerset, Wiltshire, Hampshire, Kent, Sussex and Essex. June saw the Western Rising (or Prayer Book Rebellion) in Devon and Cornwall, while in July Norfolk, Suffolk, Cambridgeshire, Hertfordshire, Northamptonshire, Bedfordshire, Buckinghamshire, Oxfordshire and Yorkshire joined the list. In August, Leicestershire and Rutland followed. In most of these counties the restoration of order was carried out by the local nobility and gentry, but troops were called in from the Scottish campaign to deal with Oxfordshire, Buckinghamshire and Suffolk and there were set-piece battles in the South-west (2500 deaths) and in Norfolk (3000 deaths).

Devon and Cornwall were among the remotest communities in Tudor England, and their isolation was accentuated by poor communi-cations and by the retention by ordinary Cornish people of their own

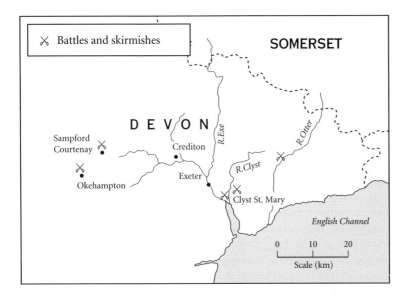

MAP 5
The Western Rebellion, 1549

Celtic language. Cornwall especially had a low standard of living and severe problems of law enforcement without resident nobles. When the Prayer Book (Western) Rebellion broke out in Devon in June 1549, it was marked by religious conservatism. The parishioners of Sampford Courtenay found the new 1549 *Prayer Book* incomprehensible and helped to swell a force of rebels including Cornishmen, who gathered at Crediton by 20 June.

Somerset's reaction was cautious: he did not see the unrest as serious and he ordered pardons for those involved in the original commotion at Sampford Courtenay. It is easy to see the sense in the Protector's stance: he was already faced with enclosure riots in a good many other areas and the French might invade at any time. Therefore, instead of intervening himself, he sent Lord Russell to the West Country to enforce order on 24 June. By August the rebels still besieged Exeter and Somerset's diary entry of 27 July betrays a certain harshness: the rebels, he wrote, 'speak traiterous words against the King and in favour of the traiterous rebels, ye shall hang two or three of them … And that will be the only and best stay of all those talks'. Ten days later Russell had breached Exeter's walls and raised the siege, while at the same time war broke out against France, thus realising Somerset's growing fear that the French might help to keep the rebellion alive. The final struggle came in mid-August when thousands of rebels died in a pitched battle at Okehampton, and the rebellion collapsed.

A study of the Western Rebels' demands shows an overwhelming call for a return to traditional Catholicism. It is clear that they misunderstood the new Prayer Book to some extent, believing that children could only be baptised on Sundays. They disliked particularly the new English language service, preferring Latin or Cornish (provoking Cranmer's comment that more Cornishmen must surely understand English than Latin). Nicholas Udall, a leading Protestant convert, maintained that the common people in these western counties had been deceived by the priests, and he and other reformers seized on the propaganda opportunity to conclude that popery led inevitably to rebellion and anarchy.

While most of the Devon Articles were religious, anti-gentry feeling creeps in here and there, although there was no fundamental attack on the gentry as a class; as with regard to religion, the social concerns were reactionary rather than revolutionary. Article 13 of the rebels' demands, for example, calls for a reduction in the size of gentry households, probably because some retainers abused the social power of the land-owning class. Article 14 urged the restoration of abbey and chantry lands which had been acquired by the local gentry and which had given them a vested interest in the progress of the Reformation. Somerset exaggerated when he said of the rebels that they 'hath conceived a wonderful hate against the gentlemen and taketh them all as their enemies'. The social radicalism he was talking of was much more evident in East Anglia, inspired in part by his own attitude to social reform.

Kett's Rebellion, which presented the authorities with an even more serious problem than the Prayer Book Rebellion, also erupted in June 1549. Times were hard and enclosures were blamed. Somerset had initiated a series of policies which encouraged this view, even though hardship was much more the result of rampant inflation owing to his further debasement of the coinage and ruinously expensive wars.

The Council had issued regulations to control prices and restrict exports, but these had not solved the problem. Despite himself having been a rapacious landlord, Somerset had fallen under the influence of the 'Commonwealth men', reformers who wished to establish a Christian commonwealth distinguished not just by its Protestantism, but also by social justice. They blamed hardship not on war but on the greed of landowners, particularly those who were thought to be out to make easy profits from sheep-farming, forcing tenants off arable land to do so and cutting the production of staple foodstuffs. In June 1548 the Council had set up a Commission led by John Hales to examine how 'Christian people' were 'by the greedy covetousness of some men eaten up and devoured of brute beasts'. The Commission was, unsurprisingly, obstructed by landowners, but it had raised expectations among tenants and labourers that something would be done. The Council now wanted to backtrack, but Somerset ploughed on, issuing a proclamation, against the Council's will, enforcing legislation against enclosure, and in July setting up a second commission with increased powers to over-awe landlords. With government policy apparently on their side, and determined to overcome what they saw as government obstructionism, people, particularly in Norfolk, took the law into their own hands.

See pages 317–18

An anti-enclosure riot in Norfolk was followed by more disturbances led by Robert Kett, a well-to-do tanner turned country landowner who brought leadership to what had been an incoherent series of violent demonstrations. By 10 July Kett was in Norwich and two days later he was on Mousehold Heath overlooking the city with no

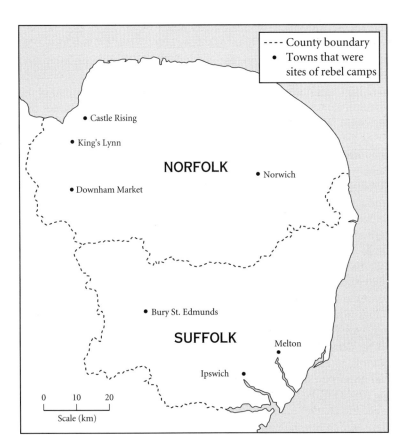

MAP 6
Kett's Rebellion, 1549

less than 16000 rebels, equivalent to one-third of all men of military age in Norfolk.

The authorities' reaction to this outrage was low key: the local gentry made little effort to disperse them, preferring either to negotiate or to ignore them. In Norwich the city fathers took a similarly conciliatory view, remembering perhaps that, unlike Exeter, their city walls were not intact. Meanwhile Somerset ordered a herald to offer the rebels a pardon if they went home. His proposal was insultingly refused and by 23 July the entire city of Norwich, the second city in the country, was in rebel hands. On 30 July William Parr, Marquis of Northampton (and Catherine Parr's brother) arrived with 14000 men, including a contingent of Italian mercenaries. After a skirmish Northampton was driven off humiliatingly and the government had to put their faith in John Dudley, Earl of Warwick, who entered Norwich on 24 August. On 27 August he brought the Kett host to battle at Dussindale when as many as 3000 rebels were killed. Kett's execution for treason on 7 December completed the repression in which 48 others are also known to have died.

It is to some extent reasonable to blame Somerset for the outbreak of the movement. His apparent concern to help ordinary folk encouraged rumours in East Anglia that he would condone direct action against enclosures. There is, however, no evidence for this latter belief

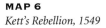

KEY ISSUE

Did the rebellions of 1549 represent a real threat to the government?

and the Kett Rebels' demands ranged much more widely than Somerset's current concerns. These did mention enclosures, but they also complained about inflation, the erosion of rights over common land and the rapaciousness of lawyers. In short their manifesto seemed to hark back to some golden age of prosperity and justice at the end of the fifteenth century, before the onset of the Price Rise, and to earlier disturbances in the county (1381 perhaps and the upheavals of 1525).

As far as religion was concerned the Norfolk peasants seem to have been unconcerned about traditional religion, for the new 1549 Prayer Book was used daily. Seven of the articles of complaint can be described as religious, all of them echoing sentiments from earlier Parliaments or Injunctions.

Yet how far is Somerset to blame for failing to stamp out the rising earlier? In East Anglia he could no more rely on the local gentry than he could in the South-west. The leading local magnate, the Duke of Norfolk, had languished in the Tower since 1547 and most of the 14 upper gentry and the 424 gentlemen who remained in the county either lacked the resources to act or deemed it prudent to bide their time and see how things would develop. It is also possible, of course, that some of them may have wanted the rebellion to run its course in order to show Somerset the danger of his social policies. Somerset's reaction to the news from Norfolk resembled his response to the Prayer Book Rebellion. He still had important military commitments in Scotland and in France, where the new King, Henry II, declared war on England on 8 August and proceeded to attack Boulogne, and he was aware of threats to law and order elsewhere in England. Hence the Protector's initial response was a conciliatory one: he offered a pardon which was rejected by Kett on 21 July.

Then Somerset authorised the sending of the forces commanded by Northampton, who was the highest-ranking Privy Councillor after Somerset himself, a relation of Henry VIII's by marriage and a veteran of the 1544 campaign in Scotland. Moreover he was accompanied by Lords Wentworth and Sheffield, who also had military experience. Following the humiliating dispersal of Northampton's forces and Sheffield's death at the hands of the mob, Somerset was stunned. He blamed Northampton for ineptitude and realised that the Kett Rebellion was a much more serious affair than he had thought; thus he decided to send Warwick to put it down. Somerset could have supervised the repression himself, but Russell had coped in Devon, and Warwick seemed up to the task in East Anglia.

An older generation of historians interpreted Somerset's apparent indecisiveness as a twinge of conscience, and for AF Pollard Somerset was choosing the path of principle over expediency. Yet Somerset's letters make clear his opposition to all rebellions. They were, he wrote, 'lewd, seditious and evil disposed persons'. His actions look more and more to modern eyes as being the only realistic military strategy, and one which seems to have enjoyed the confidence of the Council for a long while during the summer of 1549. After all, Kett was not physically threatening the government unlike the rebels in 1381, 1450 and 1497; nowhere in the rebels' demands was there talk of releasing the King from the grip of evil ministers. Unfortunately for Somerset, the Kett rising would bring about his fall by October 1549. Criticism of him was building up in the Council and elsewhere as this letter shows, written to him by William Paget, one of his closest advisers, on 7 July 1549:

> I told your Grace the truth, and was not believed: well, now your Grace sees it, what says your Grace? Marry, the King's subjects out of all discipline, out of obedience, caring neither for Protector or King, and much less for any other mean officer. And what is the cause? Your own levity, your softness, your opinion to be good to the poor. I know, I say, your good meaning and honest nature. But I say, sir, it is great pity (as the common proverb goes) in a warm summer that ever fair weather should do harm. It is a pity that your so much gentleness should be an occasion of so great an evil as is now chanced in England by these rebels ... Consider, I beseech you most humbly, with all my heart, that society in a realm does consist and is maintained by mean of religion and law ... Look well whether you have either law or religion at home, and I fear you shall find neither. The use of the old religion is forbidden by a law, and the use of the new is not yet printed in the stomachs of the eleven or twelve parts in the realm, what countenance soever men make outwardly to please them in whom they see the power rests. Now, sir, for the law: where is it used in England at liberty? Almost nowhere. The foot taketh upon him the part of the head, and commons is become a king, appointing conditions and laws to the governors, saying, 'Grant this, and that, and we will go home' ... I know in this matter of the commons every man of the Council hath misliked your proceedings, and wished it otherwise.

Q
1. *What qualities of character is Paget criticising in Somerset?*
2. *How fair are Paget's criticisms of Somerset's policy?*

Somerset's fall came soon after Warwick's suppression of the Kett rebellion, which had represented at the very least a blow to his prestige as Protector. By the end of September 1549, a majority on the Council wanted to remove him, and the only way to achieve this was through some form of conspiracy. On 5 October, the Protector issued a proclamation calling all loyal subjects to rally to the King and the Protector at Hampton Court. Eighteen Councillors, including Russell and Herbert, issued counter-proclamations, and by 14 October, Somerset was in the Tower. The reason for his fall was, as much as any other factor, his political isolation which sprang from his autocratic methods, his abrasive arrogance and his high-minded pride.

KEY ISSUE

How far was Somerset responsible for his own downfall?

5 ⌐ GOVERNMENT, POLITICS AND FOREIGN POLICY UNDER NORTHUMBERLAND

Somerset's successor was John Dudley, Earl of Warwick (normally referred to as Northumberland, as he was raised to that Dukedom in

October 1551). Having enjoyed a successful military career under Henry VIII, he emerged as a force to be reckoned with under Somerset, as shown by his suppression of Kett's rebellion. After intense political manoeuvres among the factions on the Council following Somerset's fall, Warwick became Lord President of the Council and Great Master

PROFILE

JOHN DUDLEY, DUKE OF NORTHUMBERLAND (1502–53)

John Dudley, Earl of Warwick, was the eldest son of Edmund Dudley, one of Henry VII's tax-collectors who had been executed by Henry VIII in 1510. John rapidly recovered the family's reputation through royal service, being knighted in France in 1523, and appointed Deputy-Governor of Calais in 1538. Four years later he was Warden of the Scottish Marches and advanced to the peerage as Viscount Lisle. He was Great Admiral from 1542–7, and Knight of the Garter and Privy Councillor in 1543. In 1544 he led the assault on Boulogne and became its governor in 1547. At the beginning of Edward VI's reign he was allied to Somerset and acquired the Earldom of Warwick. He was responsible for the defeat of the Scots at the Battle of Pinkie Clough. After Somerset's apparently feeble response to Kett Rebellion in 1549, Warwick, who had been responsible for restoring order, challenged Somerset's leadership, overthrew him, and became Lord President of the Council and in 1551 Duke of Northumberland.

While Northumberland had shown no sign of having extreme Protestant views before acceding to power, he supported the radical 1552 *Prayer Book* and attempted to stave off the accession of Mary Tudor as the extent of Edward's final illness became clear. Anxious to place his son Lord Guildford Dudley and his daughter-in-law Lady Jane Grey on the throne, he secured letters patent from the sickly Edward for a 'limitation of the crown' (the so-called 'Devise') to alter the succession. Most of the political nation saw through this obvious self-advancement and rallied to Mary on Edward's death.

Northumberland died on the scaffold for actively resisting Mary's assumption of the Crown, and, rather improbably, converted to the Roman Church at his execution. Historians have, however, increasingly found much to recommend him, and his stock has risen while that of Somerset has fallen. In particular his financial caution contrasts strongly with Somerset's recklessness, and his willingness to make peace with both Scotland and France has earned him some praise. Perhaps he does indeed deserve to be set in a line of cautious administrators, who cut their teeth in Henry VIII's reign, and to be seen as part of that successful tradition of administrative competence throughout the mid-Tudor period which prevented the government being overwhelmed by the so-called 'Mid-Tudor Crisis'.

of the King's Household. He had seven key supporters on the Council, including Cranmer, who favoured a further radical religious reform. There were 14 Councillors who favoured a more conservative position and a deal with the Emperor Charles V. The balance, however, began to shift. The conservative, Wriothesley, accused of plotting a second coup, was dismissed from the Council together with his leading supporter the Earl of Arundel. Following the fiercest struggle for power since the fifteenth century, Warwick, soon to be Duke of Northumberland, now had a majority of the Council behind him, including the Marquis of Dorset and the Bishop of Ely.

Northumberland's adverse reputation as the supplanter of the 'Good Duke' of Somerset and as the cynical schemer trying to deny the throne to Mary in 1553 has recently been challenged by historians. Certainly in financial affairs he could be seen as modestly successful after the near bankruptcy that had marked Somerset's period of office. While he raised government revenue in many traditional ways – selling Crown lands, confiscating lead, coining bullion from Church plate and seizing bishops' lands – he was also more vigorous than his predecessor in collecting Crown debts, pruning government expenditure and instituting regular audits. Above all perhaps, in March 1552 he appointed a Royal Commission to investigate the work of the revenue courts. Thus men who were to include key servants of Elizabeth I, such as William Cecil and Thomas Gresham, cut their administrative teeth on what Elton has called 'a genuine reform administration'.

Gresham was exceptionally useful as an exchange manipulator and agent in Antwerp where many of the government's loans were raised. He was able to ensure that the government's foreign loans were punctually renewed or paid out of new loans. While he could do little to reduce the total owing at Antwerp (£132 000 was still outstanding at the end of 1552, with a further £109 000 owing at home), he could derive some satisfaction from negotiating an interest rate of 14% when Charles V was having to pay 16%.

See page 336

The link between the royal finances and foreign policy is an obvious one. Clearly Northumberland's careful administration would only succeed if he also ended Somerset's wars. On 24 March 1550 England and France signed the Treaty of Boulogne, whereby France was to keep the town in return for £133 333, English troops were to leave Scotland, and no marriage was to take place between Mary, Queen of Scots and Edward VI. A further treaty at Angers arranged for Edward to marry Henry II's daughter, Elisabeth of Valois, for a dowry of 200 000 crowns. The peace settlement was no doubt inglorious (Pollard called it 'the most ignominious signed by England during the century') but it showed realism in cutting England's losses. If the wars had gone on, it might have led to an intolerable strain on England's social fabric. The 1549 upheavals were a very recent memory.

A strong case could also be made out for the success of Northumberland's administrative policy. While Somerset had neglected the Council, Northumberland revived it, giving it an influx of new blood – 12 Councillors were appointed in 1550, all of course pro-Northumberland. Provincial administration was improved through extending the network of Lord-Lieutenants, first appointed in 1549 following a precedent of Henry VIII to control the levies of troops in the shires. Thus the Earls of Huntingdon and Westmorland enhanced their local standing through their Lieutenancies, but were rarely able to attend the Council. In these ways the administrative machine first expanded by Thomas Cromwell in the 1530s was revitalised and prepared for its role in keeping government going during the ups and downs of the next ten years.

Even Northumberland's social policy has come in for praise. The background of the 1549 disturbances, three further poor harvests aggravated by bad weather, soaring wheat prices (from 9 shillings a quarter in 1548–9 to 15 shillings a quarter in 1549–50 and 19 shillings a quarter in 1551–2) and a slump in the cloth trade in 1551 struck fear into the government. Northumberland realised that if disorder were to be avoided, the authorities would have to show some concern for social justice and try to alleviate the effects of economic trends. While some measures to encourage a return to arable farming were abandoned, and also the Enclosure Commissions were wound up, the number of prosecutions of landlords for driving tenants off their estates increased markedly. In 1552 two Acts of Parliament were passed on social issues: one to protect arable farming and to stop usury (money lending often at extortionate rates of interest), the other a new Poor Law to collect funds for the relief of the 'deserving' or 'impotent' poor. It seems, therefore, that Northumberland's concern for social justice was more effective than Somerset's better-known measures.

KEY ISSUE
How effective was Northumberland in administration and other aspects of government?

6 ⌐ NORTHUMBERLAND AND RELIGION

Northumberland's personal religious views are an enigma. In some ways he had seemed to be a conservative, although he had tried to bring members of all factions together to oppose Somerset. Yet this was the same man who had tried to persuade both Wriothesley and Arundel that he wanted to stop further religious change, and perhaps even to go back on some of the Protector's reforms. Certainly he was no scholar and it may be that he was swayed by the arguments of Protestant zealots, or that he came increasingly to see the best chance to preserve his own power was by pushing the Reformation on.

The first sign of the religious climate came in May 1550 with the issue of a new Ordinal, the service book used at the ordination of new priests. It showed its radical tone by doing away with the minor orders of sub-deacon, acolyte etc., and by urging new ministers to preach the gospel. It was first used at St Paul's in June 1550 when John Foxe was ordained priest by the new Bishop of London, Nicholas Ridley.

Ridley was one of a number of unashamed Protestants who were appointed to bishoprics under Northumberland. He set about at once to impose a more radically Protestant stamp on the diocese. Altars were replaced by Communion tables in the centre of the church rather than at the east end in almost every London church by the end of the year. Such a change of location may seem unimportant, but to sixteenth-century Protestants it was vital to make clear that the congregation was participating much more closely in religious ritual than in a Catholic church.

Other episcopal appointments included Hooper, who was nominated as Bishop of Gloucester in July 1550. Hooper, who had recently returned from exile in Strasbourg and Zurich, was a far more extreme Protestant than Ridley and indeed he at first refused consecration at Gloucester as he would have to wear what he described as 'popish' vestments. Cranmer and Ridley refused to consecrate him if he continued to insist on scriptural justification for any ceremonial, and Hooper spent a short term in jail before he agreed to go through with the original ceremony. Once installed as bishop, Hooper was extremely active, administering the Church courts and conducting exhaustive tours of the diocese. The worst problem that he faced was the ignorance of the clergy: in 1551 to his horror he found that 168 out of 311 of his clergy could not repeat the Ten Commandments, let alone preach effectively to their congregations. He knew the Reformation would not thrive until the clergy were better educated.

Such ardent reformers often received their opportunity through the removal or resignation of their conservative predecessors: Heath of Worcester, Gardiner of Winchester, Day of Chichester, Tunstall of Durham, Rugge of Norwich and Vesey of Exeter were replaced, ensuring that, by late 1551, new bishops were installed, keen for further religious reform.

That reform was not long in coming, for in 1552 the Second Edwardian *Prayer Book* was published. In every way it marked a radical revision of the 1549 Book, as it manifestly broke the earlier compromise between Protestant doctrine and Catholic form by insisting that only forms of worship derived from Scripture were valid. Even the terms 'matins' and 'evensong' disappeared to be replaced by 'morning prayer' and 'evening prayer'. Yet the real touchstone of the new book's religious tone was bound to be its treatment of the Mass. In fact the word 'Mass' was dropped in favour of 'the Lord's Supper' or 'Holy Eucharist', and the priest's familiar medieval vestments were abolished in favour of a plain white surplice. The crucial change, however, came in the words of administration: where the 1549 Book had 'The Body of our Lord Jesus Christ which was given for thee preserve thye body and soul unto everlasting life', the 1552 Book substituted 'take and eat this in remembrance that Christ died for thee and feed on him in thy heart by faith with thanksgiving'. The Catholic doctrine of transubstantiation, which held that a physical change took place in the bread and the wine once they had been blessed by the priest, was definitively excluded and the only possible interpretation was a purely spiritual presence of Christ. Meanwhile altars became Communion tables and, to satisfy some Protestants' anxieties, the so-called 'Black Rubric' was inserted by order of the Council to affirm that kneeling at Communion in no way implied adoration or any sort of real, i.e. physical, presence.

Like its predecessor the 1552 Book was accompanied by an Act of Uniformity to enforce its use:

> … that from and after the feast of All Saints next coming, all and every person and persons inhabiting within this realm or any other of the King's Majesty's dominions, shall diligently and faithfully, having no lawful or reasonable excuse to be absent, endeavour themselves to resort to their parish church or chapel accustomed, … and then and there to abide orderly and soberly during the time of the common prayer, preachings, or other service of God there to be used and ministered; upon pain of punishment by the censures of the Church …
>
> And by the authority aforesaid it is now further enacted that if any manner of person or persons inhabiting and being within this realm or any other of the King's Majesty's dominions shall after the said feast of All Saints willingly and wittingly hear and be present at any other manner or form of common prayer, of administration of the sacraments, of making of ministers in the churches, or of any other rites contained in the book annexed to this act than is mentioned and set forth in the said book or that is contrary to the form of sundry provisions and exceptions contained in the foresaid former statute, and shall be thereof convicted according to the laws of this realm before the justices … by the verdict of twelve men or by his or their own confession or otherwise, shall for the first offence suffer imprisonment for six months without bail …, and for the second offence being likewise convicted as is above said imprisonment for one whole year, and for the third offence in like manner imprisonment during his or their lives.

Q

1. How does the first paragraph suggest opposition to the 1552 Prayer Book, or simply religious indifference, might be expressed?
2. Account for the level of severity of the penalties fixed in the second paragraph.

Northumberland's religious reforms were completed by Cranmer's 42 Articles which represented a decisively Protestant interpretation of the Christian faith. Clerical marriage was allowed in a bill passed in 1549, and the removal of married priests in Mary Tudor's reign a few years later gives some idea as to what extent this was taken advantage of: 88 out of 319 in Essex, one in three in London, a quarter in Norwich, about 70 out of 616 in the Lincoln diocese and one in ten in the York diocese. Not all were necessarily keen Protestants, for clerical marriage had its practical and personal aspects: sons to till the glebe, and a wife to be a companion, to satisfy physical desires legitimately, to order the household, to tend the poultry and to organise relations with female parishioners. But, whatever their original motivation, married clerics would nonetheless have a vested interest in the preservation of this aspect at least of the Edwardian Reformation.

Much had therefore been enacted in Northumberland's period of office in the area of religion, but even the most resolute Protestants wondered sometimes whether they had the time or the manpower to carry out the root and branch Reformation for which so many of them yearned. Some changes indeed had to be shelved through constraints of time and opposition, such as the projected cleansing of all taints of Catholicism from canon law (the law of the Church).

How Can the Success of the Edwardian Reformation be Measured?

The short answer to this question is no doubt 'with difficulty'. For a long time the leading historian of the Reformation was AG Dickens, who argued in *The English Reformation* (1964, revised 1989) that the Reformation was essentially a grass roots movement, i.e. a reformation from below. He traced this development from the early years of Henry VIII's reign, as Protestant preachers began to arrive in England from Lutheran parts of Germany. The trickle, he asserted, became a flood as Henry quarrelled with the Pope in the 1530s and established the independence of the English Church from Rome by 1536. Dickens' case is essentially that the Roman Catholic Church was unpopular in England long before Henry's spat with Rome, and that radical Protestant preachers received a favourable reception from a disillusioned people. Edward VI's reign, in Dickens' view, was the culmination of a long developed reformation from below, and thus substantial progress was made during this short period towards a reformed England.

This view came under heavy attack during the 1980s and 1990s, as a triumvirate of scholars examined both the alleged defects of the Roman Church at the start of the sixteenth century and the proclaimed vitality and popularity of Protestantism in Henry VIII's reign and beyond. In 1984 Professor JJ Scarisbrick argued in *The Reformation and the English People* that the Catholic Church in England, far from being moribund, was building new colleges and houses of every kind right up to the dissolutions of the monasteries and the chantries. This view received support from Christopher Haigh who expressed doubts about the rapid success of the Reformation in *The English Reformation Revised* (1987) and *English Reformations* (1993). Finally the Cambridge historian Dr Eamon Duffy produced convincing evidence of the popular attachment to Catholic practices and church furniture – the statues of saints, the wall paintings, the side altars – in *The Stripping of the Altars* (1992) and *The Voices of Morebath* (2001). Thus scholars have recently found little difficulty in showing that ordinary churchgoers, especially in the more remote counties like Devon, held on to traditional practices long into Elizabeth's reign, and that the full flowering of the Reformation may well not have occurred until the 1580s. In other words they see it as a Reformation (or reformations) from above whose impact was bound to be delayed. How then would it be possible to judge the Edwardian Reformation to have been a success, in the face of this well-researched and determined assault?

See pages 433–5

No doubt the Reformation (and, for that matter, Mary Tudor's counter-reformation) needed both time and manpower. Edward's reign after all only lasted five years, hardly long enough even for able preachers and prelates like Latimer and Ridley to make much of an impression. Moreover Bishop Hooper of Gloucester's visitation report suggests that the lack of learning among the clergy, at least in the Gloucester diocese, would seriously hamper either Reformation or Counter-Reformation. The number of Protestant martyrs fleeing England on Mary's accession barely numbered 800 out of a population of 3 million. Sustained preaching and missionary work would clearly be needed over a much longer period of time to ensure the success of Protestantism.

Some historians have made much of the preambles, the introductions, to wills made in the sixteenth century. A traditional (i.e. Catholic) will dedicated the document to 'The Blessed Virgin and the Saints', while a Protestant will might well delete that phrase. Thus it has been shown that the traditional preamble became less prominent as the sixteenth century progressed. It may of course also show that Protestant lawyers in the prosperous South-east managed to persuade even conservative clients to use the new fashionable formula. And it needs to be remembered that only a small minority of citizens possessed sufficient property to make a will worthwhile.

Meanwhile the many bequests to religious houses up to the eve of the Reformation also cast doubt on the idea that Protestant thinking was quickly established. As usual in the Early Modern period the essential problem is the lack of sources, particularly those left by the vast majority of common people, and a reasonable supposition is that many lay people and clergy alike wished to obey royal commands, avoid trouble, and bend in whichever direction the religious wind was blowing. Further research may challenge the formidable results of recent revisionism. But the abiding impression of the Reformation in the minds of many parishioners by 1553 was, in Jennifer Loach's words: 'looting and sacking, and the stripping by the state of the objects of beauty which bound them to their locality and to its past'. Maybe we should not be too surprised if many of them were prepared to welcome Queen Mary and the restoration of Catholicism in 1553.

KEY ISSUE

How far had England become Protestant under Northumberland?

7 ↫ THE FALL OF NORTHUMBERLAND

Edward VI had enjoyed a fairly healthy childhood, contrary to the myth of a boy sickly since birth, but early in 1553 he showed signs of incurable pulmonary tuberculosis. Now Northumberland realised that he would have to work fast in order to prevent the accession of Mary Tudor, which was likely to reverse his religious changes and to spell the end of his power, career, and possibly his liberty. Edward VI himself seems to have been a party to this 'Devise for the Succession' as it was termed, whereby the provisions both of Henry VIII's 1543 Act of Succession and of his will were set aside in favour of Lady Jane Grey, the grand-daughter of Henry's younger sister Mary. Such an arrangement ignored not only Mary Tudor's claim; it also by-passed the Stuart line of succession descended through the line of Henry VIII's elder sister Margaret. In addition, Northumberland had ensured that Lady Jane Grey should marry his own son Lord Guildford Dudley – thus the 'Devise' came more and more to look like a crude plot to secure Northumberland's continued control in the likely event of Edward's early death.

Events unfolded rapidly as the King's health worsened during the summer of 1553. On 21 June 1553 letters patent declared the Princesses Mary and Elizabeth to be bastards, and defied the claims not only of Mary Queen of Scots, but also of Lady Jane Grey's mother Frances who was still alive and who should enjoy a stronger claim than a daughter of hers. On 6 July Edward died and three days later Queen Jane was proclaimed.

Mary Tudor reacted quickly to the threat, leaving London where she would have been in danger of arrest and going to Kenninghall in East Anglia from where she mustered her forces at Framlingham in Suffolk. Over the next few days the conservative East Anglian gentry who had rallied to her initially were joined by national figures like Bath, Sussex and Derby, and even Protestants such as Sir Peter Carew in Devon and Sir Thomas Wyatt in Kent. Some nobles' rivalry with the Grey faction led them to take Mary's side – the Hastings family of Leicestershire would be an example of this. On 14 July, as his support dwindled, Northumberland left London for Cambridge and on the 19 July Mary was proclaimed Queen in the capital in what Bindoff described as 'the greatest mass demonstration of loyalty ever accorded to a Tudor'. One by one the Privy Councillors had begun to swing her way. On 24 July Northumberland was arrested. The Tudors had survived their greatest crisis.

Why then did Northumberland fail to hold on to power? One reason was certainly a practical one; he had paid off the Italian and German mercenaries whom he had hired to put down the 1549 risings. But probably more important was the respect for Mary's legitimacy. The 'Devise' looked like blatant interference with the legal succession, a fact recognised even by many confirmed Protestants such as those who listened to a sermon of Bishop Ridley's on 9 July 1553 in which he tried to justify Northumberland's scheme. There may well have also been a popular element, hatred of Northumberland for his role in putting down Kett's Rebellion. Yet at the same time it is striking how many nobility and gentry rallied to the new Queen. The allies Northumberland had were too recently established and lacked status. Two other factors are worth mentioning: while there was an awareness that Mary Tudor was a Catholic in doctrine, it was not clear that she was a 'papist' any more than her father, Henry VIII. It was not known she would re-establish papal power in England or act repressively against Protestants.

KEY ISSUE

Why did Northumberland fail to hold onto power in 1553?

And, in any case, much of England was still conservative in its religion. Finally there is no doubt that Northumberland had laid his plans too late; there is no evidence of a long-term plot on his part. Thus came to an end the rule of the man whom many historians now regard as an able ruler.

8 ⌐ BIBLIOGRAPHY

**CSL Davies *Peace, Print and Protestantism 1450–1558* (Paladin, 1977), see Chapter 9. It has remained the most admirably concise and detailed survey of the entire period. **J Loach *Edward VI* (Yale, 1999), completed by Penry Williams and George Bernard after Jennifer Loach's untimely death, an excellent and up-to-date biography. *AGR Smith *The Emergence of a Nation State: the Commonwealth of England 1529–1660* (Longman, 1984), see Chapters 8 and 9. A formidable textbook, with especially useful data listed at the back. SJ Gunn *Early Tudor Government, 1485–1558* (Macmillan, 1995), use the index for Edward VI. It is useful for the key topic of administration throughout the Early Tudor period, if quite dry. **D MacCulloch *Tudor Church Militant* (Penguin, 1999) is a convincing recent interpretation of religious change in Edward VI's reign, and *D MacCulloch *Thomas Cranmer* (Yale, 1996), see Part III, and Part IV, Chapter 12. It is a fine biography of the leading force in Edwardian church reform. WJ Shiels *The English Reformation 1530–1570* (Longman, 1989), see especially pages 37–47. An inevitably brief survey of the three main attempts at 'reformation'. **A Fletcher and D MacCulloch *Tudor Rebellions* (Longman, 1997), see Chapters 5 and 6. The standard work on the risings, brought up to date in its fourth edition. N Heard *Edward VI and Mary: A Mid-Tudor Crisis?* (Hodder & Stoughton, Access to History 1990), see Chapter 3, sections 3 and 4. A useful examination of a once controversial theory, and designed for sixth-form study.

(*Recommended. **Highly recommended.)

9 ⌐ STRUCTURED AND ESSAY QUESTIONS

A *Structured questions*

1. (a) What innovations were there in religion in the reign of Edward VI?
    (b) 'A successful reformation imposed from above.' How far do you agree with this assessment of Edward VI's religious policy?
2. (a) How close to success were the two main rebellions of 1549?
    (b) 'Somerset was idealistic but a failure; Northumberland was unimaginative but effective'. How far do you agree with this assessment of Somerset and Northumberland?

B *Essay questions*

1. Compare Somerset and Northumberland as effective rulers of England during the reign of Edward VI.
2. How far did the problems of his reign stem from Edward VI's minority?
3. Was England in the reign of Edward VI governed well or badly?
4. Why was there so much upheaval in the short reign of Edward VI?
5. What basic weaknesses in Tudor government were exposed under Edward VI?
6. What progress had Protestantism made in England by 1553?

10 ⤙ EXERCISE – RELIGIOUS GEOGRAPHY

Draw a map of Tudor England and on it mark London, Oxford, Cambridge, York, Winchester, Norwich, Lincoln, Gloucester, Canterbury, Rochester, Worcester, Durham, Essex and Nottingham. From sections 3 and 6 in the chapter mark on the map any area identified at any point in the text either with Protestantism or Catholicism under the following headings:

(a) Earnest Protestant bishops like Cranmer, Ridley, Hooper and Holgate.
(b Catholic bishops deprived of their Sees like Bonner, Gardiner, Heath, Day and Tunstall.
(c) The universities and the reformed London churches under continental figures like Bucer, John a Lasco, Peter Martyr Vermigli and Bernardo Ochino.
(d) The areas with high and low proportions of married priests.
(e) Areas for which there is information about the religious complexion of wills, e.g. Kent, Nottinghamshire, Yorkshire.
(f) Magnates and their areas of influence and religious views: e.g. Derby in Lancashire and Cheshire, Arundel in Sussex, Shrewsbury in the northern Welsh Marches, Pembroke in Wiltshire and the Duchess of Suffolk in Lincolnshire.

Q

How far was reforming activity of all kinds concentrated in one region of the country? How do you explain any such concentration?

7

Mary Tudor 1553–8

See page 319

INTRODUCTION

Mary was the third but only surviving child of Henry VIII and Catherine of Aragon. Having received a humanist classical education, she was made Princess of Wales at Ludlow in 1525, but in 1533, the year of her father's marriage to Anne Boleyn, she was declared illegitimate. She refused to accept the Royal Supremacy, even though this may have put her life at risk, but in 1536 she compromised, while clinging to the essentials of her Catholic faith, and was reconciled to Henry following the execution of Anne Boleyn. She remained illegitimate according to law during the remainder of her father's reign, but the Succession Act of 1544 declared that she was capable of inheriting the Crown after Henry's legitimate heirs. In fear of a disputed succession and the chaos that would bring, the Act came to be seen as sacrosanct.

On the day of Edward VI's death, 6 July 1553, Mary was on her way to visit her half-brother at Greenwich. Hearing the news at Hoddesdon in Hertfordshire, she at once decided to return to Kenninghall in Norfolk, one of her own manors surrounded by sympathetic gentry. She immediately began to act as Queen: for example on 9 July she addressed a message to the Privy Council in London setting out her right and title to the throne. On 19 July, Mary was officially proclaimed in London, which she entered on 3 August, becoming the first woman to occupy the throne in her own right since Matilda in the twelfth century. Northumberland, who had tried to divert the succession to his daughter-in-law, Lady Jane Grey, went to the block with several of his henchmen, but Lady Jane's life was spared. Mary had staged what CSL Davies has called 'the only successful rebellion in Tudor England', but Englishmen were as yet unclear about what Mary would now do with her power.

Until relatively recently Mary was seen as an almost complete failure. The two best-known features of her reign have always been the burnings of several hundred Protestant heretics and the loss of Calais at the end of a disastrous war fought against France in alliance with her husband's kingdom of Spain. The early twentieth-century historian Pollard summed up the period as one of sterility and stagnation, only rescued by the accession of Elizabeth on her death in 1558.

This picture of failure has been challenged by a later generation of writers who have sought to find some positive achievements. They have pointed to Mary's initial success in taking the throne under difficult circumstances in July 1553, and to the setting up, immediately after her accession, of a strong Council, less divided by faction than that of the

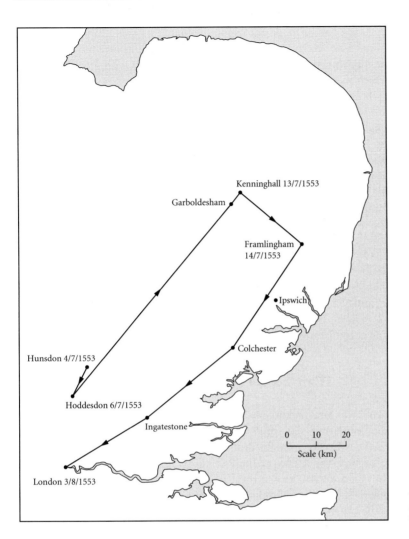

Kenninghall 13/7/1553

Garboldesham

Framlingham
14/7/1553

Ipswich

Colchester

Hunsdon 4/7/1553

Hoddesdon 6/7/1553

Ingatestone

London 3/8/1553

0 10 20
Scale (km)

MAP 7
Mary's Route on her Seizure of Power, 1553

two previous reigns. It is of course true that Councillors offered conflicting advice on the marriage question: some favouring the Spanish match and others an English suitor, but Mary reached agreement with her Council on the marriage terms with Philip of Spain and survived a serious rebellion in 1554, which whipped up anti-Spanish and anti-Catholic feeling.

Mary's determined efforts to restore full papal Catholicism ultimately failed, if only because her early death in 1558 left the way open for the accession of a declared Protestant, her half-sister Elizabeth. However, there is little doubt that the religious temper of England was largely conservative in 1553, and most of the **political nation** was prepared to accept a return to a Catholic order, provided that nothing was done to restore former monastic lands. The burnings did arouse opposition, but they were by no means the focus of popular resistance.

Political nation those people whose political opinion mattered – Councillors, courtiers, well-connected nobles and gentry in the shires, and leading figures in the City of London and other major towns

A case can be made out to suggest that Mary was a capable administrator. Her reforms of customs rates, coinage and revenue courts may be unglamorous, but they did provide Elizabeth with a good basis on which she could build.

It is hard, nevertheless, to say much that is positive about Mary's foreign policy. The marriage agreement of 1554 specifically stated that England's foreign affairs would not lead to war on Spain's side. However, Philip's second visit to England in 1557 succeeded in persuading Mary and her advisors of the need to embark on war against Henry II of France. The war was not – at least initially – unpopular in England, for it enabled a large number of formerly suspect nobles to prove their loyalty. Yet the loss of Calais, England's only remaining possession on the continental mainland, was to be the lasting legacy of her marriage and the Spanish alliance.

Clearly Mary's reign is never likely to be seen as a great chapter of national history. There were undoubted failures and even those policies that seemed to be showing some success were cut short by the Queen's untimely death at the age of 42. This should not overshadow, however, her relative popularity on her accession and her painstaking care over dull administrative detail.

PICTURE 17
Mary Tudor, *anon.*

1 ⁓ FACTION AND POLITICS

Mary was understandably determined to fill the Council with loyal appointees but she could not prevent the rivalry between Gardiner, Lord Chancellor until his death in November 1555, and Paget, who was to become the Keeper of the Privy Seal. This emerged, for example, in the discussions over the royal marriage in 1554, when Gardiner proposed Mary's English relative, Edward Courtenay, as the bridegroom, while his rival argued for Philip of Spain, the only working Councillor to do so. It is easy, however, to exaggerate the importance of this rift. After all on many matters the Council maintained a united front. Some Councillors, including perhaps Gardiner, were to have doubts over the effectiveness of the burnings of heretics, but they seem to have kept such doubts largely to themselves.

Despite the reservations felt by some Councillors at some of Mary's policies, she did emerge successful in obtaining agreement for three key controversial steps: the full return to Rome in religion, her marriage to the heir to the Spanish throne, and then the declaration of war against France in alliance with Habsburg Spain. No doubt Mary was also influenced in these, and perhaps other policies, by the advice that she received from two key, if unofficial advisers: Simon Renard, the Imperial ambassador who represented Philip's father, the Emperor Charles V at the English Court; and Philip himself, who for all his inability to read and understand English and his infrequent visits to England must have made his views plain to his wife.

Thus we are struck by a relative lack of division in the highest ranks of government, and even by a continuity from previous reigns. Not only are there a number of familiar faces from the 1540s and early 1550s, there is also some continuity into the future. The most remarkable example of this is perhaps Winchester, who served as Lord Treasurer from 1550 to 1572.

The same continuity can be detected in Mary's relations with her Parliaments. No less than five Parliaments were held during the reign: in 1553, twice in 1554, in 1555 and in 1558. Opposition was expressed from time to time to certain of Mary's policies: to the proposed Church lands settlement, to the plan to crown Philip and to the idea of removing Princess Elizabeth from the succession. There was, however, no sense of mounting opposition. Professor Tittler, one of Mary's most recent biographers, writes of 'a genuine spirit of compromise and co-operation which has not generally been observed either in the history of Tudor parliaments or of Mary's reign'.

> **KEY ISSUE**
>
> *How far did Mary's accession lead to an upheaval in government personnel?*

2 ↶ THE SUCCESSION PROBLEM AND THE SPANISH MARRIAGE

Mary was crowned and anointed by Gardiner on 1 October 1553 according to the old Catholic rite. Then the problem of the succession and her marriage loomed to haunt the new Queen. She was determined on two things: to marry and to bear children, and to keep her half-sister, the Protestant Elizabeth, from the throne. The first question was: whom should she marry?

Two candidates presented themselves: an English suitor in Edward Courtenay and a foreign one in Philip of Spain. At first sight Courtenay's credentials looked impressive, for he was of royal blood, a great-grandson of Edward IV. His father Henry, second Earl of Devon and Marquis of Exeter, had been a devout Catholic and a confidant of Mary herself. He had paid for his indiscretion with his life in 1538. Edward was 27 years old (compared to Mary's 37) and his claims were advanced in the Council by Gardiner who was keen to avoid a foreign match. However, the Courtenay candidature presented significant difficulties, not least because it opened up the danger of reviving factional quarrels, as any English husband would be expected to reward his own supporters at the expense of others. Moreover his personal qualities suggested further disadvantages: he was intellectually astute but socially awkward, unreliable in religion, debauched, weak and lacking in common sense.

Mary herself much preferred a Spanish marriage. She was after all half-Spanish herself, and Philip of Spain, the heir to the Emperor Charles V, seemed to offer so much more than Courtenay. He was 26 years old, a widower with one son by his former marriage, and had government experience as Regent in the Netherlands in 1549–50 and as Regent of Spain itself since 1551. He was also a Catholic, and supported as a candidate by Paget and by his father, the Emperor. Charles, who was later to divide his huge territorial responsibilities between his brother Ferdinand (who got the German lands) and his son Philip (Spain and the Netherlands), was keen to strengthen Philip's inheri-

PICTURE 18
Philip II, *anon.*

tance by the addition of England. Philip, with Spain on the southern border of France and the Netherlands to the north, would be in a better position to counter-balance the power of France if he was King of England too.

The official Spanish proposal of marriage was presented to Mary by Simon Renard, the Imperial ambassador, on 10 October 1553. At the end of the month Mary formally accepted the proposal and gazed longingly at a Titian portrait of her husband-to-be, pending Philip's arrival in England.

Mary had, unfortunately, failed to anticipate the furore that the Spanish marriage proposal stirred up in England, Spanish power being seen as a threat to English liberties and commercial interests. There is little doubt that a majority of Councillors opposed the match, and in November a parliamentary delegation tried to dissuade her. Eventually both the Council (on 7 December 1553) and Parliament (in April 1554) accepted the marriage treaty. Philip's title was to be that of King, but he was not to enjoy the full prerogative. (Symbolically, he was to sit on a throne, but a smaller one than Mary's.) No foreign followers of Philip were to hold office in England, and England would not be expected to join Spain in a war against France. As for the succession, the eldest surviving child of the marriage would succeed to both England and the Netherlands. If Mary were to die before Philip, then he would have no further claim to the English throne. Finally, if Don Carlos, Philip's existing son, died childless before Philip himself, any child of Mary's would inherit the whole Spanish Empire, including the Americas and much of Italy.

Philip himself was a good deal less enthusiastic about the idea than either his father or his future bride. He seems to have been determined not to be bound by the terms, and he was somewhat slow to arrive in England to claim his bride. He was never crowned King of England and he never seems to have taken to England, regarding it perhaps in Professor Loades' words as 'a chilly land of barbarous heretics'.

> **KEY ISSUE**
>
> *Why was it Mary's preference to marry Philip of Spain, and what was agreed to make it acceptable to Council and Parliament?*

See pages 319–21

3 ～ WYATT'S REBELLION

The Spanish marriage was largely responsible for the one major disturbance of the reign, Wyatt's Rebellion from January to February 1554. Professor Wernham has described it as 'a protest designed to prevent the adoption of a particular policy, a protest made in advance. It was an attempt to join in the debate about what foreign policy should be. This was something new in English affairs'. There had in fact been plots and rumours of plots since the autumn of 1553 to engineer a Protestant succession and to secure a marriage between Courtenay and the 20-year-old Princess Elizabeth. The former seems to have been thrown into the plot by his petulance at being passed over by Mary in favour of Philip, but, unstable as ever, he divulged the details of the conspiracy to Gardiner.

By December 1553 plans had been laid for simultaneous risings to erupt on 18 March 1554 in Kent, Hertfordshire, Devon, Leicestershire, and the Welsh borders. The French ambassador, Antoine de Noailles, was also involved, promising naval support in the Channel and help in securing ports in the South-west. Unfortunately the scheme went awry as the government got wind of the plan in mid-January 1554, and Devon and Hertfordshire failed to rise. In Leicestershire only 140 joined the Duke of Suffolk, one of the conspirators, who was quickly arrested by the Earl of Huntingdon, his neighbour and rival, who had remained loyal to the Queen. That left Kent where Wyatt was forced into premature action.

Wyatt had first come to prominence in 1549 as the author of a plan presented to Protector Somerset to create a regular militia, with groups of trained men in each county under a paid professional. Like other of the conspirators, he now seemed worried about further advancement under Mary. For Wyatt, his county Kent was a good source of support, close to London and more advanced in Protestantism and suspicion of Catholic foreigners than most areas of the country. Wyatt himself, a large landowner in the county, had originally declared for Mary, but in January 1554 he managed to assemble a force of between 2500 and 3000. Wyatt whipped up anti-Spanish feeling by playing on fears of being dragged into war on Spain's behalf and of imminent arrivals of Spaniards in Kent. He posed as the rescuer of the Queen from foolish advice, but beyond this he appears to have left his aims deliberately vague.

Wyatt's plan might have had some chance of success if he had moved quickly on London, either to compel Mary to abandon her plans or to replace her by Elizabeth, who was still legally the heir until Mary had children or Parliament decided otherwise. As the rebellion progressed, the slow government response also gave him opportunities, for Arundel and Shrewsbury (both known opponents of the marriage) failed to move, and the elderly Duke of Norfolk, recently released from the Tower, returned to Court having failed to block Wyatt's advance to the capital. Meanwhile the London militia confronted Wyatt from the left bank of the Medway but then moved over to his side. Wyatt, who had by now acquired ships and cannon, seemed to have an excellent chance of success. Why then did he fail?

Part of the answer lies in Mary's own response. She refrained from appealing to Charles V, realising perhaps that the presence of foreign troops would have played into Wyatt's hands. She also remained in London, despite Gardiner's advice to take refuge in Winchester, and ordered the fortification of the city. If she had left the capital, she would have left it vulnerable to attacks from other directions. On 1 February Mary issued a personal appeal from the Guildhall. She played on Londoners' fears of an incursion into the city by armed men, who would bring destruction in their wake, and she received support from the more neutral Councillors like Pembroke and Bedford. Above all she benefited from Wyatt's error in diverting his forces on 30 January to take Cooling Castle, held by Lord Cobham. The castle surrendered, but Wyatt had lost a whole day. He therefore arrived too late to cross the Thames at Southwark, where London Bridge was reinforced and held out against the rebels. Wyatt did not cross the Thames until 6 February, at Kingston much further to the west; on his approach to the city he was defeated by Pembroke. Meanwhile on 9 February Princess Elizabeth was arrested for alleged complicity in the rebellion.

Paget urged leniency for the captured rebels, while Renard by contrast wanted the deaths of both Courtenay and Elizabeth. The latter two were spared in the absence of hard evidence to implicate them, but 100 perished including Lady Jane Grey, her husband Guildford Dudley, Suffolk and Wyatt himself. The bulk of the captured rebels numbering around 600 were freed, and Elizabeth served a brief prison term before being sent to the royal manor of Woodstock. While the repression was harsh it was not vindictive.

Several questions still need to be asked about the rebellion. Firstly were the motives more complex than mere anti-Spanish xenophobia, sowing distrust of Philip and raising fears of increased taxes for foreign adventures? Professors Tittler and Dickens see religion as an important ingredient, especially as Kent was known as a Protestant stronghold. Professor Thorp has examined the religious leanings of several leading rebels, and out of 14 he has found no Catholics, eight definite Protestants, three probable Protestants and four whose religious sympathies are unknown. There were also nine clergy involved, all of whom seem to have been Protestants. It is also worth remembering that Kent later in the reign produced no less than one-sixth of the Marian martyrs, those who were burned for heresy under Mary. It seems therefore that a distinct Protestant strand ran through these upheavals, although it is not possible to list Wyatt himself as Protestant.

Finally did the Wyatt movement suffer from serious initial weaknesses? Certainly Wyatt found out the hard way that hostility to the Spanish marriage was strong, but not that strong when other factors were brought into play. The one major aristocrat involved in the plot, the Duke of Suffolk, could only raise a paltry force. It is also the case that the orthodox Protestant leadership refused to get involved, and some even refused to be released from prison by the rebels. Thus a conventional domestic revolt had little chance of success against a monarch whose right to rule was generally recognised.

> **KEY ISSUE**
>
> *What caused Wyatt's Rebellion and why did it fail?*

4 ⌐ ROYAL FINANCES

See page 106

Recent writing on Mary's reign has commented favourably on Mary's success in the vital if unglamorous area of financial administration. The most famous such measure is the amalgamation of the revenue courts in 1554 when the responsibility for First Fruits and Tenths and for Augmentations passed to the Exchequer, making this body responsible for most royal revenues for the first time since the fifteenth century. Such streamlining may well have been in line with the long-term aims of Thomas Cromwell, but it was put into effect during Mary's reign by Winchester and Mildmay who also introduced advanced methods of auditing and accounting. The net yield of the former Court of Augmentations doubled, while a new survey of royal lands increased their revenue by more than £40 000. Meanwhile Sir Thomas Gresham's services were retained, manipulating foreign exchange rates and negotiating favourable foreign loans.

See page 336

Mary is also given credit for the issuing of a new book of customs rates in 1558. The background to this is a serious rise in the general costs of government at a time of pronounced inflation, warfare, greater government activity in other areas and the expense of maintaining an impressive Renaissance court. The sale of Crown lands, offices and monopolies went some way towards solving the problem as a short-term expedient. Likewise parliamentary subsidies brought in ready cash for a short time, but there would be increasing resistance if Parliament was called on to raise taxes too often. Thus the government's attention turned to the customs duties which were still being levied according to the 1507 Book of Rates, with minor increases from 1536 and 1545. Indeed many goods remained wholly untaxed, and inflation quickly made the rates on those that were taxed obsolete. The average increase in valuation over the 1545 revision was nearly 120%, and the modest yield of £29 000 for 1558 rose to £83 000 in 1559. Indeed the Marian Book survived until 1604, giving Mary greater success in this area even than Henry VII or Edward IV. Two important new principles had also been established: that rates could be determined by the Crown alone, and that the Crown could impose new export duties without Parliament's consent.

At the same time the government actively fostered trade, seeking alternative ports to Calais such as Bergen, Bruges and Middleburg in the Netherlands. English attempts to break into the lucrative Spanish New World market were however thwarted, and commercial attention turned elsewhere. Following Willoughby and Chancellor's voyage to Russia in 1553 the Muscovy Company received its charter in 1555 and contacts developed with Morocco and Guinea in West Africa. The fact that traders did not protest at the higher duties in the new Book of Rates may well suggest a new alliance between the monarchy and commercial interests.

All of this would seem to challenge the view of an older generation of historians led by Pollard who wrote of the 'sterility' of Mary's reign. Despite some severe social and economic problems, including perhaps up to 200 000 deaths from the 1558 epidemic of sweating sickness, there were no violent uprisings arising from hardship and no air of continuing crisis like that which hung over the reign of the incompetent Henry VI in the previous century. It would nonetheless be wrong to see Mary as a great innovator in government. There was no sharp break with the past: rather Mary operated within a traditional framework of ideas. Hence the historian is entitled to wonder how far Mary herself can take the credit for the success of her government's financial management and how far it may be due to those more professional administrators who were ultimately the legacy of Thomas Cromwell.

KEY ISSUE

How effective was the administration of the royal finances and the economy under Mary?

5 ∽ RELIGION

A *Early moves towards Catholicism*

Mary's first proclamation on religion, issued on 18 August 1553, was remarkably tolerant. She deplored the diversity of religious opinions, but she promised that there would be no pursuit of heretics for the time being as she was convinced that no coercion would be necessary. The Queen believed that most apparent Protestants were really Catholics who had been led astray during her half-brother's reign and that true Protestants were only a tiny minority of fanatics. Hence she was sure that the restoration of the old faith would be easy to carry out. She also realised that little could be done to persecute Protestants, even if she wished to do so, without Parliament's approval to restore the fifteenth-century heresy laws. For a full return to Rome a special Papal Legate would also be required to absolve England and return it to the fold.

Some measures could, however, be taken at once. Seven bishops were removed, four of whom were imprisoned including Cranmer, Hooper, Latimer and Ridley. Three of them had to face debates against Catholic theologians in Oxford in April 1554 when it was expected that they would be humiliated and ridiculed. In this the government's hopes were dashed because, while Cranmer performed poorly in the debate and Latimer refused to dispute at all, Ridley managed to confound no less than 33 opposing theologians. Clearly the intellectual battle against Protestantism and its champions would be harder than the authorities had envisaged.

Around a quarter of the clergy were deprived of their livings, mostly because they had married when permitted to do so during the previous reign. Of these 2000 clergy most were, not surprisingly, in the South and East – 243 deprivations in the Norwich diocese, for instance, and 150 in London – while only 10% of clergy lost their livings in the North. There was also a significant emigration of foreign Protestants, like John a Lasco, Peter Martyr Vermigli and Bernardo Ochino, that aggravated the Church's serious manpower shortage.

Mary's first Parliament (October 1553) repealed most of the reforming legislation from the previous reign including the two *Prayer Books* and their Acts of Uniformity, permission for clerical marriage, Communion in both kinds and the 42 Articles. The forms of worship in force in 1547 were re-established. None of this happened without opposition, however, as between a quarter and a third of the Commons voted against these proposals and in Mary's second Parliament (April–May 1554), while the Spanish marriage was approved, members refused to re-enact the Act of Six Articles or to punish those who refused to attend church. The Royal Supremacy had also yet to be annulled, and to her embarrassment Mary remained 'Supreme Head of the Church of England', which she abbreviated to 'etc.' after her secular titles.

Mary's cousin, Cardinal Pole, was to be the Papal Legate who would receive England back into the Roman Catholic fold. While he waited for the official invitation to visit England, the Imperial ambassador Simon Renard wrote to the Emperor on 3 September 1554 to outline some of the difficulties which he foresaw in implementing the full rigours of pre-1529 Papal Catholicism which Mary seemed determined to re-introduce:

> Cardinal Pole presses for an answer whether or no he is to be received here as Legate, and writes that he wants a definite reply so that he may either go back to Rome or proceed on his journey. Of course one must take it for granted that zeal for religion alone moves him, but still doubts assail me. Affairs are not settled here yet, and the King has only been a few days in the realm. The Spaniards are hated, as I have seen in the past and expect to see in the future. There was trouble at the last session of Parliament, and disagreeable incidents are of daily occurrence. Only ten days ago the heretics tried to burn a church in Suffolk with the entire congregation that was hearing Mass inside …
>
> On examining the brief sent hither by the Cardinal and intended to dispense those who hold Church property, I have noticed that it is not drawn up in a suitable manner … It is my duty to inform your Majesty that the Catholics hold more Church property than do the heretics, and unless they obtain a general dispensation to satisfy them that their titles will never be contested they will not allow the Cardinal to execute his commission; and he certainly will not be able to do so until the question has been submitted to Parliament, former Acts of which have vested the title of Supreme Head of the Church in the Crown, the right of which to deal with all religious questions consequently stands firm.

Q

1. *How reliable do you think Renard was as an observer of English affairs?*
2. *Summarise briefly the reasons, drawn from Renard's observations, for Pole to be cautious.*

Pole's arrival in the country of his birth was delayed until November 1554 partly because Charles V wanted his son to establish himself first and because Mary herself wanted to be strong enough to dissuade him from restoring all former Church lands. Pole arrived at Westminster to find Mary's third Parliament convened and prepared both to abandon Royal Supremacy over the Church and to repeal the Act of Attainder hanging over him. On 28 November 1554, Pole addressed both Houses of Parliament and was reported as saying:

> … his principal business was to restore the nation to its ancient nobility. To this purpose he had an authority from His Holiness to make them part of the Catholic Church. That the Apostolic See had a particular regard for this island, and that to this, the Pope seemed to be led by the directions of Providence, which has given a preference to this country by making it one of the first provinces that received the Christian faith. …

If we enquire into the English revolt we shall find … avarice and sensuality the principal motives, and that was first started and carried on by the unbridled appetite and licentiousness of a single person. And though it was given out that there would be a vast accession of wealth to the public, yet this expectation dwindled to nothing. The Crown was left in debt, and the subjects generally speaking more impoverished than ever. And as to religion, people were tied up to forms and hampered with penalties and, to speak plainly, there was more liberty of conscience in Turkey than in England.

… The Church of Rome might have recovered her jurisdiction by force, and had an offer of the greatest princes in Europe to assist her pretensions. However, she was willing to waive this advantage, and apply to none but friendly expedients.

PROFILE

CARDINAL POLE (1500–58)

Reginald Pole was born in Worcestershire in 1500 the son of Sir Geoffrey Pole and Margaret, Countess of Salisbury. His mother was the daughter of George, Duke of Clarence, making him a great-nephew of Edward IV. After higher education at Oxford and Padua in Italy he returned to Italy as an exile, having quarrelled with Henry VIII over the King's 'Great Matter' in 1532. That way he avoided the fate of his mother and brother, who both suffered the King's vengeance and went to the block. In the 1530s Pole's reputation was that of a humanist and advocate of Church reform. Indeed in 1536 he collaborated on the famous 'Consilium Delectorum Cardinalium De Emendanda Ecclesia', whose report recommended far-reaching changes in the Catholic Church. He was promoted to Cardinal in 1536, and in 1545 he was chosen as one of three Cardinals to preside over the Council of Trent. In 1549 he failed by only one vote in the College of Cardinals to become Pope. Thus on the eve of his return to England in 1554 he was a respected senior churchman, an authority on pastoral care and clerical education and a respected diplomat. He had, however, incurred the undying hatred of the violently anti-Spanish Caraffa, who himself was to become Pope Paul IV in 1555, and who then summoned Pole back to answer heresy charges in Rome. It is ironic, therefore, that Reginald Pole should have among Protestants the reputation only of a thoroughly reactionary Catholic prelate for the part he was to play in the Marian persecutions.

Two days later on 30 November 1554 Pole formally granted absolution to the whole realm and restored it to papal obedience. Parliament went on to revive the anti-Lollard heresy laws of 1382, 1401 and 1414 and to repeal all acts passed against the Papacy since 1529. Now Pole could work fully as Papal Legate, although he was forced reluctantly to agree to concede lay ownership of Church lands given out after the Dissolution of the Monasteries. The lay peers, supported by Paget, who himself owned former monastic land, opposed Pole's initial idea to restore monastic lands for obvious material reasons, and also because they feared a revival of abbots' seats in the House of Lords which might well lead in turn to a renewed clerical majority there.

Pole's strategy for the re-Catholicisation of England emerges from the London Synod of 1555 when he tried to grapple with the Church's organisational and financial problems. He urged bishops to undertake regular visitations to detect non-residence, pluralism and tithes impropriated (taken over) by laymen, but even with the most able bishops, this would take time, especially as some of the most senior prelates like Gardiner and Heath were often preoccupied with state affairs.

Gardiner, Tunstall and Bonner, all former bishops under Henry VIII, returned to their Sees, while there were other new, vigorous men appointed. But few were outstanding and in any case they lacked the time needed for their labours to bear fruit.

Fourteen seminaries were set up to train priests, but Pole turned down the Jesuits' offer to organise a mission in England, as they recognised only the Pope as their master and would not necessarily conform to his requirements. He set greater store by the visitations he made to the two universities, and he became Chancellor of both. He encouraged the founding of two new Oxford colleges, Trinity and St John's, but he was to find few scholars to replace the likes of Bucer, Martyr or Fagius. While the MA degree course was shortened, the colleges would need much more time to become effective centres of Catholic renewal.

The same difficulties afflicted the attempts to bring in new books to counteract the effects of the Protestant Bible. A Catholic New Testament, a Book of Homilies (a collection of official sermons) and a new **Catechism** were prepared but there was little time to implement them. There was probably more success in restoring features of Catholic worship in churches: altars, rood-lofts and images reappeared, together with vestments and the paraphernalia of the Mass. Indeed Dr Eamon Duffy's work on the village of Morebath in Devon shows the persistence of Catholic church furniture in a more remote corner of the land. However, the Injunctions of Archdeacon Nicholas Harpsfield of Canterbury on the condition of parish churches in his area in 1557 underscore the sorry state of many parish churches there and the decay of church furniture necessary for Catholic worship.

The effectiveness of Pole's efforts was weakened partly by failure to motivate or inspire his subordinates or to understand the hostility to the Catholic Church that had erupted during his exile. It also suffered from the changes in his status in England. After Cranmer's death he became Archbishop of Canterbury in 1556, but the deaths of Popes

KEY ISSUE

Why could Mary attempt to re-Catholicise England only in stages? What were those stages?

Catechism a teaching manual of religious beliefs in the form of question and answer

Julius III and Marcellus II in 1555 brought his arch-enemy Caraffa to the papacy as Pope Paul IV. In April 1557 he withdrew Pole's legatine authority, summoned him to Rome to face charges of heresy and refused to confirm his episcopal appointments. Although Mary prevented his return to Rome, the Cardinal's effective period as Papal Legate had lasted little over two years.

B *Censorship and writing*

Mary's government was prepared to use censorship on the lines of the Roman Counter-Reformation itself. In 1553 she issued decrees against seditious rumours, in 1555 an Index of proscribed writers was drawn up, and in 1558 the death penalty was prescribed for those involved with prohibited books.

These measures were hampered partly by the pre-existence of around 19 000 copies of the outlawed 1552 *Prayer Book* and the continued output by Protestant writers at the height of the Marian persecution. Even Latimer and Ridley somehow managed to write from their Oxford prison.

Some Protestant writers hurled invective against Mary to undermine her credibility and to sustain the faith and hopes of Protestants by urging purely passive disobedience. Some, like Becon and Scory, enjoined obedience to the Queen, interpreting her reign as punishment on the faithful for their sins. Others encouraged non-attendance at Mass and the continuation of Protestant rites to keep up the spirits of the faithful.

There were, however, a few writers who developed theories of active disobedience, and these were to be important developments in political thought. Christopher Goodman, minister of the English exiles in Geneva, published in 1556 *How Superior Powers ought to be Obeyed*, described by Professor Tittler as 'one of the most politically practical of such statements in the literature of sixteenth-century political thought'. Goodman put forward a limited concept of monarchy in which the sovereign held his or her authority from God, but only through a covenant or contract whereby the people 'elected' the monarch. It followed, according to Goodman, that the king must fear God, respect his Word and refrain from ruling by coercion. Equally the people must obey a godly monarch, but enforce God's will against an ungodly ruler. Goodman held that the magistrates – meaning nobles, Councillors and judges – must act against a tyrannical sovereign. If they failed to do so, then the people should take matters into their own hands.

Ponet in his *Short Treatise of Political Power*, published in 1556, also argued against the absolutist nature of royal authority and stressed the ruler's obligation to protect the common weal. He did not, however, describe the specific means whereby a ruler like Mary might be brought to justice.

Finally, and with less lasting effect in political thought, John Knox's chief theme was the illegitimacy of women rulers by natural law, and in *The First Blast of the Trumpet Against the Monstrous Regiment of Women* (1558) he ascribed the calamities that had befallen England to God's displeasure at the unnatural choice of Mary Tudor as queen. In 1558 he also published in Geneva *The Appellation of John Knox* urging the over-throw of women rulers. This was to become embarrassing in the reign of the Protestant Elizabeth I.

In contrast to the Protestant theorists, Catholic publications seem much more lightweight. The government could have made much more use of the opportunity to sponsor Sunday sermons at St Paul's Cross: Nicholas Harpsfield, the Archdeacon of Canterbury, preached there only twice – once to praise the royal marriage and once to give thanks for the Spanish victory at St Quentin – while Gardiner only spoke there in 1554, to praise Philip and to announce the reconciliation with Rome. The authorities could have made greater use of an important platform to propagate their views.

Of the Catholic writers only Miles Huggard, John Christopherson and Thomas Watson are at all well known. Clearly Mary failed to inspire the intellectuals, few of her advisers had studied abroad and most of the really bright sparks were Protestants anyway. The Christian Humanist vitality of the early sixteenth century, exemplified by Erasmus and Thomas More, had died out. In any event about half of all publishers had left England, and those who remained were kept busy by Pole printing the various church service books, for which there was a ready and profitable market. Thus they were less willing to produce and sell polemical works with a more limited readership.

C *The persecution of Protestants*

Only two religious extremists had been burned in Edward VI's reign: George van Parris, a Flemish surgeon who denied Christ's divinity, and Joan Bocher, an ex-Lollard turned **Anabaptist**, but, once Mary's third Parliament had restored the heresy legislation in January 1555, the way was open for the burnings of Protestants which is such a notorious feature of the reign.

The zeal for the executions seems to have come partly from Mary herself, urged on by her Spanish confessor, Carranza a Castro, and Pole himself. Gardiner apparently became more sceptical just before his death in November 1555, and Simon Renard's dispatches to Philip suggest that he was also doubtful of the wisdom of the burnings. For example on 5 February 1555 Renard wrote to Philip to describe the death of John Rogers, the biblical translator, at Smithfield the previous day. Renard records a strongly emotional reaction from the crowd with weeping, prayers, the gathering of ashes and bones, and threats directed against the bishops. Indeed the authorities seem to have become aware that the burning policy might be counter-productive and in London efforts were made to ensure that apprentices and servants stayed away from executions.

There were approximately 300 victims, including 50 women, with most in the South-east. There were for example 67 martyrs in London, 58 in Kent, 39 in Essex, 23 in Sussex and 18 in Suffolk. Only two took place north of the Trent and very few in the West or in Wales. Certainly

See pages 381–2

KEY ISSUE

How effective were Pole's policies?

Anabaptist Anabaptists were religious radicals who denied the need for infant baptism. It made it seem as though membership of the Church would therefore be voluntary, which was deemed deeply subversive. Both Catholics and Protestants were happy to see them burned.

PICTURE 19
*The execution of Latimer
and Ridley*

the zeal and effectiveness of the regime was greatest in the South-east
and there had been more Protestants there anyway.

The best-known deaths were of course those of Ridley and Latimer
in Oxford on 16 October 1555, and of Cranmer also in Oxford on 21
March 1556. In all 21 clergy died, but later victims tended to be hum-
bler: artisans, labourers, yeomen and husbandmen. Their courage too
impressed onlookers and Protestants became convinced that these must
be God's chosen.

How far can the Marian burnings be compared with persecution
before or since, either in England or abroad? It may be that mid-Tudor
England was less used to violence. After all, Henry VIII had put only 12
Protestants to death. Yet in France more died in the persecution of
Protestants from 1547 to 1550 than under Mary, and of course it was
ultimately the Protestants who wrote the received version of the events
of Mary's reign. John Foxe's best-seller *Acts and Monuments* (better
known as *Foxe's Book of Martyrs*) was published in 1563 and added significantly to an emerging English identity as a Protestant nation and to
the 'Black Legend' of Spanish wickedness.

See page 431

Protestants themselves did not disagree with the burning of heretics;
they quarrelled only with the definition of heresy. Indeed, among the
Protestant martyrs under Mary, Philpot and Rogers had both accepted
the need to burn Anabaptists. It also needs to be stressed that capital
punishment was a frequent occurrence in sixteenth-century England,
where no less than 700 were sentenced to hang after the 1569 Northern
Rebellion and where between 17 and 54 death sentences were handed
down annually in Essex alone in Elizabeth's reign, often for small-scale
theft.

About 800 Protestant men and women went into exile abroad to escape the persecution, most in Switzerland or Germany. The largest group were gentlefolk of which 166 have been identified, including Sir Francis Knollys and Sir Anthony Cooke. There were even two nobles: Francis, Earl of Bedford and Katherine, Duchess of Suffolk, who made a stately journey from her Lincolnshire seat to Gravesend accompanied by six servants. Of the rest, 67 were Protestant clerics, 119 theology students, 40 merchants, 32 artisans, seven painters and six 'professional men'. Among the women, 100 were wives accompanying their husbands, and 25 were women on their own; there were also 146 children and 45 servants. Few of the exiles were labourers or husbandmen, no doubt because of the substantial resources needed to go into foreign exile.

In the long run the exiles' prolonged and direct contact with the second generation of continental reformers, who were running their churches without bishops, contributed to religious debates in Elizabeth's reign. They also had plenty of time to ponder Protestant theories of political opposition applicable to English conditions.

See page 216

Finally, despite the persecution, quite a large Protestant underground remained in England. In London inns and private houses, congregations of up to 200 listened to preachers of the calibre of Scambler, Fowle, Rough, Bernher and Bentham, many of whom appeared on Elizabeth's first bench of bishops. There were also similar congregations as far afield as Sussex, Kent, Hertfordshire, Essex, Suffolk, Lincolnshire, Leicestershire and Lancashire. There were even a few open preachers, of whom the best known is George Eagles (alias 'Trudgeover') who roamed over East Anglia until his capture and execution in 1557 at Colchester. When Paget suggested to William Cecil that Mary's prospects were good, he replied, 'My Lord, you are therein so far deceived, that I fear rather an inundation of the contrary part, so universal a boiling and a bubbling I see'.

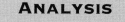

KEY ISSUE

What was the effect of the burnings?

What Had Been the Chances of Success in the Attempt to Restore England to Roman Catholicism?

ANALYSIS

Mary and her supporters had reasonably expected a full restoration of Catholicism, the one exception being a return of Church lands which the vested interests of their new owners, the aristocracy and the gentry, would never permit. However, in matters of faith, there was a widespread and genuine religious conservatism, which had hardly been touched by the Edwardian experiment in Protestantism. Most people shared an unintellectual and instinctive feeling for the familiar, traditional Catholic ritual and belief. Most people in 1553 anticipated, and indeed hoped for, some sort of restoration of Catholicism, most likely that kind which prevailed in Henry VIII's latter years.

Protestantism had its problems too. In England it was identified with faction, corruption and economic crisis, while on the continent it seemed to have shot its bolt. The first wave of reform was over: Luther died in 1547, and the Emperor Charles V's crushing victory over Protestant forces at Muhlberg in the same year subdued the adherents of reform. Moreover, the second wave of Reformation, that of Calvinism, could not yet be foreseen. Catholicism was meanwhile preparing itself to recover lost ground, as the Counter-Reformation proceeded, with new missionary orders founded, such as the Jesuits; doctrine and discipline renewed at a General Council of the Church, the Council of Trent, and a reformed Papacy. CSL Davies concludes, 'Far from Marian Catholicism being a symptom of hopeless, anachronistic reaction, as it may seem to us, to contemporaries it represented the flow of the current'.

However, in a reign that only lasted, in the event, for five years there was a limit to what Mary and her advisers could achieve to restore the Roman Catholic faith. Delays at the beginning of the reign meant that the effective period available was more like three years. Mary died childless and the throne passed to her half-sister, the Protestant Elizabeth.

It is however still doubtful whether, given more time, Mary could in fact have achieved more in religion, for few of those directing religious policy really understood contemporary English religious sentiment. Neither Mary herself nor her husband were ever really in touch, and Pole tended to think of the England that he had left in 1532. Despite more positive developments in the continental Counter-Reformation, which Pole himself had participated in, the tone of policy under Mary remained negative, lacking positive missionary zeal and failing to make use of native English spiritual or intellectual traditions. In any case, while in some churches the statues of saints were brought out of storage and put back in their place of honour, in others traditional Catholic cults had declined under Edward VI and could not easily be restored. Moreover, there was little compelling literary expression on the Catholic side and there was little money available in the difficult circumstances of the 1550s. Thus Mary's attempt to re-found the monasteries produced only 100 monks and nuns in six houses by 1557. Finally, Mary was left with most of the same clergy who had served under Edward VI, as even former married priests could officiate after putting their wives away and doing penance. There must have been many who were prepared to conform with every shift of religious flavour. If England was far from being a Protestant state in 1553, it was also far from being universally Catholic in 1558.

6 ∽ FOREIGN POLICY

The first half of Mary's reign saw England neutral in the great Habsburg–Valois conflict that had pitted France against Spain ever since Charles VIII's invasion of Northern Italy in 1494. These so-called 'Italian Wars' flared up into actual fighting from time to time, relieved by periodic truces, one being for five years solemnly agreed at Vaucelles in February 1556. In that year Philip II succeeded his father as King of Spain, Duke of Burgundy (which meant ruler of the Netherlands), ruler of much of Italy and a good deal else besides. In September 1556 Philip's armies under the Duke of Alva invaded the Papal States, provoking the furiously anti-Spanish Pope Paul IV to promise Naples to Henry II of France if he would help to drive Spanish forces out of Italy. By February 1557 war had resumed between France and Spain, and Philip looked to England for support, especially for naval supplies, funds and the presence of an English fleet in the Channel. Mary's Councillors, however, were anxious to avoid antagonising the French who were useful trading partners and who could stir up trouble for the English on the Scottish border, in Ireland or in the Pale of Calais.

See pages 60–3

Luckily for Philip, Henry II's tolerance of English Protestant exiles and his willingness to allow them to use France as a base from which to attack England, forced Mary into the war. The Dudley Conspiracy of 1556, when de Noailles, the French ambassador, encouraged Sir Henry Dudley to attack Yarmouth Castle in the Isle of Wight, was followed in 1557 by Thomas Stafford's voyage from France to Scarborough with arms provided by Henry. He declared himself 'Protector of England' before his defeat by the Earl of Westmorland. Stafford's escapade revived traditional English fears of French expansion northwards and made English participation in the war inevitable.

The omens for the war seemed good at first, especially as the 1557 harvest promised to be good after disastrous ones in 1555 and 1556. War also provided a chance to unite a divided realm, not least giving Protestants an opportunity to show their loyalty in service against a traditional enemy. Francis Russell, the second Earl of Bedford and a Wyatt conspirator, fought valiantly at the Battle of St Quentin in 1557, while others implicated in the Wyatt rebellion, such as Cuthbert Vaughan, Sir James Croft and Sir Peter Carew, also joined up. The most conspicuous example of loyalty was by the three surviving sons of the late Duke of Northumberland, Harry, Ambrose and Robert, who, pardoned in January 1555, all fought for Mary in France. Catholic and more neutral nobles were no less keen to serve, and Pembroke, Rutland, Montague, Shrewsbury, Westmorland, Clinton and Grey of Wilton all joined up for honour and profit.

In October 1555 Mary's navy was in a parlous state: she could deploy effectively only three warships, in contrast to the 21 which Henry VIII could command in 1547. By 1557 there were once again 21 men-of-war and five further ships, and during 1558–9 as much tonnage of shipping was built as during 1583–8, the height of the struggle against Spain. At the same time the administration of naval finances was entrusted to

Lord Treasurer Winchester, who with Benjamin Gonson, the Naval Treasurer, had from 1557 a regular peacetime allocation for the fleet's upkeep that varied between £14 000 and £20 000 per year. Elizabeth I was to be glad of the fleet that Mary left her for use in her Scottish campaign of 1560.

Prior to 1558 the recruitment of land forces was to be achieved by two methods: a feudal knights' levy and a national militia system, both of which had fallen into decay. Mary's Militia Act of 1558 required the ten newly appointed Lord-Lieutenants, JPs and Commissioners of Muster to raise a militia. Thus Mary laid the foundations of the Elizabethan military system.

War was declared on 7 June 1557, and on the same day Mary issued the following fulsome proclamation of war aims:

> Although we, the Queen, when we first came to the throne, understood that the Duke of Northumberland's abominable treason had been abetted by Henry, the French King ... we attributed these doings to the French King's ministers rather than to his own will, hoping thus patiently to induce him to adopt a truly friendly attitude towards us. More, we undertook heavy expenditures to send our ambassadors to assist in peace negotiations between him and the Emperor; but our labours met with no return from the King ... He has also favoured pirates, enemies of Christendom who have despoiled our subjects.
>
> We realise that nothing we can do will induce the King to change his methods. The other day he sent Stafford with ships and supplies to seize our castle of Scarborough, not content with having intrigued so long with a view to getting possession of Calais and other places belonging to us across the seas and having financed counterfeiters and encouraged them to put false coin into circulation in this country.
>
> For the above reasons, and because he has sent an army to invade Flanders, which we are under obligation to defend, we have seen fit to proclaim to our subjects that they are to consider the King of France as a public enemy to ourselves and to our nation, rather than suffer him to continue to deceive us under colour of friendship.
>
> We therefore command all Englishmen to regard Henry, the French King, and his vassals as public enemies of this kingdom and to harm them wherever possible, abstaining from trading or any other business with them. Although the French King has molested our merchants and subjects, without declaring war, we have seen fit to allow his subjects and merchants forty days to leave this kingdom with such property as the law permits them to export.

Q

1. *Comment on the tone adopted in this document towards the French King.*
2. *Are there any other war aims not mentioned here?*

Historians have usually seen the Anglo-French war of 1557–9 in a harsh light. For Elton it is 'the most disastrous of the century', while Tittler writes, 'it is hard to think of any subsequent English campaign which has resulted in less material gain and more loss of face'. However, there was success in a number of theatres, the navy performing particularly well. All French shipping was cleared out of the Channel, thus guarding Philip's supply lines to the Netherlands. Naval units also carried Pembroke and his army of 7000 across the Channel, and escorted the Atlantic fishing fleet, the Spanish bullion fleet and Sussex's expedition to Ireland. The Battle of St Quentin fought on 10 August 1557 was another success when Pembroke's detachment of 5000 English played their part in Philip's victory over the French. Finally the southwards march of the Scots, in support of the French, was halted by bad weather and divisions within the Scots army.

By the autumn of 1557 Philip seemed to have all northern France at his feet. It came as a shock therefore to hear the news of the French seizure of Calais and its hinterland on 1 January 1558 by the Duke of Guise. Thus France gained the last English enclave on the French coast, and not only the port of Calais itself, but also an area of land measuring 20 miles by 6 miles including the strategic forts of Guisnes and Hammes. Where then does the blame lie for such an unmitigated defeat? Certainly Wentworth, the English commander at Calais, and the Council must bear some of the responsibility for failing to reinforce the English garrison and for laying up the English fleet for the winter. However, there was by this stage a wider lack of enthusiasm for the war, shared even by Philip himself, leading to low morale. It may well be that sheer bad luck played a part too, and, possibly, treason.

How serious was the loss of Calais? The economic loss can be exaggerated, as the staple for cloth exports to the continent was already in decline, numbering only 150 merchants as long ago as 1540. Yet the loss to morale was considerable, and for Protestants the defeat symbolised the dire penalty imposed by God for Mary's rule and the hated Spanish link. When Mary died the conflict was not yet resolved. The war, which had been a rallying point for the nation to begin with, was far from that following the loss of Calais, and the recruitment system had proved sadly deficient.

KEY ISSUE

Is it correct to describe Mary's foreign policy as 'a complete disaster'?

7 ∾ MARY'S LEGACY

Mary died at St James' Palace on 17 November 1558; by coincidence Cardinal Pole died later the same day at Lambeth. She was childless, despite a phantom pregnancy and her ardent hopes for a child and heir following her marriage to Philip II. Shortly before her death Mary acknowledged Princess Elizabeth, thus confirming both the 1544 Succession Act and Henry VIII's will. She dreaded the accession of her Protestant half-sister, daughter of the hated Anne Boleyn, but the Act which had ensured she, Mary, would reign still commanded near universal respect, and Elizabeth was unequivocally next in line. In any case, the next claimant by blood may have been a Catholic, Mary, Queen of Scots, but she was married to the son and heir of Henry II of France, with whom England was still at war.

Since her death Mary has had a bad press. Protestant propagandists under Elizabeth vilified her, and Victorian historians followed suit, stressing the importance of the reign of Elizabeth as a restoration of English liberty. Hence both groups tended to see Mary's reign as an aberration in the even flow of English history, and presented it as an object lesson in the perils of Catholic and authoritarian rule.

There remain further difficulties in arriving at a balanced interpretation. Mary spent much time at the start of her brief reign establishing her regime, and her task was all the harder as she was attempting a sharp about-turn in religious policy. In short she had to reward supporters, deal with opponents and re-weave the nation's whole political fabric at the same time. In a sense, therefore, it is hardly fair to ask even whether there was a distinctive Marian regime, as it was still being formed in 1558. Elizabeth after all took ten years to create an identifiable Elizabethan regime.

For all that, it may be possible to see Mary as a strong monarch with a relatively successful Council and a fair grip on the administration of justice, even though many of her policies were unfinished or unfulfilled by 1558. Many of her measures were brought to fruition under Elizabeth: the search for new trade routes, coinage reform and the revival of the navy. Too often these have been held up as accomplishments solely of Elizabeth I's rule. At the same time Mary survived early threats to her authority and carried through several significant policies like her marriage, the return to Rome and the declaration of war. In fact she was defeated on only one main plank of her platform, namely her husband's coronation.

Despite all this, the bad press Mary has received is not without foundation. Pre-existing religious divisions deteriorated under her, and intolerance and xenophobia increased. Yet, in a curious way, Protestantism benefited from her reign. Under persecution, the reformed faith could prove its religious credentials while much of the blame was directed at foreign influence as a result of the Spanish marriage. Mary's reign ended just in time for a moderate Anglicanism to be possible, and her main legacy in religion may indeed be that she weakened and divided religious conservatism. Yet it remains probable that the main causes of her unpopularity lay outside religious policy. At the time of her death, the Spanish marriage and the French war cast a longer shadow than her religious persecution.

> **KEY ISSUE**
>
> *How far does Mary Tudor deserve her bad reputation?*

8 ↜ BIBLIOGRAPHY

**P Williams *The Later Tudors, England 1547–1603* (OUP, 1995), see Chapter 4. An inevitably brief survey in a magisterial work which, along with **CSL Davies *Peace, Print and Protestantism 1450–1558* (Paladin, 1977), pp. 291–316, are the best places to start. **R Tittler *The Reign of Mary I* (Longman, 1983) is the best short, specialist account of the reign, with useful documents, while **DM Loades *The Reign of Mary Tudor* (Benn, 1980) offers more detailed information. *J Loach (ed.) and R Tittler *The Mid-Tudor Polity* (Macmillan, 1980): see all chapters except Chapter 2. This comprises a useful collection of essays, with especially good coverage of the French war by CSL Davies. *C Haigh *English Reformations* (OUP, 1993) See Part III, chapter 12. This is a lively and polemical work by a leading revisionist of sixteenth century religious history. SJ Gunn *Early Tudor Government, 1485–1558* (Macmillan, 1995): use the index for Mary. It is useful for the key topic of administration throughout the Early Tudor period, if quite dry. **A Fletcher and D MacCulloch *Tudor Rebellions* (Longman, 1997) is the standard work on the risings, brought up to date in its fourth edition. N Heard *Edward VI and Mary: A Mid-Tudor Crisis?* (Hodder & Stoughton, Access to History 1990) is a useful examination of a once controversial theory, and designed for sixth-form study.

(*Recommended. **Highly recommended.)

9 ✎ STRUCTURED AND ESSAY QUESTIONS

A *Structured questions*

1. (a) What was achieved in administrative, economic and fiscal policy under Mary?
   (b) To what extent was Mary herself responsible for these achievements?
2. (a) What aspects of Catholicism did Mary try to restore?
   (b) Did religious or foreign policy contribute more to Mary's unpopularity?

B *Essay questions*

1. 'Her marriage to Philip of Spain was Mary Tudor's worst mistake.' Discuss.
2. Account for Mary's popularity in 1553 and her unpopularity in 1558.
3. How firmly was Protestantism established in 1553 and to what extent was it weakened by the policies of Mary Tudor?
4. How far can Mary Tudor's government be described as 'efficient but reactionary'?
5. What was Mary I's legacy to her successor?
6. 'Mary I proceeded cautiously, pursuing policies which showed her to be fully aware of the extent of religious turmoil which the English had experienced in the years before she came to the throne.' How far do you agree with this interpretation of Mary's religious policy?

Advice – discussion essays

Questions often ask a candidate to comment on a particular view of an individual's achievements or of a topic more generally. An example above is: ' "Her marriage to Philip of Spain was Mary Tudor's worst mistake." Discuss.'

In order to make a judgement you need to clarify other possible views. It may be that Mary's marriage was not so great a mistake after all. It may be that other mistakes were more significant. It would be best to break the question down into further questions to help you structure your answer:

- In what ways was the marriage a mistake?
- Insofar as it was ultimately a mistake, how fundamental an error was it? For example, how far was the marriage doomed to be a disaster, or how far was it later events which made it problematic?
- How far did the marriage bring benefits? How do these weigh against the problems it brought?
- What were Mary's other mistakes? How fundamental were they in comparison?

Having reviewed these questions, you will be in a position to decide broadly whether you agree or disagree with the view put forward in the question. In writing your answer, you will then be able to offer a clear argument one way or another, but rather than just agreeing or disagreeing, you will also be able to show you understand the strengths and weaknesses of alternative perspectives.

10 ⌐ EXERCISE: WAS THERE A MID-TUDOR CRISIS?

The idea that there was a 'crisis' in mid-sixteenth-century England, rather on the lines of the alleged seventeenth century crisis, does have some obvious appeal. Among historians who have suggested this perhaps the best known is WRD Jones who entitled his book published in 1973 The *Mid-Tudor Crisis, 1539 to 1563*. Jones detects a serious threat to the continuity, security and power of the Tudor monarchy in the combination during the period of severe difficulties in four main areas: the royal succession, religion, foreign policy and the economy.

There is no doubt that the period saw considerable dynastic problems for the Tudors. Edward VI succeeded as a minor of 10 years old and died before reaching his majority or producing an heir. His half-sister Mary seized the throne in 1553 in what many historians regard as the only successful rebellion during the period, but she died after only five years, failing to leave an heir. Finally Elizabeth acceded in 1558 as a young unmarried woman challenged by her cousin Mary Queen of Scots.

A study of religious developments reveals a similar whirlwind of changes. Henry VIII's 'Catholicism without the Pope' was rapidly altered under his son, as a more and more Protestant policy emerged under both Somerset and Northumberland. Mary reversed this trend dramatically and attempted a root and branch return to the old faith. Elizabeth tried to impose a moderately Protestant settlement in 1559. Religious fanaticism was a characteristic of the entire period and religious issues featured in several revolts. The Western Rebellion of 1549 was caused almost solely by religious changes, Kett's Rebellion had strong Protestant overtones, and so did Wyatt's Rebellion in 1554 – the only one of the three to mount a serious challenge to the government and dynasty.

In foreign policy Henry's military adventures against France and Scotland spilled over into Edward VI's reign. Much of the Crown's windfall profit from the Dissolution was squandered on warfare, and debasement of the coinage stoked the fires of inflation. Northumberland's pragmatic policy of financial restraint and appeasement of England's traditional enemies was reversed by Mary who embroiled England in a futile campaign against France that lost Calais and further discredited the already unpopular Spanish alliance.

Finally, serious economic problems exacerbated general poverty, and combined with natural hazards like poor harvests and disease to demoralise the mass of the population. Prices rose sharply, especially in foodstuffs, where costs doubled between 1540 and 1560. Rents also increased as landlords tried to escape from the inflationary spiral while manufacturing and exports declined, particularly in the vital cloth trade. Under these circumstances unemployment soared, and Professor Bindoff's 'dangerous corner' was reached with a series of disastrous harvests, especially those of 1555 and 1556 – the worst of the century. Influenza epidemics hit a population weakened by malnutrition and at the most conservative estimate no less than 6 per cent of the population died of disease between 1556 and 1560. Kett's Rebellion of 1549 stands out among a widespread network of revolts across southern England and the Midlands caused by economic and social grievances.

The crisis only came to an end, according to Jones, in 1563 when Elizabeth was beginning to establish herself on the throne following a successful religious settlement in 1559, the expulsion of the French from Scotland in 1560, and the introduction of a re-valued coinage in 1561. Meanwhile she embarked on a more cautious semi-isolationist foreign policy.

There are however substantial objections to this view, and it has to be said that few recent historians have been convinced by it. The crisis theory overlooks the fact that the government never lost control, even in 1549. This may have been partly because the two rebellions in 1549 had limited aims and did not intend to topple the government. The Council functioned effectively from 1540 despite undoubted factional turmoil from time to time. At the centre, ministers like Cecil, Paget, Gresham and Mildmay kept the show on the road, assisted in the provinces by the mass of JPs. The governing élites survived the most dangerous moment in 1553 when they decided to back Mary's legitimate descent rather than flirt with Northumberland's 'devise'.

If there was no real crisis for the authorities, what about the people? One wonders whether ordinary people were aware of a continuous crisis over the whole period, or even just between 1547 and 1558. Perhaps it is more reasonable to speak of a series of short-lived crises of the kind that may have been normal for any country at any time.

The foreign policy 'crisis' theory can also be challenged as there was never a real danger of foreign invasion, and even religious tensions can seem to look less threatening. There may well have been as much compromise as confrontation among the English élite in their approach to religion, and there can be little doubt that apathy and indifference to religious questions characterised the approach of many ordinary people to rival religious enthusiasms. The zealots on either side were a small minority.

AGR Smith is among contemporary historians who have been sceptical of the 'Mid-Tudor Crisis' idea. This is his conclusion:

> The death of Mary can be seen as marking the end – or the beginning of the end – of the 'mid-century crisis' of Tudor England. But should we talk in such apocalyptic terms? It may be that the application of the word 'crisis' to a period of at least eleven, and in the case of some historians (WRD Jones covers the period 1539 to 1563) of over twenty years, obscures as much as it illuminates. It seems essential at least to distinguish in discussion between the English people and the English state. There is obviously much to be said for the view that the middle decades of the century were a period of crisis (or perhaps better of crises) for the people of England. The years 1540–60 saw unprecedently rapid changes in the economy and in religion, arguably the two areas which affected most intimately the lives of ordinary Englishmen; historians are now emphasizing the profound psychological as well as material shocks which these upheavals must have meant for hundreds of thousands of men and women who had been accustomed to much less volatile conditions. It is doubtful, on the other hand, if the Tudor state was ever in quite as serious difficulties as the word 'crisis' implies. Between 1540 and 1558 the throne was occupied successively by a sick and rapidly ageing bully, a boy who was too young to rule and a woman of limited political abilities. In these circumstances what is significant and remarkable is not the weakness of government, but its relative strength. At no time during the period, except perhaps at the end of Somerset's Protectorate, was there a serious threat of the breakdown of administration, surely the fundamental test of a 'crisis' in the life of a state. The middle decades of the century certainly produced severe difficulties for the governments of the time, but the English State which Elizabeth inherited in 1558 was a fully functioning polity.

Q

1. *What do you understand by the word 'crisis'?*
2. *Summarise the case for the 'Mid-Tudor Crisis' in about 100 words.*
3. *Similarly give a summary of the case against the theory in about 100 words.*
4. *How far are the different aspects of the 'crisis' – dynastic, diplomatic and military, religious and social/economic – separate themes and how far are they inter-related? Look back over the previous two chapters to get ideas for this.*

Elizabeth I: The Government of England

8

Elizabeth I became one of England's most remarkable monarchs. Yet, when she ascended the throne in 1558 few, if any, could have anticipated her successes. Her kingdom was still at war with France, but her Exchequer was empty. The Crown had been weakened by the succession of a young boy, Edward VI, followed by a woman, 'Bloody Mary', who had become increasingly unpopular. Elizabeth herself was disadvantaged by her inexperience in government, and even by her gender.

Yet Elizabeth possessed formidable qualities which allowed her to wield authority effectively over her kingdom. Her personality mattered a great deal because, without a sizeable bureaucracy or standing army, the good governance of England depended on her management of the ruling classes. Elizabeth successfully presented herself to her subjects, great and humble, as a powerful monarch. She gathered round herself a Privy Council of sage and influential men to advise and assist her with the daunting responsibility of governing her realm. By and large, Elizabeth was well advised, by William Cecil in particular, yet she never relinquished her power to her Councillors. They were left with no illusions as to their subservient role within her system of government.

Elizabeth summoned Parliaments as infrequently as she could afford to. When Parliament was convened the Queen used it to bolster her government with financial subsidies and with its approval for her government's legislation. Elizabeth's Parliaments were strikingly co-operative with their Queen. Such rare occasions as parliamentarians dared to offer her advice about marriage, the succession or religion inevitably ended in failure. Elizabeth had no intention of surrendering her royal prerogatives to any subjects.

Elizabeth's subjects wished her to provide stable government and they co-operated with her to sustain it. That willingness to support the monarch was encouraged by propagandists, and the Church, but it was strongly reinforced by the skilful deployment of royal patronage to reward loyalty and good service. Though Elizabeth lost some of her popularity in the final, difficult decade of her reign, she succeeded in providing stable and effective government for her kingdom despite the challenges posed to good order by religious controversy, rebellions and hard-fought wars with Spain and with Irish confederates. Hers was no mean achievement.

See pages 319–20

PROFILE

PICTURE 20
Elizabeth I, *Nicholas Hilliard*

THE YOUNG ELIZABETH TUDOR

Elizabeth was only three years old in 1536 when her mother, Anne Boleyn, was executed at the instigation of her father. She never wrote or spoke about that traumatic event in her life, though one is tempted to suggest that it may have influenced her later decision not to marry. The young girl saw little of her father until 1542 when Henry VIII was belatedly reconciled with his daughters. In 1544 the King had them both formally restored to the royal succession, following their younger brother, Edward. Thereafter Elizabeth basked in her father's affection, and forgot his earlier neglect. She grew in confidence as the daughter of Henry VIII, and began to nurture an extraordinarily high opinion of her father and the God-given authority of the monarchy. She brought that remarkable confidence to the Crown when she became Queen in 1558. Contemporaries were struck by her self-belief and strength of will. She also had a formidable temper which intimidated anyone who ever dared challenge her.

The young Elizabeth was tutored by some of Cambridge's best graduates, most notably William Grindal and Roger Ascham. She was well taught and became a talented linguist, but she was not trained to be the monarch. It was accepted that Elizabeth would marry a foreign prince in due course. David Starkey has suggested one key formative influence on the young girl – her step-mother, Catherine Parr, acting as Regent while Henry VIII was engaged in war in France. That strikingly capable woman may have given Elizabeth a role model of a woman wielding authority over the greatest men in England. In the reign of her half-brother, Edward VI, the more negative lesson of the dangers involved in personal relationships among those close to the throne was reinforced. She lived with her step-mother, Catherine Parr, who was re-married to Thomas Seymour, brother of the Lord Protector. Seymour seems to have made sexual advances to the teenage princess, and there were rumours he had made her pregnant. This was held against him in his later trial for treason, and Elizabeth found her reputation tarnished.

The accession of Mary to the throne in 1553 brought Elizabeth herself closer to the possibility that one day she might be Queen. But Mary had her own mother's marriage declared valid, a move which invalidated Henry's second marriage, to Elizabeth's mother. Relations between the half-sisters cooled, though Elizabeth was politic enough to conform to the political and religious requirements of the Marian regime. She was, however, suspected of being involved with Wyatt's rebellion in 1554, and was sent to the Tower. It is likely that she knew that a rebellion was planned and had failed to report it, but nothing could be proved. Some of Mary's advisers wished to see her executed. but Mary held back. Elizabeth was moved from the Tower – terrified, believing that she was being taken to a place of execution – to be held under house arrest at Woodstock. There, denied writing materials, she scratched on a window pane with a diamond ring: 'Much suspected by me, Nothing proved can be, quoth Elizabeth prisoner'. After a year Elizabeth was released, and for the remainder of Mary's reign, she waited passively to see what fate held in store for her. She witnessed Mary's hopes for happiness in marriage, and children, being sorely disappointed. Then Mary died of cancer in November 1558. Elizabeth could be forgiven for seeing the hand of God in the events which brought her to the throne. Elizabeth's coronation, at the age of 25, was widely welcomed following her unpopular sister's death. Her right to rule was accepted by the vast majority of her subjects. She could also count on a reservoir of goodwill among her people. They wanted her to provide strong and stable government.

1 ⌐ THE MONARCH AS GOVERNOR

Elizabeth recognised the need to project the glory and splendour of the monarchy. Expenditure at Court and the size of its inner circle, the Household, were smaller than under Edward and Mary, out of financial necessity. But shrewd use of the money available meant that there was no decline in the opulence of the Tudor Court. The brilliance of the clothes, jewellery and tapestries and of the frequent tournaments, plays, pageants, banquets and other entertainments, the grace and charm of Elizabeth, the rigorous attention to etiquette, and the frequent attendance of the great aristocrats created an impression of royal magnificence among all who came into contact with the Queen and her Court. The fact that she went 'on progress' to most of Central and Southern England – although never to the North or West – exposed the glittering array to the gaze of a significant proportion of her people. And, of course, the courtiers carried to their localities news of the majesty which they associated with Elizabeth.

Poets praising the Queen as Gloriana or the goddess Astraea and a vast number of portraits of Elizabeth appearing in paintings, miniatures, medallions, woodcuts and engravings created 'the cult of Elizabeth'. Notwithstanding the propagandists, it was on her performance as the head of government that Elizabeth's success or failure ultimately depended. That performance was manifested in national policy, and subsequent chapters will assess the merits of her religious policy and foreign policy. Elizabeth had a large capacity for work and involved herself in the smallest details of government. This could annoy her ministers but it kept them on their toes and it developed in Elizabeth a considerable knowledge of every issue. She also possessed sound political judgement, though her most notable quality was her strength of character, which was the basis of her domination of the political system. She had vices, too: she could be unreasonable and self-centred, and her wilfulness often resembled blind obstinacy. Nevertheless,

See pages 393–8

it would be churlish indeed to deny that Elizabeth had the personal qualities of an effective ruler.

Elizabeth had a clear idea of her place within the English constitution. The Privy Council had an important and valued advisory role, but she asserted that the power to command was entirely hers. In contrast, humanist theory at this time was advancing the idea of the state being something separate from the ruler, and that the advice of the Council was something more than just optional advice; it limited the sovereignty of the ruler. William Cecil believed that; the Queen emphatically did not. (As John Guy comments: 'Historians have conventionally treated Elizabeth and Burghley [Cecil] as if they were two halves of a pantomime horse. The reality is that they were virtually different species'.) Cecil kept quiet about his views. Elizabeth had such a forceful, intimidating personality that no Councillor never dared to question her authority openly. Similarly, Elizabeth did not permit Parliament to make decisions on national affairs, and denied its right, with mixed success, even to discuss 'matters of state' without her consent.

In the early 1630s, Sir Robert Naunton recalled that:

> The principal note of … [Queen Elizabeth's] reign will be that she ruled much by faction and parties which herself both made, upheld, and weakened, as her own great judgment advised; for I dissent from the common received opinion that my lord of Leicester was absolute and above all in her grace … [When he presumed to threaten one of her officials with dismissal] she replied with her wonted oath (God's death!), my lord, I have wished you well but my favour is not so locked up for you that others shall not partake thereof; for I have many servants unto whom I have and will at my pleasure bequeath my favour and likewise resume the same. And if you think to rule here I will take a course to see you forthcoming. I will have here but one mistress and no master … which so quelled my lord of Leicester that his feigned humility was long after one of his best virtues …

On some points the Queen resisted clear majorities within the Council and Parliament, and would not change her course. The demands of the **Puritans**, many of them supported by her leading Councillors, never persuaded her to alter the religious settlement of 1559. Her deep suspicion of rebels and instinctive resistance to any proposals of war delayed for many years England's joining the Dutch rebels against Spain, despite a clear majority in the Council. The following examples of Elizabeth's strength are drawn from an area in which her jealous protection of the royal prerogative was probably most complete: the related questions of the succession, Mary, Queen of Scots and her marriage.

In October 1562, Elizabeth nearly died of smallpox, raising the spectre of civil war in the event of a disputed succession. She came under intense pressure to name her successor, but Elizabeth knew that men could rally to the nominee, and might even plot treason to secure an early succession. She told the Commons:

Q

1. *What light does Naunton throw upon the personality of Elizabeth?*
2. *Why was it important that Elizabeth's 'favour' should not be given to one man but to her 'many servants'?*
3. *Why must one question Naunton's reliability when he relates a story which promotes the idea of Elizabeth's greatness?*

Puritans those who wished to make the Church of England and English society more completely Protestant

> I am well acquainted with the nature of this people; ... I know what
> nimble eyes they bear to the next succession ... When my sister Mary
> was Queen, what prayers were made by many to see me placed in her
> seat ... Now then, if the affections of our people grow faint ... In how
> great danger shall I be ...? Assuredly, if my successor were known to
> the world, I would never esteem my state to be safe.

In spite of strong pressure year after year from her Councillors,
successive Parliaments, and the nation at large, Elizabeth never gave her
decision on the issue. It was a remarkable example of her obdurate
strength.

In 1567 Mary, Queen of Scots, was deposed. Indignant at the liberties taken by the Scots with a fellow monarch, Elizabeth protested
vigorously against Mary's imprisonment and dethronement, without
reference to her Council which for the most part welcomed Mary's fall.
The Scottish Queen's arrival in England in 1568 to seek refuge raised
problems, though, from the beginning. She was suspected of plotting
against Elizabeth, but Elizabeth refused even to agree to a Bill to bar her
from the English succession. In fact, only Elizabeth's determination to
protect her cousin stood between Mary and the scaffold. Elizabeth did
not wish to set the uncomfortable precedent for the execution of a
monarch. Thereafter, Mary figured prominently, though for the most
part passively, in the treasonous plans of English Catholics and their
Spanish, French and papal allies. It took irrefutable proof of Mary's
complicity in the Babington Plot of 1586 to destroy Elizabeth's resolve,
after almost 20 years, and permit the Council to decide the issue, which
led to Mary's execution in 1587. However, although she signed the
death warrant, it was despatched without her consent and she flew into
a great rage when she found out – although perhaps relieved that she
could not be held fully responsible for the execution of a fellow
monarch. Though ultimately defeated on this, the affair as a whole
bears eloquent testimony to her dominant role in the decision-making
process.

See page 254 for
Walsingham's role in this

MARY, QUEEN OF SCOTS (1542–87)

PROFILE

Mary became Queen when only a week old, on the death of her
father James V. Her mother, the French aristocrat Mary of Guise,
arranged for her to marry the Dauphin, the son and heir of King
Henry II of France, and at the age of five Mary was taken to France
where she grew up. The following years were unsettled in Scotland
as the Reformation took hold there; and there was much political
conflict between the leading Scottish nobles and Mary of Guise, as
she struggled to maintain control with the help of her French relations. In 1559 Henry II was killed in a tournament, so Mary, by
now married to the Dauphin, became Queen of France. She was
also, since the death of Mary Tudor and the accession of Elizabeth,

the next in line to the throne of England, through her grandmother Margaret, Henry VIII's sister. Her French husband, Francis II, however, died the following year, so in 1561 Mary returned to her Scottish kingdom.

She was French by culture, Catholic in religion, and impulsive in personal relationships. This was to be explosive politically in Scotland, although she maintained stability to begin with by recognising the Protestant religious settlement which had been established in her absence and supported by English force of arms. As with Elizabeth, the question of her marriage became a dominating political issue, although she made a mistake which her cousin never did, and married a handsome nobleman, Lord Darnley, in 1565. As well as being sexually attractive, he was prone to jealousy, arrogant and a drunk. In 1566 with a group of other restless noblemen, he broke into the Queen's apartments and murdered her secretary, David Riccio, whom he suspected of adultery with her. The Queen was pregnant and gave birth to the future King James of Scotland and England three months later.

She by now hated Darnley and took the unstable, but again attractive, Earl of Bothwell as her lover. Early the following year, the house in which Darnley was staying was blown up; he was found in the garden, presumably trying to escape, and had been strangled. It was assumed Bothwell was the murderer, but this did not prevent Mary from marrying him soon afterwards. A rebellion ensued, and Mary was captured and forced to abdicate in favour of her son, James. In May 1568 Mary escaped from the castle where she had been held on an island in Lochleven (her charm had overcome her jailer) and raised support to try and regain power. She failed and fled to England.

For the next 19 years, her cousin Elizabeth held her under house arrest; they never met. There was proof, in the form of the so-called Casket Letters, that Mary had been complicit in the murder of Darnley. She also became the willing centre of numerous plots and schemes to depose Elizabeth and put her on the throne of England, from the Ridolfi Plot in 1571 to the Babington Plot uncovered in 1586. Elizabeth, however, resisted all advice, particularly pressed on her by her more Protestant Councillors, to put Mary on trial. She had no wish to set the precedent of putting a sovereign queen on trial. Only when war with Spain made Mary potentially far more dangerous as a Catholic alternative to Elizabeth, and also when Elizabeth's indefatigable spy-master Walsingham had at last gathered incontrovertible proof against Mary, did a trial take place. Mary was convicted and executed at Fotheringhay in 1587.

Elizabeth's marriage and child-bearing would have solved many of these problems. The inevitability of the Queen's marriage was generally taken for granted in the first decade of the reign. Mary's experience with Philip showed that the English would not easily accept a foreign king, and the choice of an Englishman would provoke jealousy. Also, Elizabeth clearly feared that a husband would detract from her power. ('I will have here but one mistress and no master.') As early as the mid-1560s, she may have decided to remain single; after this, she reaped the diplomatic benefits of courtships with foreign princes, but she did not intend to complete the process. The candidature of Austria's Archduke Charles was favoured by Norfolk, Sussex and Cecil, but Elizabeth found it easy, in December 1567, to latch onto the Protestant scruples of the Leicester circle to reject the suit. There were subsequent discussions about marriage to two French princes, brothers to the King – the Duke of Anjou in 1570–2, and in 1578–82 the Duke of Alençon (also known as Anjou after his succession to his brother's title). The early proposals got nowhere principally owing to the Queen's lack of serious intent, despite the efforts on the first occasion of a significant portion of her Council. There was also the sticking point of religion, given that the most influential suitors were Catholics and insisted on continuing in their religion after marriage.

See pages 251–3

Elizabeth only treated the final proposal by the (second) Duke of Anjou, under discussion from 1578 to 1582, with any seriousness. Anxious for an alliance with France, and in her mid-40s apparently enjoying the romantic possibility of the match, she alarmed many Protestants that she was going to bring what they saw as the contagion of Catholicism back into England with this husband. One Protestant pamphleteer, Stubbes, went too far in attacking the Queen's marriage policy. Against all advice she insisted his hand be cut off as a punishment and savage warning to any others who might meddle. But the marriage negotiations collapsed nonetheless, to the relief of the more Protestant Councillors who had been behind much of the public agitation, and from that time the image of the Virgin Queen really took hold.

Elizabeth was no autocrat. She could not govern without the co-operation of the propertied classes, and both the Privy Council and Parliament had indispensable roles. However, the institutions of government existed more to serve than to restrict her power.

> ### KEY ISSUE
> *How successfully did Elizabeth establish her personal authority?*

2 ⌐ PATRONAGE

Elizabeth governed England through the voluntary efforts of the men of substance. To reward loyal service the Crown had at its disposal a vast array of patronage: a large number of offices in the legal system, the Church, the armed forces, the central bureaucracy, local administration, and at Court; honours such as peerages and knighthoods; favourable treatment regarding the payment of taxes and debts; the capacity to sell or lease Crown lands cheaply (though Elizabeth gifted very little land); customs farms, licences and monopoly rights; pensions and annuities.

The Queen sought to satisfy the aspirations of as many substantial figures as possible. The 200 positions at Court, for the most part, had more to do with securing loyalty and gratitude than with administration. At the lower levels, patronage might yield a modest income, along with status and the ability to use one's position to assist friends and neighbours. For a few, it meant a great deal more. Most Crown appointments carried poor pay. The Secretary of State received £100 a year, the Attorney-General £13 6s 8d, and the Solicitor £10. But official positions also yielded set fees for business completed, and gifts and gratuities from those who depended upon one's decisions. Gratuities were essentially bribes, but were regarded by society as due payment for services rendered, and were indispensable in view of the pitifully low official salaries. Only in the 1590s, when the expense of war meant that royal patronage flowed less freely, and inflation ate into other sources of income, did wholesale corruption set in.

Robert Cecil used his position as Master of the Court of Wards to extract £3000 a year, of which only £233 was made up of his official salary. Additionally, the successful courtier might hope for other forms of patronage like a **monopoly** or a **customs farm**. Great wealth was attainable. Under Elizabeth, the Dudleys re-emerged to claim a vast fortune, and the Cecils rose from the ranks of the gentry to become a great aristocratic dynasty. Many others made considerable if less spectacular fortunes.

The Queen derived much advantage from the patronage system. Loyal and reliable men could be placed in sensitive positions in every aspect of government and part of the country. The receipt of favour created gratitude and dependence. Hopeful suitors were respectful, flattering (Elizabeth craved outlandish praise), and generous with their New Year gifts. However, there were problems too. For patronage reasons, men were given **sinecures**. Others either neglected their duties or delegated them to deputies who were not accountable officials. Inevitably, the prevalence of favour, gratuities and other inducements meant that many decisions appeared unjust. Many wardships, for instance, were granted to anyone prepared to pay Robert Cecil for the privilege of extorting the wealth of the ward. Frequently, ability failed to secure appointments, a situation which not only blighted the careers of talented men but also acted to the detriment of royal administration.

The men who acquired influence over the Queen's distribution of patronage acquired also legions of expectant or grateful friends. As Neale wrote, 'Success not only meant money: it meant power. On it depended the quality and size of a statesman's faction – his entourage of household servants, followers and clients, thronging his chamber and constituting a minor court within the Court proper. The world saw his greatness reflected therein'. When Dudley won the Queen's affection, 'Men of all ranks turned to him to obtain personal favours from the Queen'. On the other hand, he who could no longer influence the flow of patronage stood to lose much; as the Earl of Essex complained towards the end of the reign when he failed to secure favour, 'Who will be desirous to come under a roof that threateneth ruin?'. His loss of the valuable customs farm for sweet wines and failure to gain the Mastership of the Court of Wards against Robert Cecil, inflicted both humilia-

Monopoly the sole right to sell a commodity or service, and so make a handsome profit by pushing up the price

Customs farm the right to collect customs duties on a particular commodity, and to retain any surplus beyond the fixed sum required by the Exchequer

Sinecure a post in government or (originally) the church without any duties

tion and bankruptcy on Essex. In 1601 he was to launch a revolt which cost him his life. Thus it may be seen that men's 'greatness', and political alliances, rose and fell according to the Queen's decision as to whom she allowed a say in the distribution of patronage.

The patronage question provoked much bitterness and jealousy throughout society. For example, the Percy family's exclusion from important positions during the 1560s created the anger which, far more than their Catholicism, led to rebellion, the Northern Rising in 1569. During the later years of the reign Elizabeth, pressed by the expense of war, greatly increased the number of monopolies to raise income. The monopolists raised the prices for many goods and services, making large profits, but consumers were outraged, the Queen's popularity suffered, and the monopolies debate in 1601 led to a unique Commons victory over the Crown.

In sum, for all the benefits patronage brought the Crown, the dangers were also considerable. Any system which often distributed great prizes according to personal whims was bound to cause difficulty. In the hands of a young, inexperienced Queen, as in her excessive favour for Leicester, and finally in the hands of a monarch in decline, as the Essex crisis shows, much damage could be inflicted. However, in the intervening years of stability, Elizabeth's judicious and even-handed approach to the distribution of patronage was not the least of her virtues.

See pages 324–6

See pages 321–4

> **KEY ISSUE**
>
> *Why was patronage necessary and in what ways could it pose problems?*

3 ⌇ THE PRIVY COUNCIL

After the fall of Thomas Cromwell in 1540, the Council was expanded to include both ministers and aristocrats chosen in acknowledgement of their status as great men in the localities. Elizabeth returned to the Cromwellian idea of a smaller, working body. She felt that 'a multitude doth make rather discord and confusion than good counsel'. Her first Council had only 19 members. That it contained several aristocrats, some of them moderate Catholics, indicates that Elizabeth did not or could not entirely forsake the benefits of a Council which represented influence and opinion. Such men would give her government more stature and authority and help her to govern their counties. Still, her priority was a Council of professional administrators, selected for their competence and reliability.

Almost immediately an inner ring of fewer than ten such people emerged, the others seldom attending. Later, the aristocrats ceased to be members, death rather than dismissal claiming a majority. In the 1590s, the membership sank at one point to as low as nine, and the regular attendance to four or five. The eleven-member Council of 1597 and the thirteen-member Council of 1601 each had only one member who did not hold ministerial office. The virtual exclusion of the aristocrats illustrates the self-confidence of the regime, but Christopher Haigh has suggested that the Council thereby became 'dangerously narrow and weak in its membership'.

PROFILE

PICTURE 21
William Cecil, Lord Burghley

WILLIAM CECIL, LORD BURGHLEY (1520–98)

William Cecil was, arguably, the most important man in Elizabethan England. Educated at Cambridge University and Gray's Inn, he entered the service of the Duke of Somerset and became a Privy Councillor under the Duke of Northumberland in 1550. Cecil was already known to Princess Elizabeth and she made him the surveyor of her estates, also in 1550. Cecil retired from high office during Queen Mary's reign, but he became a member of Elizabeth's inner circle. In November 1558, on her accession to the throne, Elizabeth appointed him as her Secretary of State and a Privy Councillor. In 1561 she also made Cecil the Master of the Wards of Court.

Queen Elizabeth valued Cecil greatly for his wise counsel and his prodigious capacity for hard work. As Principal Secretary, Cecil was the Queen's chief adviser and controlled all written access to the Queen. He was expected to deal with all matters of state. Thanks to his experience of government under Somerset and Northumberland Cecil knew the business of government inside out and helped to get Elizabeth's reign off to a successful start.

Cecil exerted tremendous influence over Queen Elizabeth, so much so that some contemporaries mistakenly assumed that he was the power behind the throne. In fact, however, his power always rested on his abilities to persuade the Queen as to what was in the national interest. He played a key role in Elizabeth's Scottish policies, favouring the Scottish Protestants against Mary, Queen of Scots, despite Elizabeth's reluctance to support rebels challenging a lawful Queen. On occasion Cecil used Parliament as an instrument to persuade a hesitant Queen to follow his advice, as happened in the events leading to the execution of the Queen of Scots.

Cecil's influence over the Queen was challenged for a time in the 1560s by the Earl of Leicester, but Elizabeth realised that he was indispensable to the effective government of her realm. He co-ordinated the Privy Council, supervised the Exchequer and Court of Wards and managed Parliament for the Queen. In 1571 Elizabeth promoted him to be Lord Burghley. In 1572 she made him the Lord High Treasurer, an office he held until his death. Cecil continued to ensure that the Elizabethan government functioned effectively. Though he struggled with increasingly poor health, he helped to ensure that England had the financial resources necessary to wage war successfully with Spain and conquer Ireland, despite the tremendous challenge posed to English rule by the 2nd Earl of Tyrone. Burghley played a decisive role in ensuring the successes achieved by his monarch, Elizabeth, before he died in 1598.

The vast majority of Elizabeth's first Council had earlier experience of high office. Some had served Henry and Edward, and ten of the nineteen had been on Mary's last Council. However, this understates the extent of the change wrought in 1558–9. Mary's principal adviser, Paget, was dismissed. William Cecil, the new secretary, was his effective replacement. The strongest Catholics were omitted. The balance shifted in favour of pragmatic Protestants like Cecil, flanked by the more radical Francis Knollys and Bedford and moderate conservatives like Winchester, Arundel, Shrewsbury and Derby. Few of the conservative Councillors (Lord Treasurer Winchester being the main exception) entered the inner circle of active ministers and none survived beyond 1572, and only two new conservatives (Croft in 1566 and Worcester in 1601) were appointed. In sum, Elizabeth's Council, especially the active element, was very much her own creation, and its Protestantism indicates that the change from Mary's Council was more than a simple matter of personnel.

During his 40 years in office as Secretary of State and then Lord Treasurer, Cecil was the Queen's most influential and reliable adviser, but he was never able to monopolise Elizabeth's favour. His greatest rival was Robert Dudley (Earl of Leicester from 1564). Though Leicester lacked ministerial office – he had only minor Household posts, as Master of the Horse and Lieutenant of Windsor Castle – he was a major political force until his death in 1588. He tried in the early years of the reign to win Elizabeth's hand in marriage, against Cecil's judgement, and their rivalry was subsequently aggravated by the difference between Cecil's moderate Protestantism and Leicester's incautious radicalism. Elizabeth's Councils included only one clergyman, Archbishop Whitgift. Initially, this probably owed much to the steadfast Catholicism of the Marian bishops she inherited, but the pattern persisted. Elizabeth's preference for active ministers over representatives of specific interests was a factor in that. Yet it may also have reflected the diminished stature of the post-Reformation Church.

A *Shaping national policy*

The Council acted as an advisory body to the Queen, taking the initiative, generally, in proposing policy. She normally took no part in the Council's discussions but received the Council's views and made a decision. Elizabeth also sought and accepted advice from people who were not Councillors at all. However, the Council was the Queen's most important source of advice.

Elizabeth respected the views of the extremely able men she appointed. And they were capable of presenting their views persuasively and diplomatically. In 1559, Cecil's arguments induced a reluctant monarch to help the Scottish Protestants to drive out the French. When Mary first arrived in England, in 1568, Elizabeth's first instinct was to help her regain the throne of Scotland. But Cecil's expression of the danger posed by a restored Mary and constant emphasis on Mary's possible guilt in the murder of her husband, as well as his secret encouragement of the Scottish Regent Moray and the Scottish Protestants to oppose restoration, checked Elizabeth (even before Mary betrayed her trust by plotting secretly to marry the Duke of Norfolk and, later, to have Elizabeth deposed).

When the Queen proved difficult to persuade, her Privy Councillors found various means to influence her. They could be skilful manipulators of public opinion. In 1560 there emerged the prospect of Elizabeth marrying Robert Dudley (Earl of Leicester from 1564). Many, however, were alarmed that, as her husband, Dudley would achieve a monopoly of influence and favour, and might even appropriate the powers of the monarchy. An explicit opposition to the marriage would have infuriated Elizabeth – she imprisoned two courtiers for their criticism. So Cecil encouraged a rumour that Dudley was plotting to poison his wife, Amy Robsart. Amy's mysterious death in September 1560 seemed to confirm the story and meant that a marriage would provoke popular outrage. It may also have been Cecil who made public in 1561 Dudley's plan to win Philip II's support for the marriage by pledging the restoration of Catholicism; causing an outcry which was fatal for Dudley's ambitions.

Councillors were often responsible for Parliament's more agitated endeavours, notably on marriage and the succession. In fact, the tendency of Councillors to manipulate information went even further: most of the correspondence sent to the Queen was received by Cecil as secretary, enabling him to keep it from her, prepare an appropriate interpretation, choose the moment of presentation, or solicit a contrary view.

The eventual fate of Mary, Queen of Scots shows that the Council could make decisions in areas where Elizabeth's will was not clearly expressed. In July 1586, Mary (allegedly) dictated the infamous letter in which she endorsed Babington's plot to murder Elizabeth, but the letter was intercepted. Mary was tried by a special commission, found guilty, and sentenced to death. Elizabeth, however, hated the idea of killing a fellow monarch so Walsingham was driven to fabricating the 'Stafford Plot' to show Elizabeth that her life remained in danger as long as Mary lived. In the end, the decision to despatch the warrant for her execution was taken by the Privy Council, and Elizabeth was informed after the deed was done on 7 February 1587. Her fury had no lasting effect, except on the ruined career of the scapegoat, the second Secretary William Davison.

The Council intervened constantly in the making of policy. However, the execution of Mary was unique; it was the only major decision made by the Council against the Queen's wishes. It was Elizabeth who made the decisions on national policy, even against the wishes of those who surrounded her. The Council had a significant role, but there is no disputing the primacy of the monarch.

KEY ISSUE

How significant was the role of the Privy Council in government?

B *Faction*

Elizabeth's Council was rarely a united body. Conflict was endemic as councillors struggled to win the Queen's favour. The honour and glory associated with a leading role in government was one incentive to competition, but control of patronage was the major prize in this political game. Policy differences also arose, though it is not always possible to separate support of a policy from the quest for favour. Leicester's backing of the Huguenots in 1562 probably owed much to his desire to match Cecil's earlier Scottish triumph; but one cannot be sure. In 1569–70, there was a concerted attempt by numerous Councillors to destroy Cecil; partly from resentment of the secretary's hold on Elizabeth's favour, and partly from the conviction that his foreign policy was placing the country in great danger. The long dispute between Cecil and Leicester on the issue of intervention in the Dutch Revolt against Philip II probably marked a genuine difference on policy; but it began as, and remained primarily, a competition for favour.

Men naturally formed alliances in the course of these disputes, but these were fluid and unstable, and historians have characterised them as factions, although even that might suggest too much continuity from issue to issue. In 1568, Norfolk was Cecil's friend and the bitter rival of Leicester; within a year he was Leicester's ally in the drive to depose Cecil. By retaining the Queen's confidence, Cecil moved from friendless isolation in 1569 to general approval in 1572. Politics which placed more emphasis on the distribution of spoils than on principle were incapable of generating lasting alliances.

Elizabeth never gave exclusive power to any single individual or faction. Whether she deliberately encouraged difference, according to the principle of 'divide and rule', is debatable. On numerous occasions she sought to resolve differences to achieve a working relationship between rivals. Yet the existence of so much conflict strengthened her hand, helping her to dominate. She sometimes appointed men of opposing factions and varying views; for example, Norfolk and Dudley were admitted to the Council together in October 1562, and Archbishop Whitgift was one of several moderate Councillors nominated in 1586 to balance the aggressively Protestant Leicester and Walsingham. Such men competed for her favours, and the Queen was able to receive varying advice, allowing her to make decisions which had the support of at least part of the Council, as, for instance, when the concurrence of Cecil, Sussex and a few others helped her to resist the pressure from a majority for intervention in the Dutch Revolt.

A Council united against her would have been a formidable prospect, but her Councillors were too ready to devour each other in order to achieve purely personal goals. In any case Elizabeth would have crushed completely any such attempt to undermine her royal prerogative.

KEY ISSUE

Did faction hinder effective government?

C *Executive role*

Councillors were more free to make decisions in the administrative role which claimed most of their attention. The Council was involved in the minutiae of everyday life to a remarkable degree. Elton cites one typical day on which 'the Council considered the Catholic Lady Stonor's house

Recusants those who refused to attend the services of the Church of England

arrest, trade with Spain, a minor land dispute in Guernsey, a poor man's complaint against the Bishop of Hereford, various matters connected with **recusants**, the report that a man had spoken in favour of [the Jesuit] Edward Campion, a land dispute between the Earls of Northumberland and Bedford, a merchant's losses through Turkish pirates, Sir Peter Carew's debts, seven passports to foreign vessels released from embargo, and the provision of post horses for a messenger'. On other occasions, the Council discussed such trivial matters as the cost of a pond in St James' Park and the alleged use of lewd words by a man from Sussex.

It would appear that no aspect of life was beyond the scope of the Council. Served by only a few clerks, it issued a constant and extraordinarily varied stream of orders to officials great and small in the provinces. It also supervised the Queen's accounts and authorised every act of expenditure by the Exchequer. In the 1580s, the campaign to suppress Catholicism saw the Council discussing the fate of hundreds of individuals. From 1585, the war against Spain was organised by the Council, a massive undertaking which included training of the militia, production of munitions, the building of ships and recruitment of privateers, and decisions about individual military operations.

The Council also had a quasi-judicial role. It investigated many crimes, especially those, like treason, sedition and popular disorder, which threatened the security or stability of the state. In addition, disputes between private individuals were often brought before the Council.

Such a centralised system imposed an enormous burden of work on the Council. In the early years, the Councillors usually gathered three times a week, in either the morning or the afternoon. Towards the end of the reign, with the war in particular adding greatly to its duties, the Council met almost every day, including Sundays, often all day. That this overloaded system yielded efficient government is eloquent testimony to the commitment and ability of the Councillors.

KEY ISSUE

How well did the Privy Council cope with the burden of business?

Cecil's role was pivotal. He was also the secretary of the Council. He procured information, set the Council's agenda, and took responsibility for the dissemination and enforcement of its decisions – across the whole, extraordinary range of the Council's business. When he became Lord Treasurer in 1572, it would appear that his involvement in administrative detail became only marginally less close and pervasive – possibly at the expense of the attention which Crown finances sorely required.

4 ⌐ ROYAL FINANCES

The Crown's finances were supervised and even administered by the Council as a whole and not merely by the finance ministers (namely the Lord Treasurer, his Chancellor of the Exchequer, and the Under-Treasurer). Elizabeth embraced the need for economy. Expenditure was kept on a tight rein. There was virtually no building; bureaucracy was not expanded; official salaries were more or less frozen at their low levels; the Household was reduced and compelled to cut its spending; gifts and pensions were much less freely given than before or after; and courtiers were instead rewarded with wardships and monopoly rights. And, of course, for most of her reign Elizabeth avoided the crippling expense of war. Not surprisingly, then, critics of the Elizabethan record on finance have not faulted her on expenditure.

Under Elizabeth, ordinary revenue increased from about £200 000 a year to about £300 000, keeping pace with inflation. With the tight control of expenditure, the Treasury was able to record a large annual surplus on the ordinary account, pay off the substantial debts (£227 000) left by Mary, and produce an accumulated cash reserve of £300 000 by 1585. Small wonder that, in 1576, Chancellor of the Exchequer Sir Walter Mildmay exultantly told the Commons that,

> Her Majesty hath most carefully delivered this Kingdom from a great and weighty Debt, wherewith it hath long been burdened. By means whereof the realm is not only acquitted of this great burden … but also her Majesty's credit thereby both at home and abroad [is] greater than any other Prince for money, if she need have, and so in reason it ought to be, for that she hath kept promise to all men, wherein other Princes have often failed to the hindrance of many.

Q

1. *Why might the Commons in particular need to be persuaded of Elizabeth's financial prudence?*
2. *In what way was Mildmay's statement influenced by the fact that Philip II had gone bankrupt in 1575?*

Elizabeth's most impressive financial achievement was the funding of the great war against Spain, from 1585, and of the hard-fought struggle (1593–1603) to complete the conquest of Ireland. In 1600 alone, Ireland consumed £320 000 out of a total expenditure of £459 840. To cope, spending in all other areas was reduced. Notably, there was a more systematic exploitation of **purveyance**. And there was a great increase in the granting of monopoly rights. Crown land worth over £600 000 was sold, including virtually all of the remaining monastic property. Parliamentary taxation was requested more frequently. Forced loans were imposed. Privateers who attacked Spanish shipping had to share the booty with the Crown. Local rates were imposed to build fortifications and prepare the militia, and **ship money** was demanded ever more widely and farther inland. In the end, Elizabeth bequeathed a debt of only £350 000 – given the financial pressures on her, a highly creditable sum achieved without having recourse to an inflationary debasement of the coinage.

All, however, was not as well as this overview suggests. Such a superficial account disguises some less palatable realities. During the reign, the overall rate of inflation was roughly 75%, but land incomes rose by only 25%, to £100 000 a year, and customs revenue barely rose at all, holding at around £90 000. The government failed to increase rents or duties in line with inflation, and land sales depleted that source of

Purveyance the Crown's right to buy goods for the royal Household at below market price

Ship money a tax originally on coastal areas for their defence

revenue. In addition, wardships yielded only a fraction of the income achieved from them in the next century. There were various forms of Crown debt which favourites were allowed to leave unpaid; thus Leicester and Winchester headed a long list with unpaid debts of £35 000 and £34 000 respectively.

The rise in the ordinary revenue mentioned earlier is attributable to such measures as diligent collection of debts (those of favourites excepted), fining recusants, and exploiting the revenues of vacant dioceses (no bishop was appointed to Oxford for 32 of the 45 years of the reign). These measures merely staved off the problems posed by inflation and the failure to act boldly on Crown rents and customs duties.

Parliamentary taxation – primarily 'subsidies' assessed on property and income – yielded about £2.5 million during the reign, a massive sum. According to custom, parliamentary taxation was to be requested only in times of war, revolt, or other extraordinary need. In normal times, the Crown's ordinary revenue was expected to suffice. Increasingly, this was an outdated idea which ignored the difficulty of meeting the rising cost of everyday government. Elizabeth frequently secured subsidies during the years of peace, and used some of the receipts for ordinary, non-military expenditure. This might have been the fundamental reform of Crown revenue which was needed, had it been undertaken systematically.

Parliamentary taxation was not efficiently administered. The collectors (subsidy commissioners) were often negligent or corrupt. Records of ownership were allowed to fall hopelessly out of date, leaving many potential payers untaxed. Above all, tax assessments were made on the basis of the payer's unsworn declaration, inviting under-valuation. The Council complained of 'the notable and evident abasing and diminution of many men's values heretofore in their assessments under all reasonable proportions, specially of men of the better state of livelihood and countenance'. Lord Burghley, the Lord Treasurer, was a prime offender, declaring an annual income of £133 6s 8d when his real income was about £4000. Consequently, without adjusting for inflation, the subsidy fell from £140 000 at the start of the reign to £80 000 at the end. This meant that subsidies had to be requested in multiples, making them psychologically less acceptable than taxes adjusted automatically to inflation.

In sum, Elizabeth and her ministers allowed the financial position of the Crown to weaken and did not attempt the reforms necessary to avoid the problem. Any conceivable policy to increase government revenue would inevitably have alienated many. In particular, tenants on Crown lands and merchants would have resented increases in rents and customs duties. The propertied classes in general would have objected to an abandonment of the idea that parliamentary taxation was acceptable only in extraordinary circumstances, and they would not have welcomed revision of the assessments. The result of reform would probably have been conflict with Parliament and obstructionism in the provinces. Nevertheless, the boldness of Henry VIII and Cromwell might have cured the ills rather better than the caution and conservatism of Elizabeth and William Cecil.

Able to employ little more than a thousand professional bureaucrats, the Crown relied upon unpaid volunteers in the provinces and, within the departments of state, on the personal servants of the officials. Their lack of direct accountability hardly ensured faultless government, but the system of rule still worked reasonably well. More serious, perhaps, were the implications for defence and foreign policy. The defences of the country were severely undermined, leaving it perpetually vulnerable. Elizabeth might have acted earlier to check the threat from Spain, had financial constraints not dictated a passive policy.

Not surprisingly, the internal politics of the country were put under strain as the government sought ways out of its difficulties. The need to employ such extraordinary measures as ship money created discontent. It was manifested in a widespread avoidance of ship money and culminated in the great dispute of 1601 over monopolies. Above all, the financial legacy of the reign was a poisoned chalice for her Stuart successors. Nevertheless, there is reason to regard the Crown's financial weakness as a blessing since it made the monarchy financially dependent on Parliament. That was the nation's principal defence against royal **absolutism**, as was argued by the opponents of the so-called Stuart tyranny.

KEY ISSUE

How well did the Elizabethan system of Crown finances work, and why did the system remain largely unchanged?

Absolutism the unrestrained power of the monarch

5 ↶ PARLIAMENT

Elizabeth summoned a total of ten Parliaments during her long reign. The first immediately after her accession met in January 1559. According to long-established principle, it voted the customs revenues for the life of the new monarch. It granted additional taxation to cover the expense of the current war against France. Finally, a new Religious Settlement was authorised; England was again made a Protestant country. Many found fault with the new Church and Protestant discontent was frequently voiced in Parliament (Catholics were excluded from the Commons from 1563). Puritan demands for further reformation were repeatedly rejected by the Queen, yet religious debate was an ongoing feature of Elizabethan Parliaments.

See pages 215–16

A *Legacy*

There was every likelihood that Elizabeth's reign would see Parliament assertive and confident. Since 1529, Parliament had met often. It had passed an unprecedented mass of legislation, particularly in connection with the Reformation, and its central role in the system of government seemed assured. Parliament offered the monarch an invaluable opportunity to sound out the governing class, the peers, gentry and burgesses, who enforced law and order, collected taxes and generally conducted the business of government. Above all, the government's measures acquired additional authority when they were agreed by the nation's representatives. In his *De Republica Anglorum* of 1565, Sir Thomas Smith described the effect:

Q

1. *What institutions was Smith referring to when he mentioned respectively 'the barony for the nobility and higher' and 'the knights, esquires, gentlemen and commons for the lower part of the commonwealth'?*

2. *Why did Tudor monarchs value the role of Parliament and how had some of the major events of the English Reformation demonstrated this?*

The most high and absolute power of the realm of England consisteth in the Parliament. For as in war, where the King himself in person, the nobility, the rest of the gentility and the yeomanry are, is the force and power of England: so in peace and consultation where the prince is to give life and the last and highest commandment, the barony for the nobility and higher, the knights, esquires, gentlemen and commons for the lower part of the commonwealth, consult and show what is good and necessary for the commonwealth ... For every Englishman is intended to be there present, either in person or by procuration and attorneys [i.e. through representatives], of what pre-eminence, state, dignity or quality soever he be, from the prince (be he king or queen) to the lowest person in England. And the consent of the Parliament is taken to be every man's consent.

The particular circumstances of the new reign made Parliament's role all the more indispensable. Certainly, Elizabeth had to secure Parliament's approval for a new Church. Parliament's co-operation would also be necessary in financial matters, given that Elizabeth inherited an empty Treasury (and an expensive war) and an inadequate ordinary revenue. Such dependence on the consent of Parliament threatened the power of the monarchy. However, Elizabeth rapidly emerged as a formidable politician who would not preside over a decline in monarchical power. She appreciated that Parliament had an important role to play, but it was to assist rather than gain ascendancy over the Crown. Parliament would not have an independent power to make decisions on national policy.

ANALYSIS

The Rise of Parliament

The rise of Parliament is one of the epic stories of English history. Subordinate to the Crown in the Middle Ages, it grew to become the dominant institution in English politics. By the nineteenth century the will of Parliament outweighed that of the monarch in deciding the policy and constitution of the government. The course of this great change is a subject which has provoked much disagreement. John Neale, notably in his *Elizabeth I and her Parliaments* (two vols, 1953 and 1957) argued that Parliament made significant progress during the reign of Elizabeth. An effective opposition arose in the Commons, inspired mainly by Puritanism. This opposition was strengthened by the development of the privileges and procedures of the Commons. It was upon this achievement that the power of Parliament was built up against that of the Crown.

PICTURE 22
Queen Elizabeth at the opening of Parliament

To make his case Neale gave an exaggerated emphasis to episodes of conflict between the Commons and the Queen. He particularly emphasised the role of Puritan MPs whom he cast in the light of an organised opposition to the Queen's religious settlement. He even suggested that the Commons ventured so far as to make votes for subsidies (taxation) conditional on government policies they wanted being agreed by the Crown. In sum, he claimed that the groundwork was laid for the successful challenges by parliamentarians to the Stuarts, leading to civil war in the seventeenth century.

Neale's argument held sway for several decades, but it was vigorously assailed in the 1970s and 1980s. It was Neale's former pupil, Geoffrey Elton, who led the way. His work and, in particular, research by Michael Graves has convinced historians that Neale misinterpreted the evidence. These 'revisionists' contend that the Commons never attempted to act as an opposition to Elizabeth, and Parliament did not rise at the monarch's expense; there is some evidence that, if anything, it entered a period of decline.

The revisionists have demolished the case that there was any extension to parliamentary privileges in Elizabeth's reign. GR Elton demonstrated that the Commons never attempted to use votes for subsidies as leverage against the Crown. On the contrary, Elizabeth's parliaments were strikingly co-operative. In part, this reflected the effective management of the Commons by Cecil, but it chiefly reflects the passivity of the Parliamentarians. Puritans did challenge the religious settlement on occasion, but they were not as popular as Neale assumed, and their opposition was often orchestrated by the Queen's own Councillors who could not persuade her by more conventional means. Graves has demonstrated beyond question that Elizabeth's Parliaments never dared to challenge her royal prerogatives. The parliamentarians were satisfied to play a very modest supporting role to the Queen as she governed her kingdom.

> **KEY ISSUE**
>
> *How, according to Neale, did Parliament develop under Elizabeth, and in what ways has his view been revised by later historians?*

B *Conflict*

Neale argued that Protestant zeal brought many MPs into conflict with the Queen. They felt passionately not only about the Church but also about the need to secure it against the Catholic threat that persisted throughout Elizabeth's reign and might all too easily prevail while the Catholic, Mary, Queen of Scots was heir to the throne. The other disruptive force identified by Neale was the growing tendency of the country gentry to acquire the representation of boroughs, displacing the townsmen who traditionally held these seats. Gentry eventually comprised four-fifths of the Commons in the later Parliaments, and a growing proportion of MPs (26% in 1563 to 44% in 1593) had some legal training, which made them more confident (and competent) law-makers. The assertiveness of such members could pose problems for a monarch determined to keep hold of the reins of power.

The religious question proved particularly difficult. The new Queen had considerable trouble in securing the settlement she wanted, for the Lords had a majority of bishops and lay peers committed to Catholicism. Neale had thought that the Puritans then in turn formed an organised opposition which devised parliamentary strategies and coordinated their activities in the Commons: 'an opposition in a significantly new sense: one with a positive programme which ... professed to aim at the fulfilment of its Protestant destiny'. Elizabeth, however, not only preserved the Religious Settlement unchanged but also denied Parliament's right to raise the question.

See pages 223–6

In 1566, 1571, 1572, 1586–7 and 1593, Elizabeth objected to Puritan bills on the grounds that Parliament had no right to raise the questions without her permission. Her displays of 'indignation' generally caused the measures to be abandoned – but not always immediately. When William Strickland proposed a bill, in 1571, to reform the *Prayer Book*, Elizabeth's order to exclude him from the Commons roused members to such angry protest that she re-admitted the offender. Though she explicitly 'commanded the House not to meddle' in religious matters, Puritan measures continued to be advanced. In 1586, she sent Cope and his Presbyterian supporters to the Tower.

Elizabeth was equally loath to allow Parliament to discuss her marriage and the succession. MPs in general, though, desperate to avoid a disputed or Catholic succession, were unwilling to leave them unsettled. The result was continual disputes. Elizabeth rebuked the Commons in 1559 for presuming to urge her to marry. In 1566 the Commons, supported by the Lords, apparently resolved to hold up the Subsidy Bill until Elizabeth settled the succession. An angry Queen duly promised she would 'marry as soon as I can conveniently' in order to have children ('otherwise I would never marry'), but 'I will never be constrained to do anything'. When she issued an 'express commandment' that the Commons should stop discussion of the matter, Paul Wentworth led the members in a famous protest in defence of 'the liberty of the free speech of the House'. Elizabeth withdrew her order and gave up one-third of the subsidy, but she refused to be bound further on the marriage and succession. Elizabeth dissolved prematurely the Parliament of 1563–7, abandoning much of her government's legislative programme 'to be rid of an intolerable House of Commons'.

The succession problem was aggravated in 1568 by the arrival in England of the legitimate but Catholic heir to the throne, Mary, Queen of Scots, and by her connections with those who organised the Northern Rising of 1569 and the Ridolfi Plot of 1570–1. In 1571, 1572 and 1584, Parliament urged exclusion or execution of Mary, or both. Elizabeth refused to accept Parliament's right to initiate measures against a fellow monarch. The successful demand for execution that was made by the Parliament of 1586–7 was the only one that did not involve conflict, for Parliament discussed the matter at the Queen's request. In 1593, a bill to settle the succession so upset Elizabeth that the Council imprisoned the MPs responsible, and their leader, Peter Wentworth, Paul Wentworth's brother, remained in the Tower until his death in 1597. Clearly, the succession was an issue which agitated members throughout the reign.

C *Free speech*

Closely involved in all of these matters was the issue of free speech. The members who raised such issues as Church reform, the Queen's marriage, and the succession encountered objections based not on the merits of their proposals but on their right to initiate discussion of them. Elizabeth distinguished between matters of 'commonweal' and matters of 'state'. The former were mostly private and local matters, or national social and economic questions, like the Poor Law. These Parliament was free to discuss (though its final decisions required the Royal Assent). Matters of state were those which belonged to the royal prerogative: religion, foreign policy, the Queen's marriage, the succession, and such Crown rights as purveyance and the granting of monopolies. Members were not even permitted to discuss these issues unless they were invited to do so by the Queen. Parliament was just expected to await the legislative proposals of the government. Only twice, in 1572 and 1586, was Parliament invited to discuss a matter of state (the fate of Mary, Queen of Scots, on both occasions) when a specific government proposal was not involved.

Some MPs, driven by Protestant zeal, went beyond this to take the initiative in matters of state. On several occasions, MPs, the Wentworth brothers in particular, explicitly took issue with the Queen's restrictive view and advanced the idea of Parliament's right to complete free speech. For example, Peter Wentworth asserted the claim in his famous speech to Parliament in 1576:

See pages 226–8

> ... in this House, which is termed a place of free speech, there is nothing so necessary for the preservation of the prince and state as free speech, and without, it is a scorn and mockery to call it a Parliament House, for in truth it is none, but a very school of flattery and dissimulation, and so a fit place to serve the devil and his angels in, and not to glorify God and benefit the commonwealth ...

KEY ISSUE

On what issues did Elizabeth find Parliament especially troublesome, and why?

But Elizabeth never acknowledged Parliament's right to unrequested discussion of questions of State. Most MP's respected the limits, and she disciplined those who pushed her too far. (Peter Wentworth was twice sent to the Tower.) Lord Keeper Puckering's famous statement of 1593 is the clearest evidence we have of her unchanging determination to hold the line in this matter:

Q

1. *What examples did Elizabeth possibly have in mind when she denounced the presumptuous efforts of 'idle brains' (line 7)?*
2. *Why did Elizabeth find no great difficulty in limiting Parliament's discussions?*

> 1 For liberty of speech her Majesty commandeth me to tell you that to say yea or no to bills, God forbid that any man should be restrained or afraid to answer according to his best liking, with some short declaration of his reason therein, and therein to have a free voice, which
> 5 is the very true liberty of the House; not, as some suppose, to speak there of all causes as him listeth, and to frame a form of religion or a state of government as to their idle brains shall seem meetest. She saith no king fit for his state will suffer such absurdities, and ... she hopeth no man here longeth so much for his ruin as that he mindeth
> 10 to make such a peril to his own safety.

D *Taxation*

Given the inadequacy of the Crown's ordinary revenues, Elizabeth had to ask Parliament to vote subsidies in peacetime as well as during the war that broke out in 1585 and lasted until the end of her reign. MPs were loath to impose new burdens on their constituents and required the Councillors to justify every demand. The holding up of the Money Bill of 1566 has been regarded as an attempt to force the Queen's hand on another issue, the succession. Neale argued that further examples of supply (of taxes) being made conditional on **redress of grievances** occurred in 1571, 1585 and 1601. In other words, the reign of Elizabeth witnessed the development of a major instrument of parliamentary opposition. In 1587, a Commons committee offered a benevolence (additional vote of money) on condition that Elizabeth accepted sovereignty over the Low Countries. She declined, but it was another notable attempt to use Parliament's control of the purse strings to influence policy. At other times, the differences over money were more purely financial. In 1589 and 1593, MPs expressed their dissatisfaction with the heavy tax burden.

Redress of grievances changing policy to remedy complaints

As matters of 'commonweal', social and economic questions could be raised, even in Elizabeth's restrictive view, on the initiative of members. This narrowed the scope for conflict. For example, the Crown accepted the Poor Law initiated by private members in 1597 as well as major additions to the government Bill which was to become the Statute of Artificers of 1563. However, the Queen's prerogative might be at stake here, too, given that such royal rights as purveyance and monopolies were major economic grievances. So, differences occasionally arose. For example, in 1563 the Commons introduced two Bills to limit the abuse of purveyance (the Crown's right to purchase goods at low, outdated prices). One bill passed through both Houses, but it was vetoed by a Queen determined to protect her prerogative powers against encroachment by Parliament. Far more important, however, was the issue of monopolies, which were a cheap way for the Crown to reward courtiers and raise money for royal needs. But monopolies artificially raised prices to the consumer. Discontent grew intense during the economic crisis of the 1590s. The Commons protested in 1597, to no avail. In 1601, the House furiously attacked the practice and the Queen, desperate to secure additional taxes, felt compelled to withdraw the most hated monopolies and submit the rest to challenge in the courts.

See page 193

E *Co-operation*

This is a substantial catalogue of conflict. It was, however, spread across a long reign of almost 45 years. Neale's emphasis on such 'dramatic aspects' has obscured the fact that co-operation between monarch and Parliament was more normal. As Michael Graves has written, 'the revisionists' study of parliamentary business places conflict in its right perspective ... an occasional isolated episode in a general climate of co-operation'.

The principal difficulty encountered by the Council was the way that the profusion of members' bills ate up the time available. Hundreds of private and local bills were proposed. Elizabeth's Parliaments considered and passed a much greater number of laws than their predecessors, averaging 33 Acts per session (out of 126 proposed), of which about two-fifths (166 of 432) dealt with private matters. This was a considerable feat of management, given that the average session lasted fewer than ten weeks.

The government's success in securing the passage of its own bills was significant. There was no substantial opposition to the great majority of its proposals. Parliament proved compliant even in areas where one might have expected members to hold strong views. For example, the money difficulties discussed above must be placed in perspective. Almost invariably, the Subsidy Bill went through easily and speedily. Alsop concluded that 'the Commons's role in initiating and deliberating on supply [of taxation] came very close to being a constitutional fiction under Elizabeth. Privy Councillors ... expected no opposition, and were generally proved correct'.

Elizabeth was never denied funds, and 1566 was the only occasion on which she felt it wise to accept a reduced sum. Parliament voted taxes in years of peace as well as war. During the war years, Parliament agreed to multiple subsidies (two in 1589, three in 1593 and 1597, and four in 1601). Such votes were unprecedented, and Parliament's ready agreement speaks volumes about its co-operative mentality.

The alleged examples of supply of taxation being made conditional on redress of grievances (in 1566, 1571, 1585 and 1601) have recently been re-appraised. Elton in particular has pointed out that, while the supply debates of those years witnessed discussion of grievances, there was no attempt to hold up supply until they were remedied. Elizabeth appeared to have less trouble securing supply of taxation than either her predecessors or the Stuarts. On the vital question of money there was harmony between Elizabeth and her Parliaments.

Parliament hardly ever intruded into the royal prerogative to conduct foreign policy, despite the high level of Protestant discontent with Elizabeth's unwillingness to support the Dutch Revolt. Domestic religious issues caused more problems, but it is important to keep these too in perspective. Norman Jones showed that it was the House of Lords, led by the Marian bishops, that rejected the original combined Supremacy and Uniformity Bill in 1559. According to Jones the new Church was established by an alliance of Crown and Commons (against the Lords).

As for the Puritan agitation of later years, the document supposedly naming a so-called Puritan 'choir', was merely a list of members appointed to consider the Succession Bill of 1563 (Elton's view) or a list of prominent personalities. Elton has concluded that 'the members of that "choir" formed no party and few of them were Puritans'. The Puritans, and discontented members in general, either acted individually or formed shifting alliances which varied from issue to issue. They pressed grievances without any thought of forming a regular opposition to the

KEY ISSUE

How far did Elizabeth find Parliament a willing source of finance?

government or seeking to assert the power of Parliament against that of the Crown. The Puritan members did become better organised in 1571, but this was under Council leadership. Above all, the Presbyterians in the Commons co-operated closely in 1584 and 1587, but they were a small minority in the House and their radical proposals were opposed by their colleagues as much as by the Queen. There is, in sum, no evidence of a significant Puritan opposition which was willing or able to lead the Commons against the Crown.

The great monopolies row of 1601 was not the work of an organised opposition movement. Similarly, the disputes over parliamentary privilege involved either spontaneous reactions to official acts or the initiatives of isolated individuals. Elizabeth quickly and sensibly defused the incidents in 1566, arising from debates about the succession, and in 1571 when Strickland tried to reform the *Prayer Book*. Peter Wentworth's call for the liberty of free speech in Parliament had a greater impact on succeeding generations than on his fellow MPs. In fact, it was the Commons that imprisoned him for four weeks for his crude and outrageous criticism of Elizabeth in the famous speech of 1576 ('It is a dangerous thing in a Prince unkindly to intreat and abuse his or her nobility and people, as her Majesty did the last Parliament'). In 1587 and 1593, when Peter Wentworth and a few allies were sent to the Tower, having pressed grievances outside as well as in the House, there was no general outcry. Most MPs who raised forbidden topics had no wish to confront Elizabeth on the principle involved and rarely persisted when the Queen indicated her hostility. Michael Graves has written that 'the Wentworths were standard-bearers without an army', and Peter was 'little more than a parliamentary nuisance'.

Finally, Parliament did not attempt to claim a role in the everyday administration of the country, nor even seek to supervise the spending of the taxes it voted or to monitor the execution of its laws. Above all, it claimed no right to control the appointment of the Queen's servants. There was no attempt to secure parliamentary government.

> **KEY ISSUE**
>
> *What limits to its role did Parliament accept?*

F *The role of the Council*

Much of the activity traditionally regarded as examples of Commons opposition involved the use of Parliament by Privy Councillors to influence the monarch, a fact which underlines the extent to which it failed to emerge as an independent power. When Councillors wished to change the mind of their obstinate monarch, they frequently tried to convince her that the political nation demanded the measures they favoured. Most of the activity associated with the so-called Puritan opposition was inspired by Councillors who shared the values and concerns of the less extreme (non-Presbyterian) Puritans.

The Queen's marriage and the succession were raised in 1563 and 1566 on the initiative of leading Councillors. The Commons petition of 1563 was drafted by a committee which was chaired by a Councillor and included all eight of the Councillors who sat in the Lower House. In 1566, Lord Keeper Bacon in the Lords and Cecil in the Commons organised the joint delegation of the Houses to Elizabeth on the succession, Cecil helped to write into the preamble of the subsidy bill the Queen's promise to marry and name a successor, and it was the Councillors and their friends who took the major part in pressing the issue in Parliament.

Similarly, the Council supported the 1571 bill to punish all who failed to take Communion within the Church, an anti-Catholic measure to which the Queen refused to give the Royal Assent. In addition, it was the Council which launched the legislative assault on Catholicism in the 1580s. This is not to say that all Puritan measures originated with the Council. The more radical bills – like Strickland's proposed reform of the *Prayer Book* in 1571 and the Presbyterian programme of the 1580s – they opposed, and these quickly failed. Again, in 1586–7, it was the Council which initiated Parliament's attacks on Mary, Queen of Scots. In the wake of the Babington Plot, the Council pressed for a Parliament in 1586 and then led the two Houses in demanding Mary's execution – this time successfully. These were by no means the only occasions on which the Council tried to use Parliament to force the hand of a Queen who liked to think that she ruled with the love of her people.

KEY ISSUE

In what ways did Councillors manipulate Parliament?

G *Control and consensus*

The Queen had means by which to 'manage' Parliament. Few MPs held paid office, but a majority prized their positions in local government and aspired to greater things. So, the possible withdrawal of favour was a major sanction available to the monarch. The Crown directly controlled the election of few MPs – most of them from the Duchy of Lancaster – but more were dependants of Councillors and loyal courtiers.

With the help of noble supporters, Burghley nominated 26 MPs in 1584, and his son Robert may have chosen 30 in 1597 and 31 in 1601. The 'great men', who generally supported the Queen's government, controlled perhaps 40% of the seats, particularly in the small boroughs whose voters could be subjected to irresistible pressure from local aristocrats. Although patronage was not sufficient to enable Elizabeth to 'pack' the Commons with nominees and other dependants, it did provide a useful nucleus of such people.

The Councillors worked hard to get the business of the Crown through Parliament. They carefully prepared their measures before Parliament met. The Speaker of the Commons was officially elected by that House, but the candidate proposed by the government was invariably elected, unopposed, so he was effectively a royal nominee. Behind the scenes, Councillors approached members to court their support or employed unofficial helpers to do so. In particular, after his own elevation to the Lords in 1571 removed the government's most effective manager from the House Commons, Burghley relied heavily on the likes of his supporters, Norton and Fleetwood, to handle affairs in the Commons. In the reign as a whole there was efficient and successful management.

The Queen could dissolve a troublesome Parliament, as she did in 1567. She could also withhold the Royal Assent, as she did more than 60 times in all. In almost every case this power of veto was used to block bills of little political importance, but the awareness that the power existed meant that bills to which she objected were often abandoned at an early stage or appropriately amended.

The Crown also used the more compliant Lords to good effect. Few of its lay members owed their place to Elizabeth, but the purge of the Marian bishops meant that all but one of Elizabeth's bishops (there were 26 at any one time) owed their appointment to her. Other peers were Councillors, members of the Household, or in receipt of some royal favour. So, dependants of the Crown constituted more than half of the 80-odd members of the Lords. Occasionally, the House of Lords obliged the government by defeating unwanted Commons bills. More often, the government introduced into the Lords those measures which were likely to meet with opposition in the Commons.

The Crown could exercise more directly coercive powers, using sedition laws or a specific law forbidding the discussion of parliamentary business outside. It was under the latter that Peter Wentworth and several others were imprisoned in 1587 and again in 1593. The possibility of such a fate may well have curbed opposition.

However, the main responsibility for the cordial relations which usually existed between Parliament and Crown lay in the view they had of their own function. Most MPs were enthusiastic defenders of local interests, and put their energies into securing the appropriate legislation. In the area of national policy, MPs were content to assist the government by passing legislation. They did not claim a right to give unsolicited advice or have it accepted. In fact, they shared Elizabeth's own view of the matter.

An awareness of the MPs' limited view of their role is crucial to an understanding of Elizabeth's Parliaments. Numerous circumstances forestalled grander ambitions. Most members came up to London from the small communities of provincial England. They were easily

TIMELINE
Parliaments under Elizabeth

1559	January–May
1563–7	January–April 1563 (first session)
	September 1566–January 1567 (second session)
1571	April–May
1572–81	May–June 1572 (first session)
	February–March 1576 (second session)
	January–March 1581 (third session)
1584–85	November 1584–March 1585
1586–7	October 1586–23 March 1587
1589	February–March
1593	February–April
1597–8	October 1597–February 1598
1601	October–December

intimidated by the splendours of the Court and the daunting presence of the Queen and her great Councillors. About half of the MPs in each House of Commons were novices who began with little knowledge of Parliament. There were numerous self-seeking men who wished to attract the favour of the monarch or another patron. Those who did attend were often keen to settle affairs quickly and terminate the expense of residence in London. An opposition could not be fashioned out of such material.

Finally, it is necessary to underline the personal contribution of Elizabeth. The Queen was so much the focus of attention and activity that her demeanour counted at times for everything. She produced displays of fury and obstinacy that indicated the hopelessness and even danger of persisting with an unwelcome measure. But she was also tactful. Her concessions to pressure – for example, in 1566, 1587 and 1601 – were well judged to curtail rather than encourage opposition. She was aware of the benefits (especially financial) of a co-operative Parliament and had the diplomatic skills to promote good relations. The first drafts of her speeches were often indignant and aggressive, but she then toned them down. Above all, she was charming, especially when addressing the 'wise and discreet men' of the Commons, and was willing and able to take advantage of men's desire to deal graciously with a woman.

For all these reasons, co-operation was the dominant theme in relations between Elizabeth and her Parliaments. Rarely did differences lead to agitation of constitutional issues which might have created deeper and more lasting rifts. Certainly, it is relatively easy to find examples of conflict under Elizabeth. But the evidence on the Commons, in the form of diaries especially, is much more abundant for her period than for the other Tudors. The apparent calm of earlier Parliaments probably owes much to the scarcity of evidence. It is not possible to compare the reigns with any certainty.

See pages 199–200

As well as the disputes over free speech, the other main issue of privilege during the reign was the Norfolk election case of 1586, when the Commons claimed the right to decide upon disputed elections to the House. The Queen insisted that this should remain the task of the Lord Chancellor in the Court of Chancery, and the Commons did not press the matter. Elton has concluded firmly that, 'The history of the Commons' privileges in Elizabeth's reign testifies neither to any growth in power nor to the forging of weapons for a fight'.

The fact that Parliament met so rarely under Elizabeth hardly suggests that it rose in power or importance. In Elizabeth's reign of 45 years, Parliament met only 13 times, each session lasted for an average of fewer than ten weeks, and an average of more than three years lapsed between each session. In 26 calendar years Parliament did not meet at all. Meetings grew in number towards the end of the reign, owing to the war with Spain and the need for taxation. Parliament's legislative role was important and not questioned by Elizabeth. But, as a cautious, conservative monarch, she made only a limited number of changes which would require Parliament's approval. As a result, Parliament largely lost the central role it acquired during the years of revolution after 1529.

KEY ISSUE

How, and how effectively, was opposition in Parliament dealt with?

6 ❦ GOVERNING THE PROVINCES

The experience of most English people was largely confined to their locality. They were only vaguely and intermittently aware of the activities of the central government in London. The Crown could not afford an extensive bureaucracy; its paid agents in the provinces numbered only a few hundred revenue collectors, customs officials and wardship administrators. So, the government of every county was principally the responsibility of voluntary, unpaid members of the local nobility and gentry.

Under the Tudors, and especially during the reign of Elizabeth, there was a substantial increase in the burdens imposed on this local governing class. This arose from the government's more active efforts to regulate the economy, deal with the poor, secure religious conformity, and promote the country's military preparedness. As the burden grew, so was the organisation of local government changed, though the Crown's shortage of money meant there could be no departure from reliance on the local élites.

At the head of each county under Elizabeth was a relatively new creation, the Lord-Lieutenant. Originally, during Henry VIII's reign, this figure was confined to responsibility for the local militia, and it was an occasional and short-lived appointment determined by military circumstances. The Elizabethan war against Spain brought it to a new level of importance. In the 1580s Lord-Lieutenants were appointed to almost every county and permitted to retain the office for life. Their duties included the levying of forced loans, enforcement of economic regulations, supervision of the Justices of the Peace (JPs), and a general responsibility for acquainting the Council with events in their county. To hold this position became a great honour. It was held usually by a nobleman, and in half the counties by a Councillor. Much of the work was done by the several Deputy Lieutenants; a post created in the 1560s which bore its own considerable prestige and was filled by the larger, resident landowners.

The JPs were both 'the mainstay of the Tudor system of law enforcement' and, increasingly, 'the general executive agents of local administration'. Their number rose fivefold under the Tudors, to an average of about 50 per county. To become a JP was to be acknowledged as a member of the leading gentry. The JP's workload grew with the great increase in statute (parliamentary) law under the Tudors. He had a major judicial role, as the magistrate responsible for deciding upon the vast majority of disputes and offences, from murder to the theft of swans' eggs. In addition, especially under Elizabeth, the JP acquired numerous administrative duties, notably in relation to the Poor Law and economic regulation, maintenance of highways and bridges, licensing of alehouses, and the management of houses of correction.

See page 357

Special commissions were set up to perform those tasks which could not be left to the existing officials. Used by all the Tudors, they appeared particularly often during Elizabeth's reign. For example, the oath to the

Royal Supremacy of 1559 was imposed by special commissions, and from 1583 staunchly Protestant commissions were deployed to enforce the persecution of Catholics. Initially, the use of these bodies was a significant departure from the principle of local men for local government, but it appears that under Elizabeth they were more often than not dominated by local men, albeit specially selected.

Below county level, in the hundred and the parish, constables, churchwardens, overseers of the poor (from 1597) and other officials carried out numerous functions, for example road maintenance, the control of vermin, policing, and poor relief, under the supervision of JPs and sheriffs. The emergence of the parish as a secular (non-religious) unit was another important development under Elizabeth. In the towns, borough councils – mostly narrow, propertied oligarchies whose members were co-opted rather than elected – appointed those who carried out a similar range of duties there.

This system of government had many imperfections. Though the office-holders at county level were formally appointed by the central government, the degree of control exerted by the latter over these mostly voluntary officials was far from complete. The channels of communication, especially with the northern provinces, were far from adequate. The fact that the JPs met increasingly often meant that they developed an esprit de corps which led to emphasis on local interests to the exclusion of wider concerns.

Not surprisingly, then, office-holders did not always co-operate with the policy of the government. The majority of JPs were relatively inactive, regarding their appointment more as a badge of honour than an obligation to serve. Some abused their positions for personal profit. According to one complainant, 'A Justice of the Peace is a Living Creature that for half a dozen of Chickens will Dispense with a whole Dozen of Penal Statutes … unless you offer sacrifice unto these Idol-Justices, of Sheep and Oxen, they know you not'. In many parts of the country, recusancy fines (for non-attendance at church) were not enforced because JPs were sympathetic to the plight of their Catholic neighbours where they were not themselves of that persuasion. Often the militia was inadequately prepared; local opposition to both service in it and the expense was shared by the gentry and prevailed over any wider conception of the national interest. The subsidy commissioners appointed to collect parliamentary taxation permitted outrageously distorted assessments which greatly diminished Crown revenue.

The problem reached new proportions in the 1590s when the country was simultaneously exhausted by the demands of war and afflicted by high inflation and (in 1594–7) bad harvests. There was resentment against parliamentary taxes, the new poor rates, ship money, militia rates, militia service, and conscription to fight abroad or, even worse, in Ireland; and it is clear that in many places the local governors shared the popular disaffection and obstructed the enforcement of these measures. National defence as well as administrative efficiency was at stake.

The composition of local power structures could also be a serious problem. Some families were of such eminence, owning vast tracts of land and exerting a perhaps centuries-old sway over the minds of all in their proximity, that they had a more effective say than distant London in the running of their counties. To try to circumvent their power would amount to open confrontation with county society.

This inability to install local governors who could check the power of the aristocrats meant that there was a danger of rebellion. The Earl of Derby's sympathy with Catholics and dubious loyalty to Elizabeth were well known, but his dominance in Lancashire had left the government little choice but to place his friends in power and make him Lord-Lieutenant – and then hope for the best when the Northern Rising broke out in 1569. The Northern Rising was a rebellion led by the Earls of Northumberland and Westmorland against the Protestantism and, even more, the centralisation of the Tudor regime which was reducing their local influence. The Duke of Norfolk and the Earl of Cumberland were others who might have raised their dependants in that year. In fact, they remained loyal, but the tension of those weeks, when Elizabeth waited for the great men of England to show their hand, bears testimony to the regime's dangerous reliance on the provincial élites not only for everyday government but for its very survival.

On the other hand, one must not overstate the difficulties. Parliament, drawing representation from every part of the kingdom, acted as a focus of national unity. For most people, local sentiment though strong did not preclude a sense of nationhood and loyalty to the seemingly age-old Tudor dynasty. 'Allegiance was not single and undivided' (Penry Williams). Tudor propaganda and Church teaching relentlessly expounded the subject's duty to obey. Above all, most people wanted the peace which quiet loyalty brought. The Pilgrimage of Grace had shown even the particularist North that rebellion was futile and disastrous.

As for the problem of ensuring good government in the more general sense, the difficulties were not insuperable. England was a small country, in terms of both territory and population. With only about 2000 families of substantial influence, the Councillors could have an acquaintance with a large part of the political nation. These people constantly travelled to the unquestioned centre of national life, London, and were often present at Court (and, less continuously, in Parliament). The industry of the Privy Council ensured a remarkably close supervision of life in England, as suggested in the previous section. The office of Lord-Lieutenant was such a great prize its holders preferred to co-operate rather than risk deprivation. The Lieutenancy, collecting information and transmitting instructions, became the major link between the Council and the provinces. The Council also had the use of the bishops, the circuit judges, and the special commissions.

Unco-operative officials could be and often were removed. Perhaps one-third of the JPs were replaced soon after Elizabeth's accession, and many more were struck off subsequently. The result for the purged official was a loss of prestige, of one's place in the all-important local hierarchy. There was usually, especially in the South, a substantial 'pool' of men who were conscientious, respected and well disposed. The

KEY ISSUE

How was Elizabeth able to govern the counties of England and Wales through largely voluntary local government officials?

patronage at the disposal of the Crown exerted a strong pull. While there could still be obstructionism, especially as we saw in the 1590s, it did not prevent the Council achieving its main goals.

Finally, it must be concluded that men of local standing were far more appropriate than anonymous bureaucrats to the government of a country so varied and of a people who spent their lives in awe of their gentry and peers. The system, as Elton put it, 'exploited local knowledge and loyalties in the interests of the state, a thing no centralised bureaucracy could hope to achieve'. In many places, government by the local squire was the best of all worlds. However, Elton may go too far in describing the system of local government as a 'success'. There was so much variation between (and within) counties that generalisation is almost bound to mislead. Certainly, some areas were badly governed, from the perspective of both Crown and people. Yet for the most part central government succeeded in having its policy implemented – rather better than the French monarchy with its 40 000 bureaucrats.

7 ⌐ CONCLUSIONS

Elizabeth needed the co-operation of her Council, Parliament, and the propertied classes of England. She ruled by consent and yet she was unquestionably a strong monarch. She controlled the policy of her government, making almost all of the major decisions. Perhaps, that simple fact represented her greatest success. Her dominance rested upon the desire of the political nation to see (and assist) effective government, on the broad acceptability of her religious and foreign policies, on her diplomatic but firm handling of Parliament, and on the impact of her daunting personality. She owed a great debt to the Privy Council which helped her to manage the system; but it was her wisdom which gave the Crown such able and hard-working ministers.

The reign was markedly less impressive in its closing years. The war, economic difficulties, the execution of the dashing Essex after his revolt in 1601 and Elizabeth's declining personal charms combined to undermine the Queen's popularity. However, one must not deduce too much from a period of extraordinary difficulty. For most of the reign, the system provided stable and effective government. It is surely unfair to denounce Elizabeth for tolerating the continuation of problems, particularly those relating to the royal finances, which were to cause insurmountable difficulty not for her, but for the less able rulers who followed.

8 ⌐ BIBLIOGRAPHY

*Keith Randell's *Elizabeth I and the Government of England* (Hodder, Access to History) is a useful starting point. *David Starkey, *Elizabeth* (Vintage, 2001) is an extremely readable introduction to the young Elizabeth. For the mature Elizabeth the most reliable authority is

**W MacCaffrey, *Elizabeth I* (Edward Arnold, 1993). *WT MacCaffrey *The Shaping of the Elizabethan Regime* (Cape, 1969) and *W T MacCaffrey *Queen Elizabeth and the Making of Policy, 1572–1588* (Princeton, 1981). More accessible, and more useful for students are **C Haigh *Elizabeth I* (Longman, 1988). **DM Loades *The Tudor Court* (Historical Association, 1989) is a key text for understanding how Elizabeth governed England. **EW Ives *Faction in Tudor England* (Historical Association, 1979) deals with a significant aspect of Tudor government which has generated much controversy. *AGR Smith *The Government of Elizabethan England* (Edward Arnold, 1967) outlines the mechanics of Elizabethan government. On Parliament see especially MAR Graves *Elizabethan Parliaments, 1559–1601* (Longman, 1987), and MAR Graves *The Tudor Parliaments: Crown, Lords and Commons, 1485–1603* (Longman, 1985).

(*Recommended. **Highly recommended.)

9 ⌒ STRUCTURED AND ESSAY QUESTIONS

A *Structured questions*

1. (a) How well did her character fit Elizabeth to govern?
   (b) In which ways did the Privy Council help Elizabeth to govern?
2. (a) What was the role of patronage in Elizabeth's system of government?
   (b) How successfully did Elizabeth deal with threats to her authority?
3. (a) Why did Elizabeth and the Privy Council find it so easy to 'manage' her Parliaments?
   (b) What evidence is there that parliamentary opposition to Elizabeth was unusual, limited and unsuccessful?

B *Essay questions*

1. Should the Elizabethan system of government be considered a success?
2. Why, and in what ways, did government operate less successfully in the last decade of Elizabeth's reign?
3. 'The history of Elizabeth's Parliaments is not one of conflict, but of co-operation and consent'. Discuss.
4. What role did religion play in causing conflict between Elizabeth and her Parliaments?
5. To what extent did the Crown remain the dominant institution in the Elizabethan system of government?

10 ⌒ DOCUMENTARY EXERCISE: AN ASSESSMENT OF WILLIAM CECIL, LORD BURGHLEY

SOURCE A

Queen Elizabeth to Cecil, 20 November 1558

I give you this charge, that you shall be of my Privy Council, and content yourself to take pains for me and my realm. This judgement I have of you, that you will not be corrupted with any manner of gift, and that you will be favourable to the state, and that, without respect of my private will, you will give me that counsel that you think best. And if you shall know anything necessary to be declared to me of secrecy, you shall show it to myself only, and assure yourself I will not fail to keep taciturnity therein.

SOURCE B

Lord Burghley to his son, Sir Robert Cecil, 23 March 1596

… I do hold, and will always, this course in such matters as I differ in opinion from her Majesty; as long as I may be allowed to give advice I will not change my opinion by affirming the contrary, for that were to offend God, to whom I am sworn first; but as a servant I will obey her Majesty's commandment and no wise contrary the same, presuming that she being God's chief minister here, it shall be God's will to have her commandments obeyed, after that I have performed my duty as a councillor, and shall in my heart wish her commandments to have such good successes as I am sure she intendeth …

SOURCE C

J. Clapham (one of Burghley's clerks), in his account of Elizabeth of England

About the fourteenth year of the Queen's reign Cecil was made Knight of the Garter, and, after the death of the Marquis of Winchester, Treasurer of England, he succeeded him in the treasureship, which office he enjoyed till his death; ordering the affairs of the realm in such a manner as he was respected even by his enemies, who reputed him the most famous councillor of Christendom in his time; the English government being then commonly termed by strangers Cecil's commonwealth … In matters of counsel nothing for the most part was done without him, for that nothing was thought well done whereof he was not the contriver and director. His credit with the Queen was such as his wisdom and integrity well deserved … the necessity of his service would not any long time permit his absence from the Court and the greatness of his place procured him the envy of those who otherwise could not but acknowledge his virtues …

Q

1. *Read Source A and B. Does Source B prove that Lord Burghley counselled the Queen as she directed him to on his appointment to the Privy Council at the start of her reign?*

2. *What do Sources A and B suggest about the minister's and the Queen's roles in decision-making?*

3. *Which 'virtues', according to Source C, gave Burghley great 'credit with the Queen'?*

4. *Drawing on the above sources and your other knowledge, discuss the view that Burghley's 'subtle and complex influence over the Queen was greater than he would ever acknowledge'. How accurate were those who called England's government 'Cecil's commonwealth'?*

9

Elizabeth I: Religion

INTRODUCTION

In 1558 Elizabeth inherited a kingdom which was overwhelmingly Catholic. The Catholic Church was the established Church of the realm and it enjoyed the support of the vast majority of the new Queen's subjects. Yet Elizabeth did away with Mary Tudor's restoration of Catholicism and replaced it with a religious settlement which reflected her own Protestant preferences. Elizabeth's Church of England matched few people's ideals, but by the time of her death it succeeded in encompassing all of the people of England and Wales, excepting only the tiny minorities of Catholic recusants and Protestant **separatists**. How the Queen's religious settlement came to be so successful is much debated by historians, especially in view of recent work by historians such as Christopher Haigh and Eamon Duffy who have revealed the continuing strength of Catholic beliefs and practices into Elizabeth's reign. It seems as though a failure of leadership on the part of the Catholic Church in the 1560s, combined with the flexibility of the Queen's religious settlement, within the limits laid down in parliamentary statutes, caused most of the English and Welsh people to acquiesce in the new religious order and gradually grow attached to it. The Queen and her bishops were able to curb the efforts of Protestant critics to force further reformation upon the Church of England and its congregations. When change did come it occurred within the structures of the Church of England and enjoyed a broad measure of popular support. By the time of the Queen's death in 1603 the Church of England was truly the Church of the nation.

1 ⤙ ELIZABETH'S RELIGION

Few did not expect Elizabeth I to change the religion of England in a Protestant direction. As the daughter of Anne Boleyn she was a living symbol of the break with Rome. Her tutor had been Roger Ascham, the Cambridge humanist of the Henrician Court, and her religion was deeply influenced by him. Elizabeth's private prayers, subsequently gathered into a very personal book by her, show clearly the depth of her Protestant faith. She saw herself as God's instrument for the restoration of the Gospel and as the mother of the Church of England, and she took her duties seriously.

Elizabeth wanted her Church to propound the theology of Thomas Cranmer, chief author of the two *Prayer Books* of 1549 and 1552, a

Separatists those seeking to establish 'purer' sects outside the established Church of England

See pages 433–5

theology which she was personally committed to and which she hoped would also be flexible enough to accommodate the wide range of religious beliefs among those with strong views as well as give direction to the large number of men and women left confused by decades of religious changes. She was anxious not to impose too restrictive a creed on her people. To be as tolerant as possible was her personal style when it came to the doctrine, not wanting, in Sir Nicholas Bacon's words, 'to make windows into men's hearts'. She herself remained attached to some traditional practices, such as priestly celibacy, and to the horror of her more Protestant supporters, she kept candles and a crucifix on the altar in her private chapel rather than a bare Communion table. But in areas of Protestant doctrine and practice she deemed essential, Elizabeth demanded obedience and outward observance, and complete loyalty to her God-given authority. Once her Church was established, she was committed to the status quo, believing that innovation would lead to instability which she had been appointed by God to guard against.

See pages 426–7

2 ⌐ THE RELIGIOUS SETTLEMENT OF 1559

Having established her Privy Council, mostly made up of Protestants such as William Cecil, who had stayed close to her during the difficult years, Elizabeth sought to revive the Royal Supremacy over the Church and reintroduce the 1552 *Book of Common Prayer* as soon as possible. This required legislation by Parliament. Meanwhile there was a danger that enthusiastic Protestants might take advantage of Mary's death to indulge in open preaching which could antagonise a populace which was still largely Catholic in sympathy. Thus, for instance, on 28 December 1558 the Queen silenced all preachers until Parliament had met 'for better conciliation and accord of such causes as at this present are moved in matters and ceremonies of religion'. This action did not appease the Catholics. Bishop White of Winchester preached at Mary's funeral that the 'wolves are come out of Geneva' to prey on the English flock. Rumours began to circulate of armed resistance to religious change and the release of heretics.

Elizabeth's first attempt to secure parliamentary agreement ended in failure. The Commons proved pliable but the Bishops and conservative peers, such as Viscount Montagu, in the Lords deleted all reference to the *Book of Common Prayer* from the proposed legislation. After some consternation and indecision the Queen and her Council responded by staging a rigged disputation between Catholic and Protestant theologians, designed to portray the Catholics as obstructive and unreasonable. More importantly, two of the leading Catholic bishops were imprisoned in the Tower of London, a move intended to overawe the Catholic party by strong-arm tactics and to undermine their voting strength in the Lords. After Easter 1559 the government presented a legislative programme to Parliament, which had been revised to calm Catholic sensitivities.

A separate Bill for Supremacy was introduced so that the Queen's Supremacy over the Church would be established, even if the form of worship were not. Significantly, though, she was not to take her father's title of 'Supreme Head' of the Church, rather she was to be 'Supreme Governor', a tactical ploy to ease the consciences of Catholics for whom the Pope was the Head of the Church on Earth. This move also placated those Protestants like John Knox who found it difficult to accept any human, and especially a mere woman, as Head of God's Church. The Supremacy Bill incorporated an oath of loyalty to be taken by clergy and officials, refusal of which would result in loss of office. The Bill repealed Mary Tudor's heresy laws, guaranteed freedom of worship for Protestants, and allowed Communion in both kinds as enacted in 1547. It also established the Commission for Ecclesiastical Causes (or High Commission) to impose order and uniformity in religion. The Bill gained wide approval in the Commons and Lords, despite united episcopal opposition. It rejected the authority of the Pope over the English Church, but without yet making it once again Protestant in doctrine and ritual.

The attempt to make the Church fully Protestant was embodied in the Uniformity Bill, which was far more controversial. The 1552 *Book of Common Prayer* was re-imposed for use in all churches upon pain of imprisonment. Church attendance on Sundays and Holy Days was enforced upon pain of a fine of a shilling per absence, to be collected by the churchwardens for poor relief. Heavy fines and imprisonment awaited those who sought to slander or libel the *Prayer Book*, or tried to prevent its proper use. Yet the 1552 *Prayer Book* was modified to calm Catholic fears about its unequivocal rejection of transubstantiation. A theological ambiguity was added with these words spoken as part of the Eucharist, which had been used in the 1549 *Prayer Book*: 'The body/blood of Our Lord Jesus Christ which was given for thee, preserve thy body and soul until everlasting life'. This modest addition allowed for a broad spectrum of interpretation concerning the Eucharist, including the Catholic belief in transubstantiation.

Another reflection of the government's anxiety to placate Catholics was the deletion of the words abusing 'the Bishop of Rome' from the Litany, a sequence of prayers. Elizabeth's Act of Uniformity was readily passed by the Commons, but the Lords passed it only by a margin of 21 to 18, with two Catholic bishops imprisoned and the Abbot of Westminster absent. The Queen and her Council had secured a narrow triumph over the conservative peers and bishops through the use of propaganda, censorship, compromise and sharp political practice.

In the 1950s JE Neale proposed that Elizabeth had been aiming merely at restoring Henrician Catholicism without the Pope, but the opposition of the Catholic bishops forced her to turn for support to recently returned Protestants, the **Marian exiles**, in the House of Commons who clamoured for a more radical religious settlement. That interpretation has since been dismissed by a number of historians, in particular N Jones in *Faith by Statute*, who have shown that the exiles had not returned in significant numbers by 1559, nor were they suffi-

See page 147

Marian exiles those Protestants who had left England during the reign of Mary Tudor, gathering in Protestant cities on the continent, such as Strasbourg or Geneva, until they were able to return to England under Elizabeth.

ciently organised to sway the House of Commons. In fact, the consensus among historians is that the Queen's tactics were clearly designed to overcome Catholic opposition to her religious settlement.

In order to reassure the great majority of English and Welsh people, who were hostile towards religious innovation and concerned about their prospects for salvation after death, Elizabeth portrayed herself as the reformer of the existing Church in England and not as the founder of a new Church. That was important in winning wide acceptance for the Elizabethan settlement. The *Book of Common Prayer* was certainly Protestant, but its scriptural basis emphasised the core beliefs common to all Christians. It contained little that was directly offensive to Catholics who could, in any case, remain as passive onlookers during Church services, except once a year at Easter when it was necessary to take Communion. Furthermore, in her **Injunctions** Elizabeth approved of the continued use of moderate ceremonial in her Church, such as the use of traditional **vestments**, and was diplomatically silent about Church ornaments and liturgical music, despite the opposition of most Protestants. Clerical marriage was discouraged by the Virgin Queen, though she was unable to prohibit it as she wished in the face of a determined Protestant preference for a married ministry.

Such outward signs of continuity, while of little theological significance, helped to convince many conservatively minded priests and people to remain within the established Church. Indeed, the decision of the vast majority of the Catholic clergy to acquiesce in the Elizabethan settlement, whatever reservations they may have felt, served to emphasise powerfully the continuity of the Elizabethan Church of England with its medieval past. The vestiges of medieval Catholicism, which Elizabeth defined as **adiaphora**, were significant in placating conservative opinion, but they would become the focus of Protestant hostility for the remainder of her reign. As time passed many Protestants, especially the more zealous Puritans and radicals, came to regard the preservation of Catholic Church structures in the Church of England, and especially the continuation of some 'popish' elements in the established Church's liturgy, as intolerable.

From the end of June 1559 the Settlement began to be implemented with the Oath of Supremacy being required by the new court overseeing religious matters, the Court of High Commission. All but one of the Marian bishops refused the Oath and were deprived of office. That gave Elizabeth the opportunity to appoint an entire bench of Protestant bishops. She chose the moderate Matthew Parker as her new Archbishop of Canterbury. He was a man with a strong sense of the past who produced a history of the English Church (*De Antiquitate Britannicae Ecclesiae*) which so emphasised continuity that the uninitiated reader would hardly realise that any Reformation had taken place in England.

Apart from the Catholic bishops, only around 300 priests, out of 8000, refused the Oath of Supremacy and were deprived of their offices in the Church. Yet, those who did refuse the oath, were drawn disproportionately from the ranks of the senior and the best educated clergy. The Catholic Church leadership in England was effectively neutered,

Injunctions official instructions on Church services and the organisation of the Church, supplementary to Acts of Parliament

Vestments the special, ritual clothing of clergy during Church services

Adiaphora matters indifferent to salvation and therefore for the Queen to decide

PICTURE 23
Matthew Parker, Archbishop of Canterbury

and its place throughout the church and in the universities was taken by Protestants. At the Convocation of the clergy of the province of Canterbury in 1563, Protestant clergymen were already in the ascendant.

Some sort of compromise had been achieved. As Conrad Russell has put it: 'as the ceremony prevented the Church flying apart at the Catholic end, so the doctrine prevented it from flying apart at the Protestant end'. Nonetheless, few were satisfied and the success of the Elizabeth religious settlement was not inevitable. The re-establishment of Protestantism was not greeted with widespread enthusiasm in the parishes of England and Wales. The Protestant exiles who returned to England after Mary's death numbered only 700, and Protestantism was largely the religion of one faction of the educated élite within the political nation and Church. The majority of the population did not want change. Their Christianity co-existed with quasi-magical sets of beliefs involving miracles and witchcraft. Replacing that concoction of faith and superstitions with an austere religion derived from the Bible only would take time.

Furthermore, Elizabeth's settlement strongly reflected her own personal inclinations and harked back to the theology of Thomas Cranmer. She refused to follow subsequent developments in Protestant theology, most associated with John Calvin at Geneva. As such her settlement was liable not only to challenge from the Catholic majority who resented having Protestantism imposed upon them, but also by the Protestant minority who regarded Elizabeth's Reformation as incomplete. As Patrick Collinson observed, 'The result must have seemed precarious and provisional, not a settlement to last for more than four hundred years'.

KEY ISSUE

In what ways, and why, was the Religious Settlement of 1559 a compromise?

3 ⌁ BUILDING THE CHURCH OF ENGLAND

It was no easy task to transform the Church of England into the Church of the English and Welsh people. Yet the Queen could count on support from a significant Protestant portion of the population, particularly in what AG Dickens termed the 'great crescent' of south eastern England, extending from Norwich to Hove and including East Anglia, London, Kent and the Thames Valley generally, with strong pockets of Protestantism in such cities as Bristol, Coventry and Manchester and in cloth-producing areas in Yorkshire. These were the wealthiest and most populous parts of England. The heartlands of traditionalist religion tended to be in the more sparsely populated and poorer highland regions in the west and the north of England. There was much traditionalism in southern England too, but it could be kept under closer official supervision and constraint in the small and compact parishes within the Protestant crescent.

Elizabeth's transformation of the Church was greatly helped by the fact that she was able to install committed Protestants on the bench of bishops, in the **cathedral chapters** and in the universities, as senior

Cathedral chapters the governing bodies of cathedrals, made up of the canons, the leading cathedral clergy

Catholic clergymen either forfeited their offices under the new settlement, or chose to go into exile. Elizabeth's bishops (17 of whom were exiles during the Marian persecution) often struggled to promote the Reformation across unwieldy dioceses, but all the further proposals to reform the Church's administrative structures were blocked by the Queen. Indeed, Elizabeth made the work of her bishops very difficult indeed by re-imposing the ecclesiastical taxes of First Fruits and Tenths, at a cost of about £40 000 in annual revenue. To make matters worse, Elizabeth took away from bishops many of their estates through the 1559 Act of Exchange which allowed her to take episcopal lands in return for spiritual revenues, like tithes, of the same value. A number of Elizabethan bishops were pushed into crippling debts which distracted them from their ministry. Bishop Bentham died after 20 years in office owing £1000 to the Crown, and £200 to his diocese. On a more positive note, the loss of their London residences compelled bishops to spend more time in their own dioceses than their predecessors had done.

Once her religious settlement had been sanctioned by Parliament, Elizabeth entrusted the governance of the Church to her bishops. Through episcopal visitations the bishops ensured that the Latin Mass and other Catholic ceremonies were replaced by the **liturgy** of the *Book of Common Prayer*. Catholic ornaments in churches were sought out and destroyed, eventually even in the most remote parishes, and the churches of England and Wales came to take on an austere Protestant appearance. The authorities in Church and state were careful not to antagonise the Catholics too much in the early years of the settlement, but as time passed there were increasing efforts made to eliminate residual Catholic practices, like praying with rosary beads. By the 1570s the aged were taking their traditionalist habits of piety with them to the grave while younger generations grew up who had not experienced the Catholic religion.

Liturgy the 'script' for church services

> ## KEY ISSUE
>
> *What assisted Elizabeth and her bishops and what obstructed them in the re-building of the Church of England?*

A *Reforming the ministry*

Elizabeth's bishops wanted to establish a preaching ministry in every parish of England and Wales (though the Queen felt that two or three per county would suffice). However, in 1559 the bishops were confronted by an acute shortage of clergymen. Recruitment to the priesthood had plummeted since the onset of religious turmoil and uncertainty over the previous three decades. The removal of Catholic activists following the Elizabethan settlement, and the very high mortality of aged priests in the great influenza epidemic of 1557–8 left many parishes without a clergyman. In such circumstances there was no question of a mass purge of traditionalists from the Church of England. Indeed, Archbishop Parker and his episcopal colleagues were obliged to ordain many unlearned men to the ministry in order to ensure a regular round of services in hundreds of parishes. In extreme instances laymen were appointed to read Morning and Evening Prayers in churches in the absence of priests.

The continuation in office of the vast majority of the Marian parish priests served to reassure the more traditionally minded parishioners.

These men smoothed the transition from Catholicism to Protestantism by using the *Prayer Book* liturgies and reading from the officially prescribed collection of sermons known as the *Book of Homilies*. Gradually, though, the Church of England evolved into a truly Protestant establishment. By the 1570s most of the vestiges of Catholic decoration and ornamentation in the churches had been obliterated.

The Church of England came to enjoy the services of more, better-educated clergy, and these gradually replaced traditionalist priests. In the diocese of London in 1560, 40% of the clergy were graduates, whereas by 1595 this number had risen to over 70%. Not every area could boast such high numbers, especially in the poorer peripheral areas, but the trend was replicated across England and Wales. In 1584, Sir Walter Mildmay, Chancellor of the Exchequer, founded Emmanuel College, Cambridge, so that 'the most noble plants of theology and learning which would be transplanted to all parts of the Church' to produce 'a faith of purest doctrine and a life of most holy discipline'. In 1596 Frances, Countess of Sussex, founded Sidney Sussex College with the same aspiration. Even Wales, following the establishment of Jesus College, Oxford, in 1571 came to experience the powerful effects of a graduate Protestant preaching ministry. It was these men who made Protestants of the average parishioner in England and Wales. Given the low life expectancy of the times, Catholicism and religious traditionalism more generally began to die with the older generations. Increasingly the men and women of England and Wales were growing up with no memory of the old religion.

There were similar changes to the outlook of the gentry. Many attended grammar schools before going to university, not necessarily to take degrees but often for a general education, and were usually exposed to Protestant ideas, some quite advanced. Quite a number of these men went on to form part of a 'godly magistracy' committed to promoting the Reformation.

It would be hard to exaggerate the contribution made to the Protestant cause by those powerful landed magnates who operated at Court and Council, including the Earls of Bedford, Huntingdon, Leicester, Sir Francis Knollys, Sir Francis Walsingham and William Cecil, Lord Burghley. Through their patronage networks, men of acceptable religious stance gained either secular or spiritual promotion. As Chancellors of Oxford and Cambridge universities, both Burghley and Leicester were prepared to appoint theologians who were more radically Protestant than suited the Queen, or promote them as Fellows or Heads of Colleges. The Crown was the largest holder of **advowsons** and the livings were distributed by the Lord Keeper or the Lord Chancellor. The committed Protestant, Sir Nicholas Bacon, was estimated to have nominated an average of 113 clerics per year as Lord Keeper. These godly magistrates were also able to use the forum of Parliament to advance the Protestant cause.

Protestantism's ultimate success owed a very great deal to the alliance between the godly gentry and the zealous cleric, seeking to build a fully reformed Church in their localities. The Elizabethan Reformation depended for its success on secular élites as well as on clergymen.

Advowson the right to nominate who would be vicar of a particular parish

KEY ISSUE

How was the quality and suitability of ministers in the Church of England enhanced?

B *Doctrine*

The doctrine of the Church of England was enshrined in the *Book of Common Prayer*. That, however, allowed for some flexibility in interpretation. It was given greater definition by the Convocation of the province of Canterbury in 1563. The Convocation approved 39 Articles of Religion, derived with very little change from the 42 Articles of Edward's reign, in line with the Queen's own religious preferences. Elizabeth quashed an attempt by Parliament in 1566 to give legislative force to the Articles of Religion. She was keen not to impose too much upon people's consciences. She was satisfied with outward conformity to her religious settlement, confident that it would take root in people's hearts in time.

Meanwhile, the settlement had its defenders against Catholics and radical Protestants, most significantly John Jewel, Bishop of Salisbury, who in 1562 published his *Apology or Answer in defence of the Church of England*. Jewel defended the Elizabethan Church by arguing that its teachings and liturgies were firmly based on the Bible. He also argued that ecclesiastical as well as secular power must lie in the hands of the Christian ruler – a view known as 'erastianism' after its originator, Dr Erastus, physician to the Elector Palatine.

Over time, though, the Church of England began to embrace much of the theology of the Geneva-based reformer, John Calvin. Calvin had interpreted the Bible as meaning that, even before birth, God predestines not just some people for salvation in Heaven but also others for damnation in Hell. This is known as double predestination, and it contrasts with the Catholic view that you will be judged according to what you do by your own free will. Double predestination became central to the beliefs of most English Protestants towards the close of Elizabeth's reign. Alongside this was a firm belief in divine Providence, that is God's plan for the world. As Protestantism became more firmly established, and particularly in reaction to the war against Spain, which was taken to represent the forces of the Antichrist, many came to believe that England was the nation God had chosen to defend the true faith against its enemies. This sense of national religious mission, reinforced by Calvinist beliefs, forged a powerful consensus that helped to hold people of varying views within the Church of England, while distinguishing them sharply from Catholics.

Calvin's views on church organisation, however, proved to be a divisive issue among English Protestants. In the Calvinist churches in the rest of Europe, such as in France and Scotland, there were no bishops. Authority in the Church was exercised by groups of ordinary clergy and leading members of local congregations, known as lay elders. This form of Church government is called Presbyterianism. There were Presbyterian campaigns in the 1570s and 1580s to do away with bishops, but the Church of England was able to maintain its ecclesiastical organisation with Queen Elizabeth's support.

By the 1590s the Church was being stoutly defended by a number of influential writers, most notably Richard Hooker. His *Laws of Ecclesiastical*

Polity refuted Presbyterianism in an effective intellectual defence of the national Church and laid the foundations for the later intellectual development of '*ius divino* episcopacy' (divine right of bishops) in the following century.

Such writers as Hooker and the bishops themselves, while supporting the Royal Supremacy and maintaining an Erastian position, did not necessarily reject the beliefs associated with Calvinism. Whitgift, for instance, produced the Lambeth Articles of 20 November 1595, in which he defined a clearly Calvinist view that 'God from eternity predestined certain men to life and condemned others to death'. Elizabeth moved quickly to prevent publication of the Articles and end potentially divisive debate. Whitgift was forced to back down, but the Articles mark a clear statement of the Church of England's Calvinist doctrine in the late years of the reign and reinforced the belief of the godly that further reform might one day be attained.

> ## KEY ISSUE
>
> *In what ways was the Elizabethan Church Calvinist, and in what ways was it not?*

4 ◦ ELIZABETH AND THE PURITANS

The term 'Puritan' is useful as a broad brush for the student of Elizabethan Protestant religion but it needs careful handling. It was not a term in much use at the time. It first surfaced in 1565 among works of Catholic exiles and was used as a term of abuse. The Puritans themselves used phrases such as 'True Gospellers' or 'the Godly' and were regarded in general as 'hotter' Protestants or 'precisians'. Many of them had gone into exile during Mary's reign and they were greatly influenced by the teachings and practices of John Calvin at Geneva. They believed in Calvinist 'double predestination' of the 'elect' (destined for Heaven) and 'the reprobate' (destined for Hell). They believed that the Bible was the only source of religious instruction in God's Word, and that a 'godly' life required total conformity to that Word. The Word had to be preached to convert the people and to uproot the last remnants of the 'Anti-Christ': the Pope and his Church (that 'rose-coloured whore seated upon the Beast'). The problem arose that many thought these criteria also applied elsewhere, to many of Elizabeth's bishops for instance.

Two issues, however, differentiated the Puritans from their fellow Protestants. Firstly, the speed at which the Church was to be fully reformed – for Puritans it was to be done as quickly as possible, irrespective of the practical problems which this might entail. Meanwhile they would adapt the regulations set down in 1559 to create a more 'Godly church' like the Reformed churches abroad. Secondly, there was the issue of obedience to the princely power – what Patrick Collinson considers 'the geological fault-line between Anglicanism and Nonconformity'. The Queen and, in varying degrees, her bishops, insisted that in matters indifferent to salvation (adiaphora), the will of the prince must be obeyed. For the Puritans, if such things were not in the Bible, then a Christian was free to ignore them. For them, loyalty to God came before loyalty to the Prince, and a truly reformed Church had to be separated from the power of the monarch.

The Puritans wished to see the hierarchical Church of England, which was subject to the Supreme Governor, replaced with a Presbyterian system which recognised no difference in authority among ordained ministers. Ministers and lay elders would lead the individual congregations in true religion, adhering as closely as possible to the Word of God in the Bible. However, while some Puritans ventured into open conflict with the Elizabethan settlement over these issues, there were a great number of others who conformed to the Church established by law while hoping for official sanction for further reformation.

A *Pressures for further reformation*

Many Protestants, and not only those known as Puritans, were not entirely satisfied with the 1559 religious settlement. They preferred to see an end to the remaining Catholic practices embedded in the Queen's Church. The 'ornaments' rubric of the Act of Uniformity, requiring the use of traditional vestments, was criticised for incorporating the 'rags of Popery' into Church services; stone altars had not been removed and a royal injunction allowed the use of unleavened wafers reminiscent of the Mass rather than ordinary bread as prescribed in the *Prayer Book*. For many Protestants the 1559 settlement was only the start of the Reformation, for the Queen it was the end.

The 1560s saw the Puritans seek further official reformation of the Church, while unofficially adapting the *Prayer Book* to create a more 'godly' Church at parish level. They took strong exception to the use of vestments reminiscent of those worn by Catholic priests and castigated the white surplice prescribed in the *Prayer Book* as the 'signs of popish priesthood'. In the 'Vestiarian' controversy, the dispute over vestments, godly ministers rejected such vestments as lacking a scriptural basis, despite Archbishop Parker's assertion (at the instigation of an irate Queen) that they were 'adiaphora'. These ministers, supported by some bishops, began to develop a pattern of godly churchmanship, rejecting also the sign of the cross on the forehead at baptism, shortening the service to allow for extended sermons, and objecting to plays and merrymaking on holy days especially on the Sabbath.

When the Convocation of Canterbury met in 1563 to define the beliefs of the Church of England, Puritans sought to promote further reformation. The Convocation agreed that 'Holy Scripture containeth all things necessary to salvation', but it did not accept the Calvinist doctrine of 'double predestination'. Even worse for the Puritans, six articles representing godly churchmanship were narrowly defeated by 59 votes to 58. Three of the six articles would have directed that the minister turn his face towards the people during Church services, that kneeling for communion (as in Catholic practice) be made optional, and that ministers need not wear vestments. These issues mattered so much to Puritans because the traditional practices of the priest facing the altar rather than the people, wearing vestments which set him ritually apart from the congregation, and communicants kneeling before him, these practices made it seem as though the priest was superior to the people, which Puritans utterly rejected.

The vote was a narrow defeat for the Puritans but the Church authorities, by careful management of elections, never again gave the Puritans the chance to attack the Established Church in Convocation. In 1566, at the Queen's instigation, Archbishop Parker published 'Advertisements' enforcing the 1559 Settlement regarding clerical dress and ceremonial. Forty London clerics were deprived of their livings when they refused to accept the orders. Parker and the Queen signalled an end to the toleration of Puritan adaptations to the *Book of Common Prayer*. The Puritans began to look to other means of achieving their further reformation of the Church.

KEY ISSUE

How did Puritans want to change the Church?

B *The Presbyterian challenge*

In 1571 William Strickland, a Puritan MP, introduced a Bill to Parliament to reform the *Prayer Book* and abolish the surplice. It was rejected, but John Field, an influential Presbyterian radical, emerged as the link between the 'godly' congregations and Puritan MPs in the Commons, under the patronage, amongst others, of the Earl of Leicester. In a related move the Queen was forced to allow the 39 Articles to be given the status of an Act of Parliament, a move she had quashed earlier, but which she now saw as necessary to contain the Puritans' challenge.

Thomas Cartwright, Lady Margaret Professor of Divinity at Cambridge, was the first establishment figure to advocate Presbyterianism, which he did in a series of lectures on the Acts of the Apostles in 1570. He called for the abolition of bishops on the grounds that they had no biblical basis for their existence, and suggested their replacement by a Presbyterian Church organisation. Although he acknowledged the 1559 religious settlement as a welcome beginning, he wanted it completed by adopting in full the teachings of John Calvin of Geneva. Cartwright was sacked for making such outrageous proposals. In 1572 Cartwright presented one of two 'Admonitions [or warnings] to the Parliament' (the other was presented by Field and a fellow Puritan minister, Thomas Wilcox) arguing that the popish hierarchy of the Church of England should be replaced by consistories (governing bodies made up of clergy and lay elders) like those in Geneva. The 'Admonitions' were rejected by the Parliament. Field and Wilcox were lodged in Newgate Prison, while Cartwright took refuge in Geneva.

In 1575 Matthew Parker died. Edmund Grindal, Archbishop of York, came south to succeed him as Archbishop of Canterbury.

It was late in 1576 when Queen Elizabeth ordered Archbishop Grindal to suppress **prophesyings**. The Queen reckoned that these religious gatherings outside the formal structures of the Church fostered Presbyterian unrest and agitation, and she wanted them closed down. Grindal, on the other hand, appreciated the value of 'prophesyings' as means of improving the quality of the parish clergy. He consulted his bishops and found, as he expected, that 10 out of 15 were in favour of

Prophesyings
gatherings of clergymen, often with some godly gentlemen in attendance, in which there was prayer, discussion of theology and pastoral issues, and exercises to improve the preaching skills of the ministers

EDMUND GRINDAL, ARCHBISHOP OF CANTERBURY (1519–83)

The appointment of Edmund Grindal as Archbishop of Canterbury in 1575 was a political move. Highly thought of by his contemporaries, he had been a Marian exile in Strasbourg and then, as Bishop of London, had helped establish London as a centre for Protestantism. In the Vestiarian Controversy he had upheld royal authority despite his sympathies for the Puritan cause and had been appointed Archbishop of York in 1569, in the wake of rebellion by the Catholic earls of northern England, to maintain the pressure on those remaining Catholic. As President of the York Ecclesiastical Commission and in alliance with the Earl of Huntingdon as President of the Council in the North after 1572, Grindal tried to entrench Protestantism in the rural, backward North. He resisted the move to Canterbury because he felt his job in the North was not finished. However, influential courtiers supported him as the one most likely to contain within the Church those 'hotter' Protestants alienated by Parker's defence of the status quo. In this way it was hoped to take the steam out of Presbyterianism, by reforming from within, and closing Protestant ranks against revitalised popery.

It looked at first that this had been the right move. Grindal encouraged the publication of a translation of Scripture known as the Geneva Bible, and ensured clergy held only one post and were not absenteeists. These were practical reforms which won wide support, and controversy between Protestants began to recede. However, the issue of prophesyings. brought about a clash between the Archbishop and Elizabeth. He refused to suppress them as the Queen demanded, and was suspended for his resistance to royal authority in this matter in the summer of 1577 until his death in July 1583.

See page 223

'prophesyings' and he refused to suppress them. He wrote boldly to the Queen on 20 December 1576 to ask 'how this strange opinion should once enter into your mind that it should be good for the Church to have few preachers'. He continued with two petitions:

> The first is, that you would refer all these ecclesiastical matters which touch religion, or the doctrine and discipline of the Church, to the bishops or divines of your realm, according to the example of all godly Christian emperors and princes of all ages …
>
> The second petition I have to make to your Majesty is this: that when you deal in matters of faith and religion, … you would not pronounce so resolutely and peremptorily, as from authority, as you may do in civil and extern[al] matters; but always remember that in God's causes the will of God, and not the will of any earthly creatures, is to take place …

Q

1. *Why was this advice so unacceptable to the Queen?*
2. *What can we learn about Grindal's religious views from the extract?*

Grindal chose, as he saw it, to obey God before the Supreme Governor of the Church. He was consequently suspended from his duties in the summer of 1577 until his death in July 1583. His suspension ended hopes of creating a consensus which could have embraced all shades of Protestant opinion within the Church of England. As such it was a sharp turning point for the Church under Elizabeth, but perhaps it should not be over-stated. 'Prophesyings' were not suppressed in the northern province of the English Church, being deemed necessary for the fight against ingrained traditionalism. Even in the southern province they subsequently re-appeared as 'lectures by combination'.

Presbyterians reacted to Archbishop Grindal's suspension by developing the '*classis* movement', which aimed to promote reform at grass-roots level despite official hostility. Owing much to Calvin's model in Geneva, the *classis* or Presbyterian meetings were organised by using Walter Travers' *Full & Plain Declaration of Ecclesiastical Discipline* (1574) in place of the *Prayer Book*. Travers' book required ministers and congregational leaders (lay elders) from a number of parishes to form themselves into a *classis* to maintain discipline and uniformity of belief. Each *classis* would elect representatives to a provincial synod and they, in turn, would elect men to a national synod. The first national synod met in Cambridge in 1582, and another in 1587 in London, to co-ordinate plans for the forthcoming parliamentary session. It was hoped that this Presbyterian system would ultimately replace the traditional system of bishops in the Church of England surreptitiously.

The coverage of the *classis* movement is difficult to gauge but appears to have been strongest in London, the south Midlands and the South-east. However, by the time of Field's death in March 1588, the attempt to establish a clandestine national Presbyterian organisation had failed due to an aggressive campaign by the Church authorities and because it was supported only by a small minority of Protestants, lay and clerical.

C *The containment of Puritanism*

The appointment of John Whitgift as Archbishop of Canterbury in September 1583, following the death of Grindal, saw a return of anti-Puritan pressure. Whitgift had come to the fore in 1570 when, as Head of Trinity College, Cambridge, he published a critique of Cartwright's Presbyterian interpretation of the Acts of the Apostles. Whitgift argued that there was no scriptural basis for Presbyterianism and vehemently defended the hierarchy as established in 1559. Yet, although he was a determined opponent of Calvinist church structures, he was a committed Calvinist in his belief in predestination.

Supported by a bench of bishops who were less sympathetic than their predecessors to Puritans, Whitgift tried to enforce uniformity and orthodoxy on the Church of England ministers, in accordance with statutory requirement. In this policy he was strongly supported by the Queen. Whitgift demanded that all of the clergy of the southern province subscribe to three articles, recognising the Royal Supremacy,

PICTURE 24
John Whitgift, Archbishop of Canterbury

agreeing to all of the 39 Articles and accepting that the *Prayer Book* contained nothing contrary to the Word of God. In other words, he demanded conformity to the established Church government, doctrine and liturgy. He intended to use the Court of High Commission to deprive any clergy of their office who would not conform. In fact, between 300 and 400 ministers refused to swear an oath that the *Prayer Book* contained nothing contrary to the Word of God and, although only a handful were actually deprived, hundreds of preaching ministers were prohibited from preaching again. A wave of protest from the Council and the counties forced Whitgift to climb down and require full subscription only from new ministers. Even so, Whitgift was appointed to the Privy Council (February 1586) as the only Elizabethan churchman to exercise significant political influence.

Puritans organised petitions to the Parliament of 1584–5 criticising Archbishop Whitgift's methods, and the condition of the Church in general. Ignoring the Queen's order that religion was not to be discussed, the Commons listened sympathetically to the Puritan complaints and demands. This was not quite the 'grass-roots' movement it might have appeared, as the agitation in Parliament was supported by powerful courtiers and Councillors who hoped the pressure would move Elizabeth towards more through-going reformation. However, the debates proved fruitless as the Queen blocked the introduction of a bill by Dr Turner to establish a Presbyterian system in the Church. Nevertheless, the Puritans persisted. A 'General Supplication' for reform, based on evidence drawn from 2537 parishes, was presented to Parliament in 1586, along with petitions complaining about the bishops' suspension of godly ministers.

See pages 203–4

On 27 February 1587 a Puritan MP, Anthony Cope, introduced a 'Bill and Book' to Parliament proposing the abolition of all existing laws and customs of the Church and the establishment of a Presbyterian system of government and worship based on a revised Genevan Prayer Book. It was a carefully prepared assault on the Church of England by Travers and Field, backed by the simultaneous meeting of the Presbyterians' National Synod in London. When the Speaker, as the Queen's agent in the Commons, warned the House 'not to meddle with this matter', four Puritan MPs still pressed for the Bill to be read. Its subsequent confiscation by the Queen caused Peter Wentworth to launch his famous attack on royal interference in Commons' business. He and his four Puritan colleagues were sent to the Tower of London charged with holding private meetings to plan parliamentary business – an offence not protected by parliamentary privilege.

See page 200

That represented the high-water mark of radical Elizabethan Puritanism. Denied again their opportunity through Parliament, the Puritans were forced back upon the unofficial implementation of their programme by godly ministers at local level, since 'seeing we cannot compass these things by suit, nor dispute, it is the multitude and people that must bring the discipline to pass which we desire'. However, circumstances prevailed against them. Foreign affairs and the Armada of 1588 rallied moderates behind the Queen, while the removal of the

Queen of Scots in 1587 as the internal focus of Catholic hopes denied the radicals a weapon with which to beat the established authorities. Even worse, the deaths of John Field and his patron, the Earl of Leicester, in 1588 were compounded by the demise of other powerful Court patrons of the Puritan cause, such as the Earl of Bedford (1585) and Sir Walter Mildmay (1589).

The 'Martin Marprelate Tracts', violent and abusive attacks on the Church of England and its bishops (1587), possibly the work of the separatist John Penry, further scandalised religious opinion and alienated political support from the Puritans. William Cecil, Lord Burghley, viewed them as subversive. That opened the way for Whitgift to launch another concerted campaign against the Puritans, one which he was to maintain until his death in 1604.

Not that the Presbyterians were the most radical of the Puritan strand of Protestantism. The 1570s had seen the development of a body of Protestants who had as little time for a Presbyterian national Church structure, as they did for the established one. These sects first developed around London after the 'Admonitions' controversy of 1571–2 and wanted each congregation to run its own affairs independently of any authority. Frustration at Presbyterian inertia led to Robert Browne publishing a 'Treatise for Reformation without Tarrying for Any' which denied the Royal Supremacy, and sought a covenant or agreement among his supporters to create a truly reformed Church within their congregations in a loose confederation.

Another separatist group later emerged in London under the leadership of Henry Barrow. These early congregationalist sects saw themselves as the 'saints' of a true but invisible church and sought separation from the 'evil' Church of England as established in 1559. To the authorities they were guilty of the same crime as Catholic missionary priests and active recusants – denying loyalty to the Queen and, through their separatism, threatening the whole social order. In 1583 two Brownists, Tasker and Copping, were hanged for treason under the recusancy laws. In 1593 Parliament passed 'An Act against Sectaries', and John Greenwood and Henry Bacon were hanged for sedition in the same year.

Presbyterianism had never been a widespread or well-supported body of opinion. It was a minority group which made an impact far in excess of its numbers through astute propaganda, shrewd tactics and sympathetic patronage on the Council, e.g. from Warwick and Walsingham. In the aftermath of political defeat, the Puritans directed their energies towards preaching, pastoral work and the development of personal piety, while conforming within the Church of England. Puritan social and moral values, and particularly the preservation of the Sabbath as the Lord's Day in opposition to the temptations of alehouse, theatre or sports, developed as the characteristics of a radical wing within the established Church. Elizabethan radical Puritanism went underground in the 1590s, to create a pressure group within the Church of England dedicated to the furtherance of the 'godly' reformation.

KEY ISSUE

How did Puritans campaign to advance their cause, and why did they largely fail?

5 ⌁ ELIZABETH AND THE CATHOLICS

The hope of the Queen and her Council was that Catholicism would quietly wither away as the old priests gradually died off and the people conformed to the 1559 religious settlement. The deprivation of the Catholic bishops and around 300 other senior priests from their offices in the Church and universities left a leadership vacuum in the Catholic community. Even the papacy failed at first to provide guidance, because Philip II wanted to avoid making an enemy of Elizabeth; it was not until 1562 that Catholics were forbidden to attend Church of England services, by which time many were in the habit of confirming, at least outwardly, to the requirements of the Elizabethan settlement. Had Elizabeth enjoyed as short a reign as her brother or sister, this stratagem could have preserved the Catholic community intact until a new, possibly Catholic, ruler ascended the throne. However, given Elizabeth's longevity, the conformity of people who were still Catholic at heart, known as 'Church papistry', actually served as a transitional phase for most from Catholicism to Protestantism.

The Acts of Supremacy and Uniformity imposed a one shilling fine for failure to attend church and loss of office for refusal to take the Oath. Celebrating Mass, or arranging for it to be celebrated, led to the death penalty. Mere attendance at Mass resulting in a crippling fine of 100 marks (£67). While the fine was levied in some cases, Elizabeth ensured that the death penalty was not implemented before 1577, partly because she thought it unnecessarily harsh, and partly from the fact that a wholehearted commitment to apply such punishments would have been beyond the government's ability to impose and would have caused serious disruption, setting Protestant against Catholic. Imprisonment was the preferred alternative, as in 1568 when a number of prominent Catholics, including Lady Brown and Lady Cary, were arrested for attending Mass.

A *Survivalism*

During the 1560s there was little threat from Catholicism. According to a 1564 Privy Council Survey many Justices of the Peace were Catholic, or at least sympathetic to the cause. Yet a minimum of conformity was almost universally observed by the heads of households, while some maintained their traditional practices behind their own doors. Several priests in the Church of England provided the official Church services in public and Catholic ones in private. Some tried to incorporate Catholic practices, such as elevating the Host, into the *Prayer Book* communion service.

See pages 433–5

During the process of gradual conformity in the 1560s, there was relatively little recusancy, though some evidence survives. The recusants were Catholics who refused to attend Church of England services or refused the Oath of Supremacy. They included priests who were deprived or resigned in 1559. Lancashire had some 40 recusant priests in the 1560s. However, the dominant trend of these early years was one of superficial conformity to the Church of England among the Catholics, their own devotions unmolested owing to the problems of enforcing penal legislation in the localities, especially in Catholic areas. This in turn meant there was little separation from parish church into recusancy.

In 1558 conservative religion was still powerful, adhered to by the vast majority of the population as the 'natural' religion. This attachment to the old religion, often under the protection of some of the gentry, formed the substance of early Elizabethan Catholicism. John Bossy, in *The Character of English Catholicism*, characterised the religion at that time as 'less concerned with doctrinal affirmation or dramas of conscience than with a set of ingrained observances which defined and gave meaning to the cycle of the week and the seasons of the year, to birth, marriage and death. This has been aptly termed survivalism'. As the years progressed this 'survivalism' was steadily eroded. It persisted most strongly in the remoter parts of England and Wales: in Cornwall, Wales and the North of England and in less accessible districts in Kent, Sussex and similar places. The external shows of this religion, such as festivals and processions, were lost, but the personal and spiritual main-stream of its faith continued in private.

> ## KEY ISSUE
>
> *How did Catholicism adapt in the early years of Elizabeth's religious settlement?*

B *Revolt and treason*

By the late 1560s the future prospects of Catholicism in England were beginning to look distinctly unpromising. However, the arrival in Eng-land of Mary, Queen of Scots (May 1568) heartened many Catholics. If Elizabeth were to die without issue then her Catholic cousin could lead the English back into the Roman fold. Meanwhile, the Catholic cause was advancing on mainland Europe with Philip II's army under the Duke of Alva crushing the Dutch Protestants. For a minority of Catholic zealots the time seemed right to strike a blow for the Catholic religion before it grew too feeble. A conspiracy centred upon Mary, Queen of Scots, was formed but, before it made any progress, the chief conspirators, including the powerful Duke of Norfolk, thought better of it and threw themselves on the Queen's mercy. Two of Norfolk's leading accomplices in the North, the Earls of Northumberland and Westmore-land, were summoned to Court to account for their parts in the con-

See pages 321–3

spiracy. In panic, and under pressure from their followers, the earls launched a rebellion in November 1569. The rebels had many motives, but religion provided the glue that held the rebellion together. It enjoyed much support in the North, but its leaders had no clear plan, and their hopes of attracting support from Philip II and from English Catholics in the South were sorely disappointed. Before the year was through the two earls fled to Scotland and the rebellion was crushed.

Then, early in 1570, mistimed to perfection, Pope Pius V issued the Bull *Regnans in Excelsis* which had been requested by the Earls to coincide with the revolt. The Bull declared Elizabeth to be excommuni-cated and deposed. By its terms English Catholics were absolved from any oath of allegiance and commanded to disobey the Queen. In practice the vast majority of Catholics ignored the Bull. However, this is to miss the point. It was a marked change in theory and that was not lost on Parliament, the Church of England nor Phillip II who criticised 'this sudden and unexpected step [which] will make matters worse and drive the Queen and her friends the more to oppress and persecute the few good Catholics remaining in England'. Obedience to Rome now meant treason towards the Queen and it was taken, in Professor Elton's words, as 'an unmistakable declaration of war' threatening to break the bonds between monarch and her people. Henceforth every Catholic was to be treated as a potential traitor.

The Catholic cause was not helped by the Ridolfi Plot of March 1571 involving Mary Queen of Scots and the Duke of Norfolk, who planned to marry and then supplant Elizabeth, backed by Spanish arms and cash. As a result the Spanish Ambassador was expelled and the Duke of Norfolk was executed for treason. New legislation, such as the Treasons Act of 1571, was passed to deal with the Catholic threat. However survivalism continued, with 'Church Papistry', outward conformity, rather than recusancy being the usual means whereby the majority of Catholic households steered clear of the new stiffer legislation. For her part, the Queen still sought to maintain her moderate policy towards her Catholic subjects and tried to control the pressure building up in Parliament for more severe legislation. Yet tensions continued to increase following the massacre by Catholics of Huguenots (French Protestants) in Paris on St Bartholomew's Eve in 1572; fears were growing of an international Catholic effort to destroy Protestantism.

> ### KEY ISSUE
>
> *How had Catholicism become an increasing threat politically by the early 1570s?*

C *The mission to England*

A seminary was founded at Douai in 1568 by William Allen to educate Catholics abroad, and then to train a new priesthood for England. Its priests were not prepared simply to maintain the Elizabethan compromise but sought to introduce a purer style of Catholicism, as agreed at a General Council of the Catholic Church, the Council of Trent, which had concluded in 1563. The intention of the mission, as Edmund Campion, a Jesuit, outlined it in 1580, was 'to preach the gospel, to minister the sacraments, to instruct the simple, to reform sinners, to confute errors and, in brief, to cry alarm spiritual against foul vice and proved ignorance wherewith my countrymen are abused'.

See page 434

From the mid-1570s onwards the Catholic threat increased as the influx of seminary priests began in earnest at the rate of about 20 per year in 1576–9, rising to 29 in 1580. In June 1580 Campion and Robert Parsons were the first two Jesuit missionaries in England, bringing with them all the determination and dedication expected of Loyola's 'Soldiers of the Faith'. These men provided the organisation and structure of the Catholic Mission which the seminary priests had failed to establish since their first arrival in 1574. The seminary priests had tended to operate as isolated individuals, often sheltering near the coast. Under Jesuit auspices, London, by the 1580s, was the nerve-centre for the shelter and distribution of immigrant priests. From 1584 Allen and Parsons were working together on the supply of priests from the Continent into England. Once arrived, a network of Catholic gentry gave them shelter in their households, though they were unevenly distributed across the country. They were concentrated mainly in the South and East, despite the best efforts of Jesuits such as Robert Southwell, Henry Garnet and John Gerard to broaden the mission's range into Yorkshire, Durham and Worcestershire.

Against the background of the Mission, the international situation seemed to suggest a turning of the tide against Protestantism. The election of Pope Gregory XIII (1572–85) strengthened the Papacy's resolve to overthrow Elizabeth 'as the cause of such great harm to the Catholic faith and of the loss of so many millions of souls'. The Jesuits and William Allen were involved in the Throckmorton Plot of October 1583, whereby French Catholic forces were to invade, backed by Spanish and papal money, and liberate Mary, Queen of Scots, to start a Catholic rising. They had come to the conclusion that England could only be made Catholic again in the wake of a foreign invasion. Inevitably the Jesuits and seminary priests came to be regarded as spies and traitors. Government fears were again intensified by the assassination of William of Orange, the Protestant leader of the Dutch, and the Treaty of Joinville between Philip II and the Catholic League in France in the following year. Furthermore, the Duke of Parma was re-conquering the Netherlands for Catholicism at an alarming rate.

Not surprisingly, this international backdrop in which forces of good and evil, Christ and Antichrist, were waging a struggle to the death, further heightened English Protestant suspicion that all Catholics were fundamentally traitorous and potential assassins, like Anthony Tyrell (1581) and Dr Parry (1584). Campion claimed the Catholics were 'as true subjects as ever the Queen had' but religion could not be separated from politics, and persecution intensified as fears increased. An Act of 1581 redefined treason to include those who withdrew English subjects from allegiance to the Queen or her Church. It was still not an offence to be a Catholic – just to become one. Recusancy fines were increased to £20 and fines were increased for hearing Mass, thereby hindering Church Papists from attending Mass privately after attending services in the local church.

In 1585 Parliament ordered the expulsion of priests, and it now became treason to become a priest, with the death penalty for those who helped priests in any way. This harsh legislation aimed to undermine the organisation of the Mission and between 1586–1603, 123 out of the 146 Catholics executed were charged under this Statute – the 'Act Against Jesuits and Seminary Priests'. Treason was extended to cover those who were the cause for which others plotted treason, specifically Mary, Queen of Scots. As part of the enforcement of this legislation a series of questions were devised in 1581 for use with captured priests. The sixth and last question became known as 'The Bloody Question':

If the Pope by his Bull pronounced her Majesty to be deprived and no lawful Queen, and her subjects to be discharged of their allegiance, and if the Pope or any other by his authority do invade the realm, which part would you take, or which part ought a good subject of England to take?

Q

1. *What precisely was meant by 'a good subject of England'?*
2. *Why were the replies published by the Authorities?*

The impact of this welter of penal legislation was varied. It was clearly an attempt by the Protestant regime to destroy the missionary priesthood and to force the Catholics into conformity to the established Church. For the priests, the dangers involved did not put them off – for such trained and dedicated men, imprisonment, torture and the traitor's death by hanging, drawing and quartering were an accepted risk. Between 1581 and 1586, 30 priests were executed and 50 were put in prison, yet a further 179 priests arrived in England in the same period. A total of 21 priests were put to death in 1588, and a further 53 between 1590 and 1603. Overall, AF Pollard observed, 187 priests died for the Catholic cause and the government was not able to halt their arrival.

As far as the Catholic laity was concerned, the increase of the recusancy laws, coupled with the impact of the mission, led to a polarisation between those who conformed fully to the Church of England, and those who shifted from outward conformity to recusancy. The evidence varies from region to region, with the greatest movement into recusancy in the North, but it was also evident in and around London and in Sussex. However, heavy fines acted as a brake on recusancy. By 1592 William (now Cardinal) Allen had accepted there would remain Church Papists among English Catholics, albeit as a declining proportion amongst Catholics.

How Successful was the Catholic Mission to England?

ANALYSIS

The success of the Catholic Mission has been much debated. Christopher Haigh has suggested that the survival of English Catholicism owed little to the missionary priests, as had been suggested by John Bossy, but owed much more to the strength of native survivalism. He has argued that the Mission did not focus its efforts sufficiently on the stronger Catholic areas of the North but rather devoted its manpower disproportionately to the needs of the wealthier South and East. After 1580, 50% of the missionary priests resorted to the South-east where only 20% of detected recusants resided. Bossy, on the other hand, argued that survivalism decayed as the Marian clergy died off, and that the evangelising role of the Mission was crucial in maintaining the 'old faith' into the next century and beyond.

PV McGrath has convincingly argued that the Mission was important, even if it failed to reconvert England or fully transfer conservatives into recusancy. For a Catholic, a priest to celebrate the Mass was essential and thus without the efforts of the seminary priests and Jesuits, Catholicism would have largely disappeared. That is effectively what happened over most of England where such priests were not available. The gentry were crucial in providing shelter, 'priest holes', and funding for priests as domestic chaplains (who cost around £30 p.a.) which could not be afforded so easily in the poorer North. The ports of entry were in the South and East, and hence London became, with its ease of communication, the focus of the organisation. The expansion of Catholicism under the greater tolerance of the Stuarts was a testament to the efforts of the mission and a measure of its achievement in nurturing Catholicism among the gentry, though it did certainly fail to maximise the size and distribution of the potential Catholic community.

It should not be imagined, however, that even committed Catholics and recusants automatically supported the Mission's aim of supplanting Elizabeth. Many were opposed to such efforts, and they showed their loyalty in not rising to meet the Armada of 1588, despite Allen's wishes. Many recusants wished to fight against the Spanish, once more illustrating that patriotism and the defence of a hereditary monarch were greater priorities than personal religious conviction. Indeed, one group of Catholics appealed against the militancy of the mission, particularly in the form of George Blackwell, appointed 'Archpriest' in 1598. This group became known as the Appellants. Not a large group, the Appellants did, however, reflect a strand of conservative English Catholicism which wished to see a return to some toleration of their faith. In a sense this marked a triumph for the Settlement of the Queen, by which loyalty was the greatest test, even though Catholicism had not withered away to the extent the Queen and Council had hoped in 1559.

By the time of Elizabeth's death in 1603 the failure of Catholicism was overwhelming. It survived, in the words of Diarmuid MacCulloch, as 'a largely upper-class sect with a faintly exotic flavour'. Its priests were supported by a scatter of gentry households, found disproportionately in the North, and acted as chaplains to their wealthy patrons and their humble dependants who were too poor to be fined by the authorities. The Church of England succeeded in holding in its embrace the vast majority of the people of England and Wales, while the Catholics stood marginalised and isolated on the outside.

> ## KEY ISSUE
>
> *In what ways did the pressures under which the Catholic mission worked reflect changes in England and abroad towards the end of Elizabeth's reign?*

6 ⌐ CONCLUSION

By the time of the Queen's death in 1603 the Church of England had been securely established and was to be governed by King James, a committed Scottish Calvinist, although one prepared to uphold episcopacy as a vital bulwark to monarchy: 'No Bishop, No King' was James I's famous reply to attempts to reconstruct the Church of England upon his arrival. The Church could still not maintain the level of active preaching ministers it might ideally have liked. But it had survived attacks from both Catholics and Puritans, and had successfully encompassed all but the tiny minorities of recusants and separatists. In this, it was a triumph for Elizabeth's religious settlement which she maintained until her death. However, in the experience of parishioners, if not in its structure, the Church in 1603 had evolved beyond that of 1559. The Queen's static view of the settlement had been challenged by moderate and radical Puritans alike who sought a continuing process of reformation until the Church of England became, in their eyes, a truly reformed Church. By the end of her reign, the Church of England had progressed somewhat along these lines. An acceptance of Calvinist 'double predestination', the development of a Puritan piety, and the growth of a teaching and preaching ministry, were all achieved informally. The Church of England represented the mainstream of English Protestantism under Elizabeth's successor.

7 ↷ BIBLIOGRAPHY

The best introduction to this subject is **C Haigh *English Reformations* (OUP, 1993). See also **C Haigh (ed.) *The Reign of Elizabeth I* (Macmillan, 1984), especially the articles by Haigh, Jones and Collinson and *N L Jones, *Faith by Statute* (Royal Historical Society, 1982). **D MacCulloch, *The Later Reformation in England, 1547–1603* (Macmillan, 1990) is focused primarily upon the processes by which England was made Protestant. His consideration of the Bossy/Haigh debate on the continuity of English Catholicism is very helpful. *John Bossy *The English Catholic Community, 1570 to 1850* (Darton, Longman and Todd, 1975) is a key text in the debate. See also *Alan Dures *English Catholicism 1558–1642* (Longman Seminar Studies, 1983). **P Collinson *English Puritanism* (Historical Association, 1983) is an important study by a leading authority on Elizabethan Protestantism. **G Regan *Elizabeth I* (CUP, 1988) includes a range of documents pertinent to the reign. **J Warren *Elizabeth I: Religion and Foreign Affairs* (Hodder & Stoughton, Access to History, 1993) can be recommended as a very accessible and balanced survey of religion in Elizabeth's reign. **Susan Doran, *Elizabeth I and Religion* (Routledge, 1994) is the best recent academic study of the subject.

(*Recommended. **Highly recommended.)

8 ⌐ STRUCTURED AND ESSAY QUESTIONS

A *Structured questions*

1. (a) Did Elizabeth get the Religious Settlement she wanted?
    (b) Why did Catholics generally conform to Elizabeth's Church of England during the first decade of her reign?
2. (a) What criticisms did Puritans make against the Religious Settlement of 1559?
    (b) How was Elizabeth able to defeat the Puritan challenges to her Church?

B *Essay questions*

1. How was Elizabeth's Church of England able to win the acceptance of the great majority of English and Welsh people over the course of her reign?
2. Account for the strange death of Catholic England.
3. Why, and with what success, did Elizabeth resist Puritan attempts to modify her Religious Settlement?
4. Which constituted the greatest threat to the Religious Settlement of 1559 – the Catholics or the Puritans?
5. How successful was the Elizabethan Reformation?

9 ⌐ DOCUMENTARY EXERCISE: ELIZABETH AND HER CHURCH

SOURCE A
Jewel writing to Martyr,
14 April 1559

It has happened that the Mass in many places has of itself fallen to the ground, without any laws for its discontinuance. If the Queen herself would but banish it from her private chapel, the whole thing might be easily got rid of … She has, however, so regulated this Mass of hers (which she has hitherto retained only for the circumstances of the times) that although many things are done therein, which are scarcely to be endured, it may yet be heard without any great danger. But this woman, excellent as she is, and earnest in the cause of true religion, notwithstanding she desires a thorough change as early as possible, cannot however be induced to effect such change without the effect of law …

We thought, until this present, that by the regard which you, being the primate and metropolitan would have had hereto according to your office ... these errors, tending to breed some schism or deformity in the Church, should have been stayed and appeased. But perceiving very lately ... that the same doth rather begin to increase ... we ... have certainly determined to have all such diversities ... as breed nothing but contention ... and are also against the laws, good usages and ordinances of our realm, to be reformed and repressed ... And, therefore, we do by these our present letters ... straitly charge you ... to confer with the bishops your brethren ... and cause to be truly understood what varieties, novelties and diversities there are in our clergy ... either in doctrine or in ceremonies and rites of the Church, or in the manners, usages and behaviours of the clergy themselves ... and thereupon ... to proceed by order ... of such laws and ordinances as are provided by act of Parliament ...

SOURCE B
Queen Elizabeth to Matthew Parker, 25 January 1565

Look upon your ministry, and there are some of one occupation, some of another: some shakebucklers [swashbucklers], some ruffians, some hawkers and hunters, some dicers and carders, some blind guides and cannot see; some dumb dogs and will not bark: and yet a thousand and more iniquities have now covered the priesthood. And yet you in the meanwhile that all these whoredoms are committed, you at whose hands God will require it, you sit still, and are careless, and let men do as they list. It toucheth not belike your commonwealth and therefore you are so well contented to let all alone. The Lord increase the gifts of his Holy Spirit in you, that from faith to faith you may grow continually till that you be zealous as good King David to work his will.

SOURCE C
Edward Dering – Sermon before the Queen 1570

Right reverent father in God, we greet you well. We hear to our great grief that in sundry parts of our realm there are no small number of persons, presuming to be teachers and preachers of the Church though neither lawfully thereunto called nor yet fit for the same, which, contrary to our laws established for the public divine service of Almighty God and the administration of His holy sacraments within this Church of England, do daily devise, imagine, propound and put in execution sundry new rites and forms in the Church, as well by their preaching, reading and ministering the sacraments, as well by procuring unlawful assemblies of a great number of our people out of their ordinary parishes and from place far distant, which manner of invasions they in some places call prophesying and in some other places exercises; by which manner of assemblies great numbers of our people, specially the vulgar sort, are brought to idleness and seduced and in a manner schismatically divided amongst themselves into variety of dangerous opinions, and manifestly thereby encouraged to

SOURCE D
The Queen's letter suppressing prophesyings, 1577

the violation of our laws and to the breach of common order, and finally to the offence of all our quiet subjects that desire to serve God according to the uniform orders established in the Church, whereof the sequel cannot be but over dangerous to be suffered.

SOURCE E
The Queen's Speech to both Houses of Parliament, 29 March 1585

Yet one matter toucheth me so near, as I may not overskip; religion, the ground on which all other matters ought to take root, and being corrupted, may mar all the tree. And that there be some fault finders with the order of the clergy, which so may make a slander to myself and the Church, whose over-ruler God hath made me; whose negligence cannot be excused if any schisms or errors heretical were suffered ...

I see many over-bold with god Almighty, making too many subtle scannings of his blessed will, as lawyers do with human testaments. The presumption is so great as I may not suffer it (yet I mind not here to animate Romanists, which what adversaries they be to mine estate is sufficiently known) nor tolerate new-fangledness. I mean to guide them both by God's holy true rule ...

SOURCE F
Sir Robert Cecil to Archbishop Whitgift, 5 December 1595

Her majesty ... hath commanded me to send unto your grace that she mislikes much that any allowance hath been given by your grace and the rest of any points to be disputed of predestination, being a matter tender to and dangerous to weak, ignorant minds, and thereupon requireth your grace to suspend them. I could not tell what to answer, but do this as her majesty's commandment, and leave the matter for your grace who I know can best satisfy her in these things.

1. *Read Sources A and B. How do these documents reflect Queen Elizabeth's concern to keep religious practice strictly within the parameters laid down by Parliament?*
2. *According to Edward Dering, in Source C, how thorough had the Elizabethan Reformation been in transforming the Church and religion by 1570?*
3. *Compare Sources D and E. What reasons does Elizabeth offer for opposing the critics of her Church?*
4. *Read Source F. Why might the Queen have wished to suppress discussion of predestination? What can we deduce about the reaction of Sir Robert Cecil, her Secretary of State by that time, and Archbishop Whitgift?*
5. *'The Queen's view of her religious settlement was essentially static.' How far do these sources support this conclusion?*

Elizabeth I and Tudor Foreign Policy

10

INTRODUCTION

Elizabeth's accession in 1558 could hardly have come at a more dangerous time: Roman Catholic militancy abroad was growing, Calais had been lost only a few months before and the war against France continued until 1559. Moreover Scotland remained a focus of attention: Mary, Queen of Scots also had a claim to the English throne, which she was able to assert even while enjoying Elizabeth's enforced hospitality in England from 1567 to 1587. One possible way out for Elizabeth was to marry and thus to strengthen her dynastic and diplomatic position, but this was a weapon that could be used only once. She was courted by two French suitors, among many others, but she was ultimately unwilling to commit herself, especially as the situation in France remained fraught from 1562 to 1598 while the so-called Wars of Religion raged there. Luckily civil strife effectively neutralized the French threat until the end of Elizabeth's reign.

However, it was relations with Spain that gave Elizabeth the greatest difficulty. By a cruel twist of fate a revolt against Spanish rule in the Netherlands from 1566 brought substantial Spanish forces dangerously near to the English coast. Now the former alliance with Spain, already hard-hit by xenophobic memories of the Mary Tudor's Spanish marriage and by religious differences, finally lapsed, and a kind of passive hostility ensued. For all Elizabeth's disdain for rebellion against lawfully constituted authority, the presence of 86 000 Spanish troops just across the Channel could only be seen as a threat – and a threat reinforced by the Papal Bull of 1570 urging Catholic powers to overthrow the heretic queen. By 1585 England and Spain were officially and openly at war: a situation provoked both by the activities of Drake and his ilk, and by Spain's intervention in the Netherlands and also in religious wars which had broken out in France.

It is easy to exaggerate the significance of the failure of the Armada in 1588. After all, three further great fleets set sail from Spain against England before 1603, but the Spanish menace was contained until the end of the reign, while Elizabeth continued to invest in the expeditions of her **privateers**. It could be argued strongly that Elizabeth achieved the modest war aims that she had set for herself. England was not invaded, Scotland remained settled and quiescent under James VI (Mary's son and the heir to the English throne), and the Northern Netherlands secured a degree of independence from Spain. England's second consecutive female monarch could not be expected to lead her forces into battle, but she was able to offer inspiring leadership, not

Privateer a pirate ship or one of its crew

least in her stirring speech to her forces massed at Tilbury on the Thames as the threat of a Spanish invasion loomed.

It is ironic that Elizabeth shared none of her father's aggressive ambitions, and yet led England into a war that not only dwarfed those fought by Henry VIII, but was one of the great wars of English history. Its most famous episode, the victory over the Spanish Armada, is a celebrated event in the country's folklore, which has contributed much to the making of Elizabeth's formidable reputation. She would have wrung a wry satisfaction from her respectable place in a TV poll of 'Great Britons' just short of the 400th anniversary of her death.

1 ⁓ EARLY DIFFICULTIES

A *The Spanish alliance*

In February 1559, Philip II acknowledged the mutual benefits of the Anglo-Spanish relationship by asking for Elizabeth's hand in marriage. In her first major foreign policy decision, she refused. She was well aware that her half-sister's marriage to Philip had been deeply unpopular among a people who considered it equivalent to Spanish conquest, and it was clear that Mary had brought England into the current war against France in order to serve her husband. The decision highlights an important element in Elizabeth's foreign policy: a determination that England would avoid both the reality and appearance of falling under the control of a foreign power.

This might appear an obvious goal. But it was one that many Englishmen feared was beyond a woman ruler and that Mary had not even attempted to achieve. Many years later, it would cause the great war against Spain. However, the refusal to marry Philip did not, and was not intended to, cause a rift between the two countries. Far from feeling rebuffed, Philip was relieved that the difficulties caused by his previous marriage were not to be repeated. The underlying reasons for an alliance of Spain and England remained compelling on both sides. Its most immediate benefit was felt in Philip's success in persuading the Pope, despite French pressure, not to declare the new Queen illegitimate and a heretic; the Pope's silence was to be a major factor in limiting Catholic opposition to the Elizabethan Religious Settlement.

B *The Treaty of Câteau-Cambrésis*

In August 1558, several months before Elizabeth's accession, the representatives of Spain, England, France and Scotland began to negotiate an end to a war that had been fought to the point of exhaustion on all sides. When the Peace of Câteau-Cambrésis was signed in April 1559, the French promise to restore Calais after eight years or forfeit 500 000 crowns was a thinly veiled English surrender, for all knew that the French intended to keep it. Giving Calais up was a realistic and necessary step, for Philip was unwilling to continue the war and England could not have continued alone. The port had been a financial drain, and, given Elizabeth's limited ambitions, it would no longer have been useful as a launching pad for aggression against France. Nevertheless, the loss of Calais was damaging. England no longer had the same domination of the narrow Straits of Dover, the principal route between Spain and the Netherlands as well as France and Scotland; one of England's levers of power against the might of both France and Spain was forfeited. Above all, the loss of Calais after over 200 years was a major blow to English prestige and in particular to the pride of a Queen who was opening her reign with this humiliating settlement.

C *Scotland*

Of course, French power was still to be feared. Henry II was 'bestriding the realm, having one foot in Calais and the other in Scotland' (Cecil), with Calais in French hands, and with the Catholic Mary of Guise Regent of Scotland on behalf of her daughter, Mary, Queen of Scots, who was married to Henry's son and heir. As Jane Dawson has written, 'An English bridgehead in France had been replaced by a French bridgehead in Britain'. It seemed likely that the French would challenge the legitimate succession of Anne Boleyn's daughter and support instead the claim of Mary, Queen of Scots, the wife of Francis, their own King's son and heir. Mary of Guise had appointed Frenchmen to numerous positions of power in Scotland, and in March 1559 launched a campaign to suppress Protestantism. In May 1559, however, the Scottish Protestants rebelled. Their speedy success, promising the institution of an anti-French and Protestant regime, was naturally welcomed in England, Elizabeth secretly sent money and arms, and some Scots even proposed a 'joyful conjunction' of the two kingdoms.

However, a very different outcome seemed likely when the French prepared to send a large army to suppress the revolt. French control would be reasserted and, even worse, this new army would be in a position to threaten England from the north. 'The old postern gate where the Scots could create a diversion had become the front door through which a French army might march' (Dawson).

In July 1559, fate dealt England a further blow. Henry II of France died after being struck in the eye at a joust held to celebrate the peace with Spain. He was succeeded by Francis II, married to Mary, Queen of Scots, but the royal couple were no more than 'flexible instruments' in the hands of the Guises, Mary's uncles. These ambitious men were determined to help their sister, Mary of Guise, assert French control of Scotland and to advance the claim of their niece, Mary, Queen of Scots, as the legitimate Queen of England. The wider context made the position ever more dire. Spain was war-weary, Philip II was now preoccupied with the Ottoman threat in the Mediterranean, and not over-enthusiastic about actively assisting the Protestant Elizabeth. England would face the might of France alone.

It was William Cecil, Elizabeth's chief adviser and secretary, with careful reasoning and a threat of resignation, who persuaded Elizabeth

KEY ISSUE

What were the strengths and weaknesses in Elizabeth's international position in 1559?

that the risk of intervening in Scotland had to be taken. Dawson has argued convincingly that Cecil had formulated a coherent, long-term 'British strategy' that aimed at ensuring England could face Europe without fear of the enmity of Scotland or Ireland. The chance to secure a Protestant, Anglophile Scotland should not be missed. 'Any wise kindle the fire, for if quenched, the opportunity will not come in our lives.' His handling of Elizabeth was masterly. She abhorred the thought of helping rebels ('It is against God's law to aid any subjects against their natural princes or their ministers'), and, far from feeling sympathy with fellow-Protestants, she shrank from the subversive brand of Calvinism of John Knox and the Scots, which justified rebellion. So, in petitions that Cecil framed on behalf of the Scots, he had them declare emphatically their loyalty to their Queen ('in no wise withdrawing their hearts from their sovereign lady', Mary) and omit any reference to religion. Elizabeth was won over, rather, by emphasising the French threat to England, and Cecil's genius was evident in his method of communicating this to her: he played upon the instances of French questioning of her right to be Queen, knowing well that her extreme sensitivity on this point made it the key to exciting her to action.

Finally, in February 1560, under pressure from the Council, Elizabeth sent Norfolk to conclude the Treaty of Berwick with the Scots rebels, and English soldiers were duly marched into Scotland. Their attempt to storm the French garrison at Leith was defeated by their own military ineptitude, the stout French resistance, and the effectiveness of the horde of Scottish prostitutes who threw stones, burning coals and wood in defence of their customers. But gales had destroyed the task force sent from France, and financial crisis ruled out another attempt at relief. The Guise faction was preoccupied at home with the opposition of other noble families and the emerging Protestant threat, and their will to continue the struggle was finally shattered by the death of Mary of Guise in June 1560. By the Treaty of Edinburgh of July 1560, both England and France agreed to withdraw their forces from Scotland, and Mary gave up her claim to the English throne; soon afterwards, the French effectively conceded self-government to the Scots, and Protestantism was established by the Scottish Parliament.

Scotland's new rulers were grateful, fellow Protestant allies of England. The 'Auld Alliance' between France and Scotland no longer existed, and a centuries-old threat to English security was, in large part, removed. 'England's postern gate was closed and the continental powers could invade her only by sea, where her naval strength must make them think twice before risking the attempt' (Wernham). The English wisely resisted any temptation to occupy or conquer Scotland, a task that Henry VIII's experience and that of the French showed was fraught with difficulty.

In the following years, events north of the border often caused concern, but the work of 1560 was never to be undone. Wernham has argued that Elizabeth's reluctance to send an army to Scotland was justified. January and February were not good months in which to march an army into Scotland, time allowed political circumstances within France to work in England's favour, and she was surely right to fear Spain's reaction to her assisting Protestant rebels. Nevertheless, Elizabeth 'trembled indecisively' (MacCaffrey) throughout, and it is hard to believe, given her natural caution and hostility to rebellion, that she would have made the necessary commitment without Cecil's and the Council's pressure. To Cecil must go the principal credit for what was one of the outstanding achievements of Elizabeth's reign.

KEY ISSUE

Was England's intervention in Scotland in 1560 vindicated by the results?

2 ᕲ OPPORTUNITIES AND MISTAKES

A *Civil war in France*

From the early 1560s, France was weakened by internal religious division. The struggle between the **Huguenots** and the Catholic majority greatly reduced the threat posed by France and instead made that country vulnerable to the intervention of other powers. The first of the French Wars of Religion began in June 1562, following the Catholic Duke of Guise's massacre of a Huguenot congregation, and the Catholics quickly gained the upper hand. Lord Robert Dudley (later the Earl of Leicester) and Sir Nicholas Throckmorton, anxious to match Cecil's recent Scottish success, strongly urged intervention on the side of the Huguenots. Without help, the latter seemed likely to collapse and a reunited France would again become a formidable enemy of England; in particular, the Duke of Guise would seek to revive French influence in Scotland through his niece, the now returned Mary, Queen of Scots. There was even the possibility that intervention could repeat the achievement secured in Scotland, for military success might give the Huguenots at least a share in the government of France. Elizabeth readily agreed, encouraged as she was by the Scottish success, eager to please her favourite, Dudley, and led by Huguenot representatives to believe that Calais could be regained. Again, there is no evidence of religious motivation in Elizabeth's policy; Cecil wrote that there were two principal goals, 'one to stay the Duke of Guise, as our sworn enemy, from his singular superiority, the other to procure us the restitution of Calais, or something to countervail it'.

Huguenots the name given to French Protestants

See page 244

In October 1562, an English army sailed to France and occupied Le Havre. Philip of Spain complained that Elizabeth was again supporting heretical rebels. As a result, she did not allow her troops to leave Le Havre to join the Huguenots. The latter were beaten at Dreux in December 1562. Many patriotic Huguenots were already alienated by England's stated desire to secure Calais, and they were now persuaded to make a peace that involved the promise of religious toleration of Protestantism in return for their joining the government forces in defence of France against the invader. The newly united French duly defeated the English, forcing the surrender of Le Havre in July 1563.

By the resultant Treaty of Troyes (April 1564), Elizabeth formally renounced the English claim to Calais. It could be argued that Elizabeth had been right to seek an advantage when the opportunity arose. Also, the enterprise usefully reminded the French that their internal divisions made England a dangerous enemy, giving rise in particular to an unwillingness to intervene in Scotland or to support Mary's claim to the English succession. But clearly the intervention was mismanaged, displaying little regard for the needs of the Huguenots, and the final result was a military debacle. Elizabeth certainly considered it a failure, and, for better or worse, she became more than ever reluctant to commit English forces in support of Protestant rebellion. As MacCaffrey wrote, Le Havre 'ended the spurt of adventurousness which had characterized the regime up to this point; the years after 1563 were ones of cautious isolationism in foreign affairs'.

B *The return to Scotland of Mary, Queen of Scots*

The remarkably favourable position in Scotland was threatened by the return of Mary, Queen of Scots, to her native land in August 1561 after the death of her husband, Francis II of France. Half-French herself by birth, she had lived at the French Court from 1548, having gone there when only five years old to escape English invaders, and she came back hoping to revive her country's traditional alliance with France. Her return, understandably, was not welcomed by Elizabeth and her government. In addition, Mary considered her claim to the English throne to be superior to Elizabeth's, as it derived from Henry VIII's sister Margaret (her grandmother), while Elizabeth was the daughter of a woman, Anne Boleyn, whose marriage to Henry no Catholic thought legitimate. Mary was sufficiently realistic to accept Elizabeth's title, but she immediately asserted her claim to be the next in line, Elizabeth's successor. Elizabeth privately recognised Mary's right.

See pages 183–4

The likelihood of a Catholic successor was bound to upset England's Protestants and encourage the survival of Catholicism, and might even tempt some of the latter's adherents into assassination or rebellion. So, both in foreign policy terms, and in relation to England's domestic affairs, Mary's return to Scotland was a potential disaster for Elizabeth.

Of course, Scotland was then ruled by a Protestant regime and Mary's return was accepted on condition that she did not try to alter the country's new political and religious orientation. Even with Mary on the throne, Scotland did not support France during the English intervention there in 1562–3. Indeed, her great desire to receive Elizabeth's nomination to the succession meant that Mary could not support the French cause or do anything else openly to oppose English interests. Elizabeth's refusal to pronounce her right to the succession, though it owed much to her natural indecision, neatly served to ensure Mary's good behaviour for several years.

In 1565, Mary married Lord Darnley. The marriage was short-lived, as was he. Mary's apparent complicity in his assassination, almost trumpeted in her marrying the murderer, Bothwell, led to a rebellion which forced her to abdicate in July 1567, and in the following year she fled to England. The restoration of full Protestant control, which had been undermined in the mid-1560s by an increasingly assertive Mary, was beneficial to England. The co-operative Earl of Moray became

Regent of Scotland, on behalf of Mary's infant son, James. But Elizabeth actually contemplated using force to restore Mary, so opposed was she to the idea that the Scots could depose their lawful monarch. Subsequently she urged the Scots to restore Mary to nominal sovereignty, a measure which past experience made unacceptable to them and to the wiser heads in her own Council.

In 1570 Regent Moray was murdered and Elizabeth, pressed by her Council, had to send forces into Scotland to bring Mary's supporters to heel. The turbulent nature of Scottish politics ensured that no English ruler could avoid difficulties there, but the essence of the achievement of 1560 remained intact. As for Mary, however troublesome she was, Elizabeth felt she had no choice. She had not been able to engineer her return to Scotland, while, as an anointed queen like herself, Mary was entitled to protection if not to freedom.

> ### KEY ISSUE
>
> *In the early to mid-1560s how well did Elizabeth manage the relationship with France and with Scotland?*

3 ⤳ THE FIRST QUARRELS WITH SPAIN

A *The arrival of Alva's army*

Spain and England found it increasingly difficult to reconcile their interests. Philip disliked Elizabeth's adoption of Protestantism and, even more, her apparent willingness to support Protestant rebels (in Scotland and France) and cause further conflict with France. He concluded that Elizabeth's regime posed a danger to Spanish interests as well as to true religion.

The first real crises between them centred upon the Netherlands. Crucially, Cardinal Granvelle, Philip's chief minister in the Netherlands until 1564, was prepared to meet Elizabeth's heretical policy with force. The efforts of English traders to spread Protestantism in the Netherlands caused him particular dismay. Also, problems arose with regard to the wool trade. The Netherlands' clothmakers resented the higher prices charged by the English merchants to cover the increased taxes of the Book of Rates of 1558, and increasing competition from improved English cloth, the so-called 'New Draperies'.

Granvelle decided to teach Elizabeth a lesson by stopping the cloth trade on which English prosperity depended and England retaliated with a ban on imports from the Netherlands. Trade was soon re-opened but English merchants were looking elsewhere for outlets, more so following the disorder of religious riots in 1566 in the Netherlands. A few merchants went to Hamburg, and, significantly, its use continued permanently. Trading links with the Baltic and Russia were also developed considerably, providing more alternatives to Antwerp. These changes to trade had a major impact on foreign policy. Anglo-Spanish co-operation no longer seemed to be quite such an economic necessity. Wernham emphasises the opportunity this gave – 'English foreign policy was to feel the benefit in a greater freedom of manoeuvre' – but neglects the risk. These events constituted, after all, a step in the direction of war with an ancient ally.

The final turning-point in Anglo-Spanish relations came in 1567. In August of that year, the Duke of Alva marched into the Netherlands at the head of a great Spanish army sent to prevent a recurrence of the unrest that first flared in the Netherlands in 1566. Philip had no intention of using it against England, whose alliance against France he continued to value, despite the recent difficulties. But things appeared very differently in England, with the historic threat to its security coming from across the Channel. Previously that threat had been French, but the presence of Alva's army created an entirely new state of affairs. The tensions of recent years had made the English apprehensive of Spanish power, but it was only when the strongest army in Christendom arrived on England's doorstep that Spain rather than France became the principal object of fear.

The religious aspect was of major importance here. Many Protestants were convinced that there was an international struggle between true religion and its enemies, and that the greatest Catholic power, Spain, would seek the destruction of Protestantism everywhere, not least in its strongest bastion, England. Once Alva's army had defeated the Netherlands' Protestants, there seemed every chance that it would be turned against England's so-called heretics. Elizabeth, although always reluctant to let religion dictate her foreign policy, shared in the general anticipation of danger.

The outbreak of the second of France's Wars of Religion, when the Huguenots rebelled in September 1567, meant that Spanish power would not be checked by that of France. Indeed, it raised the possibility of victory for the pro-Spanish Guise faction and a united Catholic effort against heretical England. The army of William of Orange, leader of the Dutch rebels, was easily defeated by Alva in 1568 and the Netherlands was so completely pacified that the day seemed to be fast arriving when Alva's forces could be deployed elsewhere. In the spring of 1568, Philip expelled England's ambassador to Spain, Dr John Man, and sent Guerau de Spes as ambassador to London, who quickly displayed his antipathy to the Protestant regime of Elizabeth by making contact with Mary and other Catholic malcontents. The changes may have had innocent reasons – Man was a Protestant zealot who informed his hosts that the Pope was 'a canting little monk', and Philip's instructions to de Spes clearly stated that he was to work for Elizabeth's continued friendship – but they nevertheless appeared to show that Philip was no longer an ally and added to the state of apprehension created by Alva's nearby presence.

B *English pirates*

Finally, another issue came increasingly to damage relations between England and Spain. The Spanish claimed all of northern and central America and attempted to prevent unauthorised trade between the settlements there and the seamen from other European countries. English sailors featured prominently among the latter, and one of the most famous, John Hawkins, had Elizabeth's support (and the investment of three of her ships) in his triangular slave trade between Africa, the West Indies, and Europe. Spain's efforts to stop this trade culminated in a Spanish squadron's attack on Hawkins's fleet in the Mexican port of San Juan de Ulua in September 1568. The treacherous nature of the attack (Hawkins received the Spaniards in peace, as servants of an allied power), as much as the losses inflicted, constituted yet another grievance between England and Spain. Initially, this was a peripheral issue, but it was to grow in significance as the struggle between Spain and England developed.

C *The affair of the Spanish bullion*

At the end of 1568, Anglo-Spanish relations were plunged into a state of crisis. The extraordinary story of this quarrel contains its fair share of mystery. In November 1568, five Spanish ships sailed towards the Netherlands carrying £85 000 in **bullion** to enable Alva to pay the costs of his massive army. Bad weather and privateers forced the ships to take shelter in Plymouth and Southampton. Elizabeth at first agreed to provide the ships with an armed escort, but she then decided instead to retain the money for her own use. The money had been borrowed from the bankers of Genoa, and legally it remained their property until it was delivered to Antwerp. Elizabeth contended that, far from stealing the money from the King of Spain, she was merely taking over the loan, a move to which the Genoese were apparently agreeable.

> **Bullion** gold or silver before coining or manufacture

It is difficult to know if the Queen's reasoning was quite so straightforward. The action may have been a response to the massacre at San Juan de Ulua, but it is unlikely that anything more than vague rumours of the incident had yet reached England (Hawkins and Drake did not arrive home until January 1569). Far more probably, she was using the opportunity to remind the Spanish that England's domination of their sea route to the Netherlands meant that the army could not be maintained indefinitely against Elizabeth's opposition. The seizure of the bullion was a lever designed to induce the army's withdrawal now that the Netherlands situation no longer necessitated its presence.

Instead, the measure did rather more to provoke Spanish hostility than achieve any goal Elizabeth might have desired. Alva's position in the Netherlands, presiding over an army owed months of back-pay, was so dire that he could only regard the seizure as the act of an enemy. Also, de Spes in London insisted that only the most vigorous response would bring Elizabeth to heel; following the ambassador's counsel, on 29 December Alva ordered the seizure of the English ships and goods in Netherlands ports and banned all trade with England. Elizabeth immediately retaliated, the conflict escalated, and trade with Spain, as well as the Netherlands, came to a halt. The English government cannot have foreseen such an outcome. In fact, a majority of Councillors attacked Cecil, the man who had urged the seizure and thereby brought England into conflict with the formidable power of Spain. Genuinely alarmed as well as hopeful of destroying Cecil's influence, they launched a major campaign for his removal. For several months, a factional struggle

KEY ISSUE

Was the seizure of the Spanish bullion in 1568 as rash and foolish as Cecil's critics claimed?

raged as Cecil's enemies sought to turn the Queen against him. That he survived is a measure of the respect she had for his abilities.

Almost certainly, Elizabeth and Cecil had underestimated the extent to which it would alienate the Spanish. The measure was a mistake. Its outcome was not as disastrous as many feared in the early months of 1569, as Philip was still preoccupied in the Mediterranean. But a traditional ally and great power was alienated and virtually nothing was gained.

D *The Northern Rising, the Papal Bull and the Ridolfi Plot*

See pages 321–3

During the succeeding, crisis-ridden years, Elizabeth paid a price for her impetuosity. In November 1569, the Northern Rising broke out in the far north of England. It cost almost a thousand lives, mostly those of the rebels. De Spes, Spain's ambassador, had played a role in encouraging the northern Earls. Three months later, in February 1570, the Pope, without reference to Philip, issued the Bull *Regnans in Excelsis* in which he called upon English Catholics to withdraw their allegiance to Elizabeth. Together, the Rising and the Papal Bull produced widespread alarm and sparked off the first wave of repression of Catholics. Finally, in 1571, Ridolfi, a Florentine banker, plotted a Catholic rising to overthrow Elizabeth and replace her with Mary. De Spes was enthusiastic, and Philip and Alva (when visited by Ridolfi) agreed to despatch an army to England once 'the first steps' were taken by Norfolk and his English Catholic allies. In the event, the plot was uncovered, thanks largely to Ridolfi's inability to hold his tongue. Norfolk went to the block, and ambassador de Spes was expelled.

These events demonstrate the harmful effects of the breakdown in Anglo-Spanish relations. A plot like Ridolfi's certainly did pose a danger, and in addition the atmosphere of panic induced by the actions of some Catholics disturbed the religious peace of the country, produc-

TIMELINE

1558	Elizabeth's accession
1559	Treaty of Câteau-Cambrésis with France
1560	Treaties of Berwick and Edinburgh
1561	Mary, Queen of Scots returned to Scotland
1562	English intervention in the French Wars of Religion
1564	England formally renounced the claim to Calais
1565	Mary, Queen of Scots' marriage to Darnley
1566	First Calvinist disorders in the Netherlands
1567	Alva arrived in the Netherlands with a Spanish army
1568	Mary, Queen of Scots sought refuge in England
	The affair of the Spanish bullion
1569	The Northern Rebellion
1570	The Papal Bull excommunicating Elizabeth
1571	The Ridolfi Plot

ing repressive measures and encouraging Puritan demands that set Elizabeth at odds with much of the political nation. The rift with the premier Catholic power inevitably gave rise to dangers and tensions in a country that was divided in its religious affiliations.

The bullion dispute had much less damaging effects on England's economy. The switch away from Antwerp to Hamburg and other ports was complete. The disruptive effect of the bullion issue was to outlast the fury it created, for it brought to an end a compelling reason for Anglo-Spanish friendship.

See page 199

KEY ISSUE

Why did England's relations with Spain deteriorate so markedly during the first decade of Elizabeth's reign?

4 ∽ THE FRENCH ALLIANCE

A *The Treaty of Blois*

The most striking departure engendered by the conflict with Spain was England's alliance with France, the traditional enemy. Catherine de Medici, the Queen Mother and effective ruler of France, was aware of France's vulnerability to English intervention in the religious strife that continued to plague her country. Elizabeth, on the other side, knew that friendship with France would force Philip to compete for her favour. Also, as Cecil especially was aware, it might help to restrain French ambition in the Netherlands. Finally, it would stave off the possibility that the two great Catholic powers would unite against heretical England – generally remote possibility, but always dreaded and a particular concern during conflicts between England and Spain.

Late in 1570, Elizabeth began to promote the idea of a marriage between herself and the Duke of Anjou, one of Catherine's younger sons. The match won the support of Cecil and others, convinced as they were of the need to settle the succession (without admitting Mary), and keenly aware of the foreign policy advantages. They were hopeful that the Duke would at least play down his Catholicism to acquire the English throne. Perhaps their enthusiasm was less wise than Elizabeth's opportunism. Probably she never really intended to enter a marriage that would have diluted her power, endangered England's independence, and provoked popular unrest (the thought of a French Catholic monarch being even more alarming than a Spaniard). She proceeded, then, to encourage the French suit, safe in the knowledge that 'the knotty point of religion' could always be used to prevent it getting anywhere.

After the expulsion of de Spes in December 1571, representing as it did a further stage in the collapse of Anglo-Spanish relations, Elizabeth proposed a formal alliance between England and France. The marriage question was shelved; the idea of a league against Spain was attractive to both sides even without a more lasting union through marriage. The Treaty of Blois of April 1572 constituted a diplomatic revolution, aligning England and France in opposition to Spain. It created a defensive alliance whereby they would help each other in the event of an attack on one by a third country. Elizabeth 'had gained a French shield' (Wernham) against the might of Alva's army, and the absence of any mention of Mary, Queen of Scots was an implicit abandonment of Mary by her former French patrons.

For all its advantages, however, the new alliance was plagued with difficulty. History bequeathed such a burden of animosity and mistrust that England and France could not suddenly live together as true and trusting friends. One source of difference was the Netherlands. Just as fear of Alva's army was the cement that held the alliance, so the question of what should follow Alva's departure served to alienate England from France. Earlier, in the summer of 1571, the Council of the French King, Charles IX, proposed a joint attack on Alva by France, England, and the German Protestants. After expelling the Spanish, the victors should partition the Netherlands, with France acquiring Flanders and Artois, England the northern provinces of Holland and Zeeland, and the Germans the rest. Leicester and Francis Walsingham (then the English ambassador to France) welcomed the prospect, in particular the 'spiritual fruit [the spread of Protestantism] that may thereby ensue'. But Elizabeth and Cecil had no desire for continental territory whose retention might be militarily burdensome and inordinately expensive.

Above all, the thought of French expansion into the Netherlands was alarming in the extreme. Their hold on the southern coastline of the Channel could be extended to embrace the land east, as well as west, of the narrow Straits of Dover. Elizabeth preferred a restoration of the traditional balance between France and Spain in an area so crucial to English security. A substantial gain by England's traditional enemy was certainly not the best solution. There was little prospect of agreement on positive action in the Netherlands. As long as the latter was the major issue of the day relations between England and France would remain brittle.

B *The Sea Beggars, 1572*

Despite these misgivings the Treaty of Blois had been signed, but the first crisis within the alliance arose only weeks later. In April 1572, the Dutch Sea Beggars, Protestant privateers, seized the port of Brill in south Holland, and launched what became the Dutch Revolt. The greatest nobleman of the Netherlands, William of Orange, put himself at the head of the rebellion and threatened Alva with an army of German mercenaries. It required only an attack by the King of France to threaten the survival of Spanish power in the Netherlands. The reaction of Lord Burghley (as Cecil had become) was revealing. He wrote on this subject in a Memorial for Matters in Flanders in June 1572:

> If ... the French begin to possess any part of ... the maritime parts, then it is like that the French ... may be too potent neighbours for us and therefore [it] may be good for us to use all the means ... to stay that course.
>
> If the French proceed to possess the maritime coasts and frontiers it seemeth to be good that ... the Duke of Alva were informed secretly

of the Queen's Majesty's disposition to assist the king his master by all honourable means she might in the defence of his inheritance, so as it may appear to her that he will discharge his subjects of their intolerable oppression, restore them to their ancient liberties, reconcile his nobility to him, deliver them from the fear of the Inquisition and continue with her Majesty the ancient league for amity and traffic in as ample sort as any others, dukes of Burgundy, heretofore have done.

> **Q**
> *In what respects could Burghley's attitude and policy be described as being very traditional and backward-looking?*

The possible resolution of England's principal foreign policy problem since 1567, the threat from Alva's army, was not to be bought at any price. Spain must be sustained as a counterpoise to French power, so strong was the continuing English fear of the old enemy.

This premise had important implications for England's long-term policy in the Netherlands, as will be seen. In June–July 1572 Elizabeth permitted Sir Thomas Morgan and Sir Humphrey Gilbert to lead substantial forces of volunteers across to Flushing in Zeeland, and the correspondence between Burghley and these men reveals that their principal purpose, in the minister's view, was to hold the port against the French. Elizabeth had already suggested to Philip's unofficial ambassador, Antonio de Gueras, that she should hold Flushing for Spain, and she warmly welcomed Alva's proposal of talks on the bullion dispute. The old allies were converging again in order to check their old adversary. In the event, a renewal of the French Wars of Religion diverted the French from the Netherlands and made this unnecessary. However, the events of 1572 served to remind the English government of the danger posed by France.

TIMELINE

1571	
Dec.	Expulsion of De Spes, the Spanish ambassador
1572	
April	Treaty of Blois with France Dutch Sea Beggars seize Brill in the Netherlands and begin the Dutch Revolt
Aug.	St Bartholomew's Eve massacre of Protestants in France

C *The massacre of St Bartholomew, 1572*

The French Wars of Religion had broken out again when, on 24 August 1572, stung by the growth of Huguenot influence, the Guise faction and its Catholic supporters initiated a massacre that claimed the lives of 13 000 Huguenots within a month. The St Bartholomew's Eve Massacre had a profound effect on English opinion. It fuelled fears of Catholic conspiracies to destroy Protestantism. Walsingham in Paris thought it 'less peril to live with them as enemies than as friends'. For religious reasons, as well as historic rivalries, England and France were not easily reconciled.

> **KEY ISSUE**
> *Why was an alliance with France to restrict the power of Spain so problematic?*

5 ⟿ ELIZABETH AND THE PROSPECTS OF A FOREIGN MARRIAGE

Within days of the opening of her first Parliament, the Commons petitioned Elizabeth to marry. The Queen's reply – 'and in the end, this shall be for me sufficient that a marble stone shall declare that a queen having lived such a time lived and died a virgin' – was not widely believed. There was the danger, however, that a foreign match would seriously limit England's diplomatic freedom of manoeuvre (and there was the loathed precedent of Mary's Spanish marriage), and that a domestic one was likely to stir up factionalism and jealousy among the nobility. However the great advantage of a marriage was the promise of an heir and thus settlement of the succession.

Early proposals came from Philip II of Spain, Archduke Charles of Austria and Charles IX of France, but all of these foundered on the rock of religious incompatibility. At home numerous courtiers pretended to be in love with the Queen, but Elizabeth's eye alighted on Lord Robert Dudley, Earl of Leicester, the younger son of the **attainted** Duke of Northumberland, and the leader of a powerful political following. Unfortunately Dudley was married already: to Amy Robsart, who was found dead in 1560 after a suspicious fall, which effectively killed off any chance of a Dudley marriage. Pressure resumed for the Queen to name a successor, and Bishop Jewel lamented in 1562, 'Oh, how wretched are we who cannot tell under what sovereign we are to live'. But Elizabeth was wise enough not to name a successor, as an opposition party could coalesce around whoever might be sure of power in the future. The heir apparent was Mary, Queen of Scots, currently back in Scotland following the death of her husband Francis II of France. Elizabeth could not bring herself to deny her legitimate right to succeed, but certainly did not want to strengthen her by naming her as heir.

The Commons petitioned Elizabeth again in 1563 to decide the succession, but only in 1570 did delicate negotiations begin for a marriage to the Duke of Anjou, third son of Catherine de Medici of France and current heir to the French throne. Again religion proved a stumbling block, as Anjou refused to conform to Protestant rites, and Elizabeth would not allow him to attend Masses in private. After Anjou's accession to the French throne in 1574, attention switched to his youngest brother the Duke of Alençon, who then himself took on the title Duke of Anjou. This plan was backed by Burghley (Cecil) and Sussex on the grounds that it would end England's isolation, and offer protection against Spanish power. Elizabeth herself was genuinely enthusiastic when negotiations began in earnest in 1578, and it was her last chance if she was to produce an heir as she was in her mid-40s. Yet many Protestants, including Walsingham and Leicester, were horrified at the spectre of a popish consort, and the Queen reluctantly dropped the idea. In any event the younger Anjou proved hopelessly irresponsible and unreliable: naked ambition drove him to fight against his brother, the French king, on the Huguenot side in 1575, and to seek power for himself in the Netherlands in 1582.

The younger Anjou died in any case in 1584, and the succession issue remained undecided until 1603. Elizabeth's availability as a marriage partner was an important card in the English diplomatic hand during the 1560s and 1570s, but it proved to be too dangerous a card to play amidst the bitter religious tensions of sixteenth-century

Attainted put under sentence of death, including forfeiture of estates

international relations. In any event, once the Queen became infertile her attraction as a bride was greatly reduced, and Mary Stuart's execution in 1587 increased the likelihood that her son James VI of Scotland would eventually succeed. Elizabeth remained the 'Virgin Queen', and the Tudor dynasty expired on her death in 1603.

KEY ISSUE

How useful diplomatically was the prospect of the Queen's marriage?

6 ⤳ THE GREAT DEBATE

The mainly Protestant rebels in the Netherlands continued after 1572 to resist the Spanish forces. For as long as it lasted, the rebellion in Holland and Zeeland preoccupied Alva and relieved Elizabeth's fear of his armed strength. Equally, France posed no threat during its civil war. England was secure. Even the capacity of France or Spain to incite rebellion within England (or Scotland) was limited by the certainty that Elizabeth could respond by intervening to aggravate their internal problems. However, it was always unlikely that both Spain and France would be weakened for good. As soon as one of them prevailed at home, England would again be faced with a powerful neighbour.

It is possible to damn Elizabeth's excessive caution, to accuse her of failing to exploit the temporary advantages of the 1570s to achieve permanent security. The latter, arguably, required bolder action to gain a favourable outcome in the Netherlands or France, or both. The perils her country encountered in the next decade may be attributable to the fact that she did not give enough assistance to the Dutch rebels and thereby allowed Spain to recover to a position of awesome, threatening power. In this view, Elizabeth must at least share responsibility for the great war that had then to be fought.

This line of criticism of Elizabeth's foreign policy has featured prominently in the work of historians, notably in Charles Wilson's *Queen Elizabeth and the Revolt of the Netherlands* (1970). In her own time, too, there was widespread support in England for the idea of military action on the side of the Dutch rebels and the Huguenots of France. The same motives had featured among Protestants from the beginning of the reign – for example, in Cecil's attitude to Scotland – but they acquired new vigour when the Dutch Revolt and the St Bartholomew's Eve Massacre initiated a period of sustained and ferocious religious conflict.

In addition to the strategic benefits of intervention, many Englishmen felt a strong obligation to help their fellow Protestants as they struggled against Catholic domination. For them, the conflicts in the Netherlands and France were the first stages of a general European war between Protestantism and Catholicism, Good and Evil. As the 'Elect Nation' England had a duty to fight the cause of true religion. Moreover, failure to join the struggle would result in the victory of Catholicism on the continent and a massive assault on the one remaining stronghold of Protestantism, England. Led by the Earl of Leicester and Sir Francis Walsingham (Secretary of State from December 1573), a majority of Elizabeth's Councillors favoured vigorous intervention for these reasons. Burghley shared their general outlook, even if a naturally moderate and defensive mentality – and possibly a keen understanding of how far Elizabeth would go – made him more cautious in practice.

The problem was Elizabeth. Demonstrating great strength of will, she withstood all the pressure for a full and open intervention in the Protestant cause. She disliked the uncertainties of war, and feared a lessening of her authority among those who would consider a female

PICTURE 25
Sir Francis Walsingham

SIR FRANCIS WALSINGHAM (*c.* 1530–90)

Francis Walsingham was born in approximately 1530, the son of a lawyer, and proceeded to King's College, Cambridge and Gray's Inn. During the reign of Mary Tudor he spent five years in continental exile as a zealous Protestant, and put this time to good use by learning foreign languages and establishing a wide range of European contacts, on whom he was to draw when he later established his spy network. On his return at Elizabeth's accession he was elected to Parliament, and was soon putting his overseas contacts to good use as an agent for Cecil.

Soon Walsingham belonged to a tightly knit group of politically motivated men, mostly Puritans, who urged a vigorously anti-Catholic policy on Elizabeth, as Mary Stuart's plots succeeded one another and as the prospect of war with Spain loomed. The group included Leicester, Mildmay, Knollys and Sidney, but Burghley usually took a more cautious line. Nevertheless they consistently urged open support for the Dutch rebels, strong backing for the piracy of Drake and his cronies and a robust attitude to Mary Queen of Scot's persistent plotting. Walsingham provided much of the intelligence for this group, often using his own financial resources to bankroll over 53 agents all over Europe.

In 1571 he unravelled the Ridolfi Plot, and in 1572 his experience as a witness in Paris of the 'Massacre of St Bartholomew' reinforced his anti-Catholic instincts. In 1581 he returned to Paris, instructed to negotiate both a marriage with Anjou, and a league against Spain. In 1582–3 Walsingham exposed the Throckmorton Plot and secured the expulsion of the Spanish ambassador Mendoza. His highly competent and committed secret service was behind the Bond of Association, a close-knit group prepared to defend the Queen to the death against the threat posed by Mary, Queen of Scots, and in 1586 he intercepted the Babington Plot to oust Elizabeth and to replace her with the Scottish Queen. In 1587 his spy network gave useful information about Spanish invasion preparations. Walsingham died in 1590, satisfied that he had overseen an efficient intelligence operation, and that he had survived the Queen's frequent changes of mood, when confronted with incontrovertible evidence of Mary Stuart's perfidy.

monarch unequal to the task of fighting one. Her sympathy with the plight of continental Protestants was undermined by dislike of their intolerant and uncompromising Calvinism. She did not feel the need to strike out in order to forestall a general Catholic onslaught, for she was more confident than her ministers that the traditional rivalry between France and Spain would keep them apart. Above all, she saw that England's national interest would be endangered by involving the country in a religious war. Secular, national interest was her prime concern. She did not share the ideological imperatives of Puritans like Francis Walsingham.

Elizabeth's instinctive loathing of rebellion made her reluctant to support the Dutch Revolt. Also, treacherous subjects were likely to be treacherous allies, as the Huguenots had proved when their fickleness led to the rout of the English army in 1563. She had to consider, too, the financial cost of a major campaign on the continent. To pay and equip an expeditionary army would entail massive expense. It would require the imposition of burdensome taxes that, for all their initial fervour, the people might come to resent and Parliament might prove reluctant to pass. Elizabeth's limited objective in the Netherlands dictated a limited commitment.

Her goal was the restoration of the semi-independent status that the Dutch enjoyed during the reign of Charles V. Alva's army must be removed and the country returned to a state of virtual demilitarisation. Philip must also restore government through the elected States General and grant religious liberty (freedom from 'the fear of the Inquisition'). She did not want to end Spain's sovereignty over the Netherlands. Possibly a majority of her Councillors wanted to expel the Spanish. But for Elizabeth (and Burghley) the Spanish presence checked French ambitions there and prevented French acquisition of the entire southern coast of the Channel. '(It is) necessary for England', wrote Cecil, 'that the State of the Low Countries (the Netherlands) should continue in their ancient government, without either subduing it to the Spanish nation or joining it to the Crown of France.' The fact that the outright defeat of Spain was not sought inevitably made Elizabeth's intervention more limited and defensive than it might have been. She had only to intervene sufficiently to keep alive the resistance of the Dutch and convince Philip of the need to conclude a reasonable settlement.

> **KEY ISSUE**
>
> *What were the arguments for and against intervention in the Netherlands once the Dutch Revolt was underway?*

7 ᴄ A LIMITED SUCCESS

The Dutch rebels survived. There was some assistance from English volunteers, and in 1574 Elizabeth granted a loan of £15 000 for the hire of German soldiers. A further loan of £20 000 followed in 1578 when the new Spanish commander, Don John of Austria, looked for a time as though he might conquer all the Netherlands, but still Elizabeth refused to go ahead with a plan to send an expeditionary force across to support the Dutch rebels directly. France remained weak and divided in the 1570s, and the Treaty of Blois, which had joined England and France in a defensive alliance against Spain, was renewed in 1575. Moreover, aware of their vulnerability to intervention, the French avoided any action in Scotland or the Netherlands that might have threatened England's interests. At one stage, in 1576, Elizabeth threatened to fight alongside the Spanish if the French intervened in the Netherlands. Maintaining the precarious balance of power was her over-riding concern.

Elizabeth exploited Spanish vulnerabilities at sea, albeit at arm's length. She allowed privateers, many of them English, to close the Channel to Philip's ships, cutting off Spain's best means of communication with the Netherlands. She formally approved (and invested in) Drake's expedition of 1577–80 to the Pacific, and probably hoped that he could seize sufficient gold and silver from the Spanish not only to fill her coffers but also to aggravate Philip's financial problems and make the Netherlands army even more difficult to sustain. All of these actions were sufficiently covert to avoid open conflict with Spain; Elizabeth later wrote of giving the Dutch 'such indirect assistance as shall not at once be a cause of war'. Her purpose was to ensure the continuation of the Dutch Revolt, and convince Philip of the need to end it by granting the sort of settlement desired by Elizabeth.

The Dutch Revolt continued, but a final settlement satisfactory to England was elusive. The Spanish, anxious to end England's troublesome interference, did concede a great deal to England, re-opening trade in 1573, settling the bullion dispute in 1574 (by the Convention of Bristol), banishing English Catholic refugees from the Netherlands, and permitting English traders to practise their Protestant religion freely. They did not, however, settle with the Dutch, except briefly and under duress in 1577. English efforts at mediation, begun in 1573, were politely rejected.

The balance of power looked as though it might be upset by the French when the Dutch, frustrated with Elizabeth's half-heartedness, turned for help to the younger Duke of Anjou, Henry III's brother, who was persuaded in 1578 to accept the title of 'Defender of the Liberties of the Low Countries', and come to their aid with a sizeable army. Though initially concerned, Elizabeth realised that Henry III of France was unwilling to risk war with Spain and would give minimal support to Anjou's 'private venture'. She decided that she could control Anjou ('her Frog') by encouraging his marriage suit; induced to hope for the kingship of England, he would not oppose Elizabeth's wishes in the Netherlands. Anjou was an erratic individual, however, and Elizabeth, ever reluctant to intervene decisively in the Netherlands, was dependent on his good behaviour, and that left England at the mercy of forces over which she had little control.

The Dutch held off the Spanish in 1578, but the latter's victory was always a distinct possibility from this point. The impressive Duke of Parma took control of the army after Don John's death in October 1578. Anjou withdrew his exhausted forces by the end of 1578. Part of the southern Netherlands, alienated by the intolerant and aggressive behaviour of the Calvinists, made peace with Parma in January 1579.

The goal of Elizabeth's policy, the restoration of the traditional status of the Netherlands, was certainly not achieved. Her Puritan critics were justified in their alarms and in their view that Elizabeth's excessively cautious approach was not sufficient to force a settlement on Spain. The policy of the 1570s was no more than a holding operation, in effect, and the failure to achieve any lasting solution in the Netherlands meant continuing and seemingly interminable danger.

KEY ISSUE

Were the 1570s a decade of lost opportunities in English foreign policy?

8 ⌒ SPAIN ASCENDANT

A *The growth of Spanish strength*

In the early 1580s a series of events enormously strengthened Spain. The male line of the royal house of Portugal died out in 1580. Through his mother, Isabella of Portugal, Philip had a claim and a Spanish army conquered the country in 1580. The two largest empires in the world became one, bringing to Spain the riches of Portugal's African and Oriental possessions. Ominously, the Portuguese navy had ten ocean-going ships. Most of Spain's navy consisted of smaller vessels capable only of sailing the quiet waters of the Mediterranean. Combined, the Spanish and Portuguese navies had an ocean-going capability that came close to matching England's, and this was bad news for the Dutch rebels.

Alarmed at the greater possibility of outright victory for Spain in the Netherlands, Elizabeth had from 1579 sought an alliance with Henry III of France, in what MacCaffrey has called 'the boldest and by far the most ambitious initiative taken by her government since the Scottish enterprise of 1559–1560'. The Queen argued that they could not 'leave the King of Spain to increase to such greatness as hereafter neither the force of France nor England nor any that may confederate with them shall be able to withstand any thing that the King of Spain shall attempt'. She pressed Henry to intervene in the Netherlands and promised secret English assistance, when three years earlier she had threatened war against him if he did so. Such was the way the balance tilted.

Ever sensitive to this balance, Elizabeth still wanted to minimise and keep secret English intervention in order to avoid war with Spain, while not encouraging French expansionism. Henry was unwilling to become Elizabeth's pawn and fight Spain alone, without even the benefit of a marriage alliance as Anjou's courtship of Elizabeth had got nowhere. So, he was not won over. Elizabeth and Henry failed to unite against the emerging Spanish threat. One view is that bolder leadership at this stage would have saved them and their countries much future pain. Another view is that a rapidly changing power balance made any irreversible moves in the diplomatic game even riskier.

To check the great Spanish general, Parma, Elizabeth became Anjou's chief backer; she funded his private ventures in 1581 and 1582 to the tune of almost £100 000. This however left him far short of the capacity to prevent Parma's continued progress. Philip, aware of her role, was increasingly convinced of the enmity of the English Queen. In August 1583 his great admiral, the Marquis of Santa Cruz, proposed that he should lead an armada from Spain to overthrow 'the heretic woman', and Philip proceeded to order the building and hiring of some large ships suitable to this 'Enterprise of England'. However, with the Netherlands still unconquered and France unlikely to remain neutral in the event of a Spanish assault on England, Philip felt unable to proceed. He temporarily turned a deaf ear to those – for example, Mary, Queen of Scots, the Duke of Guise, the English Jesuits, and his own ambassador to England, Bernardino de Mendoza – who manufactured a series of plots against Elizabeth.

The possibility of a Spanish attack on England was increased further by the turn of events in the Netherlands and France. In 1582–4, Parma re-conquered most of Calvinist-held Flanders and Brabant. Anjou, cash-starved, ineffective, and reduced to war against Dutch allies who could not trust a papist Frenchman, withdrew again in June 1583 and died a year later. Then, in July 1584, William of Orange, the military strongman among the Dutch rebels, was assassinated. This heralded disaster for the Dutch cause. The Union of Utrecht became a 'headless commonwealth' that seemed likely to fall apart for want of an agreed leader. The menace of a victorious Spanish army seemed closer than ever before.

B *The rise of the Catholic League in France*

Almost simultaneously, England's 'French shield' was removed. Alençon's death and Henry III's childlessness made Henry of Navarre the legal heir to the French throne. Henry, as leader of the Huguenots, was unacceptable to the French Catholics. A Catholic League was founded under the leadership of the Guise family. They prepared to fight to force Henry III to disinherit Navarre and to destroy the Huguenots once and for all. To this end, the Catholic League (which commanded greater support than the King) called on aid from Philip and Spain. By the Treaty of Joinville of December 1584, they acknowledged Philip as their protector and received his promise of assistance. Philip now knew that he could deal with England without fear of the reaction of France.

England's position was one of great danger. There was every likelihood that Spain would soon be able to deploy both a large navy and an unbeatable army against England. France, in which a renewal of civil war appeared inevitable, could offer no protection. Indeed, if the Catholic League took over the government, France would be ruled by Philip's grateful and dependent ally. Spain threatened to become the dominant power in all of western Europe. England would be at its mercy. This was the great crisis of Elizabeth's reign.

KEY ISSUE

How did the balance of power change in favour of Spain in 1580–5?

9 ⌐ THE OUTBREAK OF WAR

Because the Treaty of Joinville between Spain and the French Catholic League was initially a well-kept secret, the full extent of the calamity was not immediately apparent in England. Elizabeth continued to hesitate, despite the increasing pressure on her from Walsingham, Leicester and most of her Councillors, convinced both of their religious duty to save the Dutch Protestants, and of the certainty that the great Catholic power would indeed try to destroy Protestantism in England. The plotting of the Spanish ambassadors, de Spes and Mendoza, and the growing mythology surrounding the Spanish Inquisition and the supposed evils practised by Catholics throughout Europe, left Walsingham and the others in no doubt of Philip's hostile intentions. They advocated a major military commitment by England to the Protestant cause in the Netherlands.

They finally had their way in the summer of 1585. For Elizabeth there no longer seemed an alternative to war. On 20 March, the Catholic League took to arms and demanded that Henry III should root out heresy, and on the same day Walsingham received word of the Treaty of Joinville. Henry submitted to the Catholic League in June. Philip's hostile intent was indicated by his seizure of English shipping in Spanish ports at the end of May. And, all the while, Parma's army was closing on Antwerp, and bringing the Dutch under control. These events, particularly Henry's capitulation to Philip's allies, brought Elizabeth and Burghley to an awareness of the awesome power Spain was acquiring and forced them to acknowledge the need for action. On 10 August 1585 Elizabeth and the Dutch signed the famous Treaty of Nonsuch, by which she became the protector of the Dutch, and agreed to despatch an army of over 7000 soldiers. The vanguard arrived in August and Leicester, able at last not only to fight for Protestantism, but also to seek the military glory he coveted, crossed over to take command in December. At the same time, Elizabeth sent Drake to attack Spain's ports to free the English ships. War, though it was never to be declared officially, had begun.

TIMELINE

1576	The 'Spanish Fury' in Antwerp
1578	Parma took over from Don John as commander of the Spanish army in the Netherlands
	Elizabeth opened marriage negotiations with the younger Duke of Anjou
1579	The Southern Netherlands made their peace with Parma
1580	Spanish conquest of Portugal
1584	Treaty of Joinville between Spain and the French Catholic League
	Assassination of William of Orange; Dutch Revolt in danger of collapse
1585	Treaty of Nonsuch between England and the Dutch
	England openly at war against Spain

| PROFILE | **SIR FRANCIS DRAKE (C. 1543–96)** |

Drake was always a potent mixture of fervent Protestant zealot (he carried a copy of Foxe's *Acts and Monuments* on every trip) and unscrupulous privateer. He cut his piratical teeth in the 1560s and early 1570s on slaving expeditions with his cousin John Hawkins to the New World, and on attempts to cut off the supply of Peruvian silver from Panama and Nombre de Dios. He made his name on his 1577–80 voyage, secretly bankrolled by Elizabeth, to find the Pacific end of the North West Passage, but it remained elusive. Nonetheless Drake plundered the Pacific coast of America, captured the treasure-laden barque *Cacafuego* and resolved on a circumnavigation of the globe, only the second since Sebastian del Cano's voyage of 1517–20. On his return in the *Golden Hind* Drake was knighted by the Queen on her deck, for he had both humiliated the Spanish and returned a useful profit for his investors.

When war erupted in 1585 Drake attacked the sea-lanes known as the Spanish Main, but captured little booty. His repeat visit in 1586 was similarly disappointing, but the attack on Cadiz in 1587 ('the singeing of the King of Spain's Beard') destroyed at least 24 Spanish ships, delaying the sailing of the Armada by a year. Moreover the subsequent voyage to the Azores (effectively a Spanish territory since 1580) afforded him the prize of the *San Felipe* with a cargo worth £140 000, and paid the costs of the expedition twice over. By 1588 Drake was second-in-command under the Lord Admiral, Lord Howard of Effingham, pursuing the Armada up the Channel and ordering in the decisive fire-ships that disrupted the Spanish formation and sent the Spanish vessels fleeing in disarray.

Drake's later enterprises seem less creditable: in 1589 he was acquitted by a court martial for allegedly disobeying his commander, Norris, and for failing to take the Azores, and he spent most of the period between 1589 and 1595 at his Devon estate Buckland Abbey. However in August 1595 he was sent to the West Indies to hold the isthmus of Panama. Drake died of dysentery at Porto Bello on this trip in January 1596. He was remembered in England as a superb navigator and a brilliant privateer, whose exploits rapidly became part of a growing English nationalist legend.

| KEY ISSUE |

Could war against Spain have been avoided?

War probably was the only option for Elizabeth, although it was her open support for rebellion within his empire which made the equally cautious Philip finally decide to invade England; detailed preparations were ordered in January 1586. It is impossible to know for sure if Philip would have launched such an enterprise had Elizabeth continued to hold the Dutch at arms length. But there was clear evidence of Philip's growing hostility to the troublesome and heretical Queen of England, and to permit him to achieve total dominance in western Europe would surely have been a mistake.

10 ⌁ THE WAR

A *The Netherlands campaign*

Elizabeth initially failed to appreciate that England and Spain were now engaged in a struggle that was entirely different from the angry encounters of the previous two decades. In her mind, the military initiative of 1585, though much more overt and substantial than earlier interventions, still did not make all-out war inevitable. She hoped, rather, that Philip would see reason and conclude a settlement with the Dutch. In 1585 and again in 1587, Elizabeth turned down Dutch offers of the throne of an independent Netherlands, and she was enraged when Leicester implied her consent by assuming the post of Governor-General soon after his arrival. Her objective remained a self-governing Netherlands under Spanish sovereignty, and she knew that acceptance of the throne would be a hostile (and entirely illegitimate) act that Spain could never accept. Similarly, Elizabeth's attitude was revealed by her continuing readiness to seek a negotiated peace; secret talks on the future of the Netherlands went on intermittently from November 1585 until mid-1588, but Spanish success on the battlefield made them unwilling to concede a settlement that could satisfy England.

Despite his urgings, Elizabeth, ever-cautious, refused to expand Leicester's original army beyond the 7000 men promised at Nonsuch. Any great increase in size would produce an escalation of the war that she wished to avoid. As one might expect, the Crown's perpetual shortage of money was another, compelling reason for the modest commitment, and Elizabeth failed to fund adequately even the small force that did exist. At the same time, for all her hopes of a limited conflict, Elizabeth was aware of the threat of invasion. She was determined that financial and military resources should not be expended in the Netherlands when they might be required in England itself. Indeed, the priority she gave to defending England was shown even in the way that the army was deployed in the Netherlands; it concentrated on denying Spain control of the major ports, leaving most of the fighting to the rather disgruntled Dutch.

English soldiers were present in the Netherlands for the rest of Elizabeth's reign. Their first leader, Leicester, proved inept, squandering money and squabbling with his officers and the Dutch; twice he was recalled in near-disgrace. However, his army played a part in halting Parma's advance in 1586, and the great Spanish gains of 1587 did not go so far as to win them Flushing or any other deep-water port in which to receive the Armada in 1588 – a crucial failure. During the next five years, harvest failures combined with the Dutch naval blockade to cause starvation among Parma's army, the Dutch and English improved their performance in battle, and (from 1589) many of the Spanish troops were diverted to support the Catholic League in the civil war in France.

The Dutch Captain-General, Maurice of Nassau, arguably the only great general of the whole war, scored a string of successes. He required

KEY ISSUE

How successful was English intervention in the Netherlands?

the assistance of relatively few men from England (only 8000 in 1589–95) but very large subsidies (£750 000 in the same period). By 1593–4, the northern part of the Netherlands was under Dutch control, while the south was retained by Spain. For most of the period until 1648, when Madrid finally recognised the independence of the northern Netherlands, the war continued. So, Spain was checked by the Dutch, and yet remained in the southern Netherlands as an obstacle to French expansion. It was not the solution Elizabeth sought before (and during) the war, but it achieved the same end in limiting the power of her two great neighbours.

B *The campaign in France*

France provided the second principal arena of the war. Elizabeth's envoys initially failed to persuade the beleaguered Henry III to back Henry of Navarre against the Catholic League. In 1589, however, the League's rebellion finally forced Henry into this alliance, he was assassinated, and Navarre claimed the succession as Henry IV (July 1589). The civil war then began in earnest. Philip gave the struggle for France priority over the Dutch war and sent thousands of Spanish soldiers to join the Catholic League, taking the pressure off the English as well. The English role in France then also became substantial. Elizabeth sent 20 000 troops and £300 000 in 1589–95. Navarre won, although to do so he had to agree to convert to Catholicism in 1593, jovially observing, it is said, 'Paris is well worth a Mass'. This was no defeat for England. By bringing peace with the Catholic League, it ensured that England's ally was now secure on his throne and could once again act as a balance against the power of Spain.

KEY ISSUE

In what ways were the civil wars in France important to Elizabeth?

C *The war at sea*

At sea, Drake and Hawkins failed to intercept nearly as much of Spain's American silver as the Queen's fast-emptying coffers badly needed. Drake did achieve a magnificent success in 1587, entering Cadiz and destroying perhaps 30 Spanish vessels – hence his boast that he had 'singed the King of Spain's beard'. It severely disrupted the Armada preparations and led Drake and Hawkins to argue that an offensive approach, deploying ships to harry and blockade the Spanish coast and search out the silver fleets, was England's best defence. But here too Elizabeth was cautious and defensive. She insisted that her ships should concentrate on forming 'the wall of England' in the Channel. She was probably wise to rein in her naval forces, even if inherent caution was more the cause than any strategic awareness. The number of expeditions that yielded little or nothing demonstrated the uncertain benefits of a long-range strategy, while the Armada threat meant that priority had to be given to securing the home waters.

The 130 ships of the first Spanish Armada, carrying 17 000 troops and intended to bring the same number of Parma's men across from Flanders to England, reached the Channel in July 1588. It was met by

PICTURE 26
The Fight Between the English and Spanish Fleets, *1588, de Vroom*

the full strength of the navy – the Queen's own ships, privateers' vessels and merchantmen – a force that just outnumbered the Armada's warships. The English ships were also quicker, and better armed with long-range guns than the Spanish. The Armada's strong defensive formation meant it lost only two ships as it passed up the Channel. Off Calais, however, the English scattered the Spanish vessels with fireships. They then ravaged the Armada at the Battle of Gravelines, sinking only four ships but forcing the northwards flight of the battered survivors. The fierce Atlantic gales encountered off Scotland and Ireland caused the vast majority of Spanish losses, with dozens of ships sinking or finishing on the rocky shores. Only half of the Armada made it back to Spain.

The defeat of the Armada fully merits its place among the great military exploits of English history. In the years after 1588, England's sailors took many Spanish prizes, and the destruction of Cadiz in 1596 was a striking success. But they frequently abandoned military advantage in order to seek booty, and they could not stop the New World silver reaching Philip in record quantities. Their raids on Spanish and Portuguese ports did not prevent the reconstruction of Philip's navy. Fortunately for the English, the armadas of 1596, 1597 and 1599 were all scattered by strong winds. These were times when the English valued foul weather. The final verdict must be that the naval war was secondary to the land war in Europe. For all its remarkable feats, the navy could not win the war for England; it could only, as in 1588, prevent invasion and defeat.

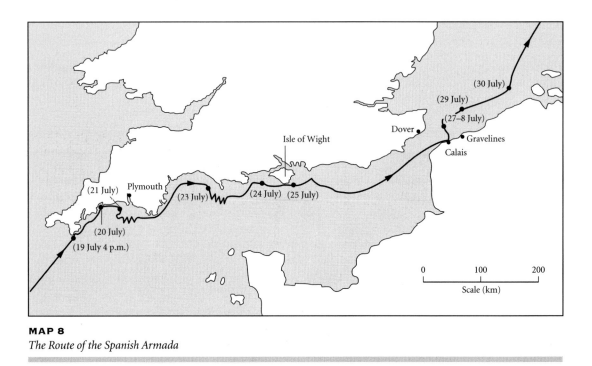

MAP 8
The Route of the Spanish Armada

See pages 297–300

The Earl of Tyrone's rebellion in Ireland in 1595–1603 made that country the fourth major, indeed the biggest, arena of warfare. The arrival of 3400 Spanish troops there in 1601 marked Philip III's willingness to respond in kind to the English intervention in the Netherlands. The Irish (and Spanish) were eventually defeated. But the struggle required the deployment of 25 000 English soldiers and a massive expenditure of £2 million, a diversion of resources that can only have damaged the war effort against Spain.

It was just as well that the other element in the 'British dimension' did not prove troublesome. Reaping the benefit of 25 years of sound

TIMELINE

1587	Execution of Mary, Queen of Scots
	The 'Singeing of the King of Spain's Beard'
1588	Defeat of the Spanish Armada
1589	Accession of the Protestant Henry IV as King of France
	Philip II concentrated on supporting the Catholic cause in France
1593	Henry IV embraced Catholicism
1596	Essex's successful expedition against Cadiz
1598	End of the French Wars of Religion.
	Philip II died
1601	Abortive Spanish invasion of Ireland
1603	Elizabeth died
1604	Peace with Spain

diplomacy, the English did not have to worry about their northern border at a time when any show of hostility from Scotland might have brought disaster. The young James VI, strongly Protestant, hopeful of securing the English succession, and attracted by an annual pension of £4000, joined Elizabeth in signing the Treaty of Berwick in 1586, making the two countries firm allies. Even the execution of his mother, Mary, Queen of Scots, in February 1587, did not break the alliance. Instead it made James the next in line after Elizabeth, and he knew that he had only to remain England's friend (and a Protestant) in order to succeed her on the English throne. This ambition was the principal basis of the alliance. But Burghley would have been justified in looking back to 1560 and musing on how different things would have been had he not driven out the Guises and created an entirely new relationship between England and Scotland.

> ## KEY ISSUE
>
> *How was the Armada defeated and what was the significance of the English victory?*

11 ᴥ CONCLUSION

Philip II having died in 1598 and Elizabeth in 1603, it was left to their heirs, Philip III and James I, to acknowledge that neither side could benefit from continued warfare. The Treaty of London of 1604 ended England's formal intervention in the Netherlands at a time when the Dutch were well capable of carrying on alone. England did not defeat

PICTURE 27
Funeral of Elizabeth I

Spain. In the first place, the military contributions of the Dutch and French surpassed those of England. Secondly, the war was fought to a stalemate, with neither side emerging as clear winners. On the other hand, the English and their allies succeeded in preventing Spanish domination of north-western Europe. Spain, for all its might, lacked the capacity to achieve this. So, the purpose for which England went to war in 1585 was, by and large, achieved, as the spectre of overwhelming Spanish power was overcome. At the end of Elizabeth's reign, the country was much more secure than it appeared in 1585. In this vital respect the war achieved much for England.

This is not to say that the foreign policy that led to war can necessarily be called a success. It was a war Elizabeth had long sought to avoid, and its occurrence must therefore be considered a policy failure. Indeed, any policy, whatever its objective, that led a middle-ranking country like England into war with the greatest power in the world must be considered a failure. Moreover, as shown in other chapters, it was a war that produced much disruption and unrest, causing as it did an oppressive level of taxation, dislocation of trade, enforced and bitterly resented military service, a profusion of detested monopolies, and widespread corruption in public life.

The war was mainly responsible for the collapse of the Queen's popularity in the last years of her reign. It threatened her authority even more directly; so dominant at home, she found that commanders like Drake, Leicester and Essex constantly disobeyed her orders – usually to ill effect. They had little respect for a woman's knowledge of military matters and were ever-hopeful that success would bring glory and forestall retribution. Of course, the war's eventual outcome was indeed in English interests but the war and the policy that failed to prevent it must not be confused.

One wonders, however, if any other strategy could have worked better. Elizabeth was endlessly hesitant in the 1570s, but she had good reasons: the fear of France, the lack of financial resources, and so on. She had more sound argument on her side than could be found among those whose views were coloured by passionate fear of Catholicism. Even if one accepts that her cautious approach owed as much to her perpetual indecisiveness as to rational calculation – and a strong case can be made – it is difficult to see how a reasoned assessment of the circumstances of the 1570s dictated a policy of war with Spain.

More recent criticism of Elizabeth, arguing that she should have taken advantage more decisively of Spain's relative weakness in the 1570s, draws heavily on hindsight. She could not have foreseen the extraordinary series of events in the early 1580s, in Portugal, France and the Netherlands, the events that forced her to go to war. It might be added that the policy of every Tudor monarch would have been wrecked by the collapse of the great rivalry between France and Spain which had been for a century England's best protection. Elizabeth had to deal with a novel and highly dangerous situation. She did so by avoiding war as long as possible and then making war when it became a necessity. Many have done worse.

KEY ISSUE

Did the results of the Spanish war vindicate Elizabeth's decision to fight?

Tudor Foreign Policy: Change and Continuity

ANALYSIS

How far is it possible to speak of a consistent Tudor foreign policy? At Henry VII's accession England ranked a very poor third behind the great powers of France and Spain, lagging behind in terms of population, naval strength, the resources of its diplomatic service and – above all – in military spending, for England was able to spend less than a third of France's military budget and less than a fifth of Spain's. However Henry did benefit from prolonged periods of Franco-Spanish rivalry from 1494 with the onset of the Italian Wars, and was able to secure a useful French pension in return for neutrality, to conclude useful trade treaties, to secure his dynasty against foreign threats and to broker significant marriage alliances for his children with Scotland, and Spain. The Italian Wars were to last on and off until 1559 and preoccupied France and Spain to England's advantage. Thus his son Henry VIII's inheritance was much more secure than his own.

See pages 36–8

Trade, most importantly in cloth, was also a concern in foreign policy. Most English trade was in turn channelled through Antwerp in the Netherlands, which was in turn part of the Duchy of Burgundy. Burgundy was also a traditional ally of England against France. Henry VII, however, faced difficulties here, as Margaret, Duchess of Burgundy, was a Yorkist and a committed enemy of his. He used trade as a weapon against her – economic sanctions are not a modern invention. But this had to be a temporary expedient if the English economy was not to be badly damaged, and good relations were restored. In 1516 the Duke of Burgundy by then (and thus ruler of the Netherlands) was Charles of Ghent who became Charles I of Spain, and later Emperor Charles V. Although there were to be reasons for discord – Charles was angered by Henry VIII's divorce from his aunt, Catherine of Aragon – these did not prevent alliance, when circumstances demanded, against the common enemy, France, and the trade links between England and the Netherlands remained of great significance. However, trade never dominated dynastic or territorial interests in foreign policy, and when England became hostile to Spanish power in the Netherlands from the late 1560s, English merchants were forced to diversify to German and Baltic ports.

In the meantime Henry VIII squandered much of his financial legacy on wars against Scotland and France. Security had been the hallmark of Henry VII's policy, the pursuit of glory that of Henry VIII. Wolsey of course preferred to play the arbiter of Europe in between outbreaks of conflict – a policy of which Elizabeth would have approved. Then with Henry's break with Rome, a new religious dimension was introduced into international affairs, reinforced by the spread of the continental Reformation. This, arguably, began to engender a new sense of English nationalism that reached a peak in Elizabeth's war against Spain. However, no

See pages 60–3

See pages 123–5

See pages 134–5

See pages 170–3

See pages 240–3

Tudor monarch engaged in conflict for religious reasons alone; dynastic and national interests were always the main motives. Henry's reign ended on a note of continuity, when he fought France in furtherance of a dynastic claim dating back two centuries. But this also closed a chapter in medieval and Tudor foreign policy – it was the last time an English monarch tried to restart the Hundred Years War (at the cost of both royal and national financial stability). Henry enjoyed vastly greater resources than his predecessors with which to wage war, thanks to his pillaging of the Church, but even so he could achieve little during the regular truces between France and Spain or in talks with a Pope effectively the prisoner of Charles V.

Edward VI's reign showed no fundamental change of direction, although there were to be no more dreams of extensive conquests in France. Protector Somerset tried to bring Scotland to heel and, in particular, to break its 'Auld Alliance' with France, which was a regularly revived threat to English security. But the ruinously expensive war achieved little except to expose England's financial vulnerability. Somerset's successor, Northumberland, pursued peace while rebuilding the finances.

Mary Tudor's marriage alliance with Philip II of Spain was broadly in line with traditional Tudor policy – after all, a precedent was the marriage of Mary's own parents, Henry VIII and Catherine of Aragon – although the marriage was deeply controversial (as shown most dramatically by Wyatt's rebellion), given anxieties about the extent of Philip's power in England and whether he might try to use England to serve Spanish interests. In the event England was indeed pulled into a Spanish war against France, but war against France was hardly a new departure and there were a number of previous occasions when England and Spain had combined against their common enemy. Had Mary survived longer, and had the war been successful, the Spanish alliance would have almost certainly endured. However, there was the beginning of a key change in England's foreign relations. Mary lost Calais, England's last bridgehead into France, before she died, and the Spanish alliance was associated with humiliating defeat and Catholic repression – the latter becoming increasingly important in memory as Elizabeth's reign wore on and Protestantism was ever more firmly established.

There was no dramatic turnabout visible at the start of Elizabeth's reign, however. Philip II, ever mindful of England's strategic role in balancing France, even proposed marriage to Elizabeth (and was politely turned down) and restrained the Pope from condemning the Protestant Queen until 1570. France, and its proxy Scotland, remained the focus of concern. Cecil's successful policy to uphold the Protestant regime in Scotland, however, barred 'the postern gate' of the Scottish border at the start of the reign (and it was to be closed permanently in 1603 with James VI's accession to the English throne as James I). A key issue running through medieval and Tudor foreign policy had now been resolved.

However, the European situation changed dramatically in the 1560s, and so did the assumptions underlying Tudor foreign policy towards its continental neighbours. In 1562 the French Wars of Religion broke out, and in 1566 the Dutch Revolt against Spanish power in the Netherlands began. Preoccupied with its own internal conflict, France was no longer the threat it had once been. However, the Dutch Revolt caused Philip II to build up his power massively in the Netherlands. Some of Elizabeth's advisers, for whom religion was the pre-eminent concern, saw this as part of a concentration of Catholic power, which would inevitably be turned against England and which required immediate military action to resist it. Elizabeth was more cautious, and her aim was to find a way to restore the balance of power as it had traditionally been in north-western Europe. She was certainly not going to go to war for religious motives, any more than her predecessors. Her method was to support the Dutch rebels as discreetly and as cheaply as possible. However, whether it was to be a cold war, as the Queen preferred, or open hostilities, a reorientation of English foreign policy was complete: Spain was now the enemy, not France.

It was to be open war from 1585 as the only way of sustaining the Dutch Revolt. The defeat of the Spanish Armada in 1588, the first time since 1066 when England had been seriously menaced by invasion, went down as a key episode in the national story, so making it look far more inevitable than it was that Spain would be a deadly enemy. Equally, the 'black legend' of Philip II put about by Protestant propagandists, made him seem hell-bent on dethroning the heretic Queen, whereas he had been as anxious as Elizabeth to avoid war and showed no signs of wishing to repress Protestantism beyond his borders until provoked into it to preserve his own security. The policy of hostilities with Spain did not long outlast Elizabeth; the Dutch in effect established their independence and peace was made by James VI in 1604. By the 1620s, his son Charles was in Madrid pursuing the idea of yet another Spanish marriage. Power politics, England's relative weakness, and the country's strategic situation off north-western Europe, rather than trade, religion or nationalistic hostility towards one or other European nation, drove Tudor foreign policy and, despite a changing European situation, account for much underlying continuity.

See pages 253–5

KEY ISSUE

How far was there an underlying consistency in Tudor foreign policy?

12 ∽ BIBLIOGRAPHY

**J Warren *Elizabeth I: Religion and Foreign Affairs* (Hodder, 2002), see especially Chapters 1 (the introduction), 5 (on relations with France and Spain) and 6 (Ireland and Scotland), designed for sixth-form study; the best starting point. A good overview is *Simon Adams *Britain, Europe and the World*, Chapter 6 in P Collinson (ed.) *The Sixteenth Century* (OUP, 2002) *S Brigden *New Worlds, Lost Worlds* (Penguin, 2000), especially Chapters 7 (1558–70), 8 (Religion in Europe and the British Isles, 1570–84), 9 (the New World and the looming war with Spain) and 11 (for Elizabeth's last years), a lively and authoritative recent survey of the period. **S Doran *Elizabeth I and Foreign Policy* (Routledge, 2000), especially Chapter 5 on responsibility for foreign policy and the conclusion. A concise volume by a leading expert on Tudor foreign policy. *S Doran *England and Europe, 1485–1603* (Longman, 1986), especially pp 63–7 in Chapter 7 on 1558–63, Chapter 8 on 1564–1603 and the assessment in Part 3. This reviews more of the evidence. *WT MacCaffrey *Elizabeth I* (Arnold, 1993), especially Chapter 6 for Scotland (1559–60), Chapters 13–17 for 1572–85 and Chapters 18–22 for the war against Spain from 1585. This is a magisterial volume from a contemporary American historian. *P Williams *The Later Tudors, England 1547–1603* (Oxford University Press, 1995), especially Chapters 8 (on the Netherlands, France and the Spanish threat) and 13 (England and the World in 1603). A masterly synthesis.

13 ∽ STRUCTURED AND ESSAY QUESTIONS

A *Structured questions*

1. (a) Account for the success of Elizabeth I's policy towards Scotland.
   (b) How significant as a threat to England was the 'Auld Alliance' of France and Scotland during the Tudor period?
2. (a) Explain how England's relations with Spain deteriorated between 1558 to 1585.
   (b) Was war against Spain inevitable?

B *Essay questions*

1. What factors enabled Elizabeth I to avoid war with Spain for so long?
2. Why did relations between England and Spain deteriorate so sharply in the years 1578–85?
3. To what extent did religion influence Elizabethan foreign policy?
4. How far did Elizabeth abandon the foreign policy pursued by previous Tudors?

14 ⌐ DOCUMENTARY EXERCISES

(i) Walsingham's analysis, October 1572

1 If her Majesty stick now to spend or put in execution all those things that tend to her safety, she must not long look to live in repose, nay, she must not long look to keep the Crown upon her head. The cause of her former quietness proceeded of her neighbours' unquietness;
5 which being removed, she must now make another account. The Admiral Coligny [the Huguenot leader] is now dead, and the Duke of Guise now liveth; the Prince of Orange is retired out of Flanders, but the Duke of Alva remaineth there still. I need not to conclude, for that to man's judgement it is apparent what will follow. Is it time now,
10 think you, Sir, to stir, or is it not time to omit any remedy that may tend to her Majesty's safety? As far as I can learn, there is none yet sent to deal with the Princes of Germany, and yet there is here almost daily conference between the Pope's **Nuncio**, the Ambassador of Spain, and them here. They omit nothing that may tend to
15 our peril. I would we were as careful not to omit any thing that may tend to our safety. It may be said that I fear too much. Surely, considering the state we stand in, I think it less danger to fear too much than too little. It may be said also that the jealousy that Spain has of the greatness of France, will not suffer him to endure to let France
20 have any footing in England, and that like affection reigning in France, if Spain should attempt any thing. I confess it to be true, and yet I see no reason but that they both may consent to advance a third person, who pretendeth right to the Crown, especially being provoked thereto by the Pope, which is my chief fear.
25 It may also be alleged that the offer of the marriage sheweth that they have no evil meaning towards her Majesty. First, it may be doubted whether, considering how nowadays their speech and meaning disagreeth, they offer as they mean ... I am now ready to think the same to proceed of abuse, only to lull us asleep in security; for any
30 thing that I can perceive, the best way not to be deceived by them is not to trust them ...

Nuncio Pope's representative at a foreign court

SOURCE A
Walsingham to Sir Thomas Smith, 8 October 1572

1 ... Can we think that the fire kindled here in France will extend itself no further? That which was concluded at the late Council of Trent [a General Council of the Roman Catholic Church which had finally condemned Protestantism], as also that which was agreed on at Bay-
5 onne [a meeting between the regent of France, Catherine de Medici and the Duke of Alva], for the rooting out of the professors of the Gospel, may in reason induce us to think the contrary. Let us not deceive ourselves but assuredly think that the two great monarchs of Europe together with the rest of the Papists do mean shortly to put

SOURCE B

Walsingham to the Regent of Scotland, 7 October 1572

10 in execution that which in the aforesaid assemblies was concluded. It is seen that when two brothers are at discord, yet when a stranger or a third person shall offer them any injury, nature teacheth them to agree to withstand the stranger.

Q

1. Which 'third person' (line 22 in Source A) did many Protestants fear would be set on the English throne?
2. What did Walsingham mean by 'the offer of the marriage' (line 25 in Source A)?
3. Why did Walsingham fear that 'the two great monarchs of Europe' (line 8 in Source B) would forget their historic rivalry and unite against Elizabeth?
4. What did Walsingham mean by his discussion of the contrasting fortunes of leading men in France and the Netherlands, and what did he think 'will follow' (line 9 in Source A)?
5. Walsingham soon wanted to do more than 'deal with the Princes of Germany'. Briefly describe the foreign policy urged by English Puritans during the 1570s.
6. Why was Elizabeth so reluctant to intervene more vigorously to assist the Dutch Revolt?

(ii) The debate on intervention in the Netherlands, October 1584

1 Dangers if her Majesty do not aid the United Provinces.

The King of Spain will overrun those countries, overthrowing their religion and ancient privileges and subjecting them to his will.

Being settled there, he will be moved to pick quarrels with this
5 country by his nearness to it; the shipping which Holland and Zeeland will yield him; his quietness in other parts; his riches from the Indies, increased by the Low Countries.

Of all which will follow a dangerous war ...

He will hope more easily to breed trouble here through the ill-
10 affected subjects when he is settled near them.

Her Majesty ... may never have the like occasion to stop the King's designs. Much better for her to keep him occupied abroad than bear the war at home, when he shall be stirred up by the Pope, Jesuits abroad, and Jesuits at home, and like enough also by the Scots Queen
15 and her son ...

Dangers if her Majesty shall aid them.

… The enterprise … will draw on a war between him and her Majesty, bringing with it great danger and inestimable charges, the burden whereof she cannot bear herself, and doubtful how her
20 subjects will like to contribute to what most will think an unnecessary war.

The offers he will make to the Scots Queen and her son to trouble her Majesty, which is more perilous than any other war, considering the readiness of their dispositions; and his stirring up evil-disposed
25 subjects to join with him.

His ability to maintain wars greater than the Queen's. Small surety to find in the Low Countries a sufficient party, or steadfastness in them … and if by the charge of the war she should be driven to leave them, then is their danger greater, for now they may make reasonable
30 composition both for their privileges and religion …

SOURCE A
Sir Walter Mildmay's opinion. Extracts from the Calendar of State Papers, Foreign Series

That it was better for her Majesty to enter into a war now, whilst she can do it outside her realm and have the help of the people of Holland and their parties, and before the King of Spain has consummated his conquests in those countries, whereby he shall be so provoked with pride, and solicited by the Pope, and tempted by the Queen's own subjects, and shall be so strong by sea and so free from all other actions of quarrels, yea and shall be so formidable to all the rest of Christendom, as that her Majesty shall no wise be able with her own power nor with aid of any other, neither by sea nor land, to withstand his attempts; but shall be forced to give place to his unsatiable malice, which is most terrible to be thought of, but most miserable to suffer.

SOURCE B
The conclusion, Burghley's Report on the Conference

Q

1. *Why did Mildmay fear trouble from 'ill-affected subjects' (Source A, lines 9–10)?*
2. *What made Elizabeth's ministers so suspicious of Philip's hostile 'designs' (Source A, line 12)?*
3. *In what ways do the above extracts suggest that intervention in the Netherlands was a very dangerous policy?*
4. *Which points in the source reveal why, nevertheless, the Council did opt for intervention?*

11

The Frontier Regions

INTRODUCTION

Historical research on the Tudor years is concentrated on the Court, the central government and what GR Elton termed the 'normal setting' of Tudor government; England south of the Trent. Yet the frontier regions in the North of England, the Principality and the border territories known as the marches of Wales, Calais and the English lordship in Ireland encompassed about half of the territories of the Tudor dominions. This chapter is focussed on the problems posed by conditions in those extensive Tudor frontiers, and examines the means by which successive Tudor monarchs sought to enhance the operation of royal government there.

The kings of late medieval England were accustomed to governing a disparate collection of territories with different nationalities, laws and customs across the British Isles and in France. However, with the loss of Normandy (1450) and Gascony (1453) the English monarchy became more insular and more 'English'. There was increasingly an assumption that there should be one law only and one culture only among the political élites across England's dominions – the law and culture of southern England. The remnants of the Crown's continental empire – the Calais **Pale** and the Channel Islands – were still regarded as England's most important frontier, bridge-heads for the recovery of lands lost in France. Nonetheless, they were no more than military outposts and possessing them did nothing to foster an acceptance of pluralism among England's élite.

Royal policy in the outlying regions of Britain and Ireland was minimalist, and they were much neglected while the Crown concentrated on the maintenance of good government in the populous and prosperous English core, while aspiring to grand conquests in France. The reformation crisis of the 1530s, however, obliged Henry VIII and Thomas Cromwell, his chief minister, to become more interventionist in the face of rebellions and the threat of imperial invasion. The extension of centralised royal control to the North of England and to Wales and the Marches, together with the progress of Protestantism and a burgeoning nationalism, paved the way for the emergence of a unified English nation state under the Tudors. However, the closer integration of the North and Wales into the Tudor state, and the loss of Calais in 1558, made Ireland increasingly the exception in its remoteness from royal authority within the Tudor dominions. Arguably, the later Tudors were too ambitious and too impatient in their efforts to integrate all of Ireland into a uniform Tudor state. By insisting on the imposition of southern English norms in government, law and culture, together with Protestantism, on people living in very different circumstances, the English Crown generated tremendous instability across Ireland, resulting in a series of rebellions which culminated in the climactic Nine Years War (1594 – 1603) at the close of Elizabeth's reign.

By the end of the Tudor era England and Wales had been welded into one of the most centralised states in early modern Europe, and relations with Protestant Scotland had become sufficiently good for the English to accept James VI as Elizabeth's successor. The capitulation of Hugh O'Neill, the Irish confederate leader, just as James ascended the English throne, left all of Ireland under English control for the first time. However, the peoples of Ireland, both the indigenous Irish population and the **Anglo-Irish** community (see map on page 281 for the Anglo-Irish Lordships and the Pale), were so profoundly alienated by the English wars of conquest, **plantations** and religious persecution, that there was to be no union of hearts and minds between the Protestant British and the Catholic Irish subjects of the Stuart monarchs.

1 ⁓ EARLY INITIATIVES

The duties of a king were essentially twofold: to preserve order within his realm, and to defend his subjects from external attack. These may seem very modest requirements, but the kings of the fifteenth century had no police force or standing army with which to fulfil these obligations. To make their rule effective in the country they had to work through those members of the aristocracy and gentry who volunteered their services as sheriffs and Justices of the Peace in the localities. This system worked reasonably well in lowland England, but proved less effective in the frontier regions.

Southern England had many large towns and thousands of well-defined, reasonably well-connected villages which facilitated centralised control and good government. It was populous and prosperous, and far too important to neglect. The frontier regions, by contrast, were less populous and poorer, and they were distant from the centre of royal power. They were more difficult to govern effectively, and the kings of late medieval England were not prepared to invest enough of their time or scarce resources in providing the same quality of governance there as was enjoyed in southern England.

Geography posed fundamental problems for royal government in the frontier regions. The Calais Pale, a tract of land only 34 km long and 12 km wide, was separated from England by the Channel and had to be strongly garrisoned in case of a French assault. Edward IV (1461–83) spent much money there in 1467 in preparation for a war to re-conquer Normandy and Gascony, which never materialised. Henry VII was less ambitious than Edward, yet in 1492 he attempted to extend the Calais bridgehead by capturing Boulogne. Henry VIII spent enormous sums on conquering and maintaining English control of Tournai (1513–18) and Boulogne (1544–50). By comparison, little

Anglo-Irish The descendants of medieval English settlers in Ireland, who continued to speak English. The native inhabitants of Ireland spoke Gaelic

Plantations estates cleared of their native inhabitants and settled by newcomers from England and Scotland. Resented by the Anglo-Irish as much as by Gaelic inhabitants of Ireland

money was spent in consolidating royal authority in the frontier regions in Britain or Ireland.

The North of England, Wales and the English lordship in Ireland were distant from London and were not subject to close royal supervision. They encompassed extensive areas of mountain, moorland and forest. The climate was cooler and wetter than that in the south and better suited to pastoral farming than tillage, giving rise to a dispersed population and few towns. Local communities were often too small to muster sufficient numbers to protect themselves from marauders. The wild and rugged terrain offered extensive areas of refuge for bandits and cattle-rustlers. Furthermore, the men of the North, who constantly readied themselves to fight Scottish invaders, were easily provoked into violence. Blood feuds were common down to the seventeenth century. In Ireland the English lordship bordered directly on independent Irish lordships from which raids and forays were common. Across the frontier regions people looked in vain to the English Crown to curb disorders and violence, and to offer redress to the victims of crime.

KEY ISSUE

What particular difficulties did the English kings of the later Middle Ages face in the government of the outlying regions?

A *North of England*

There was a dilemma in choosing those who would exercise authority on the king's behalf in the North. Either he would be a royal official or a southern nobleman, who had no local power base and was therefore dependent on the Crown; but, without local support, he could be ineffective. Or a nobleman with extensive estates in the area and local followers to command could be appointed; he would get things done, but not always as instructed by the king.

Edward IV chose to delegate his authority in the North to dominant aristocrats of the region. He made the powerful Earl of Warwick the Captain of Calais and Warden General of the Marches bordering Scotland. However, Warwick turned against the king and exposed the dangers of entrusting too much power in the hands of 'over-mighty' subjects. Following Warwick's death at the Battle of Barnet (1471) Edward IV sent his own brother Richard, Duke of Gloucester, to the North to strengthen his authority there. He appointed Gloucester as Warden of the West March and he granted him half of Warwick's estates, making him the greatest landowner north of the Trent. Gloucester cultivated an extensive network of patronage, or affinity, which bound the gentry throughout much of the North to his service.

See pages 17–18

There were three Marches, border regions adjacent to Scotland: the West March encompassed much of Cumberland and Westmoreland; the East and Middle Marches (which were always held by the same man) included almost all of Northumberland. The Warden was responsible for protecting his March from the Scots. He was, in effect, the military governor of a border zone. However, apart from the small garrisons in the royal castles in the March, he had no professional soldiers with which to repel an invasion. The defence of the realm was dependent on the Wardens drawing heavily on their private resources.

When war broke out with Scotland in 1482 the Duke of Gloucester became Edward IV's Lieutenant in the North, with full authority over all royal officers north of the Trent. As Justice of the Peace for the North (or High Commissioner, as he became known) Gloucester took an active interest in improving the quality of royal government in the North. He set himself against corrupt and incompetent judges. He arbitrated in legal disputes between local communities.

The presence of so powerful and active an agent of the Crown in the North as Gloucester, brought greater stability to the region. However, the authority of the sheriffs and Justices of the Peace was limited in parts of the North by the existence of numerous **liberties** and **franchises** in which they had little or no jurisdiction. The king's writ did not run at all in the County Palatine of Durham, nor in a number of smaller franchises held by the Archbishop of York and some northern monasteries. There were other secular liberties too where at least serious crimes could be tried by the king's courts. However, the king's officials had to depend on the lord of the liberty to serve royal writs and execute the Crown's decrees. There were occasions when lords failed to hand over their relatives or retainers for trial and punishment.

Liberties and **Franchises** areas largely independent of royal administration and the royal courts

When Edward VI died in 1483 Gloucester had himself crowned as Richard III instead of the King's son and heir, whom he murdered. He appointed the Earl of Northumberland as the Warden-General in July 1484, with responsibility for the three Marches on the Scottish border. However, he did not allow Northumberland to dominate the North as an 'over-mighty subject', as he himself had done. He appointed his nephew John de la Pole, Earl of Lincoln, as the King's Lieutenant in the North and placed him at the head of the King's Council of the North, a royal court of justice. This council was intended to guarantee the Crown's authority in the North and to provide good government there. Since its records have not survived it is not possible to assess the effectiveness of this first Council of the North. With the usurpation of Henry Tudor to the throne in August 1485 the Council ceased to exist.

Henry VII appointed the Earl of Northumberland as the King's Lieutenant in the North and Warden of the East and Middle Marches in January 1486. He was given no provincial council. He was directed simply to defend the realm from the Scots and to crush any sign of insurrection against the new régime. Henry VII was wary of Yorkist dissension, but the risings which broke out in the North in 1487, 1489 and 1492 were motivated by economic rather than political grievances. The progress of enclosure generated great resentment which broke out in armed rebellion. The Earl of Northumberland was killed by a mob revolting against increased taxation in 1489.

To strengthen his authority in the North, without creating an 'over-mighty' subject, Henry VII appointed a southerner, the Earl of Surrey, as his Lieutenant in the North. Henry appointed his eldest son Arthur as Warden-General, with Surrey acting as Lieutenant-Warden for the East and Middle Marches and Lord Dacre of Gilsland for the West March. Henry VII established a council modelled on that devised by

Richard III to assist the Earl of Surrey and to maintain his own authority directly. The Council of the North became a Court of Requests, that is a court addressing the grievances of the poor folk oppressed by the rich and powerful. As such it did much good work. However, the lords of the North were antagonised by its interference in their affairs. When Henry VII died in 1509 they successfully petitioned the new King for the dissolution of the Northern Council.

It was at Wolsey's instigation that the Council of the North was revived in 1525. The tax revolt of that year had exposed the weakness of royal control north of the Trent. Henry VIII, therefore, made his illegitimate son, Henry Fitzroy, Duke of Richmond, the Lieutenant in the North and Warden-General of the Marches. Richmond was directed to supervise the government of all of the shires north of the Trent, except Durham. Richmond's Council made good progress in improving the government of Yorkshire, but failed in its attempt to rule the border shires. In 1528 the East and Middle Marches were once more entrusted to the Earl of Northumberland, while Lord Dacre returned as Warden of the West March. The North remained a more troubled region than southern England, but it was certainly more subject to royal authority than theretofore.

B *Wales*

Wales, like the North of England, had an unenviable reputation for crime and disorder. In part, this was because there were few villages in much of Wales, and criminals could avoid capture in wild and desolate terrain. The problem was exacerbated by the multiplicity of legal jurisdictions among the Marcher lordships along the borders of southern and eastern Wales, which hindered the apprehension of felons who disturbed the peace of the Principality and the bordering shires of western England. Lawlessness, and not nationalist discontent, posed the greatest challenge to English government in Wales at the end of the Middle Ages.

Having relied at first on William Herbert, Earl of Pembroke, to maintain his authority in Wales, Edward IV, after recovering his throne in 1471, granted to his nine-month-old son the Principality of Wales, together with the Duchy of Cornwall and the County Palatine of Chester. A council was set up to manage these estates on behalf of the infant Prince. Edward IV sent the Prince of Wales and his mother to the Welsh border in the spring of 1473 in the hope that, as in the North, the presence of senior members of the royal family would generate greater loyalty towards the Crown in a troubled region.

The Principality was effectively governed with the co-operation of some of the Welsh gentry. Sheriffs and Justices of the Principality were normally appointed from among the English Marcher lords, but their deputies were often Welshmen and the coroners and lesser officers were usually Welsh. While it is true that the 'mere Welsh' suffered an inferior legal status compared with English people, it was possible to purchase letters of denizenship (naturalisation) to acquire the same rights as an

Englishman. Indeed, the Herberts and Tudors demonstrated that Welsh blood did not automatically disqualify one from promotion to a peerage – nor even from the Crown of England itself.

The Council of the Prince of Wales was originally intended to do no more than administer his estates. However, when the House of Commons complained in 1473 that crimes were going unpunished in Herefordshire and Worcestershire, Edward IV directed the Prince's Council to address the situation and do anything that was required to improve the effectiveness of royal government in those two shires, and subsequently in adjoining counties.

Though Henry VII's claim to the Crown was open to challenge, his position was reasonably secure in his native Wales. It was only after the council he established in the North had proved itself successful that he addressed the problems of his home region. In 1493 Henry VII gave Arthur, Prince of Wales, possession of the Principality of Wales and a number of the Marcher lordships which had come into the Crown's hands. He established a Council for the young Prince and made it responsible for overseeing the administration of justice in the Principality and Marches of Wales, and in the adjoining counties of Shropshire, Herefordshire, Worcestershire and Gloucestershire. Unfortunately, little is known of the work of the Welsh Council during Henry VII's reign.

Henry VIII was far more concerned with winning glory in France than he was in providing better government for his subjects. However, the King's demand for heavy taxation to finance his foreign adventures in 1523–5 exposed the weakness of royal government in the outlying regions. Wolsey attempted to address this problem by despatching Princess Mary to Shropshire to head the Council in the Principality and Marches of Wales, as he had sent Henry Fitzroy, his illegitimate son, to Yorkshire to head a newly established Council of the North. Princess Mary's Council was presided over by John Veysey, Bishop of Exeter. Like its counterpart in the North, the Welsh Council enjoyed a qualified success in improving the provision of justice in its area of jurisdiction, but was unable fully to quell the disorders afflicting the Welsh borderlands.

KEY ISSUE
Why was disorder such a problem in Wales and the Welsh Marches, and how did Edward IV and Henry VII seek to bring it under control?

C *Ireland*

The English lordship in Ireland posed a particular problem for Henry VII on his succession. It was governed by a local nobleman, Garret Mór FitzGerald, Earl of Kildare, a resolute Yorkist. But it would have been extremely difficult to replace him. With an annual revenue of only £900 and a garrison of 300–400 soldiers, the King's Deputy in Ireland, in effect a viceroy, could govern only by deploying his own resources. As the greatest nobleman in the Pale, and holding the office of Deputy, Kildare wielded tremendous power and influence there. Through marriage alliances and the development of a very extensive patronage network he also exerted great influence across Ireland, not just in the outlying territories of the English lordship but among Gaelic Irish lordships too.

See page 35

Kildare and the colonial administration at Dublin were slow to recognise Henry VII's accession to the throne. However, the new King was not in a position to intervene in Ireland while his hold on the English Crown was still unsure. He left Kildare in charge of the colony. Early in 1487 a young boy, Lambert Simnel, set up to impersonate Edward, Earl of Warwick, arrived in Ireland. He was crowned as Edward VI in Dublin by the colonial élite and was provided with an army comprised of about 4000 Irishmen, together with some English Yorkists, and Germans sent by Margaret of Burgundy. With this force 'Edward VI' invaded England, but was routed at the Battle of Stoke in June 1487.

Despite that enormous provocation Henry VII decided to be lenient with Kildare in the hope of avoiding a military commitment in Ireland. He maintained the Deputy in office and issued a general pardon to the colonial élites. However, in November 1491 Perkin Warbeck arrived in Ireland, claiming to be Edward IV's second son Richard. Kildare did not support him, but neither did he exert himself against him. Henry VII sent a small army to Ireland which expelled Warbeck. He dismissed Kildare from office and appointed two local notables to govern the colony. When Warbeck threatened to return to Ireland, the King sent Sir Edward Poynings to the colony as Deputy with a small army in September 1494.

Poynings proved to be an effective governor. He protected the Pale and he saw off Warbeck and his forces. Poynings strengthened the Crown's control of its lordship in Ireland through a parliament he convened at Drogheda in 1494–5. That passed an important statute, subsequently known as 'Poynings' Law', which forbade the holding of any Parliament in Ireland without the prior consent of the King, and which prevented the Parliament from considering any bill which had not received the King's sanction. Effectively, Poynings ended Ireland's legislative independence from England. The Parliament also granted a new annual subsidy and a new customs levy to bolster the finances of the colonial government. By the time Poynings was recalled in December 1495 he had strengthened the Crown's control over the colony. The threat from Yorkist pretenders was ended: when Warbeck returned to Ireland in 1499, he was universally spurned.

Henry VII re-appointed Kildare as Deputy in Ireland in August 1496. The King is reputed to have said that 'If all of Ireland cannot rule this man, then he is meet to govern all of Ireland'! Kildare repaid the King's trust by giving Henry VII what no one else could – an efficient administration in Ireland which was entirely self-financing. When Henry VII died in 1509 the English Crown no longer had an 'Irish problem'.

Garret Óg FitzGerald, 9th Earl of Kildare from 1513, inherited his father's enormous power and prestige and the Deputyship. Henry VIII was content to permit the status quo in Ireland until the loss of Tournai dashed his ambitions in France. The King then looked to Ireland for some great achievement. In May 1520 he appointed Thomas Howard, Earl of Surrey, as Lieutenant of Ireland with instructions to consider how all of Ireland might be brought under English rule, preferably 'by

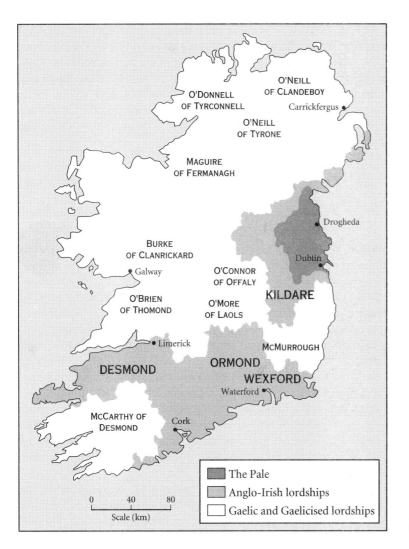

MAP 9
Ireland in 1485

sober ways, politic drifts and amiable persuasions founded in law and reason': that is, cheaply. Surrey, however, reckoned that Ireland could only be brought under English rule by conquest over many years and at enormous expense. As it was, Surrey's garrison cost the Crown £10 000 a year simply to defend the colony from Irish attacks. Surrey was re-called.

Despite Surrey's failure Henry VIII and Wolsey were anxious to demonstrate that they could govern the lordship in Ireland without Kildare. Over the next ten years there were eight changes of Deputy as the King vacillated between accepting the efficient and economical government of Kildare, and expensively demonstrating that the Earl was dispensable. The cumulative effect of the Crown's inconstancy was to weaken the colonial administration and destabilise relations with the Irish lords.

TIMELINE

1487	Lambert Simnel in Ireland
1491	Perkin Warbeck in Ireland
1495	Poynings' Law passed by Irish Parliament reinforcing royal authority
1496	Kildare re-appointed as Deputy
1520	Henry VIII replaces Kildare's son as Deputy by the Earl of Surrey

KEY ISSUE

Why was it so difficult to replace Kildare as the King's Deputy in Ireland?

Overall, one can see that the early Tudors were able to exercise royal authority across the frontier regions and ensure that they did not undermine the dynasty, as had happened to the last Yorkist kings. Real progress was achieved in enhancing the government of the North and of the Principality and Marches of Wales. In Ireland, however, the reluctance of Henry VIII to accept the Kildare ascendancy after 1519 began to threaten the progress made since the 1470s in strengthening the English lordship in Ireland.

2 ⤳ CROMWELL AND THE UNITARY STATE

See page 109

GR Elton argued that Thomas Cromwell achieved a 'revolution' in the administration of England, implementing many important reforms designed to transform the Tudor domains into a unitary commonwealth. Other historians dispute the extent to which Cromwell's changes may legitimately be termed revolutionary. Nonetheless, Cromwell certainly wished to ensure that the King's government functioned effectively throughout the realm. Through the 'Act for Resuming Certain Liberties to the Crown' (1536) he destroyed the privileges of those areas where the King's writ had not run or was strictly limited. The Lords of Liberties and Franchises were deprived of their jurisdiction in criminal causes. From 1536 only the Crown could appoint judges and Justices of the Peace in any part of England and Wales. The system of government was now much more uniform in these parts of Henry's dominions, and a first major step towards the creation of a unitary state had been taken.

Yet Cromwell's initial efforts to improve the effectiveness of the King's government in the outlying regions were strikingly conservative; in effect he did little more than change the personnel in charge. However, the break from Rome created widespread disaffection and resistance, which was particularly open where the Crown's authority was at its weakest. In Ireland in 1534–5, and in the north of England in 1536–7, Catholic hostility to religious innovation was demonstrated in armed rebellion. Fear of rebellion was not Cromwell's sole motivation in strengthening royal authority in the periphery – but it highlighted the need for more radical approaches to these areas than the minister may previously have considered.

A *The Calais Pale*

The break from Rome exposed England to the possibility of attack by Catholic European neighbours. Calais became the country's first line of defence. It had to be well governed and well guarded. In August 1535 Cromwell sent a royal commission to Calais to investigate how best to organise the outpost. The resulting 'Calais Act' (1536) entrusted the government of Calais to an executive council headed by a Deputy.

Strikingly, Calais was granted the privilege of sending two MPs to the House of Commons to represent its interests. That is remarkable since it meant, in effect, that the territory was incorporated into the kingdom of England. This strongly suggests that Cromwell had no time for Henry VIII's delusions about winning possession of French provinces, if not the Crown of France itself, into which Calais would have been absorbed.

Henry VIII captured Boulogne in 1544. However, when the town was liberated by the French in 1550, England was left with nothing to show for the £3.5 million spent on Henry's war with France. When, in 1557, England joined Spain in invading France, the French King, Henry II, took his revenge by capturing Calais. On 1 January 1558 a large French army penetrated the outer defences of the Calais Pale. Within eight days England lost Calais, her last possession on mainland Europe.

B *Wales*

To strengthen the Crown's authority in Wales, Cromwell appointed Rowland Lee, Bishop of Coventry and Lichfield, as President of the Welsh Council in 1534. Lee believed that the Welsh could only be governed through fear, and he governed with ferocity. The bishop boasted of having hanged 5000 men in his first six years in Wales – an incredible tally given population levels at that time.

In 1536 Cromwell initiated a revolution in the government of Wales. It seems likely that Cromwell was influenced by Sir Thomas Englefield, a member of the Council in Wales, into establishing a uniform system of government in Wales, as in England. In a statute of 1536 Justices of the Peace were established in the counties of the Principality of Wales, and in the Crown lordships of Pembroke and Glamorgan, with the same powers as their English counterparts. More importantly, the English Parliament in 1536 enacted the 'Act for Laws and Justice to be ministered in Wales in like form as it is in this realm':

Albeit the dominion, principality and country of Wales justly and rightly is, and ever has been, incorporated, annexed, united and subject to and under the imperial Crown of this realm [of England], ... whereof the King's most royal majesty ... is truly head, King, lord and ruler; yet notwithstanding, because in the same country, principality and dominion diverse rights, usages, laws and customs be far discrepant from the laws and customs of this realm, and also because the people of that same dominion have and daily use a speech nothing like, nor consonant to, the natural mother tongue used within this realm, some rude and ignorant people have made distinction ... between the King's subjects of this realm, and his subjects of the said dominion and principality of Wales, whereby great discord, variance, debate, division, murmur and sedition have grown between his said subjects. His highness, therefore, of a singular zeal, love and favour that he bears towards his

Q

1. *What reasons does Cromwell give for passing this so-called Act of Union?*
2. *Judging from these extracts what advantages and what disadvantages would this Act bring to the people of Wales?*

subjects of his said dominion of Wales, minding and intending to reduce them to the perfect order, notice and knowledge of his laws of this his realm [of England], and utterly to extirpate, all and singular, the sinister usages and customs differing from the same ...

That his said country or dominion of Wales shall ... continue forever from henceforth incorporated, united and annexed to and with this his realm of England; and that all and singular person or persons born, or to be born, in the said principality, country or dominion of Wales, shall have, enjoy and inherit all and singular freedoms, liberties, rights, privileges and laws within this his realm ... as other the king's subjects, naturally born within the same, have, enjoy and inherit.

By the 1536 Act the Welsh shires were each given the right to elect one MP to the House of Commons, while the boroughs of each shire could vote collectively to elect a second MP. A second statute in 1543 defined the union of Wales with England in much greater detail. The Welsh Marches were merged into new shires, each entrusted to a sheriff and JPs, as in England. However, the whole of Wales, excluding Monmouth which was transferred to England for administrative purposes, remained outside Westminster's system of court sessions until 1830.

The Council of the Principality and Marches of Wales was re-organised as a permanent bureaucratic institution to direct and supervise the government of Wales and the adjacent English shires of Cheshire, Shropshire, Herefordshire, Worcestershire, Gloucestershire and Monmouthshire. Through the Council all royal proclamations were made and orders transmitted to local government officers in the region – in Welsh translations wherever necessary. The Council continued to act as a judicial court, though the destruction of the privileges of the liberties and franchises made the task of law enforcement in the region much easier than in the past.

The reformed Council in Wales made a significant contribution towards the effective enforcement of English law in the region. No less important, were the two so-called Acts of Union which allowed the Welsh landowners and burgesses to participate in local and national politics to a degree never previously possible. One indication of the success of these developments is the fact that, despite the religious and economic upheavals which led to rebellions elsewhere in the Tudor domains, Wales remained peaceful into the seventeenth century.

KEY ISSUE

What was changed by the Acts of Union with Wales, and how successful were Cromwell's policies in this regard?

C The North of England

Henry Percy, Earl of Northumberland, was appointed Lieutenant in place of Richmond in 1533. As with Kildare in Ireland, Henry VIII resented his dependence on the 'over-mighty' subject, but he was not prepared to spend the money needed to govern the region directly from Westminster. However, Henry Percy was childless and heavily in debt. At Cromwell's suggestion Percy's debts were acquired by the Crown and used as a lever to force the Earl to bequeath his estates to the Crown in

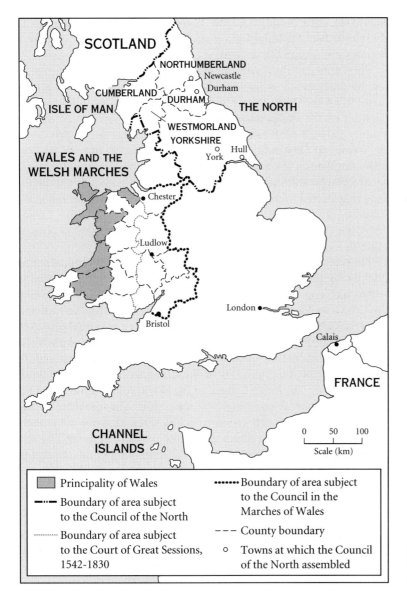

Principality of Wales

-·-· Boundary of area subject
to the Council of the North

·········· Boundary of area subject
to the Court of Great Sessions,
1542-1830

······· Boundary of area subject
to the Council in the
Marches of Wales

- - - County boundary

o Towns at which the Council
of the North assembled

MAP 10
Tudor Territories, 1540

his will. An Act of Parliament confirmed this transaction in 1536. Cromwell planned to exploit the Percy estates to strengthen the Crown's position in the North.

The impending destruction of the Earldom of Northumberland alienated the wide-flung network of Percy supporters. At the same time, the Crown's religious policies, most especially the suppression of the monasteries, were deeply unpopular in the North. Opposition to these two developments coalesced in the uprising known as the Pilgrimage of Grace. This uprising made it necessary to reform the government of the North more radically than was originally intended. In autumn 1537, after the Pilgrimage was over, Cuthbert Tunstall, Bishop of Durham,

See pages 312–16

was made Lord President of the Council of the North. Henceforth, the North was no longer governed by a great nobleman, but by a permanent bureaucratic council.

The Council of the North was made the supreme executive authority for the shires north of the Trent – excepting the royal Duchy of Lancaster. With the Percy estates in the Crown's possession, and the suppression of the independent liberties and franchises (except for the County Palatine of Durham which retained some minor privileges) there were no outstanding obstacles to the operation of royal government throughout the region. The Council of the North was the sole agent through which all royal proclamations were made, all royal orders were transmitted to sheriffs and justices, and all demands for collecting subsidies were issued. After the Pilgrimage of Grace the Crown employed the Council of the North to enforce its religious policies as much as its political policies.

The records of the Council of the North reveal that it was active in disciplining sheriffs and Justices who failed to perform their duties as well as was required. It ensured that the northern bishops implemented the Crown's religious policies within their dioceses. At its general sessions the Council sought to administer speedy and impartial justice to rich and poor folk alike. By addressing such issues as enclosures, food supplies, and the maintenance of private armies the Council was able to answer many of the grievances of the common people. Rachel Reid, in her study of *The King's Council in the North*, concluded that the reconstituted Council was singularly successful. The problem of the North, she declared, had been solved at last, although it was not entirely without its disturbances. The revolt of the northern earls in 1569 was an echo of earlier times but its rapid collapse reflected the realities of royal authority in the North in Elizabeth's reign.

KEY ISSUE

How did the Pilgrimage of Grace stimulate improvements to government in the North?

See pages 321–4

D *Ireland*

As was the case in Wales and the north of England, Cromwell's initial strategy to strengthen the King's government in Ireland was conservative. As Wolsey had done before him, Cromwell decided to detain Garret Óg Fitzgerald, ninth Earl of Kildare, in England and appoint an Englishman as Deputy of Ireland in his place. The new Deputy was Sir William Skeffington, a relative nonentity who had tried to govern Ireland briefly in 1530–2 and failed. Skeffington was given command of a paltry army of 150 men, and supplied with copies of a pamphlet entitled 'Ordinances for the government of Ireland' which advocated traditional remedies to longstanding problems. It is difficult to see how Cromwell's strategy could have achieved any progress.

Kildare was detained on arrival at Court in May 1534. On learning of his father's detention, Kildare's son, Lord Offaly, ostentatiously resigned as Vice-Deputy on 11 June 1534, and denounced the King's political and religious policies before the Council of Ireland. He then launched a full-scale rebellion, claiming to lead a Catholic crusade against the heretical King. The Kildare rebellion was spectacularly successful at first. The Kildare network of supporters and dependents was very extensive, and the appeal against English mis-government and religious innovation was very popular. The clergy were widely involved in mobilising support against the heretical King and his minions. However, contacts with Catholic dissidents in Wales and the north of England did not result in uprisings there. The Emperor and Pope gave the rebels their prayers but failed to provide any military support.

After months of prevarication, Skeffington finally landed near Dublin with 2300 soldiers in October 1534. The Pale gentry abandoned the rebellion in the face of such an overwhelming force. The Earl of Kildare, as Offaly became on his father's death, fought on until surrendering on 24 August 1535 after being promised that his life would be spared. The young Earl was, in fact, executed along with his five uncles in the aftermath of the Pilgrimage of Grace. The rebellion cost £23 000 to suppress and left the colonial administration in disarray. Cromwell was forced to recognise the need for more thoroughgoing reforms than he had previously envisaged.

On 1 January 1536 Lord Leonard Grey was sent to Ireland to govern the colony. Four royal commissioners were sent to investigate the problems facing the colonial administration. Following their recommendations Cromwell directed that the Dublin administration extend its government to the full extent of the colony. Fortifications were to be constructed, but peace was to be negotiated with the bordering Irish lords wherever possible. Yet, Henry VIII was determined that the Dublin administration be self-financing, which was impossible if it was to extend its control over all Ireland as Cromwell wished.

Deputy Grey tried to subdue the Irish lords beyond the colony but he succeeded only in forcing them into a national league hostile to both his militarist policies and the attempt to export the Reformation from England. The league launched a large-scale assault on the Pale in 1539. That was repulsed, but it maintained the struggle, approaching the King of Scotland for support in Spring 1540. It became clear that Grey was endangering the English colony in Ireland and, in April 1540, he was dismissed from office. He left behind him an impoverished administration in Dublin, a country in turmoil and a longing for the relatively peaceful and prosperous days of Kildare. Ireland had bucked the trend towards a centralised English state under Cromwell's direction.

> **KEY ISSUE**
>
> *Why were Cromwell's efforts to reform the government of the English colony in Ireland so unsuccessful?*

3 ⇜ THE IRISH CONSTITUTIONAL REVOLUTION

In June 1541 Ireland's constitutional status was changed from that of a feudal lordship, subject to the English Crown, into what seemed to be a sovereign kingdom. It was a central part of the 'constitutional revolution' conceived by Sir Thomas Cusack, an official in the colonial administration. Cusack wanted to see the government of Ireland reformed so that the native Irish and the Anglo-Irish colonists could live harmoniously together within a common political framework –

just like the Welsh and English since the 'Act of Union' (1536). Cusack's dream might never have had a chance of becoming a reality but for the support he won from Sir Anthony St Leger, whom Henry VIII appointed as his Lord Deputy in Ireland in July 1540.

The constitutional revolution got underway with the sitting of the Irish Parliament on 13 June 1541. The Parliament declared that Ireland was, in fact, a kingdom, and Henry VIII was its King. The preamble to the 'Act for the kingly title' (1541) stated that the 'lack of naming the King's majesty and his most noble progenitors as kings of Ireland … hath been great occasion that the Irishmen and inhabitants within this realm of Ireland have not been so obedient to the King's highness and his most noble progenitors, and to their laws, as they of right and according to their allegiance and bounden duties ought to have been'. The Act abolished the constitutional and juridical division of Ireland between the Anglo-Irish colony, the Pale, on the one hand, and the independent Gaelic lordships on the other. It made all of the Irish into subjects of Henry VIII, with the same rights and privileges as the King's English subjects. Henry was now honour-bound to dispense justice and good government throughout his Irish kingdom.

The Irish Parliament of 1541–3 was historic in that an Irish noble-man, MacGilpatrick, Baron of Upper Ossory, attended the House of Lords for the first time ever. Many other Irish lords attended as observers. Their presence was a revolutionary innovation. It signified that in the future the Irish Parliament would become the representative assembly of all the people in Ireland – Gaelic Irish and Anglo-Irish alike. By involving the two communities in the government in this way St Leger and Cusack hoped to break down the barriers between them.

With the constitutional framework in place, St Leger set about solving the most difficult issue dividing the Irish lords from the English Crown – the question of land tenure. To address this issue Cusack and St Leger devised the policy known to historians as 'surrender and regrant'. In essence, this involved the Irish lords surrendering their territories to the Crown, in return for them being formally regranted with a title valid under English law. This formula was designed to regularise the relationship between the Crown and the greatest Irish lords. It also began the process by which the independent Irish lordships were transformed, more or less as they stood, into feudal lordships held of the Crown of Ireland. As part of 'surrender and regrant' each Irish lord had to agree to assist and obey the King's officers, perform military service for the Crown and pay taxes. Furthermore, each lord was to speak English and adopt English clothes and customs, and reject the Pope's authority. In return, the title to his lands would be more secure, and he would be entitled to the King's support and justice in his courts.

St Leger realised that his revolution could not be achieved overnight. He worked to bring about change peacefully. The first breakthrough came in January 1541 when James Fitzgerald, eleventh Earl of Desmond, was formally reconciled to the English Crown, and brought his many underlords with him. As Cusack observed, 'the winning of the Earl of Desmond was the winning of the rest of Munster at small charge'. Progress with the Gaelic lords was necessarily more difficult and slow. Yet in September 1542 Conn O'Neill, Lord of Tyrone and descendent of the ancient Kings of Ireland, travelled to the English Court to become the first Earl of Tyrone. On 1 July 1543 Murrough O'Brien, Prince of Thomond, travelled to Court to become the first Earl of Thomond. With him went Ulick MacWilliam Burke, a great lord from south Connacht, who became the first Earl of Clanricard.

The Cusack-St Leger initiative was making remarkable progress towards a peaceful settlement of the political divisions in Ireland when it was suddenly suspended in July 1543 because Henry embarked on a war with France and Scotland. The war dragged on and, after Henry VIII's death, St Leger was replaced as Lord Deputy by Sir Edward Bellingham who abandoned the constitutional experiment in favour of brute force.

Historians have debated the extent to which the Cusack–St Leger initiative constituted a revolution. No one denies that the programme was very ambitious. If it had succeeded the independent Irish lords would have become the King's vassals and loyal peers. The political disorders in Ireland would have been brought to an end, and the new kingdom could have become an asset to the English Crown, rather than the financial liability it was destined to be. However, so little was actually achieved before it was suspended that the programme seems more revolutionary in its implications than in its implementation. The Dublin administration, for instance, was neither reformed nor expanded to deal with its greatly increased responsibilities. The Irish were not granted political and legal rights equal to those of Englishmen. The title King of Ireland was a legal fiction. The change in Ireland's constitutional status led to no recognisable improvement in the disposition of Henry VIII towards Ireland.

Nonetheless, the Cusack–St Leger initiative remains one of the most significant developments in sixteenth-century Irish history. Because of it, most of the Irish lords acknowledged the sovereignty of Henry VIII as King of Ireland and in the case of those lords whose status had been regularised by July 1543, the extension of royal authority was very real. The Earls of Clanricard and Thomond were especially noteworthy for their co-operation with the Crown during the remaining decades of the sixteenth century. The progress achieved by St Leger in the first three years

TIMELINE

1535	Rebellion in Ireland put down; young Earl of Kildare executed
1536	Calais Act
	First Act of Union with Wales
	Lord Grey sent to Ireland as Deputy
1537	Council of North replaces government through local nobles
1540	Grey dismissed having provoked an attack by a league of Irish lords
1541	Cusack and St Leger attempt constitutional revolution in Ireland
1543	Renewed war with France brought the constitutional experiment in Ireland to an end; repression the only policy left
1543	Second Act of Union with Wales

of his Deputyship suggests that the subsequent resort to conquest and colonisation was unnecessary. The Tudor wars in Ireland were appallingly costly in terms of Irish lives, and English money. Brendan Bradshaw is certainly correct in seeing the aborting of the revolutionary initiative in July 1543 as a terrible tragedy whose consequences affect us still.

The years of promise during St Leger's first term of office in Ireland were succeeded by years of turmoil and confusion. From 1547 English policy towards Ireland became increasingly aggressive with attempts made to extend English power by military action. Yet, for all the blood shed, Crown policy lacked direction. During Edward VI's short reign alone there were no less than six changes of governor in Ireland. The Irish lords were confronted by a colonial regime which behaved violently and erratically.

Lord Fitzwalter, Earl of Sussex from 1557, was appointed as Deputy in 1556. In spite of massive subsidies from England, Sussex achieved little during his long term in office. He failed repeatedly to expel Scottish settlers from north Antrim. His plantation of Laois and Offaly proved to be an expensive failure. He alienated the Anglo-Irish from the Dublin administration by excluding them from office and influence, and by imposing very high levels of cess on the Pale – a practice whereby the Crown requisitioned provisions from landowners, and subsequently paid for them at prices which usually bore little relationship to market prices. Sussex seriously undermined the Irish economy through the constant wars he provoked, and by debasing the Irish coinage to help finance his wars. Eventually, in response to local complaints, a royal commission was set up to investigate Sussex's administration. The Earl took 'sick leave' in May 1564 and never returned to Ireland. The two decades following the aborted constitutional revolution had made the Irish question more irresolvable than ever.

KEY ISSUE
How close did Ireland come to a 'constitutional revolution' in Ireland in the 1540s, and why did it fail?

4 ⌁ THE TUDOR REFORMATION AND IRELAND

Recent work has highlighted similarities in the conditions of the late medieval Church in England and in the most anglicised areas in Ireland, and in the early Reformation experiences on either side of the Irish Sea. The Church in Gaelic Ireland may have had distinctive features, but English influences were very strong in the English lordship with several bishops of Irish sees being Englishmen, and the great majority of the higher clergy of the Pale having attended Oxford or Cambridge universities. Forms of popular piety, especially in the towns, were largely drawn from England. To Irish-speakers the imposition of the English Reformation was much more likely to be experienced as cultural imperialism, but it was certainly possible that the Anglo-Irish élite, whose speech and identity were English, could have embraced the Tudor Reformations.

Unfortunately, only one Irish diocese, Armagh, still has episcopal registers from the sixteenth century which are comparable to those available to English Church historians. They show that Armagh was well administered on the eve of the Reformation through annual diocesan synods, regular visitations and a consistory court which operated very much like its counterparts in southern England. Other dioceses, particularly those in Gaelic and gaelicised regions, were not as well-ordered as Armagh, but throughout the Pale and in the towns the Irish Church seems to have been in relatively good order. Lay support for the Church was certainly strong, as is shown by the striking levels of investment in new church buildings and friaries up to the eve of the Reformation, by the number of chantries being founded (paralleling a pattern also found in northern England) and by the generous benefactions to the Church in many lay people's wills. This new work on the Irish Church in the colony echoes revisionist findings for the English Church, such as those of Eamon Duffy. Yet England's Reformation experiences suggest, by analogy, that a popular attachment to Catholic beliefs and practices was not sufficient, in itself, to ensure the survival of Catholicism as the religion of the people of Ireland.

See pages 416–20

The Kildare rebellion dramatically demonstrated the extent of Irish hostility to Henry VIII's religious policies. Some of the colony's best educated and most senior clerics promoted the rebellion as a Catholic crusade against the heretical King. However, the Irish 'crusade' got no support from English Catholics, nor from the Catholic powers of mainland Europe, and consequently it failed. Several of the leading crusaders were killed in the revolt, and the presence of a large garrison of English troops in the Pale ensured that Henry VIII's wishes could not be ignored. The Reformation statutes were endorsed by the Irish Parliament of 1536–7, not without clerical opposition, but with the support of a body of Anglo-Irish reformers. These men had encountered humanist ideas while studying in England and they hoped that Henry VIII would implement a thorough reform of the commonwealth in Ireland. As in England, the sharing of the spoils from the Dissolution of Monasteries won support from among those who received a share.

To spearhead the Henrician Reformation in Ireland, Henry VIII made George Browne, a former English friar, Archbishop of Dublin in March 1536. Browne was no zealot but he promoted the Royal Supremacy and the Crown's religious programme throughout the ecclesiastical province of Dublin. The clergy generally offered no more than passive resistance, refusing to preach or promote the Royal Supremacy. Very few openly condemned the innovations or suffered imprisonment. However, once the Act of Six Articles in 1539 made clear the Catholic nature of the King's religion much of the bitterness began to fade.

See page 96

St Leger applied his consensus approach to enforcing the Henrician Reformation in Ireland. In effect, he dissociated the Royal Supremacy from any need to do away with hallowed rituals and beliefs. He committed his administration to supporting the Church authorities against aristocratic interference and exactions. He also employed political pressure to persuade the bishops to take the oath of Supremacy. This combination of practical support and coercion succeeded in getting

24 of Ireland's 30 bishops to take the oath by the end of Henry VIII's reign. When the first Jesuit mission was conducted in Ireland in 1542 it met with a frosty response from the Irish lords engaged in negotiations to secure the benefits of 'surrender and regrant'.

The Edwardian Reformation was imposed on the colony in Ireland with energy. The first *Book of Common Prayer* was introduced into churches throughout English-speaking districts. The English Privy Council authorised the publication of an Irish language version of the *Prayer Book* in 1551, but nothing materialised. With no Protestant-Irish clergy available the Crown appointed Englishmen to the sees of Armagh, Kildare, Leighlin and Ossory. One of those bishops, John Bale of Ossory, was a zealous preacher and, despite the opposition of the local clergy, he built up a following among the young people of Kilkenny. Generally, though, hostility to the Edwardian Reformation was widespread in Ireland, if muted. As soon as Mary ascended the throne the Reformation came to an end, even in Kilkenny, before it had a chance to win committed converts.

Mary's reign was universally welcomed in Ireland. Catholic services were spontaneously restored in the English-speaking districts where the *Prayer Book* had been used. The few clergy who had married under Edward VI were soon weeded out. Local Catholics were installed in all of the dioceses and parishes, with the exception of Hugh Curwen, one of her chaplains, whom Mary appointed as archbishop of Dublin. The Irish Parliament of 1557–8 formally completed the work of restoring the Roman Catholic Church in Ireland.

However, the Irish Parliament of 1560 endorsed the Elizabethan Settlement in the remarkably short space of three weeks. Some bishops actually voted in favour of the ecclesiastical legislation in the House of Lords while only three are thought to have opposed it openly. It is thus clear that, while there was a preference for traditional Catholicism, a militant Counter-Reformation had not taken hold in Mary's reign. The ecclesiastical bills were endorsed because the colonial élite felt that they had little choice in the matter, as subjects of the Crown, and they had won concessions allowing the retention of Latin in Church services where English was not widely spoken, and the continued use of the rituals of Catholic worship in the 'reformed' Church of Ireland.

The colonial community generally conformed to the Elizabethan settlement, attending Church services though they often refused to receive the Anglican Communion. Even clergymen with conscientious objections mostly conformed and adapted the *Prayer Book* services to make them as Catholic as possible. Some priests read 'little or nothing' from the *Book of Common Prayer* and regaled their congregations with stories of St Patrick or the Blessed Virgin. Nonetheless, as long as the colonial community conformed there was the possibility that it might be won to Protestantism in time – as happened in Wales and the conservative north of England.

A key failure of the reformed Church was its inability to provide schools good enough to compete with those run by recusant priests. The Catholic priest-teachers may have saved the Catholic faith in Ireland by inspiring the younger generations with a tremendous commitment to Rome. Many scholars from the recusant academies went on to study in Catholic colleges on mainland Europe, among whom a high proportion returned to Ireland as Jesuits or seminary-trained priests.

Unable to recruit more than a handful of Irish Protestants into its ministry, the Protestant Church of Ireland began to employ English clerics. Some of these men preached zealously among the English-speaking townsfolk though, with the exception of Galway, apparently to little effect. However, the intrusion of English Protestant ministers proved very unpopular. Englishmen were already gaining a virtual monopoly of high office in the civil administration in Ireland, and they showed themselves greedy for a share of Irish land and commercial opportunities. Even the long-established, English-speaking Anglo-Irish community came to regard religious changes as part of a wider English Protestant assault on their heritage. Resistance intensified when the English administration in Ireland made extortionate demands for tax on the colony to finance the wars it was fighting against the Gaelic Irish, while Irish seminary priests returned from mainland Europe to propagate the Counter-Reformation.

The seminary priests were drawn mainly from the patrician class in the Irish towns. They used their backgrounds to win the commitment of the urban élites in Ireland to the Catholic cause. The priests demonstrated such zeal and courage in their ministry that they commanded respect even from their adversaries. The following extract is from Edmund Spenser's book, *A View of the Present State of Ireland* (1596). The book is based on his first-hand experiences as an English planter in Ireland. While reading the extract, it is important to remember that Spenser was a Protestant, and was strongly opposed to the Catholic Church:

> ... it is [a] great wonder to see the difference which is between the zeal of the popish priests and the ministers of the gospel; for they [i.e. the priests] do not hesitate to come from Spain, from Rome and from Rheims, by long toil and dangerous travel to here, where they know peril of death awaits them, and no reward nor riches is to be found, simply to draw the people to the Church of Rome; whereas some of our idle ministers, having a way of credit and esteem thereby opened onto them, and having the livings of the country offered onto them, without pain and without peril, will neither for the same nor any love of God, nor zeal of religion, nor for all the good they may do by winning souls to God, be drawn forth from their warm nests to look out onto God's harvest, which is ready for the sickle, and all the fields yellow long ago.

Q

1. What comparison does Spenser draw between the Catholic and the Protestant clergy in Ireland?
2. What might Spenser have hoped to achieve by making this comparison?

The newly arrived Jesuits and seminary priests quickly set up a Church structure parallel to that of the State Church. Recusancy on a massive scale followed. The congregations which had attended Protestant services simply deserted *en masse*. In Cork city, for instance, Bishop William Lyons complained that whereas previously hundreds of people had attended Protestant services, by 1596 there were only a handful. The borough, with a population of 2000, had ten Catholic priests who openly celebrated the Mass and other Catholic ceremonies. Protestant ministers were shunned; people labelled them 'devils' and hurried past them in the street, making the sign of the cross for protection against diabolical contagion. The scale of the Protestant collapse in Cork, and everywhere else throughout the colony where the Reformation had been imposed, was overwhelming.

One may conclude then, that the Catholic Church in Ireland, despite its failings, enjoyed much support from the laity before the Reformation. Nonetheless, as happened in England, the majority of people in districts under royal control conformed to the early Tudor Reformations. There was, though, one over-riding cause of divergence between the progress of the Reformation in England and Ireland; the Irish Church produced strikingly few Protestant preachers. In the absence of native Protestant clergy the Protestant Church in Ireland was obliged to resort to employing Englishmen, at a time when English rule in Ireland was increasingly characterised by wars of conquest and colonisation. That served to emphasis the alien nature of the State Church in Ireland. By the early decades of the seventeenth century, the Protestant clergy, who were virtually all English (or Scottish), abandoned hope of converting the Irish to 'true religion' and took refuge in the Calvinist doctrine of predestination: the Irish were simply predestined to Hell.

> **KEY ISSUE**
>
> *Why did the Reformation make only limited progress in Ireland?*

5 ⌁ THE CONQUEST OF IRELAND

A *Government of Ireland under Elizabeth: repression and resistance*

On 13 October 1565 Sir Henry Sidney was made Deputy of Ireland. He had gone to Ireland with Sussex in 1556 and served as Under-Treasurer. From 1560 he was also President of the Council in Wales. In *The Elizabethan Conquest of Ireland*, Nicholas Canny argued that Sidney's appointment marked 'a new departure' for Tudor policy towards Ireland. The new Deputy accepted office only when Elizabeth agreed to endorse his programme to subdue the country in three years if the Queen provided him with an army of 1500 men, financed directly from England.

Sidney arrived in Ireland in January 1566 and immediately set about reforming the administration of justice in Leinster, the province around Dublin. By April he was ready to establish a Provincial Council in Munster. Unexpectedly, this idea was opposed by the Earl of Ormond who feared having his independence curbed in the Palatine County of Tipperary. Ormond – known affectionately as 'Black Tom' by his cousin Elizabeth – persuaded the Queen to scupper the Council before it was even launched. Sidney suffered another setback when obliged to engage in war with Seán O'Neill, the greatest lord in Ulster, who sought to overthrow English rule in Ireland. By October 1567, after O'Neill's death, Sidney had to travel to Court to negotiate new terms for his programme.

Sidney returned to Ireland as Deputy in April 1568 with a revised programme for conquest. The essential elements of the original scheme were retained but he now intended to promote private plantation ventures to help anglicise Ireland quickly. In September and October 1568 the Deputy examined the east coast of Ulster to assess the scope for colonising the area. However, Seán O'Neill's successor in Ulster, Turlough Luineach O'Neill, lord of Tyrone, employed hundreds of Scottish mercenaries to defend his territory from English aggression. Sidney bided his time, formally recognising O'Neill's position in Tyrone, while secretly promoting the establishment of colonies in eastern Ulster, and plantations elsewhere. These ventures were directed against the old Anglo-Irish community. Unsurprisingly, they generated great anxiety and fierce opposition. In 1569–71 serious disturbances were provoked by the newly established Councils in Munster and Connacht which rigorously imposed English laws and customs, and Protestantism. Martial law was declared over wide areas and suspected rebels were ruthlessly slaughtered. By April 1571 a kind of calm was imposed, but Sidney was recalled from Ireland.

Between 1568 and 1571 Sidney's administration had cost £147 000, yet his programme was in disarray. His Provincial Councils and plantations had sparked off widespread rebellions. Elizabeth came to the conclusion that programmes of conquest were simply too ambitious. The next Deputy, Sir William Fitzwilliam, set himself the modest goals of improving the quality of royal justice in Leinster, while delegating responsibility for the other provinces to the local nobility. Nonetheless, Sidney's plantation schemes dogged the new deputy.

Further plantations by English adventurers were attempted, such as the scheme of Walter Devereux, Earl of Essex, to colonise Antrim in August 1573. It soon faltered as Essex's followers deserted him when they discovered that Antrim was not quite the paradise they had been promised. Essex's entire fortune was tied up in the venture and he grew increasingly desperate as his money was spent. He carried out some appalling atrocities – most notoriously the indiscriminate murder of the entire population of Rathlin. Fitzwilliam disapproved of the enterprise and did little to salvage it. By 1575 the whole sordid affair was brought to an end.

While not his fault, Fitzwilliam's standing suffered through the failure of the plantations, and Sidney was restored to office. Sidney was anxious to redeem his reputation by succeeding in Ireland. He arrived in September 1575, determined to avoid his previous mistakes. He recognised Turlough Luineach O'Neill as Lord of Tyrone. He travelled through Connacht and Munster to reassure the gentry that they had nothing to fear from his administration: there would be no more plantations. He persuaded them to agree to disband their private armies and to agree a modest new tax to finance the Provincial Councils. Encouraged by success in Munster and Connacht, Sidney sought to impose the new tax on Leinster also. Landowners there refused to endorse an extra-parliamentary tax peculiar to Ireland. They petitioned the Queen asking for a change of governor, insisting that Sidney was likely to provoke another general revolt. Sidney was ignominiously dismissed from office in late 1578. Sidney's programme for conquering Ireland was finally abandoned.

By 1579, however, the English administration in Ireland included several 'New English' men, zealous Protestants who regarded Catholicism as an abomination. These same men typically possessed an understanding of cultural evolution which predisposed them to regard the Irish people as barbarians who could be dispossessed or killed without any qualms of conscience. Many English colonisers regarded the Irish, like native Americans, as an inferior people who might be 'civilised' only through the use of terror. Edmund Spenser, the famous English poet and planter in Ireland, went so far as to advocate genocide against the Irish. With such men in power in Ireland both resistance and bloodshed were inevitable.

On 17 July 1579 James Fitzmaurice Fitzgerald arrived in Ireland with Dr Nicholas Sanders, a leading English Catholic, together with 60 soldiers from a larger force financed by Pope Gregory XIII. They called on the lords and people of Ireland to rally to the papal banner against the heretical Queen of England. In response, thousands of soldiers were sent from England to reinforce the colonial regime. On 3 October 1579 Sir Nicholas Malby, recently appointed military governor of Munster, defeated the Catholic confederate army at Monasternenagh, County Tipperary. The confederates were forced into south-western Munster while the more vulnerable estates of the Earl of Desmond were systematically burned and all of their inhabitants, men, women and children were slaughtered. Munster was systematically destroyed by the English army to create a famine in which the confederate soldiers would starve to death along with the civilian population.

Arthur, Lord Grey, was appointed Deputy of Ireland on 15 July 1580. Almost immediately there was a further revolt, this one led by Viscount Baltinglass, a lord on the borders of the Pale. When it was revealed that William Nugent, brother of Baron Delvin, was involved in the Baltinglass insurrection Grey had the baron himself and the Earl of Kildare and many other Pale gentry arrested, and ordered 20 of them killed before the English Privy Council intervened. In fact, the gentry of the Pale had been very hostile to Baltinglass' rebellion and its consequent disorder, however much they sympathised with his motives. Grey's executions profoundly alienated the Palesmen from the Dublin administration. The 'New English' administrators, for their part, were convinced that the old Anglo-Irish community were in fact treacherous papists who posed a greater threat to Protestant English power in Ireland than did the Irish.

By November 1582 the Catholic uprising was crushed. After a period of ominous calm Sir John Perrot was appointed Deputy in January 1584 with a new programme to impose English control throughout Ireland. Perrot summoned the Irish Parliament to meet on 26 April 1585 and he laid before it a number of bills prepared in England to endorse

TIMELINE

1565	Sir Henry Sidney appointed Deputy of Ireland
1571	Sidney recalled to England after his attempts to reform the judicial system and impose plantations with new settlers had led to fierce resistance
1575	Sidney restored to office
1578	Sidney finally dismissed following threat of rebellion against his plans for taxation
1579	Attempted Catholic rising crushed; Munster laid waste
1582	Further Catholic rebellion crushed
1584	Sir John Perrot arrives as Deputy. Seizes rebels' and others' land for plantations of new settlers
1590	Three provinces in the south of Ireland occupied by English troops

the plantation of the estates of Catholic confederates in Munster, to ratify new taxation for the whole of Ireland, and to enact harsher legislation against Catholics. Acts of Attainder declared the confederates traitors and confiscated their lands. However, the opposition to the taxation and anti-Catholic bills was overwhelming. The old Anglo-Irish community in Ireland rallied openly behind the twin causes of Catholicism and constitutional separatism. They declared themselves loyal to the English Crown, yet argued that Ireland was constitutionally autonomous from England. They were also zealously Catholic.

Through the Acts of Attainder a total of 574 645 acres in Munster were declared forfeit to the Crown. Detailed plans were drawn up in England to settle 8400 English people on the confiscated estates, but too little care was taken to ascertain exactly what land was confiscated, and what was not. Many innocent landowners were dispossessed along with confederates. By 1590 the plantation of Munster was functioning with about 2000 settlers. The native population was forced to accept a servile status on their former lands. Few of the innocent victims of the plantation were compensated.

By the beginning of 1590 three southern provinces had been effectively occupied by English troops. The colonial administration was determined to subdue Ulster as soon as possible. Hugh Rua MacMahon, lord of Monaghan, was invited to talk with government officials in Dublin but was executed there instead, and his lordship was broken up. Similar action was taken against other lords. Bingham took possession of Sligo Castle, which guarded the western gateway into Ulster. With other English garrisons at Carrickfergus, Newry and Blackwater Fort, a ring of steel was steadily tightening around Ulster.

> **KEY ISSUE**
>
> *Why did English policy fail in Ireland during the first decades of Elizabeth's reign?*

B *The Nine Years War*

Hugh O'Neill, Earl of Tyrone, watched the English penetration of Ulster with some anxiety. He had been educated in the Pale, and Elizabeth expected him to strengthen English power in Ulster. Tyrone offered to govern Ulster on behalf of the Queen, free of supervision from Dublin, but the colonial governors strongly opposed his proposal.

With that rejection, Tyrone was faced with a dilemma: how could he hope to resist an English army if his autonomy was threatened? Enniskillen was occupied by English troops in 1593 but Tyrone covertly supported Hugh Maguire, lord of Fermanagh, in besieging the garrison. When an English battalion tried to break the siege in June 1594 it was repulsed by Tyrone's brother. Tyrone tried to negotiate with the colonial administration in Dublin for responsibility for Ulster. Still they spurned his proposal. Finally, in May 1595 the Earl went to war with England.

By 1595 Tyrone was well prepared for war. He had employed English and Spanish captains to train the men of his lordship in modern warfare. He employed gunsmiths at Dungannon to produce armaments. He imported large quantities of guns and ammunition to equip his soldiers. Tyrone's chief ally, the lord of Tyrconnell, fielded a much less modern army, but employed large numbers of Scottish mercenaries. The Ulster confederates formed an army of 1000 cavalry, 4000 musketeers and 1000 pikemen – the most formidable and professional army ever fielded by Irish lords. However, they knew that they could not expel the English without military assistance from Spain. In response to their requests Philip II of Spain sent a great armada of 100 ships to

PICTURE 28
English troops campaigning in Ireland

HUGH O'NEILL, 2ND EARL OF TYRONE (1550–1616)

Tyrone presented Queen Elizabeth with the greatest challenge of her reign. His grandfather, Conn O'Neill, became the first Earl of Tyrone in 1542 under the terms of 'surrender and regrant'. Conn nominated his illegitimate son, Mathew, as his heir and successor. However, Mathew, and his eldest son, Brian, were killed by a rival O'Neill, leaving a younger son, Hugh, as the heir apparent to the earldom. For his own safety, the 11-year-old Hugh O'Neill was entrusted to the care of an English planter family in the Irish midlands. There he was groomed to be an English gentleman. O'Neill was promoted as baron of Dungannon in 1567. As an English protégé he established himself in south-east Ulster and built up a close network of relationships between northern Irish lords and northern Pale gentry. O'Neill presented himself as Elizabeth's loyal subject in Ulster, and in 1585 he became the 2nd Earl of Tyrone.

O'Neill's dominant position in Ulster came under challenge from the Queen's administration in Dublin who were concerned lest he become an 'over-mighty' subject. Dublin's increasing interference in Ulster seems to have prompted O'Neill to rebel to defend his own autonomy. His rebellion became a determined fight for Irish independence against Protestant English rule. O'Neill prepared well for the 'Nine Years War' and looked poised to overthrow English power in Ireland. He won some spectacular victories over the English, most notably at the Battle of the Yellow Ford. He always realised, however, that significant Spanish support would be needed against England's overwhelming military might. Storms kept the Spaniards at bay until a small Spanish force landed on the south coast of Ireland late in 1601. O'Neill's attempt to link up with the Spaniards so far from Ulster ended in catastrophic defeat at the Battle of Kinsale (1601). O'Neill surrendered to Lord Deputy Mountjoy in March 1603, within a week of Elizabeth's death. His submission was to mark the completion of the Tudor conquest of Ireland.

Ireland in October 1596, but the fleet was overwhelmed by a tremendous storm. Thirty-two ships were sunk, and the remainder struggled back to Spain. Late in October 1597 a second armada was sent to Ireland, but it too was forced back to Spain by dreadful storms.

The war in Ireland escalated gradually as the English Crown sent more and more troops there to crush the confederates. The Ulster lords stoutly defended their province and won a series of stunning victories against the English, most notably at the Battle of Clontibret in February 1595 and at the Battle of the Yellow Ford in August 1598. The victory at the Yellow Ford was spectacular: an English army of 4200 men was

TIMELINE

1593	Tyrone launched his rebellion
1595	Battle of Clontibret – rebel victory
1595	Battle of the Yellow Ford – rebel victory
1596	A new Spanish Armada was sent to assist Tyrone but was scattered by storms
1597	Yet another Armada scattered by storms
1599	Essex's campaign in Ireland failed
1600	Lord Mountjoy arrives as Deputy
1601	A Spanish force landed in Ireland; while trying to link up with it, Tyrone routed at Battle of Kinsale.
1603	Irish resistance crumbled and Tyrone surrendered

See page 325

smashed. The English garrisons elsewhere lost heart while the Irish everywhere were inspired. Tyrconnell gained mastery over Connacht. The midlands plantation and the plantation in Munster were overthrown. English power in Ireland seemed to be on the verge of collapse.

In March 1599 Robert Devereux, Earl of Essex, was made Lord Lieutenant of Ireland with a force of 17300 men, the largest English army in Elizabeth's reign. Essex proved to be no match for the Irish lords and, on his first encounter with Tyrone, he agreed to a truce. Essex rushed back to Court to justify his actions to the Queen. But the truce was his undoing. Humiliated, he staged a foolish coup and was beheaded.

In February 1600 Charles Blount, Lord Mountjoy, became Deputy of Ireland. He was a very able, if ruthless general, and deployed his superior forces skillfully. He set up a string of garrisons around Ulster, and established a fort behind Tyrone's lines at Derry. He made Sir George Carew president of Munster, and gave him a force of 3000 men. Without strong local leadership against Carew's army the Irish confederates soon lost control of Munster. When Mountjoy attempted to invade Ulster though, he was repulsed at the Moyry Pass.

On 21 September 1601, 3400 Spanish soldiers landed at Kinsale, County Cork. The Spanish force was smaller than expected, but it did represent a tangible contribution to the Catholic cause by Spain. Therefore, though it was mid-winter, the Ulster lords marched their forces almost 500 km southwards. Between the Irish armies and the Spanish force in Kinsale was the English Deputy, Mountjoy, with 7000 troops. On 21 December 1601, Tyrone was in the process of deploying his forces into their battle positions when the English struck. The Irish were caught off-guard and were routed. The Spanish force played no significant part in the fighting. They surrendered on 2 January 1602.

The battle of Kinsale was decisive. Tyrconnell went to Spain to secure more assistance, but it never came. Within Ireland the confederate cause crumbled. The English army penetrated Ulster's defences and systematically destroyed the province. There were mass killings of civilians by the sword and man-made famine. Tyrone held out until 30 March 1603 when he was offered his life, and very generous terms. Though he did not know it at the time Elizabeth had died six days earlier.

KEY ISSUE

Why did the English find it so difficult and so costly to subdue the Irish in the closing years of Elizabeth's reign?

6 ∾ EPILOGUE

On 24 March 1603 James VI of Scotland became King of England and Ireland. In England he inherited a kingdom which was internally peaceful and united. The King's writ was almost as effective in the north of England as it was in Surrey. The Welsh élites had been successfully assimilated into the English system. Throughout the mainland Protestantism was well established. In Ireland, however, the situation was very different. Large parts of the kingdom had been devastated. The population had been decimated by famine caused deliberately in order to subjugate the Catholic confederate forces. The economy had been severely disrupted, the Irish coinage was so debased as to be worthless, and the towns were in decay. The Catholic faith was banned, yet the Protestant Church of Ireland enjoyed virtually no support in the country. The people of Ireland, needless to say, were not impressed by the legacy of the Tudors.

Steven Ellis has remarked that by setting himself realistic goals Henry VII enjoyed greater success in his policies towards Ireland than did any other Tudor monarch. Admittedly, the Crown's authority beyond the Pale and the towns was tenuous. However, under the great Earl of Kildare the colony in Ireland financed itself, and showed definite signs of progress. After the Kildare period the government of the colony fell to too many men who had unrealistic expectations about what could be achieved. More than anything else, it was the determination of the English Deputies to force the pace of change in Ireland which resulted in such turmoil and bloodshed.

The introduction of the Tudor Reformation into an already difficult political environment was certain to be resisted, particularly by the Irish whose loyalties to the Tudor Crown (assuming they had any) were far less strong than their commitment to Catholicism. In the climactic Nine Years War Ireland was finally conquered, but only at a cost of £2 million and countless thousands of lives. Yet, the long-established Anglo-Irish community, as well as the Irish, were left profoundly alienated from the English administration in Dublin. The Anglo-Irish élites developed a new understanding of themselves as being 'Old English'; Catholic, yet loyal to the Crown and the rightful representatives of English interests in Ireland. The enforcement of the 'penal laws' against the Catholic religion in the seventeenth century, together with a range of policies to dispossess the Catholics of Ireland of their properties and political rights, eventually forced the Old English to make common cause with the Irish against the predatory Protestant establishment. The Irish were not to be politically assimilated to the English regime as the Welsh had been. English Protestantism and ideologies of colonisation predisposed Ireland's new rulers to regard the Catholic Irish as being inferior to themselves. The sectarian and racialist elements in British thinking about Ireland would hinder Anglo-Irish relations for centuries to come.

> ## KEY ISSUE
>
> *What were the long-term consequences of the English conquest of Ireland?*

7 ⤳ BIBLIOGRAPHY

**SG Ellis *Ireland in the Age of the Tudors, 1447–1603* (Longman, 1998) is the best survey available for Tudor Ireland. It is comprehensive and well judged. A summary of his views is **SG Ellis 'The Limits of Power: The English Crown and the British Isles', Chapter 2 in P Collinson (ed.) *The Sixteenth Century* (OUP, 2002). **C Brady *The Chief Governors: The Rise and Fall of Reform Government in Tudor Ireland, 1536–1588* (CUP, 1994) offers a meticulous survey of Tudor government in Ireland across most of the sixteenth century. Progress on the Tudor reformations in Ireland is slow but see **HA Jefferies, 'The early Tudor reformations in the Irish Pale' in *Journal of Ecclesiastical History*, 52 (2001) for a survey which relates Ireland's reformation experiences to that of England. For more detail see a case study in *HA Jefferies *Priests and Prelates of Armagh in the Age of Reformations* (Four Courts, 1997). For Wales in the Tudor period see **T Herbert and G Elwys Jones *Tudor Wales* (Open University, 1988), and for a longer sweep by a great authority on Welsh history see **G Williams *Recovery, Reorientation and Reformation: Wales c.1415–1642* (Clarendon, 1987). **FW Brooks 'The Council in the North' in J Hurstfield (ed.) *The Tudors* (Historical Association, 1953), is still an excellent account of the provincial council established in the North of England. Tudor Calais receives little attention from English historians but see *CSL Davies 'England and the French War, 1557–59' in J Loach and R Tittler (eds) *The Mid Tudor Polity, 1540–1560* (Macmillan, 1980).

(*Recommended. **Highly recommended.)

8 ⤳ STRUCTURED AND ESSAY QUESTIONS

A *Structured questions*

1. (a) What problems confronted the early Tudors in the frontier regions?
    (b) 'The poor quality of government in the frontier regions was chiefly the result of royal neglect'. Discuss.
2. (a) What role did religion play in distinguishing Ireland's experience of English rule from that of Wales or the North of England?
    (b) 'The Irish constitutional revolution shows that the subsequent resort to wars of conquest was unnecessary'. Discuss.

B *Essay questions*

1. How successful were the early Tudors in strengthening their authority in the outlying regions?

2. To what extent were Cromwell's efforts to secure royal authority in the frontier regions brought about by the Henrician Reformation?
3. Did Elizabeth's policies in Ireland make rebellions and wars inevitable?
4. How grave a threat to Elizabeth's rule was posed by Hugh O'Neill, Earl of Tyrone?
5. 'Success in Wales and the North; abject failure in Ireland.' Is this a fair summary of Tudor government of the frontier regions?

9 ↩ DOCUMENTARY EXERCISE: TUDOR GOVERNMENT OF IRELAND

Forasmuch as the king, our most gracious dread sovereign lord, and his grace's most noble progenitors, kings of England, have been lords of this land of Ireland, having all manner kingly jurisdiction, power, pre-eminence, and authority royal, belonging or appertaining to the royal estate and majesty of a king, by the names of lords of Ireland ... and for lack of naming the king's majesty and his noble progenitors kings of Ireland ... hath been great occasion that the Irish men and inhabitants within this realm of Ireland have not been so obedient to the king's highness and his most noble progenitors, and to their laws, as they of right, and according to their allegiance and bounden duties ought to have been. Wherefore, at the humble pursuit, petition, and request of the lords spiritual and temporal, and other the king's loving and obedient subjects of this his land of Ireland, and by their full assents, be it enacted, ordained, and established by authority of this present parliament, that the king's highness, his heirs and successors, kings of England, be always kings of this land of Ireland.

SOURCE A
An Act that the King and his successors be kings of Ireland (1541)

I recognise his royal majesty to be my most serene lord and king, and I swear to be a faithful, loyal and obedient subject to him and his heirs and successors, kings of England, France and Ireland.

I openly renounce obedience to the pope of Rome, and forsake his usurped authority, and I recognise my most serene lord as supreme head under Christ of the Church of England and Ireland ...

I, the aforesaid, Conn O'Neill, confess myself to have offended his majesty and so implore his grace and mercy, and beg him to grant me his pardon for my offences.

I humbly implore that on this account it may please his excellence to accept, regard and reckon me as one of his most faithful subjects, and that order be given to all his subjects of this kingdom to accept, regard and reckon me as such and in the same fashion.

I offer and pledge myself to live under the laws of my most serene lord ...

SOURCE B
Conn O'Neill's Terms of 'Surrender' to Henry VIII (1541) whereby O'Neill became the 1st Earl of Tyrone.

The lord deputy and council of the realm [of Ireland], having such care as becometh them, for the universal good government of this her majesty's realm, and finding that the remote parts thereof have, of long time, by lack of justice and administration of laws, continued in great disorders, and ... no means can be found more meet, to reduce the same to order, for the honour and service of almighty God, for obedience to the queen's majesty, for the recovery and conservation of common peace and tranquillity, and finally, for to breed and establish all good civility, than to have justice indifferently applied and administered to all states and sorts of people, have, for that purpose, certified the same to the queen's most excellent majesty: who having no less princely and natural regard to her said universal realm, and to the people thereof, than ever to her realm of England, ... hath ... given commandment to her said lord deputy and council of her realm, according to their advice, to erect and establish by her commission, special councils in sundry remote parts of her realm.

[Munster] was a most rich and plentiful country, full of corn and cattle ... yet before one year and a half they [the population of Munster] were brought to such wretchedness as that any stony heart would have rued the same. Out of every corner of the woods and glens they came creeping forth upon their hands, for their legs could not carry them; and they looked [like] anatomies of death; they spoke like ghosts crying out of their graves; they ate dead animals, [and were] happy where they could find them; yea, and one another soon after, insomuch as the very bodies they spared not to scrape out of their graves; and if they found a plot of watercresses or shamrocks, there they flocked as to a feast for the time, yet not able long to continue withal; that in [a] short space there were none almost left, and a most populous and plentiful country [was] suddenly left empty of man and beast; yet, sure, in all that war there perished not many by the sword, but all by the extremity of famine ...

1. That the catholic, apostolic and Roman religion be openly preached and taught throughout all Ireland, as well in cities as borough towns, by bishops, seminary priests, Jesuits and all other religious men.
2. That the Church of Ireland be wholly governed by the Pope.
3. That all cathedrals and parish churches, abbeys and all other religious houses, with all tithes and church lands, now in the hands of the English, be restored to the Catholic churchmen.
4. That all Irish priests and religious men, now prisoners in England or Ireland, be set at liberty, with all lay Irishmen that are troubled

for their conscience, and to go where they will, without further trouble ...

8. That the governor of Ireland be at least an earl, and of the privy council of England, bearing the name of viceroy.

9. That the lord chancellor, lord treasurer, lord admiral, the council of state, the justice of the laws, Queen's attorney, Queen's serjeant and all other officers appertaining to the council and law of Ireland, be Irishmen ...

14. That no children, nor any friends, be taken as hostages for the good behaviour of their parents and, if there be any such hostages now in the hands of the English they must be released.

15. That all statutes made against the promotion of Irishmen, as well in their own country as abroad, be repealed ...

18. That all Irishmen, of what quality they be, may freely travel in foreign countries for their better experience, without making any of the Queen's officers acquainted withal ...

SOURCE E

The demands of Hugh O'Neill, 2nd Earl of Tyrone (1599). Tyrone's articles of 1599 represented the conditions under which he, and the other Irish confederates, would accept Elizabeth's claim to sovereignty in Ireland.

Q

1. *Read Sources A, B and C. What claims are made for English royal authority in Ireland in these sources?*

2. *How might 'surrender and regrant', as reflected in Source B, have reconciled the independent Irish lords to the Tudors' claims to authority over Ireland?*

3. *Compare Sources C and D. How did the experience of Tudor government in Munster differ from the instructions set out in the order establishing the Provincial Council for Munster?*

4. *What does Tyrone's demands for changes to English rule in Ireland in Source E tell us about how Irish people's experience of Tudor government may have alienated them from England's monarchy?*

5. *How far do these documents support the view that a war of conquest by the English in Ireland was inevitable?*

12 Tudor Rebellions 1485–1603

INTRODUCTION

It is perhaps unsurprising that such a turbulent epoch as the Tudor period should see repeated rebellions. The Tudors themselves came to power through the 1485 campaign, nothing less than a military rebellion against the crowned monarch, Richard III, and the Cornish Rebellion of 1497 represented the last gasp of Yorkist attempts to supplant the new dynasty. Other risings may also be considered successes: Henry VIII dropped the plan for the 'Amicable Grant' in 1525, and Somerset's fall in 1549 was a direct (although, no doubt, an unintentional) result of the two commotions in that year. The most obvious example of a successful revolt must be Mary Tudor's thwarting in 1553 of the Duke of Northumberland's plan to deny her the throne in favour of his son and daughter-in-law. Dramatic religious changes were involved in the Pilgrimage of Grace in 1536, and in the Western Rising (or 'Prayer Book Rebellion') in the South-west during 1549, while important social issues appear among the grievances in 1525 and 1549. Occasionally rebellions threatened to display that potent union of aristocratic discontent and popular commotion that was to find its fullest expression in the English Civil War – the Pilgrimage of Grace in 1536 and the Revolt of the Northern Earls in 1569 would be good examples of this. In contrast Essex's rising at the end of the Tudor century seems much more like an ego trip by one disgruntled courtier: this last rebellion went out less with a bang than a whimper, and is testimony to the durability of the regime.

At first sight potential rebels would seem to have many advantages over a usurping and insecure dynasty, which still lacked a standing army and had to rely on nobles and gentry to maintain its writ over distant corners of the land. Yet, as we shall see, rebellion was abhorred in the prevailing intellectual climate, and baleful penalties could be applied to those who tried and failed. Moreover the folk memory of the fifteenth century wars served a further warning. In any event, few of the 'stirs' during the Tudor period involved the intention to achieve what would now be called 'regime change'. Often they were merely an opportunity to air grievances, and to negotiate with government from a position of strength.

The historian is struck by the relatively few rebellions in the latter part of the period. Perhaps Henry VIII and his successors had learned some of the lessons of the earlier decades of the sixteenth century: indeed Henry embarked on an elaborate progress through the north in 1541, no doubt in an effort to heal the wounds of the Pilgrimage of

Grace. Two further points can usefully be made: first, the relative lack of violence compared to previous periods (in the fifteenth century five English peers were murdered by mobs, only one perished in the sixteenth – by combat), and second, the almost complete absence of overt class conflict. The Tudor period may not always have seemed like 'Merrie England', but society was far more homogeneous than some writers would allow. There was the ever present threat of riot, sometimes revolt, but never revolution.

1 ⌐ THE YORKSHIRE REBELLION 1489

Henry VII was bedevilled in the early years of his reign by threats to his throne. The exploits of Lambert Simnel are well known. In 1487 Simnel was presented by dissident Yorkists as 'Edward VI', the son of the Duke of Clarence and Isabel of Warwick, and hence the nephew of Edward IV. Crowned King of Ireland, he crossed the Irish Sea and was defeated in June at the Battle of Stoke, which can be seen as the last battle of the Wars of the Roses. Indeed it was the last occasion when a reigning king had to take the field in person against a rival claimant to the throne.

See page 35

The Yorkshire Rebellion, by contrast, can be seen as a classic example of a 'loyal' rebellion. Parliament granted Henry a subsidy of £100 000 to enable him to intervene on Brittany's behalf against the French Crown, and it fell to the fourth Earl of Northumberland to collect it. The population of the northern shires had suffered a poor harvest in 1488, and it was, in any case, unaccustomed to heavy taxation.

On 28 April 1489 Northumberland tried to explain to a mob at Topcliffe, near Thirsk, the need for the tax. Abandoned by his retinue, he was assassinated and the rebels went on to take York. Localised rioting continued, and Henry made plans to come North, but the rising was crushed by the Earl of Surrey before the King could arrive.

Surrey hanged several ringleaders, but Henry never received the bulk of his subsidy, and this method of raising money was never tried again. The incident had shown the fragility of public order, but it had never posed a serious danger to the monarchy or to Henry VII in person. The rebels wished to express a localised grievance in a way respectful to the King, if not to all his tax collectors. Henry, however, rated his financial needs and authority above popular consent.

> **KEY ISSUE**
>
> *In what sense was the Yorkshire Rebellion a 'loyal' rebellion?*

2 ⌐ THE CORNISH REBELLION 1497

The second popular disorder of Henry VII's reign was a much more serious affair than the Yorkshire Rising and overlapped with the second dynastic threat to his throne, when the Flemish Perkin Warbeck tried to impersonate Edward IV's younger son, Richard, Duke of York and to seize the throne with help from Ireland, France, Flanders and Scotland.

The Cornish Rising stemmed from Henry's need for money to deal with the Warbeck threat, and in 1497 he was granted an unprecedented parliamentary grant of £88606. While Cornwall's MPs had voted for this exaction in Parliament, the Cornish people felt that a war in Scotland was too remote a cause for them and they began a march to present their grievances to the government. Under the leadership of Flamank, a Bodmin lawyer, and Joseph, a blacksmith from St Keverne in the Lizard, they marched via Exeter, Wells, Salisbury, Winchester and Guildford to Blackheath, a traditional gathering place for aggrieved peasants. On the way they managed to pick up a peer, Lord Audley, long disappointed that the King had not rewarded him better. The Cornishmen were careful to stress that their complaint was not against the King, but against his 'evil counsellors' Morton and Bray. This was not mere rhetoric, but a genuinely felt grievance against unpopular ministers. Henry's reaction was swift and decisive. On 16 June 25000 royal troops put the Cornishmen to flight, killing up to 1000 of them. Audley, Flamank and Joseph were all executed and their dismembered heads were set up on London Bridge.

The revolt was not, however, in vain, for Henry came to terms with James IV at the Ayton truce and sought to run down his expensive commitments on the continent. The people of Cornwall had shown that they were not yet wholly absorbed into the nation.

> **KEY ISSUE**
>
> *Did the 1497 Cornish Rebellion achieve anything?*

3 ✎ RESISTANCE TO TAXATION 1523–5

The third rebellion reverts to the tradition of simple resistance to taxation, of which the Yorkshire Rising had been an example. In 1523 Wolsey tried to raise a substantial sum: this time he asked for £800000. Despite the opposition of the House of Commons, who offered half that sum, he had collected £136578 of the subsidy component of £151215 by the spring of 1525. This represents the largest grant in taxation in the whole period from 1485 to 1543.

See page 67

At this point Wolsey decided to push his luck by sending out commissioners to collect the so-called 'Amicable Grant' of 1525, which was really a non-parliamentary tax based on 1522 valuations. Commissions were sent out in late March to nobles and clerics in each county to levy the grant, but in Professor Scarisbrick's words they 'came upon lambs already close shorn'. Archbishop Warham of Canterbury reported the refusal of the Kentish clergy to pay, and the commissioners encountered similar difficulties in Norwich, Ely, Reading, Essex, Huntingdonshire, London, Warwickshire and elsewhere. The opposition seems due partly to the unpopularity of Wolsey's foreign policy, and partly to a genuine inability to pay.

The most serious opposition to the Grant came, however, from the Lavenham and Sudbury areas of Suffolk, from where the Dukes of Norfolk and Suffolk wrote to Henry urging concessions. Wolsey urged strong measures to enforce payment, but he was overruled by Henry who ordered the abandonment of the Grant, claiming that he had been unaware of it. Furthermore, in a carefully stage-managed display of clemency, Henry pardoned the ringleaders of the Suffolk rebels after their appearance in Star Chamber.

For once a rebellion had been successful and Wolsey's enemies rejoiced to see his discomfiture at having to save Henry's face by accepting responsibility himself. Henry knew that his kingship rested ultimately on a partnership with the tax-paying classes, and that this vocal extra-parliamentary opinion would make an impact on his foreign policy. Three main factors seem to account for this result: London, usually loyal, was adamant and courageous in its resistance; opposition to the levy was spread widely over several counties, and rumours of opposition in one county encouraged refusal elsewhere; and those Councillors charged with the collection of the Grant, like Warham, Norfolk and Suffolk, were quick to report the opposition to it.

KEY ISSUE

Why was the 'Amicable Grant' withdrawn?

Types of Rebellion and Contemporary Attitudes to Them

ANALYSIS

Contemporaries identified two principal kinds of rebellion during this period. The first was an overt attempt to seize the Crown by supplanting the incumbent, or by seeking to replace 'evil counsellors' around the monarch. The attempts to press the claims of Lambert Simnel and Perkin Warbeck would come into this category, as would Northumberland's replacement of Somerset in 1549, Wyatt in 1554, the Northern Earls in 1569 and Essex in 1601. The second was a local protest, often involving a demonstration in force, but not involving any attempt to move on the centre of power, London. This category would therefore embrace the Cornish Rebellion of 1497, the protests against the 'Amicable Grant' in 1525, the Lincolnshire Rebellion and the Pilgrimage of Grace in 1536–7, and the two risings in 1549, the Western and the Kett Rebellions.

Neither was acceptable to contemporary intellectual opinion. The political theorists of the age – Cromwell, Morrison, Starkey, Barnes, Cheke and Nichols – all urged non-resistance as the only reasonable reaction in connection with perceived grievances. For anyone to challenge anointed monarchs with all their powers of patronage was both treasonable and unwise. Sir John Fortescue described the political order as a 'Great Chain of Being'; to disturb one part of it was to threaten the entire edifice. Moreover Protestant theologians concurred: Latimer recommended suffering in the face of injustice as the Christian's only justified response, despite the assertion by some Calvinists that resistance could be reasonable under certain circumstances. Paget underlined the view of the intellectual and religious establishment in his letter to Somerset at the height of the 1549 disturbances: 'society in a realm doth consist and is maintained by means of religion and law'.

Further practical points could be added to reinforce the argument. Danger from abroad might well coincide with domestic upheaval. A contemporary remarked in 1536, 'If Lincolnshire seek to destroy England, what wonder is it if France and Scotland sometime have fought to offend me?'.

Contemporary commentators frequently referred to the dread consequences of past rebellions: Morrison in his 'Lamentations' scoured the fourteenth and fifteenth centuries for examples, while Cranmer in a sermon of 1549 cited the Old Testament and the 1525 Peasants' Revolt in Germany when 100 000 are said to have died. Judicial punishments were also harsh. Capital punishment was commonplace: out of 883 accused under the wide-ranging treason laws between 1532 and 1540 no less than 38% were executed. Prison, torture, mutilation or the galleys beckoned those who escaped block or gibbet. The frenzied reaction of the political community to the non-existent Oxfordshire Rising of 1596 underscores the seriousness with which the merest hint of revolt was treated.

KEY ISSUE

On what grounds was the act of rebellion condemned by contemporaries?

See page 89

4 ⌁ THE LINCOLNSHIRE RISING 1536

The fourth major Tudor rebellion introduces, for the first time, an element of opposition to the religious changes being introduced in the course of the Henrician Reformation. In September 1536, three sets of government commissioners were at work in Lincolnshire: Vicegerent Cromwell's commissioners to dissolve the smaller monasteries following the 1536 act; royal commissioners assessing and collecting the 1534 subsidy; and Bishop Longland of Lincoln's agents enforcing the Ten Articles Act. It was widely believed that Longland was responsible for Henry VIII's divorce from Catherine of Aragon. Although the Bishop was doctrinally conservative, he was also a strict disciplinarian and determined to enforce current legislation.

In this atmosphere rumours abounded: church jewels and plate would be impounded; gold was to return to the mint for testing; taxes would be imposed on horned cattle, baptisms, marriages and burials; no church would be allowed within five miles of another; the eating of white bread, goose or capon was to require a tribute payable to the King. The fears of the beneficed clergy of the diocese were further aroused by fears of the confiscation of glebe (the farm land of a village priest) and tithes and their replacement by fixed stipends.

As the rumours spread, the clergy gathered at Louth, Caistor and Horncastle. A rousing sermon preached at Louth on 1 October inflamed the several hundred beneficed clergy gathered there, and on the following day, the Bishop's registrar, arriving to carry out a visitation of the clergy, was seized by townsfolk guarding the church treasure house. Meanwhile, a leader emerged in Nicholas Melton, a shoemaker ('Captain Cobbler'), whose supporters seem to have been paid from church funds; but a more striking development from 4 October was the emerging leadership of at least 18 local gentry in the rising. Their role was to give the movement an air of legitimacy, turning a plebeian riot into a demonstration against royal policies, and after the murder of Dr Raynes, Longland's hated chancellor, and the distribution of his money and clothes among the crowd, the gentry were able to present their articles of grievance.

Their manifesto included the following demands: the King should abandon the subsidy; the abbeys were to be untouched and the Dissolution commissioners Leigh and Layton to be punished for their inquisitorial methods; the Church's 'ancient liberties' to be restored; and 'heretical' bishops like Cranmer and Latimer were to be removed. There were also two secular demands which seem to reflect gentry aspirations: that the **Statute of Uses** be repealed and that 'base-born' Councillors, like Cromwell and Rich, be punished. The sheriff had to explain to the commons what the Statute of Uses was. It also seems unlikely that Lincolnshire peasants were familiar with Cromwell or Rich. It is perhaps significant that the rebels apparently accepted the Royal Supremacy; denial of this would after all have been treason.

Armed with this list of grievances 10 000 rebels marched to Lincoln joined by monks from three monasteries which feared dissolution: Barlings, Bardney and Kirkstead. Lord Hussey, the principal noble in the county, defected to them as the host approached the county town, damaging three of Longland's properties on the way and sending a revised set of their articles to London. The royal reply reached Lincoln on 10 October, threatening punishment if the rebels failed to disperse. Indeed, Henry had little good to say for the county and its inhabitants, describing them as: 'the rude commons of one shire, and that one of the most brute and beastly of the whole realm'.

Meanwhile a royal army under the Duke of Suffolk arrived at Stamford, 40 miles away, and the moment of decision for the 18 gentry rebels had arrived. They decided that further resistance would be treason and sued for pardon. Clearly when it came to the point, no gentleman would appear in arms against his lawful sovereign. On 11 October Lancaster Herald (the bearer of royal instructions) arrived and persuaded the remaining rebels to go home. By 18 October the rising could be said to have been over.

What then was the movement all about? It seems clear that there was a substantial element of religious conservatism articulated by priests and monks and accepted by the commons. Most historians are also convinced that the lead given by the gentry was significant. Substantial gentlemen like Willoughby and Dymoke had had earlier favours from the Tudors, but now they feared the Duke of Suffolk's attempt to create a powerful Brandon interest in the shire, with royal backing. Charles Brandon, Duke of Suffolk, was after all Henry's brother-in-law and boon companion, who, following the death of his royal wife, married

Statute of Uses law passed to prevent the evasion of death duties through the legal loophole of handing the ownership of property over to trustees

See page 352

Katherine Willoughby in 1534 and then resisted all claims to the Willoughby inheritance from male members of the family. Hence the Willoughby participation in the rising seems readily explicable.

After the collapse of the rising the expected retribution followed: over 100 death sentences were handed down for treason of which 57 were carried out. Significantly perhaps the clergy were dealt with especially harshly. Once purged, on 14 November 1536 Lincolnshire received a royal pardon. By the end of the reign, however, it could be argued that the rebellion had eventually achieved some success: in 1540 the Statute of Uses was abandoned, to be replaced by the Statute of Wills; and two Lincolnshire gentry families enjoyed some favour, William Willoughby became a peer and Edward Dymoke was appointed treasurer of Boulogne.

KEY ISSUE

How far was the Lincolnshire uprising of 1536 a 'popular' rebellion?

See page 89

5 ↰ THE PILGRIMAGE OF GRACE 1536

While the Lincolnshire events were serious, the rising in counties further to the north between October and December 1536, over apparently similar issues, was the greatest expression of opposition that Henry VIII ever faced in England, and indeed the most dangerous of all the unsuccessful rebellions in the Tudor period. It began in October when Robert Aske, an astute and successful lawyer, organised musters in the East Riding of Yorkshire on his return from visiting the Lincolnshire rebels at Caistor. On 16 October a force of 10 000 rebels took the city of York, and both Hull and Pontefract fell soon afterwards.

The first version of their demands issued at York bore a close resemblance to those of the Lincolnshire rebels, attacking the Dissolution of the Monasteries, heretics, base-born royal Councillors and the Statute of Uses. For their banner they chose the potent symbol of the Five Wounds of Christ, to which they added a marching song, the word 'pilgrimage' to describe their movement and the following oath:

Q

1. Why did the rebels choose the word 'pilgrimage' for their rising?
2. In what ways could the oath be regarded as loyal to the King?

Ye shall not enter into this our Pilgrimage of Grace for the Commonwealth, but only for the love that ye do bear unto Almighty God his faith, and the Holy Church militant and the maintenance thereof, to the preservation of the King's person and his issue, to the purifying of the nobility, and to expulse all villein blood and evil councillors against the commonwealth from his Grace and his Privy Council of the same. And that ye shall not enter into our said Pilgrimage for no particular profit to yourself, nor to do any displeasure to any private person, but by counsel of the commonwealth, nor slay nor murder for no envy, but in your hearts put away fear and dread, and take afore you the Cross of Christ, and in your hearts His faith, the Restitution of the Church, the suppression of those Heretics and their opinions, by all the holy contents of this book.

Meanwhile, rumours similar to those that had circulated in Lincoln-shire were spread throughout the North – perhaps deliberately by the clergy – that there would be taxes on baptisms, marriages and burials, on cows and sheep, and a prohibition on poor men eating dairy prod-ucts or white bread. Simultaneously, risings appeared elsewhere in the North: in Northumberland and Durham and in areas of Yorkshire. All these areas rose on or around 11 October 1536, usually under noble or gentry leaders: thus Lord Latimer, a Neville and member of the Council of the North, and Sir Christopher Danby took Barnard Castle and entered York. In Cumberland musters were held at Kirkby Stephen and Penrith and in Westmorland, but Lancashire stayed loyal when the Earl of Derby declared for the King and prevented rebellion from spilling over into Cheshire and North Wales. A few pockets of loyalty held out within the main rebel area: Scarborough, Skipton Castle, Berwick and Carlisle.

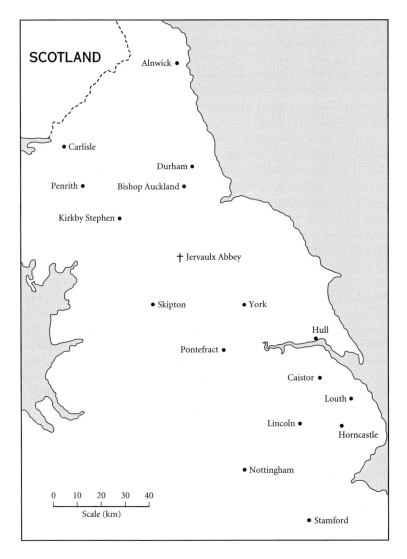

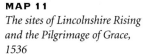

MAP 11

The sites of Lincolnshire Rising and the Pilgrimage of Grace, 1536

Such widespread disturbances caught the government unawares. The Duke of Suffolk was preoccupied in Lincolnshire, and the Earl of Shrewsbury awaited Henry's orders at Nottingham. Lord Darcy, holding Pontefract for the King, appealed for assistance but surrendered after a week's siege, claiming that he had run out of supplies and gunpowder. As Darcy is known to have felt disgruntled at his exclusion from office, and to have opposed both Henry's divorce and the Royal Supremacy, this may be a thin excuse.

At this stage Aske's intentions seem to have been to overawe the government with a show of force and thus to get it to grant his demands. He had no plan to form an alternative regime or to remove Henry VIII; rather he seems to have wanted a greater say for the North in the nation's affairs, to remove Cromwell and to reverse certain policies of the Henrician Reformation. In order to achieve these aims he would need substantial noble support, and he spent several days at Pontefract from 19 to 21 October, arguing the Pilgrims' case to Darcy, Edward Lee, Archbishop of York, and an assortment of knights and gentlemen. This case was now put forward in the form of the 24 Pontefract Articles, which were later put to Henry and which developed those presented at York, to include a demand for the return of a limited papal spiritual supremacy, a list of heretics, complaints about **entry fines** and enclosures and a demand that Princess Mary be restored her rights to the succession.

> **Entry fines** extra payments to a landlord made by a new tenant or heir to a tenancy on taking over land

The Pilgrims presented a petition to Henry at Doncaster. His reply of 2 November was to reject the demands, but he promised a pardon for all save ten ringleaders. At this stage Henry seems to have felt that the rebellion would now collapse and he would be able to save face and maintain his prestige without making any concessions.

Henry's reply was regarded with suspicion by the Pilgrims, who now proposed a second meeting at Doncaster, having clarified their manifesto, which Henry had found 'general, dark and obscure'. On 3 December Henry instructed Norfolk to grant a general pardon, prolong the truce and promise a Parliament. On 6 December Norfolk met a delegation of Pilgrims, to whom he promised that most of their articles could be discussed in Parliament, and that a compromise could be arrived at on the abbeys, which would surrender to the King's commissioners and then be restored until Parliament met. Aske announced these terms to 3000 followers at Pontefract on 7 December, and on the following day the Lancaster Herald formally read the King's pardon to the rebels who began to disperse. Aske submitted at Doncaster, kneeling in Norfolk's presence, abandoning the title of 'captain' and removing his badge.

Henry had won: he had stood by Cromwell and the 'heretic' bishops, neither ratifying nor repudiating the terms, which were in any case never written down. Thus ended the largest popular revolt in English history up to that time, or indeed ever, in terms of numbers and geographical range. The King had survived the greatest crisis of his reign by keeping a cool head and playing for time.

The problem remains, however, of establishing the cause or causes of the rising. Was it a popular rebellion of the North as a whole against the

Henrician regime? Was it a feudal or neo-feudal phenomenon, a reaction by old-established and over-mighty families of the North to Tudor centralisation? Or was it, as Professor Elton has claimed, an attempt by a defeated faction at Court to create a power base in the North to achieve a political victory over the centre? It appears that most of the grievances of the rebels were the concerns of the gentry, and that the issue of the Dissolution of the Monasteries may have been exaggerated – after all, the Pilgrims made little effort to restore dissolved houses, of which only the smaller had anyway yet been affected. There is certainly evidence of incitement by gentry who used the same muster techniques as for war against the Scots, and no doubt many leading families, including the Percies, did have genuine complaints. Darcy, Constable and Hussey had a history of opposition at Court, all were religious conservatives, and all had been in touch with Chapuys, the Imperial ambassador. Moreover Aske's links, both with this group and with the Lincolnshire rising, are clearly established. Was the Pilgrimage therefore a pre-planned coup by a tightly knit group of disaffected conservative gentry?

To answer this question it will be necessary to examine a number of possible causes of unrest, and to address first the suggestion that there may have been economic grievances affecting ordinary people. Recent taxation measures had no doubt been unpopular, particularly after two years of dearth, bad weather and poor harvests, but there is no evidence that this was a major grievance. Another possible material complaint was enclosures, but these were only resented in certain valleys of the West Riding of Yorkshire, the uplands of the Lake District, the Vale of York and a few other areas. Entry fines were exacted west of the Pennines by the Cliffords and Nevilles, but they were not a serious problem elsewhere. Tithes were attacked in parts of the North-west. All told, however, it is hard to see that economic troubles, while no doubt serious, could have been by themselves a sufficient cause of a major rebellion.

How popular a rising was the Pilgrimage? Certainly the mass of the lay people do seem to have opposed threats to traditional rituals, practices and beliefs. They cherished local religious festivals and church ornaments, and they were easily alarmed by the kind of rumours that spread so easily in 1536 about imminent confiscations and taxes. Moreover, monasteries were popular institutions, dispensing hospitality and education, maintaining vital public works, distributing alms and offering employment. However, it is worth pointing out that they were also valued by the gentry for lucrative monastic stewardships. Yet the Pilgrims only attempted to restore 16 out of 55 dissolved religious houses in the North, and there is considerable evidence of clerical, rather than popular, pressure to express religious grievances. It would seem reasonable, therefore, to seek for further motives to explain the Pilgrimage as a whole.

Can the movement be seen as a feudal rising by the Percies or other northern noble families? Henry Percy, 6th Earl of Northumberland, was the head of the most powerful noble family, with estates in

Northumberland itself, Yorkshire and Cumberland. He was, in addition, Warden of both the East and Middle Marches, Lieutenant of Yorkshire and Sheriff of Northumberland for life, but he suffered from a serious weakness: the lack of an heir. Accordingly, in an extraordinary gesture, he made Henry VIII himself his sole heir, and thus he was in no position to lead the rising once it had begun. Hence he seems to have remained aloof while other members of his family, his brother Sir Thomas Percy for example, expressed their fears of the extension of royal power into the North-east rather more actively. Indeed Sir Ingram and Sir Thomas Percy fought for their own inheritance rather than for any grandiose 'Percy interest', but there were also many Percy tenants who joined the rising as captains, including four members of Northumberland's council such as Aske himself.

It may, therefore, be possible to show that something of the old Percy network remained to figure in the rising, but what of other families? The Duke of Norfolk might have sympathised with the rising as an opponent of Cromwell and the 'heretical' bishops, but expediency and calculation seem to have kept him loyal – after all, this could be a chance for the Howards to spread their power and landholding from East Anglia to the North. The Earl of Shrewsbury was another religious conservative, but he had done well out of Henry VIII, and his firm stand stiffened the resolve of others like Rutland and Huntingdon. The Earl of Derby, as we have seen, ensured that all of Lancashire, south of the River Ribble, stayed loyal. For all their dislike of the Statute of Uses, therefore, many great nobles either supported the King or did nothing.

Finally, what can we make of the theory that the Pilgrimage was the result of a plot by members of the defeated Aragonese faction at Court? It is true that Hussey had been Mary Tudor's chamberlain and that Darcy had long plotted with Chapuys. For such men the chief enemy was perceived to be the upstart Thomas Cromwell, and the chief aim to restore Mary in the succession and to reverse the result of recent faction infighting at Court.

It is difficult, in the light of recent research, to regard the Pilgrimage as a truly popular or spontaneous rising; that there must have been some form of conspiracy is now beyond doubt. Yet the conspiracy theory is not able to provide a complete explanation of the outbreak of the rising, still less of its subsequent spread.

The North did not settle down with Aske's surrender, for Sir Francis Bigod's rebellion broke out in the East Riding in January 1537. He was captured in Cumberland the following month and suffered execution at Norfolk's hand with 177 of his supporters. Fellow victims included Lord Darcy, Sir Thomas Percy, and Robert Aske.

When it was all over, Henry also re-organised the Council of the North, choosing first Bishop Tunstall, then Archbishop Holgate as its president, while he appointed a mere gentleman as Warden of the West March, Sir William Eure. The Crown had won a significant victory in the North in the 1530s, but the 1569 rising was to show that it would require more than one success to carry out a permanent change there. The extreme north remained both a military and an administrative problem.

> **KEY ISSUE**
>
> *What evidence is there that the Pilgrimage of Grace was a pre-planned conspiracy?*

6 ∾ THE WESTERN OR 'PRAYER BOOK' REBELLION 1549

It was not until 1549 that the spectre of rebellion arose again in England in two simultaneous, but unconnected risings.

See pages 138–9

The writ of Tudor government was always more difficult to enforce in the 'dark corners of the land': the Marches of Wales, the extreme North-west, the North-east and the South-west. The Western Rebellion erupted as a result of the attempts of Protector Somerset to compel all parishes to use the new 1549 Prayer Book, which represented a discernible shift towards Protestantism. On Whit Monday the parishioners of Sampford Courtenay in Devon objected to their priest saying the new service and forced him to say Mass in the old style, describing the new liturgy as 'but like a Christmas game'. By 20 June, a force of rebels from Devon and Cornwall gathered at Crediton where they were promised a general pardon on Somerset's behalf if they would disperse. At the same time the government ordered a Devon gentleman, Sir Peter Carew, to investigate the situation. By 23 June the rebel army had moved to Clyst St Mary, and Carew was on his way to London to report serious disorder.

The Protector's forces were already stretched with enclosure riots breaking out in Somerset, Wiltshire and Hampshire and in parts of the Midlands and the South-east. At the same time danger could always threaten from overseas to embarrass a regime beset by internal difficulties: either or both of the Scots or the French could invade. Nevertheless Somerset, who was later rather unfairly accused of lack of resolution in the 1549 disturbances, sent the Lord Privy Seal, Lord Russell, to put the rebellion down. On 16 August the rebels were annihilated by him at Okehampton, where as many as 4000 may have died on the rebel side.

Does the Western Rising merit its alternative title: the 'Prayer Book Rebellion'? Certainly of the 16 demands almost all are religious, demanding the renewal of Henry VIII's Six Articles Act, the Latin Mass, and a partial restoration of the monasteries. They must have been written by clerics who believed that no religious changes could legally take place while Edward VI was still a child – in other words the 1549 *Prayer Book* was the work of 'evil counsellors'. Only one article is clearly secular, demanding a limit to the size of gentry households, and the absence of gentry support for the movement is telling – in contrast, of course, to the Pilgrimage of Grace. Most of the rising's leaders were yeomen or tradesmen; in other words from just outside the gentry class. The western gentry supported the Crown, perhaps because of a vested interest in the progress of the Reformation stemming from their possession of former monastic lands.

KEY ISSUE

Why did the Prayer Book Rebellion of 1549 occur in the West Country?

7 ∾ KETT'S REBELLION 1549

While the Western Rebellion was at its height, a series of anti-enclosure riots in Norfolk rapidly grew into a major protest. Robert Kett, a well-to-do tanner turned landowner, encouraged disturbances against a

See pages 140–2

neighbouring rival, Sir John Flowerdew, despite Kett's own record as an encloser of common land and a purchaser of former monastic property. By 12 July 16 000 rebels had set up camp on Mousehold Heath, just outside the city of Norwich. Neither the local gentry nor the city authorities were able to compel them to disperse, but on 21 July the King's representative, York Herald, offered them a pardon if they would return home.

The rebels' reply was to attack Norwich and to overwhelm its feeble defences. On 30 July, William Parr, Marquis of Northampton, arrived with a force of 14 000 troops, including some Italian mercenaries and Suffolk gentry, but on the next day Northampton was obliged to abandon the city. The rebellion was finally put down by John Dudley, Earl of Warwick, who arrived with 12 000 men on 23 August. Four days later at Dussindale about 3000 rebels were killed and Kett was captured to be condemned to death for treason and hanged with 48 of his accomplices in December.

What then were the causes of the Kett Rebellion? Somerset himself has often been blamed for inciting the movement through his social policy, and it is quite true that he had set up a commission on enclosures which was still at work. Some of the rebels do seem to have believed that they were doing no more than anticipating government policy; in other words, that they were doing what the authorities wanted them to. Only one article of grievance refers specifically to enclosures, but there are plenty of references to the burden of rent increases, to wardships, common rights and foldcourse (where landlords could pasture their own flocks on tenants' land or common land). Two articles mention lawyers' seizure of, and speculation in, land, one criticises the unfair distribution of common land, and one urges freedom for serfs, of which there were still a few in Norfolk on the Howard estates.

The religious temper of the rebels was decidedly Protestant: the new 1549 *Prayer Book* was in daily use, while four of the articles of grievance were on religion, demanding better preaching, condemning non-residence among clergy, asking for clerical teaching of poor children and calling for tithe reform. Time and again the Kett rebels harked back to some golden age during Henry VII's reign. This was a protest of a local community mainly directed against the exactions of landlords, and thus it was difficult for it to evoke a national response.

Somerset's priority was to establish garrisons to deal with the French and Scottish threats before turning to internal disorder which had in any case broken out all over the country. Thus his initial response to Kett was conciliatory, while making clear that he had no time for rebels, 'lewd, seditious and evil disposed persons', as he put it. It was, after all, Somerset who sent Northampton to overawe the rebels and who was stunned by his failure. He now saw that this required a substantial military effort. If Russell had not put down the Western Rebellion, Somerset would probably have sent Warwick to Devon and given himself the Norfolk command. As it was, Warwick was now available to suppress Kett, and Somerset had to face criticism from his enemies on the Council of alleged weakness and hesitation in dealing with the crisis.

With the advantage of hindsight Somerset's approach looks eminently reasonable. The Kett rising was serious, but it did not physically threaten the government unlike those of 1381, 1450 and 1497, for there was no plan to march on London or to release the King from the grip of evil ministers. Indeed, as we have seen, many of the rebels seem to have seen themselves as pro-government, merely pre-empting measures which they expected Somerset to take anyway.

KEY ISSUE

How far is it reasonable to describe Kett's Rebellion as 'conservative'?

8 ⤳ THE ACCESSION OF MARY TUDOR 1553 AND WYATT'S REBELLION 1554

Mary Tudor's seizure of the throne after her half-brother's death has some claim to be seen as the only successful rebellion in the entire Tudor period, leading Dr Loach to call it, 'one of the most surprising events of the sixteenth century'. It certainly contrasts sharply with the failed popular risings of 1549.

see page 154

However, Wyatt's Rebellion showed that Mary's position on the throne was not immediately secure. With this rebellion we are back on familiar ground, for the early months of 1554 saw the first attempt since the days of Perkin Warbeck to unseat a reigning monarch, when Sir Thomas Wyatt, a Kentish gentleman, tried to mount a rebellion using the issue of Mary's projected marriage to Philip of Spain. Wyatt's plot was part of a wider network of risings planned at the end of 1553, involving Hertfordshire, Devon and Leicestershire, as well as the French ambassador Antoine de Noailles.

See pages 158–60

Eventually only Wyatt managed to raise realistic support and he decided to pose as the rescuer of Mary from foolish advice, stirring up very effective anti-Spanish propaganda over the marriage issue. Little was said at first about more far-reaching aims, but it is fairly clear, at least, that Wyatt kept open the option of replacing Mary by Elizabeth if he could not compel the Queen to abandon her marital plans. However, owing to his own errors and Mary's courage in remaining in London to rally resistance, Wyatt was defeated on the outskirts of the capital in February 1554.

Historians have been divided as to the weight which they place upon religious or political motives in Wyatt's Rebellion. Clearly Wyatt tapped a rich vein of anti-Spanish xenophobia and he received support from those who preferred an English bridegroom, Edward Courtenay perhaps, and who feared entanglements in French wars if the links with Spain were further reinforced. There is quite strong evidence that many of the rebels were Protestants, including some of the leaders, although it has not been possible to establish that Wyatt himself was Protestant.

What is clear, however, is that a good many of Mary's subjects were sufficiently disgruntled with her policies after the first few months of her reign to contemplate open rebellion and, moreover, that Wyatt came nearer than any other Tudor rebel to removing a monarch from the throne. While Wyatt involved fewer men than in the 1549 rebellions, his proximity to London and his clear intention to take the capital made him infinitely more dangerous. The danger was enhanced because it was a quarrel within the ranks of the political community, rather than a threat to the whole social order when the élite would tend to close ranks. It could also be seen as a violent attempt by a section of the political nation to interfere in the formulation of foreign policy, and this was new.

Fortunately for Mary, loyalty to the Tudor dynasty, pure chance and abhorrence of all rebellion came to her aid, and of course it is now clear that Wyatt suffered significant weaknesses from the start. Opposition to the Spanish match may well have been strong, but it was not that strong. Wyatt only managed to involve one important noble – the Duke of Suffolk (successor to the duke who had been Henry VIII's old friend) – and he failed to raise a worthwhile force. Finally, for all the Protestant zeal of some of those who did choose to take part, the orthodox Protestant leadership refused to get involved, fearing perhaps to challenge a legitimate monarch and hoping that Mary's religious policies would

PROFILE

KEY ISSUE

Why did Wyatt's Rebellion of 1554 come so near to success but ultimately fail?

SIR THOMAS WYATT (C. 1521–54)

Wyatt was the son of Sir Thomas Wyatt, the poet and courtier. A veteran of Henry VIII's French campaigns of the 1540s, he devised the scheme for a local militia in the face of the 1549 rebellions – ironically in view of his prominence in the so-called Wyatt Rebellion of 1554.

His renown as a Kentish gentleman and his proximity to London should have helped him to rebel in 1554, ostensibly on the issue of Mary Tudor's plan to marry Philip II of Spain. However other participants in the plot failed to deliver, and Wyatt proceeded alone, making serious tactical mistakes and losing valuable time on the way to London. He was captured in London and executed at Tower Hill later in 1554.

Yet Wyatt came nearer than any other sixteenth-century rebel to deposing an anointed monarch. He cleverly resisted the temptation to declare his rising a Protestant one, remembering perhaps that Mary had gained strong support the previous year by stressing her political legitimacy and downplaying her Catholicism. Religion was clearly a very divisive issue, and Wyatt preferred to concentrate on the issue of the Spanish marriage which Mary intended to contract. Indeed he is said to have told one Protestant supporter, 'You may not so much as name religion, for that will withdraw from us the hearts of many'. Asked by another supporter, 'Sir, is your quarrel only to defend us from overrunning by Strangers?', Wyatt apparently replied, 'We mind nothing less than any wise to touch Her Grace'.

While Wyatt may have almost succeeded in toppling Mary, his tactic looks – with hindsight – patently bankrupt. For future rebels his example was likely to prove less of an inspiration than a warning.

turn out to be more moderate than they did. A conventional domestic revolt had little chance of success against a monarch sustained by enough aristocratic support. Nevertheless Wyatt's Rebellion came nearer than any other Tudor rebellion to toppling the monarch.

9 ⌐ THE REVOLT OF THE NORTHERN EARLS

There were no further uprisings in Mary's reign, and Elizabeth had a chance to establish her regime before a rebellion emerged once again in a familiar area – the North-east – led by the Earls of Northumberland and Westmorland.

see page 230

In 1568 Mary, Queen of Scots fled to England in the aftermath of her defeat in Scotland, and over the course of the next 20 years she was involved in numerous plots against Elizabeth to restore Catholicism and to place herself on the throne. Almost all of these conspiracies were uncovered and the chief plotters dealt with before they could be put into effect: the Ridolfi Plot of 1571, the Parry Plot of 1585 and the Babington Plot of 1586 all ended in this way. The only one which became a rebellion as such was the Northern Rising in 1569.

Mary, of course, was a danger, partly because of her Catholicism and partly because of her claim to the English throne – all the more a danger while Elizabeth remained unmarried and the succession question remained very much alive. A plan emerged to marry the Duke of Norfolk to Mary: this would, it was argued, cause the overthrow of Elizabeth's Protestant minister Cecil; settle the succession problem; and ensure peace with both France and Spain, thus ensuring that England would no longer be isolated in Europe. The plan had some appeal to Protestants like Leicester, Pembroke and Throckmorton, who saw it as a way of reducing the potency of Mary's own commitment to Catholicism, as Norfolk was a Protestant himself. It had, of course, rather less appeal to Elizabeth who foresaw that Mary would soon become recognised as her heir, that an ultimate Catholic succession would therefore be inevitable, and she would have to dispense with the loyal and able William Cecil.

On 6 September 1569 Leicester confessed his involvement, and on 16 September Norfolk left Court for his estate at Kenninghall in Norfolk, the natural assumption being that he had gone to raise the North. It is doubtful, however, if a coherent plan existed at this stage, partly because papal approval for a Catholic conspiracy in the form of the Bull *Regnans in Excelsis*, which proclaimed Elizabeth deposed, did not appear until 1570, and partly because of the weak link in the form of the Earl of Northumberland, who sympathised with the outlines of the plan, but urged Mary to marry a Catholic like Philip II of Spain.

The Percy family had been restored to their ancient dignity as Earls of Northumberland in 1557 and to the Wardenships of the East and Middle Marches. While their prestige was not what it had been, they still owned 40 townships, two key castles at Alnwick and Warkworth, and had 2000 tenants scattered over the far North-east, Yorkshire,

Cumberland and Sussex. But the Earl's doubts were compounded by Norfolk's indecision.

Norfolk was aware that his own gentry and tenantry in East Anglia would be reluctant to rise, and on 1 October 1569 he sent his brother-in-law Charles, 6th Earl of Westmorland, a message urging him not to rebel. He then returned to London to throw himself on Elizabeth's mercy, thus placing the two northern Earls, Westmorland and Northumberland, in a dilemma, from which they tried to extricate themselves by assuring the Earl of Sussex at York on 9 October that they had no part in any plot. Sussex seemed convinced by this for he reported on 13 October, 'all is very quiet here and the time of year will shortly cool hot humours', but Elizabeth summoned the two lords to appear before the Council in London with a fuller explanation. Meanwhile Northumberland hesitated, and Mary and the Spanish ambassador, de Spes, urged caution.

Yet during the first week of November both Earls came to the conclusion that they had to rise as all other avenues had failed to change the Queen's policies. Their Catholic followers were urging them to rebel, and the formidable Lady Westmorland reinforced this advice with her own pressure. They were also naturally worried by Elizabeth's insistence that they should come to Court. Thus on 14 November they made their first demonstration at Durham Cathedral when all evidence of Protestantism was removed and Mass celebrated according to the old rite.

Sussex viewed events with concern and on 16 November wrote to the Council about the difficulties in raising troops, and on the same day the Earls issued this proclamation:

Thomas, Earl of Northumberland and Charles, Earl of Westmorland, the Queen's most true and lawful subjects, and to all her highness' people, sends greeting: Whereas diverse new set up nobles about the Queen's majesty, have and do daily, not only go about to overthrow and put down the ancient nobility of this realm, but also have misused the Queen's majesty's own person, and also have by the space of twelve years now past, set up, and maintained a new found religion and heresy, contrary to God's word. For the amending and redressing whereof, diverse foreign powers do purpose shortly to invade these realms, which will be to our utter destruction, if we do not ourselves speedily forfend the same. Wherefore we are now constrained at this time to go about to amend and redress it ourselves, which if we should not do and foreigners enter upon us we should be all made slaves and bondmen to them. These are therefore to will and require you, and every of you, being above the age of sixteen years and not sixty, as your duty to God doth bind you, for the setting forth of his true and catholic religion; and as you tender the commonwealth of your country, to come and resort unto us with all speed, with all such armour and furniture as you, or any of you have. This fail you not herein, as you will answer the contrary at your perils. God save the Queen.

Q

1. What attitude towards the Queen is revealed in this passage?
2. What arguments are used in the passage to justify rebellion?

By 22 November the rebels had reached Bramham Moor near Tadcaster with roughly 5400 men while Sussex had less than a tenth the number. He was therefore surprised to hear that on 24 November the rebels had turned back to Knaresborough. This move was, however, partly to consolidate their strength and partly to await Spanish help in the North, where they believed their strength to lie. Rumours abounded of the approach of fresh royal forces, and the rebels feared the imminent removal of Mary to Coventry in the hands of the loyalist Earl of Shrewsbury. Support from Lancashire and Cheshire was also missing as both the Bishop of Carlisle and the Earl of Derby (Lord-Lieutenant of Lancashire), who had remained loyal, were popular with local Catholic gentry. Finally they were disappointed by the failure of their appeals to Catholic nobles and by the lack of Spanish help. The Duke of Alva apparently thought that the whole venture was unsound and that he was better occupied in putting down the revolt in the Netherlands.

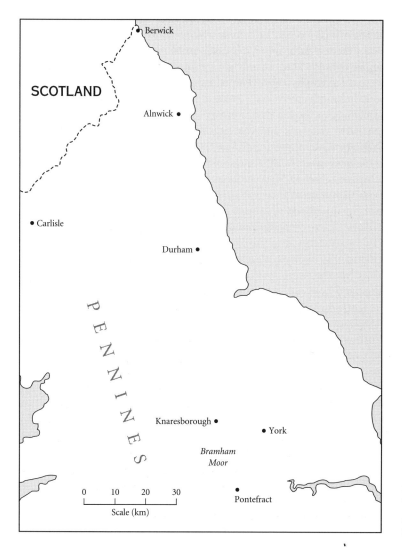

MAP 12

The sites of the Northern Rebellion, 1569

By December 1569 it was clear that the royal forces, using the new militia system, would soon wear down the rising, and by the end of the month both leaders were safely over the border in Scotland. Their rising had failed through its incoherence and aimlessness, its lack of clear articles or demands, its limited geographical support, the failure to mobilise fully the resources of the two Earls or sympathisers, and a confusion over their precise religious aims. Elizabeth sought revenge, but many of the 700 death sentences were commuted. Westmorland died in exile, his lands confiscated and his title abolished, while Northumberland was betrayed into government hands and was executed at York in August 1572.

What caused the Earls to embark on such a desperate adventure? Personal resentment of the encroachments of the Tudor regime must have played a large part: Northumberland had been deprived of the Wardenship of the Middle March in favour of his arch-rival Sir John Forster, and Elizabeth's cousin Lord Hunsdon was given charge of Berwick and the East March. Westmorland's feelings were similar: he felt impoverished, he had recently lost the title 'Lieutenant General of the North' which he had held under Mary Tudor, and his wife, Norfolk's sister, exerted pressure of her own, exclaiming of her brother, 'What a simple man the Duke is, to begin a matter and not to go through with it; we and our country were shamed for ever, that now in the end we should seek holes to creep into'. Bastard feudal allegiance still counted for something in the far North: gentry involved in the rebellion were often the Earls' retainers and the largest groups of supporters came from Brancepeth, Raby and Topcliffe, all either Neville or Percy areas.

Religion also played a major part: two of the four main agitators for rebellion, Thomas Markenfeld and Dr Morton, had both just returned from trips abroad fired with enthusiasm for the Counter-reformation, and Northumberland himself had converted to Catholicism as recently as 1567. There was also resentment at the apparent influx of militant Protestant clergy into the Durham diocese led by the puritan Bishop Pilkington. Perhaps Professor Lawrence Stone is right when he describes the rising as 'the last episode in 500 years of protest by the Highland Zone against the interference of London'.

The long-term settlement of the North does suggest that the traditional autonomy of the region had finally withered. The Earldom of Northumberland passed in 1572 to Sir Henry Percy, who never held office in the North and lacked a clientage network there, preferring to live at Petworth in Sussex. The Council of the North was reconstituted in 1572 under the Puritan 3rd Earl of Huntingdon, the Queen's cousin and an outsider with no local ties, to include Durham, Northumberland, Cumberland and Westmorland in its area of responsibility. Aristocratic territorial power seemed a growing anachronism in Elizabethan England.

> ### KEY ISSUE
>
> *Was the Northern Earls' Rebellion of 1569 doomed from the start? How far was its suppression a turning point?*

10 ↠ THE ESSEX REVOLT 1601

The last Tudor rebellion was an almost farcical attempt by a disgruntled and over-mighty subject to seize power. As the 1590s wore on, the Earl of Essex felt increasingly both that he was thwarted in his own advancement by Burghley, and that his personal following would melt away if he could not sufficiently reward his clients. Indeed, when Burghley died in 1598, Essex's worst fears seemed to be realised: Burghley's son Robert Cecil became both Chancellor of the Duchy of Lancaster and Master of the Court of Wards, and one of his protégés, Lord Buckhurst, became Lord Treasurer. Essex had triumphed in 1596 at Cadiz, but in 1599 he had returned to Court from Ireland having failed to put down the Earl of Tyrone's rebellion. When Elizabeth destroyed Essex's credit structure in September 1600 by refusing to renew his patents on the import of sweet wines, Essex was faced with two options: retire and economise, or try to seize power by force.

ROBERT DEVEREUX, EARL OF ESSEX (1566–1601)

Robert Devereux, 2nd Earl of Essex, seems rather out of place in the sixteenth century, seeming perhaps more suited to be an over-mighty subject in the previous one. Born to wealth and privilege, he attended Cambridge University (of which he became Chancellor in 1598). He rose to be Elizabeth's favourite in the late 1580s. The ageing Queen enjoyed the attentions of this attractive and impetuous young man, and he ignited a passion in her she had only felt before for the Earl of Leicester. He was made Master of the Horse in 1587, awarded the Order of the Garter in 1588, and appointed to the Privy Council in 1593. Essex had a stormy relationship with the Queen, and there were frequent rows. When he was counselled to be more respectful, he replied, 'She doth not contradict confidently, which they that know the minds of women say is a sign of yielding'. He did generally get his way, to the alarm of competitors for favour, principally Sir Walter Raleigh, and to policy-makers, mainly Burghley, who feared his schemes for war and glory. He did win glory in the assault on Cadiz in 1597, and he was advanced in the following year to be Master of the Ordnance and Earl Marshal. However, he was growing over-confident and even unstable. In a row with the Queen over patronage in July 1598, he turned his back on her. She boxed his ears and he, briefly, went for his sword. He just held himself back, and Elizabeth forgave him, but he was pushing the limits even of the infatuated Queen's tolerance. In 1599 he was appointed Lieutenant and Governor-General in Ireland, where he failed utterly to subdue Tyrone's rebellion. Against Elizabeth's strict orders, he returned to Court. Elizabeth's determination to rule finally overcame her affection: 'By God's Son, I am no queen; that man is above me'. Essex was banished from Court and faced personal and financial ruin. He launched his abortive rebellion in 1601, and the inevitable consequence followed. He was executed on 25 February, watched by the Captain of the Guard, his old rival Sir Walter Raleigh.

PROFILE

PICTURE 29
The Earl of Essex, *anon.*

It came as little surprise when Essex went for the second option, to seize power together with a group of disgruntled noblemen, all like himself deeply in debt, and including three other Earls, Southampton, Bedford and Rutland. Thus Essex assembled a coalition of impecunious, disaffected place-seekers, whose motives were largely personal. There was for example no religious unity in the group, for many supporters of Essex were Catholics while Essex himself was a Protestant. Foreign policy was perhaps more a genuine bone of contention, as Essex favoured a more vigorous, daring policy in the Netherlands, in France and at sea, while Burghley and his son Robert Cecil were keen to reduce commitments.

The rising itself was all over in the course of a few hours on the streets of London on 8 February 1601. Essex himself was captured and shortly afterwards executed. What is not clear is how far Essex might have got, if he had been more astute politically. There were many more rumblings of discontent, among noblemen and gentry starved of patronage, outside his small coterie of supporters. As Christopher Haigh has put it: 'the causes were structural, and arose from the difficulty of reconciling the costs of war with necessary patronage and political expenditure'. However, the plot had ended ingloriously; the technique of palace revolution was not feasible as an instrument of Court politics, even as the popularity of Elizabeth's regime sank. By this time, all hopes were pinned on the rising sun of the Stuarts. But they were to have their own difficulties.

> **KEY ISSUE**
>
> *Was Essex's Revolt just about his personal power and position?*

11 ⤖ CONCLUSION

Is it possible to reach any sort of general conclusions from such a disparate set of events? The historian is struck first perhaps by the refusal of most rebels to challenge the Crown directly. The aura of monarchy and the widespread belief in theories of obligation usually prevented explicit criticism of the monarch. Even Wyatt's Rebellion shows this, for while Wyatt himself had a coherent plan to remove Mary Tudor, many of his supporters saw the main motive as to stop the marriage. Rebels preferred to seek a scapegoat like Cromwell in 1536 or Cecil in 1569. and to protest their loyalty to the Crown. This tactic made it harder to convict them of treason, although this does not seem to have forestalled royal vengeance on the rebels once they had been defeated.

Second, it is clear that each Tudor monarch faced at least one serious revolt and that they encountered significant military problems in suppressing them. The Duke of Norfolk was nervous about engaging his troops in 1536, and in 1549 Somerset had to resort to foreign mercenaries, when his difficulties were exacerbated by the absence of a leading nobleman in each of the areas of revolt: in 1549 Norfolk was in the Tower and the Earl of Devon was absent from the West Country. Certainly the authorities were worried in 1549 that society itself was about to collapse, although this was an extreme and most Tudor revolts were conservative in their views of the social structure. In 1549 Somerset complained, 'All have conceived a wonderful hate against gentlemen and taketh them all as their enemies', and Cranmer had this to say of the Western Rebels, 'standeth it with any reason to turn upside down the good order of the whole world, that is everywhere and hath been, that is to say the commoners to be governed by the nobles and the servants by their masters?'. Mary Tudor could not have survived Wyatt's Rebellion in 1554 without the loyalty of several key nobles and their retainers, and the need was seen for more effective propaganda and some kind of national militia. In the short run Mary enhanced noble power, at least in the North, by restoring Northumberland to his estates as a bulwark against Scottish incursions in 1557, but in the longer term Elizabeth began the construction of a northern security system that did not rely on over-mighty nobles, having crushed the northern Earls.

Third, it is difficult to detect a clear link between poor harvests and outbursts of rebellion. Burghley declared, 'there is nothing will sooner lead men into sedition than dearth of victual', but many historians will agree with Professor Hobsbawm, that people who are hungry are so concerned with finding food to live, that they have no time for anything else. In fact none of the major disorders was directly occasioned by dearth: the 1535 harvest was poor but that in 1536 was good, there was a straight run of good harvests from 1546 to 1548 and the three that preceded the 1569 rebellion were all bountiful too. The worst harvests were from 1555 to 1557 and from 1594 to 1598 when no revolts occurred.

Fourth, amazingly little violence was inflicted by the rebels, although of course the government's revenge was frequently savage. In 1536 the Lincolnshire rebels only killed two people, and, in general, outbursts of violence and victimisation were isolated incidents in what were essentially movements of peaceful resistance to specific policies of the government. In Kett's Rebellion, Matthew Parker escaped with nothing but a bad fright after preaching on disobedience. French peasant upheavals were by contrast much more violent.

Fifth, the relative lack of resistance to taxation demands, with a few obvious exceptions like 1525, also contrasts markedly with French experience. The principle of tithe-paying was never challenged; indeed a conservative resistance to disturbance in the pattern of traditional Catholic worship looms much larger as an issue. There were, moreover, no extreme radical Protestant sects involved in disorders, unlike in Germany.

Sixth, one cannot but be struck by the provincialism of most rebellions. Almost every rising was the response of a local community to purely local grievance, and hence co-ordination with other areas hardly ever happened, if it was even tried. Peasants were reluctant to stray far from their fields, especially at harvest time. Only the gentry could have organised a more widespread uprising, and as we have seen, gentry leadership of popular revolts was by no means universal.

Finally, did Tudor rebellions achieve any of their aims, or restrain the actions of either the monarch or the ruling élite? The 1525 reaction to the 'Amicable Grant' was successful in the short run, but it had no permanent effect in restraining Henry VIII's demands for more revenue, and the 1549 rebellions led to Northumberland's triumph over Somerset, uniting the ruling class and ensuring firmer government control. It is true that the Statute of Uses, which featured as an issue in 1536, was partially revoked by the later Statute of Wills, but it could be argued strongly that the sixteenth-century rebellions tended to strengthen, as well as to restrain, the Crown. The Crown had a chance to eliminate, or at least to discipline, some of its main opponents, and to improve military recruitment and installations. Under Elizabeth more draconian treason laws were passed and the landed classes' fears may well have disposed them to greater loyalty to the established order. From the vantage point of 1603, the Crown seemed to have ridden the storms of the previous 120 years very well.

> **KEY ISSUE**
>
> *Why were Tudor rebellions so limited in their effects?*

12 ᕯ BIBLIOGRAPHY

**A Fletcher and D MacCulloch *Tudor Rebellions* (Longman Seminar Studies, fourth edition, 1997). The standard book on the rebellions, now in its fourth edition, and designed for sixth-form and college studies. **CSL Davies *Peace, Print and Protestantism* (Paladin, 1977). An admirably succinct and well-detailed survey of the whole period. *J Guy *Tudor England* (OUP, 1988). A magisterial survey of the whole Tudor period by one of its outstanding scholars. *RW Hoyle *The Pilgrimage of Grace* (OUP, 2001). A re-appraisal of a complex event by a specialist in agrarian history. P Williams *The Tudor Regime* (OUP, 1979). Concentrate on Chapters 4, 7, 10 and 11. It examines the ways Tudor institutions responded to each crisis. J Youings *Sixteenth Century England* (Penguin, 1984), see especially Chapter 9; this makes clear the social background to rebellion.

(*Recommended. **Highly recommended.)

13 ᕯ STRUCTURED AND ESSAY QUESTIONS

A *Structured questions*

1. (a) Which Tudor rebellions achieved success?
    (b) Why did most rebellions fail during this period?
2. (a) What brought about the Pilgrimage of Grace in 1536?
    (b) Which were the most dangerous rebellions in the Tudor period, and why?

B *Essay questions*

1. Why did the Tudor dynasty experience so many rebellions?
2. Were the disorders between 1549 and 1554 part of a continuing crisis?
3. Did sixteenth-century rebellions strengthen or weaken the Tudor regime?
4. Were Tudor rebellions 'conservative' or 'radical'?
5. Why were rebellions against the Tudors almost always unsuccessful?
6. 'Despite the government's fears, by the end of the sixteenth century the threat of rebellion had much diminished.' Discuss.

14 ✑ ANALYTICAL EXERCISE: WHY THE REBELLIONS FAILED

In the provinces, people must be able to feel that they had access to the king's Court through the great men of their area; they must have confidence in royal courts of justice; they must also be confident that their views would be heard in parliament. Parliamentary representation much increased under the Tudors, both in the number of borough seats and in the area which representation covered. Through the sixteenth century the overall number of commons representatives increased by more than 50 per cent, from around 300 to 462 in 1601.

SOURCE A
From A Fletcher and
D MacCulloch
Tudor Rebellions *(1997)*

In retrospect, it was Henry's success in defeating the Pilgrimage that made the English Reformation possible, for this was England's War of Religion. Opposition to religious change over the next two decades was muted. The defeat of the commons owed nothing to the king, but was made possible by their manipulation by the gentry and nobility of the North, many of whom were as appalled by the innovations of the mid-1530's as were the commons themselves. But one of the most striking features of that decade is the way in which the nobility and gentry exhibited solidarity with a wayward monarch. In the autumn of 1536 and the winter of 1537 they did the king a great service, in which they placed their king before their God. They were, perhaps, better servants than the king deserved.

SOURCE B
From RW Hoyle The
Pilgrimage of Grace *(2001)*

SOURCE C

*From A Fletcher and
D MacCulloch* Tudor
Rebellions *(1997)*

Thus, in the reign of Elizabeth the yeomen leadership of low politics was becoming closer to the gentry than to the class below. Literate culture was the culture of the powerful. Yeoman society began taking on the ways of the world of power; for instance, the inventories of their possessions on their deaths and their wills reveal musical instruments like virginals in their homes. Many of them took with enthusiasm to the new respectable activism of Puritan religion. They were also less inclined to use violence to express their anger; they would take their grievances to the royal law courts, and turn up in their hundreds even thousands to vote in county elections to parliament. There might be plenty of excitement and brawling on an Elizabethan election day, but it was a far cry from the slaughter of Kett's army on Mousehold Heath.

1. *What points in these extracts explain why the authors believe the rebellions failed? Does your reading of this chapter reinforce these arguments?*
2. *What other factors not mentioned in these three extracts from modern books emerge in the chapter to explain the failure of all the rebellions?*

The Economy and Society of Tudor England

13

INTRODUCTION

In 1348 a disease as terrifying as anything a bio-terrorist could dream up swept across Europe. It was plague, the Black Death. It is estimated it killed a third of the population of England at that time. Resistance to the disease was likely to have been weakened as food production had not kept up with population growth, and as the plague returned in epidemic after epidemic, the population could not recover for over 150 years. Then the grip of the plague slackened, and renewed growth in the population, sustained to the present day, began in the Tudor period. It brought with it renewed economic growth, but also much unsettling change.

Inflation, the Tudor Price Rise, got a grip by the middle of the century. The causes were much debated by contemporaries, and still are by modern scholars. But inflation did not worry those getting a better price for their goods. Taking the century as a whole, overseas trade flourished. Explorers laid the groundwork for new trade routes and colonies, and merchants brought home spices and luxury goods from around the globe. Mining and the fisheries flourished. More importantly, although there were occasional slumps, cloth remained in great demand on the Continent and improvements to its quality boosted its value; cloth production was the major industry of the country and its biggest employer after agriculture. Many towns grew, most spectacularly London, which by 1603 was on its way to being one of the leading cities of Europe. But others towns, by-passed by markets and trade routes, declined.

In the country-side those with sufficient land were able to sell surplus produce for higher prices, but others were hard-hit, they had little to sell in the good years, and were forced to buy at spiralling rates in order to eat when harvests were bad. Many could not keep going and abandoned the land, making vagrancy and poverty an increasing feature as the Tudor years passed. These developments alarmed the authorities. Their aim was to maintain the status quo and, when problems were apparent, the tendency was to blame the individual for exploitation or idleness. Largely with a view to resisting change, this became one of the first great ages of government intervention – 300 statutes dealt with economic and social affairs during the century, and many more proclamations. There was no faith in, and little understanding of, market forces. The government tried to fix both wages and prices, and failed. It resisted changes to the land market. Commentators at the time blamed sheep-farming, and the enclosure of land for that purpose, for destroying the more abundant food production and livelihoods that went with arable farming. But enclosure was a local phenomenon, much exaggerated in its effects, and the changes in the rural economy continued.

The authorities wanted everyone to know their place and the social order to remain unchanged in its hierarchy from the peers at the top, through the knights and gentry, the yeomen and other more substantial farmers, to the cottagers and finally at the bottom the landless labourers in town or country. But population pressure and economic change led to migration, a disruption of the social order associated with crime and unruliness which terrified the government. Migrants without obvious means of support were feared as 'masterless men', labelled vagrants and subject to penalties of increasing savagery. The government recognised, though, that poverty was a distinct and increasing problem and could not be addressed solely through the traditional means of voluntary donations, alms-giving. A series of Poor Laws were passed to make parishes look after the poor systematically, the greatest of these culminating in 1601, which established the system which was to last until the nineteenth century.

Contemporaries understood the problems facing them much more in moral than in economic or social terms, and the moral landscape was indeed changing. Property brought with it responsibilities – serving the government as a Justice of the Peace (JP) or other official, for instance – but those responsibilities were being modified as a notion of private property took greater hold. The medieval tradition of hospitality had demanded that a lord look after the interests of those on his manor and that he entertain strangers and his neighbours in his house. That tradition declined as lords and landowners withdrew into more private quarters. As individualism began to develop, with people supposed to look after their own interests rather than depending on the community, it was not just that the demand for charity went up under economic pressure, but it was becoming more likely that it would be refused.

This social strain lay behind many witchcraft accusations as house-holders, newly afflicted by illness or misfortune, mulled over the curse, usually by an old woman, which had followed the refusal of help. The fear of witches was not new and there was no 'witch craze' in Tudor England, but the increasing rate of accusation and prosecution was symptomatic of difficult social and economic changes, and the employ-ment of traditional beliefs to come to terms with them.

A further such change was in the status of women. This had been in part enhanced by the Protestant belief in the importance of women in the godly household, but this was entirely a domestic role. In addition, economic opportunity for women declined if anything during the sixteenth century. A good wife was supposed to stay in the home as far as possible and defer to her husband in all things. This was patriarchy – the man was the ruler of his family.

Change in Tudor society and the economy was disruptive, hard for contemporaries to understand, and their reaction was mostly one of deep conservatism. However, it was an immensely dynamic period and laid the basis for the dramatic economic and social developments which were to follow in the coming centuries.

1 ∽ POPULATION

There are no exact figures for population levels in Tudor England, because no national census existed on which we can rely. Yet a growing amount of evidence provides the basis for a clear pattern in which the Tudor years witnessed a phase of demographic growth starting around 1500, gaining momentum after 1540, and lasting into the mid-seventeenth century.

English population statistics	
1450	*c.* 2.1 million
1525	*c.* 2.3 million
1545	*c.* 2.8 million
1603	*c.* 3.8 million

The impact of this increase in numbers was wide-ranging and central to economic and social developments in the period. A rising population rate averaging 1% a year out-stripped a supply of foodstuffs which expanded much more slowly if at all, causing prices to rise as demand out-stripped supply. An increasing supply of young labour out-stripped an insufficient number of jobs, which held down wage rates as job-seekers were prepared to accept lower rates of pay to secure employment. Looking back from 1584, Richard Hakluyt remarked that 'through our long peace and seldom sickness we are grown more populous than ever heretofore'. The rise in population may have been caused by a falling mortality rate, as plague epidemics returned less frequently, and at first increasing fertility, the result of a long-term trend of prosperity.

The population estimates are the result of investigations into other matters. The first comprehensive valuation of lands and personal wealth took place in the 1520s, for taxation (1522 Subsidy) or military service (the 1524 Muster lists to show all able-bodied men). The densest areas of population were East Anglia, Essex, Devon and Cornwall, with Kent as the most populous. Least dense were the west Midlands, the North-west and West, and over 90% of the population of England and Wales was rural. The population was small compared to that of France at *c.*15 million, so that a French herald in 1549 concluded that there were 'more labourers of vines in France than people of England of all estates'.

The chief source is the parish register of births, marriages and deaths required by Thomas Cromwell from 1538 onwards, but few examples survive until the second half of the century, and they are not uniformly reliable. Enough material, though, does survive to provide us with a rough picture. The average family size was 4–5 members and some 40% of the population were under 16 years old. Life expectancy was about 35 years, though much less in the towns, and higher in the 'healthy' periods between the arrivals of the killer diseases, bubonic or pneumonic plague.

Continued harvest failure, another regular occurrence, seriously endangered those living close to subsistence level, for example in 1527

KEY ISSUE

What brought about the rise in the population of Tudor England, and what limited it?

and 1594–8. A string of poor harvests combined with sickness, as under Mary I, or from 1594–8, dented the population rise by trebling the mortality rate. Yet from 1538, existing parish registers do show an excess of births over burials as a general trend. Between 1575–84, in a sample of 400 parishes the ratio between births and deaths was 3:2.

Fertility rates were rising at the start of the sixteenth century, suggesting better, more abundant food and a higher standard of living. They declined from the middle of the century, but mortality rates had declined faster. However, these figures are tentative and reflect the experience of the 'better off' in Tudor society. By the late 1580s and 1590s the fall in wage rates was leading to later marriage and a decline in the birth rate while wars, famine and plague caused a higher mortality rate. The ratio of births to deaths in the last decade was around 1.2:1.

2 ⏴ THE PRICE RISE

The Tudor period witnessed a rise in the general price of goods and foodstuffs, although its exact impact and its causes have long been under debate. Professor RB Outhwaite has concluded that inflation before 1510 was gentle and mainly centred on agricultural prices. It was the unusual jump in these prices in the 1520s which sparked the Price Rise, and with it the end of a long-time stability in wage rates.

In 1509–10, wheat prices were at their lowest for 200 years. People were full of 'belly-cheer', allowing seed-corn, crucial for the next harvest, to be regularly kept back and not eaten. By the 1520s a rise in prices is discernible, e.g. the doubling of oats and oxen prices (1500–35) and general prices not falling back to old levels. It is possible that such inflation was not serious enough to be noticed until the 1540s, when rumblings among contemporaries do appear to have gathered pace, but by 1550 the average price of all grains was three-and-a-half times that in 1500. In the closing decades of the century, prices continued to rise with a crescendo reached in the last two decades when corn prices doubled between 1586 and 1596.

The general price rise was therefore not a steady, continuous rising curve, but included better years interspersed with periods of high inflation. Although it is impossible to establish with certainty how far prices did rise under the Tudors, rise they did, cereals leading the way with a six or sevenfold rise in the average price of all grains.

However debatable its long-term significance, debasement of the coinage was certainly a cause of inflation in the middle years of the century. The Crown's need for cash to finance the wars under Henry VIII and his son increased the need to expand the supply of coin, the equivalent of 'printing money'. A small debasement in 1526–7 was the precursor to the 'Great Debasement' of 1544–51, which perhaps doubled the volume of coins in circulation. The coincidence of poor harvests during the 1550s served to worsen the situation and caused the high price inflation of the 1540–60 period. The influx of foreign bullion began to increase in the second half of the century, to replace coin lost

The Causes of the Price Rise

The causes of the Price Rise have been ascribed either monetary or physical reasons. Monetary inflation occurs when too much money is chasing too few goods, so the price of the goods rises. Contemporaries, who had little to record on the issue before the late 1540s, emphasised the monetary cause in the debasement of the coinage – the fall in its precious metal content and subsequent value. This was the result of the Crown minting more coins with less silver in them to meet short-term needs for war expenditure. Between 1541 and 1551 there does appear to have been a near 50% fall in the exchange rate between London and Antwerp. This monetarist argument held sway until after 1945, bolstered by another group of historians for whom, however, debasement was not the issue. American historians such as Earl J Hamilton (1928) and JU Nef (1941) emphasised instead the impact of the influx of bullion from the New World – principally silver from Peru – on the European economy as a whole, including England. The switch to seeking the prime cause of the Price Rise in agricultural, industrial and demographic trends (the physical causes) came about in the 1950s in the work of historians such as Phelps-Brown and SV Hopkins. They saw monetary developments as of secondary importance to the trend towards an imbalance between population and resources under the Tudors. It was too many people chasing too few goods which was the enduring cause, rather than too much money. Professor RB Outhwaite and Professor DC Coleman have argued similarly, but have attributed to the monetarist argument the role of a catalyst. Debasement and bullion simply increased the pace of price inflation generated by the physical factors.

or exported to purchase ornamentation for house or church. Once American bullion began to arrive in sizeable quantities into Seville, it spread quickly throughout Europe by trade and Spanish armies. England's own domestic inflation was probably worsened by importing the European inflation which ensued. Sir Thomas Gresham, founder of the royal Exchange, wrote to Queen Elizabeth I:

It may please your majesty to understand that the first occasion of the fall of the exchange did grow by the king's majesty, your late father, in abasing his coin from six ounces fine to three ounces fine. Whereupon the exchange fell from 25 shillings and 8 pence to 13 shillings and 4 pence, which was the occasion that all your fine gold was conveyed out of this your realm. Secondly, by reason of his wars, the king's majesty fell into great debt in Flanders. And for the payment there of

Q

1. *What does Gresham argue were the reasons for inflation?*
2. *To what extent does Gresham's argument support a monetarist interpretation of the Price Revolution?*
3. *What are the problems of this source for the historian?*

they had no other device but to pay it by exchange, and to carry over his fine gold for the payment of the same. Thirdly, the great freedom of the Steelyard and granting of licence for the carrying of your wool and other commodities out of your realm … it may plainly appear to your highness as the exchange is the thing that eats out all princes, to the whole destruction of their common weal, if it be not substantially looked unto; so likewise the exchange is the chiefest and richest thing only above all other to restore your majesty and your realm to fine gold and silver, and is the means that makes all foreign commodities with all kinds of victuals good cheap, and likewise keeps your fine gold and silver within your realm …

PROFILE

PICTURE 30
Sir Thomas Gresham,
Robinson

SIR THOMAS GRESHAM (C. 1519–79)

The Greshams were a well-established merchant dynasty in the City of London. Thomas was educated at Cambridge and Gray's Inn and worked in the City, before first making his mark as an agent of the Crown from 1551 in the Netherlands, where he organised loans and procured armaments. Huge rates of interest were being paid on the war debt under Edward VI, and the value of English currency had spiralled downwards. Through manipulating trade flows, Gresham restored the exchange rate of the pound over two to three years from 16 Flemish shillings to 22 shillings. He took little notice of rules and regulations when they obstructed him; he once smuggled bullion out of the Netherlands under a cargo of harnesses and always made a point of getting amiably drunk with Customs House officials so they would turn a blind eye. He was a Protestant and therefore was suspect under Queen Mary's regime, although when his successor in the Netherlands could only obtain loans at a rate 2% higher than he had achieved, Gresham was reinstated. He really came into his own on the accession of Elizabeth, and was knighted in 1559. William Cecil was a close friend. He put forward a successful five-point plan to build up England's economic strength: (1) restore the coinage; (2) deprive foreign merchants of their privileges in England; (3) grant few licences to trade freely; (4) borrow at home rather than abroad; and (5) maintain good credit with English merchants. His name was also given to Gresham's law, the economic principle that 'bad money drives out good', that is, when debased coinage is put into circulation alongside money with a higher content of precious metals, the good money is withdrawn from circulation by hoarders.

Gresham returned to the Netherlands, much to the distress of his wife, who, he wrote, 'molests him dayly for [his] coming home, such is the fondness of women'. There he assured England's defences by devious as well as fair means. He spread a rumour that Elizabeth had 200 ships ready to fight off any Spanish force. He exported weapons as 'velvets' and even managed to acquire 2000 corslets from the Spanish armoury. The only problem was gossip in London which almost betrayed him and his accomplices in the Customs House. Gresham did not just cheat the Spanish. Through creative accounting he made a great deal of money out of the Crown. Auditors tried to reclaim it, but Elizabeth, recognising his worth to the government, over-ruled them. By 1565 he was in a position to realise a dream of his father's, to build what became the Royal Exchange, as a focus for all business in the City of London, and which was to become one of the foundations of the City's pre-eminence in European and global finance. He persuaded the City authorities and the Mercers Company to give him the land for it on the agreement that he would pay for the building and leave it to them in his will. He did, but his last trick was to specify that the rent was not theirs to spend but had to be devoted to the establishment of Gresham College to provide learned free lectures for the City; the Gresham lectures still take place. He died of a heart attack in 1579.

Yet it was the steady, constant increase in the population which gave the inflationary period of the sixteenth century its characteristic length, and helps to explain the marked difference between the cost of food, which was the prime need of an increasing population, and that of manufactured goods, which rose only two or threefold. And cheap grains rose fastest in price, as families, with more mouths to feed, consumed those rather than more expensive foods.

The Price Rise had a vital impact upon Tudor society and was the underlying cause of many of the economic and social developments. To survive inflationary pressures, some extended the cultivation area to include more marginal, less productive land; others were forced to become landless labourers hiring out their services in the locality if it could support them, while a third group migrated to the towns. Speedy changes to productivity levels were unlikely, given the basic nature of agricultural technology and the cost of land reclamation or use of marginal land. As the expanding population steadily increased demand for foodstuffs in short supply, the Price Rise was the inevitable result of such market forces. In manufacturing, the growing labour supply depressed wage rates, which made it all the harder to make ends meet.

Sustained harvest failure could lead to real hardship, without the insulation of wages inclusive of food and drink, the dual economy (workers doing two jobs) and bartering. By contrast the better-off were protected from inflation by income from production, tithes, **demesne** produce kept for their own consumption, and by rents in kind, i.e. produce rather than money. Population growth was the driving force then behind the Price Rise, but debasement of the coinage and the import of bullion provided added momentum, along with natural disasters like harvest failure. It is against this backdrop that the Tudor economy and social policy must be understood.

KEY ISSUE

What were the causes of the Price Rise in the sixteenth century, and what were its principal effects?

Demesne the 'home farm', the land farmed directly by the landlord rather than let to a tenant

3 ⌐ OVERSEAS TRADE

The expansion of overseas trade during the Tudor century marked a significant step forward for England on the international stage. At its outset, the country was a minor player in international commerce; by the close, English ships were to be found engaged in trade war over much of the known world, with London at the centre.

The early part of the sixteenth century was not free of regulation, but the contrast between this and the later period is clear. The 1485 Navigation Act sought to encourage English shipping and seamanship by forbidding the import of wine in foreign vessels. The dominating export commodity of the first half of the century was woollen cloth, which boomed under the early Tudors to reach 130 000 cloths a year by 1550, some 75% of the value of all exports. Cloth export was regulated by Henry VII in 1485 to include only those unfinished cloths of low value, so that finer cloths could be domestically finished and thus sold abroad at higher value added. Woollen cloth was the lynchpin for Henry VII's 'Magnus Intercursus' (1496) establishing the London–Antwerp trading axis in unfinished broadcloth and the lighter cloth known as kerseys. Customs revenue consequently rose from an average of £33 000 a year (1485–95) to £50 000 (1518–20), before settling at around £35 000 under Henry VIII whose wars did little to improve trade.

At the hub of activity were the trading companies: the Merchants of the Staple (London and Calais) who had the monopoly of woollen cloth (granted in 1550), and the Merchant Adventurers who dealt in everything else. They became the most powerful English business organisation, controlling entry to trade and pursuing **protectionist** policies (as Wrightson points out, adventurers they were certainly not), although foreign merchants, e.g. the **Hanseatic League** of North German merchants, still controlled a sizeable portion of trade (40–50%).

The importance of cloth for customs revenue clearly became central but there were also a wide range of imports in early Tudor trade: for instance, wine and wood from France, and herring, cod and dried fish from Scandinavia. The Company of Fishmongers had six separate halls in the City and by 1532 were ranked fourth among the guilds of London merchants, the livery companies. Wrought iron was brought from Spain, barley and malt sent to Flanders in return for sweet wine, glass, raisins, paper, dyestuffs and manufactured goods. The prospect of new commercial markets encouraged Henry VII to promote the explorations of John and Sebastian Cabot to Newfoundland (1496) and to Hudson's Bay (1506). In the 1530s William Hawkins penetrated Upper Guinea (West Africa) for pepper and ivory, later extending out to Brazil for dyewood in return for slaves.

The London–Antwerp cloth axis which so dominated the years 1485–1550 was much less influential during the latter half of the sixteenth century. Clashes with Spain and the closing of Antwerp's Scheldt river, all contributed to the search for new foreign commercial centres. It is this period which witnessed the growing regulation and intervention of the Crown through the Privy Council. The withdrawal of privileges in

Protectionist restrictions on trade designed to give the home country advantage

Hanseatic League the Hanse was a powerful association of trading ports along the coasts of Germany and Scandinavia, and in the Baltic. Hanseatic merchants co-operated in trading ventures in various parts of Europe

See pages 261–2

the 1550s afforded to foreign traders such as those of the Hanseatic League, based in the Steelyard area of London, was supported by a Crown needing money from customs revenues and with a vested interest in promoting native trading companies. The development of lighter, more, colourful cloth mixtures ('New Draperies') and a growing demand for them in the Mediterranean also helped to diversify away from the Netherlands, which had hitherto had pretty well a monopoly on imports.

New trading companies were established by 'new men' readier to take risks than established merchants; they were centred on London, given monopoly control and backed by the government. From 1555–87 the Muscovy Company, the first **joint-stock company**, was founded to trade with Russia and was heavily backed by the Court. In 1579 the Eastland Company was chartered to import goods from the Baltic, the Levant Company was founded to trade with the Ottomans in 1581, and the East India Company, destined in future centuries to rule much of India, was founded in 1601 to trade directly with oriental countries in spices and pepper.

Merchant shipping increased quite dramatically under Elizabeth. In 1560 there were some 70 ships between 100–199 tonnes and six over 200 tonnes – by 1582 they numbered 155 and 18 respectively. Privateering (licensed piracy) in the Caribbean at the expense of Spain provided a commercial benefit as Drake's exploits at Nombre de Dios testified, as did his voyage round the world in 1578–80. Between 1584–7 there was a failed attempt in America to settle Roanoke Island off Virginia, to provide raw materials, to promote Christianity and to challenge Spain by driving them 'out of trade to idleness' (Sir Richard Hakluyt).

The profit motive led English merchants to cut out foreign middle-men wherever possible, whether Italian, Netherlander or Hanseatic, and to trade directly in finished goods. The economic theory behind this was **mercantilism**. By 1600, unfinished Old Draperies were still at the 1540 figure (125 000 cloths a year), whereas New Draperies had grown proportionally to represent 20% of total exports. However, it was growing domestic demand for foreign luxury goods such as Spanish leather, French wine, Portuguese and Levant spices, sugar from Morocco (Barbary Company 1585–97) and fashion, which provided an added incentive since profit margins were high.

Martin Frobisher's search for a North-west passage to the East and its spice trade was similarly motivated. It was built on the search for fish which had taken boats to Newfoundland and beyond. By 1603 overseas trade looked to wider horizons than in 1485 and the English presence in world trade was much greater and over longer distances. At the centre of business lay the City of London, grown enormously in size and influence at the expense of the old traditional 'outports' like Southampton and Hull, whose late medieval heyday, continuing under the early Tudors, had gone.

Joint-stock company
the pooling by a group of merchants of investment, risk and profit on a lasting basis, rather than just coming together venture by venture

Mercantilism the economic theory behind protectionism in the sixteenth century, based on the belief that the economic power of a country could be measured by the amount of bullion it amassed. This led to export drives, discouragement of imports and Navigation Acts designed to restrict trade as far as possible to English ships

KEY ISSUE

What were the main sources of England's wealth in overseas trade?

4 ⌐ TOWNS

Towns were small by comparison with Europe, except for London which grew from a population of 50 000 in 1500 to 100 000 by 1570, and 200 000 by 1600. Norwich came in second with only 13 000 at the end of the sixteenth century. Bristol, Newcastle and Coventry numbered some 10 000, Northampton and Leicester perhaps only 3000. Only about 10% of the population were urban dwellers, with country towns often numbering hundreds only. The major urban areas were mainly located in the south and eastern half of the country, thus contributing to the long-term migration from the north and west to the south and east.

A significant development was the growth of London during the sixteenth century, part of a process which saw its population grow from 2% of the total population in 1520, to 11% by 1700. This growth resulted from foreign and native rural immigration in search of employment, plus the greater opportunities for begging, crime and poor relief. London's magnetic attraction was based upon its strengthening position as the country's trading and financial centre. Its very size attracted service

PICTURE 31

Elizabethan London: Londinium Feracissimi Angliae Regni Metropolis (1572) in Civitas Orbis Terrarum, *Vol. 1612–18*

industries and the food and fuel distribution trades. Spices, dried fruit and luxuries such as silks and calicoes were sold by a burgeoning number of middlemen. Above all, London was the centre of the cloth trade.

London's rise to pre-eminence did cause its problems. A rising volume of death from starvation or disease (as shown in 1563 when around 20 000, in the region of one in five of the population, died from the plague) was matched by rising unemployment and house prices. Already, by 1550, Robert Crowley complained of landlords raising rents 'some double, some triple and some four-fold to that they were within these twelve years past'. Religious radicalism was spawned from the prevailing conditions, helped by the capital's role as an educational centre through the Inns of Court, and as a centre for book publication. It was the first town or city to have an organised scheme of Poor Relief (1547), itself a measure of the problems it faced. What is surprising given the extremes of economic and social conditions, is the relative dearth of riot throughout the sixteenth-century boom years for the capital.

Outside the town walls usually lay an area of shacks (the suburbs), whose populace was frequently outside the legal jurisdiction of the town authorities. Within the walls workshops were situated either inside or in front of the houses with rarely more than four or five employees per workshop. Many townspeople had a plot of land as well, and **partible inheritance** was the norm rather than **primogeniture**, which was normal amongst landowners. Conditions were often dirty and cramped, with a growing number of poor, both able-bodied and 'impotent', seeking alms, work or relief in all Tudor towns, a problem which was to worsen by the 1590s. Between 1532–42 over 1400 apprentices were attracted into Bristol from the West Country, and such an influx of migrants could cause higher house prices. In 1534 the Worcester authorities had to institute a rent freeze.

The 800 or so market towns and cities were centres for a wide range of occupations. By 1525 Norwich, admittedly the second city, had over 80 different crafts and trades. Most large towns were similarly structured, though often built around one specialist craft or trade e.g. cloth (Lavenham in Suffolk) or leather (Nottingham). Other common urban occupations were metalwork, building and food distribution, though over 40% of urban workers seem to have worked in textiles in the 1520s, highlighting the centrality of cloth.

The guardians of craft traditions and the welfare of their members were the urban gilds, which sought to control entry to the craft or 'mystery', keep an eye on production levels and quality, enforce apprenticeship regulations, and set wages and prices. The gilds were, however, in general decline under the Tudors, the result of changing trading patterns, an increasing labour supply, new industries creating alternative employment, and increasing state regulation. Gilds, however, maintained their role as networks of social privilege. London's 150 gilds included the 12 Livery companies which were all well-trodden paths to power within the City. The ruling urban oligarchies were usually self-perpetuating within the one or two leading families.

KEY ISSUE

What were the consequences of the growth of London in the sixteenth century?

Partible inheritance is when the land is divided among all the sons of a land-owner on his death

Primogeniture is when all the land goes to the eldest son

Some towns were facing a crisis in the first half of the sixteenth century. Disease, the loss of trade to London, competition from other areas or from outside the town's immediate jurisdiction and even the clothier's **'putting-out' system**, all contributed in some part to the urban decline. In his Discourse of the Common Weal (1549), Sir Thomas Smith highlighted that 'not only the good towns are decayed sore in their houses, streets and other buildings, but also the country in their highways and bridges'. Old clothing towns suffered (e.g. Lincoln and York), as well as the outports.

By the early years of Elizabeth a degree of recovery was visible. In Norwich greater diversification into clothes had begun to take place. Building and allied trades were expanding, as was the supply of imported luxuries. A similar story can be seen in York, Bristol and Exeter as they developed as provincial capitals, with gentlemen building town houses requiring service industries, and new occupations such as vintners and brewers being established. There is evidence then of urban renewal generated by the growing wealth of the local landowners, by the end of the century.

> **Putting-out system**
> industrial labour practised at home usually in rural areas rather than in a workshop in a town; the merchant would bring the raw materials and collect the finished product afterwards, so keeping a firm control on the profits

5 ～ THE DOMESTIC ECONOMY

A *Infra-structure*

The vast majority of trade during the period was undertaken within the country, perhaps between 90 and 95%. Much of it travelled by roads suitable for droving cattle or pack-horses, by river, and by coastal shipping. Goods made their way to market towns or to ports for shipment to London or abroad; inward cargoes were broken up at main centres and then distributed out across the country to reach small towns and villages.

Coastal trade was massive in volume, comprising both foreign and domestic goods such as grain and coal, and transported via head-ports like Bristol and York. Coal from Newcastle in the 1590s went overwhelmingly for domestic use, as did Cornish tin. To ease transport problems and in typically regulatory fashion, the Tudors passed eight Acts of Parliament to help improve or maintain rivers. Apart from the Thames, the three other great trading rivers were the Great Ouse, the Severn and the Trent. The use of roads was much less economic for bulky transport. They were primarily for droving animals, carrying carts, and for people, enabling traders to meet at the fairs of many of the market towns in England and Wales. The first road map of nine long distance routes out of London was published in 1541.

B *The role of foreign investment and expertise*

To compensate for England's backwardness in commerce and industry the early Tudors, especially Henry VII, attracted foreign immigrants to introduce new processes, and to stimulate native production. Many of the foreigners wanted to make profits in a relatively undeveloped commercial nation, or were seeking religious or racial refuge. Before 1550, around 40 per cent of the cloth trade lay in the hands of the Hanseatic merchants, Flemings, Italians and French, centred on the Blackfriars Liberty and the Steelyard area, both outside the City of London's jurisdiction. The 3000 alien craftsmen of 1500 had risen to 10 000 by 1540. However, there were political pressures on the Crown from English merchants and gilds which led to restrictions whereby no alien was allowed to own land, had to pay twice the amount of tax, and were only allowed to exercise their crafts and trades in a specified area. In 1534 aliens were prohibited from work as pewterers, printers and bookbinders as the Crown sought to protect and stimulate native employment in this area. The revocation of the Hanseatic League's privileges in the 1550s at the request of the trading companies was similarly motivated. Some aliens did seek 'denization' (naturalisation) which could lead to an easing of these restrictions.

Foreign expertise often lay at the heart of new developments in manufacturing. A Frenchman, Peter Bauck, established an iron-smelting industry in the Sussex Weald and also produced a bronze cannon for Henry VIII in 1533. Foreigners introduced the notion of mixing wool with silk to create the New Draperies, and established paper-milling. What these new industries all had in common was the support of the Crown, unlike the restrictions placed on older industries where there was more competition from English interests, as cited above. The Crown protected and regulated the new industries by issuing patents giving a temporary monopoly and, therefore, high profits. It was a crude but quite effective way of stimulating domestic production and employment, advancing native manufacturing and of reducing foreign imports with their detrimental effects on the balance of payments at a time of high inflation.

C *Government intervention in the economy*

One notable feature of the Tudor economy was the growing level of government involvement to regulate and stimulate it. There was certainly no really coherent economic policy behind this interventionism, it was much more a series of ad hoc responses to circumstances and problems, and as the Tudor era wore on, examples of government intervention grew in number. Between 1485 and 1603, over 300 Acts of Parliament were passed to regulate economic affairs. Most of these laid down penalties for stipulated offences, and the rest were permissive laws allowing or prompting specific economic behaviour. Supervision of laws was patchy and sporadic, however, with local constables sometimes reticent to hand matters over to the Justice of the Peace, and they in turn were sometimes reluctant to enforce regulations if unemployment might result. Much of penal enforcement relied heavily upon the testimony of 'promoters and informers', often of the 'meaner sort' who would receive a proportion of the fine upon conviction.

The Crown also used its powers of patronage to control and promote activity through the grants of licences, patents and monopolies. Licences often exempted individuals from statutes or proclamation, such as that which allowed Robert Dudley, Earl of Leicester, to import cloth; or else they were used to appoint agents for the Crown, as with Seler's licence to develop a salt industry. Patents were granted by the Crown to help new industries, providing a temporary monopoly in return for cash. Soap, glass, paper, saltpetre and playing cards were all examples of such, although by the end of the sixteenth century patents were open to corruption, often relating to existing industries rather than encouraging innovation, and offering profitable benefits to courtiers. Monopolistic control of goods and processes by courtiers caused much hostility after Robert Bell's protest in the 1571 Parliament. It returned again in 1592, and became the main issue of the 1601 session, calling into question the Queen's prerogative and forcing a measure of retreat by the Crown when the 1602 *Darcy* v. *Allen* case, over the monopoly of playing cards, found against such a use of monopolies.

Government intervention was also required to regulate and control the food supply. Good harvest years left the country with a sufficiency, but poor years meant a huge deficit with more mouths to be fed. Statute was used to control the export of grain. Until 1534 a fifteenth-century law setting a threshold price of 6s 8d per quarter, above which export was forbidden, was applicable, and this was raised in 1563 and in 1593. Shrewsbury Council imported 3200 bushels of corn from the Baltic through the Eastland Company in 1596, to provide bread for the poor, and local officials generally were empowered to search for grain supplies following a poor harvest.

While boroughs regulated their markets for prices, weights and measures, Crown action was required to deal with supply problems in the corn areas, ranging from the hoarding of grain to forestalling (buying grain before it came on the open market). Corn merchants or 'badgers' were closely monitored and a statute of 1532 required a badger to be licensed by three Justices of the Peace, and from 1563 the licence was to be renewed. Crown supervision up to 1563 relied on local Justices of the Peace, sheriffs and town councils for information, but thereafter detailed supervision was given over to a Commission for grain. Price fixing on a national scale, as Henry VIII had attempted on meat, beer, wine and sugar, was not resorted to (except on wine), during the Elizabethan years, when market price and a degree of regulation were preferred.

D *The significance of the cloth industry*

England's reputation as a key primary producer of raw wool was superseded after 1500 by her status as a supplier of woollen cloth. Cloth was the commodity which kept idle and poor hands busy, becoming the undoubted pillar of the economy. Between the mid-fifteenth and the mid-seventeenth centuries, the value of English textile exports rose five to six times in real terms, i.e. taking inflation into account. The industry employed many thousands of mostly part-time employees, and in 1555 the cloth entrepreneurs (clothiers) were prohibited by the Weavers Act from centralising looms in one place to cut costs at the expense of jobs for the poor out-workers. Central to the industry was the 'putting-out' system, whereby clothiers hired out looms to a large number of families to produce the cloth from wool. Thus agrarian employment was combined with manufacturing, and, according to Wrightson, this was one of the major economic developments of the period. Within the family, children carded the wool, women spun and men wove and did some elementary finishing. Despite this more efficient division of labour, the workforce made up 60% of costs.

The main production areas were the West Riding, the West Country and above all East Anglia, which contributed 25% of national production. The core area of south Suffolk and north Essex around Lavenham became the densest area of population in Tudor England, after London. Traditional 'Old Draperies' of white, undressed, woollen cloth comprised the short broadcloth of the North and the finer kerseys of the South. Success in turn attracted more people to swell the labour supply, causing industrial growth, but a trade depression in cloth, as in the 1550s, or a run of poor harvests, could quickly cause unemployment and starvation, which would ripple back to wool supply areas e.g. Wales or Lincolnshire.

The New Draperies marked a further development in the cloth trade and were the result of diversification after the depression of the mid-century. Government support for skilled foreign immigrants with new technology attracted Protestant refugees from the Netherlands during the 1560–70s, who settled in East and South-east England. They brought continental techniques and styles, mixing worsted yarns – even silk – with the wool, to produce lighter, more colourful and cheaper cloths such as 'bays and says'.

E *Mining, the fisheries and building*

Mining industries also began to be exploited more intensively. In 1500 the rich mineral resources of tin, lead and coal were hardly scratched. Major sources were the Northumberland and Durham field, centred on the outport of Newcastle, and in north Lancashire and the Forest of Dean. The income generated did not just go to merchants but also to nobles, such as the Percy family, and Thomas, Lord Darcy, in Yorkshire.

Lead and tin were mined from the Pennines, the Mendips and Cornwall, both metals being in high demand in Europe. Cornish tin production doubled from 1490–1550. Iron-smelting, producing cast-iron in new blast furnaces using charcoal from the Sussex and Kent Wealds, was another notable development to meet the demands of naval dockyards. The three furnaces of the 1530s had grown to 26 in 30 years, and the industry spread to the Forest of Dean and to the west Midlands around Dudley, to produce cannon, shot and wrought-iron. Some deforestation, e.g. in the Weald, was caused by the expanding need for timber to make charcoal, itself a growing industry.

Ship-building and fishing were large employers of labour, especially on the east coast. Henry VII encouraged the building of a merchant fleet by giving cash support (1488–91), and a dry dock was built at Portsmouth (1495–7). His son established naval dockyards at Deptford (1513) and these gradually grew in importance, owing to the improved navigability of the Thames, and their proximity to London.

One of the liveliest industries under the Tudors was the building trade and allied occupations, e.g. quarrying. In the 1570s William Harrison was told by old men of his parish that, along with improvements to bedding and the use of pewter instead of wood bowls, the third thing 'marvellouslie altered' was 'the multitude of chimnies latelie erected'. Some people at least could afford not to be smoked. Evidence from parish churches clearly suggests a great deal of building between 1480–1540, and a growing use of stained glass, mostly funded by wealthy local families. Both Canterbury Cathedral and Bath Abbey contain significant amounts of work from this period, emphasising that monasteries were adding to their buildings and were increasingly important local employers until the 1530s. Furthermore, the houses of the wealthy élite were changing from a primarily defensive role, to one of peaceful, leisured residence, though this was less the case near the Scottish border. The early Tudors witnessed the dawning of the English Country House of two or three storeys. Bradgate (Leicestershire) and Compton Wynyates (Warwickshire) are both good examples. Henry VIII's own expenditure on such buildings as Hampton Court was over £60 000 between 1536 and 1539.

F *Employment and wages*

The Tudor governments took responsibility for establishing hours of work, wages and employment conditions. They took it that a fair day's work for a fair day's pay (as defined by the authorities) was a matter of moral order as much as an economic issue. By a statute of 1495, hours of work were regulated into a national pattern. From March to September a 14–15 hour day was worked, at other times dawn until dusk. This pattern was kept constant throughout the Tudor era and lasted until the nineteenth century. A 65–75 hour week was balanced by the slow pace of work and over 50 holidays in pre-Reformation England, reduced to 27 by the Protestant regime in 1552, who took exception to holidays 'spent miserably in drunkenness, in glossing, in strife, in dancing, dicing, idleness and gluttony' (Hugh Latimer).

Under the early Tudors, government and local corporations shared responsibility for setting wages. A 1389 law empowered JPs to assess wage rates within government prescribed limits. This was re-enacted in 1514, with some adjustment to reduce the growing disparity between wage levels. Wages varied between trades, and between craftsmen and labourers. Wages could often include meat and drink and the money wage would differ accordingly. In 1519 labourers were to be paid 1 penny per day, with meat and drink, a vital advantage in later years of inflation, while master craftsmen were to be paid 6 pence per day, exclusive of food and drink, and semi-skilled labour received 4 pence per day. The average income of the lowest class of wage-earner must have been between £2 and £2 10s per year for those in continual work, out of which was to be found rent, fuel, light, clothing and food. Inflation ate away at these fixed rates, and by mid-century the wage rates for agricultural labourers had fallen by possibly 40% in real terms.

The great landmark of government regulatory policy for employment and wages, indeed one of the major statutes of the Tudor era, was the Statute of **Artificers** (1563). It set out to enforce a universal obligation to work and to provide employment for that workforce. The background for the Statute was the commercial crisis of the 1550s, particularly the decline in woollen cloth exports which caused unemployment. There were also the economic consequences of an epidemic of the 'sweating sickness', the virulence of which created short-term labour shortage and applied an upward pressure on wage rates. Enormously comprehensive in its range of regulation, the Act targeted the young, single and full-time worker rather than the casual or part-time labourers (who were not dealt with until a statute of 1598).

Under the 1563 Act, all able unemployed persons were required to seek work and had to accept the offer of regular employment: men in farming, girls in service. All unmarried persons under the age of 30 were forced to serve any employer who needed them for agriculture and food production at harvest, and they were to be trained and employed in a craft. All males between 12 and 60, and women up to the age of 40, were to work on the land unless gentry born, heirs to lands worth more than £10 p.a. or to goods above £40 p.a., or else involved in occupations such as a skilled craft, education, mining, metalwork, seafaring or the grain market. To restrict migration and vagrancy, binding contracts of service of one-year hire minimum were imposed on servant or workman, with testimonials required before leaving the parish and only with 'due cause'.

The impact of the Statute was not as profound as the government had hoped. Its creators underestimated the enormous volume of unemployment generated by the economic conditions of the last third of the century; they were reacting to mid-century experiences when price inflation had only recently been grasped. The Act did not provide fair wages much beyond the short term, but held them down relative to the inflation of the 1560–1600 period. The prohibition of wages 'in kind' in 1566 removed a hedge against inflation and forced the labourer into the full blizzard of the money economy. Furthermore, assessments were generally made in the summer before harvest, thereby condemning wage levels to lag behind prices. Such was the distress caused by the calamities of the 1590s that the authorities in Chester increased its wage assessment by nearly 20% between 1593 and 1597.

Artificer a craftsman

G *Conclusion*

The many stresses and strains in society as the economy developed, the volatility in prices, the growth in trade and investment in cloth and other industries, the expansion around the globe in search of new sources of wealth, the accelerating expansion of London, and the anxiety which brought about intervention by the government, were the

Subsistence production for home consumption rather than sale on the open market

KEY ISSUE

In what ways did the domestic economy develop in the Tudor period, and what were the stresses and strains involved?

birth pangs of a modern capitalist market economy. This was to be accompanied by the development of individualism, profit-seeking and risk-taking, as opposed to communal solidarity, a **subsistence** economy and the traditional way of doing things. The market economy was only just stirring under the Tudors and was to gather force through the remainder of the Early Modern Period, but as Keith Wrightson asserts, it was overall 'a period of change just as momentous as the later era of industrialization'.

6 ↷ THE STRUCTURE OF RURAL SOCIETY

The source of all social, military and political power and wealth was the ownership of land, and the greatest landowner was the monarch. In addition the Crown enjoyed full ownership of land, and therefore all landowners held their land by some form of tenancy, if only from the Crown, technically in return for military service, although this had largely lapsed. Land-owning contained certain seigneurial rights, e.g. the holding of the manor (leet) court, of fairs and markets, of exploiting mineral wealth and water rights. Tudor England was divided into approximately 50 000 manors, the majority having an absentee landlord and being run by his steward.

At the head of the social structure was the peerage. Numbers for the sixteenth century were fairly constant at around 50–60, once the early Tudors had established themselves. There was a wide variation in income, but under the early Tudors the wealthiest were the Duke of Buckingham (£6000 a year) until 1521 and the Archbishop of Canterbury (£5400), down to just below £1000 at the bottom, based on the 1523 Assessment. Peers were privileged to enjoy trial by their equals, not to be arrested for debt or petty crime, nor to suffer branding. They sought to keep their ancestral lands intact, to provide for a son's patrimony and a daughter's dowry, and to avoid the dangers of attainder with the confiscation of family estates by the Crown. Equally damaging was dying without male heir, which often caused partition of estates, or with young children under the age of majority, which led to wardship. In 1510 and 1533 the so-called sumptuary laws regulated what social classes could and could not wear, further distinguishing the peerage. Another distinguishing feature was the right of 'retaining' followers, 'fee'dmen' (men paid a fee) wearing a lord's uniform or badge, his livery.

Knights made up the next stratum of society, again varying in wealth, but according to Professor Hoskins averaging about £200 a year in the early Tudor years. In 1600, Thomas Wilson estimated the number of knights at around 500, though around 350 might be more accurate. Knighthood was not a hereditary right but had to be confirmed, usually by the ruler, and was distinguished by the right to use a coat of arms. Also, with the right to wear armorial badges, were the squires, owning at least one manor, if not several, with an income of around £80 a year, and numbering perhaps 1000 in Henrician times. Along with the squires were the gentry, without the right to wear arms, but generally recognised to be landowners of substance, of honest reputation, who were allowed to call themselves 'gent'. Together the squires and gentry made up around 3000 men, many being the younger sons of peers, knights and squires, or of rich merchants and lawyers. Gentry were expected to own lands above £10 a year in value.

Below the gentlemen were the yeomen, difficult to define precisely except that they were solidly wealthy, made a decent living from farming a substantial acreage, but did not have sufficient land or reputation to enter the gentry lists. The yeomen were the economic backbone in the agricultural economy, producing a surplus and so in a position to accumulate capital as prices rose. Wrightson has stressed their importance to the market economy which was to develop in England in the Early Modern period and transform the country in the centuries to come.

See page 348

The middling farmer of the Tudor era, known as a husbandman, farmed perhaps 10–30 acres held on a variety of leases, with little if any of his own land, while the cottager farmer had smaller acreage and often undertook some form of extra cottage industry to supplement and regulate income levels. When harvests were bad, they had to buy food and were hard hit by rising prices. At the bottom of the social scale were the many landless labourers, who hired out their labour in return for wage payment, and the bondmen, still technically serfs. Their numbers were reducing during the century. In 1500, in Fawcett in Norfolk, there were eight bondmen of the Duke of Norfolk, but by 1575 none existed. That same year Elizabeth I gave 300 of her bondmen to Sir Henry Lee who arranged for them to purchase their freedom.

Relationships within the working structure of rural society were cemented by the system of landholding. Large landowners would hold land as tenants of the Crown 'in capite', in return for a nominal rent but allowing the Crown to maintain its medieval dues and customs such as wardship. Within the manor there existed free tenants, customary tenants and leaseholders. Free tenants enjoyed absolute security, paying a token or 'quit rent' to the lord, unchanged since medieval times, and could do what they wanted with the land. Customary tenants were the most numerous by far, and in the Henrician period constituted some 60% of the whole tenancy according to Tawney. Land was held according to the custom of the manor and a copy of the lease was held in the Manor Court, hence these tenants were known as copyholders. Those copyholders who held land by inheritance were in the strongest position, paying a fixed annual rent and a fixed level of entry fine (i.e. payment when first taking over the land) at a time of rising income for them as producers. Other copyholders held land for two or three named lives or for a specified number of years, all with fixed or variable fines payable to the lord on entry to the land. This majority lacked the guarantees and protection afforded by manorial custom and depended ultimately upon the lord's goodwill and market conditions. At a time of land shortage, unfixed entry fines or annual rent levels meant a higher price for the tenant to find once the copyhold expired.

As the population and prices rose, the terms of tenancies became more difficult, entry fines increased, and periods of leases were shortened as landowners exerted more pressure at first to defend their own real income in the face of inflation, but as customary rates and limits weakened in the process, more and more on the look-out for increased profit. This gave rise to social discontent. In 1536 the rebels of the Pilgrimage of Grace wanted entry fines limited to two years' rent.

Finally, among the tenantry, the tenants-at-will held their land at the will of the landlord and could be summarily evicted, with no protection in common law or manorial custom. Usually they were made up of the poorest cottagers and over the century faced a rise in rentals with which their income could not keep pace.

KEY ISSUE

Which social groups were most resilient, and which most vulnerable, in Tudor rural society?

7 ↳ ENCLOSURE

The vast majority of the Tudor population was involved in some form of farming. Agriculture remained mainly conservative in its style for most of the period, but there were changes and these were a source of intense controversy for contemporaries. The conflict centred upon the issue of enclosure. In 1497 an Italian visitor remarked that English farmers were 'so lazy and slow that they do not bother to sow more wheat than is necessary for their own consumption; they prefer to let the ground be transformed into pasture for the use of the sheep that they breed in large numbers'. Perhaps not the most reliable, unbiased view.

Enclosure was not new; it had been practised long before the Tudors. The loss of up to a third of the population from the Black Death of the mid-fourteenth century, and the slow rate of recovery, had meant that many farmhouses had fallen into ruin in the meantime. Wars and plague made tenants difficult to find and landlords laid grass as the best alternative solution, being less labour intensive, less costly because wages were relatively high, and easier to maintain with sheep cropping the grass and fertilising the land. Demand, firstly for raw wool and then for woollen cloth for export and home consumption, made pasture farming more profitable than arable, and this provided the incentive for some of the Tudor enclosures.

For its detractors, enclosure was responsible for many of rural society's problems – high prices of grain, depopulation, unemployment and starvation threatening law and order. Some of the criticism was justified but much was over-done. Enclosure often took place by mutual agreement between landlord and tenants. It was not a national phenomenon but concentrated in various regions. The particular areas prone to enclosure were those areas of the country of mainly mixed farming (cereals and livestock) in the Midlands and the South-east.

Enclosure was a wide term used to include hedging and cultivating waste ground, consolidating the arable strips of the large open fields and dividing common pasture. However, it did also include the extinction of common rights over a piece of land by hedging or fencing, and this caused problems in times of rising population when the use of ancient common land was at a premium. Common rights of pasturage were essential to manure arable fields, and to provide grazing opportunities for the livestock of small cottagers or husbandmen. Here lay the battleground between sheep and grain, landlord and tenant.

Furthermore, the nature of land tenure in the area was important. Customary tenants were protected by manorial courts, but tenants-at-will and copyhold leaseholders were not. It was they who were more easily evicted or who could not pay the higher rental for a new lease. They had to rely on government action, look to rebellion or add to the swelling number of unemployed and wage labour. They had powerful sympathisers who gave enclosures a bad press for its negative effects on the whole community. Thomas More complained in Utopia of that 'covetous and insatiable cormorant' the encloser, and that sheep did 'eat up and swallow down the very men themselves'. Later in the century there were the 'Commonwealth Men', who urged economic as well as religious reformation, including the cleric Hugh Latimer, the pamphleteer Robert Crowley, Thomas Smith and William Cecil.

Tudor government tried to control and regulate the excesses of changes to land use. Between 1485 and 1597, 11 Acts of Parliament were passed against depopulation and enclosure, eight Royal Commissions investigated illegal enclosures, and a welter of proclamations was issued too. The problem of government ministers was to balance the profitability of the cloth industry with the need to feed and employ the rising population. As landowners themselves, their interests could conflict. Much illicit enclosure since 1488 was discovered, but the cost of litigation and the threat of eviction caused only one conviction out of 22 cases brought to court in Leicestershire, a problem area.

Enclosure and depopulation, according to peasants, preachers and pamphleteers, became the cause of uprooting husbandmen, destroying farmhouses and causing a shortage of grain. Sheep became the symbol of such discontent, and the new Protestant regime of the Protector Somerset could not afford economic disturbances to threaten its political and religious policies. Commissions were sent out in June 1548 to gather evidence of enclosure, the closing off of land for a private park or hunting ground (emparking), the combination of two or more farms into one (engrossing), and conversion from arable to pasture, all perceived sins against the Commonwealth and the causes of grain shortage and rising prices. The only Commission to complete its work was in the south Midlands, which made a point of principle by having a furrow ploughed across the Earl of Warwick's lands.

See page 140

To stimulate a return to arable farming a tax on sheep was introduced for a short time from March to November 1549, charged at 1 pence per sheep over 150, and 8 pence per £1 on every cloth in store. In the same year one of the Commonwealth Men, Thomas Smith, argued in his 'A Discourse of the Common Weal of this Realm of England' that the government should promote 'every man to set plough in the ground, to husband waste grounds, yea to turn the lands which be enclosed from pasture to arable land; for every man will be the gladder to follow that wherein they see the more profit and gain'. However, the mid-century collapse in the cloth market led to a reduction in the controversy, and the rising price of cereals made enclosure less attractive under Elizabeth until the disastrously poor harvests of the mid-1590s led to the highlighting of the issue once again. Acts of Parliament in 1595–7 required lands which had been arable for 12 years before conversion to be restored to arable.

The enclosure controversy was substantially, if not entirely, a problem of Norfolk and the south and east Midlands, and although it reached its height in the early sixteenth century, much of it had already taken place before 1485. Some half to three-quarters of a million acres were enclosed, of which a large percentage was arable land, but it did not happen quickly or uniformly. And enclosure did not always mean a permanent shift from arable to sheep farming. In the later period the desire for convertible husbandry (land which could be switched between arable and livestock use), stimulated enclosure as arable prices rose to generate higher incomes for producers.

Enclosure did signify an underlying shift in values. Land was increasingly viewed as an economic investment for profit under the Tudors, rather than as a basis for subsistence and military service. Enclosure marked a shift from 'strip'-based communal farming to individual farming, and it did facilitate innovation and increase land values, if at the cost of dispossessing vulnerable tenants who swelled the ranks of landless labourers or, when times were hard, beggars and vagrants. But, for landowners, enclosure had clear benefits, and there were a growing number in the period who sought to consolidate their holdings and maximise their profits from land.

KEY ISSUE

Why was enclosure so explosive an issue in the sixteenth century and why was it so difficult to control?

---

8 ↰ THE LAND MARKET AND SOCIAL MOBILITY

Land only slowly became something that was commonly bought and sold. Under the Tudors of the early sixteenth century, there was little activity in the freehold land market, in part because of the widespread implementation of the 'use'. To avoid having to pay a sum of money to the Crown when an heir succeeded to an estate, and to avoid becoming a ward of the Crown, landowners by knight-service employed a body of trustees ('feoffees to use') to look after the lands, while reserving to himself and his heirs the 'use', the annual income. Consequently, no freehold estates passed down upon the owner's death, thus avoiding liability for feudal dues. By the 1536 Statute of Uses this was not prohibited, but liability for the feudal dues fell on the trustees, thus making the process ineffective and it more likely that land would have to be sold. By the Statute of Wills (1540), two-thirds of such knight-service land could be handed on to younger sons, rather than necessarily all passing to the eldest, and this too was a likely cause of fragmentation of estates and an impetus to the land market.

There was a flood of land onto the market following the Dissolution of the Monasteries. Later, chantry, collegiate and episcopal sales or exchanges further stimulated the flourishing land market as people sold on lands and consolidated their holdings. The monarchs too provided a stimulus by selling their own royal estates. Between 1536 and 1554 the Tudors raised £1.25 million in this way and Elizabeth liquidated £860 000 in three stages.

In addition, landowners found that the increasing demand for land from a growing population meant that they could charge much higher rents at full market price (rack-rents). Rents on the Herbert estates in Wiltshire rose from 13 pence to 20 pence per acre per year between 1535 and 1550, and to 28 pence by the 1570s. For the landowner, rising income levels and the restriction on labour costs meant a growing amount of wealth to be spent on further land acquisitions or on conspicuous consumption.

A familiar pattern emerges upon investigation of the land market. There were relatively few speculators and profiteers, but the market largely consisted of established landed families of moderate means or their younger sons who, faced with a small patrimony, made their fortune in government, land or commerce in London or the large provincial towns, and then purchased land of their own. Sir Ralph Sadler, Master of the Wardrobe to Henry VIII, was such a man. Yet there is also evidence of social mobility through the acquisition of land. In 1577 William Harrison suggested that yeomen were buying up the lands of gents in trouble, and then providing the education necessary for their sons to become recognised as a bona fide gent. Half of Yorkshire's new gentry were yeomen: while William Stumpe began as a clothier, his son became a knight. But it was the gentry who made the most of the land market, consolidating their economic position alongside their social and political position as Justices of the Peace.

It was argued by Tawney and others that the Tudor period saw 'the rise of the gentry' at the expense of the nobility (and that this social change, and the tensions it brought, was a principal cause of the English Civil War in the mid-seventeenth century). Lawrence Stone labelled it a 'crisis of the aristocracy'. A long debate over this has now died down. Dr Palliser, for example, has concluded that what happened was 'less a decline of the nobility than an expansion of the gentry, within which the nobles formed a smaller proportion'. The 50 peers of 1450 had grown to around 60 by 1560, some rising by land purchase (e.g. the Spencers of Warwickshire), others by office or marriage (William Cecil, Lord Burghley's grandfather, had been a yeoman-gentleman). Henry VIII and Edward VI created or restored nearly 50 peerages, some from gentry backgrounds, although the peerage's size became much more static under Elizabeth. The Crown aimed to discipline individual members of the nobility, but was not hostile to the peerage as a class.

The peerage continued to be deeply involved in the land market, as one might expect, and although the numbers of manors held by the peerage dropped from 3400 (1558) to 2200 (1600), they were purchasing regularly into the 1590s. There is evidence of many of them rationalising their landholdings by selling off unwanted manors, and of some embracing the profit motive once thought to be the preserve of the gentry. Income was

> **KEY ISSUE**
>
> *Who made the most out of the expanding land market in Tudor England?*

also sought from sources other than land, such as trade or law, or usually through office and the Court. The peerage's share of national resources may have been less proportionally by 1603, but its interests and social relationships, through inter-marriage, for instance, identified it closely with the gentry. There had been some social mobility in the Tudor period, but there was no question of social revolution.

9 ⌐ HOSPITALITY

Social change was not just an issue of economics and landholding. It was also a question of values. In 1595 the Lord Keeper of the Seal made a speech calling for household charity to be renewed. This was, in part, an appeal to restore a golden age of social solidarity which had never fully existed, an appeal prompted by the harvest failures of the 1590s and fears that the hungry would rebel; but in part there was real cause for anxiety about the dying away during the Tudor age of an ideal of hospitality.

This ideal prescribed that when a stranger appeared at the gate, he must be fed and watered. This was a unifying popular concept, applying to the cottage and the great house. It was symbolic of the code of hospitality that the gate was kept open during the day to all comers, except at meal times. The host's welcome to the guest was as important an exchange as money in other circumstances – the guest received sustenance and in return the host gained in honour. And, as Felicity Heal has put it, hospitality was 'a coded language, designed to articulate both power and magnanimity'. The more public hospitality a host was able to offer, the more influence he could wield in his community.

By 1600 the old inclusive ideal of hospitality was being much modified, especially in the upper reaches of society. This could be seen in the layout of great houses. All meals had been taken in the Hall where the master presided over his household and guests, rich and poor. Having retreated first into a semi-private chamber, more and more of the nobility and gentry during Elizabeth's reign were cutting themselves off in private dining rooms. There were still occasions for public hospitality, such as the Christmas gift-giving from tenants to lords in return for beer, bread and broth, but most hospitality was confined to social equals. It was not just a matter of being social equals by birth or economic status, however important these were; by the mid-Tudor period an increasing number of gentleman hosts expected guests to have the same cultural background acquired through a humanist education.

The Reformation also, of course, played a role. Protestant doctrine took away any virtue from the giving of alms, and hospitality was, in part, displaced by organised charity. Instead of the reciprocal exchange of host and guest and the absorption of the poor into households, the Poor Laws of 1597 and 1601 separated out the giving and receiving. And the stranger at the gate became the vagrant to be whipped back to his own parish. Organised charity was only for the really destitute; the able-bodied individual had to look after him or herself.

See page 357

Increasing commercialisation and social mobility were fostering individualism at the expense of communal solidarity. It was therefore in areas in the North, in Wales and in Ireland, more remote from the centres of commercial development, that the old culture of hospitality survived more nearly intact, and still does in some areas where tourism has not dealt it a final death blow.

The decline of traditional hospitality meant the disappearance of a code giving clear guidance to people's behaviour. This cultural uncertainty led to many social stresses and strains, the needy nursing resentments as they were turned away from the door and the householder being confronted by guilt for having done so. It certainly added to economic pressures in making poverty in the Tudor period an ever more difficult problem.

10 ✑ POVERTY

Inequality was a traditional and accepted feature of English society. A large percentage of the population earned little, rented their houses and had little to fall back on in a bad year. It was this sector which was increasingly subjected to poverty in the Tudor years, who suffered most from plague and hunger when harvests failed, and whose money wages often had to be supplemented by barter after the 1540s.

The causes were demographic in the long term, as more labour chased employment in a land where opportunities were becoming relatively scarce. Enclosures, short-term trade depressions and the demobilisation of soldiers all played a role sporadically. The Dissolution of the Monasteries further worsened problems by creating unemployment among the estimated 10 000 religious, and by opening up monastic lands to the more grasping demands of the laity, who did not have to keep up the traditional obligations to the poor made by the Church. By 1549 half the endowed institutions, the monasteries and chantries, which had cared for the poor were closed.

The picture which emerges is that of a society gradually polarising under the Tudors, the rich becoming richer, the poor poorer and more numerous. Those with sufficient land to become suppliers to the market, or at least to be self-sufficient, survived and improved their position, while those who were consumers but had little or nothing to sell faced continuing pressure on their finances and were most likely to slide into poverty through eviction and migration. Poverty became an increasingly serious urban problem, with pressure placed on town services by non-productive consumers, and causing a worsening of the quality and cost of housing. Widows appear to have made up a large proportion of the urban poor, often running alehouses or brothels, yet there were also families facing temporary hardship.

The burden of looking after the poor was readily shouldered neither by Tudor secular society nor by government. Early Tudor legislation was similar to the medieval laws of Richard II in the twin aims of keeping the poor immobile, and by deterring the able-bodied unemployed from idleness by severe punishment. The central problem was the migrant unemployed who were on the road for a variety of reasons, up to 20 000 of them in bad times – some were rogues, some were honest men and women fallen on hard times, some disbanded soldiery – but they were uniformly feared and stereotyped as 'sturdy beggars'.

Until the last quarter of the sixteenth century only those physically unable to work were regarded as deserving of relief. Poverty itself was not a qualification. The population shrinkage caused by the Black Death of the mid-fourteenth century meant that vacancies for employment had exceeded the demands of the labour force, driving up wage levels and preventing widespread poverty. As poverty became an issue under the Tudors, a variety of solutions were tried, many designed to create fear and injury. The major objective of the authorities was to maintain law and order, prevent crime and uphold security. In 1495 a new law required beggars and the idle to be put in the stocks for three days, to be whipped and then returned to their original parish. The demarcation between 'impotent' beggar, those suffering physical disability, and the 'idle', i.e. able-bodied but unemployed, was a central feature of Tudor policy. The legislation suffered from a lack of enforcement, partly due to the difficulties of establishing the original parish, but it did illustrate the simplicity of contemporary attitudes to the poor and the ad hoc nature of the government's response.

In 1531 a depression in the cloth trade, following the severing of relations with the Netherlands, caused a rise in unemployment, despite an order to clothiers to maintain employment levels. The new legislation of 1531 introduced a licensing system through JPs permitting the impotent poor to beg, with the usual prescription of whipping for the able-bodied who were unemployed. As a result, able-bodied, unemployed poor were forced to break the law or starve. An enlightened scheme of public works on roads and harbours was suggested by William Marshall in a failed Bill of 1535.

A further Act of Parliament in 1536 broke new ground by ordering parishes or town authorities to take responsibility for the impotent poor, and the apprenticeship of children.

By 1547 the economic difficulties of the time, along with the rising threat of social disorder, led to the infamous legislation of that year. With frightening severity the Edwardian legislation tried to hand out a short, sharp shock to any person likely to cause disruption. A vagrant was defined as an able-bodied person lacking support and unemployed for more than three days. The first conviction for vagrancy meant being branded with a 'V' on the chest and being given to the informant as a slave for two years. Vagrant children could be seized by anyone prepared to teach them a trade, with boys kept until the age of 24 and girls until 20. Enforcement fell upon the parish constable, but the law proved to be too extreme to be effectively enforced and the legislation was repealed in 1550 in favour of a return to the 1531 Act.

Urban authorities had already established compulsory poor rates by mid-century. The driving force was Puritans drawing on continental models, and hostile to begging and its association with Catholic almsgiving. London (taking action in 1547), Norwich (1549) and York (1551), met their own specific problems of unemployment and poverty through contributions which varied according to wealth. London acquired St Bartholomew's Hospital from the Crown (1546–7), Bethlehem Hospital (Bedlam) for the insane, and Christ's Hospital for orphans (1552). Bridewell Palace became a house of correction for employing the able-bodied poor.

A watershed came in 1572 when legislation based upon the Norwich scheme (1570) was enacted on a national basis, creating a universal statutory obligation on parishes for the first time. The Act at last recognised the concept of 'able-bodied unemployed'. Demobilised soldiers and sailors were licensed to return home and were exempted from the penalties of the Act, as were harvest workers and evicted servants. JPs were to assess the cost of relief for the local poor and compulsory weekly contributions were exacted for the aged and impotent, who were forbidden to beg unless the parish could not support them. Unlicensed begging resulted in burning through the right ear, in 1593 amended to be imprisonment. Surplus funds were to be used to build houses of correction for rogues and vagabonds. The new office of Overseer of the Poor in the parish was unpaid and was appointed annually by the JP from among substantial householders. This legislation signified a major change; until then only those physically unable to work had been deemed deserving, whereas now the existence of deserving unemployed, fit and willing labour who could find no employment, was recognised.

The last decade of the century saw a large number of able-bodied jobless swelling the ranks of the young, aged and disabled, as urban poverty escalated beyond the expectations of the 1570s, due to the impact of war on trade and the further growth in the population. Between 1593 and 1597 a series of disastrous harvests across Europe meant that wheat was priced at 80% above its norm, leading to famine. Riots, caused by dearer bread, broke out in London, Oxfordshire and Norfolk, forcing Parliament to be recalled in October 1597. Of the 17 Bills introduced, 11 were related to the relief of poverty.

Most important were the Poor Laws of 1597 and 1601. They contained little that was new, but codified comprehensively the Tudor regime's attempts to deal with the issue. The duties of the Overseer of the Poor were defined, including the power to set children and those with no assets to work. Churchwardens were to help with the assessment and collection of the Poor Rate. Materials were to be provided for the poor to work on, funded from taxation, while children were to be apprenticed – boys until the age of 24, girls until 21. The problems of collecting sufficient funds were also realised. Overseers were to meet monthly and to submit annual accounts to the JP. If a parish was unable to cope with the burden, the rates were to be spread over the surrounding district, the hundred, and other parishes were asked to contribute. Refusal to pay the Rate meant possible imprisonment and goods could be seized. Begging was henceforth regarded as unnecessary and the equivalent of vagrancy. This parish-based legislation remained in force until 1834.

KEY ISSUE

How did contemporaries analyse poverty in the sixteenth century, and how effectively did the government cope with it?

The effectiveness of poor provision is difficult to evaluate. Rural parishes appear to have produced very low levels of subsistence, just enough, along with charity, to survive the shortages of the 1590s crisis years. Informal and ad hoc almsgiving continued on a large scale and voluntary private gifts probably exceeded the levels of statutory relief. The causes of poverty were not really understood sufficiently to be addressed and therefore little was done to ease poverty in general. Private endowments for charity were of vital importance, rising according to Professor Jordan from £227000 (1541–60) to £634000 (1601–20). Given inflation, this marked a decline in real terms over the period, but together with the Poor Rate it was enough to cope with most conditions. As Dr J Pound has concluded, 'both poverty and vagrancy were fairly well contained, and to say that either created a dangerous national situation would be to strain the evidence'.

11 ⌐ CRIME, LAW AND ORDER

Tudor governments relied heavily upon a combination of statutes, proclamations and licensing to maintain law, order and stability. It was in the nature of sixteenth-century states that the writ of central government did not run very far, and depended upon the co-operation and involvement of the local political élites. Economic and social difficulties made the task harder, forcing constant vigilance and a steady stream of legislation and directives. Nevertheless, it was an impossible task to suppress violence completely, especially in times of dearth. An effective legal machinery was yet to appear, and corruption and vested interest were difficult to combat.

Central government, perhaps not surprisingly as representatives of the land-owning classes, tended to intervene on those matters which were deemed to be dangerous to the Commonwealth, a threat to land-owning interests or to be socially unacceptable. The Tudors were aware that they needed to work with the political nation, and that this relationship needed nurturing. The issue of retaining highlights the point. There was no attempt by the Tudors to destroy retaining, rather they sought to control and contain it, through the use of a Crown licence (1504). But as late as the last quarter of the century, feuds were alive between retaining nobles in Herefordshire and Wiltshire.

See page 45

There was also an attempt to define, clarify and extend felonies (crimes punishable by death), particularly in the Henrician period. Hunting at night, poaching, abducting women (1487), theft from masters, homosexuality (1534), witchcraft (1542) and poisoning (1531) were all defined as felonies, though they tended to be short-term reactions to contemporary events and many were later repealed. 'Benefit of clergy', whereby penalties could be waived for crimes by clerics, was limited so that it could only be claimed once by an individual. Psalm 51, verse 1 (the 'Neck verse') had to be read to qualify, and after 1489 branding on the left thumb with an 'M' (murder), or 'T' (theft and other felonies), was introduced. About 20% of felons obtained benefit, the ability to read at all often being sufficient to to count as a cleric and escape hanging. An increasing number of crimes, such as highway robbery or other crimes against property, were steadily excluded from benefit under the Tudors as the Crown sought to strengthen their grip on society and maintain law and order.

The core problem for Tudor central government was local **particularism**. Landowners in the localities were not prepared always to prosecute an offender with the full weight of the law, and there was no police force. Additionally, there were privileged quasi-independent areas where the Crown's writ was limited, before Cromwell's reforms. Even if a case was brought to court, juries were often made up of the 'poorer sort', open to corruption and frequently ill-educated. The Crown resorted to the quicker and less formal Court of Star Chamber and the Councils of the North and Welsh Marches to enforce laws more speedily.

Punishment was brutal. Retribution and deterrence were the only aims; rehabilitation was not yet thought of. Imprisonment was viewed as a lenient sentence, despite the terrible conditions, and in any case there were few prison places. Physical punishment was the alternative. There were 800 executions in 1600, for instance. Hanging sought to strangle slowly rather than to break the neck, and afterwards goods were forfeited to the Crown. Refusing to plead or remaining silent meant being crushed to death, while for some crimes physical mutilation provided a public warning – for example, forgery and perjury meant the loss of both ears and being branded on the face.

By the late sixteenth century, disorder still prevailed, worsened by the population pressure and economic privations of the 1590s. The search for food and employment, as well as the presence of disabled soldiers, led to rising violence among the lower classes, with the dagger or staff favoured weapons, so that by 1600 there is evidence of travellers on highways carrying personal weapons in secret to combat mugging.

There was an increase in the number of cases being brought to the courts. While 67 cases came before Star Chamber in 1559, over 700 were dealt with in 1603. Sir William Herbert was fined 1000 marks for condoning violence, seriously damaging his local reputation and standing. Piracy was another violent crime often carried out under landowner protection. An increasing volume of the rising coastal trade was hit, with local coastal villages happy to share in profit and gain. The Crown tried to suppress piracy by statute in 1536, making it a felony, and then by two later commissions (1563 and 1577), but successes were rare. The Crown could occasionally discipline local élites, but, while the poor suffered the full severity of the law, the government had to compromise with political realities when facing those who held the reins of power in the localities.

Particularism loyalty focused on the local community and local institutions, put before loyalty to national institutions

See page 41

KEY ISSUE

Why did the Crown find it so difficult to control crime?

12 ⌐ WITCHCRAFT

One of the most feared crimes of all was that which involved supernatural forces – witchcraft. On 8 March 1579 the four-year-old Susan

Webbe died. Death in infancy or early childhood was all too common, but on this occasion the cause was reckoned to be witchcraft. And the guilty one seemed obvious. Ellen Smyth was the daughter of a condemned witch; her stepfather had become ill after a quarrel over an inheritance; she had a familiar, people said, a toad which, when burnt, caused Ellen pain; her son described her three spirits kept in bottles and in a wool-pack discovered in her house. She had another familiar, a black dog, which sent Susan Webbe's mother mad. Ellen Smyth was tried, found guilty of witching Susan to death, and hanged.

It was cases like this which characterise English witchcraft. There was no witch 'craze' or sudden flare-up of prosecutions – such cases as Ellen's were commonplace, although the bulk of them were in the later Tudor and early Stuart periods. Nor did prosecutions lead automatically to conviction because of the overwhelming hysteria usually depicted in plays or films on the subject. Witch cases in England were tried by Assize judges, who were often sceptical of the village quarrels which lay behind accusations. In one sample of 474 cases on the Home Circuit, 104, that is 22%, were sentenced to death. (In contrast, in some parts of Germany and France, there could be far higher conviction rates where judges were local worthies, rather than professionals, and susceptible to local scares.) Also, cases tended to fail where a village was divided in its views, and respectable people could be found to testify on behalf of the accused.

In England there was none of the paraphernalia of continental witchcraft and the folklore which has come to represent it. There were no supposed flights by broomstick; witches like Ellen operated alone and not in covens enjoying a witches' sabbath. There were few reports of sexual excesses with an 'incubus' (i.e. the Devil playing the male part) or any bewitching of genitals, a fear of which, presumably for personal reasons, obsessed some continental commentators on the black arts. Although as the century wore on more was thought to be the responsibility of the Devil or his servants as on the Continent, in England there was generally just **maleficium**, the doing of harm to people or property. What the **cunning folk** could do for good, the witch could do for ill. The standard pattern was that a neighbours' quarrel would lead to cursing. If injury or damage followed, and the one cursing had an evil reputation usually built up over years, then witchcraft would be talked of. If there was sufficient support from other villagers, this might turn from gossip into an open accusation.

Ellen Smyth's case was typical of this pattern in most respects, except that Susan Webbe died almost immediately. Witchcraft was most often thought of when there was a lingering illness, with plenty of opportunity to reflect on what had caused it and time to try to do something about it. But Ellen did have her familiars which are the most distinctively English feature of witchcraft. Familiars hardly figured in witchcraft on the Continent, except some instances in the Basque country. And the black cat was not necessarily the standard familiar. Ellen had her toad and black dog. One Joan Prentice was famous for her Bid the Ferret, which livened up the pamphlet account of Joan's witchcraft by being able to talk.

Maleficium physical harm achieved through witchcraft rather than by direct violence

Cunning folk those who would be consulted for their understanding of supernatural forces, often healers or advisers on how to retrieve lost or stolen property

The first reaction of anyone fearful of malice from the like of Ellen or Joan had usually been to employ counter-magic. Cunning folk could help identify – or rather confirm suspicion of – the source of *maleficium* and perhaps provide a charm or advice on how to combat it. (To make a witch cake, for instance, mix some grain with the urine of the bewitched person and then burn it on a fire; the witches feel the fire in their genitals and come running to stop the burning, and so betray themselves.) Help was nearby; it has been calculated that in Essex nobody was more than ten miles from the nearest cunning man or woman. The pre-Reformation Church had also been a rich source of counter-magic with its exorcisms and holy water and other ritual devices. Only in the last resort did the supposed victim of witchcraft resort to the law. That last resort, however, became more common as pre-Reformation rituals were suppressed, and Puritan **demonologists** condemned cunning folk as even more the servants of the Devil, whatever the seeming good intentions, as they drew people away from right religion.

There were a series of statutes relating to witchcraft. Henry VIII's 1542 statute connected it with heresy but this was repealed in 1547. Another was passed in 1563, a reaction to fears of Catholic plotters against Queen Elizabeth employing witchcraft. Finally, the 1604 statute under James I, who thought himself to be an expert, was yet more severe, imposing the death penalty on a second offence for simply intending injury.

> **Demonologists**
> students of how the Devil or supernatural evil operates in the world

ANALYSIS

Was There a Pattern to the Outbursts of Witch-hunting?

Recourse to the law became ever more common in the latter half of the sixteenth century and on into the seventeenth. It was not just because of these new statutes – where injury or damage could be proved, it had already been possible to bring cases against witches. According to Keith Thomas the law filled the gap when the Reformation stripped most of the devices used in counter-magic from the Church. That does much to explain the timing of witchcraft accusations – they increased in number as the Reformation became established. It is also the case that Puritan preaching emphasised much more the active role of the Devil in the world, and, as Puritan preachers and Catholic missionary priests battled over men's souls, they developed their roles as exorcists casting demons forth and combatting witchcraft. But this was in the background rather than explaining the specific timing of more intensive prosecutions. Trevor-Roper argued that witch hunting was part of the hysteria generated by conflict between Catholics and Protestants, but there is little correlation, at least in England, between an increase in witchcraft cases and intense periods of religious conflict. Nor were witches used as scapegoats in bad times. In the late 1590s, despite disastrous harvests, there was no surge in prosecutions. In Essex, an example exhaustively studied by Alan MacFarlane, there were notable increases in the 1580s and 1640s, but he argues these resulted more from one or two determined prosecutors than from general conditions. Witchcraft accusations were not like an epidemic disease breaking out occasionally. They were a regular part of village life.

In Essex over half the villages had at least one witchcraft case in the Tudor and Stuart period. An Essex clergyman, George Gifford, who wrote two books on witchcraft in 1587 and 1593, quoted one character as saying

1   I was of a Jury not many years past, when there was an old woman arraigned for a witch. There came in eight or ten which gave evidence against her … One woman came in and testified upon her oath that her husband upon his death bed, took it upon his death, that he was
5   bewitched, for he pined a long time. And he said further, he was sure that woman bewitched him. He took her to be naught, and thought she was angry with him, because she would have borrowed five shillings of him, and he denied to lend it to her. The woman took her oath also, that she thought in her conscience that the old woman was
10 a witch, and that she killed her husband … Then followed a man, and he said he could not tell, but he thought she was once angry with him because she came to beg a few pot-herbs, and he denied her: and presently after he heard a thing as he thought to whisper in his ear, thou shalt be bewitched. The next day he had such a pain in his back,
15 that he could not sit upright: he said he sent to a cunning woman, she told he was bewitched, and by a woman that came for pot-herbs … Then came in two or three grave honest men, which testified by common fame that she was a witch. We found her guilty, for what could we do less, she was condemned and executed: and upon the
20 ladder she made her prayer, and took it upon her death she was innocent and free from all such dealings.

Q

1. *In both the specific accusations cited here what did each victim think started the chain of events leading to their being bewitched?*
2. *What is meant by the 'common fame' referred to in lines 17–18 and what made it believable?*
3. *Analyse the reasons why the accused came to be thought a witch.*

Village communities were very tight knit and conformity to precise roles was demanded. Some would not, or could not, conform. The cackling old hag cursing the ordinary villagers is an over-drawn, fairy-tale image but it has something in it. Witches did tend to be women past child-bearing age – that could make them marginal, of little further use to the future of the community, and they might understandably have shown resentment at being pushed aside. Many cases, like Ellen Smyth's, involved a vulnerable child, with a mother as accuser and a post-menopausal woman as the accused. A mother's anxieties could amplify fears of witchcraft. Also, some witch accusations may have been part of an attempt to reassert patriarchal authority over 'unruly women'. This does not mean that all witches were old and were women, nor that all accusers were men – women were more likely to make accusations. Neither the court statistics nor the pamphlet literature of the time suggest that witchcraft was only something women could be guilty of – it was not gender specific – or that being old was an absolute prerequisite. Witchcraft accusations were not part of a war of the sexes. However, it was older women who were often the most dependent on their neighbours; and where they were too demanding, tensions could grow over time, sometimes decades, and lead to quarrels and then to accusations of *maleficium* when something went wrong.

Surprisingly few supposed witches came from the poorest sections of the community, although they were usually poorer than their accusers. Possibly the poorest were too thoroughly under the heel of the rest of the community, whereas one almost universal characteristic of accused witches was a willingness to make a nuisance of themselves, to the point of cursing. It was a way older women could exert power. Where men might resort to their fists, women were more likely to employ the power of speech, whether in argument, gossip, or spitting out curses. An old woman might welcome the reputation as a witch; if her neighbours were afraid of her they would be more likely to do what she asked. Susan Asmussen has described witchcraft as 'invisible violence'. And nothing, it seems, led to cursing and witchery more quickly than being turned down when requesting traditional, neighbourly charity.

Traditional hospitality seemed to contemporaries to be in decline in the Tudor period and other forms of charity were being neglected. Alan MacFarlane sees in this the gradual rise of individualism at the expense of the old, closed, mutually supportive life of traditional communities. Village life was being disrupted by the economic and social changes of the early modern period – inflation, more trade, more movement up and down the social and financial scales, more migration from place to place, and particularly from villages to towns. With individualism developing as part of these changes, so neighbours were expected more to fend for themselves or rely on official sources of support, such as the parish. Also, since the Reformation the giving of alms had not been seen as a way of earning reward in Heaven. So there were ever more scenes where 'five shillings' or 'pot-herbs' would be denied to the old woman who asked for them, while the old moral imperative to give to neighbours still hung on in the background as a part of the inherited culture.

The result was that the one who requested charity, and was refused, felt a right had been denied, and consequently she might well curse or try to frighten her way into getting what she asked for. (And the historian can never know how many 'witches' there were who were not prosecuted simply because they were successful in terrifying their neighbours into giving them what they wanted.) Equally, the neighbour who had denied a request might well feel guilty and seek to dispel that

See pages 364–8

KEY ISSUE

What were the social characteristics of a witch?

KEY ISSUE

What were the common causes of witchcraft accusations?

guilt by proclaiming the disappointed and angry old woman to be a witch. This 'charity refused' model of a witchcraft accusation is most evident in South-east England, such as Essex, where the cases MacFarlane studied come from. James Sharpe has shown that this was not so common in northern counties, such as Yorkshire, where the economy was less developed and individualism not so far advanced.

Witchcraft accusations could only take place, however, not merely while there were accusations but also while the courts were prepared to take them seriously. Although there was scepticism about individual accusations, there was general acceptance of witch beliefs among judges and the élite in general in the sixteenth century, with just a few exceptions. One was Reginald Scott, who published *The Discovery of Witchcraft* in 1584. He asserted that the supposed power of witches belonged only to God, and that to think otherwise was 'popish trumpery'. He argued that those 'commonly accused of witchcraft are the least sufficient of all other persons to speak for themselves, as having the most base and simple education of all others: the extremity of their age giving them leave to dote, their poverty to beg, their wrongs to chide and threaten (as being void of any other way of revenge), their humour melancholical to be full of imaginations … that they can kill children with charms, hinder the coming of butter etc.' This is an acute analysis of the social and psychological features involved in witchcraft accusations, and in the accused deluding themselves that they had magical powers – so that they might even believe their own bizarre confessions. Historians writing today follow many of Scott's arguments. But very few believed him at the time, and even fewer would have dared to admit it, for a century or more.

Apart from an upsurge in the chaotic 1640s, witch prosecutions, however, gradually declined through the seventeenth century, until finally in 1736 witchcraft legislation was repealed. Partly this was because of the triumph of rationalism and the belief in a mechanical universe, partly that witchcraft beliefs in the élite became associated with reactionary politics, and partly sheer snobbery – witchcraft beliefs had been identified as vulgar, rural superstitions. Popular beliefs changed more slowly. Lynchings of supposed witches continued after the repeal of the law, the last known instance being that of Ruth Osborne at Tring in 1751. (The usual story – she had been refused buttermilk by a farmer who subsequently fell ill.) And witch beliefs survived even longer, continuing in some rural areas well into the nineteenth century and beyond.

13 ↜ GENDER AND SEXUALITY

A *The role and status of women in the sixteenth century*

In the sixteenth century, in theory, women were entirely subordinate to men. Science justified it – the ancient Greek philosopher, Aristotle, had described women as incomplete men, and the classical medical authority, Galen, characterised women as hotter and moister as a result of the **four humours**, and so more lustful and generally less in control than cooler, drier and therefore more rational men. Religion justified it – Biblical texts were used to assert that women should be submissive to men, preferably staying within the home and silent when not. A woman ruler, such as Elizabeth, caused problems for this general theory, but she was regarded as an exception. On her accession, Calvin wrote from Geneva with the comfort that this 'deviation from the primitive and established order of nature' was a divine reprimand for sin, much like slavery.

The 1562 homily on marriage (a sermon prescribed for all churches) taught that women 'be sooner … prone to all weak affectations … more than men be, and lighter they be and more vain in their fantasies and opinions'. Books of conduct, written mostly by Puritans as moral guides, urged obedience by women: a woman must 'submit and apply herself to the discretion and will of her husband, even as the conduct of everything resteth in the head, not in the body' (Dod and Cleaver in *A Godly Form of Household Government*). A woman should obey her husband (or father) as a subject should obey the magistrate. She did not own her own body. Vives wrote in 1541 of a woman who committed adultery as 'the more wrong to give away that thing which is another body's without the owner's licence'. That was the origin of the 'double standard' whereby adultery was more serious when committed by a woman than by a man.

Women were in many respects the property first of a father, then of a husband. Property needed to be protected which was the origin of a 1487 Act of Parliament against 'Taking Away of Women against Their Wills', which was designed to protect heiresses. (It did not work; kidnapping and forced marriage continued.) Wardship made heiresses a bargaining counter in property deals and family alliances; the Duke of Norfolk paid £1000 for the wardship and marriage of one of Lord Marney's daughters. The existence of women, except as mother, was almost ignored in the common law, and the legal union of Wales with England in 1536 made it worse for women there, who previously had stronger rights.

It used to be thought that the Reformation had improved the position of women, by replacing the denigration of women by a celibate clergy with the reformers' esteem for marriage and a new emphasis on companionship and shared responsibilities between husband and wife, plus an increase in basic education for women so that they could instruct their children in religion. But historians since the 1960s have emphasised that the authority of the celibate priest was simply replaced by the father in the family and that **patriarchy** was reinforced by the Reformation, as in the sermons and books of conduct exemplified above. It is also the case that the dissolution of the nunneries with the Reformation did away with the only institutions where women governed their own affairs.

As for education, there was progress after 1500 when almost no women were literate, or at least able to sign their names, but the literacy

Four humours
according to Galen, the characteristics of an individual depended on the balance of the four 'humours' or physical elements in the body: these were choler (hot and dry, like fire), blood (hot and wet, akin to the air), phlegm (cold and wet, like water) and melancholy (cold and dry, akin to the earth)

Patriarchy social dominance by men

rate for women rose only to 10% by the time of the Stuarts. Women might participate in elementary education at 'petty schools' alongside their brothers, but thereafter stayed at home to learn the household tasks which would qualify them as house-keeper, wife and mother. There were highly educated women – outstanding examples were Mary Tudor and Elizabeth, and Thomas More's daughter, Margaret – but that was unusual even among the élite. The Protestant educator Richard Mulcaster in 1581 urged that women be taught to read for religion's sake, but as 'an accessory by the way' and not to interfere with domestic duties. Needless to say, women were not permitted to attend grammar schools or universities, although boarding schools for girls were to appear in the following century.

Throughout the period, irrespective of the Reformation, women were seen as being wayward and needing to be kept in order by men. From the mid-eighteenth century until well into the twentieth, women were characterised as passive objects in sexual relationships. This was a complete reversal of the view held in the Early Modern period and before, when women were seen as incurably lustful unless contained within the patriarchal family or respectable widowhood. There was a medical assumption that women had to have regular sex or would become ill.

Female sexuality was taken to be a general symptom of women's tendency towards disorder, and there were various ways they could be controlled. Corporal punishment was regarded as normal. As a proverb at the time put it: 'a woman, a spaniel and a walnut tree, the more they're beaten the better they be'. The right of a husband to beat his wife was not finally rejected in law until 1891. This did not mean that violence against women was regarded as unproblematic. There was much anxious commentary at the time about abuse by husbands, and women could obtain legal separations from their husbands on grounds of cruelty. But it was a very brave woman who took this step and found herself on her own.

There were also more public sanctions against women who were reluctant to conform. They could be satirised in Carnival processions as 'unruly women', usually portrayed by men in drag, a distant ancestor of the pantomime dame. A woman who argued or nagged, in a less extreme example than witchcraft, was seeking to employ the power of speech when men might resort to their fists. She could be reined in, literally, by a bridle, which bit into her tongue, or subject to the ducking-stool in the village pond. Or there was a cucking-stool, a chair on wheels or a cart, on which to drag its mocked female victim round the village. One was made for the village of Morebath in 1557, and Eamon Duffy sees this as a 'coarsening of social fibre' since the Reformation which, despite the Marian restoration, had stripped away much of the communal celebrations and activity familiar in the pre-Reformation church. It had reduced the role of women in the parish who had previously collaborated much more fully in the life of the church and raised money (the Maidens' store) in order to adorn the statues of the Virgin and other saints.

It was regarded as unnatural that an older woman should marry a younger man, and there was an instinctive defence of the fertility of the community. The unhappy couple could be forced to face a charivari – public, satirical abuse with cat-calling, raucous noise ('rough music') and a procession led by mimics of them. Likewise an unfaithful wife and her betrayed husband, scorned as a 'cuckold', could be given similar treatment, or a couple where the woman ruled the roost. The 'woman on top' was taken as an insult to traditional values. Women would themselves join in a charivari, having internalised such traditional values and the righteousness of the subjection of their own sex.

The theory supporting the subjection of women and the sanctions which could be used to discipline those who failed to conform should not be taken as a clear indication of what happened in everyday life. Keith Wrightson stresses that whatever public appearances, in private more commonly husband and wives worked in partnership. It was only practical. As Sir Anthony Fitzherbert observed in 1523, a husband seldom thrived without the support of his wife. Foreign visitors frequently commented on the relative freedom of English wives to order their own lives. While a marriage was also an economic settlement dominated by the husband – a woman brought with her a dowry, the more substantial it was the better her marriage prospects, and on marriage her property passed under the control of her husband – in practice a woman often dealt with property matters herself and had a regular share of the family income. And, while most women had the legal status of 'femme covert', i.e. their property being subject to a husband, about 20% had the status of 'femme sole', that is head of their own household and able to dispose of property through sale or wills as they saw fit. Usually a 'femme sole' was a widow, who was entitled to her dower share of a third of her husband's property. The downside of this, apart from bereavement, was that widowhood might mean economic independence for some women, but poverty for others.

Women sometimes appear as traders or owners of workshops in the City of London or other towns, although less frequently than in the later Middle Ages. In 1574 in Chester five of the blacksmiths were widows. Much of the economy around 1500 was based on the household, and where a woman ran the household she might therefore exercise more general economic power. If she worked outside it, though, she would certainly receive lower wages than men for equivalent work. However, as the market developed and enterprises grew in size there was a clearer distinction between work-place and home, and given the emphasis on women staying at home, unless they were in domestic service and thus in another household, that meant a decreasing role in the economy at large. The evidence is thin in connection with a definite deterioration of the economic status of women in the sixteenth century, but the economically active woman was certainly disparaged. A fish-wife was to be despised as the byword for vulgarity and coarse behaviour, and the spinster, who stayed at her spinning wheel, rather than getting married, was to be pitied and treated with condescension.

Women, however, also had access to other forms of power, particularly if they belonged to the élite. This is most obvious in connection with the Tudor queens, but more generally an aristocratic woman might command her male servants and inferiors. Women could on occasion even nominate members of Parliament where a borough was under the control of the family, as did Dame Elizabeth Copley in the 1550s while her son was underage.

Women lower down the social scale had other ways of exercising power. There were riots led by women, for instance, particularly where it was felt unjust prices were being charged for food or to defend the community under attack. In Exeter in 1535 Protestant workmen were dismantling the roodloft of a priory church, a priory noted for its charitable works; enraged women, armed with spikes, shovels and other tools, trapped them and stoned one so that he leapt from the roof and broke a rib. The women were only dispersed when the mayor arrived with an armed posse.

Informal power could be exercised through gossip, and, where a situation lent itself to it, a woman could shame a man. A 'wittol' was a man who discovered his wife's infidelity, but begged her to keep it quiet for the sake of his honour. A man's power was not unassailable, particularly if his honour could be compromised.

The history of gender is not simply the history of the subjection of women and of male power. Men were constrained into gender roles as well, from at least when they were put into breeches at about the age of six and taken away from their mother's control. If they failed to demonstrate their manhood through physical prowess and the domination of women, if their honour was damaged, they would be subject to ridicule and exclusion.

B *Sexuality*

There were attempts to regulate sexuality, but the endless Puritan tracts trying to bring about a **'reformation of manners'** and bring it under control show that it was an unending battle in much of rural society. Pre-marital sex, 'bundling' as it was known, was tolerated, as long as there was an intention to marry and certainly an acceptance of it in the event of pregnancy. As Reay comments, 'We know from the court records that couples had intercourse in meadows, in ditches, under hedges, up against stiles, in barns and dairies, in their masters' houses (many were servants), in the woods, at the backs of inns and alehouses, in churchyards, in the homes of the women's parents'. To avoid pregnancy, though, couples often avoided full intercourse, or primitive condoms were used, such as pigs' bladders, known as 'Venus gloves'. Illegitimacy was relatively rare, 2–4% of births, and where it did occur, court records suggest that around a fifth of cases were serving girls impregnated by their masters. The rate increased in the 1590s as adverse economic conditions delayed marriage. But marriage was not at so young an age anyway – on average the couple would be in their mid-twenties, although the legal age was 12 for girls and 14 for boys. They would have needed to wait until they had the means to support themselves and start a family.

KEY ISSUE

What social and economic restrictions were imposed on women in the sixteenth century, and were the restrictions becoming easier or tighter?

Reformation of manners a Puritan attempt to tighten up moral controls in general, not just in relation to sex, which led to a considerable volume of legislation: between 1576 and 1610, along with nine Acts of Parliament dealing with illegitimacy, there were six against swearing, nine against work or play on the Sabbath, and 35 against drunkenness.

Marriage was not simply the formal event in front of the priest and congregation in church. Technically it could be contracted anywhere by the couple alone declaring themselves to each other to be man and wife. However, the usual practice was for the espousal to take place, followed by the public announcement, the reading of the banns in church, and then the formalisation of the contract in the marriage itself. The espousal was the key moment. By the time of the marriage, in Devon 30% of brides were clearly pregnant, although in Yorkshire it was 13%. A marriage was not complete without the physical consummation but that most often preceded the marriage.

Lawrence Stone argued that marriage was principally a working relationship and that only towards the end of the seventeenth century was there the emphasis on romantic attachment and affection which is regarded as ideal today. Nor, he argued, was there the emotional investment in children; perhaps because of the high infant mortality rate, parents hardened themselves. This view, however, is not generally accepted, as it may just reflect a relative scarcity of evidence of affection in the earlier part of the period. The evidence there is – such as the Paston letters from the fifteenth century – suggest close bonds between family members. Certainly, however, marriage failure is not new to the modern period. Despite all the legal difficulties, separations did occur. Roughly 10% of noblemen in the Elizabethan period were estranged from their wives, although they were even more likely to have married for economic and dynastic reasons than their social inferiors.

Sex other than between courting or married couples was frowned on, but was a recorded feature particularly of urban life. In the towns could be found the brothels. In London they flourished south of the Thames on Bankside beyond the reach of the City authorities, along with public entertainment loathed by Puritans: theatres, gambling and bear-baiting. Prostitutes clustered around the palace of the Bishop of Winchester in Southwark and were known as Winchester geese. Noblemen took brothels under their protection. A Mrs Higgens operated one in the London house of the Earl of Worcester, who sued the City constables when they closed it down. The time for Earl or commoner not to be in a brothel was on Shrove Tuesday. As part of the community's ritual purification as it began the season of Lent, it was the practice to attack them.

Sex is not just the pursuit of instinct. It is also socially constructed, that is shaped by what is thought about it, how it is categorised, and how it is controlled. A good example of this is the Tudor attitude towards homosexuality. There was no conception of a gay man or woman, no conception of sexuality defining someone's identity. There were just homosexual acts, and it was thought that a man of loose morals was as likely to go for boys as for women. As Reay has put it, 'Men were punished for buggery and sodomy, but these were considered to be the excess of mankind in general rather than the practices of a specific group'. There was no association of effeminacy specifically with homosexuality. A man who gave in to passion, whether for a woman or a man, was thought to be in danger of 'un-manning' himself. And homosexuality referred to men as far as the Tudor age was concerned – there is scarcely any reference to lesbianism in the records of the period.

People who do not conform can be scapegoats in any society, and diverse fears can be projected onto them. In the later Tudor period the fear of homosexuality was often identified with a fear of popery. The propagandists working for Thomas Cromwell attacked the monasteries as centres of sodomy, and John Bale more generally the Catholic clergy: 'within the bounds of sodomy, doth dwell the spiritual clergy, Pope, cardinal and priest'. A law against sodomy was enacted at the same time as the Reformation legislation of the 1530s. It prescribed death for the offence, but it was rarely enforced except when rape was involved. The law had been passed because of the general scare whipped up by propaganda; it did not mirror social assumptions. The headmaster of Eton, Nicholas Udall, lost his job, when he was forced to admit having sex with one of his former scholars. But it scarcely affected his career thereafter, and he ended his days as headmaster of Westminster School.

As we have seen, any sex, including homosexuality, outside the bounds of married life and the courtship which preceded it, was regarded with suspicion, but under the influence of Renaissance classicism, same-sex affection was idealised and physical attraction sublimated. Roger Ascham, who had been tutor to Queen Elizabeth, wrote letters to male friends which were expressions of love, based on classical examples. He celebrated the intimacy of two men sharing a bed and reading together. Poets made depictions of homosexual love 'safe' by writing not about mortals but about Zeus and his love for his cup-bearer, Ganymede, a shepherd boy he had kidnapped. Shakespeare wrote not just sonnets addressed to a Dark Lady, but also others which are complex, ambiguous expressions of desire for a man. It is impossible to separate out the history of sexuality in the Tudor period from the history of politics, mentalities and culture more generally.

> ## KEY ISSUE
>
> *What were the prevalent views about sex outside marriage and about same-sex relationships in Tudor England?*

14 ⤳ CONCLUSION

Like a large jigsaw with a sizable number of pieces missing, the complete picture of the economy, society and practices of Tudor England is impossible to appreciate, but a pattern does emerge. The central problem facing the historian is the difficulty of finding source material which is both continuous over a period, and comprehensive. Contemporaries also found it difficult to understand the diversity of their world. With hindsight, regional and local evidence can be used to suggest a national picture – but it must be remembered that it is often tentative and open to huge variations.

However, certain things are clear. The years between 1485 and 1603 witnessed remarkable progress in many spheres of economic activity. Population growth, the expansion of trade caused by the voyages of discovery of other Europeans, and not least the tensions created by religious turmoil during the Reformation, were examples of major changes during the sixteenth century which exerted a serious impact upon the country and the Tudor regime. The Crown's response was twofold: first, to take advantage of changing circumstances where it could, and to create further opportunities; second, to regulate and control, thereby increasing government intervention. If the growth of London, the expansion of trade at home and abroad, and the increase in consumption and landholding among the political élite, all displayed the fruits of opportunism, the enormous rise in the use of statute, proclamation and licence, coupled with the burgeoning responsibilities of the JP, all testify to the growing involvement of central government. Undoubtedly the English economy of 1603 was more complex and sophisticated when compared with that of 1485.

This does not, however, make the Tudor period straightforwardly more progressive than the Middle Ages which preceded it. Much of material life was still recognisable as it had been lived through the previous 500 years. In such areas as the increase in witchcraft prosecutions or the role of women, there was nothing which could be remotely thought of as modern. And there was great poverty and deprivation. As part of England's national story, the Elizabethan age gleams, but as Tawney put it, it 'gleams against a background of social squalor and misery'.

15 ⟿ BIBLIOGRAPHY

**N Heard *Tudor Economy and Society* (Hodder & Stoughton, Access to History, 1992) and **AL Beier *The Problem of the Poor in Tudor and Early Stuart England* (Methuen Lancaster pamphlet, 1983) are two user-friendly topic books. There is also much in *P Williams *The Tudor Regime* (OUP, 1991), best accessed by careful use of the index, and in the chapter by J Sharpe in **P Collinson (ed.) *The Sixteenth Century* (OUP, 2002). More specialist material can be found in Keith Wrightson *Earthly Necessities: Economic Lives in Early Modern Britain* (Yale University Press, 2000) and Barry Reay *Popular Cultures in England 1550–1750* (Addison Wesley Longman, 1998). *James Sharpe *Witchcraft in Early Modern England* (Pearson Educational, 2001) is an excellent brief account.

(*Recommended. **Highly recommended.)

16 ⟿ STRUCTURED AND ESSAY QUESTIONS

A *Structured questions*

1. (a) How severe was price inflation through the sixteenth century?
    (b) What impact did the Price Rise have on Tudor society and the economy?

2. (a) How did Tudor government try to deal with the problem of poverty?
   (b) Why did the problem of poverty grow more pressing during the sixteenth century?

B *Essay questions*

1. What were the effects of population growth in Tudor England?
2. Why, and with what success, did Tudor governments attempt to control enclosure?
3. With what degree of success did the Tudors cope with England's social problems?
4. Explain how and why the English economy developed between 1550 and 1603.
5. Why did the number of witch trials increase in the latter part of the sixteenth century?

17 ⌐ DOCUMENTARY EXERCISE: THE PROBLEM OF POVERTY

Decade	Money wage rate	Cost of living	Purchasing power
(1450–99	100	100	100)
1540–9	118	167	71
1550–9	160	271	59
1560–9	177	269	66
1570–9	207	298	69
1580–9	203	354	57
1590–9	219	443	49

100 = the base rate

SOURCE A
Wage rates and their purchasing power 1540–1609. Purchasing power of agricultural labourer

And I may justly say that the infinite numbers of the idle, wandering people and robbers of the land are the chiefest cause of the dearth, for though they labour not, and yet they spend doubly as much as the labourer does, for they lie idly in the ale houses day and night eating and drinking excessively. And within these three months I took a thief that was executed this last assizes, that confessed unto me that he and two more lay in an ale house three weeks, in which time they ate twenty fat sheep whereof they stole every night one; besides, they break many a poor man's plough by stealing an ox or two from him, and [he] not being able to buy more, leases a great part of his tillage that year. Others lease their sheep out of their folds, by which their grounds are not so fruitful as otherwise they would be ...

SOURCE B
Edward Hext (JP) – letter to Burghley 25 September 1596

Whereas the strength and flourishing estate of this kingdom hath been always and is greatly advanced by the maintenance of the plough and tillage, being the occasion of the increase and multiplying of people both for service in the wars and in times of peace, being also a principal means that people are set on work, and thereby withdrawn from idleness, drunkenness, unlawful games and all other lewd practices and conditions of life; and whereas by the same means of tillage and husbandry the greater part of the subjects are preserved from extreme poverty in a competent estate of maintenance and means to live, and the wealth of the realm is kept dispersed and distributed in many hands, where it is more ready to answer all necessary charges for the service of the realm ... be it enacted by the authority aforesaid, that if any person or body politic or corporate shall offend against the premises, every such person or body politic or corporate so offending shall lose and forfeit for every acre not restored or not continued as aforesaid, the sum of twenty shillings for every year that he or they so offend; and that the said penalties or forfeitures shall be divided in three equal parts, whereof one third part to be to the Queen's Majesty, her heirs and successors to her and their own use [and] one third part to the Queen's Majesty, her heirs and successors for relief of the poor in the parish where the offence shall be committed ... and the other third part to such person as will sue for the same in any court of record at Westminster ...

SOURCE C
Act for the Maintenance of Husbandry and Tillage 1598

Be it enacted ... that the churchwardens of every parish, and four substantial householders ... shall be called Overseers of the Poor of the same parish, and they or the greater part of them shall take order from time to time ... for setting to work of the children of all such whose parents shall not by the same persons be thought able to keep and maintain their children, and also all such persons married or unmarried as having no means to maintain them, use no ordinary and daily trade of life to get their living by: and also to raise weekly or otherwise (by taxation of every inhabitant and every occupier of lands in the same parish in such competent sum and sums of money as they shall think fit) a convenient stock of flax, hemp, wool, thread, iron and other necessary ware and stuff to set the poor on work, and also competent sums of money for and towards the necessary relief of the lame, impotent, old, blind and such other among them being poor and not able to work ... And ... it shall be lawful for the said churchwardens and overseers, or the greater part of them, by the assent of any two Justices of the Peace, to bind such children as aforesaid to be apprentices, where they shall see convenient, till such man child shall come to the age of four and twenty years, and such woman child to the age of one and twenty years ...

SOURCE D
The Poor Law Act 1597

SOURCE E

*Act for the Punishment of
Vagabonds 1598*

... And it be enacted ... that every person which is by this present Act declared to be a rogue, vagabond or sturdy beggar, which shall be, at any time after the said feast of Easter next coming, taken begging, vagrant, wandering or misordering themselves in any part of this realm or the dominion of Wales, shall upon their apprehension ... be stripped naked from the middle upwards and shall be openly whipped until his or her body be bloody and shall be forthwith sent from parish to parish by the officers of every the same the next straight way to the parish where he was born, if the same may be known by the party's confession or otherwise; and if the same be not known, then to the parish where he or she last dwelt before the same punishment by the space of one year, there to put him or her self to labour as a true subject ought to do ...

Q

1. *Compare Sources B and C. What do they tell us about the impact of enclosure?*

2. *To what extent does Source A help to explain the problems referred to in Sources D and E?*

3. *'The threat to law, order and social stability in the 1590s forced the Tudor government to intervene directly in local affairs.' Using the sources and your knowledge, comment on this view.*

Culture and Society Under the Tudors

14

See page 419

INTRODUCTION

Culture has often been taken to mean only high culture, the arts. Historians in recent decades, learning from anthropologists, have gone beyond this and recognised the importance of popular beliefs and customs which cut across class boundaries and which played a part in structuring people's views of the world and each other. The history of Tudor culture is not just that of the portrait and the sonnet, but also of magic and astrology. The whole community turned out for popular festivities and processions. The distinction between popular and élite culture is not clearcut.

This was, however, the age of the Renaissance, a remarkable cultural flowering most accessible to an expanding literate élite. What enhanced the significance of Renaissance classical studies in Tudor England was the introduction of printing to England by William Caxton in the late fifteenth century and the extension of formal education beyond the clergy to include a fair proportion of the nobility and gentry. Kings before the Tudors had had to win credit with their subjects through displays of piety and feats of arms. Henry VIII was the first king who saw the need to show the world how learned he was.

The culture of the élite took on particular importance under the Tudors, as did popular culture, because of the Reformation. This fundamental event of Tudor England was not just a religious and political watershed. It was also a cultural crisis. The leading writers of the age – men called humanists because of their training in the classics – had varying attitudes to the Reformation. The Tudor regime thought it vital that they should support the break from Rome, that their writings should legitimise the Royal Supremacy. The recent work of Alistair Fox and John Guy have shown the complexities and importance of this cultural struggle in Tudor England.

The Reformation destroyed much of the medieval cultural tradition. But the image of a newly austere religion cutting away the cultural luxuriance of the old is belied by the Protestant culture which grew up at the Tudor Court. This reached its height under Queen Elizabeth, with poetry and ceremonial produced by courtiers, surrounding her with a cult which made use of Renaissance symbols to bolster the Royal Supremacy and portray the justice and glory of the godly state of England. Frances Yates did more than any other historian to reveal this cultural programme of Elizabeth's courtiers. Its residual power is evident in the way that people today, who may know nothing of Elizabethan government, still have an impression of Elizabeth presiding over a golden age as 'The Virgin Queen', as 'Gloriana' or 'Astraea'. More recent historians, however, have emphasised the limitations to the cult of Elizabeth and how much the enduring vision we see had been subject to political pressures and changed over time during the Queen's reign.

The other great icon of our cultural heritage originating in the late Tudor period is William Shakespeare. His genius is felt by many to transcend history, to articulate what is universal in human experience. But no man is free from history: Shakespeare's writings are embedded in the particular cultural context of late Tudor and early Jacobean England. EMW Tillyard sought to lay bare this context in his *The Elizabethan World Picture*, published in 1943. This outlines the structure of ideas which conditioned the educated mind of the period, but again there were changing political pressures and social circumstances which meant that it did not apply to everyone in an unchanging way. Some more recent literary critics and historians, such as the so-called 'New Historicists', prefer to investigate the competing, changing ideas of the time rather than to try to identify a static 'world picture'; they are looking for all the tensions and complexities in a period's thought, for the struggle rather than the structure.

1 ⌒ MAGIC AND POPULAR BELIEFS

There is nothing ridiculous in a belief in magic. Men and women always have wanted, and always will want, to control their environment; unable to do so themselves, they defer to experts apparently qualified by a special knowledge of how the world works. Today we have a blind faith in scientists; in Tudor England people turned to experts in magic, the 'cunning' men or women. Scientists, of course, are supposed to work on the basis of experimental fact and demonstrable cause and effect. However, our trust in them is another thing: a placebo, for instance, can apparently effect a cure whether it is prescribed by a modern doctor or a Tudor cunning man or woman. For most people (now as then) it is the authority which counts.

Magic was very often used for healing. A jumble of herbal recipes and incomprehensible incantations were available for the treatment of every problem. One Elizabethan wizard would cure the toothache by writing down on a piece of paper the names of the spirits he identified as causing the malady, whispering some spells (all the more powerful because secret) and then burning the paper. Many healers used touch as part of the cure. One particularly macabre example is the lifting up of sufferers from goitre (caused by iodine deficiency) to be touched by the dead hand of a freshly hanged man. But an example of great political importance was the touching for the King's evil, the power, supposedly granted to both the kings of France and England, to cure scrofula, a skin disease, by the laying on of hands. This apparently supernatural gift bolstered monarchical authority.

These healing spells and practices may seem absurd. However, as Keith Thomas argues, the drama and the symbolism of it all could work very well as a sort of primitive psychotherapy, and magical treatment could be more benign than the contemporary 'scientific' treatment by Tudor physicians with their purging and leeches. Herbal remedies were often very effective and, as forests and thousands of species of plants disappear in the modern world, it is increasingly and belatedly understood how much modern medicine can draw on them. Tudor herbalists did not understand in our terms how their remedies worked – they believed that every herb had a 'signature', an almost mystical characteristic which revealed its properties – but long practice and trial-and-error had enriched traditional lore and made much of it effective.

Divination, the revelation of hidden knowledge, was another task of cunning men or women. The location of a lost object might be pointed to by shears and sieve, or key and book. Criminals could be identified: the skill of the diviner was, of course, to give the name of someone already suspected. In a 1590 arson case, one Thomas Harding accused a cunning man of fraud because he refused to identify those he, Thomas, had already said were guilty. Reassurance, the firming up of intuition, serving the preference to take some sort of action rather than do nothing in the face of adversity – these psychological and social needs were answered by the cunning folk.

The telling of fortunes was even more important in a period when natural or personal disaster was ever threatening. The fame of some seers spread far and wide beyond any single village. Elizabeth Barton, the Holy Maid of Kent, for instance, made herself very unpopular with Henry VIII by prophesying that he would die young if he married Anne Boleyn. A backhanded compliment was paid to the power of her prophecy (which was being exploited by those who opposed the Royal Supremacy) when she was executed in 1534.

Living prophets could be dealt with through the harsh rigour of the law but, unfortunately for the authorities, the popular imagination was host to a whole range of legendary prophets whose sayings were held to have contemporary force. Although there were those, including Caxton, who doubted that King Arthur ever existed, Merlin was still often quoted as an authority on present and future events. He was a danger to the state in that his name could be used to foster Welsh resistance to the Saxon – English – invader. There were numerous rhymes and riddles involving mythical or heraldic beasts such as the Red Dragon or the Boar of Cornwall. They could be interpreted to give legitimacy to more or less any political cause. Henry VII was astute in co-opting the Red Dragon of Wales to his own cause against Richard III. In an age lacking any concept of progress, such a cause had to be wrapped up in some sense of the restoration of a lost age or the force of destiny. Indeed prophecies multiplied during times of disturbance. The Earl of Northampton in the late 1500s observed of a century earlier: 'When the Civil War was hottest between York and Lancaster the books of Beasts and Babies were exceeding rife and current in every quarter and corner of the realm, either side applying and interpreting as they were affected to the title.'

Less dramatic but perhaps more pervasive in its effects was astrology. It made sense that the stars were placed in the heavens for a purpose,

Cosmology academic study of the universe

See page 405

Neo-Platonism Plato was the classical Greek philosopher who believed that material appearances reflected underlying, ideal forms. The neo-Platonists were the Renaissance thinkers who developed his ideas. For instance, 'Platonic love' was seen as a spiritual attachment rather than merely physical desire

Alchemy arcane science trying to transform material substances – most famously the quest to turn lead into gold

KEY ISSUE

Why were magical beliefs so important in this period?

and the unsettling emotional effects of the moon seemed obvious. The learned **cosmology** of the time, placing the heavenly bodies in their various spheres, was perfectly in harmony with the notion that they should influence natural and human events. And astrology had the great advantage of prestige in its being classified as a learned science at the same time as it could be easily, and profitably, popularised in the form of almanacs, which were pamphlets recording broad predictions and specifying which days of the year would be best for sowing or reaping, wooing or marrying, or whatever activity might be of concern. The casting of individual horoscopes also made many astrologers both busy and rich.

The triumph of the Reformation did not spell any quick end to magical beliefs or astrology either. If anything, astrology was resurgent by the middle of the sixteenth century, having been much more neglected in the early, pre-Reformation years of the century, and it has by no means disappeared in the modern world. Science too was not necessarily an enemy to magic; on the contrary it was allied to it in the sixteenth century. Magic depended on an animistic view of the material world – that is, the belief that all the matter around us is moved by spiritual forces which humans can harness through spells and rituals. Some significant science in the later sixteenth century, in line with **neo-Platonism**, a philosophy developed in Renaissance Italy, also worked on the principle that matter was imbued with spirits. Advances in mathematics grew from beliefs in the mystical qualities of numbers and not just from disinterested enquiry. The alchemist, with his repertoire of strange symbols and ritual incantations was not simply to be overthrown by the modern scientist, not even in the following century as the Scientific Revolution gathered momentum. Isaac Newton is famous as the father of modern physics – but he spent just as much of his time and intellectual energy on **alchemy**. So, just as the chronology is not simple, there is no simple division here between 'irrational' popular belief and 'rational' élite learning.

Magic, of course, was eventually to decline but not just because the clergy and (eventually) the scientists told the people to stop believing. Economic changes making existence less precarious, population movement into towns causing natural spirits to seem increasingly remote and, above all, the displacement of magical practices by modern technologies led to a gradual decline in magic and the animistic belief system which supported it. In the end it made more practical sense to drain and fertilise fields properly than to sprinkle them with holy water. Keith Thomas argues that magic declined before these material changes really got going and that it was therefore the belief system that changed first. But it is difficult to find evidence to support his claim that there was a 'trickle down' effect in beliefs from newly enlightened scientists other than among the educated classes. And, although magical practices start to disappear from the records by 1700, that may be because the élite became dismissive of it rather than because magical practices ceased to exist. Magic can easily disappear simply by being recategorised as folklore or the superstition of the ignorant.

2 REVOLUTIONS IN LEARNING – PRINTING AND EDUCATION

See page 420

Mystery plays popular theatre on the streets and in the churches of towns, portraying Bible stories, put on by representatives of gilds. A 'mystery' was a trade or craft

The popular culture examined in the last section and elsewhere was not just the preserve of the lower orders. From **mystery plays** through belief in the powers of cunning folk to witches, the display, the pleasures and the values of popular culture were shared by a full cross-section of society, despite the clergy sometimes being suspicious of areas of communal life they could not control. However, although popular culture endured as a common stock of ideas and motifs, in the sixteenth century a more distinctive élite culture began to emerge which eventually led to the spurning of much popular culture as being vulgar. (The history of the word 'vulgar' itself charts this change in attitude. It originally just meant 'of the people'; by the seventeenth century it had taken on the current meaning of 'coarse, lacking in good taste'.) This élite culture was made possible by the printed book and by education. It was the culture of the gentleman.

It is difficult to assess how deep this cultural change went. The gentleman might be able to adorn his library with books but he did not necessarily read them; and while his son was likely to attend Oxford or Cambridge or the Inns of Court he was equally likely to dedicate himself there to riotous living as to the pursuit of learning. (In Elizabeth's reign William Harrison complained that when charged with disorder such roisterers 'think it sufficient to say they be gentlemen which grieveth many not a little'.) A distinction must be drawn between a show of culture which is made to win status, and culture which involves real participation.

It is also the case that ordinary people were not necessarily excluded from the printed word and education. Elementary education was widely available in 'petty' schools and there were charity schools, such as Christ's Hospital in London, open to the poor. Nonetheless, there is much debate about literacy rates. At the beginning of Elizabeth's reign about 20% of men and 5% of women were literate, on the evidence that they were able to sign their names. However, Thomas More estimated that about half of the population were literate. This could be a quite accurate impression, although it may apply only to London. The tradesmen and craftsmen of the capital were much more likely to be literate than the inhabitants of a remote rural community. And More can only have been referring to men. It also depends what More and historians mean by literacy. Petty schools concentrated on reading, not writing, so many of those who could not even sign their names, may nonetheless have been able to read. In Middlesex in the late 1500s 32% of those accused of crimes bearing the death penalty got off by reading a verse from the bible and claiming benefit of clergy. That, if anything, was an acid test of literacy. But literacy was subject to great regional and social variations and it would be hard to generalise even if the statistical evidence was clear.

Despite the statistical uncertainties Lawrence Stone argued that the dynamic growth of literacy in the late Tudor period, coupled with the

KEY ISSUE

What are the problems in assessing literacy in the sixteenth century?

growth of schools and higher education, amounted to an 'educational revolution' lasting from 1560 to 1640. David Cressy's researches have supported this view, suggesting that there was an upsurge in literacy to about 30% of men and 10% of women by the mid-seventeenth century. However, this still leaves the cultural impact of such a revolution unclear. Literacy, for instance, might have enabled an apprentice or a yeoman to read a ballad or an almanac but these were extensions of popular, oral culture, not displacements of it.

A *Printing*

William Caxton set up the first printing press in England in 1476. This was some 20 years after printing with moveable type had been developed by Gutenberg in Mainz. Such a time-lag suggests it was not so much a technological breakthrough as a businessman's judgement that there was sufficient demand for books which spurred on the development of printing. Caxton's press was certainly a wise investment and flourished under his careful assessment of the cultural market and that of his successor, Wynkyn de Worde. They published mainly religious works and chivalric romances such as Malory's *Morte d'Arthur*.

Caxton's printing press did not lead to immediate cultural change. Much of what he published was the same as the texts copied by scribes in a monastic scriptorium. However, although the contents of books might not have been immediately affected by the advent of printing, a new consumer came into existence. There had been private libraries before printing – the most famous is probably that of Duke Humphrey of Gloucester, a brother of Henry V, who donated his great collection to the University of Oxford – but most books were in abbeys and most scholars were monks. Literacy amongst the gentry had already started to improve in the fifteenth century but books had been scarcely affordable. Printing brought learning within their reach.

The debate on the effect of printing and education at the start of this section focused on the horizontal division in society between the gentleman and the lower orders. However, it should not obscure what happened to the vertical division between lay people and clergy. Aside from some merchants and courtiers and religious enthusiasts such as the Lollards, the clerical monopoly on learning was so definite an assumption that it was sufficient to prove that you could read to claim 'benefit of clergy' and escape the full rigour of the secular law courts. Now, even before the Reformation weakened the division between the clergy and the rest of society, printing had done much to break their monopoly and open up the world of learning to the lay people.

Printing brought a new freedom of ideas, and this could be a challenge to the state as well as to the clergy. It led to repeated attempts by the government to control the presses. The year 1529 saw the first list of prohibited books in reaction to the upsurge of Protestant literature, and in 1538 censorship was extended to secular as well as religious works. Finally, in 1557 the Stationers were incorporated as a company entrusted with the policing of printing in return for a monopoly of licensed presses in London, leaving the only competition in Oxford and Cambridge. Commercial incentive proved the most effective means of censorship.

For the state, printing was not, of course, just a threat. It furthered its development towards the modern state we know today. Administration was made easier – the latest statutes, for instance, became more accurately and quickly known when printed. Government propaganda could be spread much more efficiently, as when Cromwell assembled a team of writers to communicate his view of the Reformation. More subtly the national state could be supported by a stronger national identity as printing helped to ensure the supremacy of an increasingly standardised English, at least among the ruling classes, at the expense of provincial dialects.

KEY ISSUE

What were the social and political effects of printing in the Tudor period?

B *Education*

Both colleges at the universities and schools had been founded in the later Middle Ages by pious benefactors to promote a godly life and sound learning. In the Tudor period there were three new impulses which were to transform the character and the quantity of English education – the 'New Learning', the Reformation and the increasingly perceived need to maintain social order.

Humanism was the name nineteenth-century scholars gave to the 'New Learning', which was the study of carefully edited Latin and Greek authors in place of the corrupt texts and arid, logic chopping disputes of the medieval scholastic philosophers. The humanists aimed not just to reflect on ideas but to use literature and rhetoric to motivate right action in the world. There is debate about whether humanism was ever a coherent movement in Italy, but English humanism did take on a definite character from the pervasive influence of one humanist – Erasmus of Rotterdam. He was the scholar of greatest international repute at the turn of the sixteenth century. He had a large following of correspondents and friends amongst England's leading scholars, such as More and Colet. Even Henry VIII felt it necessary to show off his Latin to him. Although he was to repudiate Protestantism, one of Erasmus' main aims was to break down the idea that only the clergy could be truly close to God. Hence he and his associates were known as Christian humanists. And he saw a liberal, classical education as the key to an improved religious life.

At the universities there were advances towards the humanist ideal of education. One of Erasmus' associates was John Fisher, Bishop of Rochester and chaplain to Henry VII's mother, Lady Margaret Beaufort. He co-operated with her in founding two new colleges to promote humanist learning at Cambridge, St John's and Christ's. There were also new foundations at Oxford, including in 1517 Corpus Christi College which established the first lectureship in Greek.

This change in the quality of learning was matched by quantity in terms of students. The records suggest the number of students matriculating, that is officially entering the two universities each year, more than doubled from 300 under Henry VIII to 700 under Elizabeth. (The conclusion has to be tentative as the evidence for Henry VIII's reign is incomplete.) Add to this the Inns of Court in London, which took 100 students per year in the first half of the Tudor period and 250 by the end of it, and it becomes clear that higher education was becoming an ever more important qualification for those with social aspirations.

The victory of humanism in the universities was, however, by no means complete. Erasmus' idyllic vision of the student like a bee sipping the nectar of humanist learning applied best to dedicated, independent scholars. Meanwhile, the curriculum remained much the same. It was divided between the trivium made up of grammar, **rhetoric** and logic, and the more advanced quadrivium consisting of arithmetic, geometry, music and astronomy. Students might thereafter move on to more specialised studies such as law or medicine while all had some acquaintance with the 'queen of the sciences', theology. The philosophical basis of most learning in the universities continued to be the medieval understanding of the ancient Greek philosopher, Aristotle, rather than Plato who was favoured by the humanists. And the humanists often had to struggle to maintain their foothold in the universities. For instance, conservative elements at Oxford sniped at the 'Grecians', the humanists of Corpus Christi. In response to their attacks Thomas More wrote his letter to the 'Trojans' in 1518, defending the new learning. More's eloquence made sure that that particular encounter was won, but humanists had to defend their position for some time to come.

Rhetoric the study of how best to use language, how to express yourself clearly and forcefully

The humanist programme was more clearly established in schools largely because of the model provided by the Dean of St Paul's, John Colet, in his foundation of St Paul's School in 1512. He was a critic of corruption in public life in church and state, and he thought virtue could be restored through a progressive Christian humanist curriculum. The school statutes drawn up in 1518 laid down very firm principles:

> A child at the first admission, once for ever, shall pay 4d. for writing of his name; this money of the admissions shall the poor scholar have that sweepeth the school and keepeth the seats clean.
> … And thrice in the day prostrate [the children] shall say the prayers with due tract and pausing, as they be contained in a table in the school, that is to say, in the morning and at noon and at evening.
> … If any child after he is received and admitted to the school go to any other school to learn there after the manner of that school then I will that such child for no man's suit shall be hereafter received into our school, but go where him list, where his friends shall think be better learning …

[Having recommended approved authors such as Erasmus, Colet continues]:

… All barbary, all corruption, all Latin adulterate which ignorant blind fools brought into this world and with the same hath distained and poisoned the old Latin speech and the very Roman tongue … I say that filthiness and all such abusion which the later world brought in, which may rather be called blotterature than literature, I utterly abanish and exclude out of this school and charge the masters that they teach always that is best, and instruct the children in Greek and Latin in reading unto them such authors that hath with wisdom joined the pure chaste eloquence.

Q

1. *To what extent was St Paul's intended to be socially exclusive?*
2. *What do the tone and content of these statutes suggest concerning Colet's purpose in founding the school?*

Colet's work at St Paul's was copied in several respects. The Merchant Taylors founded a school in 1560 and copied the St Paul's statutes almost word for word. Of even more far reaching importance was the grammar of William Lily, the first master of St Paul's School. In 1540 Henry VIII proclaimed: 'We will and command … all you schoolmasters and teachers of grammar as ye intend to avoid our displeasure, and have our favour, to teach and learn your scholars this English introduction, here ensuing, and the Latin grammar annexed to the same, and none other'. This is an example of something like a National Curriculum, with a government feeling the need to intervene in a time of flux and uncertainty. The grammar schools were at this time comprehensive in ability, and this was taken into account by the addition of vocational subjects alongside the classics. In 1596 the statutes of Northampton Grammar School specified that the scholars should be taught to 'cypher (handle numbers) and cast an account, especially those that are less capable of learning and fittest to be put to trades'.

The Dissolution of the Monasteries and the re-assignment of their lands appeared to promote education with the founding of 18 schools under the authority of Henry VIII between 1535 and 1547, and bishops were instructed to establish schools in their dioceses. But the bishops rarely carried out the instruction and the apparent gain of Henry VIII schools must be set against the losses of monastic schools. Other schools also lost endowments which meant they could no longer offer free places.

See page 137

The dissolution of the chantries in Edward VI's reign at first had even more mixed effects with many schools supported by chantry funds being threatened by the confiscation of endowments. However, there was a pressing need to educate youth in Protestant thinking and avoid any relapse into popery owing to ignorance. That ensured the re-foundation of schools in nearly every part of the country, and they were often less haphazard in the way they were organised than when so much had depended on the very variable skills and commitment of the chantry priests. The Edwardian initiatives in education continued – in Elizabeth's reign there were 136 foundations of endowed grammar schools.

Little was done to inspire the schoolmaster or raise his status; he was paid as little as half what he could earn as a clergyman and, with one assistant, he might have a class of 140. Instead the state sought to control him. From 1559 on, bishops were instructed to examine schoolmasters, and controls became tighter as the reign wore on with growing fears of hidden Catholics. However, although school-masters could be forced to conform, they could not be forced to teach well. There was much learning by heart, where the sense was not understood, and there was much beating inflicted on those who failed to learn, which scarcely enhanced love of the classics. One contemporary, Roger Ascham (a great scholar and Queen Elizabeth's tutor) observed that 'any learning learned by compulsion tarrieth not long in the mind'. Dean Colet had wanted to spread virtue through education; for many teachers the aim was the narrower one of obedience.

The third impulse in educational reform, alongside humanism and the Reformation, was the increasing concern for the common good – that the state should be administered by those sufficiently educated, that schooling should help to alleviate the poverty and idleness which might breed disorder, and that the economy in general be well served by training and education. The keeping of official parish records, for instance, began under Cromwell and that required an educated clerk. The Royal Injunctions of 1536 declared that 'through sloth and idleness diverse valiant men fall some to begging, some to theft and murder ... where, if they had been well educated and brought up in some good literature, occupation or mystery, they should ... have profited ... to the great commodity and ornament of the common weal'. One educational theorist, Juan Luis Vives, suggested that students 'should not be ashamed to enter shops and factories, and ask questions from craftsmen, and to get to know the details of their work'. The idea of work experience is not entirely new. While it remained most important to ensure through education that the people were godly, for which read Protestant, the expanding administration of the realm and the increasing commercialisation of English society were certainly connected with the upsurge in education. The need for a well-educated ruling class was apparent.

Vernacular the native language, rather than classical Latin or Greek

See pages 365–6

Having passed through a grammar school and a university or one of the Inns of Court, a gentleman could discourse with his peers in a refined **vernacular**, and confirm that he was truly a member of an international cultural élite if he also had an acquaintance with French, the Latin of the humanists and perhaps some Greek as well. (And it was normally a man, with exceptions such as Mary and Elizabeth Tudor.) He could demonstrate his judgment by 'exempla', instances drawn from classical literature of good and evil men and the consequences of their actions. This was a far remove from the pre-Tudor period when formal education had been the preserve of the clergy, and the sons of the nobility and gentry learned only by a sort of apprenticeship to their fathers or elder brothers, or by being farmed out to other households of the same rank. By 1600 there had been a huge increase in the numbers of gentlemen attending the universities and the Inns of Court.

However, the gentleman's education was not just acquired at school or university. In 1531 Sir Thomas Elyot published *The Governour*, the leading handbook for a gentleman's education. It drew heavily on *The Courtier* by Castiglione, the great work of the Italian Renaissance which laid down not just the book learning but also the manners (at table, for instance) and the pastimes (such as hunting or dancing) necessary to life in an aristocratic society. This is a vital part of what Norbert Elias identified as a civilising process in Europe, which brought order to an otherwise unruly nobility. Certainly Elyot saw the dangers of a lack of order leading to 'perpetuall conflicte'. And Elyot's extremely thorough scheme of education had one central aim that noble children 'may be found worthy, and also able to be governors of the public weal'. The nobility and gentry were not just qualified by birth to rule. It was education, and at least acknowledgement of the culture which arose out of it, which secured to them the position of a ruling class.

KEY ISSUE

What were the most significant changes in education in the sixteenth century?

3 ⌁ HUMANISTS AND POLITICS

Sir Thomas Elyot regularly dedicated his books to the King. He was seeking patronage and political advancement. Indeed he was rewarded with a brief period as ambassador to Emperor Charles V. In return for preferment he offered counsel to the King and, perhaps more importantly, added intellectual prestige to his Court. Lord Mountjoy, an eminent humanist, wrote of Henry VIII: 'Our King is not after gold, or gems, or precious stones, but virtue, glory, immortality ...' These words, certainly exaggerated and in most respects untrue, only make sense in the context of culture having become a part of political competition. Henry's real qualities were of little importance as long as he could compete with his fellow European monarchs. That was why he was very keen for the universally respected Erasmus to settle in England rather than in France or the Emperor's dominions.

Politically motivated patronage often just produced standard eulogies, praising the subject's forebears and deeds, and making ludicrous comparisons with classical heroes. History writing was very often pure propaganda about the present, with chronicles or the great classical historians, such as Livy or Tacitus, raided for useful sound-bites. Sometimes, though, works of greater substance were created. An outstanding example is the history of England finished by the Italian humanist Polydore Vergil in 1512. Although the use of the evidence is variable, there is a departure from medieval history writing in that the uncritical reporting of supernatural occurrences was spurned and a clearer sense of how events were connected through time was established. Along with its literary quality this ensured that Polydore Vergil's work remained one of the standard sources for English history for centuries. He aimed to show how the moral order of the country was restored by the advent of the Tudor dynasty. In carefully structured prose he showed, for instance, how the fatal flaws of Edward IV's character – his proneness to lust and his oath-breaking – undermined his otherwise benevolent traits and plunged the country into renewed moral chaos resulting in the tyranny of Richard III. The country could only then be rescued by the accession of Henry VII. This was still very partial history. But it was, and is, great political literature and enhanced the legitimacy of the Tudor claim to the throne.

The game of patronage was a difficult one for the aspiring humanist to play. However high the quality of his work, the political situation often led to disappointment for the ambitious writer. Paradoxically, this frustration could give rise to great creativity. An example is the satire of John Skelton, an inveterate enemy of Wolsey, fulminating against him from sanctuary in Westminster Abbey. Despite often very complex allegory his portrayal of character in *Speke Parrott, Collyn Clout* and *Why Come Ye Nat to Courte*? is unforgettably vivid and precise.

PROFILE

SIR THOMAS WYATT (C. 1503–42)

Frustration was a source for the creativity of Sir Thomas Wyatt who was one of the two leading poets of Henry VIII's reign, along with the Earl of Surrey. He fell in love with Anne Boleyn, which posed political, as well as personal, difficulties. Wyatt had been responsible for introducing the sonnet, devised by the Italian Petrarch, into England, and he sublimated his doomed love in poems lamenting the cruelties of fate and his mistress. He did, however, have extraordinary luck mixed in with his ill fortune. Implicated as a suitor of Anne Boleyn he escaped with his own life, despite having been forced to witness her execution. Rehabilitated by his friend Cromwell, he became ambassador to the Emperor (clearly a job where cultural prestige was a valued qualification), but when Cromwell fell from power it came out that Wyatt had been in contact with the 'traitor', Cardinal Pole. Having had to witness his friend Cromwell's execution, Wyatt then just escaped with his own life once more, this time owing to the intervention of Queen Catherine Howard, on condition that he returned to his wife, whom, sadly, he loathed. He wrote the Penitential Psalms and died – of natural causes – in 1542, having once again been restored to the King's favour. (His son, another Sir Thomas Wyatt, led an abortive rebellion against Mary Tudor and was executed; politics did not run easily in the family.) Wyatt's career may be exceptional, but political disaster was common enough for writers.

See page 320

Critical political thought under the Tudors was not just invective against individuals, as with Skelton. It could draw on fifteenth century authorities, and in particular Sir John Fortescue, who had been Henry VI's Lord Chief Justice. He had argued in his *Praises of the Laws of England* that the authority of the English king was 'politicum et regale', meaning that the king had to take account of political consent and could not just depend on his regal powers. The king could not, for instance, 'at his pleasure change the laws of the kingdom'. This did not mean that Fortescue suggested any practical way of forcing the king to take advice and seek consent, but he urged he should do so as a matter of honour and duty. One role of humanists was, very cautiously, to remind a king and his servants of their duty. It was also in the fifteenth century that the Earl of Worcester had absorbed the ideals of Cicero with regard to civic virtue. The key word here is Commonwealth, meaning the common good. The 'Commonwealth Men' such as John Hales were to attach this concern to the Reformation, wishing to reform society as well as the Church. Hales was to head Somerset's enclosure commission in a quest for social justice.

See page 140

The politics which writers had to cope with was not just that of the Court. They jockeyed for position intensely amongst themselves. Fierce debates sprang up which were by no means just scholarly. Even the pious Fisher became involved in a vitriolic dispute with the French humanist, LeFevre d'Etaples. Erasmus despaired of such behaviour: 'What ill spirit is it that troubles the tranquillity of studies by polemics of this kind? How much better it is to wander in the gardens of the Muses and to live in good understanding.' Again, Erasmus' idyllic vision did not fit the realities of his world.

Added to the politics of state and the political wrangles amongst scholars themselves, there could be conflicting political ideas which an individual writer had to struggle to make sense of. An example is *The History of King Richard III*, written by Sir Thomas More between 1513 and 1518. More was, albeit often unwillingly, a professional politician.

See page 87

At various stages he was Speaker of the House of Commons, Under-Sheriff of London, an ambassador, royal advisor and finally Lord Chancellor in succession to Wolsey. In Richard III he was trying to write a humanist history which followed the convention of contrasting good and evil. However, the contrast kept dissolving as his narrative charted the effects of power on politicians. Even Cardinal Morton, a great and respected influence on More, is shown to have been crafty and ruthless in luring the Duke of Buckingham to his destruction. More never finished his history, and Alastair Fox argues that it is because of this conflict in his ideas. More wrote of the politics he was describing: 'And so they said that these matters be Kings' games, as it were stage plays, and for the more part played upon scaffolds. In which poor men … that sometime step up and play with them, when they cannot play their parts, they disorder the play and do themselves no good'. More was to be a regular actor in the political theatre, and in 1535, having refused to declare acceptance of the Royal Supremacy, he was finally to play his part upon the scaffold. He knew that humanists could never write the political script, for all their intellectual prowess. He could, however, perhaps in compensation, create the perfect republic in his imagination – *Utopia*, which he wrote in 1516.

Alistair Fox has categorised works produced by the likes of Skelton, Wyatt and More as 'the literature of anxiety'. He argues that it constituted the last really imaginative writing before the emergence of Shakespeare and his contemporaries towards the end of the century. In between came the Reformation with its demand for propaganda and a disavowal of complex personal writing in favour of simple public messages.

There is a debate as to whether the influence of humanist scholarship languished as much as did imaginative literature owing to the

Reformation. Certainly the executions of More and Fisher in 1535, and the decline, and then death, of Erasmus in 1536 seem to form a natural break in the development of humanism. Christian humanism, the emphasis these men placed on the reform of the Church through satire, moral example and Scriptural knowledge, was obviously displaced by the more radical programme of the Reformation. However, the intellectual struggle involved in the Reformation put a high premium on the literary and scholarly skills of humanists.

With regard to the Divorce some humanists lined up with Catherine of Aragon and some with Henry VIII. (On the Continent yet more lined up with Emperor Charles V as he was the highest bidder in terms of patronage.) As the King moved towards the break with Rome, humanist lawyers such as Christopher St German, drawing on the work of Sir John Fortescue, supplied him with a theory of statute which under-pinned the Acts of the Reformation Parliament. A team of scholars, probably led by Edward Foxe, assembled historical sources called the *Collectanea Satis Copiosa* which made clear Henry's imperial sovereignty.

An example of one of the humanists who identified himself with the Reformation is Thomas Starkey. By 1535 he was chaplain to the King and one of Cromwell's most able propagandists. He was a thinker of considerable depth, as was shown in the *Dialogue between Reginald Pole and Thomas Lupset*. This discussion of different forms of government was not just abstract theorising – his ideas concerning the need for education and support for the poor in order to preserve social order were very much in tune with Cromwell's thinking. And it was part of a tradition of social commentary stretching back to the fifteenth century and the Earl of Worcester's reading of Cicero and civic virtue, and stretching on later to the Commonwealth Men, such as John Hales. However, in the end, Starkey's personal influence had little effect. In 1536 his old patron Pole came out decisively against the King and that helped to end Starkey's career. In any case the urgent political dictates of the 1530s ruled out any of the long-term reforms which were envisaged in humanist thinking.

Humanism was of great use to politicians but it had little independent political force. Yet its very breadth and neutrality helped to preserve the achievements of the New Learning. There was no imperative to uproot it from the education system when political circumstances changed and one set of ideas fell out of favour. And even contacts with European humanists remained fairly open. For all the upheaval of the mid-century, humanism remained the basis for the great cultural flowering to come in Elizabeth's reign.

> **KEY ISSUE**
>
> *What was the political significance of humanism in the early Tudor period?*

4 ↩ THE IMAGE OF ROYALTY

In England there was no standing army to shore up royal authority. A revolt such as the Pilgrimage of Grace or that of the Northern Earls showed just how easily the monarch's authority could be disrupted and that made the image of royalty all the more important. In the absence of coercive power the majesty of the Crown had to be self-evident to make obedience at least more likely.

A late medieval king such as Edward IV drew on a European tradition of chivalry, largely in the form of the pageants and tournaments developed by the Dukes of Burgundy. It was a culture of violence tempered by Christian virtues, the ideal of which was the heroic, selfless knight. Edward placed himself at the heart of this culture when he built St George's Chapel, Windsor as the church of the knights of the Garter. This was part of the revival of the Order of the Garter which had been founded in the previous century by Edward III. Each of the knights, the élite of the realm, was bound to the king by ties of loyalty and comradeship.

Henry VII appeared to be more remote and calculating than chivalric but he knew how to employ symbolic display for political purposes, and contrary to his reputation as a miser, he spent a lot of money on it, especially on building projects such as the continuation of King's College Chapel, Cambridge and the chapel at Westminster Abbey in which his magnificent tomb was to be constructed. In 1486 he conducted a royal progress, receiving the ritual submission of the cities on his route. During this, the Tudor rose made its appearance – the red rose of Lancaster united with the white rose of York to represent dynastic peace. Another device which Henry employed was the Red Dragon. This was the emblem of the Welsh prince of the Dark Ages, Cadwalader, who had prophesied that a hero would return to restore the British race. Henry used this mythical connection to consolidate support – it was unlikely to have been coincidence that his route through Wales to England and Bosworth fitted closely to the bards' tales of Cadwalader and that he unfurled the standard of the Red Dragon on the battlefield.

Henry VIII brought a new dynamism and character to the royal image; it became co-terminous with his own ego. Henry both sponsored chivalric tournaments and fought real wars so that he could bask in glory. In contrast with his careful father, Court festivities under the young King were more elaborate, colourful and costly. He much enjoyed being a player in scenes of courtly love, the medieval tradition of lovelorn suitors using all the devices of poetry, song and dance to win fair but disdainful ladies. A variation on this theme was an entertainment put on for the Imperial ambassador in 1522 by William Cornish, the highly skilled Master of the Revels. It showed eight beautiful ladies, the personifications of virtues, imprisoned in a castle, the 'Schatew Vert'. Henry appeared as 'Ardent Desire' (prophetically so – one of the imprisoned ladies was played by Anne Boleyn) and with his friends attacked the castle with oranges and dates. The ladies retaliated with rose water and the evening concluded with the triumph of the suitors and with dancing.

Such display can sound rather ludicrous now but the civilised quality of his Court had played its part in winning Henry VIII the reputation he desired. Francesco Chieregato wrote to Isabella d'Este: 'In short, the wealth and civilisation of the world are here: and those who call the English barbarians appear to me to render themselves such ... [Pre-eminent amongst the English] is this most invincible King, whose acquirements and qualities are so many and excellent that I consider him to excell all who ever wore a crown'.

The diplomatic value placed upon extravagant, competitive display can be seen with the Field of the Cloth of Gold, Henry VIII's meeting with Francis I, which took place on neutral territory in northern France in June 1520. Henry attempted to outclass Francis' splendid pavilion by erecting a prefabricated palace, complete with fountains which ran with wine or beer whenever the French were near enough to be impressed. The theme of the meeting was peace and brotherhood, although the suspicions and quarrels over precedence showed how skin deep this was. In fact the whole event was an elaborate bluff as Henry moved closer to Charles V.

See page 61

The palaces that Henry built were like stage sets for his courtly display. By the time he died he had over 60 houses, with 2000 tapestries, 150 easel paintings, and 2000 items of plate. He could put on a good show. Nonsuch, begun in 1538, was intended to compete with Francis I's Fontainebleau, and under the supervision of the Italian architect, Nicolò da Modena, it did achieve grandeur. Like many houses from this period through to 1603, it was traditional English Gothic in plan, with classical decoration in the Renaissance fashion: personifications of the liberal arts and the cardinal virtues, figures of the Roman emperors and the labours of Hercules, all within a very English setting. As David Howarth has observed: 'The Tudors were after all new and they needed to be bedded into tradition'.

The palace of Whitehall in contrast appeared to be little more than houses strung together; in response to an impatient King, it had been constructed far too fast. The interior of Whitehall, however, was another matter. There were elaborate carvings, much covered in gold leaf, and fine tapestries. Above all there was the **fresco** which dominated the Privy Chamber, the heart of Henry's private and his political world. It was the portrait by Hans Holbein of Henry VIII and his third wife, Jane Seymour, along with Henry VII and Elizabeth of York. Painted in 1537, it was destroyed in a fire which consumed the palace in 1698, but it is known through a complete copy and also a surviving cartoon by Holbein of the left half containing Henry VIII and his father. The fresco as a whole propagates the stability and power of the Tudor dynasty but it is the portrait of Henry VIII which was the pattern for a multitude of copies and has endured in the popular imagination. As Roy Strong put it: 'No one ever thinks of Henry VIII in any other way than as this gouty, pig-eyed pile of flesh'. He also asserts that this is where royal portraits as 'propaganda in the modern sense of the word begins'. This is indeed the foundation of our image of Henry VIII, but how far it was propaganda has been disputed. The fresco itself, being in the Privy Chamber, would have been seen by relatively few people. They were important people, admittedly, whom it was important to impress, but this was not 'modern' propaganda intended for public display. There were to be many copies but these were not officially produced.

Fresco a painting on fresh plaster

PICTURE 32
Henry VIII and Henry VII from
The Tudor Succession,
Hans Holbein

As a visual celebration of the King's power, nonetheless, the Holbein fresco in 1537 marked a highpoint for Henry VIII. The Pilgrimage of Grace had been crushed the year before, there was no foreign threat and Prince Edward was born in the October. But gone were the revels of the first half of the reign. Not only was the King ageing but the

Reformation had made the royal image an ever more serious matter as a means of consolidating royal authority. In the words of John Guy, 'the Renaissance prince had become the Reformation patriarch'. He was pictured as Solomon, by Holbein again, receiving the Queen of Sheba; she is allegorical of the Church, gratefully paying tribute to Henry. Solomon became increasingly important as a symbol of royal religious leadership. Henry was no doubt flattered in the comparison, but perhaps also the flattery had the additional purpose of persuading him to carry the Protestant Reformation further. He appears on the frontispiece of Miles Coverdale's translation of the Bible in 1535, with sword drawn to defend the Church and handing the Bible to his bishops. (The sword and the book became the great symbols of the Tudor Supremacy.) Interestingly, this was not an authorised translation, so the frontispiece was a statement of what its sponsors, who included Cromwell, wanted the King to do – authorise an English Bible and advance the cause of Protestantism. It is not art which was simply flattery or official propaganda, but an attempt at persuasion. As we shall see also with Elizabeth, the royal image was the result of a process of negotiation and not just a 'top-down' propaganda exercise.

The attempt at persuasion worked. Henry authorised the Great Bible of 1539, the frontispiece showing him ensuring that the Word of God reaches his people, via the social hierarchy, through bishops to clergy on the one side, and Councillors to gentlemen on the other. The people at the bottom are left in a passive role, listening to the Bible being read to them, and chanting, 'God save the King'. In this portrayal the royal and divine images almost become one. Stephen Gardiner wrote that God set princes on earth as 'representours of His Image unto men'. This was perhaps the most important royal image of all. This Bible was to be placed in every parish church. In reaching the people of England as a whole, it was only to be equalled by Foxe's *Book of Martyrs* in Elizabeth's reign. As Sidney Anglo has stressed, the complex symbolism present in the woodcut images in these books, painstakingly unravelled by modern historians, could not have been understood in detail by more than a tiny number of contemporaries. But it would have been generally understood at the time that these books were an expression of the Royal Supremacy.

In the mid-Tudor period there was nothing of the vigour of Henry VIII in the projection of the royal image. Indeed there was an incident under Mary which showed how difficult the control of an image could be. When Philip II made a formal entry into London following his marriage to Mary, the City Fathers commissioned the usual artists to prepare the pageantry, artists who happened to be Protestant. Philip II noticed that on one street corner there was a portrayal of Henry VIII, holding the Bible labelled 'the Word of God', a clearly Protestant statement. Too late, a furious Bishop Gardiner ordered it removed. Painting and the other arts under Elizabeth were also sometimes intended to send coded messages to her, but it was always subtle, and her role as a symbol, even an icon, for her people, gave rise to a huge outpouring of cultural creativity.

See page 430

KEY ISSUE

What was the political significance of the royal image under the early Tudors?

5 ⌒ THE CULT OF ELIZABETH I

In the first decade of Elizabeth's reign there was no sign of this cultural distinctiveness. For instance, portraits of her were standard, even second-rate and show an intelligent but unexceptional young woman. There were predictable representations of her: great anxieties were aroused by the notion of a woman again occupying the throne, given prevalent views of the subordinate role allotted to women, so Elizabeth was portrayed as Deborah, the successful woman judge in the Old Testament, and as other Old Testament heroines. She was occasionally referred to as a Virgin Queen. It was partly to be taken literally, in the expectation that as a nubile woman she would soon change her status, marry and beget an heir; and partly it was a conventional representation of a queen, applying to Mary Tudor before her and even to Anne Boleyn. Elizabeth herself did make references to her own virginity as something to value, but this was defensive, and failed to alter the general belief that she must marry to secure the succession.

It was in the 1570s that the cult of Elizabeth was first developed. There had been the revolt of the Northern Earls in 1569, the papal excommunication in 1570 and the plots surrounding Mary, Queen of Scots. To combat the insecurity these gave rise to, and the fear that the Elizabethan Settlement might have been only a temporary respite, Elizabeth's ministers and courtiers competitively commissioned and encouraged artists and poets to turn the Queen into a timeless symbol of peace, justice, stability – and love. Elizabeth left artistic patronage largely to her ministers and courtiers. It was cheaper for her, but also it reflects the extraordinary relationship which had built up between Elizabeth and her Court. She had turned her sex, seen as a weakness, into a political asset. As Francis Bacon observed after her death, she had 'allowed herself to be wooed and courted, even to have love made to her' and 'such dalliances detracted but little from her fame and nothing at all from majesty'. She was the unavailable mistress idealised in the poetry of courtly love, and her courtiers competed to show their lovelorn loyalty. The Queen frowned on the expression of enmities, and open discord at Court was, at that point in the reign, suppressed. As Susan Brigden put it: 'irony replaced invective'. Sir Philip Sidney and Edmund Spenser, both frustrated in their political ambitions, sublimated that into literary expressions of frustrated love; they wrote poetry rather than polemics. To change the Queen's policy, she had to be wooed. And she played hard to get, maintaining her freedom of manoeuvre through her renowned hesitancy.

As the cult of the Queen was built up, two fundamental causes of social anxiety were transformed triumphantly into sources of confidence. Firstly, the destruction of the images, processions and ceremonies of the pre-Reformation Church left behind much disorientation and few physical expressions of communal identity. From the 1570s the gap was filled by images, processions and ceremonies associated with the Queen. Secondly there was the continual worry over Elizabeth's marriage. At first it had been the urgent desire for an heir to calm memories of the Wars of the Roses and the uncertainties of the mid-Tudor period. However, from 1578 to 1582 the Queen was negotiating a marriage with the Duke of Anjou, feared by many of her subjects as a French Catholic. Suddenly her earlier stated preference for virginity was taken up, and she was portrayed with enthusiasm as the Virgin Queen – preferable by far to a French Catholic marriage. This seems first to have appeared in entertainments at Norwich when a royal progress took her there in 1578, and the theme was then developed in portraits of the Queen as a vestal virgin and with similar images of her in poetry. This portrayal became ever more popular as she passed any chance of bearing a child. It was a comfort: her purity and chastity would safeguard the realm whatever the insecurity of the dynasty. The Queen accepted this adulation, but it should be noted she was not the origin of it; it had emerged from sublimated opposition to her policy. As Helen Hackett has stressed, it arose from these very specific historical circumstances and was not simply the replacement of the Virgin Mary by the Virgin Queen, as has been commonly assumed. In Elizabeth's remaining years her cult continued to grow up around her, partly to flatter her and partly to push her in a political direction she may have been reluctant to go. As we saw with images of Henry VIII, it was not all top-down propaganda.

Celebrations of Elizabeth grew more elaborate. Before the Reformation the calendar had been structured by saints' days. They were replaced by festivities associated with Elizabeth, in particular her Accession Day on 17 November. It became one of the great events of the year, patchily at first – in some areas it was marked only by minimal bell ringing, and parishes with many 'Church Papists' would not have been enthusiastic – but with the patriotic fervour of war against Spain from the late 1580s, it became fully established. By then, in churches up and down the land, sermons were preached stressing the importance of that day for the preservation of the realm and of true religion. They drew heavily on Foxe and his imperial theme (Elizabeth was identified with Constantine), the Queen ushering in a golden age and renewing the Church; the idea was spread of history beginning again with the Accession. In stark contrast the Pope was pictured as the seven headed beast of the Apocalypse or the Whore of Babylon, with only the Queen to fend off the darkness. Such sermons played an invaluable role in consolidating the Elizabethan Settlement and provided the form in which the image of Elizabeth entered the popular imagination.

See page 431

At Court a resurgence of chivalry characterised the Accession Day celebrations. From about 1572 Sir Henry Lee, the Queen's champion, began to stage the Accession Day Tilts. There was nothing new about tournaments, of course, but the Tilts took on a specific character and importance. They were not just contests of martial arts but another occasion when the Queen herself could be made the focus of all attention, as the fair lady to whom all the knights dedicated themselves. (Elizabeth, however, could show a refreshing indifference to eulogies – on one occasion, when she was bored by endless dedications, she said she would not have come had she known there would be so much talk of her, and went to bed.) The Accession Day Tilts incorporated new cultural elements. Onto the Burgundian traditions of the tournament were grafted Italian devices known as imprese. They were emblems made up for the occasion and could often carry a significant, coded political message, such as the impresa Essex, who wanted war, used in order to represent his contest with Robert Cecil, who urged policy – it showed a pen on some scales outweighing a cannon. In devising the Tilts, Lee also took care to represent England's Protestant mission. How far that mission was progressing was shown by Lee at his retirement Tilt in 1590 when he showed the **Pillars of Hercules**, representing the potential for maritime expansion of Protestant England in the aftermath of the Armada. The new chivalry was backward looking in some of its forms but not necessarily in its themes.

The resurgence of chivalry went beyond the Accession Day Tilts. Edward VI had tried to do away with the tradition of St George as yet another popish superstition. Following Edward IV, Elizabeth very deliberately revived the cult of that saint and the ceremonials associated with the Order of the Garter. It was useful not only to consolidate the loyalty of the English élite, with the Queen very obviously the fount of honour, but also to cross the religious divide for diplomatic reasons, as when Charles IX and later Henry III of France were invested with membership of the Order.

Frances Yates has characterised all this as the 'imaginative re-feudalisation' of culture. It was not just true of England in the sixteenth century – a number of European regimes used 'the apparatus of chivalry and its religious traditions to focus fervent religious loyalty on the national monarchy'. Sidney Anglo and others have criticised this view of the creation of a national monarchy through culture, arguing that the involved symbols which Yates decodes were obscure to all but the most erudite scholars, and in any case the culture Yates writes about did not penetrate much beyond the Court. Even the fabled royal progresses Elizabeth undertook to show herself to her people were confined to the South-east and East of England, and in her last years to the Home Counties. Anglo is right that this culture was largely created within and for the Court. However, it was not confined there. As we saw, it was the Norwich pageants for the Queen which gives us the first evidence of her cult as a Virgin Queen, and the chivalric culture Yates analyses was known at least by many of the provincial gentry through their visits to Court and other contacts with it. As every stately home of the period still shows, portraits of Elizabeth multiplied, and while not every symbol will have been understood by a provincial gentleman, they were evidence of the Queen as a national symbol to which her leading subjects showed their allegiance and which in turn bolstered their prestige. Accounts of pageants and ceremonies were printed and circulated, in nowhere near the profusion as in Valois France, but in England it was not by order of the Crown but consumer demand. The chivalric cults around Elizabeth were not built up by an efficient state propaganda machine, admittedly, but they were a focus of national loyalty for the political nation.

Pillars of Hercules they are the rocks marking the straits of Gibraltar dividing the Old World of the Mediterranean from the New World of the Atlantic

Two poets who contributed greatly to the development of the chivalric cult of the Queen and who also encoded some criticism within the adulation, were Sir Philip Sidney and Edmund Spenser. They were austerely Protestant in their doctrinal views and yet managed to express their principles in the colourful forms of chivalry and pastoral romance; there was a fertile ambiguity in the bringing together of these diverse elements. Sir Philip Sidney was a courtier and diplomat, well connected through his uncle, the Earl of Leicester. He was also at the centre of a group of aristocratic poets. He wrote *Arcadia* which portrayed a land of pastoral allegory and shepherd knights in which Sir Henry Lee, the Queen's champion, would have felt at home. Indeed one of the events in *Arcadia* is a tilt between Philisides and Laelius in the presence of Queen Helen of Corinth – no reader could have failed to see Sidney, Lee and Elizabeth transported as these characters into an ideal world. However, Sidney began *Arcadia* while in exile from the Court in 1579, following his forceful criticism of the Queen's proposed marriage to the Duke of Anjou. His idealisation of the Queen was in opposition to her actual policy, just as the pageant-makers of Norwich had been in 1578. But once the proposed marriage was abandoned and nothing more than a memory, it was the idealisation which survived.

Much poetic imagery was given life in chivalric events organised by Lee. For instance, he entertained Elizabeth at Woodstock in 1575 and one of the characters appearing in the entertainment was a Faerie Queene. Edmund Spenser was to take this image and put it at the centre of the greatest epic poem in English. The first three books of Spenser's *The Faerie Queene* were published in 1590 with a dedication to Elizabeth. Spenser's declared intention for his poem was to 'fashion a gentleman or noble person in vertuous and gentle discipline'. But he also wished to portray in allegory the religious and political struggles of his age. His belief was that poetic images could plant virtuous responses in men's minds. In Book One, for instance, there is Una, the one signifying undivided imperial authority as exercised by Elizabeth; in contrast there is the false Duessa, 'clad in scarlet red', representing the Pope, usurping imperial authority and bringing disorder to the world. Hopes for the triumph of good over evil are pinned on a series of knights but also on various manifestations of Elizabeth. She appears as the fiercely anti-Papal Virgo but also in the neo-Platonic form of Venus. Elizabeth's public virtue is pictured in Gloriana's just government and her private virtue is seen in Belphoebe's chastity. This was 'the most stupendous exercise in flattery that British literature has ever seen' (Alistair Fox); it was a bid for patronage as well as an exercise in Protestant virtue. But in the later parts of the poem, not published until after the Queen's death; she is pictured as Cynthia, the changeable goddess of the moon. By this stage Spenser was disillusioned by Elizabeth's policy in Ireland, which he thought should be more aggressive, and it surfaces in his poetry. But a character, far less ambivalent, which is the cornerstone of the poem, and of the whole cultural project surrounding the Queen, according to Frances Yates, is Astraea.

In classical myth Astraea was the last of the immortals to leave the earth during the world's decline into the age of iron. She is portrayed as the Just Virgin holding an ear of corn and thus, while barren herself, promotes fertility. In Dante's *Monarchia*, which 300 years previously had condemned papal usurpation of imperial authority, Astraea was the Imperial Virgin. In restoring the Royal Supremacy, Elizabeth, as Astraea, was restoring a golden age in which peace, justice and all the virtues could flourish once again. One of the poets who dedicated much of his work to Elizabeth as Astraea was Sir John Davies. This is the last verse of an acrostic (which like all the others in a series of them spelt out *Elisabetha Regina*), written near the end of the reign:

> Rudeness itself she doth refine,
> E'en like an alchemist divine,
> Gross times of iron turning
> Into the purest form of gold,
> Not to corrupt till heaven wax old,
> And be refined with burning.

For all its celebration of the golden age brought by Elizabeth as Astraea, notes of an underlying anxiety can be detected. No taint of corruption could touch Elizabeth but it was still thought to be rife amongst government servants, and while Heaven might be ageless, the Queen herself was not, however much rhetoric there was about her eternal youth. And although political and religious struggles could be seen as a refining fire, that did not promise an easy time ahead.

Visual images of Elizabeth could be seen everywhere. Cut-out patterns were issued in the 1570s to serve the needs of provincial painters and she appeared in engravings and woodcuts and on coins and medallions. As her father had been portrayed in the frontispiece to the 'Great Bible' so she became more familiar through the 'Bishops Book'.

The portraits of Elizabeth increasingly followed poetry in showing her laden with symbols of justice and all the virtues, a phoenix for renewal or a moon for imperial chastity and dominion over the seas, black for her constancy and white for her purity. The Renaissance theory of the portrait went well beyond the importance of a recognisable like- ness; its purpose was to perfect nature and so elicit from the viewer a virtuous response. In studying the portrait of a ruler the viewer, aided by symbols, should see through the individual to the inner, neo-Platonic ideal of a monarch. That theory was known in Elizabethan England, although there was little evidence of Renaissance artistic techniques in Elizabeth's portraits which lacked the subtleties of perspective or the careful modelling in light and shade of contemporary Italian art. This was partly because of the lack of artistic education in England (there were few skilled or distinctive English master painters in the sixteenth century, apart from the miniaturist, Nicholas Hilliard), but it was also

See pages 409–15

related to the purpose of the portraits. They were icons to be revered and therefore little Renaissance naturalism was called for.

As Elizabeth's reign wore on, any attempt at portraying the reality of her changing appearance was abandoned. Instead what was presented was the famous mask of youth established by Nicholas Hilliard. This was not just convention or the Queen's personal vanity (which was considerable) but a matter of political concern given that the war against Spain made the Queen's image ever more important as an enduring national symbol. In 1596 the Serjeant Painter was to order the destruction of unseemly portraits and in 1600 the Privy Council was trying to call in portraits which did not comply with the official pattern. Robert Cecil in particular was co-ordinating the projection of the royal image through the poetry of Sir John Davies and the portraits of Marcus Gheeraerts, the most accomplished painter of the latter years of the reign. In paintings such as Gheeraerts', the mask of youth served its purpose of representing unchanging stability, but such symbolism could only paper over the financial and political cracks brought on by the strains of war against Spain, Europe's greatest power, and, although the mask of youth promised eternal stability, it could only have that meaning as long as the Queen lived. She defied mortality as best she could. She would have no mirrors in her chamber so she avoided seeing herself as an old woman. She would not acknowledge death by planning a tomb as her predecessors had generally done. She tried desperately to live up to her motto, *semper eadem* – always the same. She was celebrated as Astraea for the last time on 6 December 1602 in an entertainment for her when she visited Cecil House on the Strand. She died the following March.

Around the image of the last Tudor monarch clustered a rich array of symbols. The Court poets and painters who employed them transcended mere propaganda in a way that the scholars and artists working for Henry VIII had rarely achieved. The Elizabethans managed to give their political and religious commitments elaborate and enduring artistic expression. Perhaps this was made possible because of the creative tensions brought about by England's vulnerable but defiant position. It remained open to European culture and politics but was separated off by its national Reformation. Or there were the ideological, as well as personal, tensions in Elizabethan Court politics. As we have seen, the cult of the Virgin Queen had its origin in Puritan fears that Elizabeth would marry the Catholic Duke of Anjou. But such tensions and ambiguities could only be held in balance by the person of the Queen. All that could follow when she had died was disappointed expectation, despite some attempts at similar myth making around James I's son, Prince Henry. The Court culture of the Stuarts, especially under Charles I, came to express rather than resolve religious tensions and to promote not unity, but the alienation of Court from country. When Elizabeth died, her image remained like a ghost to haunt her Stuart successors and to taunt them with their inadequacies.

See the Ditchley and the Rainbow portraits on pages 414–15

KEY ISSUE

What brought about the elaborate cult which developed around Elizabeth? Did it always serve her purposes?

Was There a Renaissance in England?

The influence of the Italian Renaissance and its re-establishment of classical rules in the visual arts was very limited in England. The Italian Pietro Torrigiano built the great tomb of Henry VII in Westminster Abbey, but that is unique. There were only two major buildings in sixteenth-century England which show the full influence of classicism in form and proportion as well as decorative detail: the original Hampton Court built for Wolsey (as recently established through archaeological research), later largely re-modelled by Henry VIII in traditional English style; and Somerset House (a predecessor of the present building), built for the Duke of Somerset when Lord Protector. What Wolsey and Somerset had in common was that they were both running the country, but in a precarious position doing so. They could not rely on tradition to bolster their political position, and they did not rely on native English tradition in their greatest architectural projects. Given their insecure status they may have all the more valued the order and serenity of classical architecture. Traditional structures and a desire to emulate the great rival of England, France, were at the heart of Henry VIII's many building schemes. The palace of Nonsuch was intended to rival Francis I's Fontainebleau, not a classical villa; it was built very fast, out of brick not stone, its towers were a chivalric fantasy with no sign of classical control, and the classical Roman role models and symbols which adorned its facade in profusion were more a humanist textbook in stone and fresco than evidence of the restrained principles of classical design. Elizabeth built nothing. There were the 'prodigy houses' put up by the newly rich to impress the neighbours, and to attract prestige and debt in more or less equal measure if the Queen chose to visit on a royal progress. They could be hugely impressive but, like Nonsuch, used classicism for decoration rather than fundamental inspiration.

Painting likewise shows little direct influence of the great Italian Renaissance. The most impressive painting of the century in England was produced by a non-Italian visitor, Hans Holbein, who rendered unforgettable images of Henry VIII and his Court. He represented the Northern Renaissance, but left no local school of painters behind him. Under Elizabeth Italian artists did visit England – Federico Zuccaro, for instance, at the invitation of the Earl of Leicester – but they rarely stayed. Their great skill was in rendering naturalism and proportion. But the Elizabethans were interested in paintings as emblems, not as representations of the real world in an artful composition. Elizabethan paintings were laden with symbols which could be read like a book.

It was literature which saw the greatest creativity in Tudor England, and here the Renaissance had a much clearer effect. There were the humanist scholars, such as Thomas More, who read their Cicero and Plato, in editions produced by Italian scholars (when not by the Dutch Erasmus). There were the poets under Henry VIII, the Earl of Surrey and Sir Thomas Wyatt, who took the sonnet form developed by the father of Italian Renaissance poetry in the fourteenth century, Petrarch, and used it to show the English language off at its best, developing a form which Shakespeare perfected. There was, however, to be a 40-year gap between their achievements and that of the next generation of Renaissance poets, led by Sir Philip Sidney and Edmund Spenser. By the 1570s, after all the uncertainties of the mid-Tudor period, the creation of a national identity had begun, based on England as a Protestant bastion, defending itself against Catholic conspiracy at home and abroad, and led by a heroic Queen. Writers started to work from Italian models once more with the confidence that they could make them English. Sixteenth century Italian Renaissance writers, such as Ariosto, had merged chivalric myth with classical forms, and this was eagerly taken up in English by Sidney and Spenser, as they sought to praise, and also to tutor, that object of chivalric adulation, the Virgin Queen. Their ambition was for England to outdo Italy in their poetry – Spenser's stated intention was 'to emulate and hope to overgo' Ariosto. These poets wished to show how the conflicts of desire portrayed in the Italian originals could be resolved through Protestant virtue. A third of all plays at this time drew on Italian sources. Shakespeare was no exception, although richly ambiguous and without the emphasis on Protestantism. However, by this stage there was also deep suspicion of Italy, arising from Protestant fear of Catholic Rome. Italians were caricatured as being prone to sodomy and duplicity. The archetype of cunning was the Italian political thinker, Machiavelli, whose reputation still in part rests on the stock, wicked character, the 'Machiavell' in many an English play around 1600. That great humanist scholar, Roger Ascham, recommended Italian authors but he also wrote: 'He that by living and travelling in Italy, bringeth home into England out of Italy, the religion, the learning, the policy, the experience, the manners of Italy. That is to say, for religion, papistry or worse; for learning, less, commonly, than they carried out with them …' Italian influences were welcome, but only when they could be safely naturalized as in the work of advanced Protestants, such as Sidney and Spenser, or seen as an exotic setting for stage plays.

There was an English Renaissance but it was confined to being decorative in the visual arts; much Renaissance influence also came from France rather than direct from Italy. It was only in literature that the Renaissance was fully absorbed. But the limited influence of Italy does not necessarily devalue English culture under the Tudors. That idea of the Renaissance necessarily spreading out like ripples from its source in Italy has recently been challenged by historians such as Peter Burke, who see it as a phenomenon which was always national or regional in identity in its various manifestations in different parts of Europe, and not to be seen just an Italian import. There was to be a purer classical style which was imported into England in the seventeenth century by the likes of the architect Inigo Jones. But that became identified with the Stuart Court, a Court which looked increasingly alien to much of England's political nation in the years before the civil war.

6 ⌁ AN ELIZABETHAN WORLD PICTURE?

In 1943 EMW Tillyard published his account of the structure of ideas fundamental to the Elizabethan age, *The Elizabethan World Picture*. Without understanding these ideas, which were the assumptions and commonplaces of the time concerning the universe and mankind, much of the writing of Elizabethan authors, such as Shakespeare, Marlowe or Jonson would remain only partly comprehensible. In particular Tillyard saw in this world picture a belief in a cosmic order and hierarchy 'so taken for granted, so much part of the collective mind of the people, that it is hardly mentioned except in explicitly didactic passages'. Certainly the ideas identified by Tillyard were of importance to the Elizabethans. They derived largely from classical authorities such as Ptolemy (for astronomy), Aristotle (for natural science) and Galen (for the workings of the human body). What remains under debate is whether these ideas were ever so coherent or universally accepted. There were new theories jostling with those of the classical authorities and also political complexities which may have radically affected the idea of cosmic order and hierarchy even during the Elizabethan period.

In Ptolemy's scheme of the cosmos the earth was at the centre surrounded by nine 'spheres' (or ten or 11 according to some versions), each enclosing the other, with the outer sphere as the 'primum mobile' determining the movement of all that lay within it. The spheres moved in perfect harmony. This was literally musical harmony – the 'music of the spheres' was the ideal which the great Tudor musicians and composers, such as Tallis and Byrd, tried to express. Beneath the outermost sphere was the firmament of fixed stars and then in the lower spheres were the seven planets, each held to its perfect circular motion. Finally, the sphere of the moon divided the incorruptible ether, in which angels lived, from the unstable, sublunar region of earth and human beings.

The hierarchy of beings which stretched from God down through the spheres to inanimate objects on the earth was the 'Great Chain of Being'. Beneath God were the different orders of the angels: seraphim in the 'primum mobile', cherubim in the firmament, and the less-exalted, angels in the sphere of the moon. Next there was mankind which shared rationality with the angels above and material existence with the creatures below. Mankind occupied several subdivisions of the Chain of

PICTURE 33
The Great Chain of Being

Being, princes at the top stretching down through nobility and gentry to the most lowly peasant at the bottom. Beneath mankind came the animals, in turn subdivided into those with memory, movement and senses, such as dogs, down to those creatures with only limited senses, such as molluscs. Plants were next, being endowed with life but without senses. Finally there were the inanimate objects which made up the earth.

The material of this hierarchically constructed universe consisted of four elements – fire, air, water and earth. Each class in the Chain of Being had a primate, something of prime importance, depending on the balance of these four elements. For instance, gold was reckoned to be the finest, most durable metal because it contained fire, air, water and earth in balanced proportion.

Each individual human being was thought to be a microcosm, that is containing in miniature the features of the universe. Mankind was unique in combining features from above and beneath the moon, from the rational command of the mind to the unstable, sublunary desires of the lower body. There was a Chain of Being in the body – the liver produced 'vegetable' spirits for the basic functions of the body, which rose to be 'sensible' spirits (i.e. mobilising the senses) in the heart and finally to the 'vital' spirits of rationality in the brain. The four elements of the universe were represented by the four 'humours' of the body. These were choler (akin to fire), blood (air), phlegm (water) and melancholy (earth). Health, according to Galen, depended on the four humours being held in balance. And someone's temperament was the result of whichever humour was dominant. For instance, if you were of a fiery disposition you were 'choleric'. In this hierarchically ordered universe it seemed everything was inter-related and everything had its place.

The implications of this for the cultural, social and political attitudes of the time were enormous. Spenser, for instance, influenced by neo-Platonic thinking, identified love as the principle of order in the universe. The four elements would be in perpetual conflict except that love 'did place them all in order, and compel to keep themselves within their sundry reigns, together linkt with adamantine chains'.

And the various ranks of society were portrayed as essential links in an ordered universe ordained by God. Where there was rebellion then chaos would surely follow – whether the rebellion was that of Satan against God; or of the stomach against the head in the microcosm, the body, during illness; or a subject against his prince. Richard Hooker, the defender of the Anglican Church against Puritan enthusiasm, put the theory at its most moderate: 'Is it possible that man, being not only the noblest creature in the world but even a very world himself, his transgressing the law of nature should draw no harm after it?'

The place of the prince in the Chain of Being was gradually elaborated by the end of Elizabeth's reign into the 'divine right of kings'. The prince, being ordained of God, could lay claim to absolute, unchallengeable authority. The development of this doctrine was probably a reaction to threats of Elizabeth's deposition by Roman Catholic forces. She herself, however, made relatively little of 'divine right', stressing her adherence to law and liberties; the first two Stuarts were to push the doctrine further and finally stimulated a dramatic reaction against it.

When ideas are abstracted it is possible to arrange them in a coherent 'world picture'. Although there were undoubtedly common assumptions and intellectual traditions, the ideas outlined above existed in the thinking and writings of individuals – individuals who frequently disagreed with one other, or who were quite happy to hold to contradictory ideas themselves. One leading example was John Dee, Queen Elizabeth's favourite philosopher.

JOHN DEE (1527–1608)

Dee was at the centre of a considerable network of intellectual life. He counted amongst his patrons a wide range of courtiers including the Sidney and Dudley families, and he served Emperor Rudolf II, as well as Queen Elizabeth. He knew or corresponded with most of the leading European scholars of his day. His pupils included those who were to be leading poets, mathematicians and explorers, possibly even Drake. The library at his house in Mortlake represented contemporary learning more completely than any other; and gatherings there brought together some of the finest minds of the period.

As a student at St John's College, Cambridge from 1542, he had studied for 18 hours a day, allowing four hours for sleep and two for food and recreation. From 1548 he travelled on the continent, giving lectures in Paris on Euclid so popular that students were hanging through the windows to hear him. Given a pension by Edward VI, he was in prison for suspected treason under Mary, and finally won the favour of Elizabeth. He had now developed greatly his interest in the occult sciences. His first service to the new Queen was to calculate the astrologically auspicious day for her coronation. In 1575 she visited him at his home at Mortlake, location of his famous library, and Dee showed her his magic mirror, a highly polished disc of 'cannel' coal. He also had a holy stone, to which he thought he had been guided by an angel; it was a polished crystal globe. A comet was sighted in 1577, and he was summoned to the Court at Windsor to provide reassurance that it portended no disaster. In 1580 the Queen visited Dee once more to examine the maps he had drawn to show her claim to territories overseas. But Dee's obsessive learning left him out of touch with ordinary affairs. The Queen had awarded him a sinecure, a post without any duties to support his studies, but he never got round to completing the legal formalities so lost £1000. Seeing himself as a good Christian philosopher, he could not understand why some people thought him 'a companion of the hellhounds … a conjuror of wicked and damned spirits'. In 1581 he fell into the company of Edward Kelly, a con-man. Kelly became Dee's 'skryer' or medium in seances. In 1583 Albert Laski, a Bohemian nobleman, persuaded the pair of them to visit Bohemia where the Emperor Rudolf had a belief in all things occult. Dee and Kelly travelled from town to town in central Europe, searching for the philosopher's stone to turn lead into gold. They claimed to have made some gold out of the remains of a warming pan. Eventually Kelly went too far (insisting on wife-swapping) and Dee returned home in 1589. His house at Mortlake had been vandalised while he was away, by a mob suspicious and fearful of his occult interests. But from 1595 to 1604 he found security as Warden of Manchester College. After that, he returned to Mortlake, and his old patron the Queen dead, he himself died in poverty, his famous collection of books sold off, in 1608.

At the heart of Dee's thought was mathematics which for him was the key to understanding the universe: 'By Numbers … we may both wind and draw ourselves into the deep search and view, of all creatures distinct virtues, natures, properties and Forms; And, also, farther, arise, climb, ascend and mount up (with Speculative Wings) in spirit, to behold in the Glass of Creation, the Form of Forms'. In his *Preface to Euclid* (published in 1570), Dee did not just write of pure mathematics but showed how it lay at the heart of music, painting and architecture. Vital to architecture, for instance, is mathematical proportion, and in that it is linked to the microcosm, the human body, which also reflects eternal proportion. This was all in accord with the Elizabethan world picture, although it had little immediate application at the time. There were magnificent **'prodigy' houses** built, such as Hardwick Hall with its novel expanses of glass, but truly classical proportions were not to be seen in England until the following century.

Where Dee's ideas did make a practical contribution was in the art of navigation. His improved charts enabled captains of the Muscovy Company's ships to leave coastal navigation in favour of more direct oceanic routes. He much influenced Richard Hakluyt whose *The Principall Navigations, Voiages and Discoveries of the English Nation* was to become the textbook account of English exploration. In 1577 Dee published *General and Rare Memorials Pertaining to the Perfect Arte of Navigation* in which he argued for the creation of a navy, along with suggestions as to how it could be financed and how it might spread Elizabeth's sovereignty across large tracts of North America. He saw the emergence of a British Empire (his phrase), both secure and farflung, as certainly as a 'Mathematicall demonstration'. Dee's *General and Rare Memorials* were not applied directly as policy but they opened up further the prospect of maritime expansion; this also subtly qualified the fixity of any 'world picture' and drove forward practical scientific enquiry.

Dee also saw practical applications of his knowledge in ways which we would dismiss as being fanciful. Number being the key to the universe, he thought that mathematical language was a means of conjuring angels and gaining universal knowledge. He was much influenced by Hermeticism, derived from the writings of Hermes Trismegistus (thought to be ancient Egyptian, actually from the later Roman period) which were rediscovered during the Renaissance by neo-Platonic philosophers. Hermeticism sought to reveal the 'sympathies' which bound the universe together. Certain colours or plants or stones had 'sympathies' with the stars and could be used by a magus with sufficient occult knowledge to channel and to store the powers of those stars. Such magical beliefs, although at one with the idea of mankind as microcosm, contradicted orthodox Aristotelian or religious thinking and Dee's growing obsession with the occult finally marginalised him.

What Dee's career showed was that there was no single, settled view of the universe. For instance, he had encountered the writings of Copernicus who earlier in the century had argued that the sun, rather than the earth, as Ptolemy had maintained, was at the centre of the

Prodigy houses the great houses built by the nobility and richer gentry of Tudor England to demonstrate wealth and influence

See page 412

See page 376–7

universe. (Ptolemy was one of the great classical authorities along with Aristotle and Galen.) Dee never explicitly agreed with this but some of his astronomical work revealed Copernican assumptions. He also assumed that there was no fixed boundary to the realm of fixed stars. Here again the Elizabethan world picture is shown to be tentative even within one individual's thinking.

Thomas Digges did explicitly embrace the new cosmology of Copernicus in his 1576 work *The Prognostication Everlasting*. He also represented the universe as being infinite rather than enclosed, and in 1577 was to observe a comet which cut across the spheres and orbited the sun. This did not mean Ptolemy's system was immediately scrapped but it was brought into doubt. Similarly, the authority of Galen had been brought into question by a Swiss called Paracelsus (who had made his point by burning the standard medical works of the time in Basle in 1527) and by his followers, a number of whom were to be found in Elizabethan England. In place of Galen's view of illness as the imbalance of the four humours, Paracelsus had argued that interacting with the four elements were three 'qualities' which in chemical form were sulphur, salt and mercury. Illness therefore required chemical treatment. This was a branch of alchemy, more usually known for projects such as attempts to turn lead into gold, but it was the beginning of the chemical medicine which is still with us today. Those who read Digges or Paracelsus could no longer accept the view of the universe embodied in the traditional authorities, Ptolemy, Aristotle and Galen.

By the end of Elizabeth's reign, empiricism, the expansion of knowledge through experiment, was gaining ground. William Gilbert published *De Magnete* in 1600 in which he demonstrated the magnetism of the earth. He had learned much from observing metalworkers and he set little store by the 'probable guesses and opinions of the ordinary professors of philosophy'. Rather than a static, received world picture, he praised a philosophy which had 'grown so much from things diligently observed'.

Elizabethan scientists continually questioned, amended and diversified their world picture. However, in terms of the circulation of ideas in the Elizabethan period, far more importance lies with the creation of theatres such as The Rose or The Globe. Plays had long existed for performance in the courtyards of inns or market places, but now for the first time in England since the Romans there were buildings dedicated to drama, which in the case of large amphitheatres such as The Globe, could seat thousands. The consequent demand for new plays was huge – there were 436 we know of between 1560 and 1600 – and the golden age of English drama, with playwrights such as Christopher Marlowe, Ben Jonson and pre-eminently, William Shakespeare, had begun. Such dramatists appeared to represent the Chain of Being as a more definite set of ideas than did scientists engaged in subtle debate or private speculation. These ideas were not just natural or traditional. Heywood in his *Apology for Actors* had argued that a purpose of plays was to teach 'subjects obedience to their king' by showing them 'the untimely end of such as have moved tumults, commotions and insurrections'. This shows that people had to be repeatedly shown the virtues of order rather than it just being taken for granted. It might also be the case that Heywood was reassuring patrons, mainly courtiers, and the royal authorities that their plays were not written to be appropriated for subversive causes. After all there was to be considerable alarm that a play about the deposition of Richard II (possibly Shakespeare's) was shown in a number of public places just before the Essex rebellion in 1601.

WILLIAM SHAKESPEARE (1564–1616)

Shakespeare's parents were John Shakespeare, a substantial trader in Stratford-upon-Avon, and Mary Arden, a farmer's daughter. They could not even write their signatures – legal documents bear their mark instead – but William was sent to the local grammar school established in Henry VIII's time. (This is perhaps the most telling example of generational change owing to Tudor education.) William left at 13 to help his father in business and in 1582, aged 18, he married Anne Hathaway. As was common, the bride was pregnant at the time of the marriage and their first child Susanna was born six months later; two more children, Hamnet and Judith, followed in 1585. It is thought the marriage was not happy, and certainly he saw little of Anne after he left for London in 1585 to make his fortune (which he was to do). He may have left because of a dispute with a local magistrate, Sir Thomas Lucy, who persecuted Catholics, among them members of Shakespeare's family. Certainly the comic character 'Justice Shallow' who appears in his history plays looks like revenge on Sir Thomas. Arriving in London, he earned his living acting and revising existing plays. He started to write plays himself for the flourishing London theatres, first of all The Rose and later The Globe, built in 1599. From 1591 to 1611, he wrote two plays a year, and 16 of his 37 plays were published in his life-time. Queen Elizabeth was particularly delighted by the character Falstaff in the history plays, and tradition has it that she asked for his reappearance in a sequel that became *The Merry Wives of Windsor*. Shakespeare also wrote other poetry, including the sonnets, some to a disdainful mistress, and some to a young man. In 1596 he returned to Stratford to bail out his father out who was being pursued for debt, and that same year his son Hamnet died. He reorganised the family's affairs and bought a major property in Stratford, New Place. The money had probably been made through his acting more than by writing. His financial success made him secure, so that he gave up both acting and writing, and returned to Stratford in 1611. He died in 1616, a solid and respectable citizen in a small market town, and the author of what was to be the most renowned literature in the English language. He bequeathed New Place to his daughter Susanna, and his second best bed and a small income to his wife, Anne.

PICTURE 34
William Shakespeare, *anon.*

The 'New Historicists', such as Stephen Greenblatt, have a more subtle account of how Elizabethan and early Stuart drama relates to social order and the powers that be. They find clues in other texts from the period, about the control of prisoners, the sick (especially from the plague) and newly discovered peoples in the New World, to suggest how power operates through drama. Greenblatt argues that 'power defines itself in the relation to that which threatens it'. He means that power only exists when it has something to suppress; it does not exist in a stable, hierarchical Chain of Being. For instance, newly discovered native Americans were studied and their ways recorded and explained so that control could be exercised by their colonial masters. Similarly in the Henry IV plays by Shakespeare, Prince Hal learned about the low life from practical experience in the company of the happily debauched Falstaff and his cronies, a low life which as king he could later condemn and thereby express his power. From this point of view the Chain of Being was evident in the drama only through its being broken. The audience's doubts, in both the Chain of Being and the monarchy it justified, were raised so that they could be contained.

The 'New Historicist' reading of Shakespeare and other Elizabethan dramatists is certainly controversial. More conservative critics complain that such historical reductionism obscures the beauty and universal truths of the drama, whereas those to the left argue that genuinely subversive voices can be heard in many Elizabethan plays, and they were not just called into existence so that they could be controlled. What the debate does make clear is that there is no single reading of Shakespeare or, for that matter, any other aspect of Tudor culture. But a historical reading is always likely to be concerned with the complex, intimate relationship between culture and the power of a Tudor state which was never fully secure and which, from the inauguration of the new dynasty in 1485 through the Reformation to the cult of Gloriana, was ever refashioning itself in the minds of the English people.

> **KEY ISSUE**
>
> *Was there such a thing as an 'Elizabethan world picture'?*

7 ⌐ BIBLIOGRAPHY

A good overview is *Greg Walker *The Renaissance in Britain*, Chapter 5 in P Collinson (ed.) *The Sixteenth Century* (OUP, 2002) **D Cressy *Literacy and the Social Order: Reading and Writing in Tudor and Stuart England* (Cambridge, 1980) is a key survey. *Barry Reay *Popular Cultures in England 1550–1750* (Addison, Wesley, Longman, 1998), see Chapter 2 on printing and oral culture, and Chapter 5 on Festive Drama and Ritual *A Fox and J Guy *Reassessing the Henrician Age: Humanism, Politics and Reform 1500–1550* (Blackwell, 1986) is complex but well worth consulting. **D Loades *The Tudor Court* (Batsford, 1986) deals expertly with the political importance of Court culture. **R Porter (ed.) and M Teich *The Renaissance in National Context* (Chapter 8 on England by D Starkey) (Cambridge, 1992) is a very readable summary and strongly argued, as is the case with everything Dr Starkey writes. *R Strong *The Cult of Elizabeth: Elizabethan Portraiture and*

Pageantry (Thames & Hudson, 1977) is still the standard account of Elizabeth's portraits, and elegantly written. **FA Yates *Astraea: the Imperial Theme in the Sixteenth Century* (Penguin, 1978) is one of the great classics of historical writing, setting the image of Elizabeth in its classical, philosophical and literary context. **Helen Hackett *Virgin Mother, Maiden Queen: Elizabeth I and the Cult of the Virgin Mary* (MacMillan, 1995) is a brilliant critique, placing the image of Elizabeth firmly within its changing historical context. S Greenblatt *Shakespearean Negotiations: the Circulation of Social Energy in Renaissance England* (Oxford, 1988) is difficult but gives an exciting theoretical perspective.

(*Recommended. **Highly recommended.)

8 ⇌ STRUCTURED AND ESSAY QUESTIONS

A *Structured questions*

1. (a) In what ways did schools and universities change in the sixteenth century?
    (b) Why, and in what ways, did education become important to a Tudor gentleman?
2. (a) How did the image projected by Henry VIII differ from that of his father?
    (b) What aspects of culture were politically important to Henry VII and Henry VIII, and why?

B *Essay questions*

1. Who believed in, and practised, magic in the sixteenth century, and why?
2. How far was English culture affected by continental influences in the sixteenth century?
3. Why, and with what result, did humanism and the 'New Learning' develop in England in the reigns of Henry VII and Henry VIII?
4. What was the impact of the Tudor Court on English culture?
5. 'A Golden Age'. How far can this description be applied to the arts in England under Elizabeth I?
6. Why, and in what ways, did 'the imperial theme' assume such importance in Tudor culture?

9 ⇌ SOURCE EXERCISE – THE MAKING OF AN ICON: PORTRAITS OF ELIZABETH I

Leaders wishing to consolidate their personal authority, and obscure any opposition, ensure that triumphant visual images of themselves are displayed far and wide. The aim is to impress the popular imagination with their charisma in a way that could never be achieved by words alone. Modern personality cults tend to be associated with totalitarian regimes and the technology of the mass media. However, the Tudors developed what might be thought of as the prototype of the personality cult in England. Its effects are still with us – the earliest royal image that springs to most people's mind is that of Henry VIII.

Turbulence in religion and foreign affairs and an insecure succession gave the Tudors and their supporters sufficient motive to make political capital out of portraiture. The originals could be viewed by quite large numbers (at least of the political nation) at Court or in great houses, but there were also numerous copies sold to be hung in mansions and manor houses up and down the country. The purpose of this exercise is to explore what political messages such portraits were intended to convey.

First review the background to them below and then, having studied the individual portraits, answer the following questions.

1 *The picture in Source A shows an anonymous Coronation portrait of Elizabeth I, date unknown. The royal insignia borne by the Queen include a crown with closed arches – a symbol of imperial authority.*

SOURCE A
(PICTURE 35)
Coronation portrait of Elizabeth, artist unknown

Does this portrait project any personal or novel characteristics, or is it purely formal?

2 *The picture in Source B shows an allegory of* The Tudor Succession *by Lucas de Heere. This was probably painted to celebrate the Treaty of Blois with France in 1572. Elizabeth brings in Peace trampling down weapons of war. Edward VI kneels before his father, Henry VIII. Behind Mary and her husband, Philip II, enters War. The inscription at the base reads:* The Quene to Walsingham this Tablet sente, Marke of her peoples and her owne contente. *Walsingham had helped negotiate the treaty, but he was also an advocate of preventive war against Spain.*

SOURCE B (PICTURE 36)
Allegory of The Tudor Succession, *Lucas de Heere*

Q

Bearing in mind Elizabeth's vulnerability as a female ruler and the recent difficulties created by Mary, Queen of Scots, how might this painting have bolstered Elizabeth's authority?

3 *Source C shows the frontispiece to John Dee's* General and Rare
   Memorials pertayning to the Perfect Art of Navigation, *1577.
   Elizabeth sits, in Dee's words, 'at the Helm of the Imperiall Ship, of the
   most parte of Christendome: if so, it be her Graces Pleasure'. Kneeling
   on the shore is 'Brytanica' and the figure standing on a rocky pinnacle
   is 'Opportunity'.*

**SOURCE C
(PICTURE 37)**

Frontispiece to the General and
Rare Memorials *by John Dee*

Q

*In what ways
does Dee's frontispiece
offer encouragement to
Elizabeth to pursue a
policy of maritime
expansion?*

4 *Source D is* The Sieve Portrait of Elizabeth I, *c.1580. There is debate as to the painter, it is sometimes attributed to Cornelius Kitel and sometimes Federico Zuccari. Sir Christopher Hatton, the likely patron, stands in the rear. A column may symbolise the chastity of Laura, to whom Petrarch dedicated his sonnets, and it may also refer to the Pillars of Hercules. On the column here is the story of Aeneas abandoning his love, Dido, to found a new empire. (The Tudors claimed descent from Brutus the Trojan.) Note also the globe.*

**SOURCE D
(PICTURE 38)**
The Sieve Portrait, *attributed either to Cornelius Kitel or Federico Zuccari*

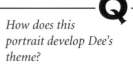

How does this portrait develop Dee's theme?

5 *Source E shows* The Ditchley Portrait *of Elizabeth I by Marcus Gheeraerts, 1592. Ditchley was the Oxfordshire home of Sir Henry Lee who had just retired as the Queen's Champion.*

**SOURCE E
(PICTURE 39)**
The Ditchley Portrait, *Marcus Gheeraerts the Younger*

Q

What is the significance of the map and the weather?

6. *Source F shows* The Rainbow Portrait *of Elizabeth I by Marcus Gheeraerts, c.1600. The rainbow symbolises peace. The serpent and the jewel represent the wisdom in her heart, and the armillary sphere (a skeletal globe) her dedication to the universe as supported by the Word of God.*

NON SINE SOLE
IRIS

**SOURCE F
(PICTURE 40)**
The Rainbow Portrait, *Marcus Gheeraerts the Younger*

Q

1. *Why is Elizabeth portrayed with eyes and ears on her golden cloak? What reference might be intended by the chivalric gauntlet on her ruff? What might be the significance of the flowers?*

2. *How might this portrait relate to the poetic image of Elizabeth as Astraea?*

Q

Using your analysis of these portraits and your reading of pages 393–8, what were the major characteristics associated with Elizabeth through her portraits, and how do they relate to the politics of the time?

15 Religion, The People of England and The Tudors

Religion is a major topic of study for the Tudor period and will have been dealt with in the appropriate chapters elsewhere in this book. This chapter sets out to cover some themes that underlie the detailed policies and circumstances of each reign. The first and last sections deal with the religious situation at the beginning and end of the Tudor period. Taken together they provide a comparison of the beliefs and practices before and after the religious changes. They also give some explanation of why and how the changes took place.

The central section looks at the role of the monarch. Royal control of the Church was an important issue even for those monarchs that did not claim to exercise Supremacy. The personal beliefs of the monarchs will be discussed and how far they had an impact on the country's religion.

1 ～ THE PRE-REFORMATION CHURCH

One of the great debates about the English Reformation is whether it was imposed from above on an unwilling or indifferent population, or whether the demand for reform already existed and all Henry VIII needed to do was to channel this dissatisfaction to his own ends. Some historians have maintained that the poor state of the Church provoked criticism and widespread anti-clericalism, and even without Henry's divorce England would have experienced some form of reformation. A leading exponent of this view was AG Dickens. In his book *The English Reformation* he set out to describe the conditions in the Church which by 1529 had created 'an atmosphere little short of explosive'. Many historians now present a much more positive point of view of the pre-Reformation Church. JJ Scarisbrick and Eamon Duffy are among those who see a church that was acceptable to the majority of its members and continued to enjoy considerable support at all levels of society.

A *The clergy*

The Church of the early sixteenth century was generously staffed. Some complaints seem to have been aimed at these large numbers, but it should be remembered that many of these clerics were not involved in what we would consider to be priestly duties. Entry to the clerical order was for some the only way to enter any form of professional or educated life. However such a large body of men could provide material for criticism.

Some accusations were about the associated abuses of pluralism and non-residence. There was some justification for both practices. Individual parishes might be too poor to support a priest adequately and so he might need to hold two livings. Sometimes the parish income supported a cleric who was at one of the universities or working elsewhere in the Church or even working for the King. On the other hand it was argued that parishioners were often left without any spiritual leadership or had to make do with a poorly paid and often inadequate substitute priest. To make matters worse, men sometimes gained their offices through **nepotism** and **simony**. Both of these could lead to the appointment of people of inappropriate character, whether as ordinary priests or bishops. Neither of them, it should be stressed, was officially sanctioned, but in an age of patronage, when so much depended on personal recommendation and the notion of reward for service, such abuses could be difficult to detect.

> **Nepotism** corrupt appointment to a Church office through the influence of a relative

> **Simony** the sale of a Church office

However, where studies have been made of different areas, using in particular records of bishops' visitations (or tours of inspection) the picture is more positive. It appears that most of the parish clergy carried out their duties conscientiously and to the satisfaction of their parishioners. In the diocese of Lincoln, for example, a study of episcopal records shows that in the years between 1514 and 1521 only 4% of parishes complained about inadequate performance of spiritual duty by their clergymen and in some cases this could be explained by old age. Inspections elsewhere have shown similar results.

Non-resident clergy were properly licensed and seem to have found adequate deputies to take their place. The parish clergy as a whole were not as ill-educated as they have sometimes been portrayed. Although rarely familiar with the latest ideas in learning, such evidence as can be gained from the books they owned and the few references to those individuals who were inadequate show a body of men who had sufficient grasp of the conventional and traditional learning to be able to cater for the needs of their parishioners.

Bishops too have fared well as a result of research. They were selected by the King, although the Pope had to approve his choice, and were often chosen because of their services in royal government. However, even when they were involved with secular tasks, they also devoted time to the administration and spiritual welfare of their dioceses. Archbishop Warham, for example, conducted a personal visitation of the Canterbury diocese in 1511–12, while still acting as Lord Chancellor of England. Even when absence was necessary, the diocese could be adequately administered by deputies and specifically episcopal functions carried out by suffragan (assistant) bishops.

> **Tithes** church taxes, a proportion of each year's produce, usually 10% of the crop in rural areas.

Some clergy were seen as too efficient. The main source of income for a parish priest was **tithes**. In addition there were fees that a priest could demand in return for services such as marriages and funerals. He could also claim **mortuary fees** from the estate of a deceased

> **Mortuary fees** death duties owed to the parish priest for performing the various religious rituals surrounding a death

Guilds religious clubs attached to a particular church, and dedicated to one or more saints

Fraternities religious brotherhoods, for worship in common and mutual support in times of illness or need

parishioner. Although some contemporaries claimed the clergy demand-ed too much in payments, and modern historians have found instances that seem to support this view, only a few cases involving such pay-ments appear in the court records. A few extreme cases have been built up to provide a misleading picture of clerical greed.

B *Popular religion*

Various sources indicate that the vast majority of people in England were more than content with their Church. As Conrad Russell has put it, the trends in popular piety around 1500 were mostly heading, not towards Protestantism, but well away from it. Evidence from wills shows money and goods still being used for religious purposes. There were bequests to orders of friars and nuns, money was earmarked for traditional practices – the saying of masses, the burning of lights before statues and altars – and the parish church especially benefited with endowments for the fabric and furnishings. Buildings themselves testify to this activity with large numbers of churches being rebuilt or improved at this period, mostly at the expense of the parishioners themselves. There was a particular growth in shrines dedicated to specialist saints, protecting fertility, for instance, or health.

A prominent concern was the provision of prayers for the dead. **Guilds** and **fraternities** flourished whose main purpose was praying for the souls of members and their families. Many of these were based on the parish church. People left money to have masses said for their souls and the rich founded chantries, leaving money or property to finance a priest to say mass for them. Another popular practice was pilgrimage, and new shrines, such as that of King Henry VI at Windsor, joined the more traditional destinations like the shrine of Our Lady of Walsingham that was visited by both Henry VII and Henry VIII.

The new printing press was producing large numbers of books aimed both at priests, to help them in instructing their parishioners, and at the lay people themselves. These included books of instructions, prayers and the lives of the saints. Sermons were of increasing impor-tance. The period saw an increase in the number of pulpits in churches, and handbooks of sermons were available for the clergy who lacked the ability or confidence to write their own.

Popular religion was also a key element in popular culture. The whole year was structured by saints' eves – perhaps 30 of them, it varied from place to place – celebrated as 'wakes' which were, in effect, all night parties, and feast days, of which there could have been as many as 95. (Much energy was devoted in the course of the Reformation to suppressing as many of these as possible.) A large number of these days were attached to specific community events. Just before the feast of the Ascension were the Rogation Days when the congregation would process around its parish boundaries – this 'beating of the bounds' affirmed the physical space occupied by the parish. Historians debate the balance between how Christian and how pagan such festivals were in the minds of people who had never received a theological education.

At least two further festivals seemed to represent the breaking out of an older, terrifying pagan vision into a Christian ordered world – St John's Eve and Hallowe'en. We still celebrate the latter, of course, although it has been locked away in the safe, commercial world of modern entertainment.

Some religious festivals also delineated a time when it was safe to 'turn the world upside down', to invert the usual social order, to let off steam. Historians have debated whether these were conservative in effect, preserving the social order by acting as a sort of safety valve, or whether such festivals could all to easily spill over into riot and threatening disorder. There was Carnival (literally, farewell to flesh), celebrated on Shrove Tuesday, the last opportunity for gluttony, drunkenness and riotous pleasure-seeking before Lent, a period of abstinence from physical pleasures. Ordinary people became Carnival kings and queens, and mockery of the authorities, the magistrates and clergy, was at such a time permissible. At Christmas there were 'Lords of Misrule', like the inverted authorities at Carnival time. Students would elect a 'lord' as part of the Christmas festivities, such as the 'King of the Cockneys' at Lincoln's Inn, one of the London communities of practising and student lawyers. Christmas was also the season of the year for plays which turned everything upside down, a famous example being the comic reversals of Shakespeare's Twelfth Night.

Pagan practices and figures could also make an appearance on the streets of sixteenth-century towns and villages. To dance around a phallic Maypole, as the return of fertility to the world was celebrated, was clearly no Christianised ritual. The 'wodevose' or 'wodehouse' would appear in Midsummer pageants, a wild man dressed in skins and foliage brandishing a torch, personifying untamed nature. This was a variant of the 'Green Man' which was sometimes presented in effigy made out of foliage, encased in branches and then burnt. The Church, even before the Reformation, distrusted but could never quite eliminate these symbolic manifestations of pagan traditions and deep responses to the natural world. Modern culture has been more successful, relegating the dance around the maypole as an asexual game for children, and reducing the image of the Green Man to pub signs.

Religious festivals expressed identity. Every individual and every group had a place within the larger community, with little conception of any personal choice. This was clearly visible in religious processions which could be read like a social map. The best example of this, at least in towns, is the procession of Corpus Christi, meaning the Body of Christ. Taking place shortly after Whitsun, the whole of a town's corporation and gilds would process in order of importance, the most eminent coming last. The dominant image was that of the body, Christ's mystical Body, which united the faithful in the celebration of the Mass, and the social body, the community in procession. The mayor was the head, with the officers and the gilds being the limbs. All would be at one in 'good unity, concord and charity', according to the Tailors of Newcastle upon Tyne in 1536, when gild brothers 'amicably and lovingly … in their best apparel and array go in the procession'. This was, at any rate, the ideal. If things went wrong there could be riots instead of concord, one gild or 'limb' against another, battling over precedence.

In many towns Corpus Christi involved more than a procession. There were also pageants made up of mimes on wagons or fullscale mystery plays as at York. ('Mystery' in this context refers to a craft rather than to the modern idea of a mystery.) Not to present a play meant that the gild would be dishonoured, and it was obvious who should present what – the Bakers, for example, were usually the choice for the Last Supper and any Watermen performed Noah's Flood. Such was the popular drama of the time where a community presented its stock characters and its values to itself.

Festivals and religious drama marked different stages of the year, but visual images, paintings and sculptures in churches, were there throughout. As we hear in *The Voices of Morebath* by Eamon Duffy, a remarkable portrait of one parish's transition from the pre-Reformation church through to the Elizabethan settlement, the material culture of the church was of great significance to parishioners, and not just as spectators. Different individuals and groups ('the young men', 'the maidens') raised money, invested in, and cared for, the vestments, the altar-cloths, the windows, the side-altars, and the statues of Virgin and saints, especially the saints of local origin or local importance. There was a church house, where 'church ales' were held, fund-raising parties when the whole community came together to enjoy itself. Following the Reformation, Morebath was to sell off its church house. The Church had provided a culture and an identity to the life of the community which was to be radically altered by the religious changes of the sixteenth century.

KEY ISSUE

What was the significance of religion in the life of local communities?

C *Criticism and heresy*

There was criticism of the Church before the Reformation, and some of it came from within the establishment. For example, in 1512 John Colet, Dean of St Paul's, preached the opening sermon to a meeting of the Convocation of Canterbury. He emphasised the need for reform in the Church and laid the blame for its current state on the clergy themselves. Colet found much to complain about, but he believed reform did not require a new system, simply the conscientious application of existing rules. His dissatisfaction was that of a highly educated scholar who wanted to update some of the practices of the Church in the light of the new ideas to which he had been exposed. Sir Thomas More was another example of humanist learning reinforcing one's faith. This learning was the inspiration of moderate reform, of deepening people's faith; it stopped well short of heresy, of challenging doctrine or the authority of the Pope.

There were more extreme voices. In 1529 the London lawyer Simon Fish produced a pamphlet entitled *A Supplication of the Beggars*. Like Colet he blamed the clergy for the problems of the Church but he thought the Church was beyond reforming itself. His solution was for the King to take action, 'to tie these holy idle thieves to the carts to be whipped naked about every market town'.

England had its native heretic tradition in Lollardy which started with the followers of John Wycliffe in the fourteenth century. Among their beliefs was a rejection of the Catholic doctrine of transubstantiation and a demand for an English Bible. They also rejected the cult of saints. One Lollard dismissed a much venerated statue of the Virgin as 'a burnt arse elf and a burnt arse stock'. ('Burnt' here refers to venereal disease.) It is generally accepted that Lollard groups survived into the early sixteenth century especially in the Midlands and the Chilterns near London. However, some identifications may have been due to over-reaction by the authorities to isolated comments or accusations about individuals who were fundamentally loyal members of the Church.

To the Lollards could now be added the followers of Martin Luther. The German reformer's books were already arriving in England by 1519. The movement was restricted mainly to areas in the east of the country which had relatively frequent contact with Germany through trade. Some interest was also shown in academic circles, especially at Cambridge where a group met regularly at a tavern called the White Horse to discuss the new ideas. There was some contact between these new reformers and Lollard groups but the Lutheran scholars could be rather dismissive of the Lollards and their inaccurate translations of the

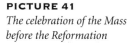

KEY ISSUE

In what ways was the Church subject to attack before the break with Rome?

Bible. However, Lutheranism had few adherents in England, and it would take more than just their efforts to change the English Church.

2 ⌒ THE ROLE OF THE MONARCH

The monarch's role in the religious changes of the sixteenth century was crucial. This was so whether it was Protestant reform or Catholic re-establishment that was at stake. Even if the religious initiative did not come from the king or queen, he or she played a central role in implementing policy and deciding what to accept or reject in the ideas put forward by others.

A *Henry VII*

Henry VII's attitude was one of conventional loyalty to the Catholic Church. He maintained good relations with the Pope, securing papal approval of his accession and support for his choice of bishops. These were generally men who had served him well in government. For example, John Morton was Archbishop of Canterbury and Lord Chancellor, while Richard Fox was Bishop of Bath and Wells as well as being Lord Privy Seal.

On a more personal level, Henry showed a special interest in the Franciscan friars and continued work on the chapels at King's College, Cambridge, and at Windsor. He combined traditional piety with dynastic propaganda when he started the process of formal **canonisation** of his Lancastrian predecessor, Henry VI, and planned a new tomb for him at Westminster Abbey. On one occasion he is said to have convinced a condemned heretic that his opinions were wrong and, although the man was still executed 'he died as a Christian'.

Canonisation the process whereby someone is declared to be a saint

B *Henry VIII*

There are two main areas to look at in Henry's Reformation: the Royal Supremacy and the doctrine of his church. In both of these areas it is worth looking at the extent to which Henry himself took control.

Henry's claim to the Supremacy arose from his divorce case. Earlier hints of such a claim were occasional and very limited in their application. In 1512 for example, Henry declared 'the Kings of England in time past have never had any superior but God alone'. He was however speaking in the context of a debate over benefit of clergy and the statement had no wider relevance. In 1521 his *Assertio Septem Sacramentorum* contained a strong defence of Catholic doctrine as it had been challenged by Luther.

The divorce changed the situation and led Henry to wider claims. He himself set out the argument that was to be followed and played an active role in the ensuing controversy. In December 1530 the Imperial ambassador stressed Henry's involvement when he commented that the King 'was minded to take up the pen against the clergy'; but his contri-

See page 78

butions had begun even earlier. In 1527 one of the first treatises defending Henry's cause contained a section drafted by the King himself.

By this time the divorce issue had broadened into the claim that Henry should exercise supremacy over the Church. He demonstrated this by more than contributing to the argument. In May 1530 he presided at a meeting of bishops and academics that discussed the heretical nature of certain imported books and, against the bishops' advice, announced his intention of authorising a translation of the New Testament. In 1531, having gained Convocation's grudging acceptance of his claim to be supreme head 'as far as the law of Christ allowed', he then went on to annotate the reforming decrees they produced later in the year.

Having dispensed with papal supremacy, Henry now took an active role in determining the practices and doctrine of his Church. He was not entirely consistent, but broadly he remained Catholic while having rejected Roman Catholicism. He clung to the essential traditional beliefs of the Church, such as transubstantiation, and would have argued that he was restoring a right order to the Church rather than ushering in an era of change in doctrine. In 1537 he had allowed the Bishops' Book to be published having 'taken as it were a taste' of it. When he finally read it, he produced a list of more than a hundred corrections and additions that would bring it into line with his own ideas. A number of these were taken into consideration in 1543 when the King's Book was published. This time Henry read through it before publication. In his corrections he often argued with Cranmer, his reforming Archbishop of Canterbury, but he also argued with his more conservative bishops. For example, Henry played a major role in the drafting of the Six Articles and most of his contributions strengthened their Catholic character. However, he refused to accept the idea that confession was required by the law of God and grew impatient when conservatives such as Gardiner and Tunstall insisted on arguing the point.

See page 96

Henry was an active head of the Church but was he always in control? He did sometimes take advice without reflection, especially when preoccupied with other matters. He disliked writing and seems to have avoided reading. Cranmer, in a letter to Capito, a continental reformer, wrote:

> The King is in the habit of handing over books which have been presented to him to one of his courtiers for perusal, from whom he may afterwards learn the contents. He then takes them back and gives them to someone else of an entirely opposite way of thinking. And when he has thus found out everything from them, and has ascertained both what they praise and what they condemn, then at length he openly gives his opinion on the same points. I understand he has done this with your book. While he was pleased with many things in it, there were also some things he did not approve. I suspect they were the statements you made about the Mass.

Q

What does this tell us about possible influences on Henry's religious opinions?

KEY ISSUE

What were Henry VIII's personal beliefs?

See page 97

One view is that the 1530s in particular were a reforming era guided by Thomas Cromwell. As Vicegerent in Spirituals, he played a leading role in implementing religious policy and he was committed to reform. This does not mean that he led the King by the nose. He has been particularly associated with the English Bible, but Henry had already indicated his interest in such a project in 1530. Reforming activity continued into the 1540s, after Cromwell's execution. The King continued to give his favour to Cranmer, although he continued to pursue reformist ideas within his diocese and in his clerical appointments, and he tolerated the reforming sympathies of his last wife Catherine Parr.

C *Edward VI*

During Edward VI's reign England became an officially Protestant country. This was not an inevitable consequence of Henry VIII's changes but the result of conscious decisions by a number of individuals, prompted by religious and perhaps economic motives. But Edward himself was a child for most of this period. How far did the policies enacted in his name reflect his own beliefs and did he have any influence on these policies.?

Some of his contemporaries had little doubt about his personal commitment. In May 1550 the Flemish Protestant Martin Micron wrote of Edward:

> Our King is a youth of such godliness as to be a wonder to the whole world. He orders all things for the advancement of God's glory. Every Sunday he has a sermon such as he used to have during Lent. I wish the bishops and the nobility were inflamed with like zeal.

Edward was brought up in an atmosphere of reform. It was, for example, a feature of the household of his step-mother, Catherine Parr. Two of his tutors, John Cheke and Richard Cox, may have been appointed because of their reputations as scholars, but were later to declare themselves openly as Protestants. Once he was king, Somerset and Cranmer played a large part in deciding who should be in his household.

Somerset's fall led to a reordering of the King's Household. However, although there was a traditionalist majority on the Council, this was not paralleled in the Privy Chamber. Cranmer played a part in this and Edward too may have had a say in keeping the reformers in the majority. The Privy Chamber was not of as great significance as it had been under Henry VIII while Edward was still a child, but it grew in importance as the King matured and began to make his own views known. The Imperial ambassador wrote in 1550 that Edward was surrounded by 'those well-known as partisans and instigators of the new doctrines'.

The same ambassador also commented on Edward's enthusiasm for taking notes on the sermons he heard. He had a special book for this, the existence of which was recorded in the early seventeenth century but which has since been lost.

Even if we knew nothing of Edward's personal beliefs, we could still assume that the reforms of his reign were acceptable to him. The 1550s in particular saw the full imposition of Protestant ideas, with the removal of altars and the publication of the second *Book of Common Prayer*. It is unlikely that Northumberland would have followed such a policy if he thought it would be rejected by Edward when he came of age in October 1553. If he did not initiate policy, the young King could still have an influence on it.

See page 147

The 1550s show Edward taking a greater role. When he heard that his sister Mary continued to have Mass said in her household he decided to take action himself. Apparently this was a change in practice since Edward told Mary that 'he had only taken a share in affairs during the last year'. He confronted his sister in a meeting in March 1551 and followed this up with an argument with his Councillors who advised him to be more lenient. The result was indecisive. Mary continued to hear Mass but there are indications that increased pressure was put on her household to conform. Edward was certainly happy to disinherit her in favour of Lady Jane Grey.

D *Mary I*

Mary's priority on becoming queen was to restore Catholicism to England, and few could have doubted her devotion to this task. She had made her position clear. In March 1551 she and her attendants had ridden through London, each openly carrying rosary beads although these had been forbidden by the Injunctions of 1547. She had insisted on having Mass said in her household and argued strongly with her brother about this. When her accession was announced there were demonstrations of Catholic piety across the country, and Mary herself set the tone in restoring the Mass which was still strictly speaking illegal.

Mary had the will to make her religious policy her own and not just that of her advisers. Back in the 1530s she had initially resisted her father's demands to accept his Supremacy. Only the threat of harm to her supporters and possibly execution for herself led her to take the oath in 1536. In 1554 she dismissed the opinion of the majority of her Council, and possibly of her subjects, when she insisted on marrying Philip of Spain, and she later disagreed with Philip himself who doubted the wisdom of burning Protestants.

Mary believed strongly that she had a personal responsibility for her subjects' spiritual welfare. In a statement to her Council outlining her intentions she wrote that she was bound 'to show such example in encouraging and maintaining these persons … that it may be evident to all in this realm how I discharge my conscience therein'.

One example she set was in her attitude to Church lands and revenues. Since the 1530s the monarchy had taken advantage of the Church financially. Mary started to reverse the process. She knew she would face overwhelming opposition if she tried to force the aristocracy and gentry to do the same, but at least she could set an example. She ordered the return to parish churches of the goods taken from them in Edward VI's reign, although in most cases it was too late since they had already been sold. She restored the lands that enabled six religious houses, including Westminster Abbey, to be re-opened and made substantial grants to a number of dioceses. Professor Scarisbrick has suggested that by the end of her reign her example may have been having some effect on others.

Mary's zeal can also be seen in the burning of Protestants during her reign. She was not alone in this. Stephen Gardiner, Bishop of Winchester, and other members of the Council initially supported the policy and so did large numbers across the country, with the initiative in individual cases often coming from the secular authorities and private citizens. Mary, however, was particularly adamant in this regard. She wrote to Bishop Bonner of London in May 1555 ordering him to be more active in taking action against heretics and pointing out that some had been condemned but were not yet burned. When Gardiner and her Spanish advisers suggested that the burnings were counter-productive and should be stopped, she insisted that they continue. In 1556 Archbishop Cranmer signed his recantation. This meant that his life should have been spared, but it was Mary who insisted that he should still go to the stake.

Cranmer's great offence was to have overseen the attempt to spread Protestant doctrine in England. In Mary's view this made him mainly responsible for leading astray many people who therefore failed to attain salvation. This was the 'iniquity' for which he had to be punished, and it was the justification for her policy. She saw it as much her responsibility to destroy anyone who might lead her subjects into eternal damnation, as it was to provide the means of attaining eternal salvation.

See pages 167–9

KEY ISSUE

What was the significance for the Reformation of Edward VI's early death and Mary I's accession?

E *Elizabeth I*

The Protestant settlement of 1559 happened because Elizabeth wanted it, and she wanted it because of her religious convictions. In strictly political terms, maintaining Catholicism was a realistic and possibly safer course to follow. Elizabeth opted for Protestantism despite the risks. As she told Parliament in 1576:

> If policy had been preferred to truth would I, do you think, even at the first beginning of my rule, have turned upside down so great affairs?

There is ample evidence for Elizabeth's religious position. In 1557 the Venetian ambassador noted that she was 'by nature and education inclined' to Protestantism. In her own words, it was the religion she had been 'born in, bred in and, I trust, shall die in'. She showed her loyalties at the beginning of her reign. Protestants were appointed to give public sermons and the procession on the eve of her coronation drew attention to her love for the English Bible – she took hold of it and kissed it – and celebrated her role as a restorer of true religion.

Recently, historians have emphasised the role of Sir William Cecil in bringing about the settlement, pointing out his experience in Edward's reign and widespread connections among leading Protestants. But Cecil would not have had the opportunity to do this work if Elizabeth had not already decided on a Protestant settlement.

It was Elizabeth's intervention that made the arrangements of her early years a permanent settlement. If her bishops and a number of her Councillors had had their way then the 1559 settlement would have been simply the starting point for further reform. They soon found that Elizabeth had other ideas. On several occasions she refused to allow Parliament to discuss any further changes in the Church even when these were supported by the bishops and members of the Council.

In 1563 she amended the 39 Articles to reinforce her own right to control the liturgy. She was still intervening in 1595 when she ordered Archbishop John Whitgift to withdraw his Lambeth Articles because she felt they would cause too much controversy. She may even have threatened him with legal action for challenging her authority.

Elizabeth had a number of motives in taking this active role:

See pages 214–15

- Her personal religious opinion: although she was a Protestant she liked some traditional elements and only agreed reluctantly to allow marriage for the clergy.
- She may have been trying to conciliate and win over the Catholics in England: too great a move towards strict Protestantism would drive too many into discontent and possible opposition.
- The desire for stability: when she condemned prophesyings she claimed that they encouraged people to be 'divided among themselves and encouraged to the violation of our laws and to the breach of common order'.
- She wanted to uphold her authority: any attempt to change the Settlement, especially if initiated in Parliament, was a challenge to her authority. The government of the Church was a task for herself and Convocation, and she had the final say.

KEY ISSUE

What were Elizabeth's priorities in making religious policy?

KEY ISSUE

In making religious policy, how far did Tudor monarchs adapt their personal beliefs to political circumstances?

3 ◦ TO WHAT EXTENT HAD ENGLAND BECOME A PROTESTANT COUNTRY BY 1603?

In one sense England became a Protestant country in 1559 when the Elizabethan Settlement made a reformed church the official religion of the country. The monarch became Supreme Governor of the English Church, services had to follow the *Book of Common Prayer* and acceptance of the new order was a condition of holding office.

In a wider sense it was not so simple. Official decrees alone are not enough to convert a nation. A survey of 1564 indicated that only 50% of JPs were 'favourers of true religion' (i.e. supporters of the established church) while 31% were regarded as 'indifferent to religion' and 18%

were 'adversaries'. Bishops' visitations in many parts of the country revealed the persistence of Catholic traditions and furnishings in parish churches until well into the 1560s, and in the dioceses of York, Hereford and Chester such practices were still being investigated in the 1580s. It would require a new clergy, the effective use of pulpit and printing press, and the passing of time to turn the English into a Protestant people. Even then, some reformers would not be satisfied.

A *The clergy*

In the 1560s there was a serious shortage of committed, Protestant clergy. In many cases known Catholic sympathisers were allowed to stay in place rather than leaving parishes vacant. Even so, many parishes remained without a minister. In 1561 in the diocese of Ely only one third of the churches had a resident minister. In south Lancashire the number of priests had dwindled from 172 in 1554 to 98 in 1563. In 1560 Archbishop Parker admitted that, to overcome the problem, he and other bishops had ordained large numbers of inadequately educated men.

The bishops' ideal was a church that was fully staffed with graduate clergy who could preach and conduct the Catechism effectively as well as lead services. This would take time and needed a reform of the universities. Oxford in particular was noted for its Catholic sympathies, but during the 1560s both universities became more Protestant with new professors and heads of colleges. Suspected Catholics were refused degrees. At Cambridge, Emmanuel College (1584) and Sidney Sussex College (1594) were founded with the purpose of providing properly educated clergy. At Oxford, the founding of Jesus College in 1571 gave a boost to providing an educated clergy for Wales.

As a result of these efforts the number of graduate clergy increased significantly. In the diocese of Canterbury, for example, it went from 18% in 1571 to 60% in 1603; in Lichfield from 14% in 1584 to 24% in 1603.

B *Preaching*

The Injunctions of 1559 declared the importance of preaching.

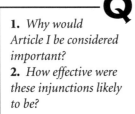

1. *Why would Article I be considered important?*
2. *How effective were these injunctions likely to be?*

(i) ... all persons having cure of souls [i.e. parish clergy] shall declare four times in the year at least, in their sermons, that all usurped and foreign power is for most just causes taken away and abolished and that the Queen's power within her realms and dominions is the highest power under God ...

(iii) That they shall preach in their churches every month of the year at least, wherein they shall purely and sincerely declare the word of God ...

(viii) That they shall admit no man to preach within their churches but such as shall appear unto them sufficiently licensed thereunto by the Queen's Majesty or the Archbishop of Canterbury or the Archbishop of York or the bishop of the diocese ...

Elizabeth herself did not like too much preaching. She once suggested to Archbishop Grindal that three or four preachers were adequate for each county. For the most part she probably thought it was enough that the parish minister read from the *Book of Homilies*, an authorised collection of sermons. She wanted the clergy and the people to accept official doctrine, not explore religious ideas with their own consciences as judge. This was not enough for her bishops or for anyone serious about spreading Protestantism.

Once again the initial problem was a shortage of properly trained clergy. In the mid-1570s only about 20% of the country's clergymen were licensed to preach, which was not enough to fulfil the requirements of the 1559 Injunctions. By 1603, however, more than 50% of the clergy were licensed. The change was due to the improved education of the clergy and to a conscious attempt to encourage a preaching ministry by both bishops and lay patrons. Members of the nobility and gentry often had the right to appoint parish clergy. As they became more committed to the new order so they chose ministers who would be effective in spreading the new religion.

A leading role was often played by town councils. Sometimes they amalgamated small town parishes into one living capable of supporting a well-qualified, preaching minister. Where this was not possible they appointed an official town preacher outside the parish system. Many towns became centres for preaching. Once a month or once a fortnight clergy from the town and surrounding parishes came together for a combination where they took it in turns to preach to an audience of clergy and lay people. The sermon was often followed by a shared meal. The whole process brought together clergy, leading townsmen and ordinary people in a shared enterprise that promoted Protestant beliefs. It became as much a part of life as going to town for market day and were perhaps some replacement for the communal life of the pre-Reformation parish.

> **KEY ISSUE**
>
> *What were the obstacles to the establishment of Protestantism, and how were they overcome?*

C *The Reformation and English culture*

The crisis of the Church in the Reformation was also a crisis of culture. The words and images the Church sanctified were a vital part of everyday life. On the one hand, the Reformation was to enrich English as a literary language with the English Bible and other texts; on the other it stripped away much of the visual heritage of medieval Catholicism.

The Lollards had had a rough translation of the Bible into English in the fifteenth century and William Tyndale's much more accurate one had been smuggled into the country from 1525, but the first complete translation published in England was that of Miles Coverdale in 1535. It was not an original translation, unlike that of Tyndale who had gone back to the Hebrew and Greek sources, but it was tolerated by the King. In 1539 Coverdale's Bible was superseded by an authorised translation known as the 'Great Bible', and all other versions were banned in the 1540s. It was also decreed that 'no woman (unless she be noble or gentle woman), no artificers, apprentices, journeymen … or labourers'

See page 95

PICTURE 42

*Frontispiece to the Great Bible
of 1539 (HM the Queen)*

should be permitted to read the Scriptures. The authorities were anxious to stop the Reformation from becoming too popular a movement and, therefore, uncontrollable. They could not, however, halt the new biblical scholarship. Exiles in Geneva during Mary's reign produced the 'Geneva Bible' which circulated widely in England in (the wealthier) private homes despite a further attempt to license just one official version in the form of the 'Bishops' Bible' of 1568. Finally, under James I the Authorised Version of 1611 was to be established as the standard until the twentieth century.

The language of these translations, honed and reworked through the sixteenth century, became the single greatest resource for English literature. Despite the restrictions under Henry VIII the Bible was the text everybody grew up with, even the illiterate as they heard it read out in church. Its vocabulary, its idioms and its rhythms were the basis, along with the classics, for the humanist trained élite, for everyday writing, such as letters and diaries, as well as the treatises and the poetry of 'high culture'. It became the core of English culture.

There were two other major texts associated with the Bible in fostering a common culture. One was the *Prayer Book*. As Cranmer put it in 1549: 'And whereas heretofore there hath been great diversity in saying and singing in Churches within this Realm … now from henceforth all the whole Realm shall have but one Use.' It was fortunate that Cranmer's English was amongst the most sensitive and elegant. The other major text was Foxe's *Book of Martyrs* which was less sensitive and less elegant but powerfully written and of enormous influence.

ANALYSIS

The Importance of Foxe's 'Book of Martyrs'

John Foxe first published his *Actes and Monuments of these latter and perilous Dayes*, commonly known as the 'Book of Martyrs', in 1563. In forthright prose it described the sufferings of Protestant martyrs at the hands of 'Bloody Mary'. It kept alive the revulsion felt towards the Marian persecution and the Spanish influence and was thereby of enormous importance in consolidating popular, emotional support for the Elizabethan Settlement. When a corrected edition was published in 1570 a copy was placed in every collegiate church in the country. It was the most widely known and influential work of the Tudor period.

Foxe is most famous for his tales of brave Protestant martyrs sustained by their faith as they faced the dreadful agonies of being burnt at the stake, but that was only one part of his work. His narrative covered centuries and told of the great medieval struggle between Emperors and Popes, which for him simply meant good against evil. Such history writing had little to do with the beginnings of critical scholarship in the Renaissance; the evidence was made to fit Foxe's schematic design, showing how the Popes gradually usurped the God given authority of secular rulers until the Reformation. Queen Elizabeth, acting as a new Constantine (the Emperor responsible for adopting Christianity as the religion of the Roman Empire), was then presented as restoring a golden age.

The ideology of an imperial monarchy obviously pre-dated Foxe but it was his work which gave it its greatest cultural impetus. And it was his imagery and language which did much to ensure that the ideology of Elizabethan Protestantism outlasted the conditions which had given rise to it in the sixteenth century. Foxe's influence could be felt right into our own era in literature and religious attitudes.

See page 394

The Reformation also had a great impact on visual culture, although in this case largely negative. The images of Scriptural figures and saints which had covered the walls of churches and cathedrals had had great staying power through centuries of medieval Christianity but did not survive the advent of Protestantism. The lives of saints and prophets were whitewashed over, and statues destroyed or decapitated. (This was not universal – some medieval images did survive until the Puritans in the English Civil War finished the job.) The Crucifix was the most striking image of suffering and the essential symbol of the Christian faith, representing the sacrifice which brings redemption. By the end of the sixteenth century it had generally been removed from the **rood screen** and replaced in many cases by the royal coat of arms. The

Rood screen the carved wooden screen separating the chancel (the more sacred space near the altar) and the nave (where the congregation sits)

KEY ISSUE

What impact did the Reformation have on English culture?

See page 419

destruction of images was not simply vandalism. It was iconoclasm, the elimination of images which might be worshipped in themselves or treated as magical objects rather than as representations of higher spiritual truths. Instead of learning from images the congregation now had to concentrate on the words of the preacher. If there was anything to be seen on the walls it consisted of verses from the Bible or the Ten Commandments. A culture of images had given way to a culture of words.

D *Popular culture and attachment to the Church of England*

By 1603 the religious life of the country as a whole was definitely Protestant. While sermons had become a feature of many towns, the old cycles of religious plays had come to an end. Corpus Christi processions were banned in 1547. These demonstrations of civic pride combined with popular religion were too closely associated with Catholicism. At first only certain plays were banned or changes made to parts of the text and in some towns new Protestant plays were put on. In York the plays were produced for the last time in1569, in Chester in 1575. Coventry's cycle may have survived until 1580 but by the 1590s across the country civic religious drama had come to an end.

The Puritans launched a general assault on popular culture. In 1585 Philip Stubbes condemned the time spent, especially on the Sabbath, on 'May games, church ales, feasts and wakes: in piping, dancing, dicing, carding, bowling, tennis-playing … in football-playing, and such other devilish pastimes'. In this general project, the Puritans largely failed, as they did in their rear-guard action against the 'lewdness' of the new playhouses, which opened up in the latter part of Elizabeth's reign. However, those sanctions against popular customs which had the force of law – banning shrines, the veneration of saints, the bulk of Church processions – did work, at least in excluding them from the church. Church Papists celebrated at home what had been forbidden in church, for instance the feast of the Purification of the Virgin Mary, or Whitsun feasts. Ronald Hutton has found evidence of this and other pre-Reformation rites and beliefs moving out of the church and onto the street as folklore or, when politic, into the privacy of home.

As a new generation grew up after the Elizabethan Settlement, attachment to these banned practices declined, or at least they lost their religious meaning, and new loyalties emerged. Familiarity with the new services led to a growing acceptance of the *Prayer Book* which now provided a substitute for the old rituals. The same feelings that moved people to resist Protestant innovation in the 1560s caused them to champion the certainties of the *Prayer Book* later in the reign. Already by 1574, for example, parishioners in Cirencester refused to accept communion from their parish minister because he did not follow the *Prayer Book*. By the 1580s and 1590s there are many examples of parishioners complaining about their ministers and sometimes going to neighbouring churches because the ritual of their *Prayer Book* was not being followed in their own parish.

Further evidence of new loyalty is in attitudes to the new Protestant Catechism. For much of Elizabeth's reign ignorance of the Catechism was not unusual and was not always seen as a major problem except by the authorities. By the end of her reign expectations had changed. Many versions were available and some ran to 30 or 40 editions. Ignorance of the Catechism had reduced considerably and an inability to recite it had become something to be ashamed of.

These works were matched by publications belonging to popular rather than official culture. Ballads and pamphlets attacking Catholicism and praising the new religion were eagerly bought, and would also be read aloud by those who could, for the benefit of the illiterate. Many of these were illustrated and these pictures, as well as prints illustrating stories from the Bible, were pinned up in private and public houses.

Records of the church courts show a much greater willingness to attend services and improved behaviour when in church. The parish communities in general seem to have co-operated with the authorities in dealing with non-attendance as well as other aspects of social and moral behaviour dealt with by the church courts. Finally, just as wills have provided evidence of satisfaction with the pre-Reformation Church, so too there are examples of bequests both to ministers and to the parish in Elizabeth's reign.

In addition to a growing popular attachment to the reformed Church of England, there were more academic works defending it. Jewel's *Apology or Answer in Defence of the Church of England* was written in the early 1560s at the suggestion of William Cecil and presented the new Church as a true church in its own right and not some kind of half-hearted compromise between Catholicism and Protestantism. In the 1590s Richard Hooker produced his *Laws of Ecclesiastical Polity*. This provided a reasoned defence of the English Church which was to be a reference point through the ensuing centuries.

KEY ISSUE
Why was there a growing attachment to the reformed Church of England, and what is the evidence for it?

E *The survival of Catholicism*

It is now clear that Catholicism survived into Elizabeth's reign much longer than used to be thought. There were the recusants, who paid their one shilling fine and stayed away from Church, and the larger number of Church Papists who conformed outwardly while continuing their Catholic devotions in private. But Catholicism was not just about survival; there was also an attempt at renewal. In 1568 William Allen established a seminary at Douai in the southern Netherlands to educate English Catholics in exile and to train missionary priests with the ultimate goal of the re-conversion of England. This mission was stepped up in 1580 when the first Jesuits, the most dedicated and politically committed of the missionary orders, arrived in England. With informers, arrests and savage penalties, the Elizabethan government tried to stem the tide but could not. With London as a centre, and protection in the houses of sympathetic gentry (equipped with priest-holes – secret rooms as hiding places) an underground network was established.

See pages 229–30

PROFILE

WILLIAM ALLEN (1532–94)

William Allen came from a gentry family in Lancashire. He took his degree at Oxford in Edward's reign, became Principal of St Mary's Hall in Mary's reign and fully supported her Catholic policies. He left his post on Elizabeth's succession, spent several years in Lancashire and Oxfordshire and was noted for insisting that Catholics could not conform in any way to the Elizabethan Church. He went into exile in 1565 and spent the rest of his life in the Netherlands and Rome.

In 1568 he founded a college at Douai in the southern Netherlands as a centre for English Catholic exiles. It provided facilities for established scholars as well as educating a new generation of Catholics. It also had a printing press. Its purpose was to help to preserve English Catholicism, ready for the day when it could be officially restored. By the 1580s it was also seen as a major instrument in effecting that restoration. The college became a centre for training the missionary priests who returned to England. Their training laid an emphasis on the Bible to prepare them for disputes with Protestants. In addition they were trained in the teaching of doctrine and in understanding the particular problems faced by Catholics in England. By 1603 more than 400 priests had gone from Douai to England.

Allen's aim was not peaceful co-existence with Protestants; his ideal was a Catholic country ruled by a Catholic monarch. He took an active role in negotiating and preparing for a number of attempts to re-impose Catholicism by foreign invasion. In particular he looked to Spain, since it was Spain which had helped in the Catholic restoration of the 1550s of which Allen had been a part. In 1587 he was made a cardinal, possibly to give him the appropriate status as England's Catholic leader if the Spanish Armada was successful. The nature of his role is indicated by the suggestion that he should study the records of Cardinal Pole's role as legate in Mary's reign. In 1588 he published his *Admonition to the Nobility and People of England*, calling on them to join the Spanish and overthrow the heretic Elizabeth.

He often claimed to distinguish between the missionary activity of his priests and political attacks against the regime. He did not see any inconsistency here. The priest's task was strictly religious and they were under orders not to meddle in politics. It was for right-minded princes and laymen to take direct action against the regime. The connection that Elizabeth's government would want to point out is that successful missionary priests would provide those right-minded laymen.

See pages 233–4

It has been debated as to whether the survival of native Catholicism or the activities of missionary priests was most important for the maintenance of Catholicism into the seventeenth century. However, this depends on the region and indeed the type of Catholicism. In the north of the country, where the grip of the Tudor state was weaker, there was greater scope for the survival of traditional Catholicism than in the more closely policed and, in terms of able Protestant ministers and preachers, the better equipped south and east. But this traditional Catholicism was a religion which clung to a set of rituals and values which were hallowed more than they were understood in theological terms. The Catholicism which was re-built by the missionary priests in the south and east was that of the Counter-Reformation, better disciplined to withstand policing by the state and the preaching of Puritans. And it was informed by the decisions of the Council of Trent – which had, at its conclusion in 1563, made absolutely clear the theology and the discipline which defined a Catholic, where before there had been much greater latitude. Traditional rituals and values still of course mattered to Counter-Reformation Catholics in the south and east, but so too did a much more dogmatic set of beliefs, a dogmatism to stand up to that of the Protestants.

Catholicism survived, and had shrunk far less than was claimed by Protestant propagandists from the sixteenth century and thought by twentieth century historians a generation ago. However, shrink Catholicism certainly did between the ends of Mary Tudor's reign and that of her half-sister, Elizabeth. For all the optimism of William Allen and his successors, there was no going back.

KEY ISSUE

How important were William Allen and other missioners to the survival of Catholicism in England?

F *Assessment*

By 1603 the majority of people conformed to the established church, and it would be fair to say that England was a Protestant country. The ceremonies of the old religion had given way to sermons and the services of the *Prayer Book*, and Catholicism and the Pope were now identified as the nation's enemies. This had huge implications for the future of the country and the way its people perceived it. As David Starkey has commented: 'At the beginning of our period, an idea of English nationhood was just formed; at the end, the English nation had emerged – so it thought – as the predestined vehicle of God's purpose on earth'.

England by 1603 was clearly Protestant in identity, but there were still limitations, however, in the understanding of the structure of beliefs which underlay that. Preachers complained frequently, and probably with some justification, of the ignorance of ordinary people. Their loyalty to the established church was based on a mixture of familiarity and conformity rather than a real knowledge of Protestant doctrine. Being able to recite the Catechism was one thing; understanding it was another. Even superficial conformity was adapted to suit popular ideas. For example, the official requirement was that communion should be received three times a year but general practice was to receive it only once, a habit that persisted from pre-Reformation days. In London parishes, around 1600, it has been estimated that only 35–75% of potential communicants took communion in any one year.

Many Protestant preachers and writers criticised the lack of commitment and true conversion. Conforming to the established church did not always mean true understanding of what Protestantism meant. They regarded unthinking loyalty to the *Prayer Book* as simply a survival of earlier attitudes to Catholic ritual. William Perkins, a radical Protestant, at the end of Elizabeth's reign wrote: 'For the remainders of popery yet stick in the minds of many of them, and they think that to serve God is nothing else but to deal truly with men and to babble a few words morning and evening, at home or in the church, though there be no understanding'.

There was some justification for this comment. Much of the change was simply conformity. As office-holding became increasingly dependant on attending church and taking communion, so more and more gentry abandoned their old loyalties. In doing so they thought more of social acceptance perhaps than of religious commitment. In contrast to those who were addicted to lengthy sermons and eagerly bought the religious pamphlets which flooded onto the market, others may have valued the rites of passage the church offered – baptism, weddings, funerals – while dozing through the sermons, wondering what double predestination might mean, and believing that just doing the right thing was the sure route to heaven. The historian can detect what people fought for, but when they quietly conformed in all outward observances, it is hard to tell what they really believed. Unlike Elizabeth, the curious historian would dearly like windows into men's souls.

> **KEY ISSUE**
>
> *What difficulties are faced by a historian assessing religious change?*

4 ᔐ BIBLIOGRAPHY

**The best overview is D MacCulloch *The Change of Religion*, Chapter 3 in P Collinson (ed.) *The Sixteenth Century* (OUP, 2002). *Christopher Haigh *English Reformations* (Oxford University Press, 1993) surveys the religious changes and considers both why they happened and their impact. The state of the church before the Reformation is studied in *Christopher Harper-Bill *The Pre-Reformation Church in England* (Longman Seminar Studies, 1989) and it provides a very positive assessment. *Christopher Marsh *Popular Religion in Sixteenth Century England* (Macmillan, 1998) is an excellent survey from the grass-roots up. A much larger work that stresses the flourishing nature of the late medieval church is **E Duffy *The Stripping of the Altars* (Yale, 1992). It also has an account of the Reformation itself that concentrates on the resistance to change. R Rex *Henry VIII and the English Reformation* (Macmillan, 1993) and *D MacCulloch *The Later Reformation in England* (Macmillan, 1990) are both excellent surveys. **D MacCulloch *Tudor Church Militant* (Penguin, 2001) is an account of the Reformation in Edward VI's reign that keeps one's attention. A fairly positive view of Mary's policies is found in Robert Tittler *The Reign of Mary I* (Longman Seminar Studies, 1983). The best brief survey of Elizabeth's religious policy is probably **S Doran *Elizabeth I and Religion* (Routlege Lancaster Pamphlets, 1994).

(*Recommended. **Highly recommended.)

5 ⇜ STRUCTURED AND ESSAY QUESTIONS

Consult the other relevant chapters before answering these questions

A *Structured questions*

1. (a) What criticisms could be made of the pre-Reformation Church?
    (b) What evidence is there for a flourishing church in pre-Reformation England?
2. (a) What is the evidence for Henry VII's conventional approach to religion?
    (b) How did Henry VIII differ from his father in this?

B *Essay questions*

1. Is it true to say that there would have been a Reformation in England even without Henry's desire for a divorce?
2. How different was religious life *c.*1603 compared to religious life *c.*1500?
3. Which of the Tudor monarchs had the most significant impact on religion in England?
4. How vital were humanism and the printing press to religious life and the Reformation in England?
5. 'Any history of sixteenth century England that failed to emphasize religion would be worthless.' Comment on this statement.

6 ⇜ HISTORIOGRAPHY EXERCISE: THE DEVELOPMENT OF PROTESTANTISM IN TUDOR ENGLAND

On the one hand there is Geoffrey Elton claiming that the advance of Protestantism owed almost everything to official coercion ... On the other there is the line pursued by AG Dickens that the new religion spread by conversions among the people and that it gained strength independently of the 'political' reformation. This view emphasizes also the debt owed by the English Reformation to continental Protestantism. Simultaneously there runs a debate concerning the pace of this religious change: Dickens's view that Protestantism made real inroads very early (so that it was a strong force by 1553) being challenged by Penry Williams, Christopher Haigh and JJ Scarisbrick, who argue, from differing perspectives, that little permanent was achieved before Elizabeth's reign.

SOURCE A
From Rosemary O'Day The Debate on the English Reformation *(1986)*

The Crown did not need to whip up anticlerical feeling; its task was to canalise, even to restrain such feeling. Anticlericalism probably owed less to the actual faults of the clergy than to a gradual shift in the attitude of lay society and to the growth of its literacy and intellectual resilience, its wealth, its political power. Lay resentment against tithes and against the moral jurisdiction and the heavy probate fees of the church courts, the rise of lay education, the import of bibles in English, the declining reputation of the Roman Curia, the survival of Lollardy and neo-Lollard anti-church opinion, the inveterate hostility of the common lawyers, the long-remembered scandal of Richard Hunne, the colourful but disastrous experiment with Thomas Wolsey; all these influences and many more had created before the meeting of the Reformation Parliament, a sharply critical atmosphere, particularly in London …

That the Reformation had already become far more than any mere act of state can be seen from that most crucial episode in the social history of the English Reformation – the conversion of an ever-growing minority among the people of south-eastern England to Protestant opinions, even while those opinions were still discouraged by the King … These quiet advances of Protestantism during Henry's last years account for the ease with which Somerset established it as the official religion from the beginning of the new reign. His championship, followed by that of Northumberland, gave it an invaluable breathing space of more than six years, during which it spread and consolidated itself beyond the likelihood of extinction by any machinery available to Tudor governments. By the end of Edward's reign it had taken full advantage of the old basis of proletarian heresy and had penetrated deeply into the working classes of south-eastern England, which supplied the great majority of the Protestant martyrs under Mary.

SOURCE B

From AG Dickens The English Reformation *(2nd edition, 1989)*

English men and women did not want the Reformation and most of them were slow to accept it when it came … To speak of a rising groundswell of lay discontent with the old order, of growing 'spiritual thirst' during the latter Middle Ages, and of a momentous alliance between the crown and disenchanted layfolk that led to the repudiation of Rome and the humbling of the clerical estate is to employ metaphors for which there is not much evidence …

As events were to prove, pre-Reformation Catholicism was vulnerable. But there is little sign of growing popular hostility towards it. And this in turn helps to explain another fact: the more we know about the spread of Protestantism in England, the more obvious it is that the process was, on the whole, slow, piecemeal and painful. Of course, it spread faster in some places than others – usually thanks to the accident of proximity to Protestant influence or the efforts of a zealous bishop, preacher or lay patron (male or female). But even in those areas where the new creed prospered most and fastest, the 'Protestantisation' of English men and women was an uphill task and never perfectly achieved.

SOURCE C

From JJ Scarisbrick The Reformation and the English People *(1984)*

The concept of anticlericalism plays a crucial role in recent accounts of the English Reformation, for it helps to explain how a largely Catholic country had a largely peaceful Reformation ... But the Reformation was not the product of a long-term clash between laity and clergy ... relations between priests and parishioners were usually harmonious, and the laity complained astonishingly infrequently against their priests ... In a frantic search for the causes of the Reformation, we must not wrench isolated cases of discord from their local contexts, and pile them together to show a growing chorus of dissatisfaction; we must not construct a false polarisation between Church and people. There was no general hostility towards the clerical estate, and such criticism as there was came from specific interest groups, especially lawyers, London merchants, and the political enemies of Thomas Wolsey. The English people had not turned against their Church, and there was no widespread yearning for reform.

SOURCE D
From Christopher Haigh's introduction to The English Reformation Revised *(1987)*

There were three political Reformations: a Henrician political Reformation between 1530 and 1538, much of it reversed between 1538 and 1546; an Edwardian political Reformation between 1547 and 1553, almost completely reversed between 1553 and 1558; and an Elizabethan political Reformation between 1559 and 1563 – which was not reversed. These political Reformations could not make England Protestant; statute by statute, however, they gave England Protestant laws and made popular Protestantism possible. What made English people Protestant – some English people Protestant – was not the three political Reformations, but the parallel evangelical Reformation: the Protestant Reformation of individual conversions by preachers and personal contacts, the reformation which began in London, Cambridge and Oxford from about 1520, and was never completed. So England had blundering Reformations, which most did not understand, which few wanted, and which no one knew had come to stay.

SOURCE E
From Christopher Haigh English Reformations *(1993)*

I have tried to tell the story of the dismantling and destruction of that symbolic world [of late medieval Catholicism], from Henry VIII's break with the Papacy in the early 1530s to the Elizabethan 'Settlement' of religion, which I take to have been more or less secure, or at least in the ascendant, by about 1580 ...

It is my conviction ... that no substantial gulf existed between the religion of the clergy and the educated élite on the one hand and that of the people at large on the other ...

It is [my] contention ... that late medieval Catholicism exerted an enormously strong, diverse and vigorous hold over the imagination and the loyalty of the people up to the very moment of Reformation. Traditional religion ... was showing itself well able to meet new needs and new conditions ... when all is said and done, the Reformation was a violent disruption, not the natural fulfillment, of most of what was vigorous in late medieval piety and religious practice ...

I have tried to demonstrate the anxiety of the Elizabethan episcopate about the persistence and vitality of the forms of traditional religion, an anxiety reflected in the determination with which they set themselves to achieve the destruction of them.

SOURCE F

From Eamon Duffy The Stripping of the Altars *(1992)*

1. Use the information in the extract to draw up a chart summarizing the different historians' interpretations of the Reformation.
   The headings you might use include:
   - Was reformation inspired by politics or religion?
   - What was the popular reaction to change?
   - How swift was the process of reformation?

Add your own headings. For example, a final column might include your own comments on the historians' views.

Professor Dickens's work has been justly celebrated, though its definitively Protestant assumptions now jar somewhat ... At one point, he praises Elizabethan puritanism for having 'taught men to see Christ through the eyes of St. Paul instead of through a cloud of minor saints, gilded legends and plain myths'. This is hardly a balanced assessment, though we can at least commend the author for not seeking to conceal his bias.

... Scarisbrick's preconceptions, like those of Dickens, arouse suspicion. We are invited to consider, for example, 'a random sample' of late-medieval wills, which are employed to make the point that people bequeathed large sums to a universally beloved church. Yet it is obvious to those with knowledge of the sources that this is not pot-luck at all (unless the pot is a jackpot), but a mouth-watering selection of the choicest morsels.

... [Haigh's] use of evidence suggests the influence of unspoken bias. For the late-medieval church, a rate of ten tithe disputes per year in the Norwich diocese is dismissed as insignificant, certainly not an indication that the laity resented the church; but in Elizabethan Essex, religious disputes in twelve parishes during an entire decade are presented as evidence that Protestant ministers were deeply unpopular.

SOURCE G

From Christopher Marsh Popular Religion in Sixteenth Century England *(1998)*

2. Read Source G. What aspects does Christopher Marsh find to criticise in the work of the historians referred to in the extract?

3. Drawing on your own knowledge and your study of all of the sources, which of the interpretations do you find
   (a) most persuasive?
   (b) least persuasive?

Glossary

Index